EL MONTE

A book in the series Latin America in Translation /

En Traducción / Em Tradução

*Sponsored by the Duke–University of North Carolina
Program in Latin American Studies*

LYDIA CABRERA

EL

MONTE

....

Notes on the Religions, Magic,

and Folklore of the Black

and Creole People of Cuba

Translated by

David Font-Navarrete

DUKE UNIVERSITY PRESS *Durham and London* 2023

Translation published by Duke University Press 2023

Printed in the United States of America on acid-free
paper ∞
Designed by Matthew Tauch
Typeset in Adobe Jenson Pro, SangBleu Versailles,
and Cronos Pro by Westchester Publishing Services

Library of Congress Cataloging-in-Publication Data
Names: Cabrera, Lydia, author. | Font-Navarrete, David,
[date] translator.
Title: El monte : notes on the religions, magic, and folklore
of the Black and Creole people of Cuba / Lydia Cabrera ;
translated by David Font-Navarrete.
Other titles: Monte. English | Latin America in translation/
en traducción/em tradução.
Description: Durham : Duke University Press, 2023. |
Series: Latin America in translation/en traducción/em
tradução | Includes bibliographical references and index.
Identifiers: LCCN 2022029291 (print)
LCCN 2022029292 (ebook)
ISBN 9781478018735 (paperback)
ISBN 9781478016090 (hardcover)
ISBN 9781478023340 (ebook)
Subjects: LCSH: Black people—Cuba—Religion. |
Santeria—Cuba. | Black people—Cuba—Folklore. |
Traditional medicine—Cuba. | Magic—Cuba. | Folklore—
Cuba. | African diaspora. | Cuba—Religion. | BISAC:
SOCIAL SCIENCE / Anthropology / Cultural & Social |
HISTORY / Caribbean & West Indies / Cuba
Classification: LCC BL2490 . C2413 2023 (print) |
LCC BL2490 (ebook)
DDC 299.6/897291—dc23/eng20221031
LC record available at https://lccn.loc.gov/2022029291
LC ebook record available at https://lccn.loc.gov
/2022029292

Cover art: José Bedia, *Animal Armado y Madre de
Guerra*, diptych, 2019. Woodcut and silkscreen on
heavyweight paper, 78 3/10 × 78 3/10 inches, edition
of 30. Courtesy of the artist.

Published in collaboration with the University of
Miami Libraries' Cuban Heritage Collection.

publication supported by a grant from
The Community Foundation for Greater New Haven
as part of the **Urban Haven Project**

·

To Fernando Ortiz, with
fraternal affection

·

Contents

Foreword

The Forest as Moral Document

....

JOHN F. SZWED AND ROBERT F. THOMPSON

It is said that the jazz style of Charlie Parker, blowing cool, blowing hot, blowing all the points in between, was so complex that several musicians, and indeed schools, were needed fully to explore his implications. This point applies to Lydia Cabrera and the richness of her Afro-Cuban scholarship. Only a task force, working day after day for years, could effect the just estimation that her work demands as surely one of the twentieth century's most important bodies of urban anthropological research. We say *urban* because the two main Cuban cultures from Africa, Yoruba and Kongo, were urban, and anciently so. The creolization of these cultures, and their fusion with elements of Spanish, French, and even Chinese in the history of Afro-Cuban art and

---

DF-N: This foreword is based on an essay originally cowritten, according to the authors, circa 1982. It was informed by conversations with Cabrera during visits to her home in Miami, where she lived with María Teresa de Rojas. Quotations attributed to Cabrera without parenthetical citation in this foreword (e.g., "so that you can write freely about our traditions") are based on personal communications with the authors. The essay was originally intended as an introduction to an earlier effort, by Eliot Klein, to publish an English-language edition of *El Monte*. The text of the essay has been adapted from a previous version published as "The Forest as Moral Document: The Achievement of Lydia Cabrera," in *Crossovers: Essays on Race, Music, and American Culture* (Szwed 2005).

music, largely took place in the port cities of Cuba—notably, Havana and Matanzas. The famed stylishness of Black Cubans is a function, we would suggest, of their tropism toward the city. Afro-Cubans, like the Yoruba and Bakongo, appreciate the parlance of the city, the verbal lore and gossip, the continual elaboration of tradition in a situation in which an artist or musician might move in a given week from Yoruba to Dahomean to Cross River Efik/Ejagham to Kongo to commercial *música cabaretera* to playing a trumpet solo at a wedding to Yoruba *bembé*. In fact, polyvisuality (a world of Catholic chromolithography and Yoruba sacred stones) and polymusicality (where Kongo society members are called upon to play Abakuá, or Cross River, drums) may well be a Black pan-Caribbean phenomenon, as suggested by Kenneth Bilby in his account of a Jamaican musician:

> Starting one morning by playing guitar in a coastal *mento* bend for tourists, he returned later that day to his rural village to join in a fife and drum performance, playing the leading drum, and then in the evening added his voice a Revival church chorus. . . . The easy movement between styles was not unusual for this man. (1994, 203)

Nor was it unusual for Lydia Cabrera. Modest, completely free of any self-conscious sense of her exalted status in Afro-Caribbean studies, she has given us a unique body of vividly written works.

In 1954, Cabrera published *El Monte*, a monumental compendium of the lore of herbal healing and associated African-influenced worship among the Black people of western Cuba. Ever since, the book has remained continuously in print. For *El Monte* (The sacred forest) has become a holy book for thousands of servitors of the Afro-American religions derived from the Yoruba, Kongo, Dahomean, and Ejagham cultures. Among other things, the book provides a key to Afro-Atlantic herbalism, not only in its western Cuban manifestation but in today's broader universe of Afro-Cuban influence, involving thousands of worshippers of Yoruba-Cuban deities and practitioners of Kongo-Cuban medicine and Yoruba-Cuban herbalism in Florida (Miami, Hialeah, and Tampa); New Jersey (Elizabeth, Union City); New York City (especially the South Bronx, Spanish Harlem, and the Lower East Side); and the Cuban and Puerto Rican barrios of other major northeastern industrial cities. The range of these religions is enormous. This book helps us comprehend them.

El Monte defines a history of brilliantly effected change whereby the worship of more than twelve major goddesses and gods (orishas) of the Yoruba (a people who live in what is now southwestern Nigeria and eastern Benin Republic) was transmuted into La Regla de Ocha, the worship of the same deities in Afro-Cuban terms and a worship also known as Santería, after the "masking" of orisha with Catholic saints (*santos*) where both shared highly similar or identical visual attributes. For example, Ogun, the Yoruba deity of iron (the charismatic metal), lord of the cutting edge, and today patron of metallic wonders like oil rigs, speeding locomotives, or taxicabs, blended with the image of St. Peter because the latter was depicted frequently in Roman Catholic chromolithographs holding an iron key to the gates of heaven. Similarly, the playful propensities on one side of the complex Yoruba trickster-deity, Eshu-Elegba, found a ready avatar in "the child of Atocha," shown with a round object which Yoruba would almost inevitably associate with *àdo*, calabashes of transforming power that are one of the deep signs of the presence of Eshu and his power to make things happen (*àṣe*, called *aché* in the creolized Yoruba of Cuba). In addition, the dreaded deity of pestilence and social conscience, Obaluaiye, blurred into the picture of St. Lazarus supported by crutches, dogs licking his numerous wounds. Meanwhile, the equally tumultuous and beautifully conceived deities of Dahomey, the *vodun*—the same deities that elsewhere in the Caribbean helped spark one of the world's most conceptually complex and misunderstood religions, Haitian Vodun—were transmuted into Arará worship, in which god and goddess again served with and without carefully selected Catholic masks and counterparts. To this day both Yoruba and Dahomean deities are worshipped with a wealth of vernacular drums, costumes, beadwork, and dance, all combined. In the process, Cuba became a marvel of the Black Atlantic world, with an elaborate and continuous tradition of decorated *batá* drums, beaded necklaces, and ritual beaded garlands (*mazos*) in symbolic colors. Yoruba is still spoken and sung in Cuba, albeit in a creolized fusion form. The Yoruba-born linguist Dejo Afolayan maintains that this fusion brings together Kétu and Ijésha dialect forms, separated by hundreds of miles in Yorubaland itself, in the strength of a reblended cultural flavor.[1]

The rise of Yoruba-Cuban and Dahomean-Cuban circles of artistic culture would be accomplishment enough, but there were two more surges out of anonymity, misery, and economic deprivation. First, there is the rise of apparently the only male secret society of African type in the New World, a transformation of the important Ejagham male society called Ngbe, from the hinterlands of the notorious slave port of Calabar. Many slaves from this part of Africa arrived in Cuba in the first half of the nineteenth century, where they were called Carabalí (linguistic metathesis transformed the word, but not to such an extent that most persons could not sense a relationship binding such

---

1   DF-N: Based on the authors' personal communication.

people to Calabar and its hinterlands). In Calabar proper, the Ejagham are known as Abakpa or Qua, and it is from the first term, almost beyond doubt, that the creole term for the Ejagham Cuban male society, Abakuá, derives. The Ejagham are famed for skin-covered masks and a supple ideographic writing system called *nsibidi* ("the dark letters," "the serious signs"), plus powerful women's arts including, again, ideography and remarkable ceremonial plumed calabashes (*echi okpere*). High-ranking initiates of the Ngbe society also used plumed drums of silence, drums to be "heard" visually at funerals and other most important events but not actually sounded. And many of these subtleties of act and envisionment passed intact to Cuba, where Lydia Cabrera for years was alone in rendering full justice to the presence of the Ejagham-derived Abakuá practices, not only in two chapters in *El Monte* but also in two later works, *La sociedad secreta Abakuá* (1959) and *Anaforuana* (1975), the latter a landmark publication in the history of the study of Black Atlantic graphic scripts and ideography. With the exception of Argeliers León and Sosa Hernández, Cabrera remains the sole and brilliant scholar of Ejagham impact on the New World, as mediated through the culture of Ejagham-influenced slaves and freed slaves, who were concentrated in the sugar ports of western Cuba (Havana, Matanzas, and Cárdenas), their environs, and the sugar plantations themselves, linked to these termini by rail and road. Finally, we are confronted by the mighty Kongo and Angola presence, less evident linguistically, perhaps, but massive and profound in the making of charms (*minkisi*), incantations (*mambu*, creolized to *mambo*, a word further borrowed to name one of the most multimetric Afro-Cuban musics of the twentieth century), and dance and musical instrumentation. That presence is especially felt in the hundreds of plants that bear creole Ki-Kongo names in Cuba and are linked with interlocking circles of Kongo-derived or Kongo-inspired folklore, without which the world would have never heard of rumba, never danced to the conga drum.

El Monte also forces the recognition of a parallel medical system in the Western Hemisphere. As Mercedes Cros Sandoval points out, most of the 400,000 Cubans now settled in Dade County, Florida, rely on standard health care systems for treatment of infections and organic diseases. But many consult Cuban-Yoruba traditional herbal medicine in dealing with problems emerging from spiritual or emotional stress.[2] For pneumonia one goes to the hospital, but for psychiatric disorders, caused by the destruction of a love affair or bitter jealousy, one goes to the herbalist-diviner. There are serious skills involved in the latter realm of medicine, for the Yoruba of Nigeria, for example,

2   JFS and RFT: For a general discussion of these matters, see Cros Sandoval (1977, 1979).

are believed to have known, classified, and used the tranquilizing properties of *rauwolfia* years before it was adopted in Western pharmacopeia. Moreover, a team of Western doctors reliably report from Yorubaland that "one can say further that the criteria employed to distinguish particular kinds of mental and emotional disturbance are very similar to the criteria employed by Western psychiatrists" (Leighton et al. 1963, 105). In other words, the folkloric substance of this book, largely rooted in herbalism, is not a quaint collection of archaic, vanished happenings but a vibrant reality, a design for right living, which exists parallel to Western diagnostic medicine in Nigeria and in the Nigerian-influenced New World. Patients involved in this popular medicine sometimes remark on their close and cordial relationships with the healer-diviners, recalling a fictionalized account of the encounter of a North American Black woman with a prophet-healer in which her consultation contrasted vividly with the relative perceived coldness of official medicine: "The satisfaction she felt was from the quiet way he had listened to her, giving her all of his attention. No one had ever done that before. The doctors she saw from time to time at the clinic were brusque, hurried, and impatient" (Petry 1946, 136).

Among the folklorists of the twentieth century, Lydia Cabrera is distinguished by her special attention to Black Atlantic herbalism. We say *Atlantic*, instead of *Afro-Cuban*, because some of the herbs she documents are linked to cognate herbs and healing practices among Afro-Jamaican, Afro-Brazilian, and Afro-American systems. Conventional wisdom cites music, dance, oral literature, religion, and revolutionary politics as the key Black contributions to world culture. But here is the beginning of understanding of perhaps the finest contribution of them all: Black Atlantic medicine. *El Monte* lists more than five hundred herbs, the ailments that they are alleged to cure, the spirits that preside over their healing powers, and the creolized Yoruba, Ki-Kongo, and Ejagham (Abakuá) words that name the leaves in Afro-Cuban terms.

In addition, we find whole legends associated with certain leaves: miniature narrations. "Truths that can be rendered in a dissociated moment," Susan Sontag points out, "however significant or decisive, have a very narrow relation to the needs of understanding. Only that which narrates can make us understand" (1977, 23). And, in fact, *El Monte* is a miracle of narration, brought into being by a woman who uniquely combined the powers of a painter, an interior designer, a sculptor (her painted stones were exhibited in New York City in the spring of 1984 at the Intar Gallery), a writer, a linguist, and a passionate student of the folkways of Black people. The result is a major work of twentieth-century Cuban literature in the depth of its vision and the quality of the writing, with interviews embedded like "found conversations" (Black Spanish phrasing and all) in the flow of her discourse and summation. It is also a major document in the history of popular Afro-American art, for no place else does one find photographs of major Kongo-influenced charms in Cuba, or photographs (in color, in the original edition) of Yoruba initiatory body painting in Cuba or the characteristic hands-crossing gestures of the Ejagham- and Efik-derived *íreme* (cf. Efik: *idem* "spirit") masker in action, or the only full-color portrait of an *íreme* showing Calabar-influenced details of appliqué and decoration. It becomes immediately comprehensible why this uniquely talented and spiritually knowledgeable woman would attract the friendship and admiration of some of the finest minds of twentieth-century literature.

. . . . . .

Lydia Cabrera was born in Havana on Independence Day, May 20, 1900,[3] the last of eight children of Raimundo Cabrera y Bosch and Elisa Macaida y Casanova. Her father was a distinguished lawyer, journalist, playwright, poet, and novelist, as well as a leader in the movement for Cuba's independence, and the Cabrera home was a gathering place for intellectuals, painters, lawyers, and politicians. It was a climate that helped shape the range of interests character-istic of her later work. Cabrera's older sister Estelle was married to Fernando Ortiz, who had published (when Lydia was six) the first major work on Afro-Cuban culture, *Los negros brujos*, a study of magic workers. Ortiz's Afro-Cuban studies had begun with the assumption (like much conservative and liberal scholarship of the 1960s in the United States) that people of African descent lacked a true culture and, if anything, practiced a culture of poverty (or a culture of pathology). But the sheer corrective power of Afro-Cuban culture fused with Ortiz's basic integrity as a scholar so that he ultimately came to spend much of his life documenting the splendor and normativeness of this culture, and what's more, to use his documentation as a means to justice for Black Cubans. Cabrera, of course, knew Ortiz's dozens of articles and books: still, her contribution was ultimately to prove of greater bite and substance, for in submitting to the responsibility, the incredible repetitiveness of her in-formant's valuable, pithy arguments, she made an even greater contribution to the cause of Afro-Cuban studies. For she collected whole texts, as it were, whereas Ortiz pigeonholed his facts and worked up essentially an etymology of the main traits of Afro-Cuban lore.

Nevertheless, Ortiz's work was something of a foundation on which the Afro-Cubanist movement of the 1920s and 1930s was built, a movement that sliced together European primitivism, Cuban nationalism, and the grow-ing thrust toward Afro-Cuban rights and freedom. It was a period that saw

3   DF-N: Regarding Cabrera's date of birth, see the introduction to this edition by Isabel Castellanos.

the writing, from the bottom up, of novels such as Alejo Carpentier's *Écue-Yamba-o*, the culturally Black poetry of Nicolás Guillén, and the composition of classical music (by Alejandro García Caturla and Amadeo Roldán) and popular music (by Ernesto Lecuona) based on Afro-Cuban folk song and dance.

In the spirit of the times, Cabrera's first works were literary retellings of Afro-Cuban folktales, works of local color. But she also knew the creolization of European surrealism and Afro-American political consciousness that had produced *négritude*: she had translated the classic of this movement herself, Aimé Césaire's *Cahier d'un retour au pays natal* ([1939] 1943, [1939] 2013), and she was friendly with the Martinican poet Léon Damas. Cabrera refers to her books of Afro-Cuban tales as fiction, with no claim to folkloric validity.[4] At best, she says, they are loosely based on Afro-Cuban originals (as are some of the stories of Carpentier), while some are totally invented, perhaps inspired—like some Afro-Haitian paintings—by Black folk song. Nonetheless, these tales and the anecdotes and dialogues within them are rooted in ethnographic realism. Indeed, the glossaries of Afro-Cuban terms that Cabrera includes with some of these books absolutely suggest a more than casual concern with accuracy. Her ear for dialogue—at the margin between fiction and ethnography—is also displayed in *Francisco y Francisca* (1976), a collection of humorous anecdotes and short tales in Kongo Cuban idiom. In fact, it is at the borders of conventional literary genres that Cabrera works most comfortably, as illustrated by *Refranes de negros viejos* (1955), a collection of proverbs; and *Itinerario del insomnio* (1977), a blend of folklore, politics, and mystical nostalgia, a literary raising of the dead in the Cuban city of Trinidad at the turn of the century.

In 1938, after years in France, Cabrera fled the rise of the Nazis and returned to Cuba to live and work, though her travels often took her back to Europe. Home again, she began persistent research in the Black barrios of Havana and Matanzas in the tradition of field ethnography. And while she has always distanced herself from anthropology (she claims merely to "repeat" culture, not interpret it),[5] she approached research on her own country in a highly sophisticated, relativistic fashion and managed to bridge the "native," the amateur, and the professional anthropological points of view. Additionally, she counted among her friends such anthropologists as William and Berta Bascom, Melville and Frances Herskovits, Alfred Métraux, and

---

4   JFS and RFT: See Cabrera's *Cuentos negros de Cuba* (1940); *Ayapá* (1971); and *Cuentos para adultos, niños, y retrasados mentales* (1983).

5   DF-N: Quotations without bibliographic citations are based on the authors' personal communications with Cabrera circa 1982, during visits to her Miami home, where she lived with María Teresa de Rojas.

Pierre Verger. In fact, it was Métraux, the distinguished French ethnographer of Haitian *vodun*, at first skeptical of her findings of African languages in Cuba ("Quelle imagination, Lydia!" he said), who aided her in confirming the Yoruba sources of the Lucumí material she had encountered, and who encouraged her to expand her research to include Kongo—that is, *palero*—material. And, for a time, the French Afro-Brazilianist scholar Verger joined her in field research, especially aiding her with photography. Most of the research was done by Cabrera herself, however, though sometimes in the company of her companion, paleographic scholar María Teresa de Rojas.[6]

In disagreement with the direction taken by the 1959 Cuban Revolution, Cabrera left Cuba for Miami in 1960. Though her exile was intended to be temporary, her Coral Gables residence became permanent. Isolation from Cuban tradition sharpened her consciousness, and like an anthropologist writing far from the field, she produced eleven more books, each breaking new ground.

Cabrera's ethnographies of Afro-Cuban religious life are the heart of her later work. These include research on the Yoruba in Cuba published as *Yemayá y Ochún* (1974), an account of the verbal arts surrounding the goddesses of the seas, sweet water, and love; *Koeko iyawo* (1980), concerning the structure of the Afro-Yoruba religion, its rituals, sacrifices, and cures; *Anagó* ([1957] 1986), a lexicon of creolized speech in Cuba; *Otán iyebiyé* (1970), on the beliefs of the priests of the orishas about precious stones; *La laguna sagrada de San Joaquín* ([1973] 1993), about the rituals of the followers of Iyalosha, the water goddess; and *La medicina popular de Cuba* (1984), a study of folk medicine among Afro-Cubans.

The seminal work on the Efik and Ejagham male "leopard society" (Ngbe) in Cuba is represented by *La sociedad secreta Abakuá* (1959),[7] an account of the myths, rituals, ideography, and organization of the Abakuá religion and their influence on Cuban religious life; *Anaforuana* (1975), offers an ideography of initiation, funeral leave-taking, and membership in the Abakuá society. Cabrera's research on a creole Kongo society in Cuba appears in *La Regla Kimbisa del Santo Cristo del Buen Viaje* ([1977] 1986), a close look at a nineteenth-century creolized Kongo-Catholic religious group and its leaders; and *Reglas de Congo* ([1979] 1986) examines the creolized Kongo-Angolan ritual, religion, ideography, and folklore of Cuba.

---

6   DF-N: It is worth emphasizing the integral role of Josefina Tarafa's photographs and audio recordings in a trio of Cabrera's most important projects: *El Monte* ([1954] 1992); *Música de los cultos africanos en Cuba* (1956); and *La laguna sagrada de San Joaquín* ([1973] 1993).

7   DF-N: For an annotated translation of this work, informed by new transnational scholarship on Abakuá traditions, see Cabrera (2020).

But *El Monte* is the centerpiece of Cabrera's enterprise. When it was first published in Havana in 1954, it was issued as part of what Cabrera called the *Colección del chicherekú* (a *chicherekú* is a wooden doll made by a *santero*); when she reprinted *El Monte* in Miami in 1968, she made it a part of the *Colección del chicherekú en el exilio*. In 1954 most Cuban intellectuals treated it as something of a national embarrassment—a tarnishing of Cuba's image as a modern nation-state. European and North American folklorists and anthropologists then, as now, took little interest in the scholarship of Cuba, so its publication went unnoticed abroad.

Yet *El Monte* was not lost, by any means. Afro-Americanists such as Melville Herskovits, William Bascom, and Roger Bastide recognized its importance and kept it alive in their footnotes as part of the growing corpus of comparativist Black studies. And Cabrera's skill with local languages and characterization did not escape the notice of Cuba's novelists, for whom she became both a model and a source. Even the folkloric content of *El Monte* influenced Cuban fiction: Alejo Carpentier's *Explosion in a Cathedral* ([1960] 1963), for instance, is indebted to Cabrera's detailed herbal descriptions and classifications.[8] Most importantly, *El Monte* was immediately recognized to be the first printed guide, the Bible, of Santeria worshippers, and began to sell widely. It has been in print now for fifty years, in several countries, an underground best seller if ever there was one, and some kind of assessment in terms of ethnographic tradition is long overdue.

. . . . . .

Just what constitutes a successful ethnography is far from obvious, even after a century of professional anthropology. Exactly what the relationship should be between a culture and its analysis and representation in a book is at best understood only in general terms by anthropologists. Beyond general strictures, disagreements persist over what ethnography should be. In part this debate is the result of the discipline's history; by and large, ethnography developed as an ad hoc discipline constructed by amateur scientists. Anthropologists such as Frank Boas, Alfred Kroeber, and Paul Radin had no social science training, and came to the discipline from backgrounds in other fields, such as geography, literature, and history. Lacking an agreed-upon firm sense of what ethnography should be and how it should be done, early anthropologists experimented with a variety of approaches and even a variety of genres for rendering the results: laboratory-inspired reports, diaries, travel accounts, native autobiographies, and even fictional forms were all tried. Much of the

8   JFS and RFT: For a guide to Carpentier's *Explosion in a Cathedral*, see Echevarría (1984).

strength of anthropology developed within this sense of experimentation and reflexivity, and the question of what makes for successful (or convincing) ethnography continues to remain in contention. For some anthropologists, an adequate ethnography would allow one the knowledge to act acceptably as a native in the society represented (needless to say, no such ethnography has yet been written for any society). For other anthropologists, a good ethnography would offer a "reading" of native texts alongside natives' readings of those texts. For still others, ethnography would set a given people, a given culture, into the comparative community of peoples within the conceptual world of anthropologists. Much of the training of anthropologists is taken up with discussions over the various merits of these and other approaches.

What, then, are we to make of *El Monte*, which is now, more often than not, very closely read by the "natives," the followers of Santería in a number of countries in the Americas? What are we to make of a book so powerful that it continues to be pirated and plagiarized year after year? A book that has left the disciplinary realms of literature, science, and folklore and has joined in the very processes of cultural influence and change itself? A book written, after all, by a native Cuban untrained either as anthropologist or as *santero*, and yet someone who is often sought after in both roles by two worlds of people? A book which, though written outside the usual academic and disciplinary frameworks, is based nonetheless on over ten years of field research and is supremely sensitive to cultural variety? Finally, what are we to make of a book whose complex literary originality is matched only by its subject, a culture so complex that it resists complete understanding by means of any known theories of cultural change?

What *El Monte* shows us is no fusion culture in which African cultural particularity is shredded and kaleidoscoped, thus remaining incomprehensible. The assault on such cultural fatalism begins on the title page. There we find a kind of cabalistic anagram of the secret cultural profundities, distinct and independent, that make up the culture of Black Cubans. The title of the book, *El Monte*, is standard Spanish for hill or mountain. But in the vernacular the term refers to the country, to bush or forest, to wild vegetation, plants growing in their natural, undomesticated state. Cabrera deepens and confirms the sylvan associations by causing the letters that compose the phrase *El Monte* to be illuminated, on the cover of both the Cuban and Miami editions, in green. And she immediately follows the symbolically illuminated letters with reinforcing glosses from the two major African languages in Cuba: IGBO (Yoruba: bush, grove for worship) NFINDA (Ki-Kongo: woods, forest, wooded country; place of the spirits of the dead [from time immemorial]). The semantic range of both these important African words makes plain that the forest in two African civilizations important to Cuba is charged with spirituality, a cathedral buttressed by the trees and lit by herbal stained glass, as it were—a cathedral such as William Faulkner glimpsed in "the big woods, bigger and older than any recorded document" ([1931] 2011, 190). And like Faulkner before her, Cabrera was guided to the forest in terms of Black culture. As she notes in chapter 1,

> An astonishingly tenacious belief in *el monte* persists among Afro-Cubans. In the woods and scrubland of Cuba, as in African forests, dwell ancestral deities and powerful spirits that today, as in the days of the slave trade, are most feared and venerated by Afro-Cubans, whose successes or failures depend upon their hostility or benevolence.[9]

. . . . . .

The book's concentration upon the healing essence of the forest, the herbs and roots, is rendered explicit by other Yoruba and Ki-Kongo phrases that illuminate the cover and the title page: EWE ORISHA (creolized Yoruba: leaves of the divinities) and VITITI NFINDA (creolized Ki-Kongo: herbs of the forest). The literal, trunkal (root, branch, twig) and herbal (the leaves) elements of the forest are involved in these phrasings, but elements of sitting, high and low, are also understood from the Ki-Kongo spatial references. Thus, in classical Ki-Kongo pharmacopeia, according to Kongo scholar Fu-Kiau Bunseki, the *makaya* (a word that turns up in Kongo-influenced Louisiana and Haiti as well as Cuba) refers to vertical leaves, fluttering high within the branches, whereas *bititi* refers to horizontal leaves attached to vines and creepers. In Cuba, however, *bititi*—creolized to *vititi*—refers simply to leaves.[10] Cabrera has said that *monte* refers to "the bush, to many plants" and that its literal meaning of mountain is not to be taken *al pié de la letra* (literally) except in a metaphoric sense of *altura*, height, ascendant source of power, a mountain mortar in which the leaves of the gods are ground and worked for the good of all humankind.

A sense of spiritualized rightness and organic sequence permeates the book's chapters, which flow from forest to herbs to doctors to fees to medicines and magical constructions, to chapters literally built around specific trees, like the turning of Afro-Haitian *vodun* dance about the trunkal middle post sited of a peristyle. Thus, chapter 1 introduces the forest and its spirituality, source of all wild herbs and roots, and chapter 2 talks of *bilongo* (Ki-Kongo: medicines) or the actual force of the forest in action. Chapter 3 introduces the spiritual lords and masters of the leaves (*oluwa ewe*); Osanyin, the

---

9   DF-N: The translation by Szwed and Thompson differs slightly from my own.

10   DF-N: Based on the authors' personal communication.

Yoruba deity of herbalism; and Eshu-Elegba, who is the spirit of the cross-roads and of spiritual communication with the goddesses and gods—great trickster and holder of the powers to make things come to pass. The divine tribute that one owes to such spirits for the privilege of plucking and working leaves unfolds in chapter 4. Then, in chapter 5, we actually learn how to make an Angolan charm (*como se prepara una nganga*) and various Kongo-influenced charms, a tour de force of magical reportage, with one informant sometimes contradicting or correcting another, until the whole point of miniaturizing the forest essences to make the healing medicines of God (*minkisi*) is memorably made plain. Soul-embedded earths and spirit-commanding objects or fluids—mercury for spiritual flash and fleetness, stones for immortal presence—are classified and revealed in long and absorbing passages about the building of Kongo charms, major charms like *mpungu*, with details that further research will probably identify as witty but culturally and historically appropriate local invention and improvisation.

There follows a brief but remarkable chapter 6 on the magical, medicinal treasury of the lord of medicine, Osanyin, and a corresponding creole Kongo figure called father of the forest (*tata nfinda*). And in these pages, among many illuminations, one learns to what extent Black Cubans believe that the forces of the forest are morally neutral, shaped by the particular character of their users, even as "a breeze is good and refreshing. But what about a hurricane? They're both wind." Then the book modulates into a tree-centered stanza of four chapters, two (chapters 7 and 8) on the cottonwood tree in Yoruba and Kongo rites, and two (chapters 9 and 10) built around the royal palm, rendered in the lore of the Abakuá and a sign par excellence of the Yoruba thunder god. Groundskeepers working in the parks of Miami today, so it is said, sometimes come across sacrificial remains at the base of the noblest and tallest royal palms.

In the climatic final section, the botanical encyclopedia, leaves themselves are listed by their vernacular Cuban-Spanish, Yoruba-Cuban, Kongo-Cuban, and Abakuá names, with legends and stories that detail the strong mystic links between the leaves and the deities of Yorubaland; for as Cabrera herself has said, "each orisha has its series of leaves which transmit its power-to-make-things-happen (*aché*)." Whence came this incredible ethnographic abundance of testimony and folkloric evidence? The answer: from an exemplary scholar-informant relationship rendered in terms of longtime mutuality of service and favor, without the self-serving fanfare that marks some scholars' attempts to set themselves up as paragons of cultural camaraderie and inside observation. After Cabrera returned to Havana from Paris, already primed to investigate more fully the Black roots of Cuban culture, she began to interview Omitomi, the Black seamstress who worked for Cabrera's grandmother.

Omitomi (Yoruba: I am satisfied with god of water) is a "water name" in Yoruba, indicating in all probability that she was a devotee of the riverine healer spirit Eyinle or Erinle, called Inle in Cuba. At first Omitomi feigned total ignorance of the Afro-Cuban world of worship: "I don't know nothing. I was brought up with white folk." Gradually it developed—and her name was a strong hint of this—that Omitomi was one of the most respected Afro-Cuban religious authorities in all of Cuba, and she introduced Cabrera to her friend Oddedei (Yoruba: the hunter has made us this). The two of them, Omitomi and Oddedei, saw to it that Cabrera traveled to Matanzas. This city, "the Ile-Ife of Cuba," was reputed to be home to the true spiritual overlords of the Afro-Cuban religion. The priests and priestesses there, many in their eighties and nineties, were deeply erudite and spoke the three major creolized African languages of Cuba. Oddedei made Cabrera swear that "no one was to touch her head" (i.e., no one was to initiate her into the Lucumí or Kongo religion, "so that you can write freely about our traditions, for once a *iyawo*—a bride of the gods, an initiate—you will never be allowed to speak").[11] And so a pact was sealed and word spread that Cabrera was a white person of distinction who truly respected Black culture and who was quite generous with her informants as regards gifts, services, and favors. As her network of informants grew in the 1940s and 1950s, she found that her house, the Quinta San José, was admirably sited, built as it was in Pogolotti, a barrio of Marianao, a western suburb of Havana. For Pogolotti is famed to this day for its African-influenced religious activities. It is the site of one of the most prestigious and culturally important Abakuá lodges. Cabrera comments: "In fact Pogolotti was a barrio entirely enlivened with Black people and culture. There were Abakuá, there were *paleros*, there were Yoruba diviners (*babalaos*), excellent people, no? I had but to cross the street to be in Africa."

These and other informants taught her that *el monte* was a Bible, that the great Kongo kettle charms (*prendas*) spoke through the bodies of their priestly mediums. Through Black friends of friends she was put in touch with perhaps the most holy—and feared—of all the Kongo *banganga* of Cuba, J. S. Baró, who worked with two or three ritual assistants in Pogolotti, and, Cabrera thinks, was descended from Black Cubans who worked on the Baró plantation in the province of Matanzas. Gradually her photographs and her documentation grew, each illustration, each legend not a coldly analyzed object but a gift, gestures of good will by Black women and men. Cabrera gave room and board to three Black elders, led by the incredible Saibeke, who was at once *mayombero*, a *lucumí*, and an Abakuá. Without question, part of the

11   DF-N: Cabrera narrates this episode first-hand in an interview (1982b).

special power of Afro-Cuban culture, the engine behind its world conquest of the dance halls of the planet, is the fluent, constant creolizing exchange between the three great African traditions that surged forth upon the island, as exemplified by Saibeke's multi-religiosity. Saibeke fell ill, and Cabrera brought in a doctor who cured him. And then one day he crossed the compound to Cabrera's door and said, "Niña, ¿tu quiere saber Abakuá? Coge libro." (Girl, you want to learn Abakuá? Pick up your notebook.)[12] And so began the lengthy seminars that resulted not only in *El Monte*'s magnificent chapters on the Abakuá and their lore of the palm tree and the cottonwood, but also Cabrera's full-scale books on the Abakuá and their ideography.

Cabrera's fluency in art and language (speaking excellent English and French, in addition to her native Spanish) prepared her for the daunting challenge of making sense of a sea of creolized Black speech in the provinces of Havana and Matanzas, where she did the bulk of the work in preparation for *El Monte*. She took down remarks and observations not only in Black Spanish, but also in creolized African languages: Yoruba (*lucumí*), Fongbe from Dahomey (*arará*), Ki-Kongo mixed with words in Black Spanish (*lengua palera*), Efik (*efí*), and Ejagham (*ekoi*). With the vision of a novelist she saw this incredible linguistic landscape whole. And, not unlike a filmmaker, she used "establishing shots" or introductory paragraphs along with moments when a single Black woman or man dominates a page with a string of texts. Her informants, working-class Black people, came to her with their noble memories and legends. She quickly recognized the strength and validity of their traditions. She saw creative vision, *grands initiateurs*, where others saw only stevedores, household domestics, common field hands, or ex-slaves.

We cannot repeat too many times that the great source of the strength of this book is linguistic, involving the patient documentation of texts and phrases from five major African languages spoken or chanted in Cuba. The author made constant contact with Black women and men, particularly in Matanzas, who spoke creolized Ki-Kongo and Yoruba fluently. In fact, so creatively challenged was Cabrera by the vibrant linguistic tumult she found about her that she matter-of-factly compiled, as parallel projects to the making of *El Monte*, lexicons of the different African languages that came to Cuba in the nineteenth-century slave trade. With *Anagó* ([1957] 1986) she rendered the lexicon of the Yoruba language spoken in creole form in Cuba. But she also published texts that established lexicons for Ki-Kongo and Ejagham/Efik creole languages in Cuba. And behind *El Monte* itself we sense the authority of carefully and painstakingly rendered documentation: myriad texts in

12   DF-N: Cabrera narrates this episode first-hand in an interview (1982b).

creolized Yoruba, Ki-Kongo, and Abakuá. Cabrera's mastery of the feel and distinctiveness of each idiom, her pride in mastering them as a genuine intellectual accomplishment, like learning Greek or Hebrew, is an important source of the authority of this book. There is such linguistic abundance, so much linguistic variety, that it is almost as if Lydia Cabrera had been confronted with Ki-Lele, as was Mary Douglas; Samoan, as was Margaret Mead; and Japanese, as Ruth Benedict might have been had she actually gone to Japan, and somehow brought together ethnographic reportage from all these languages within the compass of a single book. Hers is an exquisite art of sharing hours and afternoons with her informants, some of them—to judge from the quality of their remarks and the fluency of their citations of folk authority in songs in Yoruba or Fongbe or Ejagham or Ki-Kongo—among the most fertile sources of modern Afro-Cuban culture. Untied to a single social scientific vogue or theory, laced with insights internal to Afro-Cuban artistic culture and its amazing languages, her work is a fabric of timeless presences.

This book establishes, once and for all, that the descendants of Yoruba, Kongo, Ejagham, and Dahomean slaves in Cuba never were in their private minds mere pawns or tokens, objects shorn of creative spirit or will. *El Monte* is a mirror of collective resistance and ingenuity by which the Black women and men of Cuba elaborated a secret island within an island wherein they were free to think and act differently from the whites around them and, more to the point of their own recaptured creativity, differently from one another as well.

Introduction

Loose-Leaf Notes on the Life and Work
of Lydia Cabrera

....

ISABEL CASTELLANOS

To the memory of María Teresa de Rojas
and Amalia Bacardí

Those who deem themselves intelligent
find that admitting to the reality of the
unreal is detrimental to their prestige.
—LYDIA CABRERA

In December 1991, a few months after the death of Lydia Cabrera, I visited the Library of Congress in Washington, DC,
to leaf through *Cuba y América*,[1] the magazine edited by Don

---

DF-N: This introduction, translated and edited by David Font-Navarrete, is
adapted from Castellanos's introductory essay to *Páginas sueltas* (Cabrera 1994).
The author was Lydia Cabrera's student and friend, and a caretaker to Cabrera
and María Teresa de Rojas during their final years in Miami. Castellanos was
also the heir to Cabrera's archive and publishing estate, which she entrusted to
the University of Miami's Cuban Heritage Collection. Cf. Cabrera (1982a, 1982b);
Cámara (2015); Castellanos and Inclán (1988); Font-Navarrete (2022); Gutiérrez
(1991, 2008); Hiriart (1978); Hoffman-Jeep (2005); Maguire (2018); Marta and
Rangel (2019); Rodríguez-Mangual (2004); and Tsang (2019).

1   DF-N: Castellanos's original Spanish essay uses the verb *hojear* (to leaf
through), evoking the botanical-literary theme that resonates throughout

Raimundo Cabrera, and to read the columns and articles Lydia wrote in her childhood and adolescence. Since I did not know the exact range of publication dates for my search, the library staff regaled me with an impressive identification document and granted me access to the labyrinth of shelves in the John Adams Building. There, I found (and later copied) all of the columns titled "Nena en sociedad" (Nena in society). Reading them, I was able to verify that the original, merry spirit that animated the Lydia I knew had already flowered in these first articles. I decided to conduct a survey of newspapers and magazines to rescue the *páginas sueltas* (loose-leaf papers) of her life's work, which were sometimes "lost" in old Havana newspapers. The fundamental guideline I have tried to follow has been to include that which will serve to illuminate the life and, above all, the work of the author of *El Monte*.

When and where was Lydia Cabrera born?

She affirmed that she was born in Havana, at her home at Calle Galiano 79, on May 20, 1900. According to the *Diccionario de la literatura cubana* (Dictionary of Cuban literature) published in Castro's Cuba (1967), she was born in New York City on May 20, 1899. I have not been able to obtain her birth certificate, but I have seen one of her Cuban passports, which clearly states her birthplace: "La Habana, Cuba." If we add this piece of information to her own testimony—along with those of her childhood friends, such as María Elena Pérez de Bandujo, who still remembered it nearly a century later—we can conclude that Lydia came into the world in Havana, the same Havana she still recalled a few minutes before dying in Miami.[2]

Her exact date of birth is a more complicated matter. Was she really born in 1900? Were her birth certificate and passport the result of a clerk unaccustomed to writing dates in a new century? Or did her vanity or imagination—or both—consider it more prudent to belong to the new century, not the nineteenth? Whatever the case may be, Cabrera was *officially* born in Havana on May 20, 1899. If so, she was ninety-two years old when she died on September 19, 1991. Lydia was the youngest of eight children. The sibling who preceded her, Seida, was eight years older.

---

both *El Monte* (1954) and *Páginas sueltas* (loose-leaf pages) (1994). Although this sort of artfully nuanced language is usually lost in translation, the Spanish and English titles share some poetry. Throughout this introduction, quotations from *Cuba y América* were transcribed by Castellanos from archival copies at the Library of Congress. In several instances, partial bibliographical data (issues, titles of articles, and page numbers) will require further archival research. The Spanish-English translations are my own. Similarly, quotations attributed to Cabrera without parenthetical citation in this introduction (e.g., "watching a light go out") are based on personal communications with the author.

2   IC: After she was already in exile, Lydia applied for and received US citizenship.

In a conversation with Rosario Hiriart, Cabrera attributes her conception to the victory of the *mambises*:[3]

> I was born at a time when nobody could imagine it. I don't think it was in my family's plans. I must have been the result of the celebration that followed the triumph of the Cuban Revolution, or something like that. I was definitely a result of the triumphant jubilation. (Quoted in Hiriart 1978, 103)[4]

From the beginning, a powerful bond was established between Lydia and her father. Lydia seldom spoke of her mother, Elisa Bilbao Marcaida, except to say that she was always a good and discreet woman. I suspect she was not very affectionate with her youngest daughter, and that she probably felt intimidated or frightened by the girl's intelligence and unconventional nature.

The earliest document of Cabrera available to us was not in her own handwriting but rather copied by her cousin, Jorge de Castroverde. It is a letter from Lydia to Jorge and his brother Eloy, written sometime around 1910—we do not know the exact date—in which she dictates precise instructions regarding their behavior in the game they would play the following day.[5] Jorge and Eloy, along with other friends, were members of the "court" created by her imagination. In fact, the earliest surviving text by Lydia Cabrera is a letter from the "Duke D'Artagnan."

There is nothing unusual about Lydia, like so many children before and after her, trying to transform the magical world of her reading into a real-life, ludic reality. It is certainly interesting to note that her alter ego was D'Artagnan, a literary figure, and that the game should be played, in part, through writing (letters to the members of her "court") and the making of works of art ("coats of arms"), two endeavors that accompanied her throughout her whole life.

---

3   DF-N: The nineteenth-century anticolonial Cuban revolutionary forces were known as *mambí* (singular) or *mambises* (plural).

4   DF-N: The idiomatic phrase *el triunfo de la revolución cubana* (the triumph of the Cuban revolution) most often refers to the 1959 revolution led by Fidel Castro. Here, Cabrera turns the phrase, using it to refer to the Cuban War of Independence (1895–98) against Spanish colonial rule; she thereby rhetorically undermines the notion that the 1959 revolution, which she detested, was a singular or defining "triumph."

5   IC: This letter is archived in the Lydia Cabrera Papers in the Cuban Heritage Collection at the University of Miami Libraries.

Cuba y América (1913–1916)

D'Artagnan grew up, and a fascination with literature made her dream of a change in profession. She decided to transform herself from a musketeer to a journalist. Haven't many children tried to do so? Nonetheless, circumstances almost always limit them to homemade productions on one or two little sheets of paper circulated within a family. But Lydia could count on her father, who owned a magazine, *Cuba y América*, and was willing to please his youngest daughter in most things. The game became a reality, and in 1913, at fourteen years of age, Cabrera published her first article as a journalist. The column was titled "Nena en Sociedad (En vez de la crónica social)."[6] For nearly three years, until May 1916, she wrote some very peculiar reviews, sheltered by the strictest anonymity.[7]

She begins the first column by explaining that Señor Cabrera has put her in charge of a society column, and she continues by praising her father without, of course, revealing their familial bond. She accepts the offer, she says, "because a man like that, who smiles and knows how to say things a certain way, is difficult to resist." Beginning with this article, the humor and irony that characterize her entire body of literary work are conspicuous:

> I will write in each issue of *Cuba y América* what I know about Havana's social life. Having said that, these pages will only include episodes and incidents in that life that have occurred before my own eyes. Nothing more than what I witnessed with my own eyes, because the rest, no matter how important it might be, will be impossible to narrate, because I do not possess the enviable gift of obiquity [*sic*] that allows the masters of the genre to attend a dozen social events celebrated simultaneously. Forgive the defects of my humble beginnings.

From the beginning, Lydia used her column to upbraid an official indifference to culture and literature. In April 1914, when she had not yet turned fifteen, she reviewed the festivities in honor of Gertrudis Gómez de Avellaneda that had been celebrated at the Teatro Payret on March 21–23. Cabrera deplored the absence of government dignitaries at the event:

---

6   DF-N: The title of Cabrera's column "Nena en Sociedad (En vez de la crónica social)" might be translated as "Nena [or Girl] in [High] Society (Instead of the society pages)." The title employs the same sensibility—ambiguous, ornately complex—that informed her densely layered title and subtitles of *El monte* a half century later (1954).

7   IC: As an adult, Lydia admitted to having been the author of "Nena en Sociedad." See also Cacchione (1988).

Where are our government officials who are always so lavish in their calls for public spirit and civility? . . . They certainly know Gertrudis Gómez de Avellaneda, because the government voted to approve funds for these celebrations.

It was the beginning of the presidency of Mario García Menocal, who assumed the office in May 1913, and Don Raimundo Cabrera was a leader of the opposing political party.

Beginning in the first months of 1915, the style of "Nena en Sociedad" began to change. Little by little, the young woman matured and distanced herself a bit from the profusion of social events and the saccharine prose of her early days. In July 1915, her primary concern was the heat! There were no weddings "because nobody can think about getting married in summer." The engagements would arrive in the fall. And, she warned, with a bit of malice, "I will save my column's wealth of adjectives until then." As time went on, the articles by "Nena" became increasingly original and more personal.

For anyone who doubts that the young writer was laughing to herself about the genre she was cultivating, here is the apotheosis of her sardonic spirit: in September 1915, she wrote a review of herself. Don Raimundo was preparing to travel to the United States on vacation. Along with his wife and his children Raulín and Seida, he was accompanied by Lydia,

the intelligent, diligent and witty Lydia, she of the special vocation for study, who received such harsh treatment and a failing grade from Doctor Eduardo Desvernine at the Instituto de Segunda Enseñanza de la Habana as a reward for her interest and selflessness, and who has now abandoned academic studies forever so as not to be subjected to the judgment of pedagogically unsound and inquisitorial courts.

Cabrera recounted the episode to Hiriart (1978, 125). The professor was one of her father's political enemies. When the young student responded orally to the third question, the examiner interrupted her in an impolite way and she was upset. Out of six questions, she failed to answer two of them, and he, ipso facto, flunked her. Don Raimundo, who was present, left the hall indignant. Orestes Ferrara challenged the teacher to a duel. Apparently no blood was shed. Lydia, referring to the incident in *Cuba y América*, used her sharp pen to obtain the satisfaction denied Ferrara with the sending of his seconds.

It is true that the twenty-seven columns of "Nena en Sociedad" lack literary merit. Nonetheless, they are essential to understanding the process that led a little girl from a distinguished family to become the writer—and, above all, the storyteller—Lydia Cabrera. The lightheartedness, the irreverence, the irony, the humor: all of the characteristics that would nuance Cabrera's prose

Lydia Cabrera in Havana. May 16, 1925. The
dedication says, "To mom, with all my heart
and soul, from her youngest daughter Lydia."
Courtesy of the Cuban Heritage Collection
at the University of Miami, Lydia Cabrera
Papers, Box No. 37, Folder No. 1.

years later are already apparent in the girl who wrote "Nena en Sociedad." Up to a certain point, "Nena" is a symbol of who Cabrera always was: extremely individualistic, but without shrillness or exhibitionism; unconventional, yet never breaking away completely from her traditions or her social class.

Lydia took an interest in Oriental [Asian] art from a very young age. Years later it would be the subject of her studies at L'École du Louvre. In June 1916, *Cuba y América* published an old Japanese story—"Leyenda de la bella cortesana Otzumi y del monje Itsari" (Legend of the beautiful courtesan Otzumi and the monk Itsari), with illustrations by "L.C." Although the magazine does not identify the translator, the style and subject seem to indicate that Cabrera was responsible for the Spanish version. The following month she illustrated the cover of *Cuba y América* and published an article titled "El teatro japonés" (The Japanese theater). We can observe that she was aware of Japanese history and culture in those days, she was up to date on French theatrical magazines, and she quoted Voltaire and Thackeray.

At seventeen years of age, another very powerful interest consumed her attention: painting. She enjoyed pencils and brushes from a very young age, and the painter Leopoldo Romañach encouraged her passion. Behind her father's back, and with her sister Emma's help, she took courses at the Academia San Alejandro for several months, where she perfected her drawing and color technique and where she met Victor Manuel and Amelia Peláez.[8] She told Hiriart that she would practice "between two and five" in the afternoon (1978, 129). Angela Elvira Machado recalls that her hand served as the young painter's model so many times that Cabrera once exclaimed, exasperated, "Ay, I'm so tired of your hand!" Even as a child Lydia would dedicate herself to a task with tenacity and discipline. If her stint as a society columnist began as a game, the "game" continued, religiously, month after month, for nearly three years. And, once she had become an adult—in Paris, just as in Cuba, then later in exile—her interest in African cultures on the island endured, despite immense obstacles, for some sixty years.

Casa Alyds and the Convento de Santa Clara (1922–1923)

In April 1922, Cabrera exhibited her paintings for the first time at the Salón de Bellas Artes (Salon of Fine Arts) during an event sponsored by the Asociación

---

8   IC: According to Lydia, she attended the Academia San Alejandro in 1914 (Hiriart 1978, 129). Since many years passed between her early youth and her conversation with Hiriart, it is possible that she sometimes failed to remember the correct dates of some events (as we will see below, with reference to the Convento de Santa Clara). Based on records provided by the late Ángela Elvira Machado, I suspect that Lydia attended San Alejandro later—perhaps in 1915 or 1916.

Wifredo Lam. *The Jungle*, 1943. Gouache on paper mounted on canvas, 94-1/4 × 90-1/2 in. (239.4 × 229.9 cm).

de Pintores y Escultores (Association of Painters and Sculptors). In a review of the event, L. Gómez Wangüemert dedicated several laudatory paragraphs to four paintings by Lydia, emphasizing, above all, her originality:

> Lydia's sketches are surprising in their original and new way of solving problems outside all rules of color and form. In each particular instance, her intelligence searches for a solution that is appropriate to the moment, far from any academic rules. And it is worth noting that the novelty and interest in her paintings is due to that personal way of working. Her audacity leads her to deal with the most difficult themes with a simple approach to her medium which is frightening and disconcerting.

In "La procesión," she creates a powerful mystical ambience, serene and sweet, on a luminous yellow surface with white and purple nun-like touches. (1922)

One month later, on May 21, 1922, a full page in *Diario de la marina* was dedicated to five photographs of Lydia, including one of her at her easel, under the title, "Lydia Cabrera, la exquisita y genial artista" (Lydia Cabrera, the delightful and brilliant artist). Everything seemed to indicate that her artistic career was on the verge of taking off. But Cabrera would not exhibit in subsequent shows. In my view, she understood that she would need to overcome the limitations of insularity in order to fulfill her artistic ambitions, expanding her horizons in Europe. She would not be able to do so until 1927, but the year 1922 proved to be decisive in her personal, intellectual, and aesthetic development.

Aside from exhibiting her paintings at the Salón, Lydia launched a commercial business with Alicia Longoria de González that was, initially, dedicated to interior decorating and importing European decorative objects. She made three drawings herself to promote Casa Alyds, the name of the new business located at Calle Jovellar 45. She also wrote seventeen "advertisements," the first few of which were rather conventional, but they quickly became brief essays in which their author—just as in her work on "Nena"—tackled a wide array of topics, always in a light, charming style.

Other establishments of the time—El Encanto and Fin de Siglo, for example—included small stories about their merchandise or other current events in their advertisements, and the first advertisement for Casa Alyds follows this custom very closely. The "furniture dealer" highlights the quality of her products, which are made with Cuban wood, among the world's finest. In later advertisements, she tries to educate consumers regarding details of a style or reiterates warnings about shoddy work common to other shops. But these vignettes quickly become more personal. In some, she relates visits to the shop made by clients and friends. In one, she conducts a sui generis "interview" with her friend Lucía Victoria "Mimín" Bacardí and, in passing, she offers a disquisition on laughter. In a few ("En guardia," "La real gana," and "Margaritas a los cerdos"), she resorts—just as in her days as "Nena"—to social satire. Tackiness, social climbing, vulgarity, and bullying are slyly but severely chastised by Cabrera, who employs the genre that would seem to be the least suitable: advertising.

The most interesting advertisements are written in a narrative style featuring characters, dialogue, plot, and even some action. They are precursors to the stories Lydia would begin writing in the 1930s. Curiously, it is also possible to discern certain features in these advertisements that would later character-ize her Afro-Cuban tales, in which it is impossible to find a truly inanimate object and it is equally possible for a king, a frying pan, or a pair of underpants to dance to the music of the marvelous Guinea Hen. In an advertisement titled "Las maderas de Cuba preservan a los libros de las polillas" (Cuban wood protects books from termites), the books are prone to nervous exhaustion, and a copy of *Cecilia Valdés* is able to beg to "not let *her* come unbound." (The strategic, ambiguous use of the word "her" forces us to ask ourselves who, in fact, is calling out: the book, or Cecilia Valdés herself?)[9] The insomniac Doña Concepción, who opens her windows "to love and to the night," is as sensual and voluptuous as Soyán Dekín, whose hair turned—in a masterful story—into the silt of the Almendares River. Obviously, the advertisements for Casa Alyds are a far cry from the mature stories written later in Paris, but the seeds of those tales are there, in those small publications whose purpose had noth-ing to do with literature.

Casa Alyds arose with a very clear commercial purpose: Lydia wanted to study in Paris, but she did not want to become a burden on her family. With the earnings from the business, she was able to live in France for several years. But the owners of Alyds were also motivated by another goal: to educate and cultivate a more sensitive aesthetic spirit among Cubans.

Indeed, Lydia Cabrera and Alicia Longoria were motivated by educational concerns, which led them to begin documenting and publicizing works of art owned by prominent Havana families. In 1922, Lydia participated in the es-tablishment of the Asociación Cubana de Arte Retrospectivo.[10] According to its bylaws, the association's purpose was to "celebrate an annual Exhibition of works constituting a Cuban art tradition, such as fans, lace, embroidery, fab-ric, clothing, jewelry, furniture, etc." Cabrera writes that the aesthetic values of a people should not be improvised. It is necessary to cultivate a love of the na-tion's arts and artisanal traditions. "It is a love for the past and an understanding of the past that prepares us and enables us to love and understand the present." According to Cabrera, in the first decades of Cuba's republic, the "ruling class," contaminated by an "unfortunate intellectual blindness," neglected the pres-ervation of what is native and only looked to what is foreign. Wardrobes and headboards made from caoba wood were being replaced by en suite "furniture sets" from the United States in which all of the pieces were perfectly matched. But some women wished "to provide an example of civic spirit" by founding

---

9   DF-N: Cabrera employs the same sort of deliberate, generative grammatical ambiguity throughout *El Monte*.

10   DF-N: The name translates literally as the Cuban Association for Retrospective Art, with "Ret-rospective" meaning antique or historical art.

groups to conserve, preserve, and protect objects and buildings threatened by "the savagery of some commercial enterprises or a government's culpable negligence."[11]

The establishment of the Asociación Cubana de Arte Retrospectivo coincided with another activity in Havana. Nuns from the Order of Santa Clara had moved to a new residence and left the Convent of Santa Clara de Asís unoccupied. The monastery's first stone had been laid in 1638, and nuns began living there in 1644 (Conde de Rivero, 1922). A small section of the old city of Havana was eventually surrounded by the convent's walls, an important testament to the country's oldest architecture. But the buildings were in poor condition, and it was decided they would be demolished to make way for "progress." As a sort of goodbye (and, perhaps for a few sponsors, a rescue attempt), a commercial exhibition was organized on the convent grounds. Important Cuban and foreign businesses would display their products. The founders of the association—especially Cabrera and Longoria—decided to take advantage of the opportunity to arrange the exhibit of fans in a section of the Santa Clara convent.

The scope of the project grew little by little. On October 14, *Diario de la marina* announced, "The sleeping city will awaken." According to a press release, a large art exhibition would be presented, in parallel to the industrial exhibition, under the title *La Habana Antigua*.[12] The organizing committee consisted of Cabrera and Longoria. For several months, Lydia dedicated herself completely to the venture, wrote articles (both signed and anonymous), and planned an effective publicity campaign. On November 8, photographs of the famous "treasure" appeared in *Diario de la marina* with the following explanation: "We are publishing a photograph of the *botijas* found yesterday next to the Casa del Marino. The photograph was taken by our colleague Mr. Buendía. Since it is supposed that treasures are buried around that house, which is known to have been the residence of a fearsome pirate of his era, investigations are ongoing."

Cabrera's motivation to organize the exhibition was driven by three basic aims: first, to showcase the artistic value of the architectural complex and ensure its preservation; second, to encourage members of the social elites to share their art collections by exhibiting them for the public; and, third, to proclaim the work of the Condesa de Merlín, whom Lydia and her father

11   IC: The bylaws were published in *Diario de la marina*, June 16, 1922. The article is attributed to Cabrera and reproduced in *Páginas sueltas* (1994).

12   DF-N: The evocative title *La Habana Antigua* could be translated as "Old Havana," "Antique Havana," "Historical Havana," or "Old-Fashioned Havana."

admired, and who had lived at the convent during her childhood.[13] The exhibition *La Habana Antigua*, which opened on November 23, 1922, was a categorical success. Although Casa Alyds already existed, the exhibition at the Santa Clara convent established a public association between Cabrera and antiques, as well as demonstrating her knowledge and taste in furniture and classic decor. From then on, preservation of her country's artistic legacy was a constant, tenacious concern for her, as we will see.

First Ethnographic Notes (1930)

From the middle of 1923 until she left for Paris in 1927, Cabrera removed herself completely from public life and her name rarely appeared in the Havana press. In one of these rare instances, she sent a letter to Jorge Mañach in support of a tribute to the painter Romañach, which was reproduced in *Diario de la marina* on March 18, 1924. In his "Comment," Mañach describes Cabrera as "the intense chatelaine of an ivory castle, who comes to her aesthetic shutter only on rare and noble occasions." This withdrawal might be attributed to the fact that the death of her father, on May 21, 1923,[14] was a terrible blow for Lydia. Don Raimundo suffered from heart disease and, some months before his death, he was given a national tribute. Lydia, who was not a fan of public flattery, was upset by the theatricality and physical toll it imposed on her sick father.[15] The writer remembered her father's death until her own last days: "Looking in his eyes, it was like watching a light go out."

Cabrera dedicated the four years preceding her departure to France almost exclusively to Casa Alyds and planning the European trip for which she

---

13 IC: For several days beginning on November 4, 1922, *Diario de la marina* began publishing reports regarding the Condesa de Merlín signed "Un Incógnito" (Anonymous). I suspect the anonymous character is none other than Cabrera. The reports promote the idea that Merlín's works, titled "Mis doce primeros años" (My first twelve years) and "Sor Inés" (Sister Inés), should be edited and published. This project was immediately undertaken by Raimundo Cabrera and Nicolás Rivero, and only a few days later—on November 24—the publications were already printed and stocked for sale at the Librería Cervantes bookstore.

14 IC: Cabrera told Hiriart that her father died on March 21 (Hiriart 1978, 141). In fact, Don Raimundo died May 21, 1923, the day after Lydia's birthday. See, for example, *Diario de la marina* (1923b).

15 IC: See Hiriart (1978, 141). Lydia was right to worry about the effects of the event on her father's health. For example, the "Comité de propaganda" published reports in the daily news like the one which appeared in the February 9, 1923, issue of *Diario de la marina*, which read, "time is dumping a few, final shovelfuls of Life's dirt on this distinguished man" (los años están echando sobre este hombre benemérito las últimas paletadas de polvo de la Vida) (1923a). Since Don Raimundo read the newspapers, he must have been disturbed by such indiscretion.

yearned. Every once in a while, she accompanied her brother-in-law Fernando Ortiz to attend an Abakuá procession, which is how Alejo Carpentier remembered her in 1936: "Sometime around 1927, when I was going around hunting documents for my book *Ecue-Yamba-ó*, I remember running into Lydia Cabrera at a *ñáñigo 'juramento'* [swearing-in, initiation] being celebrated in the middle of a forest near Marianao" (Carpentier 1936, 40). In January 1923, together with her niece Isis Ortiz Cabrera, Lydia attended the inaugural session of the Sociedad del Folk-Lore Cubano (Cuban Folklore Society), which was presided by Fernando Ortiz. The meeting was attended by Alfredo Aguayo, Emilio Roig de Leuchsenring, Carolina Poncet, José María Chacón y Calvo, Joaquín Llaverías, Eduardo Sánchez de Fuentes, and many other intellectuals and artists. Although Lydia had not yet discovered her vocation for the study of Afro-Cuban religions, her presence at these events is symptomatic of a certain curiosity about the popular culture of her country. After all, that interest ran in the family: Fernando Ortiz was her brother-in-law, and her brother Ramiro had written and delivered conference presentations on the popular music of Cuba (e.g., R. Cabrera 1922).

In 1926, she spent a season in Madrid, where she struck up a close friendship with Federico García Lorca. And in 1927, she finally established herself in Paris, in a flat near the Place du Tertre in the Montmartre district. For several years, she studied Oriental [Asian] art at L'École du Louvre.[16] She also enrolled in Ferdinand Léger's Academie Contemporaine, where she took classes with the Russian painter Alexandra Exter, who would become a friend and maternal protector for Cabrera.[17]

Lydia had met Teresa de la Parra in Havana in 1924. Their friendship was rekindled in Paris in 1927, and it lasted until Parra's death in Madrid in 1936.[18] During her first years in Paris, Lydia returned to Havana several times to visit her mother. In 1930 she spent a season in Cuba and established her first contacts with her informants: Lolita "La Cabezona," José de Calazán Herrera (Bangoché), Calixta Morales (Oddedei), Teresa Muñoz (Omi Tomi),

---

16 IC: L'École du Louvre lost all documentation of its students during World War II. Therefore, I have been unable to find a copy of Cabrera's records or thesis. I am grateful to Isabel Malowany, who kindly assisted this research.

17 IC: See Blanc (1988). The influence of Exter and Léger's constructivism on Cabrera's painting can be observed, primarily, in the illustrated manuscript of Francis de Miomandre's *Theophanie* (1933), now in the University of Miami's Cuban Heritage Collection.

18 DF-N: According to the biographical timeline offered here by Castellanos, Cabrera and Parra had an intense relationship that lasted nine years (1927–36). During those years, Cabrera was between twenty-seven and thirty-five years of age, while Parra was between thirty-eight and forty-six. The impact of Parra's untimely death is not discussed in detail here, presumably to avoid dwelling on a very intimate and painful subject.

and others. Three primary factors drove Lydia to cultivate her interest in *lo negro*. First, as she always insisted, her studies of Oriental [Asian] art led her to ask herself how much *lo africano* had penetrated the nation's soul—and let's not forget that she had already witnessed public Abakuá rituals. Second, Africa was a powerful influence on European art and literature between the two world wars, precisely when Lydia was living in Europe. Many years later, in exile, she wrote,

> This discovery of Africa also opened new horizons for aesthetic understanding. In the first two decades of our century, before and after World War I, artists like Derain, Matisse, Vlaminck, Modigliani, Juan Gris, Picasso, Braque, dazzled by African masks, and one poet, Guillaume Apollinaire, contributed to ascribing top ranking among the world's art to sculpture they could no longer call "savage."
>
> Africa also influenced literature—in surrealism, which insisted on removing all the barriers of convention—once the immense wealth of its oral literature became known, along with its folklore, which was among the world's richest.[19]

In Paris, Lydia attended exhibitions of African art, and she could not escape the attraction to the "primitive" and "exotic" that permeated the intellectual environment of the time. Finally, the influence of Teresa de la Parra was decisive in Lydia's definitive orientation toward literature and Black culture.

Teresa de la Parra was also attracted to popular culture and individuals from humble backgrounds, like the character Vicente Cochoco in her story "Memorias de Mamá Blanca." Getting close to Black Cubans in 1930 in order to learn something from them—especially details regarding their religion, which many considered to be mere superstition or *brujería* (witchcraft, sorcery)— was not viewed favorably by Havana's high society. The understanding and support Cabrera received from Parra, finding an interlocutor in whom she could confide her enthusiasm and details of her search, defined her development as a researcher.

Her first ethnographic notes reveal her method, the approach Lydia always followed to obtain information. Her first index cards are less concerned with the formal aspects of Afro-Cuban religions than with the *individuals* who practice it. And that is why the style of these initial notes is almost narrative. (From the beginning, ethnography and storytelling are intimately entwined in her.) A clear protagonist—Calixta Morales—appears, along with a series of

19 IC: See "La influencia africana en el pueblo de Cuba" in *Páginas sueltas* (Cabrera 1994, 541–50).

secondary characters: Herrera, Teresa Muñoz, Leonorcita Armenteros . . . At first, Calixta seems suspicious and reluctant, until Lydia, the white "girl," sits at a table to share lunch with her and Calazán at Omi Tomi's home.

For Cabrera, who lacked professional training in ethnology, the scientific method of participant observation came spontaneously, almost intuitively. If her visits to Pogolotti were a cause for consternation among the white Cubans around her, they certainly provoked surprise among the neighborhood's Black residents. An index card about Calixta reads,

> Regarding her friendship with me: "At a wake, [they said] 'Now that you're with your white woman, and one from up high, you act like you don't know us anymore.' I've always been around white people, and not dirty whites. People are envious. . . . Today, when I'm sad, what shade of color am I? Word has spread all over Pogolotti . . . that an upper-class white woman visits me."

In 1930, then, in the home of Teresa Muñoz, Cabrera's *El Monte* and *Cuentos negros de Cuba* began to take shape.

Calixta Morales's "birthday throne" is the altar before which Sanune regained consciousness in "Bregantino Bregantín," the first of *Cuentos negros*. Let us compare the descriptions. The ethnographic note on an index card reads,

> At night, the altar is already set up. Two wildcat pelts embroidered with cowrie shells. On the floor, a great cooking pot filled with rice and beans and popcorn. Two lit candles. The altar is also saluted by touching the ground with your hand and kissing your fingertips. . . . The small room smelled of guayaba [guava].

And in "Bregantino Bregantín" we read,

> Sanune touched the ground and kissed it on her fingertips; prostrated around the feet of those men, she lost consciousness. . . . When she opened her eyes, she was in a room surrounded by the night; the scent of warm greenery and Guayaba fruit hung thick in the air . . . before an altar, which consisted of two branches of Álamo, freshly cut, leaning against the wall, and two wildcat pelts. On the ground, several covered soup tureens, a horseshoe, two big cooking pots of rice, beans, and popcorn. (Cabrera 1940, 22)[20]

---

20 DF-N: The translations here are my own. Cf. the English translation by J. Alberto Hernandez-Chiroldes and Lauren Yoder in *Afro-Cuban Tales* (Cabrera 2005).

Lydia Cabrera was at once an ethnologist, storyteller, and painter. And these three aspects of her work animate her *entire* body of work. The painter imprints numerous visual details on her ethnography and stories, adding light and color to the environments she describes. The storyteller incorporates many tales into a tome like *El Monte*, making its structure twist around a single, central thread: nature, and—more specifically—the magical Afro-Cuban world of plants. The storyteller benefits from the profound understanding of the rituals and practices acquired through informal research sessions.

By the time Cabrera returned to Europe after her vacations in Cuba during 1930, her direction was clearly defined. She then began writing her first *Cuentos negros*, which would be published in a French translation in 1936, then later in their original Spanish in 1940. In a letter from Teresa de la Parra dated 1931, we read, "Your story about the tortoise is beautiful! Do you know the music? Can you sing it to me when I see you?" (Hiriart 1978, 134). In another, sent from Leysin, Switzerland, on May 1, 1933, Parra writes,

> Cabrita, your story about the silt in the Almendares river is *gorgeous*. The other one is very charming, but that one about the *mulata* makes me recall La Argentina's *marvelous* dances.[21] The popular is stylized with real skill. The image of the *mulata* sinking into the circles of water in your story reminds me of the dance embroidering the music, the intimate harmony of the two rhythms. The call to the mother is quite evocative, and it paints a vivid portrait of anguish. Does it have music? I enjoyed the story very much, and it is different from the other ones. You realize they have an extraordinary variety? I imagine them in a handsome book. (You have enough material for several volumes.) What happened to the one you started on the Richmond and read to me in fragments? I want to *reread* it. I congratulate you on today's and *all* of them. You are a small, portable church organ: you have such a huge range!
>
> You are a Cabra *harmonium*.

The 1930 trip to Havana ended up defining the Cuban writer's future agenda. She collected data, stories, and music, and she established close relationships with her first informants. As to the songs we find frequently in her stories, Lydia took them directly from her Black informants' mouths, and sang them often until her dying day. She managed to collect so many that she apparently intended to transcribe them in a book she never published, but

---

21 IC: See Hiriart (1978, 174). Parra is referring to the dancer Antonia Mercé, La Argentina. Cf. "La Vase d'Almendares" (in Cabrera 1936), "El limo de almendares" (in Cabrera 1940), and "The Green Mud of the Almendares" (in Cabrera 2005).

which she titled *Barril-agua (Colección de canciones de cuentos afro-cubanos)*, for which she registered the author's rights on July 1, 1930.[22] Later, I will refer to the creation of *El Monte* in some detail; it is worth noting here that its composition also seems to have begun in Europe, although it would only see the light of day in Havana many years later, in 1954. As Parra's diary notes in an entry from January 24, 1936, "Lydia is working in earnest all afternoon on her ethnology book" (1982, 465).

Lydia Cabrera and Wifredo Lam (1942–1946)

Four years after her return to Cuba, Lydia Cabrera had her first encounter with Wifredo Lam in Havana.[23] The relationship between these two artists had important consequences for both of them, and especially Lam. Despite enormous differences (in race, social class, and political inclination) that separated the painter from the writer, a profound affection grew between them. They were both, to use Lydia's word, *desterrados* (exiles) from Paris. She had lived ten intellectually and emotionally intense years in the French capital.

Lam had left Cuba eighteen years earlier, in 1923, bound for Madrid. He spent three lean years in France, but that is where his painting achieved the level of maturity and recognition that had eluded him up to that point. He established contact with Pablo Picasso, and his first Parisian paintings display a marked influence from Henri Matisse and the cubists. Indeed, it was difficult for him to liberate himself from the stigma of Picasso's influence. For example, a 1942 article in *Art Digest*—just before Lam created *La Jungla*—deplored what it called "the Picassolamming reverence" in the Cuban painter's work (quoted in Stokes Sims 1992, 72–73).

In France, Lam also penetrated the orbit of the surrealists, and the synthesis of cubism and surrealism turned out to be decisive in the development of his visual language. Events in Europe forced many intellectuals and artists to

---

22 IC: The document—number 1808 in the *Registro General de la Secretaría de Agricultura, Comercio y Trabajo de la República de Cuba*—was signed by the chief registrar, Luis O. Rodríguez. It was presented at 10:05 a.m. on July 1, 1930. The original is archived in the Lydia Cabrera Papers at the Cuban Heritage Collection. In response to a question from Rosario Hiriart regarding the music we frequently find in her stories, Lydia explains,

> I had written down the music [lyrics] from all the songs, not just the ones in the stories, but many, many more. And I still remember many, but they stayed in Cuba and I don't have the slightest idea who might have them. (Quoted in Hiriart 1978, 84)

23 DF-N: On Lam and Cabrera, see Cernuschi (2019), Cuervo Hewitt (2007), Kubayanda (2002), Museum of Modern Art (n.d.), and Sotheby's (2020).

leave France. Lam and his partner, Helena Holzer, left Paris for Martinique with a group of friends that included André Bretón, a leader in the surrealist movement. In Marseille, Lam worked on the beautiful illustrations for Bretón's *Fata morgana*.[24] Finally arriving in Cuba after a long and perilous journey, the painter found that he needed to begin his life all over again, since he had lost everything, including his paintings, during his escape. The initial encounter with Cabrera took place in the midst of that initial confusion. Cabrera immediately recognized her compatriot's enormous talent, and she and María Teresa de Rojas helped him find adequate lodging and offered economic support.

In 1942, Cabrera wrote an article in *Diario de la marina* in which she introduced Lam to the Cuban public. The painter and Helena were frequent dinner guests at La Quinta San José, the historic home Cabrera shared with María Teresa de Rojas in the Marianao neighborhood of Havana [see below]. For two years, Helena assisted María Teresa de Rojas in the transcription of documents from the Archivo de Protocolos de La Habana (Archive of Protocols of Havana) (Rojas 1947). Meanwhile, Cabrera and Lam exchanged ideas and attended Afro-Cuban rituals. She was writing *El Monte*, a very peculiar ethnography whose North Star is the sacredness of the vegetal world.

For Lam, the return to Cuba was an encounter with his roots: the light, the plants, the colors, and the magic of his country. He began painting like never before. And that is how Cabrera describes him in a second article written in 1944:

> The two years of exile in Cuba . . . have been extremely beneficial, possibly decisive, in the work of Wifredo Lam. . . .
>
> Wifredo Lam, on his own in the land "whose silt he was made from," has been able to collect himself and express himself with absolute freedom. Returned to the country where he was born, this land of his awakens new aesthetic concerns: the warm music of its harmony continually arouses new problems which throb in his consciousness, demanding an immediate response. And the light of his home country suddenly begins shining in his paintings: a poet, who is also a naturally gifted painter, dreams of the tropics in dazzling tropical light. Black, ancestral, millenarian deities,

24 IC: Lam's work for Breton's *Fata morgana* comprises six drawings in *tinta china* (India ink). One drawing from Lam's time in Marseille, clearly dated 1941, was given to Cabrera and María Teresa de Rojas by Lam and Holzer. It now belongs to the Lowe Art Museum at the University of Miami. The Lowe loaned it for an exhibit of works on paper by Lam that took place in Barcelona from January 21 to March 21, 1993. The drawing is reproduced on page 107 of the catalog; see Lam (1992).

withdrawn in the soft and enveloping light of Europe, obsessed him there, but here they appear *tangible* in their true light, resplendent in perennial summer, and in every instant, in every corner of the landscape, in every tree-god, in each fabulous leaf of his garden in Buen Retiro, which has also begun flowering on his canvases.[25]

In 1943 Cabrera and Lam collaborated on a Spanish edition of poems by Aimé Césaire titled *Retorno al país natal* (Return to the native land).[26] Helena Holzer Benítez recalls that the Martinican poet sent them a copy of the work with a request that Helena translate it to Spanish. Although she spoke the language well, Helena thought a poetic text of such magnitude was beyond her abilities, so she asked Lydia to translate it (Herzberg 1992, 50–51n50). Lam designed the cover and created drawings to illustrate the text. This collaboration is symbolic of the personal circumstances surrounding both Cabrera and Lam. Both of them, like Césaire, had returned to their home country to confront their own identity. It must have been a traumatic period of adjustment for both of them. Lam returned poor, just as his career was beginning to take off in Europe, where he belonged to a group of intellectuals and artists among whom his race and nationality were incidental. In Cuba, he found himself isolated, once again in the midst of a racist society (*un medio social pigmentocrático*) in which people of color were not necessarily treated as equals, no matter how talented they might be. He arrived with a white woman—without yet having married her. Old prejudices crept up on him again after eighteen years of amnesty in the old continent.

The return must have been just as difficult for Cabrera—in fact, it is no coincidence that she uses the word "destierro" (exile) to describe it. Clearly she did not suffer the sort of discrimination and rejection faced by Lam, but she did experience severe hardship and problems, since she found herself in an environment that was not sympathetic to her research projects and lifestyle. Her mother had died in 1932 and, subsequently, the old family home no longer existed. Her inheritance had been mismanaged in Cuba and vanished, which placed her in a precarious state of dependency and created serious tensions within the family. Her sister Seida had taken her in, but Seida's intense social life and constant visitors disturbed Lydia and prevented her from writing. Moreover, her desire to study Black people's religions was neither understood nor accepted. If she had, as in the past, spent a few months visiting Pogolotti

---

25 IC: Emphasis in the original. "Wifredo Lam," published in *Diario de la marina*, January 30, 1944. Reproduced in *Páginas Sueltas* (Cabrera 1994).

26 DF-N: Originally published in French as *Cahier d'un retour au pays natal* ([1939] 1943, [1939] 2013). See also Maguire (2013).

and compiling information about *brujería*, it might have been tolerated, with an indulgent smile, as *cosas de Lydia*—the eccentricities or poor manners of a spoiled child. But for a woman of her class and age to try to treat visiting humble Black people as an important project, regularly sharing meals with them, was beyond the acceptable limits of eccentricity. Cabrera was fortunate enough to very quickly find refuge and support with María Teresa de Rojas and her widowed mother, Doña Teresa García de Lomas. Lam found spiritual shelter in his painting, and in the friendship of a reduced group of artists and intellectuals.

In 1942, Cabrera and Lam were working on the exact same subject: the magic of *el monte*, the sacred realm of orishas and duendes.[27] One of them described it in the pages of what would become an ethnographic treatise, while the other expressed it on canvas and paper. As Julia Herzberg explains, "Cabrera and Lam shared many experiences during those six years, beginning in early 1942, when they would attend *bembés* [ritual celebrations] together in Pogolotti and Regla" (1992, 39). Critics now accept that many of the titles of Wifredo Lam's paintings were provided by Lydia Cabrera. According to Helena Holzer Benítez, "Cabrera would suggest titles because the images in the paintings brought to mind specific experiences she had documented" (Stokes Sims 1992, 73).

After *La Jungla* (1942–43)—was this painting once known as *La Manigua* and the word *jungla* (jungle), so seldom used in Cuba, merely a translation from English or French?—Lam decided to make another painting along similar lines as a gift for Cabrera. Based on her suggestion, he included the small figures of *chicherekues*, the magical dolls of the Lucumí, which have practically disappeared from the popular imagination. Although she was not a *creyente* (believer, devotee), the oracles had determined that Lydia was a daughter of Yemaya, the aquatic goddess par excellence, so the hair of one of the painting's central figures transforms itself into two streams of water. The painting was titled *Omi Obini*.[28] Even the initial sketch made in the painter's small notebook was dedicated to his friend. The painting was one of the sixteen in Lam's first exhibition in Cuba, which took place at the Lyceum on April 11–19, 1946.

27   IC: Although Cabrera did not publish *El Monte* until 1954, we know it was composed very slowly, since an initial version was published in 1947 in *La revista bimestre cubana*. See "Eggüe o Vichichi Finda," in *Páginas sueltas* (1994).

28   DF-N: The painting's Lucumí title translates most clearly into English as "Water Woman." Translating the title more literally, according to the grammatical conventions of Lucumí and Yoruba, *omi* would be a possessive adjective of *obini* (analogous to *obirin, obinrin,* etc.)—i.e., "Woman's Water," "Water of Woman," or "Woman Water."

(*Left*) Wifredo Lam. *Omi Obini*, 1943. Oil on canvas, 72 × 49 in. (182.9 × 124.5 cm).

(*Above*) Wifredo Lam. Untitled sketch for Lydia Cabrera ("Para mi amiga"), 1982. Charcoal on paper, 19-1/8 × 12-5/8 in. (48.6 × 32.1 cm). The dedication reads, "For my friend Lydia Cabrera. Paris 9 1982." Courtesy of Lowe Art Museum. © 2022 Artists Rights Society (ARS), New York / ADAGP, Paris.

The painting's title and ownership were clearly identified in the exhibition's catalog ("Prop. Lydia Cabrera. Habana").

When Cabrera left Cuba again in 1960, *Omi Obini* remained, hanging on one of the walls of La Quinta San José. We have learned that it had mysteriously arrived in the United States and formed part of a private collection for many years. It was sold to a European gallery not too long ago. Lydia died without knowing where her "lost Jungle" ended up, and she often lamented its absence.[29]

---

29 DF-N: The story of the painting Lam made for Cabrera is still unfolding. On June 29, 2020, in the midst of the COVID-19 pandemic, *Omi Obini* was sold at an auction by Sotheby's for \ US$9,603,800\. Sotheby's record of the painting's provenance names Cabrera as the first owner; the second owner is identified as Osuna Art, a Washington, DC, gallery owned by Cuban-born

Time and distance conspired so that Cabrera and Lam never saw each other again. Every once in a while, she and María Teresa de Rojas (or Titina, as she was affectionately known), would receive a catalog from a European exhibition or a small drawing in the mail. Of course, the Cuban revolution opened an ideological abyss between the two friends. Lam defended the revolutionary cause, and Lydia and Titina embarked on the path of exile in 1960. Yet, in the modest apartments of their *destierro*, they were always accompanied by Lam's work: seventeen drawings, many of them with dedications, and a beautiful portrait of Titina, pale and remote, sitting in a rattan rocking chair.[30] (Minutes after her death, Titina's profile acquired, almost miraculously, the exact same facial expression captured in Lam's portrait of her.) In 1982, already sick, Lam decided to bid Cabrera farewell. He sent her a sketch he had drawn in charcoal, with an unsteady hand, showing a bird-woman with an Elegua in her hand. Beneath the figure, he wrote, "For my friend Lydia Cabrera, Paris 9 1982, Wilfredo Lam." He died a couple of months later.

From La Quinta San José (1945–1954)

In 1937, following the death of Teresa de la Parra the previous year and facing the uncertainty of events unfolding in Europe, Lydia Cabrera returned to Cuba.[31] When she arrived, she wanted to continue the work she had begun seven years earlier, which had allowed her to publish her first collection of stories in Paris, in a translation by Francis de Miomandre. The reception was extremely warm, and the echoes from Paris even reached Cuba by way of a

---

Ramón Osuna, who died in 2019. Galerie H. Odermatt-Ph. Cazeau in Paris subsequently acquired the painting from Osuna at an unspecified date, then auctioned it through Sotheby's in 2020. The latest buyer has not been publicly identified yet. In a bitter irony, Sotheby's web page promoting the auction is punctuated by Cabrera's loving description of the painting that was stolen from her:

> She is the river, Omí Obiní, woman of water, she is the Lady of Fresh Waters who fertilizes the earth and dances, dispensing life. She slips and slides among the reeds, alongside the flanks of the bodies that rock and sway, transported by the miraculous rhythm of the wave; and her shining arms and knowing hips undulate in time with the water. Her long wake is frothy; the merry water breaks, boils, and splashes back against her starched petticoats. Her body gleams with springs and currents. (Sotheby's 2020)

30 ic: All of these works now belong to the Lowe Art Museum at the University of Miami.

31 ic: According to Lydia, she returned to Cuba in 1938, but her story "Susundamba" (which later became part of *Por qué*) was originally published in a 1938 issue of *Estudios afrocubanos*. At the end, the date and location where she finished the story are clearly written: "San José de los Maizales, August 1937."

Lydia Cabrera and Titina in the courtyard of the Quinta San José. Courtesy of the Cuban Heritage Collection at the University of Miami, Lydia Cabrera Papers, Box No. 40, Folder No. 9.

review by Alejo Carpentier in *Carteles*, which remains one of the most penetrating analyses ever written about that work.

As I have already noted, once she disembarked in Havana, Lydia first stayed with her sister Seida, and later moved to the home of María Teresa de Rojas and her mother, Doña Teresa García de Lomas. As part of an inheritance from her first husband, who was a member of the Pedroso family, Doña Teresa had received a large old colonial home in the Marianao neighborhood. La Quinta San José (or San José de los Maizales, as Lydia referred to it in the first years) had been constructed in the eighteenth century as a country home for the mayor of Havana, Don Mateo Pedroso y Florencia. Over the years it underwent various modifications. Shortly before she died, María Teresa Rojas shared a few details about La Quinta with me. The tower and lower structure were part of the original construction. In the nineteenth century another section was added, and the facade was subjected to several transformations throughout the century. When Lydia arrived in Cuba, the house was in poor condition. She and Titina decided to restore it and make it their permanent residence. Thus, Lydia picked up her old passion for preserving buildings and collecting and documenting antiquities. Moreover, the location turned out to be very convenient for her fieldwork, since only one street separated the Quinta

San José from the neighborhood of Pogolotti, where she had established her first contacts with elderly Blacks in 1930.

Lydia and Titina attacked the work of reconstruction and decoration enthusiastically. They replaced destroyed doors with others salvaged from mansions being demolished in Havana. They repaired the roof of the lean-to in the garden with antique wood. The coffered ceiling from the Santo Domingo convent, which would later become the headquarters for the University of Havana, was saved from demolition and installed in the tower. They repaired the original iron gates and fences, and they installed others from the ancient Havana jail. Fortunately, the magnificent red, yellow, white, and blue stained glass windows had been preserved. They decorated the hallways with colonial-era tiles, and the iron lantern at the entrance was brought from the main residence of Don Mateo Pedroso on Calle Cuba 64, which also belonged to Titina and her mother. Finally, they furnished La Quinta with carefully chosen items. Despite being a true museum of antiques and craftwork, photographs show an inviting creole interior, as well as a marvelous informal courtyard.

Once the restoration was completed, Doña Teresa, Lydia, Titina, and Julia García de Lomas—an orphaned cousin of Titina's—abandoned the centrally located neighborhood of Vedado and went to live at La Quinta San José. The quinta's tranquility proved beneficial to both Lydia and Titina. From the 1940s until their 1960 departure into exile, Titina dedicated herself, with Benedictine patience, to the task of photographing, transcribing, and publishing the documents from the Archivos de Protocolos de La Habana. The condition of many of the papers in the archives—especially those from the sixteenth century—was deteriorating due to their age, the appetite of bookworms, and a combination of indifference and neglect on the part of official institutions.

For her part, Cabrera rekindled her contacts with her old informants and expanded her circle of friends among the *negros*. She worked every day, writing, asking questions, attending rituals, hosting visits from [J. S.] Baró or José de Calazán Herrera. (Calixta Morales had died, but Teresa Muñoz was still fit, despite being a centenarian. Her story is told in "Eggüe o Vichichi Finda" and, later, in *El Monte*.) Lydia continued editing *El Monte*, which still lacked a definitive title. And she wrote many more stories, such as "Susundamba" (Congo: owl), which was later included, with minor changes, in *Por qué*.

In 1947, Lydia had gathered enough material to publish a long essay full of footnotes and titled "Eggüe o Vichichi Finda" (Congo and Lucumí: plants). It is, without a doubt, an initial version of *El Monte*. The two works begin with a similar phrase. In "Eggüe o Vichichi Finda" we read, "The spirituality of the forest is an ancestral concept that persists deep in our [Cuban] Black people." The book, published seven years later, begins with a statement that reveals the development of Cabrera's thinking: "Among Black Cubans, the belief in the spirituality of *el monte* persists with an astonishing tenacity."

In 1954, Cabrera finally found the word that defines the title of the book and the concept which turned into its axis: *el monte* conceived as Afro-Cuban temple. The writer went round and round before settling on precisely the right term. Although she uses it several times and quotes it as spoken by *negros* in her 1947 essay, as we have just seen, she prefers to refer to it there as "the spirituality of the forest [*bosque*]." Even as late as 1950, when she published an excerpt of her future book in *Orígenes*, she called it *Vititi Nfinda y Ewe Orisha* (see Cabrera 1950, 16n1), terms that would become part of *El Monte*'s subtitle. It is surprising, then, that Wifredo Lam's *La Jungla* has not been known by its most fitting name, *El Monte*, because there is no doubt that Cabrera's *monte* and Lam's *jungla* are one and the same.

To this day, the word *monte* is so precise and fits so well that it becomes untranslatable.[32] No English word—"bush"? "Forest"? "Jungle"?—manages to include the full range of meanings evoked by the word—not its definition in Spanish, but its meaning in a Cuban sense. Of course, *monte* is hill, mountain. But in Cuba, it also signals a wild thicket, a combination of vegetal wilderness, the product of the divine hand, as a counterpoint to urban spaces, a product of human hands. (An old creole song says, "I'm going to *el monte*, today's my day.") In the end, *monte* is virgin nature, populated by gods and spirits about which the Senegalese poet Birago Diop sang masterfully in a 1975 poem ["Breath"], which Lydia later translated into Spanish:

> . . . the dead are not in the earth:
> they are in the tree that stretches itself out,
> they are in the wood that moans,
> they are in the water that flows,
> they are in the water that sleeps . . . (Diop 1975, 45)[33]

· · · · · ·

---

32   DF-N: In the original version of this essay, Castellanos presaged the title of this edition: "The future English edition of the book (if the legal mess that has prevented it for so many years is somehow untangled) will have the same title: *El Monte*" (Cabrera 1994, 55).

33   DF-N: The excerpt from Cabrera's unpublished Spanish translation reads,

> . . . los muertos no están bajo la tierra:
> están en el arbol que se estremece,
> están en la madera que gime,
> están en el agua que corre,
> están en el agua que duerme . . .

In 1954, Cabrera published another essay in *Orígenes* on Cuba's religious syncretism. It is a shame that the text has not circulated widely, because its first few pages truly illuminate the relationships between Catholicism, Afro-Cuban beliefs, and spiritism in the formation of a popular religiosity.[34] It has been frequently affirmed that the identification of Catholic saints with African orishas was nothing more than a ruse by slaves and their descendants to mask their religious beliefs, thereby protecting themselves from official persecution. There is no doubt that the identification was employed to those ends. But Cabrera provides oral documentation demonstrating that the process of assimilation had taken place *earlier* and at a much deeper level of consciousness. Africans taken to Cuba could only understand the "white" religion imposed on them from the perspective of their own mystical interpretation of the universe—from their peculiar conceptualization of the predominant natural forces in their vision of reality, which, as we know, was strongly colored by elements of polytheism. Moreover, it was psychologically important for slaves to feel their deities had accompanied them in the diaspora, that gods were the same everywhere, for both white and Black people, and that the differences between saints and orishas were purely accidental—mere variations in manifestations or "paths." Cabrera clarifies all of it by employing her characteristic method: having her informants explain it in their own words.

Any discussion of the period at La Quinta San José must include Lydia's work on the Abakuá secret society. We already know the author had attended public *ñáñigo* processions. But it was not until her return from Paris that she took advantage of the opportunity to establish contact with Saibeke and the other Abakuá informants. Saibeke lived in Matanzas, but he stayed in the Quinta San José when he visited Havana. Mercedes Muriedas, Cabrera's secretary during the 1950s, remembers him very clearly, chatting with Lydia daily in the courtyard or the office, sipping on coffee the author asked to have served—for both of them—in the afternoon, despite the objections of the white servants, who resented having to serve an old Black man.

If the wealth of information she obtained from members of the Regla de Ocha is surprising, the data she unearthed among the hermetic Abakuá, who exclude women from their rituals as a matter of religious principle, is even more so. Cabrera managed to have them describe what they had heard regarding the origins of their organization and the land of their elders, their "geography by way of memory." She reproduced the gorgeous myth of Sikanekue,

---

34 DF-N: Here, the Spanish term *religiosidad popular* is akin to "folk religiosity," "religion of the people," or "common people's religious traditions." That is, *popular* (like *pueblo*) implies cultural and/or national identities, as well as socioeconomic class.

Lydia Cabrera with her father, Don Raimundo Cabrera, ca. 1910. Courtesy of the Cuban Heritage Collection at the University of Miami, Lydia Cabrera Papers, Box No. 39.

the ideological *clave* (cornerstone) of the society,[35] and she figured out the extremely complex hierarchy of ritual positions and functions, which are intimately woven together with liturgical objects and moments or episodes of the origin myth. She also compiled an extensive vocabulary, which she published in exile years later as a 530-page book (1988a, 2020), and obtained unique photographs, including one of the Ekue.[36] Moreover, she managed to document a huge number of ritual drawings, or *firmas*, which later saw the light of day in her book *Anaforuana* (1975). Lydia was especially proud of her studies of the Abakuá, since it was the least accessible Afro-Cuban group.

The political situation in Cuba at the end of the 1950s deeply concerned Lydia. As was her custom, she occupied herself with manual labor and, to keep herself "entertained," she started decorating images of virgins (Las Mercedes,

---

35 DF-N: The term *clave* is translated as cornerstone, but it also means key, keystone, code, codex, primer, nucleus, core, and crux. The term's rich musical meanings are not directly relevant here.

36 IC: The Ekue, the sacred drum of the Abakuá, remains hidden in the *famba* shrine room.

La Caridad del Cobre, La Virgen de Regla) with "pearls" and "precious stones" she bought in bulk on Calle Muralla in Havana. At the same time, Lydia and Titina started building a new house from antique materials and decorations, since certain zoning regulations in Marianao were threatening La Quinta San José. The Cuban revolution happened suddenly in 1959, before the work on the house was finished. Like so many other Cubans, Lydia Cabrera and María Teresa de Rojas left their country forever on the ferry which traveled between Cuba and Key West. In an old trunk, in photographs and notes made with pencil and paper, memories of José de Calazán Herrera (Bangoché), Francisquilla Ibáñez, Calixta Morales (Oddedei), and Teresa Muñoz (Omi Tomi) arrived too.

Exile (1968–198?)

Like the majority of Cubans who abandoned their homeland in the first year of the 1960s, Lydia Cabrera and María Teresa de Rojas believed their exile would be brief.[37] They dedicated themselves completely to hastening the conditions that would have allowed them to return to a free Cuba. The failure of the Bay of Pigs invasion in April 1961 made them suspect, for the first time, that their stay in the United States might be prolonged indefinitely. For many years, it was impossible for Lydia to work on new books. It is true that her notes had accompanied her into exile, but the memories of her old friends were still too alive, too painful for her. The first decade of her exile was marked by a prolonged silence. She lacked both the will and the means to write and publish.

Eight years later, in 1968, Lydia edited a new edition of *El Monte*, which relied on the economic support of her friend Amalia Bacardí. That same year, some French colleagues invited her to Paris to participate in a conference on possession trance cults attended by distinguished Africanists, including Roger Bastide, Luc de Heusch, and Pierre Verger. The title of Lydia's talk was "Le guérisseur noir de Cuba" (The Black healers [or diviners] of Cuba). Much later, Cabrera would return to the subject with her book *La medicina popular de Cuba* (1984).

In 1970, ten years after her departure from Cuba, Cabrera took up her pen again, this time for good, and published her first book in exile: *Otán iyebiyé: Las piedras preciocas*. In 1971 she published *Ayapá*, in which she compiled nineteen stories circulating around the central character, the mischievous Jicotea (Turtle or Tortoise), who is sometimes male and others female. Like all of

---

37   IC: Readers are advised that the dates in the section headings only correspond to the composition and publication of the works discussed therein.

Lydia's stories, these have often been misunderstood. At first glance, a superficial reading might suggest it is a collection of folkloric myths, more or less adapted and embellished by the collector. Although she clearly and frequently incorporated materials taken from Afro-Cuban oral tradition in her stories, those themes were, fundamentally, used as motifs and stimuli to awaken the creative imagination of the artist. Gastón Baquero is correct when he writes,

> The work of this woman—studious, very modest, working silently—is, in its depth and form, a work of true poetry, of genuine creation. Her work is so creative that, at first glance, it appears to be a simple, mechanical compilation of words, customs, and folktales. The author's hand is invisible. And it is easy to overlook the mastery of this invisible writer who manages to re-create something that actually happened, making it seem anonymous and popular, and giving it a pure, authentic flavor. It is typical that the process of making great art usually remains unseen. The genius of Leo Frobenius's achievement when he wrote *The Black Decameron* has also been achieved absolutely by Lydia Cabrera, by knowing how to get out of the way of what she is narrating, composing it with such a strong mark of spontaneity that the reader never sees the author, but rather believes they are listening—truly and directly—to the voice of an African culture, a powerfully unique and authentic human group, or a folkloric myth from before the dawn of time. In reality, all of these pleasures are due to the most difficult art of "impersonating others," of deeply being others, which is the secret of great works and great authors. (1982, 5–6)

In fact, pretending that Cabrera's stories are mere "folktales" would be like insisting that Mario Vargas Llosa's *La tía Julia y el escribidor* (*Aunt Julia and the Scriptwriter*) is an autobiography rather than a novel.

Don Fernando Ortiz was the first person responsible for this confusion. In his foreword to the first Spanish edition of *Cuentos negros de Cuba* (1940), he affirms that the book is "a rich contribution to the folkloric literature of Cuba" and explains—in all seriousness—that some of the stories include "curious and very significant examples of the phenomenon of cultural transition; for example, when the narrator appoints gods to the offices of Chief Justice of the Supreme Court and Captain of the Firefighters Brigade." Ortiz's foreword has been quoted left and right, and it has been used more than any other text as a means to misinterpret Cabrera's stories. The second person to blame for the misunderstanding is Cabrera herself, who never bothered to clarify the matter. On the contrary, she was pleased to have "pulled the wool over the great Fernando Ortiz's eyes." (Lydia was very pleased that her brother-in-law would comment, very solemnly, on the novelty of a "myth" "discovered" by Cabrera in which Obá-Ogó made humans "by breathing over his own poop.") We insist that the purpose of Lydia Cabrera's ethnographic work was the faithful, detailed study of Afro-Cuban religious transculturation. Her stories, on the other hand, are pure literary fiction, even if they are sometimes based, with more or less fidelity, on myths or genuine *patakies*. Sometimes a song would suggest the tale, as in the case of "Arere Marekén" (Hiriart 1978, 84).[38]

Lydia tended to affirm that she had never broken with the imaginative and fantastical world of her childhood. Beyond the memories of specific stories told by Tula and her other Black *tatas*—and she is sure to have heard some, though, according to her, the nannies preferred reciting "Cenicienta" ("Cinderella") or "La cucarachita Martina" (The little cockroach Martina)—the adult writer remained under the influence of a diffuse "reality of the unreal," which overwhelms children and inspired her writing from such a young age. As she confessed to Rosario Hiriart, her stories arose from "a reencounter with the world of fantasy of my earliest infancy, from which I never broke away" (1978, 75). On the other hand, *El Monte* is the product of "the blinding illumination that *real* and unforeseeable world, of beliefs, legends, and . . . poetry produced in me" (1978, 79). Cabrera undoubtedly enjoys herself, having fun, playing with the possibility of creating a *magical-real* reality.[39] It is a reality that is just as immediate and genuine for her as it is for a child living in the imaginary universe of her games, and it is just as authentic and positive as the precepts of magic are for believers, with which they can subvert and re-create the established logical order. It is a narrative reality in which animated and rational characters such as Brother Dove and Sister Hen, the governor's nine unmarried daughters, His Majesty the King of Spain, Sir Christopher Columbus, His Holiness the Pope, and One-Footed Osain can coexist. It is an ethnographic reality in which nature is permeated by mystical essences that can be manipulated by humans by way of orishas or the spirits of *muertos* (the dead) that reside in stones, waters, trees, and vines of an enchanted *monte*. This fascination with what Cabrera has called "the reality of the unreal" evolved into the

---

38 DF-N: *Lydia Cabrera: Between the Sum and the Parts* (Marta and Rangel 2019) includes a full-color reproduction and English translation of "Arere Marekén," including the illustrations by Alexandra Exter (also known as Aleksandra Aleksandrova Ekster). The original illustrated manuscript, archived in the Lydia Cabrera Papers at the Cuban Heritage Collection, has been digitized and made available online. An audio recording of an interview with Cabrera, archived at the Library of Congress, includes her own recitations of sections from "Arere Marekén"; it has also been digitized and made available online (1982b).

39 DF-N: Returning to the theme established by her epigraph ("the reality of the unreal"), Castellanos draws our attention to the dynamic interplay of magic and reality as a central theme in Cabrera's life and work, above and beyond her often unacknowledged role in the literary genre known as magic realism.

driving force and central theme of all of her work, both scientific and literary, in her anthropological treatises as much as her books of *cuentos negros*.

In 1972, Lydia and María Teresa moved to Madrid, where Amalia Bacardí had lived for some time. There they collaborated on an edition of the writings of Don Emilio Bacardí, Amalia's father. In Madrid, Cabrera wrote three of her best books. *La laguna sagrada de San Joaquín* (The sacred lagoon of San Joaquin, [1973] 1993) is a long, nostalgic, and poetic essay that is her most personal and intimate work. The text seems to be the result of a sort of catharsis, a painful evocative experience by which she regained the ability to return to her ethnographic work after a long period of mourning. *Yemayá y Ochún* (1974) followed, a magnificent treatise on the two water goddesses and the initiation rituals in the Regla de Ocha. In Spain, she also composed *Anaforuana* (1975), in which the author collects the Abakuá ritual drawings and offers detailed explanations of the Abakuá secret society's process of initiation. Describing *Anaforuana*, Robert Farris Thompson notes, "I estimate there are approximately 512 discrete signs documented in this important text, a landmark study in the history of Black Atlantic writing systems" (1983, 299n10).[40] If we are surprised by the fabulous, overflowing imagination of Cabrera's stories, in which the boundaries of conventionally recognized categories disappear, her research astounds us with the abundance and depth of its information, which is strictly and verifiably true and documented.

In 1974, Lydia and Titina returned to Miami, where they would reside until the end of their lives. Lydia collaborated on the sixth volume of the *Enciclopedia de Cuba*, contributing a valuable essay on San Lázaro, Babalú Ayé, a few children's stories (unique in her literary corpus), and a series of "myths and legends." She later wrote and published numerous books, including *Reglas de Congo* ([1979] 1986), *La Regla Kimbisa del Santo Cristo de Buen Viaje* ([1977] 1986), *Koekó iyawó* (1980), and *Los animales en el folklore y la magia de Cuba* (1988b). She also edited a number of articles and presented various conference presentations. In 1976, Florida International University hosted a tribute to her that was organized by José A. Madrigal and Reinaldo Sánchez.[41] This was followed by Cabrera being awarded various honorary doctoral degrees, from Denison University in Ohio, Manhattan College in New York City, and the University of Miami.

At the beginning of the 1980s, Cabrera's eyesight began to fail as the result of progressive macular degeneration. It quickly became impossible for her to read, write, or paint, the three things she considered her greatest "diversiones" (hobbies). Despite her advanced age and limited eyesight, she managed to

---

40 DF-N: Scans of the drawings are archived at the Cuban Heritage Collection.
41 DF-N: See Sánchez et al. (1978).

edit several manuscripts for publication. On January 25, 1987, María Teresa de Rojas died. They had shared more than fifty years together. A few weeks later, Lydia became gravely ill, but she managed to recover and survive for almost five more years. Finally, at 8:00 p.m. on September 19, 1991, she died, calmly and peacefully, sitting in her *poltrona* (lounge chair). She remained conscious to the very end, with the same sense of humor as ever. One of her last recollections was of the Havana where she was born. In keeping with her will, her remains were cremated, and her ashes now rest next to María Teresa de Rojas's coffin in a Miami cemetery. Lydia Cabrera was unable to return to a free and happy Cuba, but her name did not disappear from her homeland. We frequently receive news of young Cubans on the island who read and admire her. Her writing has inspired artists who are just starting out. As I write these lines, José Bedia, a painter who arrived from Cuba by way of Mexico, is exhibiting a painting titled *Homenaje a Lydia Cabrera* at the Art Museum in Fort Lauderdale.[42] A few months ago, Arturo Lindsay, a young Panamanian painter, exhibited a series of canvases inspired by *El Monte. Cuentos Negros and El Monte, Ayapá, Anaforuana, Por qué*, and *La laguna sagrada de San Joaquín* are and will remain part of a heritage for future generations. The year 1994 commemorated the fortieth anniversary of the publishing of *El Monte*, that seminal work of Cuban culture, and its author, a model of intellectual dedication, genuine modesty, and human integrity.

42 DF-N: The museum is now known as the NSU Art Museum Fort Lauderdale. In 1994, at the time of Castellanos's writing, it was known as the Museum of Art, Fort Lauderdale.

Translator's Notes

Reading El Monte *in the Twenty-First Century*

....

DAVID FONT-NAVARRETE

This book's subject—the African cultural legacy in Cuba—has been studied by cosmopolitan artists and scholars like Lydia Cabrera for more than a century, and it is arguably the world's most iconic, prominent symbol of the African diaspora. Depending on your historical orientation, narratives of Afro-Cuban traditions might illustrate: retention or survival of African culture in the Americas; cultural adaptation and mixing; and/or transnational identities that resist the ruptures of slavery and modernity. At the beginning of the twenty-first century, nearly seventy years after *El Monte* was first published, Afro-Cuban traditions have also become increasingly prominent emblems of national identity in Cuba, and they have been transplanted from Cuba to Mexico, the United States, and Venezuela. Afro-Cuban cultural traditions thrive in disparate communities around the globe, leading some scholars to approach them as a world religion.[1] Meanwhile, Cabrera's approach to those traditions—in *El Monte* and throughout her work—remains at the cutting edge of art, ethnography, folklore, and literature.

El Monte is unruly, organic, and forbiddingly complex. Regardless of cultural or linguistic background, every reader will find unfamiliar and disorienting moments in these pages. This

---

1   See Olupona and Rey (2008).

is intrinsic to the book and its subject matter, both of which resist all but the crudest or most abstract sort of cartography; put another way, maps are often less useful in *El Monte* than concepts and techniques. Cabrera anticipates postmodern and experimental approaches to translation and ethnography by several decades, making her contributions seem, in retrospect, more radical than ever.[2] The following notes offer readers a handful of frameworks and tools to navigate this long overdue English-language edition of *El Monte*.

Cabrera resolutely insisted that she was neither a scholar nor a priest. In fact, she did not teach or hold university faculty positions, nor did she publish her work in peer-reviewed academic journals or through presses, and she was not initiated as an *olorisha* or *yaya nkisi*. Rather, she was, in the words of her friend and colleague Pierre Fatumbi Verger, a "quasi-iyalorisha," meaning she was analogous to a priest (≈), but not one (≠). Likewise, she was a quasi-academic, esteemed as a colleague by professors though she never held a university position, and she was resistant to being identified with the scientific ambitions of ethnography and anthropology. Certainly she was a writer, an artist, and a translator.

In *El Monte*, Cabrera also works as a quasi-folklorist or quasi-documentarian. When she claims to offer "material for specialists that has not passed through the dangerous filter of interpretation" in the preface, she appears blind to the processes of filtering and interpretation she performs in *El Monte*, which is inherent and inevitable, which is always not equal to the original text. Paradoxically, her hyperbole draws contemporary scholars' attention back to the fundamental nobility of her ideal: maximum fidelity to her human subjects, whom she describes as *documentos vivos* (living documents).

In the context of Cabrera's numerous publications, three of her other major works from the 1950s are natural counterparts to *El Monte*, namely:

---

2 Fortunately, Cabrera and her work continue to receive attention from remarkably diverse quarters, and *El Monte* certainly lends insight into Cabrera's cultural milieu. For example, at the nexus of avant-garde and ethnographic writing, this edition can be usefully juxtaposed with three other genre-bending manuscripts published the same year as *El Monte*: William Bascom's "Four Functions of Folklore" (1954); Eleanor Smith Bowen's pseudonymous *Return to Laughter* (1954); and Amos Tutuola's *My Life in the Bush of Ghosts* (1954). At a much more local level, *El Monte* can also be placed in direct dialogue with Nicolás Angarica's *Manual de Orihate* (1955).

The single most closely related counterpart to this edition might be the English translations of Pierre Verger's encyclopedic *Ewé: The Use of Plants in Yoruba Society* ([1995] 2007), republished, along with an anthology of Verger's articles (2007), by Black Madonna Enterprises.

Various other seminal English-language publications offer more or less direct parallels and dialogues with Cabrera's work, including Bascom ([1969] 1991, 1976, [1980] 1993); Césaire ([1939] 1943, [1939] 2013); Chief FAMA (1993, 2001); Hurston ([1938] 1990); Gleason (1973, [1987] 1992); Leiris ([1934] 1988, 2017); MacGaffey (1991); Thompson (1975, 1983); Verger (1956); Warner-Lewis (1990, 1996, 2018); and Wenger and Chesi (1983).

Música de los cultos africanos en Cuba (ca. 1956), *Anagó* ([1957] 1986), and *La sociedad secreta Abakuá* (1959). Additionally, *La laguna sagrada de San Joaquín* ([1973] 1993) can be read as a coda to this set of publications, a nostalgic, post-exile meditation on Afro-Cuban devotional traditions. The book was Cabrera's first ethnographic work in exile, written in Madrid twelve years after she left Cuba for the last time. According to Isabel Castellanos, Cabrera described the process of writing *La laguna sagrada* as a reckoning with exile as the author emerged from a decade-long depression, finally accepting the fact that her life in Cuba would remain in the past tense.

I have supplemented translations of Cabrera's footnotes with my own annotations to offer contextual information and commentary, along with references to Cabrera's subsequent publications and other related literature, with special attention to newer English-language publications.[3] With a few notable exceptions, most of Cabrera's publications have yet to be translated into English.[4]

Beyond Cabrera's subject matter (and the confines of artistic or scholarly disciplines and genres, which she ignored and/or obliterated), the act of writing was at the heart of her work. Officially, she was not an anthropologist, a linguist, a botanist, or a theologian. She referred to reading, writing, and painting as her "hobbies," yet they were obviously her primary tools and means of expression. A close reading of any section of this book makes clear Cabrera's sensitivity to the fact that writing words down transforms them as radically as any translation between languages.

---

3   Among a vibrant body of English-language scholarship on Cabrera, see Cabrera (2020); Gutiérrez (2008); Maguire (2018); Marta and Rangel (2019); Otero (2020); and Rodríguez-Mangual (2004). For a formidable contemporary counterpart to Cabrera's ethnographic and botanical approach in *El Monte*, see Martínez Betancourt (2013).

Meanwhile, a slew of unauthorized editions of Cabrera's massive bibliography continues to be published in small-run editions, often poorly edited, and often neglecting to credit the author. More broadly, Cabrera's work circulates within a vibrant Afro-Atlantic cultural network of independent publishing that confounds even the most sophisticated notions of genre and authorship (Font-Navarrete 2021). Inevitably, this edition will circulate within that network in unpredictable ways, especially in digital form.

For a contemporary musical soundtrack to the book, see *Música de los cultos africanos en Cuba*, Cabrera and Tarafa's massive collection of audio recordings , ca. 1956 (Cabrera 2001a, 2001b, 2003; Font-Navarrete 2022), Celia Cruz and La Sonora Matancera's *Yerbero Moderno* (1955), and Francisco López's *La Selva* (1998), among many others.

4   See Cabrera (2005, 2020) and Marta and Rangel (2019). Other long-overdue translations and collaborative research projects based on Cabrera's work are forthcoming, in collaboration with the Cuban Heritage Collection of the University of Miami Libraries, which has managed Cabrera's archives and publishing estate since they were transferred to the university by Cabrera's heir, Isabel Castellanos.

Describing *El Monte* as a "holy book," the foreword by John Szwed and Robert Farris Thompson makes it clear that the book contains a singularly robust body of evidence for a diversity of African ritual traditions and identities on the island of Cuba. This particular constellation of African antecedents documented in *El Monte* places it within a growing body of research on the Afro-Atlantic. It also reminds us that the broad Congo and Lucumí "ethnic" designations often obscure a much, much wider variety of distinct Afro-Cuban identities, and it underscores the potential insights to be gained through new tools in linguistics and/or genetics. Similarly, Cabrera makes it clear that other broad African groupings—Abakuá, Arará, Gangá, Mina, and others—often contain multiple, more local identities that would have been more salient in the colonial era, and that a great many of the African captives were always already multilingual and "multiethnic" before they were taken to Cuba.[5]

This book itself is the product of a transatlantic network of scholars, artists, and priests. In 1955, Cabrera sent a letter from Cuba to her friend Verger, who was then living in Oṣogbo, a West African mecca of orisha traditions in present-day Oṣun State, Nigeria. Cabrera describes the reception of their respective books among her Afro-Cuban "informants" in rural Matanzas, Cuba:

> When I'm with these friends, who remain more African than the ones I have in Havana, I don't feel jealous of your good luck for being in Africa. . . . The ones who know how to read all ask me for my "ewé wélo," my book. Inside santería, among the Padres and aborissás it's been received very well, "because of the respect with which the white woman speaks."
>
> *Dieux d'Afrique* [Gods of Africa, Verger's book of photographs from Benin and Nigeria] provokes mad enthusiasm. I always bring it with me, since they come specifically to see it. Fortunately, I have two copies. One for them to paw at, and another untouchable one for me.
>
> It will be interesting to compare the vocabulary with the dictionaries you have, and with the living dictionaries . . . I limit myself to the translation they offer me, and to writing the words the way they sound; it is not a scientific system in any way. I do nothing more than repeat what is spoken by Black people. It is a shame that an oniyé moyé—lorí dára dára, "a sage"—has not come to study these African survivals which are so rich and strong in Cuba. (Cabrera and Verger, 2011, 18–19)[6]

---

5 On African ethnic designations in Cuba and the Afro-Atlantic, see Law (1997); Matory (2005); and Miller (2004).

6 The Spanish-English translation is my own.

Cabrera's longing for "a sage" evokes contemporary networks of Afro-Atlantic scholars and ritual experts whose exchanges often establish parameters for ethnographic authority and ritual orthodoxy. The exchange reflects dense patterns of cultural circulation and transformation: oral traditions and multimedia documents inform one another; ethnographic scholarship, art, and ritual knowledge blur together; cultural authenticity and ritual authority constantly intersect and overlap; and it all happens in a matrix that moves constantly between nations and languages. Then and now, in Africa or Cuba, ritual experts' prestige is still liable to be established, reinforced, compounded, or compromised by collaboration with foreign scholar-artist-devotees like Verger and Cabrera, and the stories of the individuals and communities documented by them are continually evolving.[7]

Most notably, however, the earnest exchange between two friends reinforces the intimate human dimension at the heart of Cabrera's work, which is epitomized by this book: she did her best to faithfully convey the traditions, voices, and genius of the real, living people memorialized herein; and the whole enterprise depended on a very real sense of trust (*confianza*) that was often navigated and negotiated at a much less intimate level. In an interview, recorded in Miami at the age of eighty-two, Cabrera distilled her research to an elegant formula:

> Of course, I didn't know anything about these things, until I went back to Cuba [from France, in 1930] and established contact with Black elders, no? When they saw that I was approaching them with great respect, well, they taught me. And that's where my books come from. Someone would say, "There's So-and-So in Matanzas, he's 104 years old and speaks Yoruba—" And I would devise some way to see them. And we would become friends. I would ask, "—your religion?" And once they could verify that, for my part, I had no intention of mocking them, they were very friendly, very welcoming. And they would talk to me, tell me things. They taught me. . . . It was a matter of demonstrating respect. . . . And they saw, the elders, that I wasn't interested in mockery. Also, there was a fear—in certain eras, they were persecuted. And they might think that I would denounce them, inform on them. But no. When they saw there was none of that, they were very, very helpful. In fact, they took great care to make sure I understood what they were explaining to me, and that I write it down. (1982b)[8]

---

7   See Font-Navarrete (2022).

8   The Spanish-English translation is my own. Special thanks to Talia Guzman-Gonzalez from the Library of Congress for facilitating the digitization of the original cassette tape recording,

Monte, Santo, Muerto, Negro, Brujo, Diablito, and Other Multivalent Terms

Even before we open its pages, *El Monte*'s ornate subtitle obliges us to interpret multiple layers of language, identity, and history: *Igbo, Finda, Ewe Orisha, Vititi Nfinda: Notes on the Religions, Magic, Superstitions, and Folklore of the Black and Creole People of Cuba*. The subtitle—which incorporates Spanish, Lucumí, and Congo terms—telegraphs the book's inherent complexity, paradox, and ambiguity, making it clear that translation is at the heart of the matter. As the preeminent Cabrera scholar Edna Rodríguez-Mangual points out,

> The first challenge presented by *El Monte* is of an ontological and hermeneutical variety: What kind of text is it? How can it be classified? The answers to these questions vary, depending on interpretation and how the text is used. The first clue lies in the title itself; rather than clarify, the title confuses the reader: the note in parenthesis indicates that the reader is dealing with a religious book, but also one that addresses magic and superstition. Religion, magic, and superstition imply three different forms of knowledge. . . . Can these categories be compared on the same level? At the same time, the book is about Black Creole folklore, but it also includes the people of Cuba as a whole. Does Afro-Cuban religion belong to blacks alone or to all Cuban people? Are "black" and "Cuban people" separate categories? Is the word "people" (*pueblo*) being used in the sense of the "popular" classes (a connotation suggested more strongly in Spanish than in English), or is it used as a common national denominator? Does this title point to a traditional ethnographic investigation . . . ? (2004, 64)

In her original text, Cabrera leaves much of the Afro-Cuban language in *El Monte* untranslated and unexplained, and she employs a number of sophisticated literary and linguistic devices in order to reveal details and nuances of Afro-Cuban traditions. The book—like its namesake subject—is intrinsically, overwhelmingly complex. Voices, languages, information, and stories are layered in ways that are disorienting by nature, thereby presenting particular challenges to translation.[9] Translation is built into this book's structure and

---

which is part of the Archive of Hispanic Literature on Tape from the Hispanic Division. The recording, which is now available on the Library of Congress website, begins poetically, with Cabrera's voice caught midsentence on side A of the cassette tape, saying, "—el monte" (1982b). Side A ends abruptly, interrupting Cabrera's recitation of "Arere Mareken" (musical refrain and all) at the end of the cassette's length of magnetic tape. Side B of the cassette begins even more poetically: Cabrera—again recorded midsentence—says, in English, "We have eternity before us."

9   Rodríguez-Mangual (2004) and Wirtz (2014, 2016) both refer to Mikhail Bakhtin's *Dialogic Imagination* ([1975] 1983). Theoretically minded readers who follow their lead will find numerous

sensibility, which are informed by Cabrera's lifelong immersion in deep translation. As Castellanos reminds us in the introduction to this volume, Cabrera's first book—*Contes negres de Cuba* (1936)—was first published (natively in translation) in a French edition, and she translated a French-Spanish edition of Aimé Césaire's poetry ([1939] 1943) more than a decade before *El Monte*.

The remainder of these notes spells out some of the ways this new English-language edition transforms and adds even more layers to *El Monte*. The outline of a technical and theoretical framework for the translation is intended to offer a measure of transparency, explaining and making explicit some of my decisions as translator. Although it is impossible to provide an exhaustive context for every reader, this edition's foreword, introduction, and notes are intended to offer useful points of departure.

Readers are enthusiastically encouraged to compare this edition to the original text; specifically, this translation is based on the 1992 edition published in Miami by Ediciones Universal. The rationale for using the 1992 edition as the primary source is based on four criteria: (1) it is the latest authorized edition, thereby reflecting the most comprehensive aggregate version of the text; (2) it is the last edition to reflect Cabrera's own editorial decisions, making it the author's most definitive version of her own work; (3) it is the edition that has remained in print the longest; and (4) it remains widely available in an edition from Ediciones Universal, Cabrera's last publishing partner.

Several features of the translation are tailored to Cabrera's idiosyncratic approach. Generally, my interpretive style is more synthetic than strictly literal, offering a version of the text that is meant to be as accessible as possible without sacrificing accuracy or specificity. At an even more basic level, this edition translates Spanish to English—that is, it substitutes English for Spanish as a lingua franca and assumes only English fluency on the part of readers. Inevitably, this version does not attempt to exhaustively translate the African and Afro-Cuban idioms into English. Instead, Cabrera's own translations of Afro-Cuban idioms are translated into English and allowed to speak for themselves, mirroring the text in a way that is as close as possible to the Spanish original. This is also intended to faithfully convey the book's esoteric nature, which is inseparable from the fact that Cabrera is often more poetic than didactic, intentionally employing artful ambiguity and obscurity.

· · · · · · ·

In virtually any cultural tradition, fundamental terms and concepts inevitably mean more than one thing, and esoteric terms are often deliberately shaded

---

facets of Bakhtin's work useful for making sense of *El Monte*, including the notions of "heteroglossia" and "chronotope."

and veiled by layers of context and ambiguity. In the context of Afro-Cuban traditions, the meanings of Spanish terms like *monte*, *santo*, *muerto*, and *palo* are always plural and fundamentally multivalent—that is, they carry multiple meanings simultaneously, all of which inform and influence each other. Therefore, a handful of Spanish terms are defined and contextualized but not translated. For example, even before we grapple with its extravagant, multilingual subtitle, the book's succinct title suggests multiple voices and paradoxes: as Isabel Castellanos points out, any single English translation of *el monte* would do more harm than good. No single English word—*forest*, *jungle*, *wilderness*—captures a rich enough spectrum of meaning; on the contrary, most would be misleading. *Monte* is perhaps closest to the English word *bush*, especially in its archaic British colonial sense, still employed in Africa and Australia, which evokes a place "outside" modern urban life, beyond the confines and safety of so-called civilization (cf. Maguire 2018). Likewise, both *monte* and *bush* suggest the sharp edges of nature, danger, freedom, and magic.

In *El Monte*, the only true authority is *el monte* itself: not any single entity or force (and certainly not humans), but a mysterious space in which nature, spirits, and humans commune. Cabrera's text is modeled on its subject: thorny, tangled, and somewhat treacherous, but also lush, gorgeous, and teeming with life. In a philosophical vein, *el monte* represents nature.

Other foundational Afro-Cuban terms convey this multivalent quality. For example, both *orisha* (Lucumí) and *nganga* (Congo) refer variously to forces of nature, consecrated objects, ancestors, deities, or deities in possession of human vessels. Likewise, the word *santo* might be synonymous with a saint, holiness, an icon, a state of consciousness, or an orisha.

El Monte virtually insists that readers cultivate an acute sensitivity to the ways a single term might convey a variety of interrelated meanings. In translation, the esoteric, mystical, and idiomatic nature of some words make tidy correspondence between languages misleading. Depending on the context, *el monte* (Spanish) might correspond well to *igbo* (Lucumí) or *forest* (English), but it does not correspond perfectly to either. Likewise, *muerto* (Spanish) might translate well as *egun* (Lucumí) or *nfumbi* (Congo) in a particular context, but it might also suggest English terms as diverse as *ancestor*, *ghost*, *spirit*, *dead person*, or *cadaver*. Depending on the context, *palo* (Spanish) might mean: a stick; a tree; the initiations and consecrations in "Congo-inspired" ritual traditions; a specific branch and/or the entire complex of Congo ritual traditions; a genre of music, poetry, and dance; and so on. Again, each of the various definitions of *palo* informs the others in a multitude of ways (trees are central in the rituals, objects, and traditions), and the term corresponds to a constellation of closely related terms (*igi*, *iki*, *nkunia*, etc.) and concepts (*muerto*, *nganga*, *fundamento*, etc.).

Meanwhile, in *El Monte*, the Spanish term *santería* evokes a very specific historical idiom. Given its ambiguous, often-negative valence at the combustible intersections of religion, race, ethnicity, and language, I do not render the term in English, despite its common usage. Several footnotes offer other examples of multiple ways to translate particular terms or passages, drawing attention to important nuances that resist or preclude translation, and encouraging readers to consider ways *El Monte* weaves linguistic and philosophical concepts together. However, like the original Spanish edition, a great many terms remain deliberately untranslated.

Cabrera's massive body of work is built on the premise that Afro-Cubans—that is, Cubans of African descent, or Black people in Cuba—are "living documents" of intellectual and philosophical wisdom, and it is worth contemplating the ways in which that premise was a revolutionary notion among her contemporaries, and the ways it remains so. Sixty years later, Cabrera's approach still seems ahead of our time, which is a measure of both her radical achievements and a dispiriting lack of human progress. Therefore, a few words regarding Cabrera's engagement with politics of race are in order.

Cabrera's primary subject is Black culture and people, and her references to *los negros* or *el negro* are categorical, generic designations for Black people. Note that these terms are linguistically gendered by the conventions of Spanish (not necessarily references to male subjects), and that *El Monte*'s subtitle refers to "los negros criollos de Cuba" (the Black Creoles of Cuba) but not Africa. Cabrera's use of "nuestros negros"—the possessive form (literally, "our Blacks")—suggests a sharp double edge that is more problematic: the term can be understood as an embrace, insisting that Black people belong to Cuba; but it can also be read as an estrangement, evoking the condescension and ownership intrinsic to white supremacy. In *El Monte*, the term *negro*—which is always already profoundly multivalent—can usually be read simply as "black." Occasionally, it is akin to the outdated English word *Negro*, which would be consistent with other archaic, mid-twentieth-century terminology in the book. While the possessive grammatical form can be read as a truly atavistic extension of the racist ideology of slavery, more contemporary translations such as "our nation's Black folks" or "our Black community" are just as accurate.

Cabrera's transliteration of so-called *bozal*—African-inflected Spanish associated with the colonial era, akin to pidgin or "broken" English—is particularly resistant to translation. First, the meanings of certain passages are often obscure and ambiguous. Even when the meaning is clear, *bozal* in translation might sound like a linguistic caricature of Blackness in English, a sort of verbal minstrelsy reminiscent of language in the Jim Crow–era United States. (See, for example, this volume's botanical encyclopedia entry for ESPARTILLO.) That said, several of Cabrera's *bozal*-style transcriptions are exquisitely rendered sketches of ritual virtuosity that represent the highest ideals of Cabrera's project: to document voices and idioms from the edges of living memory, now receded into history, except when they are adopted in dramatic historical reenactments, theatrical and artistic productions, and/or in the context of possession trance.[10] For example, compare Cabrera's transcription of invocations in the botanical encyclopedia entry for LAUREL and the transcription of a masterfully crafted *mambo* in Ochoa (2010).[11] Wherever possible, I translate passages that might be called *bozal* in a neutral, unaffected style; for example, in chapter 9, I translate "Olofi mayor, jefe tropa lo Changóse" as "the senior Olofi, the war chief of all the Changós." Otherwise, I leave *bozal* passages untranslated, sometimes with explanatory footnotes. Occasionally, I alter Cabrera's spelling of transliterated Afro-Cuban terms to reflect English orthography (for example, from "Changóse" to "Changós").

The racial vocabulary of *El Monte* reflects its time and place, yet it seems relatively wholesome compared to Cabrera's quasi-scientific, racist turns of phrase (in the preface) associating Black people with an "extraordinary proclivity for autosuggestion" and general "atavism" (*atavismo*). While it is Cabrera's own language and views in that passage that now seem primitive, a close reading makes it clear that she considered millenarian "superstition" (that is, "irrational" or "magical" thinking)—rather than Blackness—atavistic. Returning to the book's subtitle for foundational context, Cabrera enumerates *religion, magic, superstition*, and *folklore* as a continuum of interpretive frameworks. Arguably, in Cabrera's formulation: religion descends to magic; (real and/or not) magic descends further, down to (false) superstition; then the phenomenon is neutralized by a more or less secular folklore.

While Cabrera differentiated herself categorically from *creyentes* (believers, adherents) of the traditions that obsessed her, she was manifestly not immune from a belief in "the reality of the unreal." Several passages describe superstitions and esoteric rituals among Euro-Cuban *guajiros* (country peasants) and members of the bourgeoisie alike in condescending terms, regarding their credulous superstition as their shared folly. In short, alongside the respect and fascination that animate *El Monte*, it is worth considering the ways Cabrera's

---

10   In Spanish, see Castellanos and Castellanos (1992, 1994). In English, see Lipski (1987, 2001); Schwegler and Rojas-Primus (2010); and Wirtz (2013).

11   The term *mambo*, used here to describe a performance of Congo-Cuban musical liturgy, is another profoundly multivalent term that has filtered into the English language; in other contexts, it also refers to: a traditionalist priest or possession mount; a raucous popular music genre (à la Pérez Prado et al.); a section of a song or performance; a genre of ballroom dancing; and so on. See Iseman (1984); Sublette (2004); and Waxer (1994).

skepticism and razor-sharp wit, eye, ear, and tongue sometimes blur lines between mordant observation, mockery, and condescension.

The terms *brujo*, *brujería*, and their derivatives present more troublesome dilemmas. Given the historical (and ongoing) repression, persecution, and stigmatization of Afro-Atlantic traditions, some readers will understandably bristle at the use of those terms in the original, as well as translations employing similarly pejorative English words like "witchcraft." For a sense of this deep-seated prejudice against Afro-Cubans and their cultural traditions, we need only recall the title of Fernando Ortiz's first major publication in 1906, which effectively inaugurated Afro-Cuban studies in a most inauspicious way by criminalizing and demonizing its human subjects: it translates literally as "The Afro-Cuban Criminal Underworld: The Black Sorcerers (Notes on a Study in Criminal Ethnology)." This stigma still echoes inside and outside ritual spaces more than a century later.[12]

Recognizing that my approach to these contentious terms cannot satisfy all readers, I have taken care—above all else—to be as faithful as possible to the text and to the people and traditions it describes. Most often, I translate *brujo* as "sorcerer" in order to convey an intrinsically ambiguous quality evoking both formidable power and danger. (The drama of the Harry Potter series is built on this ambiguity, and even the Disney-produced vignette of Mickey Mouse as the Sorcerer's Apprentice in *Fantasia* conveys it instructively.) On the positive end of the spectrum, numerous other English words work just as well in various instances—for example, "priest," "wizard," "medicine man," or the more esoteric, glamorous-sounding "magus" (Cabrera 2020). But it is important to underscore the negative valence of the word, especially in the context of malicious, unjust, covert, antisocial, and/or destructive behavior. In several instances, I translate *brujería* as "witchcraft" to reflect a somewhat more manifestly negative context, similar to distinguishing between "curse" or "hex" on the one hand, and "magic" or "ritual" on the other.

Connecting passages like these, readers might discern the outlines of philosophical principles elaborated by Afro-Atlantic traditions, and—just as important—individuals' varied approaches to them. If we follow Szwed and Thompson's suggestion to read *El Monte* as a "moral document," we seldom find simple, straightforward ways through it. The book's discussions of moral,

---

12 A 2019 newspaper headline reported, "Encuentran 42 cráneos, 31 huesos, un feto y un altar en una casa de Ciudad México" [42 skulls, 31 bones, a fetus, and an altar found in Mexico City] (*La Vanguardia*, 2019). A few months later, a *New York Times* headline announced "Two Men Are Accused of Stealing Skulls from Florida Cemetery"; the article noted that "the men said that they took the skulls to use in religious practices of Palo Mayombe, an African-Caribbean religion related to Santería, according to the authorities" (Díaz 2021).

amoral, and immoral behavior often obviate simplistic, binary notions of good and bad. For example, Cabrera's fulsome, loving portrait of José de Calazán Herrera (aka Bangoché, El Moro) emerges from a composite of numerous passages in the book, and it offers an intimate celebration steeped in ethical and moral nuance. On the whole, consent (or lack thereof) emerges as a crucial factor in distinguishing good from bad, and "religion" from "witchcraft."[13] In chapter 5 we read about ways the spirit ("soul"?) of a dead person might be enslaved, thereby becoming the captive of a sorcerer's will. Yet the legitimacy of the ritual operation rests on whether or not the spirit agrees with the "arrangement," explicitly consenting to a mystical pact. Similarly, ritual action based on negative and harmful intentions might be justified as a mystical or pharmacological use of force, especially if it is framed as justifiable or necessary self-defense, and it is distinguished from covert, nonconsensual, and antisocial acts.

The word *brujería* is given an explicitly negative, pejorative valence in many, many examples throughout *El Monte*. For example, the story of Omi Tomi's first-born daughter (in chapter 2) describes the real-world consequences of harmful, covert ritual action in heartbreakingly vivid detail. Even brief notes in the botanical encyclopedia refer to frankly destructive intentions: for example, a ritual formula in the CALABAZA entry is reportedly "able to 'ruin' a home down to its very foundations." Descriptions of poisons, which are more pharmacological than symbolic, abound. The entry for BEJUCO VERRACO reads, "It is poisonous for livestock. 'Yes. And, from time to time, for two-legged animals too.'" And the entry for BEJUCO ZARZUELA quotes another informant verbatim:

> "It's called Bauba, and its roots and leaves are used to *nsaranda*, to work over the cauldron and bind a child in its mother's belly, so it can't be born. This is revenge work. Parents' vengeance and quarrels are the downfall of many innocent little angels."

Numerous formulas discuss ways to abort pregnancy, suggesting women's reproductive autonomy and/or ways to covertly "spoil" a pregnancy. The difference—consent—marks one sort of action from another. In these contexts of negatively charged and socially illicit ritual actions, translating the term *brujería* neutrally as "sorcery" or "ritual" (rather than "witchcraft" or "curses") would be misleading. Of course, this is still unintentionally pejorative for English speakers who refer to themselves proudly (if somewhat ambiguously) as

---

13 For ethnographic approaches to "sorcery," see Evans-Pritchard (1937); and Stoller and Olkes (1987).

"witches" to embrace an empowered, mystical kind of femininity, not to mention their Spanish-speaking counterparts who embrace formidable personae under the epithets *brujo* or *bruja*.

Moralistic vocabulary in *El Monte* occasionally takes the form of demonization. Discussions of the iconic Abakuá masquerades known as Ireme and/or *diablitos* (literally, "little devils") offer one example, yet translating *diablitos* into English would flatten the vocabulary (such as referring exclusively to Ireme), and it might even mislead readers; therefore, the word is italicized as a discrete foreign term. On a graver note, Cuban Congo traditions in particular are often framed as amoral (and more susceptible to immorality), and traditions regarded as *judío* (literally, Jewish) are frequently even more literally demonized.[14]

The encyclopedia entry for CIPRES (the Chinese weeping cypress) describes blood oaths and an obscure connection between the Cuban Congo tradition known as *mayombe* (whose practitioners are referred to as *mayomberos*) and a European book of spells:

> The relationship between the Cypress and "the one the *mayomberos judíos* call the Devil, and evil spirits," might have its origins and establishment in one popular treatise on magic, which is still being edited and sold because "the *conguería* worked with him a lot, and he's a genie for *mayomberos*." Even if there is no romantic cypress tree growing in a cemetery, every other tree, herb, and shrub within its walls is useful for black magic.

The passage contains an explicit formulation in which Congo traditions and people—in the words of one of Cabrera's anonymous informants, *la conguería*—are consistently, literally demonized. Likewise, the term *magia negra* is translated literally as "black magic," and it should be read with a keen sense of the ambiguous resonances between morality and race. Indeed, the discussion of *mayomberos judíos* is based on a patently anti-Semitic formulation, inherited from the Spanish Inquisition and *reconquista*, that is still used colloquially in Cuba and beyond.

Invoking the European language of "the Devil," the least pejorative interpretation of *mayombero judío* might be "practitioner of unorthodox Mayombe," but the terminology itself—which I italicize without translation—explicitly equates Jewishness with amorality and evil, forcing us to contemplate a tragic confluence of two diasporas. In chapter 2, a dramatic revelation by Calazán's tutelary orisha makes the negative quality of *judío* clear:

---

14   For a discussion of various intra-African ethnic stereotypes and hierarchies in Cuba, see Capone (2000).

That is how Changó took possession of Calazán at one of those unforgettable gatherings, revealing something that the old man had kept hidden from me: that he—his horse Bangoché (Calazán)—was a *mayombero judío*, "as evil as the devil himself." And he ordered us to tell him "that he was tired of his shamelessness, and that he would make him eat dirt before sending him to Ile Yansa," the cemetery. "Kuruma koi ina koi mowi." (With him, Changó, disagreements are tragic.)

Besides its frankly sensationalistic tone, the passage offers layers of commentary on racialized notions of good and evil, and it identifies layers of identity and moral hierarchy (in ascending order of authority: person, priest, and orisha). The passage also illustrates Cabrera's artful, oblique approach to translation: for example, Ile Yansa is—more literally—"home of the mother of nine" (i.e., the orisha Oya), and it only translates as *cemetery* (*cementerio*) idiomatically, in the context of Lucumí mythology and symbolism.

Like so much else in *El Monte*, the passage about Calazán's possession elaborates a partial, oblique, and poetic sense of meaning, and it can be read as a provocative invitation for readers to join in her process of documentation: the parenthetical commentary on the Lucumí phrase "Kuruma koi ina koi mowi" (With him, Changó, disagreements are tragic) is not a translation either; rather, it is a literal quotation of commentary, a sort of summary, synthesis, or moral of the story offered by an anonymous elder (possibly Calazán himself). It is an invitation to join Cabrera in deciphering literal meaning, mythological and ritual context, and philosophical principles for ourselves.

Clearly, though, the term *mayombero judío* is defined by shame and dishonor. Savvy readers wonder—along with Cabrera—whether the term might merely masquerade as a religious affiliation, perhaps functioning as an anti-Semitic catchall for unorthodox or unconscionable ritual action. Likewise, as she navigates the negative ends of the moral spectrum, Cabrera's descriptions of ruthless cruelty can be shocking by any measure, and the sensational nature of episodes she narrates might even provide fuel for racist caricatures, stigmatization, or persecution. That said, some of these horrifyingly dramatic accounts of occult rituals might "work"—in social, psychological, and/or mystical ways—as competitive counternarratives: portraits of adversarial foils ("Those people are savages") and/or belligerent, intimidating self-mythology ("We don't give a f——").

As the botanical encyclopedia entry for CAFE (coffee) notes, "Offerings to the *muertos* never lack the cup of coffee they always enjoyed in life." Additionally: "'It's the great intermediary for sorcery,' and there are places where one should not drink it." This is a warning: the strong taste, dark color, and thick texture of coffee can mask or hide other substances mixed into it, making it ideal for the covert delivery of poisons and potions. (See also the entry for CHICHARRON DE MONTE.) In Cuba, where coffee is ubiquitous, seeing every cup as a source of existential danger leads to a hypervigilance that might be regarded as paranoia and/or common sense. More broadly, the passage on coffee is only one of countless ways to read *El Monte* as a historical case study of nineteenth- and early twentieth-century Cuba, a time and place in which living memory was saturated by the chaos of slavery, colonialism, and civil war—chaos that was, in turn and in no small measure, animated by a modern global market for sugar, tobacco, and coffee.

En lengua: Translation, Transposition, and Transliteration

The confluence of Afro-Cuban languages in *El Monte* presents one of its most valuable contributions, as well as some of the most severe challenges to translation. The elderly priests meticulously transcribed by Cabrera were one or two generations away from Africa, and their words contain a wealth of detail that is extremely valuable to readers interested in the linguistic dimensions of the African diaspora. Of course, the linguistic richness of the book can also make it daunting. According to Rodríguez-Mangual, "The only informed reader who might be able to understand all the different registers would be a specialist who knows not only Spanish, of course, but also the Cuban syncretism of Lucumí, Congo, Arará, and the Ñáñigos. Some religious prayers fill long paragraphs. They are citations of other voices, in another language, where oftentimes the language is not identified and no Spanish translation is included" (2004, 89). This point is crucial and insightful: *El Monte* is obscure by nature, and Rodríguez-Mangual's example of the "different registers" in Cabrera's text illustrates the virtual impossibility of any individual interpreting the full spectrum of those registers.

The following example, which consists of several lines of a Lucumí invocation for the orisha Elegua, illustrates how meaning can become obscure or lost in translation. Rather than quoting the passage verbatim, Rodríguez-Mangual mistakes a few syllables of Lucumí words for Spanish homonyms, then translates those words into English. Cabrera's original text reads, "Elegguá tubo cosi laroye aquí bollú Baba" (1992, 92–93). In Rodríguez-Mangual's English-language monograph, the passage is nearly identical: "Eleggua *had almost* laroye *here* bollú Baba" (2004, 89, emphasis added). As a linguistic formula, small but significant errors introduced by the translation can be visualized as follows:

tubo cosi (Lucumí) ≠ *tuvo casi* (Spanish) ≠ had almost (English)
aquí (Lucumí) ≠ *aquí* (Spanish) ≠ here (English)

In this instance, a discrete cultural and linguistic form (Lucumí) is inadvertently mistaken for a hybrid (Cuban syncretism, acculturation, etc.). Misunderstandings of crucial details like these might thereby lend support to theoretical frameworks (syncretism, acculturation, etc.) that are contrary to the evidence in Cabrera's text (linguistic survivals, etc.), inadvertently distorting linguistic data, not to mention readers' perspectives. The first task, then, involves distinguishing Afro-Cuban terms and Spanish terms. Despite my best efforts to read more closely, conduct research, reflect, and—most important—solicit input from a cohort of expert readers, errors like these undoubtedly lurk in these pages. Subsequent editions will hopefully offer even more refined versions of the text. And despite its quasi-biblical status, Cabrera's original text undoubtedly contains many such misunderstandings and errors.

African (or Afro-Cuban, African-inspired, etc.) language is referred to generically as *lengua* (literally, "tongue" or "language"), which is analogous to the use of the term *nación* (literally, "nation") as a generic reference to African-born people. Indeed, the term *en lengua* recurs throughout *El Monte*, invoking both literal African languages and/or mystical languages of liturgical ritual and possession trance, the latter being more explicitly idiomatic, poetic, idiosyncratic, and interpretive. But both *lengua* and *nación* illustrate ways that Africanness and mysticism tend to define each other, in Cuba and elsewhere (see Maguire 2018; Miller 2004; and Wirtz 2007a, 2007b, 2011, 2013, 2014). How did Cabrera write out Afro-Cuban vocabulary in the original text? The question—whether technical, linguistic, or philosophical—is inseparable from historical context. For example, a great many African-born people in Cuba (*gente de nación*) undoubtedly spoke several languages before being taken across the Atlantic Ocean—primarily, in *El Monte*, the languages of the Òyó, Dahomey, and Kongo colonial-era African empires.[15] As Cabrera

---

15   A fourth, quasi-ethnic branch of African tradition in Cuba—Abakuá—features prominently in *El Monte*, and it is the focus of chapters 8 and 10. Paradoxically, Abakuá tradition simultaneously includes and excludes a general public. On one hand, it is a tradition based on continually encoding (and restricting) culture according to an Afro-centric, exclusively male ritual affiliation: the culture of Abakuá can be forbiddingly hermetic and obscure. On the other hand, as a cultural and historical phenomenon, the virtuosic performances of African heritage by Abakuá members connect Cuba to the broader historical Afro-Atlantic: for example, if we consider the words *chévere* and *asere*, it is arguable that Abakuá branches of Afro-Cuban tradition have installed themselves even more profoundly in the collective cultural consciousness than the Lucumí, Congo, or Arará branches. Cf. Cabrera (1950, 1959, 1975, 1982b, 2020); virtually the entire bibliography of Fernando Ortiz, starting with *Hampa afrocubana* ([1906] 1973); Brown (2003a); Miller (2000a, 2000b, 2004, 2009, 2016, 2020); Sosa Rodríguez (1982); and Thompson (1983).

makes clear, the book—and her entire Africanist agenda—wrestled, continually, sometimes intimately, with the legacy of tragic cultural loss of slavery. A nostalgic sense of cultural loss (and preservation) extends to a concern for innumerable other, less prominent African languages, dialects, and traditions erased from the Cuban landscape within a generation of the transatlantic slave trade.

In the early twentieth century, Cabrera and a handful of her contemporaries were the first to document substantial portions of Afro-Cuban vocabulary in writing, effectively rendering an oral tradition as a literary one for the first time, and their methods were essentially experimental: the pronunciation of Afro-Cuban words was rendered phonetically using Spanish orthography. In this edition, my approach to Afro-Cuban language is based on a translator's version of the Hippocratic oath: to do no harm (or, more accurately, do as little harm as possible). It is also based on a rejection of categorical distinctions between African and Creole traditions (see Akiwowo and Font-Navarrete 2015), and it represents an effort to move away from characterizing Afro-Cuban traditions in terms of diasporic "loss," "corruption," "adulteration," "decay," and so on. Indeed, the idea that African "originals" became inferior Creole derivatives is often naturalized and taken for granted. For example, contemporary Cuban scholars often express this negative formulation of African legacy using the quasi-scientific turn of phrase *sufrió una metamorfosis*, meaning that African culture "suffered" a radical transformation.

Instead, my treatment of Afro-Cuban terms represents an embrace of a fundamental correspondence between various African and Creole traditions that share intimate relationships across space and time. Ultimately and truly, Changó is Shango is Xangô is Ṣàngó; *orisha* is *oricha* is *òrìṣà* is Ocha; *prenda* is *nganga* is *fundamento*; and so on. In that sense, I hope students of Afro-Atlantic languages and liturgies will be able to read the Afro-Cuban terms in this edition as a skeletal "clean slate," an active surface to annotate and build upon. (Soon enough, I expect, we will be able to explore *El Monte* in digital, hypertext-style editions and formats.) Built on polyvocal and nonlinear frameworks that underlie much of Cabrera's work (and arguably, the Afro-Cuban traditions she studied and her generational milieu), a more open model incorporating various translations would be much better suited to the book's nonlinear qualities (and theoretically, would allow readers to access and connect various passages, languages, and interpretations).

In order to convey the sound of the language as faithfully as possible according to English orthography, I have transliterated (or transposed) Cabrera's Spanish-based phonetic versions of Afro-Cuban language into homologous English-based phonetic versions. This intervention attempts to account for two vexing linguistic problems: (1) diacritical marks perform fundamentally different functions in Spanish and West African languages; and (2) this new edition is meant to be accessible to readers who are fluent in African languages and English but not Spanish. In practice, the English-based versions here are intended to sound as close as possible to Cabrera's Spanish-based versions. In the passage cited by Rodríguez-Mangual, Elegguá—which could also be spelled phonetically in Spanish as Elegüá, etc.—becomes Elegua; *cosi* becomes *kosi*; *aquí* becomes *aki*; and *bollú* becomes *boyu*. In this instance, readers with a keen ear for pronunciation and accents will note that Spanish speakers might pronounce *ll* sounds in a variety of ways, emphasizing *j* or *y* fricative sounds to different degrees. Likewise, readers will also notice that the English versions of these words lack diacritical marks (for example, *aquí* becomes *aki*, not *akí*). The decision to remove diacritical marks from Afro-Cuban terms is based on careful consideration, and it merits explanation.

Although Spanish orthography is generally more uniform than English, Cabrera's Spanish-based phonetic versions of Afro-Cuban terms are exceedingly varied and inconsistent. Consequently, my most notable interventions involve diacritical marks. Spanish orthography uses diacritical marks to indicate stress or emphasis. For example, Spanish speakers pronounce *cosi* as "KO-si" (as in "coat" and "see"), *bollú* as "bo-YU" (as in "boat" and "you") or "bo-JU," and so on. But many African languages, including modern standard Yoruba, use diacritical marks to indicate tonality, not stress. In order to avoid further confusion that would be caused by combining different linguistic conventions and pronunciations, I transliterate Spanish phonetic versions of Afro-Cuban language into English phonetic versions.

A handful of examples from the encyclopedia entry for ALGODON (cotton) illustrate my approach. The entry is dedicated almost entirely to the "owner" of cotton, the orisha Obatala, and it contains various accounts, many of which contradict each other; names, identities, and genders blur together, forming a composite image that is characteristic of the book's inherent complexity, paradox, and ambiguity: the orisha is one and/or many, male and/or female, and so on. To reinforce this overall quality, Cabrera's informants—some quoted or cited, others not—often disagree with one another: "'They say the female Odua, known here as Santa Ana, is called Oduaremu? I disagree! She is called Oño oro.' ('Ena oro,' Manuela, a Changó mount, corrects.)" The most common Spanish version of the name—Obatalá—indicates stress on the final syllable; although it does not indicate tonality, most Spanish speakers inflect their pronunciation with a two-tone melody (mid–mid–high). The Spanish version is equivalent to the way Yoruba speakers might pronounce the written Spanish version if they mistook one orthography for another. Yoruba speakers, however, would take care to write and pronounce it as Ọbàtálá, specifying a distinct ọ sound (as in "awe," not "over") and three-tone melody (mid–low–high–high) that is at odds with the most common Cuban pronunciation.

Even when Cabrera is relatively consistent in her transliteration, her spelling allows for considerable variation in pronunciation. For example, she writes the name of one of the paths or avatars of Obatala as Alláguna, except for a single quotation in which she omits the diacritical accent. Regardless of the diacritical accent, the pronunciation remains ambiguous: the consonant *ll* might be pronounced along a spectrum between *j* and *y*, allowing for a difference between Ayaguna or Ajaguna that would be significant to West African speakers in both the nineteenth and twenty-first centuries. These examples illustrate how even the most sophisticated readers might mistake one set of linguistic convention for another, effectively misinterpreting, mishearing and/ or misunderstanding vital antecedents.

On a similar note, the Lucumí word *ire*—written and pronounced according to Spanish orthography as *iré* ("ee-REH")—is usually understood to mean a blessing, good luck, a good thing, and/or a state of goodness. In chapter 9, however, Cabrera's informants use *ire* to mean a taboo or prohibition.[16] The lexical ambiguity of the word *ire*, which can be used to convey two contrary meanings, is an especially significant example of Lucumí vocabulary whose meaning depends on context and/or tonality. Similar in ambiguity are *osa* (divination sign, deity, nine), *ilu* (town, a people, drum), and *oko* (hoe, stone, husband, name, farm, penis).[17] The diacritical marks indicating tonality in Samuel Crowther's Yoruba dictionary distinguish *íre* and/or *ọre* ("goodness; favour; benefit; a blessing; well-wishing") from *ìre* ("curse; execration; imprecation") ([1854] 1913, 138). The exquisitely fine, possibly melodic line distinguishing the meaning of one (positive) *ire* from another (negative) *ire* is a linguistic detail that might shed a unique historical light on fundamental cultural values and philosophical principles.

Cabrera was evidently conscious of the ways meaning might be misconstrued, but she sometimes inscribed her critical interpretations in obscure ways. For example, she sometimes uses the editorial interjection "(*sic*)" as

---

16   Like other passages that refer to informants generically, the sources for these linguistic details remain anonymous. In a characteristic example, Cabrera quotes a source who glosses the Lucumí term *iré* as "mal visto"—literally, "seen as bad," but largely understood as "regarded negatively," a Spanish idiom referring to something disreputable, frowned on, and so on—and accounts for the testimony in a passive voice: "se dice lo siguiente"—literally, "the following is said" (Cabrera 1992, 235–36; see also 271).

17   Alberto Quintero, my primary mentor in orisha ritual traditions, described this prismatic, fluid sense of textual meaning in Lucumí liturgy as a *criptograma* (cryptogram)—i.e., a mystical, linguistic, and symbolic puzzle (personal communication, 2003). See also Quintero and Marcuzzi (2015).

a cautionary note, indicating a conceptual or theological error rather than a misspelling or grammatical error: in chapter 8, she refers to "The Old God, 'the creole Christ' (*sic*) Abasi Okampo"; presumably, "(*sic*)" clarifies that Abasi Okampo is not—strictly or literally speaking—"the creole Christ." Likewise, in chapter 9, Cabrera quotes an anonymous informant: "'Just like a *muerto* is called by the earth from their grave or anything else that belonged to them—their hair, nails, bones, anything that really hangs on to their *vaho* [vapors, odor]' (*sic*)." Again, "(*sic*)" seems to indicate a conceptual error—in this case, an error regarding the nature of the relationship between a *muerto* and their *vaho*. Elsewhere, Cabrera also uses "(*sic*)" to indicate an apparent mispronunciation of a word whose conventional or common origin remain obscure; for example, in chapter 9, she refers to "*concumitancia* (*sic*)," but it remains unclear what the ostensibly correct word might be, much less what it means.

A few notes specific to the botanical encyclopedia merit explanation, all of which are organized in Cabrera's original order—that is, alphabetically according to plants' Spanish names.

In references outside the encyclopedia entries, I have retained the Spanish names of plants in order to allow readers to more easily cross-reference various entries. For example, in the entry for ALBAHACA, I list "basil" as the plant's English common name, along with Cabrera's list of Latin botanical and Afro-Cuban names. Outside the entry, I refer to "albahaca," sometimes adding "basil" in brackets. While this approach makes certain passages less elegant, it is intended to make data in the encyclopedia clearer and more consistent, thereby avoiding a number of more serious pitfalls, and it accounts for the fact that the encyclopedia section is ordered by plants' Cuban names. Within encyclopedia entries for plants that have clear English analogs, I use the common English name to help the prose flow a little more smoothly. For example, in their respective entries, *algodón* is cotton, *calabaza* is pumpkin, *coco* is coconut, *perejil* is parsley, and so on.

In the botanical encyclopedia Cabrera documents numerous African translations of plants' Cuban Spanish names—not necessarily, as we might assume, historical African names for plants. For example, the Congo, Lucumí, and Spanish names for *mariposa* (*Hedychium coronarium*, the butterfly lily), are all literal analogs; all three can be translated into English as "butterfly."[18] It is easy

---

18 In *Anagó*, Cabrera ([1957] 1986, 198) translates the Lucumí word *labé labé* as "mariposa" (butterfly), while Crowther's Yoruba dictionary ([1854] 1913) translates *labalába* as "butterfly." In Cabrera's *Vocabulario Congo* ([1984] 2001), *kanda* is translated as "family," "ceiba," "skin," "paper," "tree bark," and "flag" (192); *fititi nkangriso* is translated as "*mariposa* flower" (*flor de mariposa*; 178); and *nkangreso* is translated as "*mariposa* bud" (*capullo de mariposa*; 251).

to imagine verbal exchanges that might have produced this ethnographic-linguistic-botanical data:

> Holding a *mariposa* leaf, Cabrera asks an herbalist, "What do you call this plant?"
> An herbalist might respond, "Mariposa" (i.e., Spanish for "butterfly").
> "And in Lucumí?"
> "Balaba [or labé labé, labalába, etc.]" (i.e., Lucumí for "butterfly").
> "And in *lengua* Congo?"
> "Fititi nkangriso" (i.e., Congo Cuban for "butterfly plant").

In other words, many of the African names for plants reflect the generative linguistic prowess of Cabrera's informants, a phenomenon that seems as interesting and significant as correlations testing how faithfully African traditions might have been preserved in Cuba. Several annotations identify other instances of these Congo-Spanish and Lucumí-Spanish translations.

· · · · · ·

Readers employing *El Monte* for critical, comparative research on Afro-Atlantic names and idioms should refer to the original Spanish edition (1992). A few details and examples of my approach to the transliteration of Afro-Cuban terms merit explanation, including a handful of notable exceptions, as follows:

+ Essential terms are contextualized in notes, with particular attention paid to Cabrera's three dictionaries of Afro-Cuban vocabulary: *Anagó* ([1957] 1986), *Vocabulario Congo* ([1984] 2001), and *La lengua sagrada de los Ñáñigos* (1988a), translated and annotated in English as *The Sacred Language of the Abakuá* (2020).

+ Generally, proper nouns presumed to have an African provenance are capitalized and transliterated into English phonetic versions (for example, *Oguere* is transliterated as *Ogere*), while Spanish proper names, proper nouns, and terms retain the conventions of Spanish orthography (for example, Rodríguez and *santería*). The term Lucumí is a notable exception: in the specific context of Cabrera's work, the diacritical mark is maintained to deliberately identify and emphasize the term's Cuban, Creole, Spanish-language context, despite the fact that Lukumi and Lucumi would both be acceptable analogs for English-language readers. Other exceptions are identified in footnotes, and Cabrera's original spelling is retained as a default wherever a word's provenance remains unclear.

- Cabrera employs capitalization inconsistently, sometimes artfully, and her use of capitalization is retained unless noted. For example, in a particularly biblical passage in chapter 3, she writes:

  > After he finished the great task of creating the world (but before he retired to heaven to avoid earthly affairs so absolutely, making Heaven itself move away from the earth because humans bothered and "debased" him), the Eternal Father distributed his children throughout the universe.

- Cabrera employs double consonants, suggesting a "hard" clearly defined sound rather than a "soft" subtle one. For example, the proper names Obbatalá, Oddúa, and Oggún suggest that a Spanish speaker should emphasize their *b*, *d*, and *g* sounds, respectively. Because Cabrera and other Spanish writers employ double consonants in an inconsistent and arbitrary way, I avoid this convention for the sake of clarity and consistency. One exception is the ritual name of Cabrera's informant, the renowned orisha priest Oddedei, Calixta Morales.

- Similarly, while double consonants are generally transliterated according to English language convention for clarity, an exception can be found in the botanical encyclopedia entry for CIRIO, a plant whose natural habitat is restricted to Cuba. The Lucumí name for the plant given by Cabrera (*enéen opa* in the original, *ene'en opa* in this edition) suggests two consecutive *eh* sounds—that is, a double vowel sound, not tonality.

- Cabrera often employs two or more ways to spell out the same name. For example, in the header for the botanical encyclopedia for CUABA, the primary Congo name is *inkita*, yet she refers to it as *nkita* within the entry. Where these differences seem arbitrary and do not affect pronunciation, I retain both, sometimes indicating correspondences and differences between them in footnotes.

- When phonetic pronunciation calls for it, the Spanish *c* is replaced with *k* to avoid its mispronunciation as an *s* sound. For example, the Lucumí name for *hinojo* (fennel) is changed from *korico* to *koriko*, but the name Coballende is changed to Cobayende (rather than Kobayende).

- As noted earlier, the Spanish *ll* is generally transliterated in English as *y* in ostensibly Afro-Cuban terms, though it might just as easily suggest a pronunciation closer to a *j* sound.

- The letter *y* can function as either a vowel or a consonant in both Spanish and English. The Spanish consonant *y* is unchanged in English, while the Spanish vowel *y* is transliterated as *i* (as in "icon").

- The letter *i* in italicized Afro-Cuban terms should be read phonetically as a long *e*, as in "eat" (not "inner" or "ire").

- The Spanish nasalized *ñ* is alphabetized between *n* and *o*. In order to avoid confusing it with various possible pronunciations (*ny*, *ni*, etc.), it is generally not transliterated. For example, Aña (Añá, Àyàn, Ayon, etc.)—the proper name given to consecrated Lucumí *batá* (*bàtá*) drums—is retained, despite the fact that it is homologous with the name Anya, and modern Yoruba writers spell it as Àyàn, Àyon, and the like. Cabrera's original text, however, includes numerous notable instances in which she writes Afro-Cuban words out using *ny* instead of *ñ*. For example, the Congo name for the *corojo* palm tree is given as *anyeta* rather than *añeta* or *anieta*, even though all three might effectively sound the same according to Spanish phonetic spelling.

- Sometimes considered a separate letter in Spanish, *ch* is placed between *c* and *d* in alphabetical order. Following this convention, Cabrera's original encyclopedia places the six entries beginning with *ch* in alphabetical order between the last entry beginning with *c* (CURUMAGÜEY) and the first beginning with *d* (DAGAME).

- The *ch*, *s*, and *sh* sounds are indicated in a variety of ways throughout the book, but it is worth emphasizing that they are often effectively interchangeable. For example, Cabrera writes the names Changó (rather than Shangó) and Oshún (rather than Ochún) regularly but not entirely uniformly, while *oricha*, *orisha*, *orisa*, and *orissa* are all used variously and interchangeably. Because these three distinct consonant sounds (*ch*, *s*, and *sh*) are conveyed equally well by English and Spanish orthography, and in recognition of the possibility that these distinctions might suggest historically meaningful dialects and accents, I generally retain Cabrera's transliteration of those three sounds.

- Changó—a doubly Cuban transliteration, with *Ch* and an accent indicating stress on the second syllable—is retained throughout (rather than Sàngó, Shango, etc.), with a few variations indicated in notes. *Kabiyesi* . . .

Lastly, it is worth noting that this edition's bibliography cross-references *El Monte* with portions of a robust, rapidly expanding body of English-language literature on Afro-Cuban language and culture, including landmark translations and studies of Cabrera's work. By definition, this edition's commentary cannot be definitive or comprehensive, and it is not meant to be. More broadly, beyond the conventions of writerly genres, this edition, which has been overdue for at least a half century, will now enter the cultural ecosystem of the early twenty-first century, designed and built—conceptually and technically, like *El Monte*—on quasi-organic, ever-evolving networks of archives. Blessedly, the internet-based digital archives and platforms that will undoubtedly shape the future of Cabrera's legacy seem extremely well suited to her massive, labyrinthine body of work.

May this edition nourish the memories and future legacies of the individuals, communities, and traditions enshrined in it.

Acknowledgments

....

DAVID FONT-NAVARRETE

My work on this edition owes a debt of gratitude to a great many people, and numerous institutions.

First, to Isabel Castellanos, loyal custodian of Cabrera's legacy, whose seal of approval and moral support were decisive. *Gracias, maestra. Ahora sí . . .*

To Don Manolo Salvat and John Szwed, true gentlemen scholars who inspired me with their work, unfailing generosity, and scrupulous honesty.

To the Cuban Heritage Collection at the University of Miami, which now safeguards Lydia Cabrera's personal archives, and especially to my research partners Amanda Moreno, Juan Villanueva, and, most especially, Martin Tsang.

To Smithsonian Folkways, Atesh Sonneborn, and Dan Sheehy.

To Elliot Klein and Morton Marks, whose dedication and hard work helped enshrine Cabrera's legacy.

To Melinda Kanner and Steve Schwerner, whose tender encouragement and camaraderie, long ago at Antioch College, endure.

To Lidia Godoi: *mi amiga, tía, y maestra, paradigma de mujer artista (y) cubana.*

To Donna Torres and Constantino (Manny) Torres, who inspire and know things about plants.

To Clara, Elías, Sabina, Stefan, and the entire Padilla Galarza family, and to Edgar and Diana Moscoso, whose support and understanding have made all the difference over many years now.

To Miguel Díaz Medina, whose virtuosic love of our native language and immutable support tend to leave me speechless. *Gracias, siempre, maestro . . .*

The staff at Duke University Press have been ideal collaborators on this project, and I am especially grateful to Gisela Fosado, Ale Mejía, Lisl Hampton, and Jessica Ryan for their graciousness and diligence. Sincere thanks also to the editorial team at Westchester Publishing Services for their patient and meticulous review of the manuscript in the crucial final stages of production, and to Judith Reveal for her rigorous and sensitive approach to the index.

I am deeply indebted to numerous other teachers, friends, and colleagues for their support and encouragement of this project: Omar Angulo, Idalberto (Puchito) Berriel, Beverly Botsford, Luis Bran, Javier Díaz, David T. Doris, Jonathan Dueck, Harris Eisenstadt, Iya Doyin Faniyi, Bunmi Fatoye-Matory, David F. García, Juan García, Sebastián Guerrero, Greta (Insky) de León, J. Lorand (Randy), Mark Merella, Ivor Miller, Robin Moore, Yaniela Morales, Melissa Noventa, Elaine Penagos, Hiram Puig-Lugo, Michael Birenbaum Quintero, Miguel (Willie) Ramos, Marc Anthony Richardson, Agustín (Billy) Sera, Michael Spiro, and Susan Thomas.

Duke University, and its Africa Initiative, Center for African and African American Research, Thompson Writing Program, and Trent Foundation, provided crucial early support for this edition, as did colleagues, including Vincent Joos, Tsitsi Jaji, Wyatt MacGaffey, Charles Piot, Luis Othoniel Rosa, and Jaki Shelton Green.

As the project developed, I also received generous support from the City University of New York (CUNY), its CUNY Research Foundation, Lehman College, and Professional Staff Congress. I also received much-needed support and camaraderie from colleagues at CUNY—most especially, Alejandro Castro, MX Cooper, and Benjamin Lapidus.

A Gerald E. and Corinne L. Parsons Fund for Ethnography Award from the American Folklife Center at the Library of Congress helped me make new connections between *El Monte* and Cabrera's other projects, and it offered precious opportunities to nourish the archive. More recently, a US Latino Digital Humanities Grant from Arte Público and the University of Houston, shared with Martin Tsang, has offered a transformative way to continue developing this vein of work.

This edition has been an act of love and devotion, and the book itself is now evidence of a tribute paid to *el monte*.

Numerous deceased friends and mentors—QEPD, *iba e*—made direct, indelible marks on me, and they shaped my approach to this edition: Michael

Marcuzzi, Akinṣola Akiwowo, Olympia Alfaro, Carolina Robertson, Robert Farris Thompson, Ángel Bolaños, Alberto Quintero, and Acelia Cebreco Clejer.

My mother, Margarita Navarrete, dedicated countless hours of hands-on work on this edition, and she deserves credit as coeditor, coresearcher, and cotranslator. She reviewed countless drafts with a sharp maternal eye, a sober, scholarly medium for Cabrera's world and words. Along the way, she shed light on countless confounding problems of language, history, and culture. I am grateful for the privilege. *Iya mi, modupue* . . .

This edition is dedicated to Denise and our children, Luna Celia and Manuel Octaviano: your well-being is my north star on the road, in *el monte*, and you paid this tribute with me. May our sacrifices be witnessed, may our work be rewarded, and may our blessings multiply and flourish. *Iba to to to* . . .

New York City
2022

EL MONTE

PREFACE

The notes that make up this volume are the product of several years of patient effort.

There is no need to underscore that I am publishing them without any hint of scientific ambition. If it is possible to speak of this book in terms of methods, even in rough terms, then my method was imposed by the explanations and digressions—each one inseparable from the rest—of my informants, who were incapable of adjusting to any plan or program. My desire to be precise might be excessive, and it might make portions of the text tedious or confusing, but I have always followed my informants closely. I have carefully avoided modifying their opinions or their words, clarifying them only when they would otherwise remain completely unintelligible to the layperson. I do not omit repetition or contradiction, because in their details, one can discern constant disagreements among "authorities" in Havana and Matanzas (the latter being more conservative), as well as between elders and youths, and between the countless *cabildos* or *casas de Santo*.[1]

---

1   DF-N: *Cabildo* and *casa de Santo* both refer to Afro-Cuban religious and cultural institutions. A *cabildo* is most often defined as a mutual aid society based on hereditary, religious, and/or ethnic identity. Based on both antecedent African and Catholic models, cabildos were most active in the late nineteenth century, generally organizing according to a shared African ethnicity (e.g., Iyesa) and devotion to a Catholic saint (e.g., San Juan Bautista). Although cabildos were most prominent during the Spanish colonial era and often relied on official status conferred by the Catholic Church and the state, several have remained continuously active, while others were established later or were reconstructed

I was able to gain the trust of these elders, many of them children of Africans, who were the most knowledgeable and respectful bearers of their traditions. Without altering their charming and peculiar forms of expression, I want to offer their words, exactly as they were spoken to me, like an ear without an intermediary, to students of a deep, living imprint left on this island: the magical and religious concepts, beliefs, and practices of *negros* imported from Africa during several uninterrupted centuries of human trafficking.

It is not easy to gain the trust of these elders, priceless wellsprings near the point of exhaustion, without having anyone feel rushed to make the most of them for the sake of our folklore. They test the researcher's patience, and they require considerable amounts of time. It takes time to understand their euphemisms and their superstitions about language. Indeed, some things should never be spoken clearly, yet it is essential to learn how to understand them. In other words, we must learn to think like these elders. We must submit to their whims, bad habits, and moods, adapting ourselves to their schedules and frustrating delays. We must pay dues, employ cleverness sometimes, and wait without any rush. They do not understand the hurrying that undermines modern life and sickens the spirit of whites: oppressive rushing, pressure, and anxiety. "Hurrying only makes you tired." And so, the researcher must assimilate their calm slowness and its great philosophical virtue: acceptance. "For everything in life, we need acceptance." And if we want to know, for example, why the goddess Naná "wants" a bamboo knife, not a metal knife? We must accept that they will respond with a story about how the worm made it rain and the spider burned all the hair on its chest. Two or three months later, or perhaps a year later, if we repeat the same question point-blank, we will be told, "Because of what happened to her with the Iron." With a few fragments of the story, we will be told the rest later. These Black elders exasperate our own bad habits as *blancos* [white people]—our mental tendencies, our need for precision, and, most of all, our impatience ("the deer and the turtle can never walk together")—which, in the long run, fail to reward us.

With all modesty and the greatest possible fidelity, my goal has been to present living documents that I have been fortunate to discover, offering material for specialists that has not passed through the dangerous filter of interpretation.[2]

from earlier models. *Casa de Santo* refers to a much more diverse set of religious affiliations: the term is most closely associated with Lucumí tradition's hierarchical initiation lineages, in which a *casa de Santo* refers to any group of devotees affiliated with a particular religious elder (i.e., a ritual "house" or family). See Brown (2003b); Lovejoy (2018); and Ortiz (2018).

2   DF-N: In *When the Moon Waxes Red* (published the year Cabrera died), Trinh T. Minh-ha offers a sharp-edged postmodern complement to Cabrera's documentary project:

I have taken care to draw a mystical map of influences inherited from the two most important and persistent African groups: the Lucumí and the Congo (Yoruba and Bantu). Outsiders have confused these groups for a long time, often classifying them under one erroneous and imprecise term: *ñañiguismo*.[3]

We will identify the Lucumí or Congo as they continue to identify themselves: according to their customs and ancestry, especially when referring to their religious affiliation.

We will employ our consultants' terminology to designate phenomena and practices. These terms are common among the people who—without racial distinctions, and often without regard to social status—regularly patronize a Babalocha or Oluborissa (Lucumí) and a Padre Nganga or Tata Inkisi (Congo).

Certainly, as one North American Africanist commented, "Cuba is the whitest of the Caribbean islands." But the weight of African influence on the segments of the population considered white is enormous, even if it might not be appreciated at first glance. It is impossible to understand our nation without knowing Black people. Today, this influence is even more evident than in colonial times. We cannot get very far into Cuban life without encountering this African presence, which is not manifested exclusively in skin color.

Even if we set aside the Yoruba and Bantu languages, which so many in this country actually speak proudly, we can note other African languages in Cuba, including Arará and Carabalí (Ewe, Bibio, Efí). I intentionally avoided having dictionaries or other reference works at hand, wrote down the voices that my informants normally use in their stories and chats, and followed the

---

Making a film on/about the "others" consists of allowing them paternalistically "to speak for themselves" and, since this proves insufficient in most cases, of completing their speech with the insertion of a commentary that will objectively describe/interpret the images according to a scientific-humanistic rationale. Language as voice and music—grain, tone, inflections, pauses, silences, repetitions—goes underground. Instead, people from remote parts of the world are made accessible through dubbing/subtitling, transformed into English-speaking elements and brought into conformity with a definite mentality. This is astutely called "giving voice"—literally meaning that those who are/need to be given an opportunity to speak up never had a voice before. (1991, 28–29)

3   DF-N: The terms *ñañiguismo* and *ñáñigo* are sometimes extremely pejorative. Historically, they are most commonly applied to members of the Abakuá society, and it frequently connotes racial stereotypes, especially criminality. The opening epigraph to Ivor Miller's *Voice of the Leopard* quotes an unusually enlightened Spanish penal officer in colonial Cuba: "Ñañiguismo ... is not a masquerade, nor a fearsome society. It is an ethnic re-importation: it is an African country that plays, chants, and dances things that in Africa must have meaning. What does it mean? Like Hamlet, I said, *That is the question*" (2009, n.p.).

pronunciation and variations of each individual. In both Lucumí and Congo groups, I have been unable to determine which words correspond to different dialects; in fact, the speakers themselves generally ignore these distinctions. These dialects were (and still are) spoken in various temples and among priestly lineages—if we may designate them as such—and their followers in Pinar del Río, Havana, Matanzas, and Santa Clara. For example, some Lucumí call a tree *iki*, while others call it *igi*; the divinities are *orisha* or *orisa*; herbs are *ewe, egwe, egbe, igbe*, or *koriko*; the rainbow is *osumaremi, ochumare, male*, or *ibari*; and an orange is *oromibo, orombo, olomba, oyimbo, osan, esa*, etc. Analogous differences reveal the dialects of Bantu spoken in Cuba. Among the Congo, we find that an elder is *angu, angulu*, or *moana kuku*; liquor is *malafo* or *guandende*; a sorcerer is *nganga, fumo, musambo, imbanda, muloyi, sudika mambi*, or *mambi mambi*; a party is *bangala, kuma, kia kisamba, kisumba*, etc.

I have rigorously limited myself to recording what I have seen and heard with absolute objectivity and without prejudice.

I accept all criticisms of this book in advance. Its sole value consists exclusively of Black informants' own direct roles in it. They are its true authors.

I want to make it clear from the outset that I do not write or use the word *negro* (black) in a pejorative sense, nor with an inflammatory or prejudiced inflection to humiliate our people of color and erase them from our language and statistics.

I express a most sincere gratitude to the spirits of José de Calazán Herrera Bangoché, also known as El Moro, son of Oba Koso; Calixta Morales, Oddedei, daughter of Ochosi; J. S. Baró, "Campo Santo Buena Noche"; Gabino Sandoval, son of Ayaguna; Nino de Cardenas, son of Ogun.[4] They were my first true collaborators. And to those who came later, lovingly opening the doors to their world, so far from my own. To Francisquilla Ibáñez, *filani oluborisa*, the epitome of African vitality and good humor, and to her *olorisha* daughters Petrona and Dolores Ibáñez. To Marcos Domínguez, *filani oluborisa*, an intelligent, thorough, and understanding collaborator.[5] To the

---

4   DF-N: In tribute to her deceased friends and informants, Cabrera uses the idiomatic phrase "las sombras de" (literally, "the shadows of"), a poetic euphemism used in spiritism to evoke the memory, soul, or spirit of the deceased. See Braude (2001); Davis (2018); Kalvig (2017); Kardec and Wood (1874); Moreman (2013); and Otero (2020).

5   DF-N: Cabrera's Lucumí-Spanish dictionary—*Anagó: Vocabulario Lucumí (El Yoruba que se habla en Cuba)*—translates *filani* simply as "chino," meaning Chinese (or more generically, East Asian) ([1957] 1986, 183). Although the literal meaning of *oluborisa* is a bit more ambiguous, it can be understood as a perfectly intelligible Lucumí term suggesting a chief or owner (*olu*) of the ritual sacrifice (*ebo*) for deities (*orisha, orissa*, etc.). *Olorisha* is a generic term for initiated priests ("owners") of *orisha*. In other words, *El Monte* describes Francisquilla Ibáñez and Marcos Portillo Domínguez (alias Até Borá) as Afro-Asian *orisha* priests. Both individuals play central roles in *La*

conga Mariate, a slave to her gods and her scrupulous conscience. To Anón, another centenarian, who only dared to go out at night to collect alms from a charitable family because children would yell at her during the day, calling her a witch and throwing stones at her. For a month and a half, she arrived punctually to talk with me in the traditional window of a house on Calle Gloria de Trinidad. To the conservative and uncompromising Enriqueta Herrera. And to those youths who preferred to remain unnamed for fear of being branded as traitors by the "*santero* syndicate"; they overcame their qualms and understandable suspicions, and they did not refuse to collaborate with me.

I also thank those who tried to trick and confuse me. They did so with much finesse, and their mystification was no less interesting or plausible.

I owe a great deal to Sra. María Teresa de Rojas, who has helped me so much in the preparation of this book. To Baron J. de Bieskeí Dobrony, who provided me with photographs that were very difficult to obtain: two *iyawos* (recent initiates) greeting the drums, and the painting on the head of a novice during the *Asiento* ceremony consecrating a "child of Santo." To Miss Josefina Tarafa y Govín, who was kind enough to accompany me on many folkloric outings in order to take most of the photographs that appear at the end of this text. One exception is the portrait of Calixta Morales, Oddedei, taken by the unforgettable writer and distinguished Venezuelan Teresa de la Parra. Teresa saw Calixta often; she enjoyed their conversations during her stay in Havana, and she retained memories of some of the old *iyalocha*'s immortal sayings, style, and courtesy. And she never forgot the inimitable actor Calazán, nor the fabulous beggar who was like a Black Diogenes and would bring her oranges as gifts. They were characters that could be incorporated directly into a novel. The writer identified them with the flesh-and-blood Vicente Cochocho from her fragrant book *Memorias de Mamá Blanca*, as well as other characters— just as interesting and likable—from her childhood at Hacienda Tazón in a Caracas full of deep eaves and kneeling windows. She would have brought them back to life in a book she dreamed of writing about colonial times.

I consider one of the photographs in this series to be evidence of support from a fearsome *nganga*, as well as a display of its sorcerer's obedience to its mandates. María Teresa de Rojas was finally able to photograph a magical container, a *prenda* of Mayombe, for me. The *ngangas*, "mounted" orishas, the stones in which they are adored, the ceremonies: none of these should be photographed under any circumstances. To date, *santeros* and *paleros* are inflexible on this point. I had forgotten that Baró had refused emphatically when I had

laguna sagrada ([1973] 1993). Até Borá is pictured in several photographs (by Josefina Tarafa) in *El Monte*, and he is featured prominently as the lead singer on the first two discs of the *Música de los cultos africanos en Cuba* collection (recorded by Tarafa). See Font-Navarrete (2022).

asked him for permission to photograph his *nganga* three or four years earlier. Then, one day, he arrived unexpectedly, carrying nothing less than his magical, sacred, and awe-inspiring cauldron hidden in a black sack. The spirit who lived in it had stated that *it wanted to be photographed*, and that it was fine for the "moana mundele" to keep the photograph. The old man was anxious to satisfy the unexpected whim of his *nganga*. Calmly, he authorized me—"with the permission of the Prenda"—to publish the photograph if I so desired.

It is the only *nganga* that has been photographed in Cuba. For the first time in his life, Baró also agreed to remain still for a few seconds in front of the lens, the unsettling "mensu" of a camera.

He had previously refused me this favor, not because he was suspicious of my good intentions, but out of fear that the image might end up in the hands of another sorcerer. A rival might use the photograph to cast a spell, killing him easily by performing rituals with needles or "lukambo finda ntoto" (in a grave). Desecration aside, his rivals would have been able to use the photograph to magically restrain and weaken his *nganga*.

In order to photograph the sacred stones of the Lucumí, the orishas were always consulted beforehand.

I would like to acknowledge Srta. Julia García de Lomas, who endeavored to decipher my tangled handwriting and copy it on her Remington typewriter. I would also like to acknowledge the workers at the superb Burgay press for the interest and care they have all invested in the preparation of this volume.

LYDIA CABRERA
from the Quinta San José, April 1954

1

....

EL MONTE

Among Black Cubans, the belief in the spirituality of *el monte* persists with astonishing tenacity. The same ancestral divinities live in the wilderness and undergrowth of Cuba as in the African bush, and just as they did in the days of the slave trade. They are the powerful spirits that are still feared and venerated, and their hostility or benevolence determines human success or failure.

Black people who enter the wilderness, who fully commit themselves to going inside "the heart of a *monte*," have no doubt about the direct contact they establish with supernatural forces. There, in the true domain of these forces, they are surrounded: because of the invisible (and sometimes visible) presence of gods and spirits, every part of *el monte* is considered sacred. "El Monte is sacred" because it is the home where the divinities "live." "The Santos are more present in El Monte than in the sky."

It is a source of life. An old herbalist named Sandoval, descendent of Egwados, tells me, "We are children of El Monte because life started there. The Santos are born in El Monte, and our religion is also born from El Monte." "Everything can be found in El Monte"—the foundations of the cosmos—"and we need to ask El Monte for everything. It gives us everything." In these explanations and others like them ("life came from El Monte," "we are children of El Monte," etc.), El Monte is related to the Earth, a concept of the universal Mother, source of life. "Earth and Monte are the same."

"The Orishas Elegua, Ogun, Ochosi, Oko, Ayé, Changó, and Ayáguna are there. And the Egun—the dead, Eléko, Ikús,

Ibayés. . . ." "It's full of the dead people! The *muertos* [spirits of ancestors, deceased] go to the wilderness."

"In El Monte, you find all the Eshu," diabolical beings. The Iwi, "the *addalum* and *ayés* or *aradyés*. The Bad-Thing, Iyondo."[1] Dark and maleficent spirits "who have bad intentions." "All the strange people from the other world," ghostly and horrible to behold. Also, otherworldly animals, "like Keneno, Kiama, or Kolofo. Aroni, may God deliver us!" Alone in the tangled wilderness, the clairvoyant perceives bizarre and astonishing forms: to the human eye, they sometimes become the elves and wild demons that Black people sense living in the vegetation.

"I swear on my soul," my beloved teacher José de Calazán Herrera confides in me. "I saw the head of a big Black man, who was hairy like a spider. He had feet coming out of his ears, and he was hanging by one foot from a tree branch." And we should have no doubt about the horrifying reality of this head, glimpsed in a thicket and formed in the mystery of shadows and fear, nor other visions produced by some sort of illusion. For a Black man of faith,[2] these visions quickly become reality, like everything he dreams or imagines. Due to an extraordinary proclivity for self-suggestion, the lies he so frequently improvises eventually impose themselves on his spirit with the conviction of a true experience. We should keep this in mind and avoid doubting his sincerity, thereby understanding him better. It is sufficient to invent a fantastic event and repeat it poetically a few times, thereby irrationally transforming it. Then the event will remain recorded as something that actually happened to him. And, while the gift of auto-suggestion is not strictly exclusive to Black people (even if it is less exaggerated among others), it explains many of the distinctive features of their souls, their religious fervor, their credulity, and—of course—the persistent and enormous influence that is continuously exerted on their lives by sorcerers and magic.

El monte is the natural domain of spirits, many of which have been seen by several of my most reliable and self-confident informants, both young and old, "with their own eyes and wide awake." Logically, it is a dangerous place for those who venture into it without taking precautions. Everything looks natural, but it exceeds the illusory limits of nature: everything is supernatural. We *blancos* tend to be truly ignorant of this truth, or perhaps we have forgotten it in this era. Like all spirits and divinities, the majority of spirits living in specific trees and brush—the great divinities that live in and control *el monte*, such as the ceiba and *jagüey*—may be benevolent or malevolent, and some of them are fearsome, but they are all extremely sensitive. I would also add, with

---

1   DF-N: In the original, "Cosa-Mala" (Bad-Thing) is a euphemism for the devil.

2   DF-N: The original phrase, "un negro creyente," might also be interpreted as "a religious Black person," "a credulous Black person," and/or "a Black devotee."

my teachers' approval, that these spirits are all extremely self-serving. It is essential to know their needs and demands, proceeding in accordance with the rules established by the spirits themselves ("El Monte has its law") and those African grandparents who taught and initiated the old Creoles. In order for *el monte* to respond favorably to humans and support their efforts, one must "know how to enter El Monte." I defer to the words of Gabino Sandoval, who takes pride in explanations that offer "a clear understanding" and knows how to choose good examples:

> Understand that Eggo, El Monte, is like a church.[3] A white person goes to church to ask for what they do not have, or to ask Jesus Christ or the Virgin Mary or some other member of the heavenly family to maintain what they have and strengthen it. They go to the house of God to attend to their needs . . . What can a human do without God's help? We go to El Monte as if going to a church, because it is full of Santos and ancestors. We ask them for the things we need for our health and our business. Now, if we're supposed to be respectful in the homes of strangers, then shouldn't we be even more respectful in the home of the Santos? White people don't go into a church carelessly, as if they're in their own home . . . What will the Santísimo [Almighty] think if you turn your back on the altar? After you've asked him to give you health, to help you, to give you this and that? Jesus Christ will be offended. If he hears you, he won't listen or pay attention. Because everything has its own way . . . and that's no way to address a Santo. Well, it's the same in El Monte, because it also has Santos, the Animas are there, and all kinds of spirits, so you don't enter without respect and composure. And that's all the more important when you go there to ask for something.

Essentially, *el monte* contains everything Black people need for their magic, to preserve their health and well-being and defend themselves from all adversity. It provides all of the most efficacious elements for protection or attack. But in order for it to consent to the taking of an indispensable plant, stick, or stone, it is necessary to respectfully request permission. It is especially important to pay religiously with liquor, tobacco, money, and—on certain occasions—the spilling of the blood of a chicken or rooster. This is the "derecho," the ritual tribute that everyone owes it. "One tree does not make El Monte." And in *el monte*, every tree, plant, and herb has its owner, and with a perfectly defined sense of ownership.

---

3   DF-N: Sandoval uses "Eggo" as a somewhat obscure Lucumí word for *el monte*, which is analogous to other Lucumí terms such as *igbo*, *ibo*, and the like.

"Without courtesy," Baró assures me, "El Monte won't even give so much as a small leaf or anything else that has any virtue." Let us not forget that our Black people humanize everything: "If you do not greet El Monte, if it doesn't collect its due, *it gets angry*."

Even the most daring thief in town would not dare to take a *bejuco* [liana vine] out in the open to prepare an amulet without uttering a reverential "con licencia" [with permission, authority], then paying the invisible and fearsome owner a few copper coins in good faith. Or, if one does not have coins, an equivalent handful of corn kernels.

M.C. visits the bush often during the full moon and always begins by saluting the Viento del Monte: "Tie tie lo masimene—good morning. Ndiambo luweña, tie tie. Ndiambo que yo mboba mpaka memi tu kuenda mensu kunansila yari-yari con Sambianpungo mi mboba kuna lembo Nsasi lumuna. Nguei tu kuenda. Cuenda macondo, nboba nsimbo. Nsasi Lukasa! Pa kuenda mpolo, matari Nsasi . . ."

God, give me permission.[4] In short, speaking in the Congo language, M.C. says to *el monte*, "See what I am giving you so you'll allow me to gather what I need for a talisman or some powders, so that I can take a stone of Nsasi."

He knows that, without this reverence, what he gathers "would have no essence." Spirit. Soul.

The role of trees and plants is too important in the religious and mystical life of Black people—and the whole of Cuba's mestizo population—for them to, in Catalino's words, "neglect El Monte."

"There is no Santo"—Orisha—"without Ewe." Nor can there be Nganga, Nkiso, or magical charms without Vititi Nfinda. Trees and plants are beings that are endowed with souls, intelligence, and willpower. Like everything that is born, grows, and lives under the sun. Like every manifestation of nature. Like everything in existence. At least, that is what my many informants steadfastly believe.

A woman complains to me, "This year, my *marpacífico* [hibiscus] decided not to give me a single flower. Not one! It's punishing me, but we'll see how we take care of it. The thing is, my neighbors asked me for a few leaves, and I handed them over without thinking. He doesn't like that. He wants to be paid. It's only fair. You know, one shouldn't give away leaves from *marpacífico* or *paraíso* for free."

Even if a particular tree is not, strictly speaking, the home or "throne" of a divinity, it possesses the virtues given to it by the divinity to whom it belongs. It has its "aché," its grace, power, and gifts.[5] Christian folk traditions

---

4   DF-N: The original phrase, "dame licencia," is a request for ritual license, permission, authority, and/or absolution.

5   DF-N: The term *aché* is analogous to the Yoruba *àṣẹ*. See Abiodun (1994).

encompass an old and universal tradition, which also knows a great deal about miraculous herbs and trees: certain plants that were born along the Calvary, healed the sores of Our Father, or were planted by the Virgin herself received their beneficial properties from these divine hands. And in others, as in all things, the Devil got himself involved.

Black people attribute healing properties and magical powers to trees and plants. They cannot forgo using and invoking the protection of plants' innate spirits on an almost daily basis. They make use of *ewe* or *vititi nfinda* in every moment of their lives. Magic is the eminent concern of our Black informants, and their greatest wish is to obtain dominion over powerful occult forces that will blindly obey them.

In many instances our Black people are *brujos* [sorcerers, wizards, or witch doctors] in an individualistic sense that is disapproved, feared, and condemned by those whose orthodox magic—that is, practices and rituals—is directed toward the good of the community

In other instances, the occasion might call for someone to be a *brujo* for personal gain and to the detriment of others: a *brujo* out of necessity, in self-defense . . . "It's very dangerous to live here without protective magic. Oh! Cuba is full of sorcery!" Facing any natural accident or obstacle that arises in their lives, whether inexplicable or . . . easily explained, they react with the same primitive mentality as their ancestors. Their way, like our own, is permeated by inconceivable magic—despite public schools, universities, or a Catholicism that perfectly accommodates their beliefs and has not altered the essence of most of the people's religious ideas. (C. asks, "Wasn't Jesus born in *el monte*, on a pile of grass? To go to heaven and become God, didn't he die in a *monte*, Mount Calvary? He was always roaming around *montes*. He was an herbalist!"[6])

Without changing the African patterns of defense (or attack), they fight against others' incessant sorcery by preparing an integral preventive technology of formulas, antidotes, counterspells, "work," "nsalanga," and "ebos" derived from the secret qualities of a tree, vine, or herb. The descendants of the Lucumí and Yoruba call leaves *ewe*, while the descendants of Congo call them *vititi nfinda*, although this latter term includes trunks, leaves, and roots. They can cure a simple stomachache or a malignant sore. And above all else, through *ewe* or *vititi* and their "secrets," they achieve a supernatural effect. They know very well that they could never achieve this effect by relying solely on their own scant powers—that is, without the resources of magic, gods, and spirits. With *ewe* or *vititi nfinda*, one can "spoil" a curse, purify or "cleanse" the macula of sorcery from an individual, conjure a bad influence, "close the path

---

6   DF-N: The juxtaposition of various meanings of *monte* (as both forest and hill) establish a consonance between African and European myth and theology.

of evil," ward off misfortune (a tragedy, or a bothersome person) from a home, neutralize the malicious actions of an enemy, or—even more practical and satisfactory—dispatch them to the otherworld.

In the fields of magic and folk medicine (which are inseparable from magic), trees and herbs respond to any request. Considering them as necessary agents of health and fortune, it is no wonder that our Black people—and perhaps we should speak of our people, most of whom are racially mixed physically and spiritually—often have great knowledge of the healing properties attributed to plants' magical powers. "They heal, because they themselves are sorcerers."

It is important to heal from an illness, but it is even more important to be liberated from a dark shadow,[7] an evil influence, a "malembo," or a "ñeke," which tends to be the cause of sickness.

Every calamity has an antidote or a deterrent in a tree or weed—and, of course, in the intervention of another spirit that works through it, fighting and defeating the adversarial spirit that produced the harm.

A "palo"—a stick or a tree—is known as *musi* or *inkunia nfinda*. One spirit attacks us and the sorcerer defends us with another. The "palo" can cause good or harm according to the intention of the person who cuts it and uses it.

The ritual, the word, the magical threat, determines its ensuing effect. And there are two roads for everything: the good one and the bad one. "One takes whichever road they want." "The palo does what it's told to do."

In the countryside—and, truth be told, in Havana itself—pharmacies have been unable to compete decisively with the natural pharmacy, which is within everyone's reach in the nearest thicket. The names given to the most common plants are picturesque, sometimes obscene.

Sodium bicarbonate does not enjoy any more prestige than concoctions made with Ogun's basil (*albahaca morada*) or Obatala's marjoram (*mejorana*). For the slightest affliction or mishap, to improve the luck of a person whose destiny has darkened, any white woman "de la tierra"[8]—without necessarily being an *iyalocha*, or priestess—will prescribe a series of herbs that inspire more confidence than the pharmacist's medicines. The medicines do not act with spiritual power in the way plants do. According to the faith and experience of our people, plants are a more effective way to combat bad luck, "la salación."[9]

---

7   DF-N: Cabrera's original phrase, "mala sombra," can be usefully understood as an evil shadow and/or harmful darkness, meaning a dark or malicious spirit. The image is a counterpoint to the positive quality implied by the phrase "las sombras de" (literally, "the shadows of"), which Cabrera uses to commemorate her deceased informants and friends in the preface.

8   DF-N: The term *de la tierra* literally means "of the land"—that is, native-born Cuban.

9   DF-N: A *salación* is a jinx, hex, or curse.

The virtues of a "Santo," a supernatural power, exist in every plant. "The medicines are alive in El Monte," one old man tells me. I was unable to convince him to be treated for a case of rheumatism, which a doctor had promised to alleviate. "I know the plant. I know which one is right for me, and I'll go get it. Take your doctor to the bush and see if he knows which plant he has to pull out to cure a cold. I take care of my aches and pains with plants, not needles." Another insists, "You can never rely on doctors." The magic formula heals: the one from the *ngángántare* or *ngángula*; the one from the *agugú*; the one from the *awo* or *babalawo*. Black people in the capital have undeniably adapted to material progress, which we proudly tend to confuse—here more than anywhere else—with culture. They are on an equal level with white people, enjoying every facet of the benefits of civilization. Nonetheless, African atavism is just as strong and irrepressible among Black people in the capital as it is among coarse, backward Black people in the country. The roots planted at the beginning of the sixteenth century remain firm and vigorous. Despite a decisive break in all direct communication with Africa during the second half of the nineteenth century, our Black people—in spirit—have not become any less African. They have not renounced the secret lessons of their elders. They faithfully carry on their old magical practices, and they keep turning to *el monte* for all of it, engaging with the primitive natural divinities their ancestors worshipped and bequeathed to them as living beings who reside in stones, cowrie shells, or trees and roots. Like their ancestors, they still speak to them in African languages—Yoruba, Ewe, or Bantu. The city dweller knows how to read and write, listens to the radio, and spends many of his evenings in a movie theater, but he also makes sacrifices to his fetish, "his prenda," just like a rustic illiterate who still lights his thatched hut in the solitary countryside with a "chismosa" oil lamp. In terms of magic or folk medicine, the latter is considered to be a purer, more rigorous repository of the tradition. Precisely because he has remained in *el monte* and preserved the "secrets" of the African elders, he enjoys the deep respect of the urbane resident of Havana. The city dweller consults with the rural provincial when they find themselves in a particularly difficult situation. And when a "palero" wants to impose his authority, he takes pride in having been the disciple or confidant of a rustic expert.

In both thatched huts in the countryside and comfortable houses in Havana, the god Elegua is represented by a stone carved in the form of a face. Covered in palm oil, he continues (and will continue) to stand guard with his cowrie shell eyes, concealed in a nightstand next to the entrances to the homes of Black people and *mulatos*. He is satisfied by being given the blood of a chicken at least once a month—whenever he does not request, from time to time, the sacrifice of a "tere" (rat) or "ekute" (hutia). All of this takes place in the same room in which a large lithograph of the Sacred Heart of Jesus hangs prominently on the wall, reading, "God bless this home." This religious syncretism does not exclude white people, reflecting a social syncretism that will not surprise anyone familiar with Cuba, and which Fernando Ortiz studied among us more than forty years ago in his book *Los negros brujos*. The Catholic Saints have always coexisted harmoniously and intimately—and now openly—with the African "Saints." In the same way, scientific "patents," penicillin, and vitamins alternate with the plants consecrated by folk healers—sorcerers. The late Calixta Morales, who could recite the Catholic Catechism from memory and was one of the most honorable *iyalochas* in Havana, said that, in the end, "The Santos are the same here and in Africa. They're the same with different names. The only difference is that ours eat a lot and need to dance, while yours are satisfied with incense and oils, and they don't dance." As for medicine, "It's herbalism in disguise"—trees and herbs. "And in *el monte*, they're all *alive and kicking*."

In short, Black people almost always turn to hospitals on the advice of Ifa or *dilogun* [cowrie shell divination]; the *vititi-mensu* or *nkala*, the magic mirror of the *mayombero*; a "Ser" (Being) manifested through a spiritist medium; or when he has no other choice. If he has gone through surgery, he boasts about it: the scar left by the operation is shown off with a certain vanity, and it has a distinctive or even sacred quality, like an "eje" (tattoo).[10] He receives the medicines from the dispensary, and he pays for them more gladly when they are expensive. (If they are expensive, he puts more faith in them.) But, deep down, he places much more trust in the grace of *ewe* or *konge*, the magical prescription of the *santero* dictated by a divinity, which is merely augmented by a physician. Deeply and in every way, he never ceases to be "a child of the Mother Jungle," the mysterious *monte* that is saturated by powerful energies and contains sacred forces. It always awakens an atavistic feeling mixed with euphoria and a profound, fearful mysticism. The holy remedy, the providential salvation, is undoubtedly still found in *el monte*: the descendants of the Lucumí call it *ileiggi, igbo, yuko, oboyuro, nguei, araoko, ego,* or *ninfei*; and the descendents of the Congo call it *musito, miangu, dituto, nfindo, finda, kunfinda,* or *anabutu*. Because the trees (*iki, nkuni, musi*) are the homes of the orishas, *mpungus*, and spirits (*ngangas*). The influences of divinities or the divinities themselves work in the herbs, which are imbued with arcane and essential virtues. They "rule the world" and the destiny of every human being.

---

10   DF-N: The word for "tattoo" is transliterated from *eye* (pronounced "EH-yeh") to *eje* in order to avoid any confusion between the Lucumí term and the English word *eye*.

BILONGO

ILLNESSES. THEIR TRUE OCCULT CAUSES. "THE TRUTH IS THAT NOT
EVERYONE DIES BECAUSE THEIR TIME IS UP." BRINGING DOWN THE
SANTO. TRANCE IN THE RELIGION AND LIFE OF OUR BLACK PEOPLE.

CHARACTERISTICS OF THE DEITIES. ORISHAS AND IKÚS LIVE WITH
OUR PEOPLE IN AN INTIMATE COEXISTENCE. THE STORY OF OMI
TOMI'S DAUGHTER: A "CURSE." THE HAPPINESS AND HEALTH OF
DEVOTEES AND OLOCHAS DEPENDS ON THEIR BEHAVIOR TOWARD
THEIR ORISHA. THE GODS' PUNISHMENTS. ANIMALS CONSECRATED
TO THE ORISHAS. A BABALOCHA OR NGANGATARE SUCCEEDS
WHERE A DOCTOR FAILS.

"There's a spirit where you least expect it." "They're everywhere." "We might not see them, but we're rubbing elbows
with *muertos* [spirits of ancestors, deceased] and the *Santos* all the time." Our Black people are convinced that we
live surrounded by spirits, and whatever bad or good that
may happen to them depends on the influence of spirits.
So they will hardly accept a purely scientific explanation for
an illness troubling them, or that natural causes might have
caused it.

Illness—*oigu, aro, yari-yari, fwa*—is the most fearsome
enemy of people's happiness, especially the poor. And experience will invariably confirm that it is the work of a "bilongo," a
"wemba" or "moruba," a "wanga" or "ndiambo," a "curse," an "ika"

or "madyafara" introduced into the body.[1] And we must surrender ourselves to evidence that it is the result of an evasive enemy's maneuvers to reach someone by way of an impalpable, malevolent energy. Of a soul. The sick person is quickly convinced of this, and a faint suspicion they could scarcely admit to themselves becomes a certainty after a "registro" or a "vista" [consultation, divination, reading] with a *babalawo*, a diviner priest in the Regla[2] Lucumí, or a Bokono from the Regla Arará-Dahomey, or a *mayombero* (the *kintuala nkisi* or *nfumo* of the Regla Conga), or a sorcerer, known generically as a *mayombero*. In the end, the people always rely on these consultations with millenary characters who fuse the roles of diviner, doctor, magician, and . . . priest. We find them at every turn in Cuba, even if they are sometimes described in a way that is not at all respectful. They will suddenly reveal the bad intentions of someone who has bewitched them, "working" or "binding" them. They will describe the physical and moral characteristics of their enemy in minute detail, identifying that enemy as the sole cause of their ills. It goes without saying that these illnesses, the constant product of witchcraft, are the ones most often cured as soon as the diviner intervenes.

---

1 DF-N: Cabrera begins her essay on *bilongo* with a definition of terms, outlining vocabulary and ideas, and including a list of rough synonyms in various languages. Her study of Afro-Cuban vocabulary became the primary subject for several other books (see Cabrera [1957] 1986, [1984] 2001, 2020), and it runs throughout *El Monte*.

2 LC: The word *Regla* [Order, Rite, Rule, or Principle] is used by the people to mean a cult or religion. It comprises the religious and magical rituals and practices from Africa that are divided into two large groupings: Regla de Ocha (Yoruba) and Regla Mayombe (or Palo Monte). In simple terms, "Regla Lukumi" and "Regla Conga" correspond roughly to the two predominant African ethnic groups according to their numbers. Their languages, music, and cults remain living representations of the Yoruba and Bantu cultures.

In other words, their priests and wizards (although our *mayomberos*—sorcerers—are not worthy of the term) "who don't stray from their Reglas" define them in moral terms, like the old *Diccionario de Autoridades* [Dictionary of the authorities]: "In this sense, they function as a way to measure actions so they might be adjusted and straightened out."

I have heard many people of color refer with absolute devotion to the Catholic religion as the *Regla* of white people. Today, some are already referring to the *Regla* of spiritism, whose popularity is booming, even among *babalawos*, *babalochas*, *iyalochas*, *ngangas*, and Madre *ngangas*.

The Regla Arará—Arará Dahomey—is smaller in Havana than it is in Matanzas, and it enjoys enormous prestige. It is considered very strict and recalcitrant about communicating its secrets to white people. The language spoken by its *bokonos*—Arará (Ewe)—is very difficult to learn and pronounce, like their liturgical chants. And it is very costly, which only increases its prestige. Its priests charge the highest "derechos." A consultation with a diviner in Regla de Ocha costs $1.05. In Regla Arará, it costs $2.05. [DF-N: Throughout, monetary amounts should be understood in historical terms; they refer to Cuban pesos in the early and mid-twentieth century, not US dollars.]

Bound by an unsuspected spell, only another spell will free one from it. *Nganga* against *nganga*! In other words, energy against energy. The "fumbis"—spirits, working in the service of a witch—do not rest. "Kindamba! The one who doesn't keep a lookout will not escape!" "A Loanda War is always sprouting up."[3] The sinister world of witchcraft is always an oppressive enterprise! But luckily, every "kindambazo" and "aye" has a remedy. "A nail removes a nail." "Mayombe shoots and Mayombe answers back." In other words, a sorcerer's work is undone by another sorcerer: "The stick that kills a white dog can kill a black dog." Unless the "curse" has been launched by a Chinese sorcerer. Chinese magic is considered the strongest and most evil of them all, and—according to my Black informants—only another Chinese sorcerer can undo it.

And here we encounter something awful: no Chinese sorcerer will undo a curse, a *"moruba,"* that has been cast by one of their compatriots! For example, we have the unfortunate case of E., the child of a *mulata* and a Chinese man, who died a few years ago in the flower of her youth. When the dying girl's father brought the doctor—also a native of Canton—to the girl's bedside as a last resort, the doctor could not free the innocent victim from the terrible curse, nor did he want to do so. Everyone seems to agree that the same indestructible Chinese "bilongo" is still affecting E.'s family. One of her nieces—who is, incidentally, a very beautiful girl, making the case even more pitiful—lies in bed without speaking or moving for long stretches of time. The family is already convinced of the impotence of doctors from . . . the "Faculty," and the power of *Santeros*. Resigned, they abstain from fighting for a hopeless cause: the girl has been "worked," cursed by a Chinese sorcerer. They all know this. In this case, medical treatment, all of the offerings that might be made to the gods in these cases, the African *santos*, the Lucumí *orisas*, Arará *vudus*, and Congo *mpungus* would all—logically—be useless.

Chinese sorcery is so hermetic that Calazán Herrera—whose name will appear continually throughout these notes, and who "walked the entire island to learn"—was never able to penetrate any of their mysteries or learn anything from them. He only knows that they often eat a paste made from ground bat meat, mixed with the bat's eyes and brains, which is excellent for preserving one's eyesight; they prepare a very strong poison with lettuce; the candle they light for Sanfankon shines but does not burn; they always keep a receptacle

---

3 DF-N: "Loanda War" refers to Congo traditions of spiritual warfare. In context, Loanda—i.e., Luanda, the port city and capital of present-day Angola—refers generically to "Congo-inspired" traditions. See Cabrera ([1977] 1986, [1979] 1986); Martínez-Ruiz (2013); Ochoa (2010); and Thompson (1981).

full of enchanted water behind their doors, which they toss behind the backs of people they want to curse; and they feed their dead very well.

The witchcraft of the *isleños*—natives of the Canary Islands—is also very fearsome. The *isleños* have passed on a great number of superstitions to us. The Islander women can fly "like the witches of Angola," although Enriqueta Herrera assures me that they do not drink blood. They slap their thighs three times and say, "Sin Dios ni Santa María. Sin Dios ni Santa María. A la zánga no má, con ala vá, con ala viene." Then they fly off.

"The Islanders can fly," my friend C. warns me. "I can swear it. They fly riding on brooms, and they fly over the sea. My grandfather was from the Canary Islands. He came to Cuba to work the land, and he bought two or three slaves, and a Black woman. And the usual thing happened . . . The Black woman woke up in the master's bed and started giving him children. That woman, a Congo from Loanda, was my grandmother. My grandfather had left a legitimate wife in the Canary Islands and forgotten all about her. One morning, when my little sister was seven years old, she woke up and said a woman she didn't know had walked into her room and told my sister to be sure to tell her father that she had been there. My mother said that man got scared out of his mind! Especially when he received a letter from the Canary Islands that said the woman had been to his house that night, and she'd seen what was going on with her own eyes, but she didn't want to harm his daughter because she was a very pretty Black girl that was completely innocent. She never came back. Of course, for her part, my Congo mother knew very well what she needed to do to make the Islander woman stop flying . . ."

And the witchcraft of Black Haitians and Jamaicans is not far behind. "They send *muertos* out with an oil lamp to torment those they want to curse. This *muerto* chases them at all hours holding the lit oil lamp in its hand." That is why it is said that the victim of a Jamaican sorcerer has "an oil lamp following them."

When it is not the product of a "kindambazo," a curse, then illness is sure to be the result of a deserved punishment (or sometimes an arbitrary one) decreed by *oru*, the sky. This invariably assumes that an offense has been committed—an act of irreverence or disobedience to the mandates of a deity.

Regarding this rather naive notion of illness that is so strongly rooted in our Black people, we cannot offer a better example than the very typical case of Teresa M., which we will refer to below. She is now a centenarian. In her good old days, she was a seamstress for many of Havana's oldest and most opulent families. She was well known as "Omi Tomi"—her secret Lucumí name— among "the cream of the crop" in those colonial times, in the celebrations of the famous *cabildo* "Changó Terdun,"[4] in the Ibeye's "Palenque,"[5] and in "Pocito."[6]

---

4   LC: The Cabildos—some of which carried on until the early days of the Republican era [after 1902], always with a religious character—were congregations of Black Africans and their Creole descendants, enslaved or free, who belonged to a shared nation, tribe, or locality. They named and submitted to the authority of a foreman and Queen, chosen according to the rank [status, title] of chiefs and princes they had in their homeland, which still bestowed real honors among them. This is like today's older, distinguished *iyalochas*, with whom younger *iyalochas* and *babas* observe an etiquette in which suggests a type of courtly reminiscence. This impression jumps out during the most solemn ceremony of the Regla Lucumí, the *Asiento*, which Oddedei describes: "To make *Santo* is to make a royalty, and *kariocha* is a royal ceremony, like those in the palace of the Lucumí Oba." This observation is interesting: "The *babalawos*, the Mamalochas, formed a court like the one over there."

With a more democratic spirit, the Capataz [leader, overseer] was also elected for their abilities and knowledge.

In the old Cabildos, the slaves—as Fernado Ortiz writes—"tried, in their celebrations, to revive the ways of life from their distant homelands." See Ortiz's "El Día de los Reyes" [1920, 6].

A deep study of these groups of slaves during the colonial period has not yet tempted any of our historians.

All the "nations" had their Cabildos. They became "temples," schools for the languages and traditions of each African group, and effective mutual aid societies, since the members of each Cabildo were obligated, by religious oath, to come to help each other face any adverse circumstances in their lives.

Limiting ourselves to a mere footnote, we will mention Changó-Terddún (Cabildo de Santa Bárbara) because it is still recalled with pride. Calazán claims his father, Tá Román, was one of its founders, known by his compatriots as the prince Latikuá Achíku Latticú.

It was a great Cabildo "until the little Creoles got in Changó Terddún, then they made two *bandos* [blocs, factions]: one with Creoles, progressives, who wanted to show off and boss everyone around; and the other with the elders *de nación* [born in Africa], who were intransigent. The *chéveres*, dandies, started calling the elders Arakisas, *onirira*" (that is, slovenly, dirty people). Around the 1870s, Changó Terddún was located in a house on Calle Jesús Peregrino. Later, in Jesús María, on Calle Gloria, between Indio and Florida. "That was when it was a proper Cabildo." The pale shadow of a Cabildo de Santa Bárbara exists or existed until recently in Pogolotti, "although Changó said he was not from Pogolotti." Dr. Manuel Pérez Beato published, in his interesting "Curioso Americano," the seal [banner] of this Cabildo, which is unforgettable for so many elderly children and priests of Changó.

5   LC: Until the 1880s it was a farm, in the municipality of Marianao, known as El Palenque, that became an African neighborhood, past La Lisa, in front of a house known as *la casa del cura* [the priest's house]. Many Lucumí and Creoles lived there, all of them "godchildren" of the then-famous Ibeyes, two twin *santeros* who were very important. They had innumerable godchildren in Havana. They were called "los Papá Jimaguas" [the Twin Fathers], Perfecto and Gumersindo.

Those who knew them assure us that they were wealthy, and they owned various houses and had a woman in each one. Ña Chucha and Ña Pilar were Gumersindo's wives. Ña Cecilia Pedroso, who was highly respected "for her *fundamento* and her air, was the wife, by legitimate sacrament," of Perfecto, and she was very demanding and conscientious about her status as "primary wife." Some of her contemporaries insist they were the property owners of El Palenque. What is certain is that they enjoyed fame and esteem among the Black people in those days, and "they were protective godparents to many high-class white people, both male and female."

19

Everyone who has been "asentado" in the Regla de Ocha—that is, those who have undergone the trials of initiation (*Asiento*), elevating them to the category of *omo orisha*, children, the *santo*'s chosen, and *iyawos* (wives), priests and priestesses—has two names: the Christian, Spanish name they receive at the baptismal font; and the African name given by the orishas, the "Angel," or the *nganga* or "fundamento" that has claimed their head.[7] They should not divulge their name under any circumstances. (It is used by sorcerers to bind their subjects more effectively, to harm them, or—in the worst of cases—to kill them.)

Teresa M. was the child of a Mina slave.[8] She was liberated at birth, together with her African mother, who was a servant. "Not in the back of the

---

The great fiesta for Baloggué (Ogun) was celebrated every year at El Palenque, the orishas installed in a rod in the earth, covered by a *ñame* [yam] vine. El Palenque was also, naturally, a sanctuary of the Ibeyi (San Cosme and San Damián), even though its principal *Santos* were Baloggué and Orishaoko, which is represented by a roof tile and farming tools. And everything was done and maintained as it was in Africa.

In El Palenque, there were only Lucumí. El Pocito, next to El Palenque, which is now a bastion of Abakuá, belonged to the Gangá, who gathered there after the abolition of slavery. The fiestas on the first day of the year were just as important as the ones for Baloggué and Orishaoko at El Palenque.

At the dawn of that day, the Gangá, their drums, and their devotees went to feed Kunanbungo—to sacrifice to the spirit of the river. Those drums were guarded religiously the whole year. They also adored Elegua, and individuals from various "nations" attended their fiestas, including the Congo and many Lucumí. There was absolutely no intransigent sectarianism among Black people, whose religiosity accepts all creeds. In terms of their thinking on religious matters, there is very little distance separating the descendants of Congo, Yebú, Oyó, or Dahomey. There are no essential differences in concept.

6   DF-N: "Pocito" refers to the neighborhood of Los Positos (Pocitos) in the municipality of Marianao. For more on the Gangá discussed in Cabrera's footnote on El Palenque, see Christopher (2013).

7   DF-N: The abundance of italicized terms in this passage becomes a dense and forbidding thicket of language, but English readers might take heart in knowing that most Cuban readers of Cabrera's original would be unfamiliar with these ritual idioms. For example, even the Spanish word *asentado* is a neologism that might be translated as "initiated" or "those with an orisha installed in them," but *asiento* refers more generally to a colonial-era system of monopolistic charters granted by the Spanish Crown. Meanwhile, *fundamento* carries a prismatic variety of connotations that evoke orthodoxy, initiation, legitimacy, spiritual depth, and power.

8   LC: As Omi Tomi explained, her mother was a Mina Popo from the Slave Coast in the west of Dahomey:

They were considered Lucumí, and they would say they were. They were very intelligent and very sophisticated. They said the true Yemaya was from the Mina territory. Very discreet, they would dispense with nosey onlookers by sending them on some errand or other when they were going to one of their ceremonies. By the time they got back, everything was already finished, so they didn't learn anything.

house, but in the kitchen and on the patio," she insists, full of pride, whenever she summons her astonishing memory, which seems to be—like her healthy, firm teeth and her unflagging happiness, despite calamities—one of the birthrights of pure Africans and elderly Creoles. "I grew up in the living room, like a young white lady," with all of the care and excessive tenderness that her mistresses—two spinsters—could possibly lavish on a daughter. And both of them loved the little Black girl—she was jet black, but she filled the void of an unsuccessful motherhood. They loved her so much that they named her the absolute, universal heir to their property.

"I was always in the living room," Omi Tomi recalls. "Mamaita and the other Lady didn't let me rub elbows with Black people. I was the little baby of the house, the apple of their eye."

I know that my father—who was already a famous lawyer, even though he was still young—felt sorry for a Black client who consulted with him one day and left some papers for him to review. The woman—whom white people had mocked in a miserable way, "as was the custom" in those days—was hoping for a miracle from the young lawyer, but it did not come to pass.

Everything had already been planned in advance. Teresa M. had been legally dispossessed of her inheritance, and litigation would have been futile.

The presence of Teresa M.—Omi Tomi—in my family dates back to that time.[9] She was my grandmother's and my mother's seamstress. She was the

---

When I was a child, they didn't really play anymore. In the Santa Rosa sugar refinery, the old man Odilo, who was a *mobwa*, said that the Mina were—like the Black people from Mozambique—very keen to learn Spanish. It was a pleasure listening to them, like the *Congos Reales*.

Lucumí, Arará, Dahomey, and Mina—they're all related. They understood each other even though they spoke different languages. But their *Santos* were similar. They went from one land to the other.

They were very valuable, but they were scarce. There were few of them, at least when I was born. They worked [performed sorcery] with water. *Cuando yo nací ya no había cepo en mi ingenio* [When I was born, there was no root (anchor, stock) at my (sugar) mill; in other words, there was no formally consecrated *fundamento* object there.]

It is interesting to ask the elders about their historical origins. Their accounts are sometimes confusing or contradictory. Others are fantastical. Calazán describes a group of African people who are all dwarves—he is referring to pygmies—and informs me that his mother had told him about them. "They had beards that grew down to the ground, and a single eye on their forehead. They climbed trees like monkeys," and they shot little magical arrows that made them invincible. "The *negreros*—captors, bounty hunters, patrols—could not hunt them down. They lived very far away, deep in the jungle, like the monkeys."

9   DF-N: As Cabrera makes clear in her preface, *El Monte* is grounded in her conversations with elders between 1930 and 1954. Roughly speaking, their accounts recall life in the late nineteenth and early twentieth centuries. Put another way, Cabrera's historical subject—the *fundamento* of her narrative—is the era immediately preceding her own lifetime, meaning the late nineteenth

one who took me to an "Asiento" for the first time, along with her dear friend, the unforgettable Oddedei, Calixta Morales. Oddedei was a slim, elegant Black woman. She was very dignified, and she came from a pure Lucumí lineage ("orile"): she was an aristocrat (like her mother, who was honored as a queen in the Cabildo de Santa Bárbara). She also dressed in white, impeccably clean, with a pearl necklace decorating her neck. I recall this luxury as a heartbreaking detail, since I met her when she was going through very difficult times, but always, as she would say, "with her head held very high."

"I don't know anything about Black people," Omi Tomi would answer when I first asked indiscreet, unexpected questions about the mythology and rites of her parents, who were also Lucumí. Her ancestry filled her with pride, "because Lucumí was the best of Africa." (The Lucumí's well-founded regard for their own race bothered the Congo intensely, and it still bothers their descendants.)

"They didn't let me get near any Black person when I was a little girl, and I always stayed close to white people! Why would I know anything about that?" Nonetheless, when she was convinced that there was no hint of contempt in my curiosity about "asuntos de negros" [Black people's affairs], that I was "not joking around about the African *Santos*" or asking "por guachánga," and that I did not believe *santeros* "sacrificed children," then she introduced me to the great Oddedei. For her part, Oddedei spent an entire afternoon observing me, extending long silences with an enviable smile that showed her small, straight teeth, or with very timely evasions. But she finally gave me her approval deep down. Everyone recognizes that Calixta Morales was the last great, schooled *llamadora de santos* [lead singer, the one who calls *santos*], the *apwonla*, who leads the ritual chants in Ocha ceremonies. "Ah! When Oddedei called the *Santos* the way she used to, up from the roots, there wasn't a single one left up in heaven!" As a result of the interview with that *iyalocha*, the two old ladies took me to the "middle day" of an *Asiento* of a *mulata* who was receiving Oshun to cure herself from some unmanageable illness or other. Oddedei stayed next to me the entire time, explaining everything I was seeing for the first time—now without beating around the bush. As for Omi Tomi— "Teresa la negrita," as she was affectionately known (and is still known in my

century. In terms of cultural memory, Cabrera relies on both first- and secondhand accounts, tracing the edges of living memory by evoking the youth and/or immediate ancestors of elderly informants. The intimately personal narrative of Omi Tomi saturates the whole of *El Monte* with bittersweet nostalgia—a chaotic intersection of historical eras, regimes, and identities that reaches a cathartic peak in *La laguna sagrada de San Joaquín* ([1973] 1993). A sense of nostalgia— both Cabrera's own and that of her informants and many of her readers—suggests an ambivalent, abstract relationship to the past.

home)—who supposedly "knew nothing, nothing at all about Black people's ways!"? The one who only danced [European-style] *lanceros* and *danzas* at the formal Sociedades de Recreo (Recreational Societies), like Bella Unión and the Centro de Cocheros—one of whose founders was José, my father's unflappable and generous driver. When it came time to leave, I practically had to drag her away from the room where she was dancing in a group of her friends and contemporaries, all of them in trance, "mounted" by the *santos*. And it was obligatory to wait until the *santo* came down and bid farewell . . . But before going any further, a parenthetical note is in order for the reader who is unfamiliar with Cuba. Being "taken by the *santo*," "the *santo* coming down," being "mounted" by the *santo*, being "knocked down by the *santo*" or "enraptured by *santo*," or the *santo* entering someone's head—all of this refers to this phenomenon which is as old as humanity. It has always been known by all peoples, and it occurs incessantly among our people. It consists of a spirit or a deity taking possession of a person's body and behaving as though it is its real owner for the length of its sojourn. That is why the person who is the object of this infiltration is called a "horse" or "a head taken by a *santo*." In the Regla Conga, those who go through the same trance are called *yimbi*, *kombofalo nganga gombe*, *gando*, *perro vasallo*, *criado*, or a *nganga*'s head. The *santo* (and the *mayombero's fumbi*) evicts or, for lack of a better term, replaces the "I" of the "horse"—that is, one's individual identity or conscious self.

According to one Black informant's own words, "the *santo* descends to mount its horse," it gets inside them, and "that man or woman who gets the *santo* inside them is no longer themselves: they are the *santo* itself." "They were grabbed" or "enraptured" by the *santo*," "they were knocked down," "overcome," "grabbed" . . . "They are with *santo*." "They have *santo*."[10]

The ego of persons possessed "with *santo*" is removed, thrown out of their bodies, or out of their heads ("*ori*, which controls the body"). The ego is nullified and substituted by the orisha, the *mpungu*, or the *fumbi*. ("And then there's no more Pedro or Juana or María. It's Yemaya or Changó or Oshun or whatever *santo* grabs them. It's Mpungu Choya Wenge, Inkita, or Dibude.") Proof of this is found—and most convincingly for Black people—in the "horse" losing all consciousness of their usual personalities. "They steal their head." The *santo*—or the spirit, *nganga*—can "come down" or "crown" someone spontaneously, surprising the "horse" even if their descent has not been provoked. (There are always warning signs of a short-lived struggle in the "horse.") They

---

10   DF-N: In Cabrera's dense montage of language associated with possession trance (*bajar, subir, montar, tumbar*, etc.), each term arguably conveys a different aspect or interpretation of the phenomenon. The term *caballo* (horse) refers to the medium—i.e., the person subject to possession trance. See Hurston ([1938] 1990) and Matory (1994).

enter or "mount," and when they leave, the "horse" is left unaware of what has happened inside and around them. After the trance, they do not know what they have said or done. "Unless they're told." Those who "come down with *santo*" never know at which moment "it gets inside them or goes away." They remember absolutely nothing. "If nobody tells them afterward, they won't know. Their heads are left a little empty, they sweat copiously, and they come back to themselves very hungry and thirsty. At first, when the *santo* starts to come down, we don't tell them about it because we don't want to frighten them." There's also a fear that the initiate might go mad, but an old *santera* protests: "How could the *santo* make the *eleda* of their *omo* crazy? Bah! That's a modern person's view. The old Lucumí never told us any of that. They didn't scare us about the *omo* going crazy if they knew the *Santo* mounted them. None of that! Lies![11] They didn't say any of that to us because they didn't want us to start faking or clowning around." Additionally, the *santo* tends to use their medium to carry out actions that are so repugnant that it is better, more compassionate, that their *omo* remain ignorant of the whole affair:

> Out on a ranch, a daughter of Changó-Onile suddenly came down with the *santo*.
>
> Mounted, she went over to the house of a sick neighbor whose legs were covered with sores. She used her mouth to pull off the scabs and wash off the pus with her tongue without spitting it out. She asked for palm oil and rubbed it on her legs. Then she ordered that nothing else be done.
>
> And that's how she cured her. After the *Santo* left her, nobody dared to tell her anything, because she was a very clean person. The disgust would have killed her. One of her family members was horrified and took her to the doctor, thinking she had contracted the illness by swallowing the pus, the blood, the scabs, everything. But nothing happened to her!

The most revolting cures are performed by M. when Ogun Arere comes down:

> One time, when he was licking a tumor, a girl who saw it was unable to contain herself and vomited. The *Santo* said to her, "What is it that disgusts you, eh? Very well, then. We'll see if everyone doesn't become

---

11   DF-N: The original quotation ("¡Farso!") is a small example of Cabrera's lexical virtuosity, which she uses to convey a generative sense of ambiguity. The exclamation might be a grammatically incorrect version of the word *farsa* (i.e., a farce, a ridiculous falsehood), but it might also be a phonetic transcription of the way the elder *olorisha* pronounced the word *falso* (false, lies) by replacing an *l* sound with an *r* sound.

disgusted by you after a while . . ." Well, the woman with the tumor was saved after that cleansing that Ogun did for her. A year later, the girl who had vomited came down with consumption . . . The poor thing coughed and coughed, and it's true, everyone avoided her. You have to be very careful to avoid offending the *Santos*, no matter what you see!

But there are ways to prevent possession. The most common way is to tie a cloth the color associated with the *santo* to whom they belong around their waist, cinching it tight. Other methods include refreshing the necklaces (*eleke*, *chire*) that serve as emblems of each Orisha and always worn as protection by the faithful; tying three knots in a handkerchief, thereby binding the "Santo"; tying a blade of grass or a strand of corn fiber around the middle finger of their foot, as is done in the Regla de Mayombe; and, above all, removing oneself in a timely fashion from whatever might convince the *santo* of one's devotion, such as particular songs and drum rhythms that call a *santo* with irresistible force.

Some are very careful to leave the room in which the drums are ringing out and the chorus is breaking out in songs honoring their tutelary "Angel," their orisha.

It is astounding how easily our Black people "come down" with *santo*—that is, fall into trance. Therefore, it seems perfectly logical that spiritism, whose centers are multiplying throughout the entire island, currently claims thousands upon thousands of believers, and thousands upon thousands of mediums. This does not entail a weakening of faith in the Orishas or a neglect of the cults with African roots: spiritism goes hand in hand with them, despite its ambitions to spirituality . . . of "spiritual advancement, light, faith, and progress." Many *babalawos*, *oluos*, *babalochas*, *mamalochas*, *mayombe-ros*, *viyumberos*, and *kimbiseros* now have "spiritual spirits"—that is, they are also spirit mediums. That is what an *iyalocha* who "works with spiritism" tells me. Both Cachita—Mamá Caché, the Virgen de la Caridad del Cobre—and the spirit of a Gangá slave manifest through her. "Ocha or Palo . . . Well, don't they amount to the same thing? They're all just spirits! Don't people come down with *santo* and *muerto* the same way?" "In religion, it's all about the *muertos*. The *ikus* became *santos*." *Santos* and spirits are everyday guests in the homes of the Cuban people. "Spiritism . . . Bah! In Africa, the *muertos* talked too. That's nothing new." One is able to speak with the goddess Oshun or with Obatala, just as one is able to speak with the Apostle Martí,[12] or with Dr. Juan Bruno Zayas, a famous, heroic, and "disembodied" doctor. And

---

12   DF-N: This is a reference to José Julián Martí Pérez, polymath and hero of Cuban independence.

thanks to the unbelievable abundance of mediums, the souls of the deceased are able to take leave from *el espacio*[13] inordinately often in order to talk with their family and friends, smoke a cigar (the same kind that was their favorite in life), offer their opinion on current events, and intervene officiously in all of their affairs. (Many "highly elevated" spirits are so political that they come from the great beyond to support an election campaign with the same passionate interest as the living. They demand votes for their preferred party in the same furious, apocalyptic tone used in the deafening oratory of flesh and blood politicians on Cuba's "terrestrial plane.")

In short, the extreme ease with which people of color and . . . whites of color fall into trance or "with *Santo*" in response to the slightest stimulus can be attributed to their predisposition to auto-suggestion, which—as we have already emphasized—is congenital among the majority. To their astonishingly childlike psychology. To their impressionable nature.[14] To their ancient religious tradition. To their truly unbreakable faith in the existence of the spirits, which drives them to accept the reality of these manifestations from the supernatural world—they are so natural!—without hesitation. To their belief in the great beyond, which is entirely tangible and evident to them. For the Black person, any abnormal psychic state supposes the interference of some strange spirit, or an orisha that penetrates into a person and takes the place of their self or—occasionally—intrudes without displacing them completely.[15] In these instances, "the *Santo* does make somebody lose consciousness. They say what they have to say without the horse realizing it." This is referred to as "having" or being a "*Santo de guardia* (guardian)." "An *omo* comes down with their *Santo* and, before departing, they declare that they will remain on guard for a few days." The subject finds themselves perfectly conscious and in a normal state of mind, "but then they'll suddenly say profound things without knowing what they've said or why they said it. It's the *Santo* that remained on guard who is speaking or mediating in the conversation."

To "retire" or "remove the *Santo*," they sit the horse down in a chair, covering its head with a white kerchief. They blow in its ears and say some words *en lengua* to the *Santo*.[16] Then they call the medium loudly by their given name,

---

13   DF-N: In the idiom of spiritism, *el espacio* refers literally to outer space, meaning the other-world or spiritual realm.

14   DF-N: Like sections of Cabrera's preface, this passage articulates a frankly condescending, elitist iteration of psychology and "modern science" in which "people of color" (notably including "whites of color") and possession trance are linked and characterized as primitive.

15   DF-N: The passage outlines a broad spectrum of influence and coexistence between a person and (ostensibly external) spirits.

16   DF-N: The idiomatic expression *en lengua*—literally, "in the tongue" or "using [special] language"—refers to African/Afro-Cuban idioms.

"so their spirit comes back in." Or they lay them facedown on a straw mat, bidding the *Santo* farewell or "sending them away" from this position.

In the past, the *Santos* were not sent away at the "fiesta" or wherever they manifested. They returned to their temples to give the horse's godmother an account of their actions. They would walk barefoot, as they were, to their godmother's home and regain consciousness after the orisha had saluted their "fundamento" and the Godmother. Similarly, if the horse was a *babalocha* or an *iya*, they would return to their own *ile* [house, home] "mounted." Even today, it is not so unusual to encounter a *Santo*—"the ones made by the elders"—that observes that same ritual. When others come to bid the *Santo* farewell, they are warned that the *Santo* will go on with their child and see themselves off later.

In the Congo rituals, they sing to the *fumbi* to make it leave. They stretch the medium's arms out and rub them down with aguardiente, sometimes shaking a rattle next to their ears. They remove the red or black cap that is decorated with jingle bells and worn during trance. They make the sign of the cross three times over the center of the medium's head and over the soles of their feet. It is not unusual for the *Santos* to manifest themselves in many individuals from a very tender age. I have personally seen many children "mounted," which obligates the parents to "asentar" [install, be initiated to] their *Santo*, to immediately recognize the *Santo* as the owner of that head, or to "scratch" them in Mayombe. Others are "born with *Santo*" and consecrated before they are born, "when they're still in their mother's belly."

Convulsions (like the ones caused by parasites, which are so common in Cuba), sudden changes in the nervous system, any sort of madness or hysteria, or the slightest bit of trouble are attributed to the meddling of a *Santo* or orisha; a *fumbi* or *katukemba*; or the soul of a *muerto*, whether it has been summoned by a sorcerer, or even if no one sent for it. They install themselves next to the subject, "sticking to them" out of mere impulse, or perhaps out of resentment, or due to an affinity. (A spirit was in love with one of Sandoval Herrera's protégées. The spirit prevented the woman from getting close to her husband. "As soon as the marriage started to evolve, naturally, into a more intimate relationship, the *muerto* made its presence felt and pulled them apart. And a lot of stuff needed to be done to drive the *muerto* away." And thanks to Sandoval's tenacity in resolving such a strange and uncomfortable situation, he was able to "reason with the *egun*.") "The *muerto* imposes its will."

"The *muerto* makes people crazy." "An undeveloped spirit will perturb persons it grabs, or even drive them crazy." The *Santo* can have this effect when *santeros* make a mistake: instead of "asentar" the *Santo* that truly claims the head of an *omo*, they "switch and mix up the *Santos*" and "give" them a different one.

Possession—whether it is due to auto-suggestion, provoked, or frankly simulated—is so common in Cuba that whoever wants to observe it will have more than enough opportunity to do so. There you have the boarding houses, the extraordinary and fantastical tenements in which it is rare for a day to go by without someone from the neighborhood going into trance. The *fiestas de ocha*, the *juegos de palo* (which are perhaps less accessible), or simply wakes, where one can attend out of a mere pretext of courtesy (which is received gratefully, even if the guests do not know the mourners personally).

A *Santo* or a *fumbi* can come down spontaneously, apart from the rituals that provoke them. (People do not go into trance at a *bangala*—the secular celebration of the Congo—the way they do at a Lucumí fiesta.) The *Santo* can surprise whomever they want, whenever and wherever. (María G. found herself in her room in a rooming house shortly after arriving from her hometown. She did not know anybody in Havana. She would not have dared to walk the city streets alone. Her husband went out to buy cigarettes at a café nearby. When he returned, she was gone. During his brief absence, María had—for the first time—"come down with *Santo*," and the *Santo* had taken her to a *toque* [musical ceremony] in honor of the Virgen de Regla—Yemaya, her orisha—at a house far away from the inn. An hour later, *un negrito* arrived to tell her husband, "on behalf of Yemaya," that he should come get his wife at a *tambor* that was being celebrated on Calle de Figuras, where the "mounted" *Santa* had taken her.)[17]

("Carmelina suddenly says to her mother Rosa, 'Mom! Listen to the drums!' 'What drums, child?' 'Don't you hear it? Mom, take me there! They're calling me! Ay! They're calling me and I need to go!' Rosa was in the middle of washing rice. 'But they're not playing, child!' Carmelina took off running. Rosa and two neighbors tried following her, but the little girl ran so fast that they lost sight of her. Far away, very far away, there was indeed a *bata*. The girl did not have *Santo* or even the ritual beaded necklaces. Nonetheless, *Santo* had come to her since she was three years old. When they arrived at the fiesta, the girl was possessed by Yemaya. It was impossible for someone to have heard the drums from where she lived!")

On more than one occasion in the neighborhood of Pogolotti, where I often got together with various Black elders at the home of Omi Tomi, I have witnessed *Santos* "come down" violently on individuals, and, on many occasions, I have seen them "jamaquearlo" (rough people up) because the conversation had turned carelessly to some episode or characteristic trait of their

---

17   DF-N: Extensive parenthetical anecdotes like the story of María G. exemplify the nonlinear, tangential narrative structures, rhetorical devices, and discursive styles Cabrera describes in the preface.

Santo. That is how Changó took possession of Calazán at one of those un-forgettable gatherings, revealing something that the old man had kept hidden from me: that he—his horse Bangoché (Calazán)—was a *mayombero judío*, "as evil as the devil himself."[18] And he ordered us to tell him "that he was tired of his shamelessness, and that he would make him eat dirt before sending him to Ile Yansa," the cemetery. "Kuruma koi ina koi mowi." (With him, Changó, disagreements are tragic.)

At the Lucumí fiestas, during drumming *toques* meant to give thanks to the orishas, where they are honored and invited to enjoy themselves, posses-sion is evoked by the drums and rattles, the songs and dances.

In this case, the *Santo* comes down to dance in the "head" of the *omo*, and the trance is provoked intentionally. The "child" of the *Santo*, the "horse," is a direct medium of communication between the deities and humans. In the homes of the *Santos*, whose doors should be opened wide for anyone who wants to take part in the fiesta, the "horses" still carry out the same social function as they would in a primitive society. Using their *omo*, or medium, the orisha speaks through them with all of their divine authority: they are asked questions, they respond to the questions they are asked, and they give advice when they are asked for it, or they give advice spontaneously. They scold, threatening a "pikuti" (a pinch, a small punishment) for those who are "stum-bling and messing around"—that is, behaving badly. I witnessed an elderly "omo" be reprimanded by a *Santo* for abusing alcohol and mistreating his part-ner. I also witnessed the shaming of one woman whom Oya accused—angrily and publicly—of having aborted several pregnancies, dragging a promise out of the woman that she would not "throw away the child she now had in her belly, or else she would take the woman to the other world." The *Santos* take matters into their hands in all of their children's affairs. Their divine, parental protection is always sought: the faithful address the *Santo* as Father, Mother, or Babami and Iyami. The *Santos* "cleanse," purifying with their touch, running their hands over the arms and bodies of their devotees. Or they rub their dev-otees' faces with their holy, beneficial sweat. They press their foreheads against that of their *omo* (which is sometimes dangerous since the *Santo*, especially Changó and Ogun, are known to deliver terrible blows with their heads). They get up and dance around, carrying their favorite "child" in their arms or on their backs. They play with children, joyfully tossing them in the air. And, as an obvious sign that a true *Santo* has come down, they ask for money and distribute it to those who need it most among the devotees, without keeping

---

18   DF-N: On the term *mayombero judío*, see the Translator's Notes.

anything for themselves.[19] They deliver messages for people who are absent, along with orders or warnings. They diagnose illness, prescribe remedies to cure them, and then rejoice in the company of their children and everyone they protect. The objective of these fiestas is to make the *Santos* happy and adulate them, dancing their dances with them.

Sometimes the dances are as beautiful as those of Oshun and Yemaya, which Fernando Ortiz poetically described as "the dance of the fountainhead." Or the hunters' dances of Ogun and Ochosi, those of Changó and the Ibeyi, the divine twins, etc. And the beauty of these dances depends on the dancer's respect for the tradition. Therefore, it should not surprise us that the elders are invariably the best dancers—their style is more pure.

The *omo* possessed by the *Santo* or Angel reflects the same personal characteristics that mythology attributes to the *Santo* possessing or "mounting" them. (Black people use the term *Angel* to refer to the *Santo*, orisha, or Congo *mpungu*, thereby finding the precise Catholic equivalent. This is the spirit "that is contained and consecrated in the head," the Lucumí angel, Eleda or Ori, Olori, the Guardian and protector of their lives.) For example, if Changó or another of the orishas known as warriors possesses a woman with a thin, soft voice, she will speak in a loud, rough way, adopt a masculine attitude, and act arrogant and confrontational. This is so much so that daughters of Changó are almost always dressed in a male outfit when he comes down and possesses them: red, decorated with jingle bells (*chaguoro*), the cuffs of *pantalones bombachos* [wide, short pants] (or "blumeros," from the English word *bloomers*, as our people now call them). This is because the *Santo* tends to rip off or lift up the skirts of the *iyalocha*, demonstrating that he is not a woman and that skirts bother him. The women Changó "mounts" will almost always pull their slips over their heads and make subversive gestures, reminding everyone of the virility of the God, who is determined to make it very clear that "he's got" what his horse lacks, "and very big. *Ekua, etie mi oko!*"

Formerly, in *Santo* houses, each *omo orisha* had the wardrobe and mask corresponding to the deity that possessed them, ready for the moment of trance and dancing. But outfits and masks were expensive, and that custom was discontinued out of necessity. Likewise, cowrie shell masks have become obsolete. In the Congo *toques de fiesta*—accompanied by the *yuka* drum, "which, in the days of my grandparents, was called *makuta*," according to O'Farril and Nino from Cárdenas—dancers in trance would wear an apron made of deer or cat skin, a belt of small bells, and a necklace of cowbells

---

19 DF-N: In other words, the legitimacy of possession trances can be inferred from acts of selfless generosity.

(*gangarria*). If an *omo-Elegua* is a serious person who is not at all inclined to clowning around, they suddenly transform into a joker, "a trickster, prankster, having a good time and fooling around to make somebody laugh at him."

But those who have been forewarned will abstain from laughing. Because Elegua "is a trickster," he provokes laughter among attendees at *fiesta de ocha* with the deliberate intention of starting a fight by pretending to be offended, alleging that they are mocking him. This *Santo*, as we know, is the first one to be honored at the *tambor*. It is advisable to bid him farewell with the drums as soon as he manifests, or to not let him come in the door. "There's one that would start acting indecently . . . but not anymore, just so you know."[20] It is also best to avoid drawing Changó's attention while he is eating, because he might obligate us to accept the food he offers with his hands, or even a plantain. This runs the risk that the *Santo* will demand payment—with interest—for his gift. "In exchange for a plantain, he might ask for a ram!" Changó has the habit of spilling his beloved cornmeal and okra, so he can eat it on the ground, then putting his devotees in a grave predicament: forcing them to accept the handfuls of food he offers them.

Refusing this food—messy and contaminated with litter—would be a sacrilege that would expose them to the effects of the god's resentment, who tests the devotion of his "children" and worshippers.

A person who abstains from alcohol might be possessed by Ogun and drink a bottle of aguardiente in a single swallow, though—theoretically—there is no drinking of alcohol at a *fiesta de ocha*. "The Lucumí Santos don't drink," like the *ngangas*. Ogun only fills his mouth with aguardiente to spray the gathering and purify it. In earlier times, no alcoholic beverages of any kind were ever offered when a *Santo* came down, as is now done in some "disorderly" houses to the shame of good Santería.

The only liturgical and traditional drink of the Lucumí *Santos* and their faithful is *chekete*, a mixture made with *naranja agria* and corn, then sweetened with cane syrup or brown sugar.[21]

If a black dog has the misfortune of finding its way into the fiesta and being seen by Ogun, the orisha will pounce on the animal immediately to bite it and suck its blood. And Yemaya will eat any cockroach it surprises.

---

20   LC: "One Elegua is very indecent. He liked to show people his private parts. But we don't allow those bad habits here." In Cuba, "that" Elegua lost—according to what we have been told—its phallic character. All of my old informants know about this, including the fact that his dances simulated the sexual act.

21   DF-N: See the NARANJA AGRIA and MAIZ entries in the botanical encyclopedia.

These, as the *Santa* herself says, are her "pork rinds" (*chicharrones*) . . . They are snacks and messengers for all the *Santos*.

("Andreíta is the fussiest woman on earth, and she is terrified of cockroaches. But when she's mounted by Yemaya, you'll see her chewing one and savoring it as if it were a chocolate bonbon. Of course, nobody's told her about it.")

Babaluaye, San Lázaro, was "Arará Dahomey by birth," according to some. According to others, "He went from Lucumí territory to the land of Dahomey." Also known as Ayanu, he is the most venerated *Santo* in the Regla Arará. He immediately makes his *omo* assume the appearance of an invalid who has been crippled and deformed by illness: he twists his legs, stiffens and curls his hands, and curls his spine down. This orisha—whose Catholic image we often find behind doors accompanied by a loaf of bread, a toasted ear of corn, or a millet straw broom—is the Owner of epidemics and illness: leprosy and smallpox, from which we no longer suffer in Cuba. In possession of his *omo*, he carries out the same repulsive acts we have already noted: he cleans sores with his tongue and "cleanses" the ailing body with a piece of raw meat, which he then eats.

"I've seen Tata Cañeñe in the countryside"—some *ganguleros* call him Futila—"roll around on a dead animal that is covered with maggots, then happily rub that putrid stuff on his face and all over his body, and I've seen him eat the secretions from the nose and eyes." Like Elegua, he also "comes down" joking around and provoking laughter among onlookers, only to punish them later. "Oshun and Yemaya play the same game. Especially Oshun, with her laughter, swagger and wisecracks, *merengueteos* and *cuchufletas*." It goes without saying that of all the orishas that "mount," Ayé (San Lázaro) is the one that inspires the most terror and respect. Black people say, "You can play a little bit with all of the *santos*, except him." Also, "Not even the Congo, who are clever devils, dare to play around with Mpungu Futila!"

A male Obatala will tremble from head to toe: they become a little old man, hunched over and walking unsteadily. Obamoro, Ochagrinya, or Agirinya always tremble. Yet this quivering old man is also a fierce warrior who stands straight up and dances, imitating the gestures of a paladin who fights vigorously.

Ayaguna—San José—dances with a machete. He is the perpetrator of the disputes between different peoples, "the one who lights the fire." He is a bit of a thug, since "in one path," during one period in his life, he was an "*ole*," a thief, *ole fiti-fiti*. Whatever is offered to him—hens, doves, or white guinea hens—needs to have been stolen. (One informant, whose Angel is Ayaguna, confides in me that this is why many of his sons are thieves. "They undress *fosas*"—which, in Caló, means they steal.[22] *Fosas* is jargon for pockets. Like Elegua, who often only wants "ill-gotten" chickens.)

Among the *santas*, Yemaya distinguishes herself with her majestic, queenly demeanor. "Yemaya *ataramagwa sarabi* Olokun." She is a lady of enormous wealth, very dry and haughty. Like Yemaya Achaba, the one "with a powerful gaze" who only listens with her back turned, or leaning over and turning slightly away. Yemaya Ogute is masculine and aggressive. And Yemaya Mayelewo gets offended if anyone touches the face of her "horse" or medium; she will be ashamed and leave the *guemilere*, the fiesta. Yemaya Ataramawa is arrogant, vain, "stylish and haughty." Yemaya Olokun, who was tied down at the bottom of the immense ocean with a chain, is too big—big like Agayu, Omiran, like Olodumare—and she does not bow her head to any mortal. On very rare occasions, a Babalawo dances her with a mask, never with his face exposed; afterward, they need to make a ritual offering immediately to avoid dying.[23] Like Yewa, her name should never be uttered without first touching the earth then kissing the remnants of dust on one's fingertips. Yemaya Olokun never allows anyone to see the face she covers with a mask; as far as I have been told, it is only seen in dreams. "It's nothing more than a round face with Lucumí markings" (*yesa*). "She has very white, bulging eyes. Brown irises and sharp eyelashes." During a new moon, the stone representing her is rubbed with *cascarilla* [chalk made from egg shells]. In short, Olokun is the ocean, "and an ocean without shores cannot fit in one head."

Oshun-yeye-Kari, or Yeye Maru, "the one with gold bracelets," and whose devotees can be maliciously described in song: "All the daughter of Yeye like other people's husbands." She is the fifth element of flirtatiousness, grace, and captivating and suggestive flattery. She is the mirror of the genuine Cuban *mulata de rumbo*, the inspiring, toned-up and decanted *mulata* from colonial times, the refined *mulata*, forgotten ancestor of some highborn families, or the secret grandmother of many recently minted magnates. Oshun Yeye Kari, the idealized brown beauty, usually "comes down" cheerful and charming, but with the arrogance, extravagance, and airs of a proud sovereign. "Es de rompe y rasga" (She breaks, rips, and tears). Yalode, Yeye Kari, *abeberiye-moro lade koju alamade oto*, her power is limitless.

---

22   DF-N: Caló is the language of the Iberian Roma, also known as gypsies, *gitanos*, etc.; more generically, the term refers to slang.

23   DF-N: On Olokun rituals in Cuba, see Brown (2003b); Ferrer and Acosta ([2012] 2015); Mason (1992, 1996); Ortiz (2018, 125); Otero and Falola (2013); Ramos (2003); and Sanford (2001).

According to the characteristics presented by the *santo* when they take possession of their chosen ones and their behavior during trance, my Black informants explain that we will be in the presence of either "a Santo or a Santico"[24] ... When the abnormal character or epileptic nature of trances— especially the violent ones in Palo Monte—becomes evident, a Black person firmly believes that the *Santo* or the *Palo*, the *fumbi*, has "come down." It is a divinity, a spirit that acts through the "horse"—one cannot think otherwise. In the Lucumí fiesta, the external individuality presented by the "horse" is that of an orisha, a true *Santo*, which "tosses them around and knocks them unconscious" when it enters them. I recall the first time I saw this phenomenon occur, which astonished and—I confess—frightened me. When the drums were beating for Changó, a very dark brown woman suddenly jumped incredibly high in the air, then fell rigid on the concrete floor, receiving a blow to the base of her skull that I naively believed to be fatal. In a split second, I imagined the unpleasant consequences that my presence at the "bembe" might have on me if that monumental woman died. The door to the room was blocked by the many participants, and no one else showed the fright my companion must have seen in my eyes when she grabbed my arm and said, "It's nothing, child. That's a real *santo*." Overcome by convulsions, that big woman snorted and hit herself in the head so hard that I thought it would smash to pieces like a fruit—a coconut or a pumpkin—thrown furiously on the floor. Then she sat up, and that roaring mass, driven by an extraordinary energy, did several somersaults with an inconceivable agility. I could not believe the nimbleness of that woman, who anyone might have assumed would be hindered by her excessive corpulence, and who in her normal state appeared so calm and unremarkable. It was even harder to believe that she had not died a moment earlier by fracturing her skull. But, fortunately, faith does not abide by logic ... The owner of the house where the *tambor* was being offered said, "That's nothing. I'm telling you, there's no reason to be scared. Her Changó is like that, a fierce Changó. And I know some that are even hotter."

On that occasion, I had the impression that I was really seeing the god of thunder and war—the irresistible "Bull of the Hill"—dance. Later, I had that impression with La Capitana, an *iyalocha* who had been a *mambisa*, fighting like a man in the second war of liberation. She would invite me to her *batas*, thanks to Oddedei and Calazán. (In order to irritate La Capitana, B.H. would refer to the war of 1898 as "su guerrita de independencia" [her

---

24 DF-N: The devastating use of a diminutive suffix (*-ico*) in the term *Santico* indicates a subpar or false possession trance. Cf. Hagedorn (2000).

little war of independence],[25] because the good one, the one that counted, the one involving the great Cubans, was the Guerra de los Diez Años.)[26]

Whenever these trances—as any observer could see—are obviously, crudely simulated without a trace of artfulness, they are contemptuously branded as "Santicos."

"There are *Santos*, and then there are lots of fake little *Santicos*." And those who only have Santico play their roles, like the worst actors. They are far from presenting the impressive, disordered, and indisputable state of abnormality that heralds a "true" *Santo*.

After attending many fiestas with an abiding desire on my part to get closer to the deities descended from the Lucumí empire, "from Ife, the home of the Lucumí *santos*," or from Gini, as the elders pronounce Guinea, you get the impression that they are no longer willing to descend every day . . . Generally—in fact, almost always—the performances of these "horses" are contrived and studied in advance, like that of spiritist mediums. The "horse" without a jockey openly perpetrates a fraud that—I dare say in good faith and with a clear conscience—is carried out collectively. I would say that every devotee in every fiesta feels a psychological need to contribute to this sort of simulation and devoutly participate in this phony *santo*. There is a need to believe the *Santos* have come down, to believe as long as the fiesta lasts, to believe and to make believe that they believe, until they have bid farewell to the last fake orisha. "*Santos* and *Santicos*!" "When the truth is absent, you need to resign yourself to the lie. That's why we say, *a falta de pan, casabe* [if you have no bread, eat cassava]." But "the old Lucumí didn't abide Santicos. They'd start beating them. Whoever started clowning around, *aboreo*.[27] They'd be beaten with leather straps. Those people . . . *Odaniko!* They hit them hard. And they kept *chuchos*—switches, thin sticks to administer beatings—in the house to punish them. Green switches. The *omo* couldn't cheat." "Whoever has real *Santo* doesn't feel or suffer pain. Nothing hurts them." Moreover, "If a *Santo* comes down—a real *Santo*—on the head of their child, everything they say

25   DF-N: Like *santico*, *guerrita* (little war) is a cutting use of a diminutive Spanish suffix (*-ita*) to indicate a small version of something. When Cabrera pivots to the next paragraph, she returns to the matter of small (i.e., fake) possession trances and quotes an anonymous informant's even more acerbic use of diminutives ("Santicos de mentirita").

26   DF-N: La Guerra de los Diez Años (the Ten-Year War, 1868–78) was the first of three major struggles for Cuban national independence from Spain. The second is commonly known as La Guerra Chiquita (the Little War, 1879–80), and the third is known as La Guerra del '95, or La Guerra de Independencia Cubana (the War of Cuban Independence, 1895–98).

27   DF-N: The word *aboreo* is Lucumí for "leather" or "hide"; in this context, it refers to leather straps or belts used to beat people suspected of faking possession trance (i.e., effectively assuming the authority of an orisha under false pretenses). See Cabrera ([1957] 1986, 23).

is the truth. Because they're all-knowing. *Oloin*: they see, they divine. Every word they say is true, and it can be verified." Let us suppose someone joins the crowd—for instance, an unknown *iyalocha* or Mother of a *Santo*, an incognito *babalawo* or *babalocha*. The *Santo* will discover them immediately, go to them, and salute them. "They will do *moforibale*,"[28] according to the hierarchy of their orisha and the number of years they have been initiated. An elderly woman will prostrate herself before a child if the child has been "asentado"—initiated—before her. "Years are counted in the religion starting on the day you are born in Ocha. A recently born initiate in the religion might be fifty years old, but their child of ten or twenty years might be senior because they were born in Oru first." On the numerous and lamentable occasions when police have interrupted a *toque* and put their hands on *omos* that are truly possessed by their *Santos*, the police can never interrupt these sacred fiestas. It is unimaginable that a Yemaya, an Ogun, a Changó, or an Oya escape, like untamed birds, shouting, "Umlo! Umlo!"[29] How could an Obakoso that fears no one and nothing rush to remove their ritual clothing, ripping off pieces of the compromising outfit to jump over a fence or up on a roof and run like a rabbit because the Achelu (police) arrived unexpectedly. This is inconceivable! Nobody has ever heard a "mounted" Ngangangombo shout, "Kisa halele masoriale!" (Run away, the cops—*masoriale*—will catch you!)

> Two civil guards went into a Santo house.[30] Yeya Menocal—a famous *santera* around the year 1890—was possessed by Yemaya, Charito by Oya, and another Black woman was mounted by Changó. The soldiers took all of the *santos* away, mounted, to the police precinct. They all went along, jabbering away in their language without a care in the world . . . Because they were real *Santos*! The first one to go in the precinct went in dancing. Francisco Pacheco was the lieutenant on duty. Yemaya was dancing and greeting everyone, "Okuo yuma!" They asked their names. "Yansa, hekua hei!" "Alafia kisieko!" They immediately left them in peace. "Get these *morenos* out of here!" "Lakue lakua boni," Yemaya said, giving thanks. And Lieutenant Pacheco said, "Fine, whatever! I don't understand a word you're saying, but get going already! Move it!"

Nothing unpleasant, much less humiliating—like being locked up in "the cage," the police car—can happen to someone who is mounted with (or "carry-

---

28 DF-N: The Lucumí term *moforibale* (literally, "I touch my head to the earth") refers to prostrating oneself to salute ritual elders and orishas. See Mason (1994).

29 DF-N: "Umlo!" is Lucumí for "I'm leaving!" or "Let's leave!" See Cabrera ([1957] 1986, 313–14).

30 DF-N: The Guardia Civil (Civil Guard) was the Spanish colonial law enforcement agency.

ing") *Santo*, "because it is not them, it is the *Santo*." Nothing can resist the *Santo*, which can control any situation. At Alambique 12, a Lucumí named Ojo had his *Santos* on the floor.[31] They had been fed that day. At three in the afternoon, he started playing his drums on the patio. "Kantankitanka!" . . . Then three loud knocks were heard at the door. They opened the door, and a civil guard went inside. "You're under arrest," the Spaniard said to Ojo. "Yes, sir. I'll go with you." But the guard went up to Changó's small wood vessel, saw money inside it, and tried to take it. Oh my! I was there and saw it myself. That Black man got furious and shouted, "Eh! Don't touch that! No! White men don't touch Changó's money, not as long as I'm around! Alafi kisieko kawo kabiesi! Grab him! Stop him, Alafi!" (Alafi is one of the names given to Changó.)

"The Spaniard jumped up, shook like a chicken whose neck had just been wrung, got possessed, and started talking. Alafi grabbed him, all right! The Spaniard got *Santo*, and the other guard standing at the door didn't dare take another step inside . . . They were watching all of this with their eyes bulging out of their heads. 'Alafi, let him go already! Make him leave . . .' They bid the *Santo* farewell and gave him some water to drink. Then the two guards left, trembling and empty-handed."

(After Independence, *santeros'* best allies were dark- or brown-skinned police officers and soldiers: devotees of Ogun or Changó, many who were "scratched" in *Palo*, regulars at the Ocha fiestas, and, often, members of the Abakuá secret society, in which white people currently outnumber Black people.)

Also, *Santos* do not allow anyone to mock them. The *santeras* Monikin and Omi Tomi recall an episode from colonial times when two *panchakaras*— *alabwa*, "cebollas" (prostitutes)—stopped their carriage in front of a *Santo* house. They looked through the iron gates covering the window at the front of the house, nosing around. Then they laughed at a Black man who looked like "a real mess, wearing a red jumpsuit." As soon as one of them said, "That man is crazy," both of them lost their minds and rushed into the house in a flash: "the *Santo* got on them." Changó took them, and they did not leave that house until they had gone through the "asiento."

Ogun Arere came down on Miguel constantly. One of his neighbors had a bad idea: to mock him, the neighbor crushed glass and surreptitiously put it in a bottle of aguardiente offered to the orisha. But Ogun, after he finished off the bottle of aguardiente, said to the foolish neighbor, "Look, son. I drank that. That other me"—the medium—"is going to *yeun* (eat) for me,

31   DF-N: Alambique 12 is a street address in the Havana neighborhood of Atarés.

and nothing is going to happen to Miguel." The next morning, Miguel woke up perfectly fine, but the neighbor woke up vomiting blood and, punished by Ogun, bled to death three days later.

The *Santo* also deals harshly with devotees who dare to provoke their descent:

A *Santo* can't be forced to come down into a head they don't claim. A daughter of Oya they called La Chinita went to a house in Puerta Cerrada where another daughter of Oya was giving a *tambor* for her Angel. La Chinita wanted her *Santo* to mount her. But then, what did La Chinita say? "I want the *Santo* to possess me, but I want to stay conscious!" You hear that, Calazán? God help us . . . La Chinita started singing. Dulce Maria, Belen's daughter, showed up to the fiesta, and a little while later Yemaya came down. Yemaya came down laughing a lot. "Hmm!"

Mother says, "I'm Yemaya, you drunk."

"Mother, we're not drunk," I said carefully.

Yemaya grabs the pestle from the mortar, dances around, and stops in front of La Chinita.

"Go on, Chinita. Sing." La Chinita was already out of sorts. "Let's go, Chinita, sing. You want to get *Santo* while you're still conscious." And Yemaya ordered them to sing for Oya, which was La Chinita's Angel. That poor Chinita! . . . It was terrible! I thought she was going to rip her own head off, that her arms would fly off her body! She destroyed her clothes, she was beating the hell out of herself. Listen, we couldn't hold her. And she herself was shouting, "Ayaga! Korin!" (Sing!) "Didn't you want a conscious *Santo?*" When it was over, my hand hurt. It seems Changó grabbed me, and Changó hit her an awful lot. It was a memorable day! Because, what's more, San Lázaro sent for a lady, his horse. They knocked on her door and she said she couldn't go, that they should tell San Lázaro that she was busy with her husband. Well, she ended up having to go practically naked. The other *Santos*, Santa Bárbara and Regla, locked her in the outhouse because San Lázaro almost killed her. The reprimands of the *Santos* in my days were savage.

They would punish us when we children gave them a reason.

In short, a fake Oya will not sit on a burning fire or a cauldron full of boiling water, or swallow burning oil that she scoops up in her bare, cupped hands. A fake Changó does not eat fire, and a fake Yemaya will not throw herself down a well, as tends to happen in the countryside when a real Yemaya "comes down."

In Havana, the goddess settles for flooding the room with buckets of water, generously soaking the attendees. In any case, there is no horse for Yemaya—or Oshun—that does not get wet.

Black people in colonial times—and, of course, those in contact with upper-class white people—camouflaged their religious practices, even when they indirectly influenced those of the white people. And let us agree that there was sometimes very little distance between the Catholicism of white people and the fetishism of their slaves.[32]

When they celebrated their rituals, "playing" *juegos* [games] from their homeland, they entertained themselves the African way. In their beliefs and cults, they were extremely reserved. This is especially true of the Congo, who—to this day—are more cautious "because they go around with *muertos*." Those Black Creole women who were secretly schooled by Africans, or who were African themselves, were also regulars in the church—"calambucas," church ladies with rosaries and prayer books in their hands if they knew how to read, and even when they did not, which was more common and normal. They never missed Sunday mass, and they forced us to recite the Our Father at night, even if we were so drowsy we were about to collapse. And they made us kiss the bread—the daily bread given to us by God—when it fell on the floor, and to make the sign of the cross every time we passed a church. Those Black women were such good, devout Catholics that many gentlemen did not have the slightest suspicion that those same women—after praying in the temple to the Virgin Mary, Santa Bárbara, or La Candelaria "like white people"—would go spill the blood of a sacrificial animal over the sacred, living stones with redoubled fervor. The stones represented the same Catholic saints from the church, except with the purely African obligations, names, and personalities of Yemu, Changó, or Yansa. (And if a white person was initiated in the faith of their slave and entrusted themselves to the African gods, which also happened quite often, they were even more secretive than their Black counterparts.) One of these old ladies tells me, "When I arrived from school, I put aside the Christian ABCs. My lessons took place on the street where La Merced lives. My father was a *mayombero*, *musunde*, and my mother was an *iyalocha*. They were waiting for me at home with the other notebook . . . the one from over there, from Aku and Kunansia. At home, I had to speak Yesa and Congo. And just as I was learning how to pray the catechism, I was also learning to salute and pray in *lengua*. And the rest of it." "We learned the stuff from here, but the other stuff from over there was also obligatory." In this same sense, our good friend Omi Tomi insists that she could not have learned

32 DF-N: On the intersection of Afro-Atlantic ritual traditions and Eurocentric notions of "fetish," see Matory (2018).

the "African notebook" because she was with her Mamita and Madrina all the time, always under their watchful eyes, so she did not have a Black man or woman to teach her properly. And so it was . . . She was forced to learn "the other stuff" out of necessity, and at the cost of great suffering. She was married without knowing "the wickedness that people of color can do," oblivious to many things that she should have learned before going out into the world. And because she did not know them, she lost her firstborn daughter . . .

After living in the spacious house with marble floors like a chessboard, and a patio and a backyard, Omi Tomi installed herself in her very decent second home—that is, one that a bricklayer could offer her. She married Miguel, a creole Lucumí like her, "by the sacrament," and he was a good, hardworking man. But before he "formalized" things with her, he had a "cohabitation agreement" with another woman. Although Omi Tomi only had a vague idea about her, the woman could not stomach being passed over. A friend of this woman, María del Pilar, came to live near the newlyweds and struck up a friendship with Omi Tomi. This was the beginning of a series of calamities that marked her first years of marriage. She soon got pregnant, but at a bad time. Everyone knows that a baby born with teeth will be a sorcerer, and that clairvoyants cry in their mothers' bellies, and that they can be deprived of their gift by being silenced. The baby she was carrying in her womb cried near the end of her pregnancy in the presence of her new friend and neighbor, who silenced the baby. The baby cried again, and—again, imperiously—the friend imposed silence on the baby. But Omi Tomi did not even know that clairvoyant babies cry in their maternal enclosure, or that every pregnant woman should take certain precautions to avoid a miscarriage. She was a legitimate daughter of Yemaya—of the Most Senior of the Yemayas, Olokun—and she should have wrapped her belly with a blue sash and seven silver coins. At the time of the birth (and thanks to the deliberate neglect of her friend), she was also lacking a prayer card or wax statue of San Ramón Non Nato (an Obatala), who helps all women with difficult labor—white and Black, rich or poor. Our people cannot do without him. (The prayer is recited, then the card is turned backward and a candle is lit. Or San Ramón is placed directly on the belly.) Speaking of San Ramón . . . A former governor of the island, General Martínez Campos, is fondly remembered. At one point, he gave the *Santo* stiff competition as the new protector of women in labor. One night, when a woman was struggling through a difficult birth, they mistakenly brought her a picture card of the general. After having the miraculous image placed on her belly, the woman was able to push out the baby almost immediately. After those anguished moments, the error was discovered. It was judged—wisely, in view of such a quick and satisfactory result—that Martínez Campos could be just as effective as San Ramón Non Nato. The portrait of the governor successfully functioned as Santo Partero in many instances, and it was employed by everyone who heard about his virtues. It remained in the hands of a midwife who took it with her wherever she lent her services.

The prayer to La Caridad del Cobre—"who is the mother of women's bellies"—is also recited for women in labor, and it is recited directly over the womb. Water boiled with a cord from the Order of San Francisco (Saint Francis)—Orula—with seven grains of guinea pepper also helps to resolve the slowest and most difficult delivery.

People resort to Catholic *Santos*—Celestial Doctors—with the same urgency that makes them run to the orishas. These *Santos* specialize in different illnesses, and they had a large following during the colonial era. Older people have not forgotten that San Gregorio el Magno and San Bernardo were popular and in demand to treat stomach disease. San Fermín and San Quintín for dropsy. San Lucio and San Bernardino de Siena contained bloody discharge. San Marcos, San Moro, and Santa Ludovina cured paralysis. Santa Apolonia cured toothaches. San Leonardo helped to treat strokes.[33] Santa Jacobo de Sales helped asthma. San Bernardino de Siena helped cure dysentery. San Servando took care of ailments affecting the feet, while San Hilario and San Leonardo helped ailments affecting the legs. San José, Santa Lucía, and San Felipe de Neri cured ears and eyes. San Blas, Santa Margarita, and Santa Ludovina were petitioned to treat ailments of the throat. San José, San Pedro Mártir, San Ignacio, and Santa Petronila lowered fevers . . .

Returning to our story: This woman María del Pilar seemed so affectionate, so willing to help Omi Tomi at any time, that she truly gained her trust and recognition during those months. She had no doubts about involving her in all of her affairs, much less did she suspect the danger to which she was exposing herself. On days when she had too much work sewing, Omi Tomi very serenely accepted that María del Pilar would cook for her or bring her food.

Finally, once Omi Tomi gave birth without any complications—without San Ramón, even—to a girl that seemed healthy and normal, María del Pilar installed herself in Omi Tomi's house. She was the one who picked up the blood and placenta from the birth (which should be buried or thrown in the ocean to prevent them from falling into an enemy's hands), and she took the bedsheets to wash them in her own home.

Three days later, there was a lot of talk in the neighborhood about a man who had drowned at the seashore, at a place they used to call La Cortina de Valdés. "The mayombero," they said, "has killed himself out of remorse." At Omi Tomi's house, visitors commented on this event, whispering discreetly,

33 LC: The Arará *vodú* [*fodun*, etc.]—orisha—Nanabuluku, which is analogous to Santa Ana, cures strokes infallibly.

out of earshot. One of her relatives insisted that the *mayombero* had thrown himself in the ocean, desperate after having committed a wicked deed. But Omi Tomi did not pay attention to what she was hearing, because she did not clearly understand what "work" they were talking about. Her good friend kept coming and going all day long, taking charge in Omi Tomi's house as if it were her own, and saving Omi Tomi from the least bit of effort.

And—as usual—no one was "loyal" enough to tell her what they all knew and whispered all around her: the sorcerer who had committed suicide was the father of her husband's former lover; the woman had been working through María del Pilar to "bring on Omi Tomi's misfortune" for a long time; and she had taken control of the blood and placenta from her daughter's birth so she could give it to the *mayombero*, which was tantamount to taking control of a woman's life. Thanks to a supernatural intervention that will become clear below, this witchcraft failed to result in any harm (*morura*) coming to her.

When the little girl Belencita started recognizing and acting cute with the people who were around her regularly, she demonstrated an open revulsion for María del Pilar, crying inconsolably every time the woman held her.

And such a noticeable dislike started troubling Omi Tomi. Her friend always wore very long dresses. Even before she was one year old, the girl's tender face would suddenly become very serious as soon as she heard the sound of María del Pilar's long dresses and bracelets approaching. If she came near enough to caress the child's face, the little girl would start pouting and trembling, rejecting the gesture out of genuine terror.

Apologizing, the mother could only think to say, "Some children are foolish like that, nobody knows what to do with them!"

Later, when Belén[34] was already walking around on her own two feet, she would run away from that woman as if she were the devil himself, hiding behind Omi Tomi's skirts. One day it seems the woman "did something" to her mouth or gave her something to eat or drink, because the girl screamed and María del Pilar—very nervous—shook her. Omi Tomi saw this and realized that the friend had restrained herself from hitting the child, and she did not like it. "With the caution of a courteous person," yet angry, she made her displeasure known.

Moreover, she "politely" indicated that María del Pilar should never set foot in the house again. Indeed, from that day, her good friend did not visit her anymore. Belencita got sick. She started vomiting, and from that day she

---

34 DF-N: Cabrera drops the diminutive suffix -*ita* here ("Belén"), emphasizing the maturation of Omi Tomi's daughter at this point in the narrative, then returns to it in the next paragraph ("Belencita"), emphasizing that she was still a young girl.

would throw up every day after eating . . . The mother ran to the doctor, and the doctor prescribed various medicines that had no effect.

For a year, some reputable, "expensive" doctors—the kind who rode in carriages and wore long coats and gold watch chains—saw the girl. She had lost the beautiful dark skin color that had given Omi Tomi so much pride, the same skin color as Yemaya. One doctor would advise donkey or goats milk, while another recommended completely eliminating milk from her diet and substituting it with rice milk or barley, and yet another would prescribe the exact opposite of what his colleague had recommended. They tried all of the remedies—expensive powders, spoonfuls of medicine, and patented French remedies—but the poor child became more ill every day, weaker, more pale, and more skeletal. Belencita died "like a skinny little chicken." Fortunately, a neighbor who overheard Omi Tomi send for the doctor advised her against such a thoughtless decision, because they would perform a "utopsy" [autopsy] on the girl, which would be "bad for the departed little angel, who wouldn't be able to fly all the way to heaven."

Two or three hours after her death, a reptile—a *jubo* or another small snake—was seen curled up asleep over the cadaver's belly.[35] This time, Omi Tomi's friends and neighbors focused her attention. "The evil . . . It's right there!" The estranged friend who had stopped visiting so diligently attended the wake. She was overtaken by terrible convulsions and died nine days after the little girl was buried. The fact is that, as soon as the girl's eyes closed for the last time, that woman suffered a horrible, relentless nervous breakdown. And Omi Tomi, who was still blind to what was really going on, felt terrible about the constant suffering of her old friend. She now regretted keeping away from her house, based only on the childish whims of Belencita and her own harsh, motherly reaction.

In the end, it was a *mulata* she knew, a fellow seamstress, who "came to tell her the whole story and open her eyes": Belencita had been killed by witchcraft, and everyone knew it except her. Then, for the first time, she went to visit a Lucumí *santera*, but the *santera* didn't want to tell her much—she obviously didn't want to reveal a secret if there was no remedy to the predicament. And that's why what the *santera* said about what the cowrie shells were saying didn't line up very well with the truth of the matter. Omi Tomi went back home crestfallen, full of doubts about the wisdom of *santeros*. But nearby, only two doors down from her, a Congo had just moved in who could "see" using a glass of holy water. One day when she was returning home from running errands, the man went up to her and said, "Come with me. I need to

---

35 DF-N: The *jubo* (*Alsophis cantherigerus*) is a small species of boa constrictor found throughout Cuba.

tell what I've seen." She followed him, putting a half *peso* down on the table between them when the Black man asked for it, and she sat down to listen to him. "Ah, my dear . . . I still get goosebumps all over when I think about it." The Congo described her husband's former lover down to the last detail, the false friend that had pretended so much affection but only served the plans of the jealous woman by stealing the blood and placenta to kill her. But the witchcraft, the "bilongo"—as is sometimes happily the case in the interest of justice—had turned against them. If the sorcerer was caught up in his own web and committed suicide, it was because his *inkiso* had "doubled back" against him, punishing him by forcing him to throw himself in the ocean. The *nganga* had drowned him. It is an end awaiting many unscrupulous sorcerers . . . Sometimes, if a sorcerer insists on doing "work" of this sort against the advice of the *nganga*, if that stubborn, wicked sorcerer ends up ignoring the advice, then they send themselves to the other world instead of the person they intend to destroy. "An Nkise must be attended to and obeyed." The danger in being a *gangulero* is that evil deeds are repaid sooner or later.

Soon after all of this, it is true that Omi Tomi learned—at the foot of Ifa, the supreme oracle, and from many elders who had known her mother—that she had come into the world with "*santo* made." Pure-blooded Africans had consecrated her *santo* in her mother's womb, and her "Santo"—Olokun Yemaya, "the *fundamento* of the Yemayas, the oldest, the deep one," which she has not abandoned during her hundred years—does not abandon her dutiful, respectful children. (In this, all the orishas are like Yemaya.) Everyone finds their way in the world according to how they behave with their *Santo*. It is a law, the elders assure us, that young people seem to have completely forgotten, only to be crushed by its weight in the end. The *santeras* of yesteryear died in old age, calmly, in their beds—they had good deaths. They did not play around with the *Santo*. Today, on the other hand, it is astounding how many die suddenly, at their peak, or still young. They are gone in a few hours, without time to feel remorse or atone decisively for their faults and misdeeds. "And that's how the world is going, upside down." She was saved by Yemaya Olokun (just as she has saved so many others), who the *mayombero* had offended knowing full well that Omi Tomi was her child and her ward. Both the sorcerer's *inkiso* spirit and the powerful orisha that protected her agreed to destroy him. But poor Belencita was bewitched, "cursed," "nsarandada" before she was born, and she inevitably succumbed to the "wemba" that was put in her mouth. Her portrait, drawn with charcoal, is still preserved: a sad infant with the mysterious, awful expression of an adult. The day that the false friend made the girl cry out, she ingested the *bilongo* that grew into a reptile in her belly, devouring her insides little by little until she was left without a single drop of blood. Regarding the principal author of this crime, which only the "Santos" judged, she was—like Omi Tomi—a daughter of Yemaya.

Therefore, her sin—in the eyes of the goddess—doubled as fratricide. Morally, the "children" of the same *Santo* should consider and treat each other like siblings. Thus Omi Tomi saw the prediction of the Congo fulfilled to the letter: that evil woman, her husband's old lover, died of severe colic some months later—a very characteristic punishment from Yemaya, who (like Oshun) regularly attacks people by way of their intestines. Nevertheless, Omi Tomi's kindness still led her to arrange for masses dedicated to the peaceful rest of that woman's soul.

How could the doctor know? How could any of the doctors in Cuba know that the true source of the little Belencita's illness was a *jubo* or another snake (in other instances, a scorpion, a tarantula, a frog, etc., will make the curse work) that was eating her guts day by day.

Her daughter's illness cost Omi Tomi a lot of money, and she ended up in debt up to her eyeballs. For ten silver *reales*, however, a diviner made her see through the thick wall that always separates people from those other mysterious realities that many white people do not know or fail to keep in mind for their own self-defense: a *brujo*, called in time, would have saved her.

Most of our Black people, the bulk of our people, go through life scared of a continual threat from some *kimbamba*, feeling that they are the playthings of numerous dark forces that intervene in unsuspected ways to twist or fatally turn their destiny.

Countless versions of stories like this one, all fundamentally identical, are repeated continually. They explain the occult cause of any illness with considerable certainty. In case of death, they never justify a hypothesis—almost always inadmissible—of natural causes. In the face of a calamity, Black people do not hesitate to resort to the same magic that can provoke illness, the timeless traditions that fear and credulity maintain so alive and strong in our people and, undoubtedly, all of the world's peoples.

If an illness is not the result of bad intentions, hate, or some unrelenting resentment that an unscrupulous *mayombero* must satisfy, then it is simply a corrective punishment from heaven that is sometimes imposed when an offense is committed: failing to repay a debt incurred with a deity, even a trivial one; an irreverence—although, sometimes, there is no one more disrespectful than a Black person with their *Santos*; an involuntary oversight; or even a mild, seemingly insignificant distraction.

We can see that the *Santos* cause different kinds of deaths: Babaluaye kills with gangrene, smallpox, leprosy; Obatala with blindness, paralysis; Yewa with consumption; Inle and Orula with madness; Ogun, Ochosi, Elegua, Alagwana—perpetrator of solitary deaths—with unstoppable hemorrhaging;

Changó with fire, suicides by fire, and burns; Oya—who is even more violent and irascible than the god of fire—with electrocution. According to Odd-edei, "Oshun and Yemaya punish the person's belly. They kill in fresh water or saltwater; they sicken with rain and humidity. Oshun and Yemaya punish the genitals and the lower abdomen; Changó and La Candelaria kill with fire: before you know it, your clothes will be on fire! Be careful with kerosene stoves and never play with fire, because she can catch you off guard with just a look. Ogun takes the blood: he'll derail a train or trolley; he punishes with the machinery in mills and refineries a lot; he kills by stabbing and cutting. Eshu, Ogun, and Ochosi behave the same way. That's why you give the machete the blood of a rooster every once in a while." The machete and the knife—like any other metal, blade, or firearm—represent Ogun. "If it's not thirsty for blood, it won't cut its owner or anybody else." According to Anita, "Elegua bars the door, keeping anything good from coming in. He doesn't let you eat or even get dressed when he's upset. He puts a weight in the pit of your stomach that gets you upset (*el mal de madre*) and makes you sick from pain and suffering; and once you're weak and malnourished, he waters down your blood."

"Oya launches a bolt of lightning, or else she kills with an electrical wire or a strong gust of wind. She takes advantage of someone being sweaty and shocks them." "Baba (San Lázaro) twists and stiffens. He afflicts people with erysipelas, sores, and venereal disease. He attacks with embolisms and small-pox." "Flies and mosquitoes are his messengers."

Nuestra Señora de la Candelaria—Oya, or Yansa Oriri, "the lady who shoots lightning"—warns her children against eating mutton. It is a taboo that must be observed rigorously. Since this *Santa* renounced the ram (*abo*) and relinquished it to her lover Changó, she abstains from eating it. I know how much it cost one daughter of Oya, whose appetite made her repeat-edly forget this strict prohibition (*ewe*) that was imposed by her divine mother.

Two years ago, I heard about the grave condition of a *babalawo* who found himself at death's door because he had recklessly provoked the fury of the Venus of the Lucumí Olympus, Oshun Yeye Kari, who is more earthly than divine. She is a lively lover of parties, but she is equally willful, terrible, and merciless when she gets angry.

This man allowed himself to pawn a *manta de burato* [embroidered shawl] that belonged to the *Santa*. He also committed another, possibly even more grave, offense when he sold a splendid peacock that had been dedicated to the *Santa*.

Animals are often used as guardians in the homes of *santeros* and devotees. "In the house of a daughter of Yemaya, the *Santa* always likes seeing a duck (*kuekueye*)." You could always find African gray parrots (*odide*), which were brought directly from Africa, and they knew how to say "okuo yuma" in the "ile" of Lucumí or their descendants.[36] It is the favorite bird and symbol of all the *Santos*: sixteen of its feathers adorn Obatala's crown—*koide.* "These days, they paint pigeon feathers, disguising them as parrots."

Changó, Ochosi, or Ogun happily accept or demand a ram or a handsome red rooster. San Lázaro, a guinea hen, a rooster with gray patches, or a pair of dogs with yellow markings. Obatala, a she-goat, a dove, or white guinea hens.

These animals—mascots whose lives are spared from sacrificial killing and consecrated to the orisha—are the objects of the most careful attention. They are especially pampered, and anything they might do is tolerated . . . "Bellita's duck is very spoiled," one of her relatives complains to us. "Now she's decided to do her business in the living room." There is no question that the location is inappropriate. And, although it is true that this family deplores the fact that this duck is now in the habit of entering the house from the patio to defecate in the most conspicuous spot in the house, no one dares to reprimand or stop her. "She's Yemaya!" Another duck—the one belonging to Alicia M.—has spent twelve years doing whatever it wants.[37] I have the pleasure of knowing her; indeed, you will not find a more insolent animal. Sorcerers pay dearly for eggs laid by these ducks belonging to Yemaya, since the goddess fills them with virtue. In general, duck eggs are valued by the people. It is believed they strengthen the lungs and cure anemia. The true owners of these animals—the *Santos*—severely punish anyone who mistreats them: hitting an animal that belongs to an Orisha is an offense that incurs their displeasure. Goats, rams, and dogs often wear a ribbon of the *Santo's* emblematic color.

The peacock—*agi, egueni olora, tolo tolo orukoye*—is a favorite of Oshun. She considers peacock feathers to be one of her most beautiful adornments.

The unscrupulous *santero* we were discussing earlier became possessed by the *Santa* on the same day he sold Oshun's peacock.[38] "Oshun descended on him." It was after eleven o'clock at night in the tranquil Havana neighborhood where he lived, and almost all the neighbors had gone inside for the night. The *Santa,* "mounted" in the culprit, went around calling everyone door by door and gathered some twenty people. More joined in as she led them to her *omo's* house to convey the following: "N. has sold my peacock . . . The peacock which was a gift from my daughter Z. And he has pawned my *manta*

---

36 DF-N: "Okuo yuma" is a Lucumí greeting akin to "Good morning."

37 DF-N: Cabrera's original description of Alicia M.'s (and Yemaya's) beloved ducks illustrates a sort of nuance that is lost—often and inevitably—in translation: "Otra pata, la de Alicia M., ha cumplido doce años haciendo su santísima voluntad."

38 DF-N: Previously, the same "unscrupulous *santero*" was referred to as a *babalawo,* despite the widely held prohibition against possession trance among *babalawos.* The initial identification was probably an error.

de burato, which my daughter X. bought for me. I want you to bring me N. to shame him in front of all of you. Go get N.!"

"You can just imagine the predicament!" A witness to this curious scene told me about it the next day. "What a dilemma: finding N. for Oshun when she—Oshun herself—was mounting N.!" Faced with this impossible demand, they explained to Oshun that the *babalocha* was far away, in the middle of the city, but nobody knew exactly where.

"Well, then I'll wait for him until he comes back." Oshun seemed to be overflowing with outrage, breathing hard, furiously stomping her foot on the floor. And it became necessary to fan her. (*Abebe*, the fan, is put into action immediately when a *Santo* shows up angry.)

The *Santa* kept repeating, "It's mine! *Temi eiye!* I want my peacock! My peacock and my *manta de burato*." Eventually, she calmed down a little bit. "We really had to flatter her, soothing and caressing Yeye!" (This is another name given to Oshun; it means "sweet.") "So she wouldn't keep waiting for N.," they were forced to assure her that they would deliver her message word for word. "Yes, Mother! He'll return your peacock and your *manta*. Calm down. We promise. You'll see. We'll tell him."

"And tell him if he doesn't bring me my peacock, he's going to *iku* (die). Who is he to take what's mine? He must think I'm a little boy, taking what's mine! If my *manta* and my *ageni* aren't here in three days, you're going to find out who Yalode really is. My little horse is going to dance! *Obisu ñaña! Niakeni! Ofofo! Atiyu! Afoyudi! . . .*" (Scumbag, queer, and other insults.)[39] And that is how Mama Cache—the familiar name Cubans give La Caridad del Cobre when this goddess of love and happiness is in a good mood—departed, without ever having unknitted her brow.

They warned N. immediately, as soon as "the *Santo* went back down." They told him about his mother's visit, and they all agreed it was the truth. Two days later, the *babalocha* was burning up with a fever. Full of dread, since Oshun had set a term of three days to return what he had stolen, he went to the pawn shop and was forced to buy a different *manta*: Oshun's had already been sold. From there he went to the market and bought a small peacock. Returning home, shivering from the fever, he went running to the wardrobe where he kept the tureen that contained the "otan" (stone) of the orisha. Apologizing, he presented the *manta* and peacock. He went to bed thinking that he had been forgiven, but Oshun came back to mount him again. This time she called the neighbors at the top of her voice from the entrance to the house. "My *ageni* was big. It was *gan-gan*," she boomed. "It was like this!" And she made

---

39   DF-N: For a primer on Lucumí epithets, several of which are frankly homophobic and remain untranslated here, see Cabrera ([1957] 1986).

an exaggerated gesture a meter above the ground. "This little thing you've brought me is a *tomeguín*![40] It's not my peacock, and I don't want it. And this isn't my *manta de burato* either. This is a used *manta*. It's dirty and broken— look where it's been mended. This crook bought it at the pawn shop." Oshun's fury reached a fever pitch, and she doubled down on her threats. Let us not tire the reader: the *Santa* forced the *babalocha* to suffer through bitter times. He became very ill. She had heralded a visit from the law, which did indeed pay him a visit in order to collect payment on furniture he had bought on an installment plan; he was forced to pay the debt quickly to avoid a brief spell in jail, since he had sold the furniture before paying it off. Oshun filled his gallbladder with stones, "chinitas." She reduced him to skin and bones. Finally, after many petitions and offerings, she tired of punishing him, or perhaps she yielded to the pleas of her sister Yemaya, who interceded on behalf of the repentant *babalocha*. She "allowed herself to be appeased" and forgave him, helping him survive an operation—which he underwent on the advice of the *Santa*—to remove the gallstones: "The same ones she'd grown in his belly."

Arsenio—the brother-in-law of the famous clairvoyant E.—was more deserving, yet he failed to obtain the grace of absolution.

His wife killed him. He practiced a *cruzada* [mixed] religion, Congo with Lucumí, and he had his *nganga kimbisa*. His *nganga* told him to leave that woman so many times! But he was in love, and he was soft. He took care of his godchildren like no one else. The protection charms he prepared for them were so good that no harm could get to them. Arsenio was a truly good man. One of his goddaughters brought him a she-goat for Oya. Oya was very happy with her goat, and she made it clear they should not kill it. But when his wife celebrated her *Santo's* feast day, she got it in her head to kill the goat, so Arsenio killed it. If my wife asked me to kill my *Santo's* animal, the wallop I'd give her . . . The thing is, she would never dare to do that. But some men are like that. Poor Arsenio! He got sick. He became bedridden. Another of his goddaughters came to visit him, also a daughter of Oya, and the *Santo* went inside him right there and then.

And Oya stayed by Arsenio's side until she took him away. The worst part is that no *Santo*, not even Obatala, stood up for him, because she was as angry as Oya. Arsenio said to his wife, "If I could get up from this bed, I'd slice you open like a pig with my *nganga's* knife, because you're the only reason I'm dying! You wretch! To get rid of me, you made me offend Oya." And the woman was quite pleased when Arsenio met his end.

---

40 DF-N: *Tomeguín* is the Cuban name for a small bird known as the Cuban grassquit (*Tiaris canorus*).

The impulsive and arrogant *babalocha* Manengue had to walk around barefoot and begging as punishment for eating a hen that belonged to Oshun. The hen would soil the whole house and break plates and glasses. "Even though he had money, because he would win the lottery often by playing the numbers 73 and 37,[41] he still had to beg for handouts to pay for the hens his *Santa* had demanded. This was only after many offerings made with the help of four *babalawos* and twenty-five daughters of Oshun, and thanks to Orula, who was his sponsor. Manengue was so close to dying that, by the time Oshun decided to forgive him and he started to recover, he had to relearn how to walk again."

Sacrificing a *Santo's* animal when the *Santo* has not demanded it is so dangerous that Omi Tomi became angry every time she recalled a *babalawo* named Patrocinio.

> I bought a beautiful *pollón* [young rooster] for Elegua, but Elegua didn't want it to be killed for him. And the *pollón* became a rooster. He was obnoxious. He broke everything. One day, Patrocinio came to visit. He saw the rooster. "Teresita," he says, "Elegua wants that rooster." "Oh no, sir. Elegua told me he wants it to be a lookout. He wants to see it alive, walking around the house." Patrocinio says, "No, no, Teresita. His time is up. Elegua wants him, and you need to do it soon." He insisted so much that his bullheadedness confused me. Patrocinio was a *babalawo*, and they know a lot. So, I offered the rooster to Elegua. Dear God almighty! I had as much work as I could handle as a seamstress. All the work stopped coming in. My husband got sick. I almost lost him. He lost his job. Back then, I lived in a house with lemon and fruit trees on the patio. To help make ends meet, I sold lemons and fruits, and that was all. They sued me and evicted me from the house.
>
> Thankfully, my neighbor held on to the pots and pans; we passed them to her through the fence on the patio. Then I bought a chicken to give its

---

41 DF-N: The numbers likely represent coded signs in Lucumí *dilogún* divination. In the symbolism of *dilogún*, the two pairs of composite "numbers" are complementary, sharing themes and principles in common (3-7 = Ogunda-Odi; 7-3 = Odi-Ogunda). See Angarica (n.d. [1955]), Bascom ([1980] 1993), and Tsang (2021). I am grateful to Martin Tsang for pointing out that the numbers might also refer to *la bolita* (also known as La Charada Cubana and La Charada China), a complex Cuban lottery system, a reference that adds another layer of symbolic meaning to this passage in the context of a numerological theme woven throughout *El Monte*. A reference guide to La Charada—which incorporates numerical, textual, and (in its iconic caricature) pictorial elements—is included in numerous ritual reference guides. See Cabrera (1994), which includes her essay "Charada para Roger Caillois"; and Espirito Santo (2018). In the symbolism of La Charada, 3 is *marinero* (sailor); 7 is *caracol* (shell); 37 is *bruja, gallina prieta, hormiga* (witch, black hen, ant); and 73 is *buey, jicotea, collar* (ox, tortoise, necklace).

blood to Elegua, and another to keep as a lookout. But what a setback, thanks to Patrocinio! He might have been a *babalawo*, but he practically buried me! Nobody knows your Elegua better than you.

The "guardian" animals are protectors and taboos that are recommended or demanded—verbally by "mounted" *Santos*, or by way of the *dilogún* [cowrie shell divination] or Ifa. They ward off Death from homes, carrying away "evil" or illness that might attack the owner or members of the family at any moment. To illustrate the benefits they bring to homes, *Santeros* tend to this well-known story: A man was the father of a large family, and he owned many animals that lived inside the house with him and his children. This man understood his animals' language perfectly, which is not so uncommon among certain individuals—in fact, it is much more common than most people imagine. Because of this, our good man remained as calm as usual when his wife became ill and the rest of the family cried uncontrollably in their desperation to save her. The man had overheard the Cat tell the Dog, "Our master's wife is very sick and she's going to die. Let's stop playing and running around. Don't bite me and I won't scratch you." Then the *quiquiriquí* [rooster] joined the conversation by responding with a guffaw: "Bah, the master's wife might be in very bad shape, but this isn't going to kill her. We have to be brave and defend her when Ikú comes . . ." All animals fear Ikú; they are clairvoyant, so the sight of her horrifies them. After a few days, during which the sick woman slowly became even more ill, Death did indeed come looking for her. Seeing her enter the house in the image of a skeleton, all the animals were frozen in terror, but each—in their own language—expressed their terror in the most strident tone.

Bewildered by all the commotion, Ikú hesitated as she took a step forward. The rooster was insolent and full of courage. While the other animals retreated, he kept yelling and rushed forward to confront Death, jumping on her determinedly. In the midst of this pandemonium, the rooster left a feather stuck in the bones of one of the skeleton's arms. Seeing that strange thing sprouting from her arm, she got scared and ran out the door, fleeing, not from the rooster, which was still plucking up even more courage, but from the feather that followed her as she escaped. No matter how much she ran, in her fright, she could not manage to free herself.

During the last days of Oddedei's life, I had the pleasure of paying her rent at a house she had converted into a sort of Noah's ark—"before I eat, I give my animals corn"—warning her godchildren and friends about the danger of humiliating or abandoning the animals. One day, as she was scolding a woman for tossing a hen out of the house by hitting it with a broom, I heard her tell this story, which she believed to be true and which certainly made an impression on her listener:

A woman went to the market to buy a chicken. "I want a cheap chicken. A *real* and a half? That's too expensive!" And after a lot of haggling, they gave her a little chicken. "There you go, take it for one *real* . . ." She bought it. She had a big backyard. But because the chicken was very small and skinny, she didn't pay any attention to it. She tossed it outside, where there were a lot of bushes. She didn't take care of the little chicken at all. It got lost out there, picking at a little bit of grass here and there, eating whatever little bugs it found. After some time—and thanks to its good luck—she became a big fat hen, and she met a rooster. She laid eggs and hatched three chicks. One day when the hen was walking along with her three children, looking very pleased with herself, the woman saw her. "Damn! That's my chicken!" She reached down to grab the hen, but the hen escaped. The woman sent her daughter to grab the hen, and the hen started talking. The girl went back to her mother and said, "I'm not grabbing that chicken. It's talking like an old Black woman." When the woman found the hen again and approached it, the hen said, "Keep walking, *atrevida!*" Can you imagine? The woman called a *babalawo*. The *babalawo* went to the yard, and this time the hen sang a song (which I did not transcribe). The *babalawo* heard the song and told the woman, "The hen has explained to me that she was happy to go home with you and help you when you bought her, but you threw her out. You never went out to the yard to give her so much as a little grain of corn. Now she has children and she's very happy in the yard, so she doesn't want to have anything to do with you, and she's taking her children and leaving." The woman said, "That's the absolute truth. It's just that she was so skinny and small." And the hen answered, "That's no excuse. When you go to the market and want a big fat hen, pay for it. Otherwise, buy a skinny one and fatten her up."

In Africa, an animal is never thrown away. That brings misfortune on you, and you'd better stop hitting that hen with the broom, or you'll regret it . . .

Another version of this story:

A man bought a small chicken. He put it in his henhouse, but then it got sick with pip and the man said, "This is no good. Let's toss him in *el monte*." The abandoned chicken became a gorgeous hen. One day, the hen went back to the farm with her chicks following along behind her. She was very proud of her children, and she started singing in front of the house of the man who had been her owner: "E mi adiye yeye kuao kuao meta emi adiye ogu meta alado eri moro." The man came outside, stunned. He was admiring the hen and asked for her forgiveness, but then she ran away with all her children. The misdeeds of men are the reason we have so many stray animals.

Santeros use a small chicken that follows behind a hen to benefit those under their protection. This is how:

You take the little chicken and rub it with palm oil, bee honey, and aguardiente. You ask Elegua if he wants its blood. Yes? You rip the head off and give him *eiye* (blood). Then you ask if he wants to have the body for three days. Yes? You leave it there for three days. No? Immediately, without delay, you burn the little chicken to make *afoche* (powder). You mix the powder from the chicken with powdered *ñame volador* and place it before Elegua.[42] You pray to all the Elders, *muertos*, and the living. You keep those powders, and every time they're needed, you add a pinch of three different kinds of ground pepper. When you want to give good luck to a godchild or some other person, as that person leaves the house of the *iyalocha*, she blows a little bit of this powder on him, saying, "As the little chick follows the hen, may luck follow you. As the Ñame Volador grows by rising up, may you rise up in your life."

When they are angry, the *Santos* dispatch not only illness, but every other sort of calamity. The elders remember the case of Papá Colás, who was well known in Havana at the end of the nineteenth century. He was "*omo* Obatala." He had the unspeakable habit of getting angry, behaving rudely toward his *Santo*, and insulting it when he had no money. I heard the story from various sources: it is well known that Obatala—the god of purity par excellence, the Immaculate, the god of whiteness, the owner of everything that is white—needs to be handled very delicately. The stone that Obatala inhabits cannot be subjected to inclement sun, wind, or night air. Obatala must always be wrapped in cotton (*Ou*), covered in spotless white cloth. In his rages, Papá Colás would grab Obatala, wrap him in a dirty or black rag, and, as a further insult, relegate it to the outhouse. Obatala is the Compassionate One, the great omnipotent Orisha who says, "I always forgive my children." But he eventually had enough of such despicable and unjustifiable behavior. One day when Papá Colás came down with the *Santo*, the *Santo* left a message for him saying that he needed to act as if he were imprisoned, remaining in his room with his orisha for sixteen days as penance for his irreverence. Papá Colás shrugged his shoulders and, far from

---

42 DF-N: See the ÑAME VOLADOR entry in the botanical encyclopedia.

obeying the will of the god, unleashed a litany of insults as he marched out into the street without even putting on an emblem of Obatala, not even a white ribbon.

"I knew his sisters, and I can vouch for all of this being true. His poor sisters were always terrified, talking about his poor conduct and waiting for the *Santo* to rough him up. Colás treated his *Santos* like a *mogrolón*,[43] and his sisters would say, 'His Angel is going to knock him down.' And that's what happened. Papá Colás slept next to the window in his room, which faced the street. Nobody knows why, but when the cart for trash collection went by his window, that Black man went crazy. He armed himself with the metal brace from his door and killed the trash collector." (Recall that Obatala, "the owner of heads," punishes by way of the head, making people insane.) "That's how a sixteen-day retreat turned into a sixteen-year prison sentence for the wayward Papá Colás." He was as well known for his blasphemy as he was for his clairvoyance; they say "his vision was so strong" that he divined without needing to consult his cowrie shells. A contemporary of this *santero* tells us that the judges were going to condemn him to death by garrote, but a council of *babalawos* met and Orula, Oshun, and Obatala refused to consent to the pleas of the other *Santos* who asked that he be pardoned. After considerable supplication, only Obatala forgave him and agreed to save his life. "When the white people wanted to sentence his *ori* (head) to death, Obatala commuted the sentence because it was a question of the head of one of his children." This Papá Colás, who left an impression on the memories of so many elders, was also famous for being queer. He surprised one naive priest by disguising himself as a woman and getting married to another queer, causing the sort of scandal one can easily imagine.

This heinous sin has occurred quite frequently in the Regla Lucumí for a long time. Nonetheless, many *babalochas*—*omo Changó*—have lost their lives as punishment from the manly and womanizing orisha Changó, who repudiates this vice. These days, the number of pederasts in Ocha seems to be so numerous that it is the subject of constant indignation among older *santeros* and devotees.[44] (This is not the case among the Congo sects, which treat them

---

43 DF-N: While the word *mogrolón* is clearly a pejorative neologism or mispronunciation of a Spanish word—Cabrera marked it parenthetically as "(*sic*)"—its precise meaning and etymology remain obscure.

44 DF-N: In this passage (including a direct quotation possibly but necessarily attributed to Sandoval), the use of the word *pederasts* ("pederastas") performs the abhorrent equation of queerness with pederasty. It is clearly a troubling historical artifact, and several quotations carry a similarly ugly stigma, punctuated by a particularly disturbing anecdote of cruel violence. While the language has been intentionally toned down somewhat here in translation, it is worth em-

with profound scorn and banish them.) "At every turn, you run into queers with their *merengueteo!*"

"There's mystery in this issue of the Addodis [gay men]," Sandoval says. "Because Yemaya had a relationship with one of them ... She fell in love with one of them and lived with him. It happened in a country called Lado, where the inhabitants were like that—fags, half men, what they call [her]maphrodites—and Yemaya protected them." "Odo is Yemaya's land. How many of Yemaya's sons are queers!" (And Oshun's.) Nonetheless, the male *Santos*—Changó, Ogun, Elegua, Ochosi, and Orula, not to mention Obatala—do not look kindly on pederasts. Not long ago, Tiyo was present at a scene that cost an effeminate man his life. He was a son of Changó Terdun they mockingly called María Luisa:

> It was a real shame, because that wretch came down with a magnificent Changó. Whenever he would give somebody lottery numbers to help them out of a tight spot, they could make the bet with the money they'd set aside for food or rent. He never let them down. That lottery number that Changó Terdun gave you would come out for sure. Ah! But Changó didn't like him being effeminate, and he'd declared publicly that he was ashamed of his son. At a fiesta for La Virgen de Regla, María Luisa was there and we were all joking around with him, making fun of him. In the middle of all that, when María Luisa was getting mounted by the *Santo*, another young Black man arrived. He was *un cojo* [a lame, disabled man] named Biyiken, and he pinched María Luisa's ass. Instantly, Changó himself turned around like an enraged bull and shouted, "Enough!" He demanded that they bring him a big bucket, then he ordered all of us to spit in the bucket, saying that whoever failed to spit in it would receive the same punishment as his son. María Luisa was healthy. The young Black man was beautiful, and kind ... What a shame! When the bucket was filled with gobs of spit, he dumped it over his own head. The next day, María Luisa woke up with a fever. Ten days later, we took him to the cemetery. Changó Terdun left him shriveled up like a little raisin.

The story of the *Santeros* R. and Ch. is just as odd and emblematic. Wearing a yellow shawl tied around his waist, Ch. was La Caridad del Cobre, Oshun *panchagara* in person.

---

phasizing that Cabrera, a queer person herself, undoubtedly found various slurs she documents in the original text particularly repugnant.

In the tenement on Calle Gervasio known as Solar de los Catalanes, he celebrated a great feast in honor of Oshun. The "plaza" he made for the goddess was splendid (*plaza* being the name given to the fruit offerings which are placed in front of the orisha's altar for a while, then distributed among the attendees at the fiesta). One witness tells me,

There were basketfuls of everything: oranges, coconuts, canistels, plums, mangoes, apple bananas, papayas. All Oshun's favorite fruits. And eggs, as well as plates of buns, *palanquetas*, *panetelas borrachas*, honey, custards, sweet cornmeal with milk and butter, raisins, almonds, and white sugar and dusted with cinnamon, and popcorn . . . Ch. had spent extravagantly for his *Santa*. The house was totally packed with people. At twelve o'clock, Ch. came down with Oshun. R. was standing at the door drunk and said, "I'm gonna get possessed by the *Santo* too, right now," and he faked it. He goes in the altar room, goes to the basket full of honey buns, and starts eating them. Ch. came in with Oshun to greet him, and R. smacked her face. When everyone grabbed him, he kicked her. We yelled at him, "R., throw yourself on the floor! Ask Mother to forgive you!"

"Bah! That's nothing but a fag . . ."

"It's not Ch., it's our Mother!"

Oshun did not move. She opened the very fine shawl that Ch. and his godchildren had given her, and she laughed. She raised her right hand and pointed it at R. Pressing her other hand to her chest, she said, "Five *irole* for my son, and five *irole* for my other son."

And that's exactly what happened.

Ch. woke up with a fever of forty degrees [Celsius] and a swollen belly. R. woke up with a fever of 40 degrees and a swollen belly . . . Five days later, they died the same day, at the same time. It made no difference that their godchildren brought a peacock and fifty-five yellow hens and everything else to make *ebo* for them. Five days later, as I attended the burial of Ch., I saw the funeral procession for R. go by the cemetery gates. Their graves were near each other. The mother of Ch.—who was also a daughter of Oshun—and twenty-four other children of Oshun from one or the other entourage got mounted, and you could see them laughing and laughing, without speaking . . . Until they shoveled the last mound of dirt, the Oshuns were lined up along the edges of the graves, and they didn't stop laughing. But it was not the joyful laugh of the *Santa*. It was a cold, mocking laugh that froze the blood in your veins, and it rang in the silence. The only other sound you could hear was the shovel digging in and the dirt falling in the hole.

Lesbians (*alakuata*) also abound in Ocha. In earlier times, their patron was Inle, the doctor Kukufago, San Rafael, "a very strong and mysterious *Santo.*" Elders recount that, in the colonial era, they would all attend Inle's traditional celebration at la loma del Angel (Angel's Hill).[45] Invertidos, Addodis; Obini Toyo, Obini Ñaña; Erón Kibá, Wassicundí, or Diánkune (as the Abakuá, or *ñáñigos*, call them); and Alakuatas or Oremi. They would meet in the neighborhood of El Angel on October 24. The balconies of homes would be decorated with drapery on the eve of the Feast of San Rafael. At night, a fish made from straw, with gunpowder and fireworks stuffed in its tail, would be set on fire; the procession and its fireworks were splendid. There, in 1887, we find "its overseer [*su capataza*], La Zumbáo."[46]

She lived on the very same hill. She would set up a table in the street and sell her famous tortillas de San Rafael.[47] (Those of her contemporary, Papá Upa, were also widely celebrated, and they are still fondly remembered by a few gluttonous old men.) Indeed, various elders have told me about La Zumbáo, a *santera* of Inle. She was a seamstress with a good clientele, and she was *muy presumida y rumbosa* [very arrogant and flamboyant].[48] Others have

---

45   DF-N: La loma del Angel is an iconic landmark in Cuban culture, beginning with Cirilo Villaverde's novel *Cecilia Valdés o la loma del Angel*, first published in Havana in 1839 and later expanded and revised in a more definitive 1882 edition. The story—a tragic love triangle with a light-skinned *mulata* at its center—is a canonical example of the *costumbrismo* genre (the depiction of the customs and manners of a particular social or cultural milieu) and dramatizes many of Cuba's racial, sexual, and social tensions; see Corbitt (1950); and Ocasio (2012). The title of a 1935 English-language edition of Villaverde's novel—*The Quadroon: A Romance of Old Havana*—foregrounds race. Beyond the original novel, the story has enjoyed remarkable longevity and continually reinforces the symbolic importance of La loma del Angel. A popular musical theater version of *Cecilia Valdés* was first performed in 1932 with music by Gonzalo Roig, subsequently becoming a quintessential example of the zarzuela genre. An epic 1982 film version of *Cecilia Valdés*, directed by Humberto Solás and starring Daisy Granados, made Afro-Cuban religious traditions a prominent part of the story, and notable new iterations of the story were published by Reinaldo Arenas (1987) and Daína Chaviano (2008).

46   DF-N: In this context, the feminine gendering of the term *capataza* (overseer, foreperson, leader, boss) should be interpreted as emphatic, since the much more common *capataz* applies equally to men or women.

47   DF-N: In Cuban slang, the word *tortilla* refers to lesbianism.

48   DF-N: The term *rumbosa*, like *la loma del Angel*, evokes Cuban *costumbrismo*. More specifically, it evokes the consummately gendered and racialized figure of *la mulata de rumbo*, famously rendered in an iconic 1881 painting by Victor Patricio Landaluze (and reiterated as a persistent Cuban stereotype ever since). Landaluze's portrait is reproduced in *Santería Enthroned* with the following caption: "The fan-holding '*mulata* of the street' was a fixture of nineteenth- and early-twentieth-century Cuban arts and letters. She provided the model for and embodied the tensions of mixed Cuban identity" (Brown 2003b, 188). I am grateful to Martin Tsang for his keen insights on this passage.

spoken to me about a supposed religious society of Alakuatas. The curious thing is that Inle—like Yewa—is such a chaste and strict *Santo* regarding the moral conduct of his children and devotees. He is mentioned as seldom as Yewa, Aboku (Santiago Apóstol), and Nana because they are all feared, and nobody wants to risk serving such severe and imperious deities. By the end of the nineteenth century in Havana, "Inle would almost never visit heads."[49] A sixty-something woman tells me that she was at the Palenque once when Inle came down. All of the *Santos* paid their respects to him, and all of the old men and women *de nación* [people of the nation; i.e., Afro-Cubans] there "were overcome with emotion, and they started weeping. Since then," she tells me, "I have not seen Inle on anybody's head again." Nor does she remember anything more from that unforgettable visit to the Palenque which was honored by San Rafael coming down, because later, after the fiesta was over, she found herself in a room at the back of the house, dazed and with her clothes still soaked with water. She deduced that "she was overcome by the *Santo*," Inle. Since it is customary, when a *Santo* manifests itself, to offer them a *jícara* full of water to drink and spray lavishly over devotees, her wet clothes and stunned, disoriented state ("sirimba") amounted to evidence of the Orisha possessing her.

In the town of Santa Clara, Inle is associated with San Juan Bautista rather than San Rafael. (Whereas San Rafael's day is October 24, San Juan Bautista's day is June 24, which is celebrated as Ogun's day here.)[50] San Juan Bautista is an adolescent, almost a child. He is offered toys, and he is so mischievous that they get him drunk on the evening of the twenty-third so he spends the next day sleeping rather than causing trouble. He wakes up refreshed on the twenty-fifth. He was the *Santo* of the famous Villa Clara native Blas Casanova, in whom the *Santo* would manifest very serenely and "look into everyone's soul."

Yewa, "nuestra Señora de los Desamparados" (our Lady of the Helpless), a virgin, prohibits her children from all sexual affairs. That is why all of her servants are always elderly women, virgins, or already infertile. And Inle—who is "just as severe," powerful, and delicate as Yewa—sometimes demanded the same from his *santeras*, who had to abstain from maintaining sexual relations with men.[51]

Among the elders of Santería, the case of P.S. is just as widely known as that of Papá Colás. P.S. was the son of O.O., one of the most respected and sought-

---

49 DF-N: The idiomatic phrases "visit heads" and "come down" both refer to possession trance.

50 DF-N: "Here" refers to the western part of the island (Havana and Matanzas).

51 DF-N: The precise wording suggests that a prohibition against sexual relations with men does not necessarily preclude sexual relations with other women.

after *iyalochas* in Havana. During a candid moment, she recounts the story as an example of the rigidness and conduct of a god that has been offended:

P.S. was, like me, a son of Changó. And, as such, he was a drummer, although he was just a hobbyist. If he picked up a wood box to play, the box became a drum. When he sang, he would bring all of the *Santos* down from heaven. But he offended Changó and became lost. At a fiesta in my own home, he told the *Santo*, "If it's true that you're Santa Bárbara, and you say you're the one that calls the shots and makes things happen, and that you're going to kill me, then get it over with and kill me already! Let's see it. Strike me down with a bolt of lightning right now! Enough talk." Santa Bárbara didn't respond. He laughed. I was stunned and ashamed by the boy's insolence. Years went by. He kept working and enjoying himself. At the *toques* I gave at my house, Santa Bárbara would collect money and give it to him.[52] Well, that made P.S. think Changó had forgotten about the incident. Another offense he committed was hitting several of Changó's daughters. I mean, considering how jealous Changó is! Add a few other things he did to the stupidity of how he behaved with the *Santo* himself, and it eventually turned out that Santa Bárbara got fed up and said he was going to make him pay for all of it, and pay dearly. Because that's one thing about the *Santos*: they wait to avenge themselves; they give people more and more rope, then they yank the guilty person when they least expect it. First, Changó made my boy dumb. Then crazy. One day, he went out in the street naked and came back covered in blood. He was bound, tied down, bewitched. He asked for forgiveness, but Changó always had the same reply: "He needs to know that my balls are bigger than his, and I may have laughed when he insulted me, but I haven't forgotten." I cast cowrie shells so I could do something for my son (*ebo*), but Changó answered that I couldn't go over his head and I should stop being so cocky. Listen, I couldn't do so much as a cleansing for my son. With my Santería, I couldn't do anything! I just suffered as a mother. When he finally died, he wasn't even a shadow of himself. He was a skeleton. When they took him away, the only weight they carried was the casket.

O.O. has remained silent regarding another unforgivable sin that her sacrilegious son committed. It was a close friend of hers that told me about what

---

52   LC: The *Santos* in possession of their children ask the attendees at the fiestas for money to give to the drummers, thereby demonstrating that the drummers have played to the *Santos'* complete satisfaction.

saddened O.O. the most. What "started her decline and crushed her" was what he did with her Oshun stone:

> O.O. had an African stone that belonged to her Lucumí godmother. Her godmother brought it when she came to Cuba, and she'd left it to her. And that stone grew. It got huge. It was the size and shape of a melon. Two men couldn't move it. That Caridad was a meter wide. There was no clay pot big enough for her.
>
> O.O. kept her in a washbasin. During a move from one house to another, P.S. threw it away. Yes, ma'am . . . A lot of people say he threw it in the river, but nobody knows exactly where La Caridad del Cobre ended up.

Yet the *Santos* are not always just in their punishments. It is easy to understand why Obatala would administer a punishment on Papá Colás that was more than well deserved, but Changó's severity in the case of Luis S. seems both excessive and gratuitous. There is no way to fight against the cruel whims of the gods, no defense against a divinity's brutal treatment of a mortal, "just because."

The evil unleashed by a *mayombero judío*—those figures who inspire such intense terror among the people and evoke such foul African memories—can be contained expeditiously. On the other hand, everything fails against the irreducible ill will of *Santos* who are "pissed off" or "turn their backs" and deny their protection or absolution to an unfortunate human whose only sin might have been "rubbing them the wrong way." It is true that the Orishas' favor can be bought, because they are very selfish, gluttonous, and susceptible to flattery. Yet when an Orisha stubbornly decides to turn a deaf ear, they will not negotiate at all. If someone has already been condemned, without recourse to an appeal, an honorable diviner or conjurer—whether they work with coconut, *dilogún*, *okpele*, *vititi mensu*, or *andile*—will not insist on offerings and sacrifices, which will be so costly that they will ruin their subject and will only benefit the diviner economically.

"What can you do when a *Santo* turns against someone?" Absolutely nothing. As the *babalawo* and the *gangangame* know, there is no remedy for these illnesses. For this individual, there is no longer any possibility of an "exchange of lives" or heads, the universal and millenarian magical procedure which consists of transferring an illness from a person to an animal, a doll made to look as similar as possible to the sick person, or another healthy person. That is why many people avoid having direct contact with or even visiting *santeros* and *iyalochas* who are gravely ill. "They avoid exchanging lives," since the stronger spirit can take over the vitality of a weaker spirit, steal their life, and recover their own health. ("That's why you'll see an old dying *santero* come back to life, just as a younger person at their side dies.")

They will not be saved by the grace an orisha has infused in a plant. Offerings, prayers, and *ebo* will be of no use. Neither will sacrifices of birds or four-legged animals, which are so effective when they are stipulated by the *Santos* beforehand, specifying their role in each case by way of cowrie shells or Ifa.

Unlike Papá Colás, Luis S. was not a *santero*. In a drumming *toque*, Changó asked him for "Agude" (plantain), but Luis either did not understand, or he pretended to be distracted. It is true that he believed fervently in the *Santos*—a crucial detail. One Sunday, he was on his way to the market when someone came up to him and spoke to him in *lengua*. He instantly lost consciousness, and they took him—still unconscious—back to his room at the *solar* [tenement]. He didn't regain his senses for another five hours. While he was passed out in his bed, his wife was "knocked down" by Changó, who directed her to her godmother's house. There the *Santo* related what had happened.

They asked, "Alafi (Changó)! What have you done?" Slapping his thigh and shrugging mischievously, the *Santo* replied, "Etie mi kosinka" (I didn't do anything).

The godmother dismissed the *Santo* from Luis's wife. They did not waste any time making an offering to placate Changó. On the advice of his wife's godmother, Luis sacrificed a gorgeous ram. But Changó—"because he's so resentful and so capricious"—was not satisfied. The man got worse. His wife could not leave his side, because Alafi would immediately toss him on the floor, leaving him dazed and motionless for long stretches of time. When he came back to his senses, he clumsily explained that a Black man kept picking him up and dropping him on the ground. "Because of Santa Bárbara's ill will and determination to kill him," Luis S. ended up dying of a syncope.

Illness might be due to an orisha's irritability, an unfair dislike, justified anger, or the hatred and hidden vengeance that a wicked sorcerer can satisfy. Illness is sometimes also due to the ill-fated effects of the spirit of a *muerto* directing their resentment or loathing against an individual. As we have seen, an *egun* or *fumbi* might attach itself to us and attempt to remove us from this world.

A *bata* drumming *toque* with its sacrifices of birds and animals, a "spiritual mass" in a spiritist center every once in a while, or a responsorial mass in a Catholic church—"Oru ile Olorun"—must be celebrated for the souls of deceased *santeras* and *santeros* nine days after their death.

The mass begins other funerary rituals—the *ntutu*, then the Lifting of the Plate—to soothe the "Egu who is still standing upright in the grave" or refuses to leave the house.

"The *muertos* need to be kept happy and in a good mood. They need to be respected as much as the *Santos*." My Black teachers emphatically underscore that the cult—or, more precisely, the reverence—of ancestors is one of the pillars of their religion. They categorically affirm and repeatedly insist that "the *Muerto*, in all of the *Reglas*, gives birth to the *Santo*." "Before saluting the *Santos*, one salutes the *Muertos*." ("Ikú lo bi Ocha," and without *muerto*, there is no Ocha.)

A *tambor*, a mass by a Father priest, or a spiritual mass "will subdue a *muerto* who has gone crazy."

In the "spiritual masses" that are so widespread nowadays, disembodied souls who still find themselves in darkness are "given light." In no way do they nullify the Catholic masses dedicated to a soul's peaceful rest: "First, the *muerto* demands a mass." The orishas recommend them constantly, and nowadays a mass at a spiritist center is added—I repeat—to the one traditionally celebrated in the church nine days after a death, as well as on the anniversary of the death of a *santero*. This cannot be circumvented, regardless of the Regla to which they belong. The spiritual mass consists of offerings of flowers and candles—"flowers attract the spirits"—to invoke a soul, discern their wishes, and carry them out, helping them if they are "disturbed," "elevating" them if they are a soul that is stuck on the earth or "lagging in their spiritual evolution." To this end, various mediums gather around a table where they place vases of flowers, glasses filled with water, and perfumes (Loción Pompeya and Agua de Florida). In addition to mediums we might describe as professionals, relatives and friends of the departed also fall into trance, as well as invited or curious guests who often turn up at these spiritist sessions "where many spirits descend," manifesting—like everything regarding the religiosity of our *negros*—immutable African depths.

Despite the high esteem with which spiritual masses are regarded, recalcitrant "brothers from space," intractable reactionaries, sometimes "refuse to show up" at spiritist/spiritual masses, despite being called. They send their mourners word by way of cowrie shells, Ifa, or the *Santo* itself in the head of one of their "children," letting them know that they do not want a spiritual mass, but a Catholic one, which is "the real one, the one with the *fundamento*." One of my elderly acquaintances tells me, "The spiritual mass is fashionable now. Well . . . I always find a way to offer my *muertos* their favorite food in a corner of the bathroom, which is where they eat, and that way I keep them happy." She concludes, on a philosophical note, "Mine haven't gotten into that trend of being given light in outer space [the otherworld].[53] I just light a little oil lamp, and that's good enough for them."

The souls of the *muertos* cannot eat inside houses, "only in the outhouse." They are given offerings on patios—the farther from the house, the better. And there is no better place to leave offerings than in the spaces between the roots of trees. They are offered water, liquor, cigars and cigarettes, and food prepared with no salt.

They eat before Elegua, apart from the orishas, at every Ocha ceremony and fiesta. "First, we need to abide by them and ask for their permission for everything we're going to do." Two days before a fiesta, a scrupulous *babalocha* will prepare food for the Ikús and leave it in the usual place so they eat the spirit of the food calmly. It is understood: "The *muertos* don't chew with their teeth, madam." The next morning, four pieces of coconut are cast, and the positions in which they fall on the ground are interpreted to determine where they want the remains of the offering to be deposited—in either the cemetery or the forest. Then they are content and grateful.

If the soul of a neglected friend or family member—or, doubly undesirable, the intrusive soul of a complete stranger to the family—"causes headaches" by being troublesome or harmful, then they are forced to leave by a ritual presided over by Oya. In the case of an unknown soul, one might also resort to fire, as some spiritists do in Santiago de Cuba. They take a bundle of *escoba amarga* grass, tie a burlap string around an end that has been soaked in alcohol, and light it. Reciting one of the many Prayers that are useful in these types of situations, the flames are rubbed over the walls of the room where the *muerto* has installed itself, "the same way you kill bedbugs and ticks." In this way, by swirling whirlwinds in the air, "lighting the spirit on fire," they are easily removed. That is how, in one bunkhouse where this violent cleansing ritual was performed, the *muerto* fled to the open patio on the way to the street, knocking down a neighbor who was in the way. The force of the impact made the neighbor have a severe nervous breakdown.

The following procedure is ill advised. If there is a capricious *muerto* in a house, Oya demands that a bonfire be made on the patio, because fire scares away and wards off *muertos* . . . "But we don't burn them! On the contrary, we plead with them." The residents of the home and the *iyalochas* directing the ceremony sing and dance as they circle around the bonfire. Meanwhile, plenty

53   DF-N: The original quotation suggests that the unnamed "elderly acquaintance" and Cabrera both regard spiritist masses (séances), their vocabulary (*el espacio*), and their popularity with a mild, sarcastic disdain: "Los míos no han entrado en la moda de que les den luz en el espacio."

of water is poured out the door to the street, and the bonfire is put out by pouring plenty of water on it.

On November 2, the Day of the Dead, all of the Souls in Purgatory—"all the *ikus*"—are offered a plate of *maíz finado* and a glass of water. Cotton wicks are placed on a ceramic plate or in a tin can full of cooking oil, and they are lit for nine days. The tail ends of candles used in funerals are kept or acquired so they can be used on this day. Whoever is too poor to buy oil or nine candles will settle for a single candle, on which they mark nine segments, burning one each night.

Regarding *maíz finado*: On the night of November 2, it was a tradition in every Cuban home to eat it with the obligatory dessert called "huesos de Santo" [Saint's bones], a dessert consisting of marzipan rolls filled with egg yolk. The *maíz finado* is prepared in the following manner: First, the kernels are put in a basin with water and ashes, then they are left to soak overnight. In the morning, the water is sometimes changed out. Then the corn is boiled. Once it is cooked, the small peel of the corn is separated from the kernel. Any vestiges of the ashes are carefully removed. An onion sauté is prepared and mixed with the corn in a saucepan, then cooked until the butter is reduced and the kernels become very soft and dry. These days, *maíz finado* is only eaten in the homes of *santeras* or *gentes del pueblo* [working-class people]. In *Santo* houses, it is offered to Yemaya, by itself or mixed with black-eyed peas.

The interesting thing is that the majority of the spirits that manifest themselves through many mediums of color, as well as so many white people who are supposed to be mediums, are the spirits of *negros de nación*, of African slaves—*congos reales* or *angungas*, all of whom were "disembodied" in the days of the slave trade and speak in Bozal. They are named Taita José, Ña Francisca, Ta Loenzo Lucumí, Juan Mandinga, or El Mina, El Ganga, El Makua.

These beings are very advanced in their spiritual evolution, and very elevated and luminous in *el espacio*. They, too, cure with plants and trees, and—aside from glasses of water, "vasos de asistencia"—they make the same prescriptions as a *babalocha* or *mayombero*. Their repertoire of "cleansings," baths, *ebos*, and remedies is exactly the same, and they, too, prepare talismans and amulets.

Sung Catholic masses for the deceased are especially valued by Black elders, at least in Havana, even if they are not practicing Catholics. According to Catalino, "It's what venerable *muertos* like best."

"African-born people—*de nación*—would spend a lot of money on Gregorian masses for the dead, which cost six cents." The *muertos*, as we have seen, sometimes demand them, and some have even resorted to tricks in order to obtain them. Let us see how one mischievous, deceased spirit managed to get thirty Gregorian masses dedicated to him. The origin of this story might not inspire much confidence. I once heard the person who told me the story narrate other tales at one of the gatherings with Omi Tomi and Oddedei. He had been a cook for the holder of an old title of nobility in Havana, but he had lost that lucrative job for rushing the preparation of a chicken pie. When his boss—a marquis who was hosting dinner guests at his table that evening—broke open the pie, the chicken emerged alive, cheeping, flapping its wings, knocking over the glasses of water and wine, and scaring the ladies in attendance "who couldn't decide whether or not they should faint from their shock." Two of the old ladies, who were regulars at these get-togethers hosted by Calazán, became indignant. "That's a lie!" "A *lie?* Take that word back . . . I have never in my life told a lie!" And in that vein, the argument became quite bitter. I had to contain my laughter, gesturing to the old ladies so they would shut up. At least, I pretended to have no doubts regarding his verac- ity. Well, this is what the old man told me, and—if you consider once again the auto-suggestion of *negros*—it might have been true. *Si non é vero e ben trovato.*[54] One of her *comadres* [close friends, associates] might have lived in a *solar* named Los Aparecidos,[55] because, as soon as night fell there, you could see lots of ghosts and hear a lot of strange noises. That *comadre* was "fond of talking with the *muertos.*" One night, she had a pressing need to go to the back of the patio. On the way back to her room, she heard a voice say, "Let's see if you're going to give me something." The Black woman replied, "Well, sir. Yes, I'll give you something if you promise to give me something too." "Thirty Gregorian masses, because I've been condemned." "Fine. Give and get." "Then look over there, under that loose tile, and you'll find what was promised."

The Black woman lifted the loose tile next to her foot and found a *real* and a half and a little bit of ashes. Given such roguish conduct, she did not feel obligated to repay him with the Gregorian masses. Over the next few months, however, she suffered being persecuted by that clever, condemned soul. As soon as she went out to the patio or found herself alone, then in dreams and—finally—at all hours, she heard the nasal voice of the *muerto* demanding, "What about my masses? My masses!" And in exchange for that coin, the Black woman worked for months and months to pay for the last of those Gregorian masses that crooked *muerto* incessantly demanded. Her friend specifies, "I helped her by giving her a *doblón* [doubloon] coin. And everyone from the cabildo helped her as much as they could."

The reader—having been warned about the source of the story—is free, as always, to believe whatever they like. For my part, I am inclined to accept

---

54   DF-N: This is an Italian aphorism attributed to Bruno Giordano: "True or not, it's a good story."
55   DF-N: Literally, The Apparitions (or The Ghosts).

it as true, because I have witnessed other incidents that would seem just as far-fetched, if not more so.

José D. was a very bright man (although alcohol sometimes dimmed his mind), but he did not believe in apparitions. When a certain *iyalocha* died, he went to her wake at the Cabildo Santa Bárbara because she was his wife's Godmother—*iyabuona* or *oyubona*.

When an *iyalocha* or *babalocha* dies, her colleagues gather next to the coffin to sing to the sixteen orishas and the orisha of the departed, "to bid the *Santo* farewell" approximately one hour before taking them away for burial. At the end, they sing for Oya, the owner of the cemetery, then to their principal *Santo*, their Parent, the "Angel" of the dead *santero*. It is the most solemn hour, when attacks of hysteria tended to happen, during which the tone of the last few songs rise as the person consecrated to Ocha has their "feet removed from the cabildo." That is the name of this ceremony: "removing the feet of the deceased" [*sacar los pies del muerto*].

The *iyalocha* at the head of the coffin passed out and collapsed in the arms of another *iyalocha* at the end of the last song. The *santeros* directing the ceremony sprinkled fresh water along the way to "refresh the arrival at la casa Santa." They shouted—"make way!"—so the attendees would leave an open path to the door, careful to avoid the spirits and not stand in their way. At that moment, José saw the *muerta* sitting on top of the coffin. When they loaded the coffin on the hearse, José saw her again, this time standing in the middle of the wide-open door of the Cabildo. Her head was wrapped in a purple scarf, and she laughed with satisfaction.

The apparition resulted in a very fortunate consequence. As mentioned, José liked to drink, and every time he bent his elbow more than he should, his wife would end up black and blue with bruises. After the *iyalocha*'s funeral, his wife simply needed to threaten him—with a dramatic gesture, and falling to her knees—by invoking the soul of her godmother: José became as soft as silk. He was terrified of that dead *santera* whom he saw—with his own eyes and perfectly sober—attend her own burial.

Another acquaintance of mine, Juan A., abandoned the army after a nocturnal tour of the province. In Sagua La Grande, he saw so many Eshus and apparitions, *Iwis* (or *makundus*, as they are called in Santa Clara),[56] along those dark roads, that he did not feel brave enough to obey an order that would obligate him to repeat such a terrible experience.

In short, it is understood that a *Santo* or a spirit, via its medium, can cure what even the most sagacious "mundele" or "oyibo" doctors cannot. The

---

56 DF-N: An *iwi*, also known in Yoruba as *iwin*, is translated by Samuel Crowther ([1854] 1913, 144) as "ghost, spirit."

doctors cannot see what is hidden behind false appearances. ("The people of this world are *burundanga*; with Mayombe, everything is known.") The doctors cannot offer remedies with their dead medicines, as my old herbalist friend refers to them. Meanwhile, the Lucumí *santero* might be completely ignorant! But he can perform divination and make the Gods dispel illness. And the Padre Nganga has an astonishing ability to counter spells produced by an *ndiambo*.

My old instructor Calazán always referred to doctors, with arrogant disdain, as "the gentlemen of the Protomierdicato."[57]

"Wherever you see a little bit of grass, that's where you can find a remedy."

For the health of his body and soul, every Black person will resort to *el monte*. "It's an instinct," says Catalino. "We're herbalists. We're pulled to *el monte*!"[58]

But the reader should not think that this word *Monte*, or bush—here, we never say "forest"—is only used to designate an expanse of uncultivated land populated by trees. In Havana, any empty field covered in plants is considered a "monte"—or even a savanna! (Just as an aguacate [avocado] or laurel tree is called a plant!) An uncultivated parcel of land in a *solar* of the most meager proportions is categorized as a *manigua* (wilderness, bush) by virtue of wild plants sprouting in it, and it will be referred to simply as a "monte" or "manigua." Every space where leaves grow dense is suitable for depositing an *ebo*, the usual "offering" in the Regla de Ocha intended for a *Santo* that is "not from the water." (Offerings for those that personify the river or ocean, like Oshun and Yemaya, are generally taken to the bank of the river or the seashore.) That way, Black people living in the capital do not need to walk very far to find a "monte."

The majority of plants that are used constantly—for bathing and cleansing oneself of bad influences, washing the floor of a home, burning as incense, or simple homemade remedies—abound in these miniature *montes*, which are so accessible and no less worthy of respect.

It is precisely the most common plants that have the most prophylactic value; they are the most indispensable for what we might call their daily, preventive magic. They protect us throughout our whole lives, which are constantly threatened by exceedingly subtle dangers. The very common *kimbansa* or *bebeke*—in Lucumí, *dede*—that we call white *pata de gallina* [hen's foot] is one of the most powerful plants for sorcery; whether it is used for good or evil, it is among the most valuable plants that sprout from the earth. Or common

---

57 DF-N: Calazán's neologism, which can be translated as "Protocrapestablishment," provides a clever, light-hearted pivot to a synthesis of many of *El Monte*'s central ideas.

58 DF-N: The original quotation in Spanish: "Es que por instinto"—dice Catalino—"somos yerberos. Tiramos pa el monte!" (Cabrera [1954] 1992, 67).

grass, which is in the same family as *pata de gallina*; likewise, it grows in any field. It has the same tenacity to live, it offers the same virtues, and it can be used in the same ways.

For witchcraft or remedies, even a sterile rock will inexplicably sprout a humble, miraculous, and everlasting plant. Due to the construction of new houses in Havana, these grassy uncultivated fields—"placeres" where our Black people's natural divinities visit or install themselves—are being reduced at an alarming rate. And even patios are being done away with in modern houses: the popular, traditional patios, which are reserves of coolness, crammed with plants and vines, where great trees sometimes grow and fill with birds.

The late Miguel Adyai—"El Lucumí," a Creole who had an admirable command of the Aku language—had all of the plants used in herbalism, all the plants for Ocha (*ewe orisha*) growing in the green, fragrant patio of his *solar*, all of it on a thoroughfare as busy and bustling as Calle San Rafael.

Without a doubt, cement condemns the living surface of the earth to a silent death, and it is the worst enemy of wild African deities. Urbanism, which lacks urbanity or faith, drives the orishas from the essence of Osain, Ogun, and Ochosi, "who need the earth's heat and energy."

Although *babalawos*, *iyalochas*, Padre *ngangas*, and Madres de Palo bring the "bush" into their homes, sometimes in the hectic heart of the city, they also gladly emigrate to the suburbs, where overgrown *solares* and houses with patios are still plentiful, or to nearby towns where they can—happily—still coexist with trees and plants. Places on the other side of the bay like Marianao, Regla, or Guanabacoa are authentic bastions of Havana's Santería.

3

....

OLUWA EWE

The Owner of El Monte

OSAIN. ELEGUA, OWNER AND GUARDIAN OF DOORS AND
ROADS. TIMES OF DAY. THE SUPREME BEING AND ELEGUA.
HIS TRICKERY. HIS IMPORTANCE. PATHS, ROADS, OR
AVATARS OF THE ORISHA. ESHU.

STORIES. HOW TO MAKE AN ELEGUA. THE IMPORTANCE
OF OSAIN. HOW TO MAKE AN OSAIN. THE IMPORTANCE
OF OSAIN IN LUCUMÍ RITUALS. "MAKING OSAIN." OMIERO.
THE PLANTS OF THE ASIENTO.

ॐ

For the adepts of the Regla Lucumí, the diviner who is the
owner of plants and *El Monte* is Osain. (Adyai pronounced it
HOH-sai.) He is associated with the Catholic saints San Antonio Abad and San Silvestre, and with one of the many names
or "roads" of Elegua, Elegbara. For many in Matanzas, he is San
Ramón Non Nato: "Because Osain is an *orisa* that has no father
or mother. He wasn't born; he appeared. He came out of the
earth. Just like plants, he's not anyone's child."

Changó was the first diviner. He owned the wooden diving tray, the *okpo* Ifa, or *fate*, which originally belonged to
Obatala and now belongs to Orumila or Orumbila, the orisha Ifa, the Diviner par excellence. All *santeros* recount that
Changó gave Orula the privilege of diving with *okwele* in exchange for the grace that characterized Orula's dancing which,

despite the fact he was an old man, aroused admiration in people, and which Changó, despite being young and very handsome, could not inspire with his own dancing.[1]

"All of the *Santos* are herbalists," but Osain is the undisputed Owner of plants, the doctor, and the botanist.

"Osain Agueniye came from the Yesa land, and he is the protector, the benefactor of the whole world." "Osain belongs to all the Lucumí: from Oyo, he went to the Arará when they received Ifa." "He's Yebu." "He is Egwado." This powerful *Santo*—a Lucumí Asclepius—only has one foot (the right one), one arm (the left), and one eye. He has one ear that is disproportionately large and cannot hear anything at all. In contrast, his other ear is very small, but it is so sensitive that it hears even the softest and most distant sounds. He hears an ant walking or the beating wings of a distant butterfly. Osain walks by hopping or hobbling, like Awo Honu Agroniga or Sodyi—the Lucumí Babalu Ayé, San Lázaro, the great *santo* of the Arará.

"This Osain Okini Gwawo Eleyo was bad: he was very angry, too hot-tempered. He fought over a woman with his brother Osain Alabio. He secluded himself deep in *el monte* for fourteen days to perform witchcraft and defeat his brother with sorcery. There, as he dedicated himself solely and completely to his own hatred and prepared his *morora* (*bilongo*), he encountered his brother's Elegua (sentinel), a *jubo* [small boa constrictor] that whistles and secretes a liquid from its tail. He fought him, and that's how he lost one of his eyes."[2]

He became even more furious after this misfortune, continuing his invocations, praying, and summoning terrible maleficent forces against his rival. He paused the magical endeavors in which he was immersed. He needed to go down to the bottom of a well, to find a hidden secret that he wanted to mix into his witchcraft.

---

1   DF-N: The disorienting variety of references in the opening passage of this chapter synthesizes Cabrera's approach to densely encoded layers of language, history, and theology in Afro-Cuban tradition. For example, Cabrera refers to "Orumila or Orumbila," then, as any devotee might, switches to "Orula" without necessarily pausing to explain that they are different epithets or iterations of a multifaceted mythological figure.

2   DF-N: In this series of stories and descriptions of the orisha Osain, which reads like an Afro-Cuban Rashomon, each narrator and narrative is distinct from the others, and the narrators sometimes expressly dispute each other. By explicitly acknowledging multiple narrators, here and throughout *El Monte*, Cabrera draws readers' attention to the constructed nature of dialogue and rhetoric, articulating what amounts to a collective, multivocal philosophical principle she considered intrinsic and essential to Afro-Cuban tradition. She spells out this principle in the preface ("My method was imposed by the explanations and digressions—each one inseparable from the rest—of my informants.... In their details, one can discern constant disagreements among 'authorities'").

He climbed on an old parapet above the well, which crumbled and fell down. In the fall, he lost an arm and a leg. Broken and bleeding at the bottom of the well, he grabbed a rat with his one hand. The rat shrieked, and it was heard by an owl, which shouted, "Aleyo! Aleyo kini ba wo!" Osain gave the owl the rat to eat in exchange for three feathers from the owl's left wing. Then he waited until daybreak and called the Vulture, asking for another three feathers from its right wing. The Vulture asked, "What for?" "For a *matari*, for *nki-simalongo*, to prepare a stone that will walk around *el monte* with a *muerto* inside. And Vulture gave him three feathers from his right wing. Thanks to these feathers, Osain flew and defeated his brother."

This account from a *palero* will be refuted categorically by any *obalofumi* who is well informed about his own religion. There is only one Osain. Osain has no siblings. Osain Okini Gwagwo Eleyo is not the name of an orisha, nor is it Lucumí. It is an invention. Osain does not have an Elegua; on the contrary, Elegua depends on Osain. That is why all of Elegua's children are protected by Osain; they are "osainistas." Moreover, according to Domingo Hernández, a conscientious *osainista*: "How can Osain fight against a brother he doesn't have? What's more, over a woman? Osain has no wife and never has any desire for women. He is a pure *santo*, so much so that daughters of Osain should not marry. And when they receive Osain, they are no longer women, because Osain wants them to be pure like him."

Osain is a hunter, like the god Ochosi. "With only one hand, he can handle a bow, arrow, and rifle, and he runs swiftly with only one leg." And another *palero*—whose authority on Lucumí topics is dubious—insists that Osain lost his missing body parts as punishment for shooting the Deer, "who bore the mark of the *santísimo* [almighty] Olofi on his forehead." Perhaps it was Changó, in one of his fits of rage, who left him so badly damaged:

Changó broke him apart in a fight by throwing rocks at him. With one rock, he took off his arm. With another, his leg. Then he blew out his eye. Changó and Oya had plotted to steal Osain's *ewe*. Oya went to ask for a few leaves, giving him a *jícara* full of liquor and a cigar—with the intention of stealing his gourd.

Half drunk, Osain fell in love with Oya and tried to woo her. That's when they started arguing and fighting. Changó came to Oya's defense. Ogun heard the ruckus and jumped in to fight for Osain. Changó launched a lightning bolt at Osain and took off one of his arms. Osain fled to hide in his hut, and another lightning bolt hit him in the leg just as he was pulling it inside the hut. He stuck his face out to look, and—bam!—Changó blinded him in one eye. Ogun protected himself from Changó's thunder stones by turning himself into an iron lightning rod, and the stone broke into pieces.[3] But Osain stayed broken.

Another of my *Osainistas* objects to this story too.

"Osain is not a womanizer, and he's always been a dear friend of Changó," to whom he voluntarily gave the gift of his magic.

This is what happened: Osain was waging war against Orula. He was doing *ika* against him, even though Orunla never did anything against Osain. Tired of so much disruption, and without knowing who his enemy might be, Orula consulted with Changó, who told him to do a *trabajo* [work, assignment] with twelve lit cotton wicks and twelve thunder stones. "And that is how you will discover your enemy," Changó told him. While Orumila was home making this *ebo*,[4] Osain was in *el monte* searching for *ewe* to harm him. As soon as Orumila began his invocations and lit the twelve wicks, a lightning bolt fell far off in *el monte*. Osain was trapped between two fires. That's how he lost the limbs and the eye he's missing.

A little later, Orula passed a straw hut and heard moaning inside. He was eager to help whoever was complaining inside the hut, and he saw that it was Osain who was burned, and that is how Orula finally discovered his enemy's identity.

An *osainista* tells us that Ifa is senior to Osain, but "Orula had to bow down to Osain. He needed an *ewe* and sent his children to *el monte* to ask Osain for it, but Osain killed all of Orula's children, and Orula had to bow his head down in the face of Osain's power."

Everyone who has seen Osain agrees that he is one-legged, one-armed, and one-eyed. "Elekan, odete, ofotan . . ."

"He has a twisted mouth and a head as big as a watermelon. His voice is nasal and he hops on his one foot."

Osain tends to appear to night owls after midnight, asking them for *ina* [fire] to light his pipe. A *mayordomo nganga* from a temple—an extended "branch" of the Regla Santo Cristo del Buen Viaje, which was founded in the nineteenth century by the *mulato* Andrés Petit, whom we will discuss below—is not a fainthearted man, but he never goes out alone late at night. This intrepid young apprentice is accustomed to jumping over cemetery

---

3   DF-N: "Thunder stones" (*oduara, edun ara, matari*, etc.) are often indigenous artifacts repurposed and reinterpreted as divine meteors from the sky and/or outer space, and/or stones created by the impact of lightning bolts striking the earth. See also chapters 5 and 9.

4   DF-N: *Hacer ebo* means to make, do, or perform a ritual offering/sacrifice.

tombstones in the dark. But, on one occasion, Osain appeared to him as he crossed a "placer" [an open field], then asked him for a flame to light his pipe, making him run away in terror until he collapsed. "The sight of him was horrifying." Every Black person fears encountering this character at night—"okani," "eleseka" [one-legged]; and "odyu oka" [one-eyed],[5] or Ogun, who also enjoys frightening people in the night. Not to mention Elegua, Eshu. His unearthly, piercing whistling scares Black people so much that they never dare to whistle alone out of fear that Elegua might respond.

Elders never forget to recommend that we avoid whistling at night or whistling too much, because "Elegua is the owner of whistles and whistling," and to whistle is to provoke him.

What happened to Clementina will serve as an example. Clementina is one of several wives of Bangoché—José de Calazán Herrera, one of my most competent informants.

In the early days of her marriage to Calazán, Clementina had the dangerous habit of "whistling like a mockingbird," or like a cigar factory worker.

"Listen! Don't get used to whistling. It's bad, and you're going to end up having a scare!" But Clementina was not paying attention, or perhaps she simply forgot the advice from her husband, "who knew the *Santos* very well." Indeed, one night when she was whistling her favorite *danzón* at full volume,[6] Elegua rewarded her with three whistles right next to her ear that were so loud they made her lose consciousness. At that late hour, they rushed to "*korobo* Elegua," gathering everything they needed to "make an offering" to appease the *Santo*, which—Calazán assures me—"wanted to take Clementina." Obviously, after an experience like that, Clementina did not whistle again for the rest of her life.

It is Elegua—Afra and Maken,[7] as he is called in the Arará cabildos, where he is not offered *han*, liquor—who whistles at street corners, in deserted spots, or inside empty houses. "And Osain whistles too." Of course, the night is the

---

5   DF-N: These two symbolic terms are more commonly rendered as *elesekan* and *oju okan* or *oyukan*, respectively.

6   DF-N: On *danzón*, see Madrid and Moore (2013).

7   DF-N: According to Galvin and Spiro (2020, 23, 102),

Afrá is the Fodu [*fodun, vodu*, etc.] of the crossroads and the first (and last) Fodu sung to during a ceremony. Afrá opens the path to all the other Foduces [plural of Fodu]. He is equated with Eleggua in Lukumí and his name from both traditions appears in the Arará Savalú cantos, demonstrating the strong syncretization of the two West African faiths as they are practiced in Cuba....

Auñoro and Makenu are the female and male avatars of the Oricha Obbatalá from Lukumí, representing age, wisdom, and calm. Arará Savalú makes a clear distinction between the female and male roads of this Fodu, or the Lukumí roads Oshanla and Ochagriña.

domain of all kinds of spirits, but there are also times of day that should be kept in mind: namely, twelve noon, when spirits roam around for a while. Elegua abandons his watch in doorways, and—even though he returns right away—houses are left unguarded at noon, as well as at six o'clock in the evening. Thanks to the fear inspired by high noon, Elegua saved Obatala, helping him escape during a difficult episode during which he lived surrounded by enemies:

> Since God made the world, noon is a bad hour. A long time ago, Elegua told all the people in town who were plotting the downfall of Obatala that they needed to close their doors at twelve noon on the dot, because a Bad Thing was going to pass, and no one should be out in the street. Taking advantage of that hour when everyone had gone home, Elegua covered Obatala with a white mosquito net and took him outside while ringing a bell—the *agogo*, with which we now call Obatala at the *ile* of the orisha. That is the hour . . . that's when the Santísimo passes by. It is a time full of mystery. May Echuni save us, like he saved Obatala!

Some lift their legs up off the ground at twelve noon—including many in the city of Bayamo, which is so infused by Spiritism—in order to "not pick up any bad influences that are sweeping along the earth, because the spirits scatter at that moment." There, in Bayamo, I overheard two young women in the street saying to each other, "Careful, we don't want noon to catch us by surprise." By midnight—the worst of all the times of day—Egun and Eshus already roam freely. "Elegua, Ogun, and Ochosi go out to take care of their business." These are the hours to deposit *ebos*, to launch witchcraft, to pick up bad influences, to stumble upon Ero and Poelí. "The spirits dance . . ."

In short, if we search—as Niní always does—for a mythical precedent for the origin and explanation behind many of our beliefs and customs, the following story will give us good reason to regard the street as a dangerous place and consider it wise to remain at home, behind closed doors, at certain times of day:

> When Obatala ruled, Ikú (Death), Ano (Illness), Ofó (Dishonor), and Eyé or Arafé (Iñá) (Crime and Tragedy) became very hungry.[8] Because

---

8   DF-N: This anonymous quotation enumerates various types of misfortune, identifies them parenthetically, and capitalizes them as proper names for characters in a mythological narrative. Within the quotation, I have retained Cabrera's original spelling and orthography for the proper names, all of which have common alternative versions or analogs. For example: *eyé* or *arafé* (crime, tragedy, etc.) is more commonly *arayé* or *eyó*; *ano* (illness) is also commonly *arun* or *aro*; and so on. As in the story, ritual recitations group the terms as a formulaic element that is contex-

nobody was dying, nobody was getting sick, nobody fought, and nobody dishonored themselves. All this happiness was good for some and bad for others. In order to survive, Ikú, Ano, Ofó, Iñá, and Eyé decided to attack Obatala's subjects. Obatala told his people that no one should go out in the street or stick their heads out their windows to look outside. And in order to calm Ikú, Ano, Ofó, Iñá, and Eyé, Obatala told them to wait, to have a little patience. But the hunger they were suffering was unbearable, so Ikú, Ano, Ofó, Iñá, and Eyé went out at twelve noon with sticks and tin cans in their hands, and they made a huge racket. Curious people carelessly stuck their heads out of their windows. Ikú cut off a large number of heads. At midnight, another deafening commotion could be heard out in the street. Some reckless people went outside, while others went running to their windows to see what was happening, and Ikú collected another robust harvest of heads. Since then, Ikú, Ano, Ofó, and Arayé have the habit of wandering the streets at noon and midnight, and that's why wise people go home.

Any observant person who spends time in Havana's poor neighborhoods will confirm that many neighbors toss water into the street to refresh evil spirits that wander around, threatening human beings' tranquility.

---

tualized negatively (*ko si*...) as misfortunes one wishes to avoid. Let us consider the following set of closely related, complementary definitions from Cabrera's *Anagó* (translations are my own, with Cabrera's original Spanish in parentheses):

Ofó: to destroy, annihilate evil (*destruir, aniquilar lo malo*)

Ofo: arrow (*flecha*)

Ofó: dirty (*sucio*)

Ofó: grief, mourning (*luto, duelo*)

Ofó: shame, disgrace due to unfortunate or tragic circumstances (*bochorno, verhuenza producida por una causa lamentable o trágica*)

Ofo achó: mourning clothes (*traje de luto*)

Ofoché: powders for curses, evil spells (*polvos para maleficiar*)

Ofódá: evil, malice (*mal, maldad*)

Ofodá: something useless, bad (*que no sirve, malo*)

Ofodá: disgrace, tragedy (*desgracia*)

Ofofó: a gossip (*chismoso*)

Ofón: throat (*garganta*)

Ofónfón: a liar, who talks a lot and does not tell the truth (*mentiroso, que habla mucho y no dice la verdad*)

(Cabrera [1957] 1986, 237–38)

OLUWA EWE

75

I do not know a single old Black man or woman who does not place a receptacle full of water behind their door before they go to bed—*omi, lango* for the Souls in Purgatory and Las Nueve de Lima, for Antonia Gervasio—*la incestuosa* [the incestuous one]—the Anima Sola, Eshu Alona or Alagwana. Spirits, whether good or bad, should not be left wanting for this liquid—but especially not the bad ones, should they enter the house thirsty. "Everyone should drop a little water on the ground when they wake up in the morning. And at night, to sleep peacefully, put a glass of water with cocoa butter next to your bed." "The *muertos* are often thirsty, and some of them are so tormented and dangerous that it's wise to quench their thirst." We often come upon a man or woman who, upon reaching a street corner, will spill water they are carrying in a tin can or a *jícara*—discreetly, if they spot white strangers. This gift of coolness is for Elegua, Laroye.

Eshu, a very dangerous orisha who runs up and down the street and stations himself—with Ogun and Ochosi—on corners, "where they work the most."

"There's a lot of coming and going of *malongo, diambos*, and *fuiris* at *pambuan sila*" (Santos, muertos, and spirits on street corners). "Kilungo goes out to stretch his legs." A little bit of food is also left there for them. It is customary to place a little bit of all the foods that have been eaten that day in a *jícara* or small pot, then take it to the Elegua at the street corner. Sharing with Eshu and "feeding the Spirits" ensures that sustenance will never be lacking at home. This ritual—an act of everyday devotion, *ebochire*—is performed regularly. The woman who explained its meaning for the first time was an *iyalocha* who, like almost all of them, never lets a single day go by without doing it. They separate a bit of each food on a plate, and when they are finished eating, they pour a little of the water that has been drunk. Before getting up, the table is struck three times, then the plate is taken to the patio or an overgrown lot nearby, and at the base of any tree, it is offered to Eshu. "Here is your food, Eshu." Very often, a domestic or stray animal will suffice for the offering, but that is not so important. Eshu allows it because the animals (there was a dog and a cat at that *iyalocha*'s house) are his messengers. Guard dogs and stray dogs "whose tongues have been blessed by Baba" are friends of Elegua, a divinity who also likes to move around in the street and "lets them eat his food." To avoid fights arising at *Santo* fiestas, food for Eshu is taken to the bush to avoid him coming to look for it and instigating conflict. And a dog that appears at the door on these occasions is given food. "He's a friend of Elegua, and you avoid tragedy that way." Moreover, that stray dog intruder might be Eshu Lele, who one must watch out for, especially at a party. A piece of meat or a bone are left for him. He is encouraged by saying, "Here you are, father. Now go." And then he is shooed away. Elegua—like San Lázaro—tends to assume the appearance of a beggar and—like Osain—disabled. That is how he punishes a disobedient daughter in one story after making her his fiancée. She was a pretty young woman who maintained relations with a man that was not good for her. In the end, she gave in to her father's reasoning and ended her relationship with the man. But as soon as another handsome man went by her window, the young woman gave herself to this new lover, who her father also disliked. This time, it was Elegua who had seduced her. He disappeared a few days after formalizing the relationship, then returned in the form of a broken, lame beggar with one arm. He claimed that she belonged to him, body and soul, and the young woman had no choice but to share the rest of her life with the mutilated, wandering villain.

It is essential to keep Elegua happy. He lies in wait on every street, determining the course of our lives at every turn and playing games with them according to his own whims. "He opens and closes the roads and doors," both in heaven and on earth, to gods and mortals, and he impulsively opens and closes them to luck or ruin. Although he is small—a "kereke," a little kid—we should definitely consider Elegua to be the most fearsome of the orishas. "He holds the key to destiny."

He is the spy and messenger of the gods. "Because of his temperament, which is that of a rebellious child," he is always willing to make mischief. As Eshu, he is also malevolent by nature—that is why some cannot be kept inside the home. He is the first orisha whose favor needs to be gained.

Luckily, since he is gluttonous, he can be bribed easily. In this, he is like the Ibeyes—the divine twins, San Cosme and San Damián, favorites of Obatala and Changó—who are also given whatever they fancy.

Elegua is everywhere, lying in wait and watching. "My father's Elegua," Calazán tells me, "had a lot of money to pay for kites that were supposed to be flown for him." That is, they would be flown in his honor, for the orisha's pleasure, because he is the owner of *papalotes*—as kites are known in Cuba. "And I would steal it. Elegua told the old man. One day the old man was going to kill a rooster for Elegua and he asked me, 'Why do you take the *owo* from Elegbara? Yeah, he told me himself that you are *ole*'"—stealing—"'and he's going to catch you flying his *papalote*. Go to the hen house and bring me *akukuo*'—a rooster. I went and brought him the rooster. 'Kneel down there.' And I knelt down in front of Elegua. He whacked me three times. And Elegua prohibited me from flying *papalotes*. He himself, who is the *papalote*, was going to throw me off the roof. That was the last time I stole money."

"Elegua guards the crossroads. He is the caretaker of *el monte* and the savanna." "He is at the entrance and the exit." The drum proclaims this clearly:

Alalubanche.[9] "With Orula, Baba, and Oya, he rules the Four Winds, and he can get in the middle of anything, make a mess, and turn things upside down. The power to destroy or save anyone is in his hands." Elegua can contradict the plans of both gods—even Olorun!—and humans. He can save Olofi with a single leaf. We should remember that he is the orisha who receives the first offering, who "eats" on the day of sacrifices, the first to be greeted—as we mentioned, after the Ikús (ancestors)—and the first to be honored in every Lucumí ceremony, in order to avoid the difficulties provoked by his displeasure. Olofi himself decreed it. "He told him, 'You are the smallest, and you are my messenger. You will be the biggest on earth and in heaven, and it will be impossible to do anything without reckoning with you.'"

This Olofi, Olorun—Babade—is the Supreme Being. One *Santera* from Matanzas defines him literally: "The one who is greater than God." And another informant, a beggar named Ciriaco, says, "He's the one who rules everything, the biggest that exists. But he's very far away. He's so far away that he doesn't understand anything, and he's so big that humanity doesn't understand anything he says. He left us on earth."

Olofi, Oba-Olorun, Olodumare (or Olodumadye), Alanu, Olonu of the Lucumí. Sambi, the Congo's "Tubisia Nsambi bisa munansulo," "the great God who lives in heaven, that is senior to Sambia mpungo bisa munantao, the other Sambia that is on earth." These are equivalent concepts of a Supreme Being in both Reglas: infinite, inconceivable, and oblivious to what happens on earth, despite it being his creation. He is "the one who nobody thinks about." ("Our heads can't cope with it. Olorun is very big"—like Sambi—"and can't fit in anyone's head.")

I have copied down these definitions of "the oldest God"—the "arubo," the "Taita God from above"—from the lips of the elders, including a centenarian on a sugar plantation in the province of Matanzas. "He is the absolute first, and he doesn't involve himself in anything." "He watches everything, but he's indifferent. He's only a presence." "He doesn't work. He's isolated. He doesn't come down to earth." "He couldn't care less about any of it." "God is the greatest, the vastness, the immensity. But we can't reach that one." The elderly woman at the Santa Rosa sugar mill says, "Ese Olóru, ese Dúddua viejo, Papa Dió del Cielo, no pasa a orí de gente. El dice tu me saluda y deja quieto yá; tu pide bendició, sigue tu camino, yo tá pá riba, riba cielo, tu ta bajo, tu son bruto, bwóbwó!" (That Oloru, that old Oduduwa, Father God of the Sky, doesn't go

---

9   DF-N: Alalubanche (Lubanche, Alubanche, Alalubanşe, etc.) refers to a *bata* drum salute rhythm (*toque*) that performs musical speech surrogacy, effectively drumming the text of the phrase. See Marcuzzi (2005); Mason (1992); Oyelami (1991); Schweitzer (2013); and Villepastour (2010).

in anybody's head. He says, "Salute me, then leave me alone already. Ask for my blessing and be on your way. I'm up very, very high in the sky. You're down there, and you're dumb brutes, all of you!")

"The greatest and oldest *Santo* doesn't deal directly with anyone." He is like Sambia, who made the sky with the sun and stars and the earth with the trees and everything that lives on her, and sent humans there, naked and hungry. "Olofi made everything. Everything is Olofi. He made the world, the *Santos*, people, the animals. Then he said, 'Now you work it out.' And he left. Olofi retired. He delegated his duties to his son Obatala, his heir, the acting Olofi." "He watches and Obatala acts." "Oloro Owa. He says, '*Emiri* . . . I just watch and nothing more. *Dubule* . . .,'" (he sleeps).

This Being is detached from his creation. We do not think about him "because we can't comprehend him," and he demands very little from us. Odd-edei explains, "He doesn't ask for anything," only respect. Like Sambia or Nsambi, "he is always named" but does not receive tribute, and "he doesn't eat or dance." Indeed, he does not intervene at all in our affairs, though he appears in the mythology maintained by the descendents of the Yoruba with all of the characteristics of a flesh-and-blood patriarch. The *taita*, "head of the orishas," is the old man who works his own fields, "his plot of land," holding the plow, the hoe, and the machete in his hands, and whose numerous offspring sometimes upset him most bitterly.

Olofi and his family, like Zeus and his own family, are omnipotent and immortal. (This Lucumí pantheon is curiously reminiscent of the Greek one.) But this family is not very different from Calazán, Calixta, Catalino, Baró, or any of these good friends who tell me their stories.

Olofi gave Elegua the privilege of eating before any other gods, even Obatala, as well as the right to refuse his consent if he is not acknowledged, regardless of whether it is the most important or most banal deed. As we have mentioned, this is because Elegua cured Olofi—the Eternal Father—once upon a time. "He saved God's life." Olofi was suffering from a mysterious malady, which became worse every day and prevented him from working his fields. All of the *Santos* had tried to at least alleviate his pain, but their medicines had no effect. The Father of the Orishas, the Creator, was so weak and wracked with pain that he could no longer stand up.

Elegua was a child. Many clairvoyants can see him sitting at the foot of their beds: small, with the face of an old child, a straw hat, smoking a cigar. And, as we know, he remains most unruly and problematic in many of his manifestations. For example, Eshu Beleke, the Niño de Atocha or Ibori— cannot be kept inside homes with children because he becomes jealous and kills them. He was so mischievous that, during the nineteenth century, they did not give him a place inside the Cabildo. Nor did they allow Mako—a thief, known in Santa Clara as Arere Obi Oke, the one who holds an adult Elegua in his arms, San Antonio de Padua—to live inside. Despite his youth, he asked his mother to take him to the house of Olofi, assuring her that he could cure the old man. At the time, Elegua's mother Oya—these divine genealogies are sometimes the subject of heated arguments between Black people—was the wife of Ogun, the god of iron, and the lover of Changó. Although the mother was not entirely convinced by the child's claims, she agreed to take him to Olofi. He did not make the child beg. It was a good opportunity to free herself from the child and spend a few hours undisturbed with her lover. (We do not know if this happened the same day Changó abducted Oya on his horse, Eshinla.)

The child picked out a few plants and used them to make an "ogbo" (a decoction). As soon as the old man swallowed the mixture, with a long grimace, he quickly began recovering and regained his strength. Olofi gratefully ordered the senior orishas to cede the first portion of every offering to Elegua. He placed a key in his hands and made him the owner of the roads. Since that day, he not only tolerated Elegua's mischief with limitless pleasure, but he made everyone else accept it, conceding—as Sandoval says—"the right to play tricks whenever he feels like it."

This mischief is suffered by debtors who do not settle their debts or neglect to give Elegua the attention he deserves as the one who is deservedly known by the moniker "Ruin and Repair."[10]

According to another version,

> At the beginning of time, Olofi became ill. In those days, Elegua ate in the trash. He ate the garbage. All the clever ones went to see Olofi. Nobody could cure him. Elegua put on a white cap like the ones worn by *babalawos* and used his herbs to cure Olofi very quickly. The old man said, "I have so many wise children, but none of them were able to do anything to help me! Elegua, ask me for whatever you want, young man." And Elegua—who was no stranger to the misery of poverty—answered, "I want to eat before everyone else . . . And I want to be next to the door so they greet me first." And Olofi said, "It will be so. And I appoint you to be my messenger."

On one occasion, Elegua saved the Creator from an encounter with a rat. The Orishas were insubordinate, and they wanted to dethrone Olofi. Knowing he was terrified of rats, they placed one at the door of his *ile*.

---

10 DF-N: In the original Spanish, "Desbarata y Compone." Alternative translations are "Spoil and Remedy," "Break and Fix," "Destroy and Create," and the like.

Olofi consecrated the rat, "and that's why Elegua eats rat. To get something big, we kill a rat for Elegua." The worst "curses" or "good works" are done by using a rat, but the slightest error committed by the *babalocha* in the course of the ritual will result in their own misfortune.

On another occasion, Elegua discovered that the diviners, the *awos*, "consulting" the oracle for the year,[11] changed the *odu* (the prophetic signs) for Olofi on the divination tray. This established a precedent: *kofibori* Eleda. That is why, to this day, *babalawos* tend to change the "signs" or predictions during *ita*, even if their lies are uncovered later.[12]

In short, "If Elegua is happy, if he's given gifts, and if all the promises made to him are fulfilled, then everything will go well." In that way, he is an inescapable and decisive factor in any situation, influencing—for better or worse—even the smallest matters.

His favor will improve even the worst destiny, but his hostility will cast a shadow over even the brightest. In one instance or another, he avails himself of a thousand tricks to help or harm us. "God wills that you are meant to be stabbed when you go around a street corner. If he wants things to work out well for you, Elegua will find a way for the assassin to be seen by a police officer just as he's raising his arm to bury the knife in your back, or for him to stumble and fall, or back out at the last moment without knowing why."

His role is to be a guardian. "That's why he is indulged so much; so he protects us." For that very reason, the Elegua that guards the home "never lacks food, so he's always comfortable there, and he doesn't abandon the home to go out to find what he needs. Or else he might take revenge by closing the door on good fortune and clearing the way for misfortune." "But it's also not wise to keep him too full, because then he slacks off." Elegua Alayeki is a Rumbero, fond of liquor, and a glutton. He is unscrupulous about satisfying his appetites, even at his best friend's expense.

Once, when he was going around partying with Osu (another messenger of Obatala), he got Osu drunk. When Osu fell asleep, Elegua took advantage of his slumber and stole a goat. He killed the goat and ate it. But the blame for the theft fell on Osu: Elegua had spilled the animal's blood on Osu's mouth, left its bones next to him, and disappeared. When Achelu found Osu with

---

11   DF-N: The original Spanish, *registrando* (translated here as "consulting"), refers broadly to divination, but its literal Spanish meaning implies a search, an inspection, an investigation, an analysis, a record, a mark, and/or "checking in."

12   DF-N: By articulating the idea that a divination "sign" might be consciously and deliberately manipulated by diviners, Cabrera delves into a subtle and contentious discourse about truth and divination.

blood all over his mouth and face,[13] it was easy for them to deduce the thief's identity. Elegua also has a very strong passion for dancing, like all *Santos* and mortals with black skin. He is capable of making all kinds of sacrifices to attend a fiesta. One story recounts that, once upon a time, he found himself more impoverished than usual—"he had no shoes and no money." He asked Obatala, La Virgen de las Mercedes, to let him clean and sweep her *ile* in exchange for a little *owo* (money).[14] For the first few days—"a new broom sweeps well"—he cleaned Obatala's house admirably. Obatala paid him, and Elegua went to a dance. The next day, he was tired from a night of partying, but he had to return to fulfill his obligation with Obatala. And since he went out drinking and dancing every night, he was weary and performed his duties very reluctantly.

As a result, the cleaning of the home of Obatala—who is the essence of cleanliness—left a great deal to be desired. Therefore, Obatala became ill. Afraid of dismissing Elegua, she consulted with Orula, who consulted his *okuele* and told her that the boy who was in her *ile* should leave as soon as possible. Otherwise, she would not recover her health. The whole place was making her sluggish; dust gathered everywhere, and trash piled up where it should never have been in the first place. But Obatala, afraid of antagonizing her very dangerous guest, did not dismiss him immediately. She waited until a new fiesta was being celebrated in *ile-ilu* Ife, then she gave him a substantial amount of *owo*, which—in those days—consisted of cowrie shells, not coins. She told him, "Take this money. You don't owe me anything. Go dance, and come visit me every once in a while." Elegua kept dancing and "acting like a dandy," since he did not need to work. And in her clean home, Obatala, La Inmaculada—*fun fun*—recovered quickly.

Gluttony is one of his most conspicuous traits. In another of the innumerable stories told about an Elegua Laroye—a "Quicio-Puerta,"[15] as the *ganguleros* refer to him—we see him mocking the great orishas, and obstructing their affairs and impoverishing them, when he is displeased or hungry:

The Virgen de la Caridad del Cobre (Oshun), La Virgen de Regla (Yemaya), and Nuestra Señora de la Mercedes (Obatala) lived in the same

---

13   DF-N: *Achelu* is one of numerous Lucumí terms for police, the authorities, and/or the law. The character's name in the story is thus Police, or law enforcement personified.

14   DF-N: Note the female gendering of Obatala.

15   DF-N: The term *Quicio-Puerta* translates literally as "Doorway," "Doorframe," or "Hinge Post"; idiomatically, it refers to a "Guard," "Sentinel," or "Gatekeeper."

"ile" in town, and the three of them divined with cowrie shells. Elegua guarded the door. People went to consult them.[16]

"Good morning, Elegua. Is Iyalode (Oshun) here?"

"Yes. Come in." And he'd open the door.

"Good morning, Elegua. Is Yemaya here?"

"Yes. Go ahead."

"Greetings, Elegua. Is Obanla here?"

"Yes, she is. *Owole*" (Enter).

"*Modu kue*" (Thank you).[17]

Those who came for divination would leave money, birds, chickens, and pigeons every day, and the *santas* ate very well. Then Changó, Ogun, and Ochosi would come over and eat with them.

They gave Elegua the bones. Meanwhile, the others would feast. Elegua said, "No, this can't go on. My teeth are going to break from gnawing on all these bones!"

They didn't send anything to Eshu, nor to the Elegua on the corner . . . not even to the one at the four corners. Elegua couldn't stand the hunger anymore! And his guts grumbled, "Ebinpami, ebinpami, ebinpami!"[18]

One stormy day, a rat ran in the house fleeing from the rain, and he caught it. "At least now I'll have something to eat for a few days . . . Today, the head, tomorrow a leg, the next day the other one . . ." And what needed to happen happened.[19]

"Good morning, Elegua. Elegua, is Regla here?"

"She's not here."

"Good morning, Elegua. Is Caridad here?"

"She doesn't live here anymore."

"Good morning, Elegua. Is La Merced here?"

---

16 DF-N: This long story is an example of Cabrera adopting or transcribing "an informant's voice." By contrast, the next story—arguably a different version of the same story—is told "in Cabrera's voice"—that is, except for a brief, direct quotation (from another unidentified informant at the beginning) and characters' dialogue in the story.

17 DF-N: This term is more commonly written as *modupue, modupe, modukpue*, and the like.

18 DF-N: The term *ebinpami* (or *ebi pa mi*)—in Yoruba, "I am hungry"—is a reasonable analog of the name of a Cuban *bata* drum *toque*, a musical motto associated with the orisha Changó. According to John Mason, "Èwì Pámi (disheartened turtle) is considered an *ègún* (thorn or prickle). In Spanish, it is called *puya* (goad, goad stick). Ṣàngó, to my knowledge, is the only òrìṣà who has rhythmic as well as sung puyas. The puya is meant to stick the òrìṣà, goading them to respond in a certain way. Puyas can be highly insulting and border on the profane. . . . There are more puyas associated with Ṣàngó than with any other òrìṣà" (1992, 29). Numerous instances of *puyas* can be found below.

19 DF-N: The original Spanish is a cascade of past-tense constructions: "Y pasó lo que tenía que pasar."

"She's traveling."

Elegua picked away at his little bit of rat, sustaining himself one way or another and chasing away the clientele. Eventually, nobody knocked on the door anymore. So, nobody went to the *santas* for divination, and the food ran out at the *santeras'* house.[20]

"Elegua, why isn't anyone coming?"

"Yes, it's very strange. Nobody's coming to the door. And look at the miserable state I'm in. Now, I don't even have the damn bones you were giving me to gnaw on!"

"What can we give you? We don't have anything to eat either!"

Changó didn't bring a single centavo with him. (Changó is a bit of a pimp. He doesn't provide for women, unlike Ochosi, who hunts birds for them even if he doesn't give them money.) Changó saw what was happening, heard the lamentations of the three *santas*, and found out that they had been keeping Elegua on a diet. He got mad and said, "It's your own fault you're hungry! For being *osiere omotiwo*" (dumb). And this business with Elegua needs to be fixed. He's the owner of the door!"

Then Oshun said, "I'll go speak with him right away."

She said to him, "Elegua, if you let somebody pass today . . . you'll eat well tonight." Elegua went to the corner.[21] The Elegua at the corner sent them a woman who wanted to be released from her husband.

"Elegua, has Yemaya come back from her trip?"

"She just got back today. Come in."

"Elegua, is Oshun here?"

"Come on in!"

Chickens, pigeons, and . . . a little black rooster arrived. Elegua got a little bit of everything. That day, the house of the *santas* filled up with birds. Elegua found himself owning so many black chickens that the *santas* themselves had to tell him, "That's enough, Elegua! Hold on. Now it's time to fatten ourselves up and rest a little."

In another story, we are told, "In the beginning, before Olofi distanced himself from the world, he gave each orisha a mission. He gave out the jobs, and Elegua—because he's such a tramp—was left without a job to do." After a while, he complained to Changó about his situation. When the jobs were assigned, Changó had been tasked with Ifa. But Changó was very

20 DF-N: In a subtle linguistic and philosophical twist, the house of the *santas* (deities) becomes synonymous with the house of the *santeras* (priests).

21 DF-N: Oshun is portrayed as a practical negotiator who breaks an impasse—that is, a savvy, cut-and-dry dealmaker.

young and too much of a *rumbero*—there were sick people in the world, but no doctor, and Changó did not worry about curing them. On the advice of his mother Yemaya, who was Orula's wife at the time, Changó handed *ifa* (*ache*, *ifa*, and *okuele*) over to Orula:

"Changó, I'm wandering around out here without a steady job. I need to beg to survive!" (Before he saved Olofi, he survived on Trash.) Changó took Elegua to Orula's house and told the old man, "This is going to be your sentinel. He'll always watch the door to your house, and, in exchange, you'll feed him." Orula took Elegua in and put him in charge of guarding the door. But it seems Elegua did not eat as much as he wanted, or perhaps he saw how much money Orula made as a diviner and became jealous, so he said, "I want to talk a little bit and make some money too."

"You have everything you need. What more do you want?"

The next day, they knocked on the door.

"Arareyi, is Orula here?"

Orula was home, but Elegua answered, "He's not here." This situation went on for many days, and Orula—who was accustomed to giving advice, curing people, and handling *owo* (money)—asked his guard, "Arareyi, how is it possible that nobody is coming to see me?"

"They come, but I don't let them pass."

"Let's see here, Elegua. Come here." And he gave him three cowrie shells. "I'll give you three 'letters'"—three cowries—"so you can speak and divine like me.[22] Do you agree?"

"That's good, it's enough."

That is how, shortly after this episode, Yemaya—the *santa* that knows the most about *dilogún* [cowrie shell divination] and *iki*—started using Orula's divination tray to "prophesy" in secret. Then Elegua notified Orula, who caught her learning about his secrets. Orula gave her seven cowrie shells, but he complained to Olofi that his wife wanted to know more than him.[23]

Another version of the *apataki*—or *pataki*, which is to say, an origin story, an ancient history—is repeated constantly by a goddaughter of the famous

---

22   DF-N: Curiously, Cabrera refers to the three "letters" and/or cowries as *Oddi*, although *Odi* is a sign in *dilogún* divination associated with seven cowrie shells falling "mouth up" or "open," while three cowrie shells would most commonly be referred to as *Ogunda* (three cowrie shells falling "mouth up" or "open") or *meta* (the number three).

23   DF-N: While this mythology invokes a straightforward sort of male chauvinism, it also outlines a critique of gender roles vis à vis divinatory knowledge, authority, and secrecy.

iyalocha Belén González.[24] It explains why Elegua "lives in the doorway and eats right there in the doorway." N. says,

Orula has an Elegua. One day, Orula got dressed up: he dressed in white clothes from head to toe, every detail just right, and, swaggering around the way *babalawos* do, he went out. Elegua thought, "I don't have a stove. I don't have *acha* (a cigar). I have no *owo*. I have no *obini* (woman). I have nothing! Orula doesn't give me anything." And he left the house too. He went to the corner. People went by looking for Orula, and Elegua told them, "He moved." When Orula came back, Elegua told him, "Nobody has come!" And time went on without anybody coming . . . Orula was inside his house and Elegua was on the corner, giving everyone fake directions to Orula's house.

San Francisco watched his bread and butter go away, and he called Elegua. "Barayiku! Listen . . . Come here and have some food. I'm going to give you a woman . . . Which one do you want? Do you want Oshun? Oya? Yemaya?"

Elegua answered, "Bring me women to keep me company, but nothing more than that. I have my woman out there in the street."

Elegua had Eson, but he was not serious about her.

Orula said, "Barayiku, I'm going to make a room for you, back there, so you can be comfortable. You can live there and eat well."

"A room at the back of the house? *Kosi!* No, sir . . . Put me right here at the door . . . Just here to one side."

"But you're going to eat all of that? Smoked fish, hutia, *epo, aguado, akuko, oti?* All of that, right here at the door?"

"Yes sir. Right here. And if you don't give me the food, I'll go out and lock the door from the outside!"

That's why Elegua lives in a little cabinet, or a little box, next to doorways . . . And if you don't honor him, he leaves and punishes you.

In another *apataki*, Elegua obtains Ifa, thanks to a scheme that leaves Orula's wife in shock:

---

24 DF-N: The Lucumí term *apataki* (story, narrative) is more commonly rendered as *pataki* or *patakin*. Meanwhile, in this context, Ifa refers simultaneously to (a) the system of divination, (b) its initiatory cult, and (c) the anthropomorphic orisha, while Orula (Orunmila, etc.) refers to the orisha and/or the deified prophet of the Ifa cult. A few lines later, Elegua is quoted as saying, "ya tengo hecho Ifa," which can be translated in a variety of complementary ways ("I now have Ifa," "I have Ifa made," "I have already been initiated into Ifa," etc.).

Elegua had asked Orunla to give him Ifa. But Orunla refused him categorically when Elegua confessed that, at that moment, he had no money to pay him.

Then Elegua jumped up in the air and landed on his own head, injuring himself with a deep wound which bled profusely. When Orula's wife saw Elegua in her house, lying in a pool of blood, she got scared and pleaded with her husband to give Elegua what he wanted.

"Give him Ifa, or else we'll get in trouble with the Law!" And Orula gave him Ifa for free, and Elegua went back to his corner happy.

Later, Olokun's son Inle passed by the corner. Whenever he saw Elegua, Inle was in the habit of saying, "Salute me, Elegua. I'm a doctor. *Ologun.*"

But this time it was Elegua who stepped forward and said, "Salute me, because I've been initiated in Ifa." Olokun's son said, "I don't believe you."

He asked Elegua to divine for him, and Elegua said, "There's a big tree at your house that fills up with birds in the evening . . ."

"Bah! Liar. You already knew that perfectly well without divination."

"Wait," said Elegua. "This morning, your mother yelled at you. She was indignant, because you grabbed her butt, then her husband surprised you."

Surprised, Olokun's son responded, "That's true. That's a secret. You couldn't have seen it, and nobody could've told you about it."

Olokun's son told his mother about the encounter with Elegua. He told her that he had resolved to become a *babalawo.* When Olokun approved her son's decision, he went to ask Elegua how much he would charge to initiate him in Ifa. "Lots of money and lots of goods!"

Olokun's son agreed to give him everything he asked for, and Elegua initiated him to Ifa. Then he paid Orula twice what Orula had asked for to make Elegua's Ifa.

Oshun, who is the owner of gold, went into Orula's room one day. She offered Elegua gold in exchange for five cowrie shells so she could speak too, and Elegua gave them to her.[25]

---

25 DF-N: The set of stories about Elegua's role in the politics and economics of initiation into divination cults outlines some of the ways divination can be a form of subsistence, making it clear that the financial cost of initiation can be significant, analogous to the costs of formal vocational certification.

Oshun—"la santa puta"—and Elegua are very good friends.[26] He protected Oshun and saved her during a very perilous episode in her life, during which she quarreled with her sister Yemaya:

Elegua is the owner of the road, so he has power over journeys. One day, Oshun encountered Changó on the road. They were alone, and he tried to seduce her. He wanted to rape her, and the two *santos* started wrestling. She defended herself; Changó was trying to dominate her. Although she would have wanted him, she did not consent because Alafi is her nephew. When Oshun felt she was losing the struggle, she shouted, "Arayeyi!" Elegua appeared and stood between her and Changó, immediately separating them.

"Get out of here, Changó! Don't take another step forward! I'm the owner of the road! Leave Oshun in peace!" And Changó, despite all his regal sovereignty, was forced to obey Elegua, who didn't let him keep going.

Elegua (Abanuke) is the best ally of Orula—the god Ifa—and, of course, *babalawos*. "He is their security." "Elegua protects the *babala* a lot." No one needs Elegua more than a *babalawo*. "Orula and Elegua are one." (The Eleguas that belong to Orula, like Laroye Biba Kikeño, have a small metal arrow on the top of their heads.)[27]

In another legend, Orula is forced to demonstrate his clairvoyance to Olofi, and he passes the test thanks to Elegua (Abanuke):

"Baba, they say there's a Black man with red skin, Orumila, performing divination."

"Orula? Bah! There's no better diviner than me."

"Well, they're saying he is, Father. They say he can see everything. He predicts what's going to happen and what happened in the past by making marks in white powder on a wood tray, or by tossing a chain."

Olofi, who was the world's most suspicious old man, wanted to confuse Ifa. "I'll find out whether or not his mouth tells lies. *Yo fémma*. I'll show them. They say old Olofi's *ñangando*. I'm going to dress up and make a face like *egun* (*muerto*). Tell them I died."[28]

---

26 DF-N: The anonymous quotation—"santa puta" (literally, whore saint)—is viscerally offensive to devotees of Oshun, myself included. Cf. Brown (2003b); Cabrera ([1974] 1980); Murphy and Sanford (2001); and chapter 2 and the encyclopedia entry for PRINGA HERMOSA in this volume.

27 DF-N: Lucumí ritual experts often distinguish between Elegua (consecrated by *santeros*) and Eshu (consecrated by *babalawos*), but that distinction is not remotely universal among ritual experts.

28 DF-N: The original reads, "Yo fémma. Tu dici viejo Olofi yá tá ñangando. Yo va sé mueca y pone como egun (muerto). Dícin que ta morío yo."

Whenever the Supreme Being speaks in one of these tales, the narrator assumes the flavor and style of speech of *negros bozales*.[29] Elegua goes everywhere, he sees and hears everything, and he gets involved in everything. He sat and listened to Olofi's conversation, then he ran to Orumila and told him everything he had heard. Soon, Orula was summoned to see Olofi, who was lying rigid on a platform surrounded by his children and his "entourage," who were all crying and lamenting over him:

> "Ay! Ay! Olofi ya okuo. Olofi! Look at him! Ya Ikú!" Then Orula arrived at Olofi's side and said, "Olofi is not *aro* (sick).[30] Olofi is *odara, agada-godo* (healthy, strong)! Olofi is not *okuo* (dead). Our Father Olofi wants to know if I'm a diviner, if I *ofe* (see), and that's why he's pretending to be dead."
>
> Then Olofi congratulated him and agreed to give Orula whatever he wanted. The first thing Orula asked for was *parubo* Elegua, the food Elegua was awaiting: "*akuku kereke* [a young rooster], *epo* [palm oil], *akute* [hutia], *eya* [fish], *obi* [coconut], *akara* [buns], *oti* [liquor], *acha* [tobacco, cigars], *atana* [candle], *aguado* [corn]. *Modije!* Thank you."[31]

Orula knows Elegua's whereabouts better than anyone. Orula once found himself obligated to prepare a great feast for all of the *ocha*, but he refused to account for Elegua. "None of the *santos* wanted to accept the sacrifice. It was a mess. Elegua went around spoiling everything and causing trouble. Oya said, 'Someone is missing here . . .' 'No, ma'am!' 'If that one doesn't come, we can't do anything.' Ifa was very upset and said, 'If he shows up, fine. If not, it's just as well.' Things got even more mixed up. In the end, he had no choice but to invite him."

On the other hand, when Ifa and Elegua are friends, Elegua performs countless crucial services for Ifa. In the relentless war that the great Osain once declared on the Supreme Diviner, Ifa owed his victory to Eshu. A *ba-balawo* recounts that, once upon a time,

> Orumbila couldn't tolerate Osain anymore. He accepted Osain's challenge and asked him how he wanted to engage in combat. Osain replied, "By burying our children. Each of us will sustain them with our power. Let

---

29 LC: *Bozal* is another name for *negros de nación* (Africans) who spoke Spanish with difficulty. In the countryside, we still find them at every turn.

30 DF-N: The term *aro* (sick) can also be *arun*. See Cabrera ([1957] 1986, 59–60).

31 DF-N: The enumeration of various offerings is a primer in both Lucumí vocabulary and symbolic ritual protocol.

them demonstrate who can withstand being buried in the earth the longest." And that's what happened. But Eshu made himself invisible and fed Orula's buried children with rooster blood. When the date they had set to disinter them arrived, Osain grabbed his whistle and Orula grabbed his *apun* (*irofa*, or *lofle*),[32] and they each called out to their children. Orula's children had been well-fed with blood, so they heard their father's call, answered him, and emerged right away.

Osain's children were exhausted, so they stayed in the ground; they didn't hear him, and they couldn't answer him. Osain was forced to surrender to Orula in order to save his children in the nick of time.

In some stories, Elegua is the first diviner and teaches Orula divination. Or, accompanied by Moedun (the monkey),[33] he discovers the tree—a palm tree that grows in the garden of Orungan (the sun at high noon) and gives the Odu, the seeds used in divination. The cowrie shells *babalochas* and *iyalochas* used to prophesy belong to this orisha. *Bake Elegua.* "He is the one with the most cowrie shells."

On the other hand, Elegua indirectly established Orumbila's authority as a diviner:

Because Elegua, secretary of God, was always a dear friend of Changó. And Changó was very good friends with Orumbila. Changó saw Orumbila go through a desperate situation. He was homeless and begging, so Changó promised that he would ask Olofi to transfer his position as owner of the divination tray to Orumbila. Changó conferred with Olofi, presenting his reasons, including—among others—that fighting wars left Changó without any time to perform divination. Olofi replied that he would first need to subject Orumbila to a very difficult test to prove that he was up to such an important position.

As soon as Changó left, Olofi grabbed raw corn and toasted corn. He planted the raw corn on a plot of land. Next to it, a palm away,[34] he planted the toasted corn. Elegua saw him do this, and he quickly went to tell Changó that Olofi would soon be summoning Orula so he could indicate where he had planted the corn. Changó warned Orula in time.

---

32 DF-N: These are ritual paraphernalia associated with Ifa divination.

33 DF-N: More literally, this would be "child (*omo*) of monkey (*edun* or *edu*)." See Cabrera ([1957] 1986, 100).

34 DF-N: A *palmo* (translated as "palm") is a unit of measurement equal to the length of a hand. Given the importance of palm trees in the Ifa divination system, the term is used in a clever play on words that works well in both Spanish and English.

Indeed, when Olofi sent for Orula, Elegua stood at the door and whispered the secret of the corn in his ear. Olofi led him to the plot of land and asked, "Orumbila, on this land . . ." Orumbila didn't let him finish.

"Babami, there in that section, on the left, no corn will grow because you planted it toasted to find out whether or not I *ofe*. But, here, where we're both standing, it will grow soon."

Osain had also gone to perform divination, and he requested the position that Changó was abandoning, but when he arrived at Olofi's door, Elegua told him nothing. Obatala was satisfied,[35] and he gave Orunla the wooden tray and the other instruments of divination, while Osain remained a clairvoyant herbalist.

Countless stories like this one illustrate the universal importance of Elegua and what is entailed in having him on our side at all times. This explains why his cult is so widespread in Cuba, and why everybody wants to have an Elegua that will protect them, assuming they do not intend for him to make mischief on their behalf every once in a while.

The *babalawo*, *babalocha*, or *iyalocha* prepare an Elegua—following consultation with cowrie shells[36]—in accordance with the tutelary Angel, divination sign, temperament, and sex of the individual to whom he will belong. The substances used to make an Elegua are as follows: soil from a crossroads, an anthill, a church, a market, a courthouse, a jail, a hospital, a bakery, etc.[37]

Three plants' leaves and seven pieces from the various "palos" belong to this orisha. The head of a turtle. A *palo* belonging to Osain. A stone from the savanna—a true *otan* of Elegua, not one formed from coral. *Afoche* of Orula, powders prepared by a *babalawo*. Twenty-nine coins of different denominations—*medios*, *reales*, *pesetas*, *dobles pesetas*[38]—gathered in the course of exchanges at seven different shops. A small batch of cement is wet with *omiero*, or sacred water (which contains rainwater, river water, seawater, and holy water from the church) and mixed with palm oil, *otipa* (white wine), bee honey, *miel de guinea*, a small piece of charcoal, and his ground leaves. The cement is then sculpted into the shape of the face that represents the orisha. This type of Elegua is known as Elegua *de masa* or *de amasijo*.[39] Once it is constructed, the *santero* buries it at a crossroads—Cuatro Vientos, "Gwagwa

---

35 DF-N: In this context, God, Olofi, and Obatala are roughly analogous.

36 DF-N: Alternatively, the divination might be performed using the distinct tools of the Ifa cult.

37 DF-N: Note that the definitive rhetoric here ("the substances used to make an Elegua are as follows") is contradicted by the dizzying variety of ritual protocols that follow.

38 DF-N: Coins from the Spanish colonial and early republican periods of Cuba's history.

39 DF-N: An Elegua *de masa* or *de amasijo* is, literally, an Elegua made of dough.

o de"—before sunrise so that the stone is imbued with its spirit, acquiring nature's internal and external power. After seven days, they will go back to collect the Elegua, digging it up and—in order to fill the hole in which it was buried—sacrificing three *gallos jiros* [white-feathered roosters], spilling the blood into the hole, then filling it with the birds, plantains, corn, bird feed, and everything that Elegua or Eshu likes.

Additionally, plenty of liquor is poured into the hole. After those seven days, Elegua's stone comes back from the four corners "alive with its own spirit." Upon returning home, the *santero* offers Elegua a goat or a rat, a black rooster, a chick, or a hutia. He is never offered pigeons; he does not eat them, and neither do his children. (But Eshu Ayé does eat them. Hens are *euo*— taboo—for all the Eleguas.)

Before offering the sacrifice, older *santeros* will recite the Apostles' Creed and an Our Father.[40]

Iyalochas are authorized to "asentar" (initiate, consecrate, install) Elegua, prepare *omiero*, and baptize his stone, "which is dark like charcoal and should be found in the savanna by the *omo* themselves." But only men go out in search of the spirit and god of *el monte*. In many rituals for this orisha, only men officiate, and the role of the *iyalocha* is reduced to bearing witness.

"The genuine stone of Elegua, the true one, only needs to be washed with his *ewe*. Elegua made with cement and sand, that's a modern thing!"

A *babalocha* in the capital—who does not actually have the authority to perform this operation, since it is legitimately the exclusive concern of *oluo* or *babalawo*—tells me how to make an Elegua *de amasijo*. Palo Santo Tomás (?). The shell of a crab. *Erun, kola,* and *obi*.[41] (These are sacred seeds which are imported from Africa. They are essential to the consecration of a *Santo*, and *iyalochas* guard them like powdered gold because of how scarce they have become and their high price within Santería.) Turtle shell. Soil from four roads, a market, and the grave of a woman whose name starts with *E* and ends with *A*.[42] A silver coin. A small knife in the shape of a sickle. Gold dust.

---

40 DF-N: The account of "older" Lucumí priests' embracing explicitly Catholic ritual elements is remarkable as one of the few instances in which notions of Catholic-Lucumí syncretism (often suggested by the term *Santería*) ring true. As Cabrera notes, a ritual visit to a Catholic church was already falling out of fashion in the 1950s, and only "older *santeros*" recited Catholic prayers before making sacrificial offerings to Eshu/Elegua.

41 DF-N: *Erun, kola,* and *obi* are, more commonly, *eru, osun,* and *obi kola*.

42 DF-N: Cabrera makes it clear that the information offered by the "babalocha capitalino" is dubious, and her mockery of his testimony is clear and merciless. By explicitly marking certain informants' testimony as suspect, Cabrera makes her respectful skepticism legible, thereby enriching readers' sense of ethnographic data and narrative. That said, her mockery—however warranted—can also be read as unkind, condescending, or even cruel. Meanwhile, contemporary

Three pieces of coral. Three cowrie shells. And a parrot feather. The stick from the *palo de Santo Tomás*,[43] dirt from the crossroads, and dirt from the bank are put inside the base of the Elegua, along with the crab, the silver coin, the three pieces of coral, and the dirt taken from ground in a cemetery next to a cadaver's feet. Meanwhile, dirt taken from the space next to the cadaver's head is placed at the height of the Elegua's eyes, which are simulated with two of the cowrie shells; the third cowrie below them simulates the mouth. The head is topped with the small knife and the parrot feather. Having done all of this, it is left to dry. Later, it is buried. Then it is taken out of the hole while saying, "I am taking a weapon so it will defend me," and it is offered a rooster, a small goat, coconut, liquor, and honey. Then a candle is lit for it. This formula provokes the indignation of a different, scrupulous informant who rejects outright that soil from a grave would be included in the "fundamentación" [foundation, genesis] of a proper Elegua.

This is equivalent to introducing the spirit of a *muerto*. Nor should a crab be included. No doubt, the young *babalocha* is steeped in Mayombe and does not know that an Elegua "never, ever carries a cemetery inside." A daughter of Echubi also voices her own opposition to what she considers "a very serious error," the horrifying notion of using Apan (or Akan), the crab: "It sets you back, like everything that walks backward, and that's why children of Elegua can't eat it." (And not only because it "sets you back": on one occasion, Ifa had thrown his *okuele* down at the bank of the river and the crab hid it for him. "Out of respect for Orula and his experience with the crab, many people are prohibited from eating it.")

Nonetheless, "Eluasama is made with *yerba pastillo* and crab. That Elegua isn't washed, and you don't look at him except when you're feeding him. He's only used for doing harm. Eluasama turns people backward and inside out."[44]

His priests and devotees do not prostrate themselves before this orisha the way they do before Changó, Obatala, and the goddesses by offering *odubale* or *ekunde*.[45] Elegua is not invoked while kneeling: "Eshu guara guara kikenya

---

olorishas reading Cabrera's gratuitously detailed description of an "unorthodox" ritual formula are liable to experience the same visceral "indignation" Cabrera describes among a more "scrupulous informant" later in this same paragraph.

43   DF-N: It is unclear which tree (*palo*) is referred to here.

44   DF-N: Cabrera's original includes a detail that remains obscure: "'Vive debajo de la horma' (de una horma de azucar)" ([1954] 1992, 90).

45   DF-N: These are Lucumí terms for kneeling or prostrating oneself as a ritual salute. The gesture is pictured in one of the photographs by Josefina Tarafa at the end of this volume. In the image, one embodiment of the orisha (in the possession mount) salutes another, elder embodiment (the lagoon). The captions reads, "The moment a *santero* intones a chant calling Yemayá, one of her 'horses' falls to the ground, possessed by the goddess."

alalarosoyo asu kama ache akue e." Nor are offerings or sacrifices made in this posture. To communicate with Elegua, his priests and devotees crouch down, never placing a knee on the ground. Upon entering the home, he is saluted the same way the god usually salutes when he "descends": putting one foot forward, he presents one elbow, then the other, then turns his back, kicks his feet back along the ground, and vigorously shakes his hips. Like Ogun, he only rarely embraces his devotees when he is in possession of one of his children at a fiesta, *guemilere*, or *bata*. He is also saluted by lifting one arm after the other with closed fists and—before turning one's back and kicking the floor, "the way dogs do with their back legs"—shaking one's hips. This is done in cases where "the warriors"—Elegua's inseparable companions Ogun and Ochosi—are also kept in the same cabinet. That way, the warriors are saluted facing forward, while Elegua is saluted by turning one's back and immediately shaking one's backside energetically.

The attention required by a domestic, "guardian" Elegua is not particularly demanding. His *otan* should be fed every Monday, which is the day governed by this orisha, or on the third of every month. Tuesdays are governed by Ogun and Ochosi; Wednesday by Babalu Ayé; Thursday by Obatala; Friday by Changó and Oya; Saturday by Yemaya and Oshun; and Sunday by Obatala and the *Santos*. But Nini and another *santera* consider that Monday, Tuesday, and all third days of the month are consecrated to Elegua and Eshu; Wednesday and the fourth days of the month to Ogun, Ochosi, and Changó; Thursdays and the eight, sixteenth, and twenty-fourth days of the month to Obatala; Saturday and the seventh, fourteenth, and twenty-first days of the month to Yemaya; Saturdays and the fifth, tenth, and fifteenth days of the month to Yalode; and Sunday belongs to all the *Santos*. Inle, Babalu Ayé, Obamoro, and Osain also rule over Fridays.

On Elegua's day, he is left out in the sun for a while and rubbed with palm oil. Once he is ready to receive his food, he is placed back in his cabinet. Water is spilled on the ground in front of him three times in a ritual used to address all *orissas*:

Omituto anatutu tutu laroye. You speak to him, asking him for health and prosperity. You pray to him in Lucumí, if you know how. One should at least know how to say *Elegua laroye asu komache icha fofa guara omi tuto anatuto tu tu babami kosi iku kosi aro kosi ofo, araye, kosi achelu kosi eun afonfo molei delo omodei.*

Immediately, you chew three grains of pepper, fill your mouth with liquor, and bathe the stone with a generous spraying. Because he is known to be a smoker, you light a cigar for him, blowing a few mouthfuls of smoke at him, then leave the lit cigar next to him. This is followed by "feeding" with small pieces of smoked fish, roasted hutia, black-eyed pea fritters, a handful of toasted corn, and pieces of coconut that are put inside or around the clay base in which he is kept. He will consume this little by little during the week. Finally, you light a candle next to the open door of the cabinet where the orisha is kept, letting it burn itself out. Once a month, the blood of a rooster (mixed, black, or white-feathered) is offered in addition to his usual food, but the bird's legs and beak are washed before being presented to him.

After putting him out in the sun from seven to nine in the morning, many owners of Elegua rub corn over him and offer three heads of herring fishes cooked in the oven with verdolaga, tete (bledo), and guayaba leaves. The three fish heads will be left on Elegua for three days. Afterward, a small chick that still follows its mother is sacrificed to him; ideally, "one that's been stolen" will be appreciated even more by the orisha.

As compensation for some blessing received or to beg for his protection, a young black goat is sacrificed for him. A *babalawo* or *achogun*—a son of Ogun, who has the right to kill in the absence of a *babalawo*—will come to sacrifice it for a fee of $3.15 per leg of an animal.[46]

The sacrifice of a pig offered to Elegua in the savanna in order to obtain his protection in some great endeavor is both solemn and dangerous for the supplicant. Immediately after performing the sacrifice, the person who killed the animal avoids their responsibility, as always, by saying, "It wasn't me! It was Ogun!"

During the presentation of food offerings to Elegua, each item should be enumerated out loud, "because it's important that he hears clearly what he's being given." This is done with all of the orishas.

Many devotees light a candle at midnight for Las Animas, "which are Eshus." The door is closed, so then no one can go out to the street under any circumstances. "This candle is not lit for witchcraft"—we will see below some of the missions entrusted to the Animas del Purgatorio, most especially the terrible Anima Sola—"but rather for personal protection. We ask them to not bring bad things our way, so they say, 'No, we're not going to that house; they always treat us well there.'"

It is advisable, as we have mentioned, that the owner of an Elegua— and anyone who frequents *casas de santo*—learn how to address him with a few "greetings" in Lucumí: "Elegua ake boru ake boye, tori toru la ya fi yoruare."

---

46 DF-N: Throughout, monetary amounts should be understood in historical terms; they refer to Cuban pesos in the early and mid-twentieth century, not US dollars. According to the particular formula outlined in this passage, the ritual fee for sacrificing and butchering a four-legged animal would be $12.60, the fee for two animals would be $25.20, and so on.

"Ala le ele kupache ago meko"[47] is a reverential formula often used to praise or "flatter" him, as the old *santeras* say.

"Ago Elegua Baba guara ago Elegua abaku maku ofonfo tube abebeniyo alanu la mu bata omo marata omo kuama du achere omo achere airku Babagua dede wanto lo kun. Elegua tubo kosi laroye aki boyu Baba guara Eshuboru, Eshu boya Eshu bochiche. Eshu Barakikenyo."

"Elegua ago laroye Eshu Beleke inka Eshu Eshu Bi mama kenya ofe mi, moforivale Olodumare bara male Babami lowo, Oli loguo, eye loguo, iguaraye abolyo kerekete."

"Elegua alaroye Echu kaika laguana un bele kun sekun loaroye un cheche anikano nikun Olorun."

"Eshu Beleke alaroye kiroche Babaguona ile orissa, modukue. Babakua elo sise kuan kuana ona Baba."

"Elegua obara ago kidua dide emi, fu mi, etie omi, tuto ana tuto Eshu bara Kikenyo anya ago, kosi aro, kosi iku, kosi eye, kosi ofo, kosi araye, kosi achelu, ire, owo ile mi."

"Okuyire Elegua. Ara inya unlo! Ara unlo. Ariku Babagua. Kosi iku, kosi ano. Achelu unlo, Araye unlo. Kua bofi gue boda? Baba laroye unsoro. Ago, koto bae, unye, chokoto, abata ile. Ago Elegua."

"Bara laroye achukai kolaguola un bele kun laroye un cheche oni koni oni kondori."

"Eshu elu kama chacha onire meni kando iye ko mo yagata Elegua iku laroye un egue niga ala roye ebelegue epopo ni pere epepe ni poreda komo da efu da komo epere enyini epere epamorugun eye oma."

"Baralayiki ene bede eka ere alamu bata alako mako atuka ma chacha enise meni konduru qye komo ya gata, epepe ni pere Elegua niga inga boye laroye ebelegun eni ada kun."

In all of these prayers—*kosi aro, kosi iku, kosi eya*, etc.—one asks Elegua to ward off illness, death, tragedy, crime, the *achelu* (the law) and procure *unyen* (*yeun dada*, sustenance), *ire* (luck), and *owo* (money).

"Elegua is the orisha of jokes and pranks"—*chefe*. These can be huge, cruel, and overwhelming. Or small, irritating, ironic mishaps. The unexpected and the unforeseen. As Oddedei says, "Elegua both brings and takes away, preparing the good and bad that is unexpected." Elegua changes a situation in an instant. He is the imponderable creator of fleeting disagreements and sudden, definitive splits. "The truest love and friendship can be turned to hate by Elegua, confusing people who really love each other." This is conveyed in a well-known "pataki" about two inseparable friends who had such similar

47 DF-N: For a discussion of the transliteration of these passages, see the Translator's Notes.

temperaments and tastes that they spontaneously came to the same decisions and opinions. These exemplary friends were known in *ile-ilu* (the town) as the best in the world. They had known each other since they were children and never argued once in all of those years of friendship. Claiming that only he could turn them against each other, Elegua appeared one day when the two friends were chatting in the street. One of the friends saw an unknown stranger who was completely bald and Black, while the other friend saw a bearded white man (*oyibo*). Elegua had shaved half his head and face, then showed each friend a different profile. The friends disagreed for the first time. "Who was that Black man?" "I didn't see any Black man. You mean that white man that went around the corner?" "That man was Black!" "He was white!" Each one insisted on what they had seen. Their voices rose in discord.

Losing control of himself, one of them shouted, "You're mocking me!" And the other one said, "I'm not going to let you insist that I'm *gueri-gueri* (crazy) or drunk. It's an insult that . . ." "I don't tell lies, and you're the one who's insulting me!" Elegua disappeared, letting those exemplary friends beat each other in the middle of the street.

In another *pataki*, Elegua causes the dispute with a hat that he made, or a horse painted white on one side and black on the other. There are many stories recalling the mockery, quarrels, and mischief of this great troublemaker, Eshu. The *babalawos* recount that a farmer had an enviable harvest, and Eshu asked to eat some of it. Unfortunately, the man did not recognize him and replied coldly that he did not give his food away to anyone. Eshu returned in costume, saying that the King had sent him to destroy his gardens because the food he was sending to the market was making the whole town very sick. The man had a violent, impulsive temper. In a furious rage, he destroyed his plants. Later he reconsidered, but the harm was already done. He went to ask the Oba for the reason behind such an unfair measure. The king let him know that he had not sent anyone, but he listened to the account of what had happened and understood. He burst out laughing and said, "This is one of Eshu's tricks because he was hungry!"

Due to the character traits of some of his many manifestations designated by the name of Eshu—not just mischievous and spiteful, but decidedly perverse and openly malicious—he is identified in a purely Christian sense with the devil.

"Eshu, the evil one." "Satan." "The Lucumí Devil." "Eshu is the very same San Bartolomé, the devil celebrated on August 24. If you don't think so, just look at the picture card: in the shadows, you can see the devil holding two daggers, hunting his prey." "That's how the feast of San Bartolomé goes: Eshu runs loose."

"Eshu is an Elegua that is only willing to do harm." "He stabs people in the back." "He lives in the dark, and he should always have a knife." But . . . "Eshu are the twenty-one Eleguas: Eshu Oku Boro, the one that mediates between life and death; Eshu Alayiki ("the greediest one"), "the one who owns the unexpected"; Eshu Latieye, "the one who wins no matter what"; or Eshu Bi, "the king of mischief." "He is one and twenty-one, the same Elegua traveling different paths."

According to Domingo Hernández and his partner Enriqueta Herrera, a daughter of Elegua, "The Eleguas from Oyo land are named Aguo-Bara, Ekileyo, Osu Kakugwo, Okokoye Biye, Agomeyo, and Baralayiki."

Sandoval and Sixto refer to other fearsome aspects presented by the multiple orisha Elegua.[48] "Didn't he burn all of his children in an oven?" They tell us about Abalonke, Baralanube, Alona, Baralagwana or Alabaguana, and Belenke ("he's very tricky"). And Eshu-Mako and Yelu.

"God, Olofi, gave Elegua to Orumbila. Eshu Male showed him where to find the seeds for divination (the palm nuts), and all of the orishas have an Elegua as a sentinel and messenger." There is one in every location. In the cemetery, he opens the gates of Oba's graveyard, "because it's not like they say in Havana. Oya's not the owner of the cemetery; it's Oba. Elegua opens the gate and digs the grave. Babalu Ayé carries the cadaver." Laroye is at the doors of houses and in the street. At the corner, Eshu Bi. At the four corners, Alalu or Achi Kualu; in plazas and markets, Eshu Ile-Oloya or Kaloya; in the hills, Agere; in the savannas, Lagwana, Obanigwana or Alagwana, the Anima Sola, Eshu of isolated places and sister of Eshu Bi, "the one that draws people to the savanna or *el monte* so that she—the Anima Sola incarnate—will kill them in the midst of that solitude." But the tragic Alagwana—misfortune and desperation—is not found exclusively in *el monte* or the savanna; it travels all over. "Ah! The person who knows how to prepare an Eshu Alagwana is stronger than any *gangulero*!"

A "male" Elegua, crafty and bloodthirsty, Eshu Oguanilebe is an inseparable companion of Ogun. He stands on corners, causing accidents, and killing. "Sometimes he's satisfied with killing a dog so Ogun can drink fresh blood when he's hungry." "He goes out and finds food for his owner, killing, and he's to blame when automobiles and trains go off course and crash," or when a distracted pedestrian dies under the wheels of a vehicle. Salako—who exaggerates his *negro bozal* style of speaking when he lectures—says, "Eshu is the

---

48   DF-N: The description of Eshu/Elegua as both singular and plural ("el múltiple Orisha Eleg-guá") and the notion that "en cada lugar hay uno" (there is one in each location) can be understood as philosophical propositions. See Chemeche, Cosentino, and Gonçalves da Silva (2013).

best friend of Oggú.[49] Ogun does *foribale* in front of him. If Ogun's belly isn't full, he calls Eshu. Eshu Bi is on the corner and a truck comes along. Eshu gets in the truck driver's head—*brán kráo!*—and he kills, then Ogun eats the spilled blood."

Alaroye, friend of Oshun, "is the one who lives behind the door in a little clay vessel." Barainye "walks" with Changó. "Ayeru is a messenger and guardian of Ifa" and his representative, the *babalawo*, who, without Elegua and Osain, "is vulnerable."

An elderly devotee, terrified, pleads with me to refrain from discussing Iyelu, the one belonging to the Arufas, or Agbanukue with "the Nazarenes" (*anochecido*), "who makes those who see him go blind."

Anyagi [Añaguí], the defense and security of Ifa, "is the finest of the legion of Eleguas. He's the most important one, because Olofi put him in charge of opening and closing the gates of the cemetery." He is the one that gives orders, naming and assigning work to the other Eleguas. And they are all messengers, "kids who run errands and obey their elders' orders"—most often, they are children, by and large, under orders from other, older Eleguas. The oldest one, before whom one should behave with the utmost circumspection, is named Elufe. His face is carved in a stone that has a base that is wide enough to keep it in an upright position inside the clay vessel or gourd that serves as his seat.

(But Sixto, an *Osainista* and a descendent of the Chággo branch of Lucumí people, tells me about Eshu Marimaye, who is even older and considered "the origin of all the Eleguas. It's him, not Anyagi, who is at the door of the cemetery, the owner of the key. He is made with rat. He's bad.")

According to Domingo Hernández, "Elufe, the oldest Elegua, lives"—is kept—"far back in the patio, because nothing dishonest can happen near him. No one can get naked, talk, do anything indecent, or even say bad words. Elufe is a very well-endowed man. He has a hernia, he's busted up, and his testicles hang down below his knees." Sixto also insists on an austere aspect of Elegua: "He never had a wife." "He never had a woman in his house. He made his house . . . then he went to live outside four walls."

"This old Elegua is given snuff. You know? Those little powders you put up your nose." (He is still offered tobacco powder.)

Alaleilu is also old. "Alaleilu is an honorific given to Elegua." He is an *awo*, "one of the great ones."

---

49 DF-N: Cabrera's original reads "'Eshu,' dice Salakó, que cuando está en cátedra exagera su habla de negro bozal, 'e mejó caraela de Oggú, Oggú li hace forivale'" (1992, 95–96). The suggestion, made in passing, that Salako is engaging in an "exagerrated" performance of linguistic Blackness is exceedingly subtle. Cf. Wirtz (2011, 2014, 2016).

"Ogiri Elu, Afra, and Keneno are Arará."

Anyangi and Alabgwana and Oguanilele are adults. Akileyo, Alayiki, Echubi are adolescents, turbulent children—and how! This Bi, the leader of the Ibeyi or twins, is a little more docile. Barainye is unbeatable when it comes to protecting his *omo*. Echerike goes around with Osain. We also have Alalu, Kinkeye, Laroye Akokelebiyu, and Aganika, who stumbles around and bumps into everything, attracting the police. (He even goes out to get them!) Osika—like Akokoribiya—is from Mina land, and he is very fond of playing with glass marbles, spinning tops, and smoking cigars. Barakenyo is the smallest one of them all; he lives in the jungle, in the brush, and he confuses and disrupts everything. Anyagi, Obanigwana or Alabagwana, Abalonke, and Alona engage in constant trade with *muertos*.

As we have mentioned repeatedly, Alabgwana is identified by *aborisas* with the Anima Sola, who is associated with most desperate and underhanded ventures. "She gave birth to Elegua, who bound her wrists in chains when he was a little boy before running rampant and growing up on his own. Ogun baptized him, and he baptized Ogun. And these two go around together, doing whatever they want."

Regarding Eshu, "He was birthed by Oya, who abandoned him in the savanna. After years had gone by, Oya wanted to acknowledge him as her son, but he refused, and he threw the fact that she'd abandoned him back in her face."

"Oya is a woman who did not want children in her home. She doesn't like children."

Anyagi, Mother or overseer of the Eleguas, appears in one story that explains the origins of the cult of Elegua. She was married to Okuboro, an *oba*, or king, with whom she conceived this son who will be called Eleguara. He was born a prince. He is of royal descent. One day, in the company of the large entourage that accompanies an Aremu wherever they go, he stopped at the intersection of two roads. There he hesitated before choosing which way to go. He took three steps back and forth three times, then continued on his way without any more hesitation until he came across a light on the ground among the plants. The light split in two, shining in two different directions, like two penetrating eyes looking at him. Elegua leaned over the mysterious lights. Full of fear and respect, he picked up a dry *obi* (coconut) from the ground. He took it to the palace and told his father about what had happened. Because he was such a mischievous trickster, Anyagi and Okuboro did not believe him. The coconut was abandoned behind a door. Then, a day or two later, at a party where all of the court was gathered, the coconut began to shine again, its light so bright and alive that it terrified them all. This phenomenon coincided with the sudden death of Eleguara.

During the entire duration of his lengthy funerary ceremony, the coconut glowed intensely.

Elegua's death was followed by an era of misery and calamity. The palace diviners gathered and deduced that the town's misfortune was due to the fear and neglect of the prodigious *obi* that the prince had left behind. Moreover, when they went to honor and perform sacrifices to it, they found the *obi* was rotten and infested with bugs. This led to another gathering of the Awos, who decided to choose an *otan*, a stone, so that the spirit of Elegua would come from the savanna to live in it—his spirit is always found in the savanna—and they nourished and worshipped him in the stone.

"Sometimes a coconut can be an Elegua." Yet despite that fruit's ageless quality, which is due to its holiness, Elegua should live in an incorruptible stone, or in a statue made from *cedro* [cedar].[50]

The Ñame can also be "baptized" and serve the function of an Elegua—that is, contain him:

> Because once upon a time this orisha went to *el monte* looking for a hutia he needed. He lay down on the ground and fell asleep. The sound of moaning woke him up, and he saw that something shaped like a foot was emerging from the earth right next to him.
>
> He asked, "*Kilonfe?*"
>
> There was no response. He heard more moaning, and it was the earth that was struggling. Then Elegua said to the yam being born, "*Dide.* Rise." And he took it out of the ground.
>
> He showed it to Orula, and Orula said, "This is Ichu, and in your absence, it will take your place. Offer it to Obatala, cooked and pounded, at the top of a hill."

The yam and coconut always accompany Elegua. Neither he nor any other orisha can be without them.

Many reasons concur to make the yam—like the coconut, as we will see below—a sacred fruit.

Elegua is diffused everywhere. "They are a web." All of them communicate among themselves, and they trick each other. "When the Elegua at the door is offered a rooster, he arranges things—the scoundrel—so he can eat it by himself by sending away the Elegua on the corner." Other times they work together in solidarity to avenge themselves: the one guarding the door will

---

50 DF-N: Tropical red cedar is pest resistant, making it ideal for ritual objects like statues and drums.

collude with the one on the corner; the one on the corner with the one at the four corners (*ota meta*); the one at the four corners (Traga-Legua) with the one in *el monte* . . . Therefore, it is necessary for the one at the door to be satisfied—"that he eats, and that he's fed before anyone else"—in accordance with the decree of Olofi (according to some versions) or Ifa, Orula (according to others). This is meant to avoid having him impede the normal course of life, to keep him from whistling to the one on the corner, an unruly troublemaker who will whistle to the one at the four corners, who will whistle to the one in *el monte*, all of them answering the call and entering the house together and causing a terrible tragedy. "To avoid these conflicts, all of them need to be fed, because they get jealous of each other until they can't stand it anymore, then we suffer the consequences."

Osain is often—inappropriately—referred to as the Guardian of Ewe. For this reason, many consider him to be another Elegua within the extensive "gang" led by Añagi. "But he is not a guardian. He is the Owner."

The symbol of Osain is a branch in the shape of a *garabato* (a walking cane or staff). "A *garabato* that comes back from *el monte* with you"—that is, one found in *el monte*. *Santeras* go to *el monte* to look for it, consecrate it, offer it sacrifices, call it Osain, and keep it in the rear of their home so it looks after them. "It whistles to warn of danger." "This *garabato* works to grab"—attract—"and it's loaned to young women so they can hook a husband."

Of course, the spirit of Osain, like all supernatural forces, can be contained in any object. But, strictly speaking, the *garabato* "belongs" to Elegua, who uses it to hook, pull, or bring himself next to whatever he needs. Osain, for his part, uses a walking stick formed by two roots that have wound around each naturally, and he uses it to dance at the *toques*.

This *garabato* is made from the wood of a yamao or—almost always—guayaba tree, since its fruit is one of Elegua's favorite offerings. It is used to invoke him and oblige him to "come down," then commit to executing delicate "work." The *garabato* is swung in the air to urge him on and compel him. "Elegua is a *Santo* that needs to be commanded with authority. When he has to work, he doesn't like to be pampered. He wants to be addressed in a strong way when it's a matter of serious issues, like getting a man out of prison or something like that." "And he acts like a Mayombero."

He is usually invoked by striking the floor firmly three times.

All of the orishas received their "ache" from Olorun—their grace, virtue, talent. Magical power.

After he finished the great task of creating the world (but before he retired to heaven to avoid earthly affairs so absolutely, making Heaven itself move away from the earth because humans bothered and "debased" him), the Eternal Father distributed his children throughout the universe.

From his hands, each one of them received—or obtained on their own, "on their own merits"—what now belongs to them. Olokun, the sea. Agayu, the savannas. Oke, the mountains, hills, and any knoll or mound. Orishaoko, the earth and farmed lands. Ogun and Ochosi, metals and *el monte*, wild animals, etc.

Osain received the secret of Ewe. The knowledge of its virtues. The plants were his exclusively, and he did not give them to anyone until Changó complained to his wife Oya, the owner of the Winds. He complained that only Osain knew the mystery of each *ewe*, so the rest of the Orishas found themselves in the world without a single plant. Oya opened her skirts and shook them violently, making whirlwinds—*fe fe*—that started blowing intensely. Osain kept the secrets of ewe in a gourd that hung from a tree. When he saw that the wind had blown it down and broken the gourd, dispersing the plants, he sang, "Ee eguero, eguero, saue ereo." He could not stop the orishas from taking the plants and distributing them. They named the plants and gave each plant one of their own virtues. And although Osain is the owner of plants—or he is at least referred to as such—every *Santo* owns their own plants in *el monte*. "And there was one who wanted to know more than him, but it turned out the knowledgeable one didn't know as much as the one who knows the most."[51]

Osain, as Lari defines him, is "the physician, administrator, and distributor of Ewe."

He is one of the great deities in the Creoles' Lucumí pantheon because, as one *osainista* tells us, "his presence is essential to everything we do in our religion. Osain discovers and gives the *ewe* that is necessary for any situation: to initiate someone, to cure them, or to make them ill." Along with Changó, he is co-owner of the drums.

Like Olokun and Orula, Osain does not "come down on anybody's head": he does not take possession of any mortal, because "nobody could withstand having *el monte* in their head." Another reason he is often confused with Elegua is that dancing in his honor—in both Lucumí and Arará *toques*—is performed by jumping on one leg, the same way San Lázaro also jumps. But it is not Osain "mounted." "You dance like Osain to honor him. In Havana, the Herbalist Santo "doesn't come up." ("He does come down" in Matanzas.)

Osain speaks from inside a gourd, "softly, in a nasal voice." "He lives in a gourd," and in a pot.

OLUWA EWE

---

51 DF-N: The original Spanish text includes an especially tight turn of phrase: "Y alguno quiso saber más que él, pero resultó que el sabio no sabía lo que sabía el más sabio." In this formulation, knowledge, knowing, and wisdom are virtually interchangeable.

The secret of this great orisha is the concern of the *babalawo*. "It is prepared by the Awo." And in Palo Monte, it is made by the Padre *nganga* in an equivalent way. "¡Cómo habla gangalan fula! He talks like us, and that's why sorcerers and herbalists say he's a gossip." He knows and says it all: "He finds out about everything: he sees and hears, then he tells his owner about it right away." (This is another characteristic that resembles Elegua.) Osain informs his owner when someone is going to visit him to "get a reading" (a consultation) and is already on the way to his house, and Osain tells him what issues worry the individual before they have even knocked on his door. The loquacity of these marvelous gourds might make skeptics think that many of the sorcerers and *santeros* who were famous and feared for their Osain were actually ventriloquists. The Congo were especially well known for being "able to produce a voice from their belly," making it seem like they had someone who spoke inside them whenever they wanted—as if, as Calazán and Catalino say, "a dwarf was hidden in their stomach." Some *santeros* claim that a few years ago, in the town of Perico, an Osain allowed his voice to be heard emanating from his gourd—which was decorated with hawk feathers—without interruption for several hours. Others insist that one still exists in the small town of Alacranes, and another in Mantilla, which is near Havana. Sometimes Osain, like Elegua, lives in a statue. "The Osain belonging to the old man Federico was a statue. The old man would sit behind his half-open door smoking his pipe. One day, I was there with him, and I heard the statue say, 'Federico, a woman dressed in white is coming to look for a cure for her husband.' There's still an Osain like that at the Central Orozco." An Elegua—an Oba Kekere or Oba Kere—lives in a cedarwood statue that is dressed in striped pants and a guayabera—the typical shirt of the Cuban peasant—and has his head covered by a straw hat made from Yarey. The renowned Aniceto Abreu had one.

"Elegua and Ogun, Ochosi, and Osain—and the Ikú—are very closely connected. They are all the right hand of the Awo, and Osain is his greatest and most profound secret."

On the other hand, elders refer to Osain—personified in the materials we will enumerate below—as "Lucumí sorcery" that belongs to the *agugu* and *oloyifo*. It is used in the same sense as the *nganga* or "Prenda" (a fetish or object associated with a supernatural power or spirit) that belongs to *paleros* or sorcerers of Congo origin and—by extension—any magical amulet. For example: a turtle shell, vulture feathers, thorns from Zarza and Cambia Voz—used to escape from the police—is an Osain. "Roughly and clumsily speaking, Osain refers to any amulet," or even a curse.

"At first, Orula—who was a beggar—was an *odosain* . . . He only used his Osain for witchcraft. As a punishment, Obatala was going to kill him, but

Changó saved him with a scapegoat ritual. Orula swore he'd do no more harm. Osain is the *agugu* or *oguni* of the *santos*."[52]

For some elders, Osain is also used to designate "witchcraft," "the secret of Osain" that Elegua kept in three gourds, "the secret that talked," "divined with words," and prophesied like the *dilogún* or *okuele*, Orula's chain. In the beginning, the Turtle—Ayé, Ayagguá Tiroko, the slave of Elegua—was a man, just like any other man. He was a "security guard" who always looked after these three gourds full of mysteries. But one day he abandoned them and, intending to betray Elegua, attended a get-together where the *santos* were celebrating. None of them knew the "tratado," the power contained in the prodigious gourds that Aya—the Turtle—revealed to the gathering of *orisas*. Olofi cursed the traitor who sold his master's secret, and that is why the orishas in *oru* kicked him out of heaven.

This explains why the turtle—"Osain is born from the head of a turtle"—is essential to its preparation, as we will see. It is also indispensable in the preparation of an Elegua, which contains an *otan* of Osain and the substances that are animated by the spirit of the divine botanist.

The old *santera* Conga Mariate—a Lucumí, despite her nickname—says, "The name and surname is Osain Agenegi Aguado Kini-kini." He is implored by singing, "Oile Sai-Sai Babalogwo oile Sai-Sai." And he is saluted with these words: "Osain agueniye eliseko eguelere nile araye obaniye." He is offered sacrifices of he-goat, turtle, and only roosters with mixed- color feathers (*akuko oriyaya*). The Osain belonging to Conga Mariate is an ancient piece of iron from Africa: a spike some forty-five centimeters long with a vague, very worn image of a face at its top end and a trident ornament sticking out from the top of its head (as far as I could tell when I saw it, with some difficulty, in the darkness of her room). A small iron trident symbolizes the Owner of *el monte*.

"They didn't know Osain in Grefe or in Dahomey, not in the same way he made himself known and took shape in Oyo, Yesa, and Takua. The *fundamento* of Osain—the real one, like the one I've conserved from my grandmother—is made of two medium-size crystal balls, one of which is bigger than the other. A small deer horn packed with its load of earth and trees, a jar with turtle blood, water from the first rains in May, seawater, river water, holy water, and guinea pepper.

To make a Lucumí—Oyo—Osain, these pieces are placed in a clay pot and buried under a *palma real* [royal palm] so that Changó transfers his power to it. Then it is buried under a ceiba so that it receives the virtue and power of Iroko, Boma, Obatala, Nana, Agayu, and all the orishas that gather there. It stays

---

52 DF-N: In Lucumí, *ogun* (*oggun*, etc.) refers to medicine or witchcraft, while *agugu* and *oguni* refer to a sorcerer, medicine man, or witch doctor.

at each of these trees for six days, accumulating power. Then it's taken to an anthill. And, finally, to four corners to gather the spirit of Elegua, the vitality of the earth, the blessing of Osaoko and Los Cuatro Vientos.

"You never leave a hole in the ground empty, so when it's unearthed at the four corners at the end of another six days, tribute is offered to Tile (the earth) by leaving a rooster, turtle, corn, white wine, and aguardiente in the hole. After this burial at Los Cuatro Vientos, Osain emerges *cristiano*, complete, and alive. Orisaoko gave it *ache*. Now it has all the powers, the strength, the life, the secret of the earth." The only thing left for the *santero* to do is recite the Apostles' Creed and the Our Father, just as he has done each time he unburied and removed Osain.

The jar, the deer horn, the balls—Osain—is kept in a pot or tureen.

The "fundamento" of an Osain in Regla de Ocha and Arará is essentially the same as a Gurunfinda, except for the inclusion of human bones. "Gurunfinda, Andudu Yambaka Butanseke in Regla de Palo Monte, is the same as Osain. The *tratado* is the same." Meaning, its components are the same. Another of my elderly informants, a *mayombero*, prepared his gourd (Osain) with the head, heart, and four legs of a turtle, parrot, and dove. The bodies of these birds are dried, toasted, reduced to powder, and placed in the gourd with Amansa-Guapo vine (to be clear: not the wood, but the vine), along with another very magical vine called Wakibanga, as well as Sapo vine. The tongue and eyes, always vigilant, of a rooster—"the guardian eyes of Akuko, which are always on the lookout." Seven or eight human teeth, "so it talks." A Cuatro-Vientos. A jawbone taken from a grave, along with some dirt and a tuft of hair from the cadaver. The full name of this *muerto* is written on a piece of paper and placed inside the gourd, accompanied by seven Spanish *reales*, which is the token "*derecho*" or payment usually received by souls who become subjects of a sorcerer. Seven live leaf-cutting ants are included in the gourd before they turn red, along with seven maté seeds wrapped in the birds' feathers. Before sealing the Osain or Gurunfinda, a half bottle of aguardiente is poured into it.[53] Then it is buried, remaining under a ceiba for twenty-one days, so the strength and powers of the sacred tree are incorporated into it. Alternatively, it is buried in an anthill, "so it learns how to work hard and persevere." A.D. tells us, however, that "Gurufinda, the Congo Osain, doesn't necessarily have a *muerto*." "It is made with birds. Birds that talk like people: the African grey parrot, *cáo, cotorra*. The *fundamento*, the main thing, is a turtle." If an Osain is intended for good, if it is an "Osain cristiano" to benefit humankind, then

---

53 DF-N: The alcohol works as an antiseptic; the other half of the liquor in the bottle is presumably either saved for later or consumed by the officiants (before and/or after the offering is poured over the ritual objects).

it is buried on a Thursday, Friday, or Saturday. If it is meant to be "judío" and used only for harm, then it should be buried on Monday, Tuesday, or Wednesday, since those are the days—according to *mayomberos*—governed by Kadiampembe, the devil, *taita* Kochano.[54] The most abominable sorcerers choose those days to practice their evil arts.

One old herbalist who teaches me insists, like most of them, that his Osain used to talk. Unfortunately, it became mute after his godfather died, the great *mayombero* Nyunga-Nyunga who had prepared it for him. "He's never made so much as a peep after that." Everything he did to reanimate it was futile: neither he nor other senior *mayomberos* could restore its eloquence, so he opted to destroy it, bury it, and pay its *derecho*.

"Prendas" lose their essence. "They get weak." The "fuiri" abandons them; the spirit leaves them and the energies contained in the receptacle are weakened if their owner does not attend to them "and if they don't eat." We will return to this subject.

Like this *palero* who extolled the loquacity of Gurufinda, I met a *babalawo* who boasted confidentially that his Osain told him—in a twangy, nasal voice—about everything that was happening around him. For my part, I have never had the good fortune to hear an Osain. *Paleros* refer to Osain as a gossip, and with good reason. It is like the mirror. "Osain says things, while the other one shows them."

"Gourds of life" is another name for the protective amulets prepared in these fruits, talismans that—in stories—often save protagonists just in time when they are about to die at the hands of a demon or witch that is determined to devour them. They are constructed accordingly.

An old man laments, "I don't know if an Osain still exists that talks and sings like the ones the Lucumí used to make. Osain was a great secret. I think our elders took it with them to the grave."

Calazán, Gabino, and Catalino Murillo clarify, "It's a secret of the Lucumí, the Dahomey, and . . . the Congo." Because the Black people from all of the different nations knew it. "Especially the Mina Afafe."

Women are prohibited from owning an Osain "because it is too strong for them."

Cape tells us, "When the magic of the gourd was first created by Osain, it was a woman who first found it, but she didn't know how to control it. She

---

54   DF-N: Cabrera's original includes seven variations of the same name in different passages: Kaddiampémbe, Kaddiampemba, Kadianpemba, Kaddiempémba, Kaddiempembe, Cáddian pémbe, and Kadiampemba. Notably, each variation is transliterated in a unique way, meaning that no two mentions of this fearsome entity are written the same way. Presumably, this represents a deliberate, artful intervention on the author's part.

didn't remove herself from it when she had her moon"—menses—"and Osain destroyed her." That is why a woman never passes under a flying Osain, the gourd decorated with all kinds of birds' feathers—especially hawk—which is always kept high up, hanging from a waxed string on a tree branch. If a woman commits this sort of carelessness, she will become sterile and "never have her period again." But it is not only women who should beware of passing under an Osain: nobody should endanger themselves by taking that sort of risk.

Nonetheless, older women, like many *santeras* of a certain age "who don't menstruate anymore," can have a "guide" of Osain, which is to say "an incomplete Osain." On this point, Cape claims this Osain-kinibo "also flies and sees with one eye," and it is the most noble. It is also hung, but lower than the one previously mentioned, and it is not decorated with feathers. (A woman's Osain lives outside the house, in the patio or in a corner. A man's in the ceiling.)

This gourd, always marked with a cross in white plaster, is fed with the blood of a black rooster, taking care not to show him the feathers. "And you need to give him money, silver, or else he'll go away and leave the gourd empty."

"When he is working on the ground, Osain works inside a turtle shell. Obatala punished Turtle for being a chatty gossip."

In the Regla Lucumí, it is not necessarily prepared by a *babalawo*. An *osainista* (herbalist), who might not be *Asentado*, is almost always a son of Changó, since Changó was the first owner of one of these prodigious gourds.

Tá R. assures me, "An *mpaka*, a horn that's prepared well like my Ngomba-sueto, can talk like Gurufinda . . . It was loaded with critters that talk, and it had brains. I'd put it next to my ear . . . Ay! My Gombe-sueto would sing to me!"

The Owner of Plants also lives in a stone, accompanied by two other stones. The stone is found in *el monte*, in the river, or on a hill. "And it doesn't go to the cemetery" in the Regla Lucumí. "The Lucumí Osain does not have a *muerto* inside."

In conclusion, Osain is of the utmost importance in all Lucumí rituals. "Without making Osain, you can't make *Santo*. Without Osain, there's no work"—magic. "Without Osain, there's no remedy"—medicine.

"As the distributor of the *ewe* of each orisa," Oluwo Ewe provides each ritual with the ewe that corresponds to each deity, as well as the most crucial ones used to make the *omiero* for initiations—the holy regenerative water used in all the consecrations in the Regla de Ocha, which is used "to wash and make *Santo*."

Omiero, the supreme cleansing liquid, is made with "water from heaven" (rainwater, *oyouro*), river water, and seawater. Water collected every year on the feast day of San Juan, at daybreak on Good Friday, and daybreak on Easter Saturday are added, as well as holy water from the church, aguardiente, bee honey, palm oil, cocoa butter, *cascarilla* [chalk made from egg shells], guinea pepper, *osu*, *eru*, and *obi kola*. Also, a burning coal is wrapped in a fresh malanga leaf and dropped into it.

The powers and vitality of the plants are concentrated in this very sacred liquid, even though it has a bad odor and an even worse taste. It is used to purify and invigorate, and it can be said that it deifies *iyawos* and neophytes during their first seven days of initiation and seclusion in the temple.

"*Omiero* is used to wash and sanctify everything: the *otan*, the necklaces, the cowrie shells, the tools." "Making Osain" involves the *santeras* responsible for this process preparing the sacramental plants, grouping them, and ripping and mashing them.

The herbalist—"one who has Osain" and has expert knowledge of plants—goes to gather them on the order of a *babalawo*, who will give them his *ache* or blessing. In Havana, they believe "the correct thing is for the *babalawo* to go and get them himself in person."

The *osainista* receives a fee of $1.05, "the *derecho* of the Ewe." The *babalawo* receives $3.15 for blessing them. The "basket bearers"—Yeya calls them *naseros*—who carry the basket to the temple or house of the *Santo* also receive compensation.

The *babalawo* hands over the plants to the first godmother or *iyare*, the owner of the *Santo* that the neophyte will receive. The plants are essential to making Osain for the great ceremony. First, they are presented to Olorun and receive an offering of coconut. They are then placed in two large bundles on a straw mat in the same room where all of the rituals, cleansings, and sacrifices of the *Asiento* will take place. The *babalawo* takes a bunch in each hand and presents them to the orishas, then he chews a leaf that he is holding in his mouth and spits on them to give them his *ache*, the gift of Orula. "Their *ache* is in the saliva."

The principal leaves of each Orisha should be there—a minimum of twenty-one in total, which get all mixed up.

A number of basins painted with the emblematic colors of each *santo* are placed along the edge of the straw mat.

The *iyalocha* who is youngest in *Santo* (the one who has been initiated the fewest years) kneels down. Using both hands, she receives two bunches of leaves from the Oriate, a *babalocha* who sits in the middle of the straw mat and directs the ritual. The *iyalocha* who is receiving the plants and kneeling then hands over the bunches, one after another, to the other *iyalochas*.

With the bunches in their hands, the *iyalochas* recite "moyuba" or "kinkamache." That is, they solicit permission—from Olodumare, God, the ancestors, the elders, and godparents, both living and dead—to undertake the work of shredding or crushing the *ewe*. They ask for their blessing.

"Moyuba Olodumare loguo Ikú embelese Olodumare. Moyuba ibae baye tonu," etc. Or, "Iba Baba, iba yeye. Iba Eshu Alagwana. Iba ile apoko yeru. Iba ita meta bara bidi ya kata. Kinkamache yoru mi kinkamache Baba mi. Kinkamache iyami, kinkamache oyubona, kinkamache mi oribobo, alaba kinkamache oru koma de le iba mi che iba mi omo ana kini, ana iba, iba mi, eba eyo, iba mi kachocho."

As the plants are passed from one pair of hands to another, they gather the blessings and the *ache* of all the *santeras* present. Once the *iyalochas* each have the bunches of plants corresponding to them, they sit on chairs (*apotie, akua tau ko*, as the elders would call them) or small stools, then proceed to rip them and toss them in the clay pots, each plant in the pot marked with the color of their Orisha.

When all of the plants have been distributed, the *iyare* and her assistant or second godmother (*Oyubona*) lift the straw mat from either end and very carefully let the residual leaves and fibers drop into the clay pots, which were already blessed by the *babalawo* and remained on the mat.

Sometimes, the *iyare* and the *oyubona* leave the room as the *santeras* begin breaking apart and crushing the plants and the *oriate* begins the singing that accompanies this ritual, to which everyone responds as a chorus. There are sixteen, seventeen, or twenty-one prayers to Osain.

That is, they perform *oro*, a call to the Orisa by means of these songs.

They begin by singing for Elegua and finish by singing to the Ibeyi, the Twin Santos.

In order to not make a mistake, the *oriate* draws a line with chalk on the floor after every *ankori*, thereby keeping track of the number and order of songs or *ankori*. (The prayers are called *suyeres*.)

Once the plants have all been broken apart and piled up, and after they have received the blessing of all the *iyalochas* (culminating with those of the *iyare* and *oyubona*), two *iyalochas* pour water into the clay pots, one after the other. Singing the corresponding songs, they wash the *otanes* or "stones of the orishas" in the following order: Elegua, Ogun, and Ochosi; Changó; Obatala; Oya; Yemaya; and Oshun.[55] The other Orishas that are not installed directly are received later. They will be washed and consecrated—it is often said that "they are baptized"—separately with their own plants. Not a single leaf should fall on the ground: "They're blessed. As they crush the

---

55 DF-N: Details have been edited in keeping with widely agreed-upon ritual norms. See Cabrera ([1954] 1992, 107–8).

leaves, the *santeras* are continually praying for health for everyone, luck, prosperity, strength."

Finally, the plants and water from all of the clay pots are gathered in a large basin. During seven consecutive days, the *oyubona* will use them to bathe the *iyawo*—the newborn in Ocha, the spouse of the *santo*[56]—and give them three sips of it to drink every morning.

Nothing compares to the vital potency of *omiero*. Everyone who attends this ceremony—the *aberi kula, eleyos, bobo kaleno, omolei*, etc.—and salutes the new *Santo* is allowed to drink it for their own well-being, if they like. With only rare exceptions, everyone hurries to do so, even if they need to hold their nose as they bravely rush a drink of the nauseating panacea, whose stench is due to the decayed plants and blood. There is no doubt about its marvelous effects on the health of the *asentado* [initiate], and even their beauty. "*Iyawos* come out of the *Asiento* with their skin smooth, fresh, and lovely. *Omiero* rejuvenates."

The uninitiated layperson—*aberi kula*—does not have access to the making of Osain, nor should we even risk sneaking a curious glance through a door, which might be left half open out of carelessness, into that room where an animated group of women sings and moves their hands quickly as they crush piles of leaves. In some temples, all of the plants—including, necessarily, those with thorns and barbs—are pounded in a mortar. "That pulls out more of the plants' goodness." Only *iyalochas* can pour water or shred the sacramental plants. To carry out this first ritual of the *kari ocha*, it would be sufficient to have two *iyas* pouring water and seven others to rip leaves and toss them in the seven clay pots. But many more attend in order to sing, lend their *ache*, and earn a little money. The presence of many *santeras*—the influence or emanation of their respective Eledas, Angels, or *orisas*—is always highly beneficial and stimulating for the development of any ritual: "More *ache* is accumulated."

A complete Osain to prepare the *omiero* for an *Asiento* is composed primarily of plants, but they cannot do without leaves from trees that have a very close relationship to the deities that the *iyawo* is receiving.

Omiero for a *medio* (partial) *Asiento* is "a necessarily silent ceremony," because drums do not intervene, and it is officiated exclusively by *iyalo-*

---

56   DF-N: Although Cabrera uses *esposo* (meaning husband), *iyawo* literally means "wife," implying a gendered, hierarchical relationship in which the initiate is subordinate to the orisha in a way that is analogous to how a wife might be considered subordinate to a husband. Cabrera's use of gender in the anecdotal narrative of "making Osain" during an initiation supposes that all of the priests are female except for the *babalawo, oriate*, and *iyawo*—in other words, her description of the ritual hierarchy and ritual labor is skewed rather severely along gender lines.

chas.[57] It consists of a sacrifice to the *Santos*, washing the head and body of the devotee with *omiero*, and consecrating an *orisha-eleke* (*añale*),[58] the symbolic necklace of their *orisa* that should be accompanied by the *eleke* of another three orishas. (This ritual is like a "marriage engagement," a first step forward into the world of the sacred. It is carried out to restore the health of a sick person—both principles of life come together in the *omiero*—or to calm the impatience of an orisha who demands their *omo* enter into religious life immediately.)

Omiero is used to consecrate or "baptize" the stones in which the orisha are venerated, and the cowrie shells belonging to each one. They are washed after receiving sacrifices—"after they have eaten"—and remain submerged in blood for several hours.[59]

Those belonging to Elegua are washed with three plants consecrated to him. Oshun with five. Ogun and Yemaya-Olokun with seven. Obatala with eight. Changó-Agayu with six. Oya with nine. Orisaoko with six. Baba, San Lázaro, with seventeen.

Omiero is used to season the food offered to the orishas: a little is always poured into the *jícaras* or tureens that serve as receptacles for the *ota-orishas* when they are going to receive blood from a sacrifice.

Omiero is sometimes still used to wash the cadavers of Mothers and Fathers of *Santo* [*olorisha*], their stones, tools, cowrie shells, and other property, "so their departure is pure." *Omiero* is inseparable from every ritual, all purification.

Because it is so difficult, or even impossible, to obtain 101 *eweko* (the different plants required for an *Asiento*), these are sometimes reduced to those considered most essential to each *santo*.

Beginning with those belonging to Elegua, these are the *ewe* and leaves of *igi* (trees) belonging to the seven orishas that are consecrated for the *iyawo*, a future Father or Mother of *Santo*.

Elegua: *grama de caballo, lengua de vaca, espartillo, abre camino, pastillo, yerba fina, guanina* or *yerba hedionda, itamo real, meloncillo, kioyo* (a species of basil with a wide leaf that the *osainista* Domingo Hernández only knows by its African name), *piñón criollo,* and *yamao.*

---

57 DF-N: The absence of drums does not imply lack of music, much less "silence."

58 DF-N: The original refers to *áñale*, also known as *iñale*. In *Anagó*, Cabrera defines *iñale* as "the leg[s], head, and mesentery of the victims—animals and birds—of a sacrifice. It is placed all together before the orisha and remains exposed several hours" ([1957] 1986, 168).

59 DF-N: According to virtually any ritual specialist, this paragraph and the next are rife with errors.

Ogun and Ochosi: *caña santa, pata de gallina, yerba de la sangre, mora, pegojo. Hueso de gallo. Adormidera* or *siempre viva. Anamú. Romerillo. Rompezaragüey, albahaca morada, palo manajú,* and *ébano.*

Changó and Agayu: *bledo punzó, atipolá* or *moco de pavo, baría, platanillo de Cuba, zarzaparrilla, paraíso, álamo, jobo.*

Oya: *yerba garro, guasimilla, baría, mazorquilla, yuca, ciruela, palo caja, cabo de hacha.*

Yemaya and Oshun: *lechuguilla, yerba añil, verbena, prodigiosa, paragüitas* or *quita solito, flor de agua, helecho, berro, lechuga, yerba buena, albahaca morada, guamá, guásima, botón de oro, yerba de la niña, coate* or *colonia, marilope, panetela, huevo de gallo, helecho de río, guacamaya, yerba mora, corazón de paloma, cucaracha, diez del día, orozú, palo canela.*

Obatala: *bledo de clavo, sauco, campana, carquesa, algodón, aguinaldo blanco, higuereta, almendro, guanábana, jagua blanca.*

Bejucos (vines) are not included in *omiero*—not even the ones that are well known, such as *guaco, tocino, peonía* (although the seed from it is included), *bejuco marrullero* (which belongs to Ogun), *tripa de jutía, verraco, batalla, trabea, enredadera coralillo* (which belongs to Oshun), nor *nígua* (which belongs to Obatala). In effect, vines "entangle, and they can tangle up someone's luck." Only leaves from trees and shrubs are used. *Santos* with similar temperaments—Elegua, Ogun, Ochosi—"lend each other their plants," and the sisters Oshun and Yemaya use more or less the same ones.

The *ewe* of Babalu Ayé—the Arará say *amasi* instead of *ewe*—are never mixed with those of any other *santo*, and they are collected and used exclusively for his rituals.[60] They are his exclusive property: the bitter *cundiamor, zargazo, zazafrá, piñón botijo, caisimón, bejuco ubí, tapa-camino, carabalí, yaya,* and *tengue.*

Some *santos* need fewer plants than others.

Let us examine a list of the *ewe* most commonly and continuously employed by *iyalochas* and *babalochas* in their *omieros* and rituals with their equivalent Lucumí names:[61]

---

60 DF-N: In Cuban Arará traditions (and Brazilian Candomblé traditions), *amasi* refers more properly to the ritual elixir; it is analogous to *omiero* (not *ewe*). I am grateful to Martin Tsang for pointing out this significant detail—one of many of Cabrera's relatively oblique references to Arará traditions. See Sogbossi (1998).

61 DF-N: This condensed, Lucumí-specific list of plants is a natural complement to the detailed botanical encyclopedia entries in the last section of this book.

Platanillo	Olubo, Ewe Afere, Oluro, Ewe Bikan
Lirio blanco, Bayoneta, Gloriosa	Peregun fun fun, Osumare itana fun
Zarzaparilla	Ateke edin, Ewe ategue, Biedu
Flor de agua	Ewe oyouro
Bledo	Ewe tete
Tostón	Atipola, Atinkuala
Meloncillo	Ewe oni bara
Helecho de río	Ewe Imo, Imo Oshun
Berro	Ewe igere, Yeye peregun
Cordobán, Zapatón	Ewe jere gun, Peregun tupa, Peregun puppua
Yerba de la niña	Ewe ñani, Ewe ñeñe
Maravilla	Ewe kua, Auema
Sanguinaria	Ewe Eye
Poleo	Ewe oki kan
Guanima	Ewe yaaso, Oyeun, Oyeusa
Yerba more	Ewe atore, Podu
Malanguilla	Ewe koko
Lino de río	Ewe eleri lodo
Serraja	Olure
Malanga	Ewe ikoku, Chika
Siempre viva, Prodigiosa	Ewe dud, Edudu
San Diego	Ewe yeye
Añil	Ewe nyi
Campana	Ewe ogogo
Granada	Yayeku, Chimini-chimini
Zargaso	Eprimocho
Zarza	Ewe tiya
Ortiguilla	Ewe eguene

Patico	Ewe yokole
Peonia	Eguereyeye
Colonia, Coate	Ewe oburo
Rompe zaragüey	Ewe tabate, Han
Adormidera, Vergonzosa	Ewe erukumu
Albahaca mora (wide leaf)	Ewe fini adache
Albahaca menuda	Ewe kini kini, Epiriki ningini
Canutillo	Ewe karodi, Kotonembo, Ewe ibakua mimokui
Farolillo	Ewebo, Ewe ona
Verdolaga	Ewe ekisan
Algodon	Ewe keoli, Ewe Ou
Alambrillo	Ochibata
Sabe lección, Mastuerzo	Ewe chini-chini, Ewe Tan
Carquesa	Ewe okikan, Eyu ovo
Serraja	Olube, Eguene, Ewe taue
Hierba fina	Ewe amo
Cundiamor	Ewe san san
Pata de gallina	Ewe eran, Oklepuese
Yerba hedionda	Ewe hara-hara, Ayegue
Cortadera	Ewe guna
Malva té	Ewe dubue, Laibo
Nelumbio	Chibata
Frescura	Ewe ru matan
Verdolaga de España	Ewe Euro
Ruda cimarrona	Ewe atopa kun
Cardo santo	Ika agogo
Boniato	Kukundu kuenden, Kukuduku
Anis	Ewe aye

Calabaza	Elegede
Yuca	Bagudan
Ñame	Ichu, Osura
Salvia	Ewe uro
Anón	Inabiri
Yagruma	Ogun gun, Ogu, Loro, Lara
Jía	Erere, Ebere
Álamo	Ofa, Abaila
Caimito	Osam, Ogoe, fuse, ayeko fole
Güira	Ague, Egwa
Ceiba	Iroko, Elueko, Araguo, Araba, Iroko tere, Iroko-Awo
Palma	Sefidiye, Ope
Agarrobo	Afoma
Almendro	Abusi
Mango	Orombeye
Goma francesa	Gogo
Fruta bomba, Papaya	Ibepe, Ibekue
Piñón	Obutuye, Olobo tuyo
Caoba	Roko, Ayan
Jobo	Erika, Igi Waakika, Aba
Cerezo	Igi Eyo
Palo caja	Igi Bire
Ayúa	Igi Oro
Jagüey	Igi igwa, Igi oke
Aguacate	Okutara itobi
Cedro	Opepe

THE TRIBUTE TO THE OWNER OF EL MONTE

Black people humanize everything around them, even the most insignificant things that might appear inanimate.[1] (They only appear that way!) They conceive the orishas or gods—personal, supernatural, and omnipresent—in their own image and likeness. *A su más pobre semejanza.*[2] They are the same in humans and in the deities whose protection they implore: the deity and the human have the same appetites and needs. What pleases the Black person produces the same material satisfaction in a god or a spirit. The following is the agreed obligatory payment, the most agreeable offering to the incarnation of *el monte* that is the god Osain (and, in general, for all of the other gods of *el monte* who are similar to Osain): a mouthful of aguardiente, the "malafo mamputo" or "oti," which they love so much "and was regarded so highly in all of Guinea"; a cigar; and some coins.

---

1   DF-N: In the chapter title, the word *Tributo* (Tribute) contains two related meanings in both English and Spanish: on one hand, praise, honor, and recognition; on the other, payment and/or offering, akin to an honorarium.

     In the first sentence, Cabrera's original use of the Spanish term *negros* (translated as "black people") seems most akin to the archaic English term *Negroes*, especially in light of the anachronistic rhetoric of this brief chapter.

2   DF-N: The phrase is ambiguous. It might be translated literally as "In their (own) (poorest/most meager) (likeness/image)."

As we already know, everyone—every herbalist or *odusain*, godchild of an *iyalocha*, assistant in a *casa de Santo*, or *babalawo* entrusted with collecting the ritual plants for an initiation and giving them "ache" (consecrating them)—"salutes and pays tribute to the Owner of Ewe, the plants, Egun, and all of the plants and trees on the earth. This is the first thing they do when they enter a *monte* or thicket."

"Osain aggeniye lese koyulese meyilo kukuru kukuru tibi tibi agwadiyera Babami sagre kere gweye Osain ibu alona."

"Osain Agwaniye Osain akkara mayi, Osain akkara heri hekua hekua heri."

Likewise, the *palero* greets Nfindo or Anabuto out loud, respectfully requesting consent to take the leaf or root he needs: he explains the reasons for his visit clearly, and the goals he wants to achieve by means of the plants' power, which are almost always ambivalent in their efforts to cause good or harm, and which—"con licencia de Nsambi"—have been stipulated by their *nganga*. Now he can confess to Nfindo that he is "looking for a tree to turn the world upside down," or "to help an *mpangi*, a brother." This is a point that the Owner of El Monte could care less about. He will give his plants with their powerful properties—terrible or beneficial—if the sorcerer pays his *derecho*. Even so, J. de R. believes that—following courteous greetings, but before paying Nfindo—it is beneficial to "specify what will be done with the trees and plants that you'll take, because El Monte should understand clearly what you want in order to facilitate the work. After all, that's why you pay."

Because his *nganga* is mixed—good, bad, or very bad, as needed—this is the recitation with which S.B. customarily addresses it:

"Buenos días pa tó basura monte. With your permission, and God's, and the Holy Virgin's, and with the permission of Tata Fumbe, I'm here looking for good and bad. Everybody wants to live under the peace of the sun that shines for everybody, and holy Santa Bárbara. Here, Father. I'm giving you your candle, your *malafo*, your *nsungu*, your *simbo*—take a good look at your *simbo* . . . Now I've paid you what I owe you: Father, look closely and see that I've paid, so I can gather plants."

The metal tribute—usually a *real* and a half ("if possible"), aguardiente, and tobacco—is placed next to the first tree the *ngangulero* comes across when they enter *el monte*, or whichever one they like best. This tree "gets paid on behalf of them all," "representing the other *nkuni* or *musi*" (trees). Once this basic requirement has been met ("out of courtesy and obligation"), the Taita *nganga* has the right and freedom to cut as many as he needs. "Without paying, you don't take a single fiber. Nifinda"—or Osain—"does not empower a tree that you haven't paid for, so that tree will be of no use to you. It is not authorized." The *conciente* [sic; conscientious] *palero* should say, "I paid, *bukota*. I gave to *musi*, under the tree."

"Girl, when I go to Nfindo, or when I go to *munanseke*"—the savanna—"I take my hat off, kneel down there, and I say good morning, and I talk. I light a candle, *echa simbo*. After I've paid, El Monte gives me permission."

To enter *el monte* or a cemetery, hat in hand, the *palero* or *mayombero* should toss a grain of corn and a *centavo* coin at each corner—"paying before entering"—then identify themselves: "Ceiba is my mother. Jagüey Macho is my father. Campo Santo is my Godmother." El Monte recognizes someone who has been initiated in its mysteries, "a child," and smooths the way over all obstacles.

The elders recite an Our Father ("but in Congo, so *el monte* understands it better"), which opens the doors to the bush or the cemetery.

This prayer is also recited—"*ngandala kufua*, from the heart"—at cross-roads, "at Cuatro Vientos, where all of the Santos and *muertos* go by, which might be an even sadder and more dangerous place to talk with the *fuiri* than the cemetery itself":

> *Tendundu Kipungule*
> *Nani masongo silabansa*
> *Sese madie silabansa*
>
> *Sese madie silanbanka*
> *Bika dioko bika ndiambe*
> *Sese madie, sese madie.*

The *gangulero*—or, as Lara calls them, the Sudika Mabi—who wants to make a *nganga* or carry out some other "work" is obligated to go to a *monte firme* to cut the wood he needs on the feast day of San Juan or Easter Saturday, then add a chicken, incidentally, to the usual tribute.

One enters *el monte* before the sun rises, a time of the day N. calls *dikolombo Dikuana*. Juan Lara calls it Kuma Kiaku. While they perform their greetings, they offer aguardiente and tobacco smoke, and they sing like one old *mayombero* who allowed me to write down his prayer:

Kasima yere	*Dame sombra palo Cuaba*
Kasimbango	*Dame sombra palo Yaba*
Yo salí de mi casa	*Dame sombra palo Caja*
Kasimbango	*Dame sombra palo Tengue*
Yo salí de mi tierra	*Dame sombre palo Grayúa*
Kasimbango	*Dame sombra palo Wakibango*
Yo vengo a buscá . . .	*Dame sombra palo Caballero*
Dame sombra Ceibita	*Yo vine a bucá . . .*
Ceiba da yo sombra	*Tengue, yaya, etc.*

The *palero* finishes their work before twelve noon. They begin gathering *vititi* at sunrise and during the waxing moon. "When they're accompanied by the stars."

Trees have particularly strong virtues at sunrise, in the light of dawn. "At twelve noon, at six o'clock in the evening, and at midnight, they're better for doing harm and they have bad *mfumbi*." In general, trees are cut and plants are pulled before sunrise and sunset. "The morning is the good energy."

"At night, the leaves are sleeping, and tree sleeps like people, so they shouldn't be woken up. Plants that are pulled at night when they're asleep are ineffective." ("No, the ones that go to sleep early shouldn't be woken up.")

When it is not possible to pay El Monte with money, it accepts the equivalent in grains of corn, *chiche aguado*. That is what Juan X.—who is distinguished by his bad temper—declares: "El Monte prefers tobacco and aguardiente. Corn is its money, and I don't give it my loose change."

The elders like to repeat that, in the past, *masango* or *aguado*—corn— regularly served in place of money if someone was unable to pay the "derecho" for a consultation with a *babalawo* or a Padre *nganga*:

> If you were going to consult with the *mayombero*, the *babalawo*, or the *mamalocha* when you were broke, indigent, then you'd put three or five little grains of corn at the foot of the Santo, one of them broken in half, in place of the consultation costs (*peso cinco*). If you had to make *ebo*? In those situations, the *santero* kept a reserve of bird heads and feathers, which were equivalent to what the person couldn't afford at that moment. And because the *ebo* was done for their own progress, he would pay what he owed later, when the Santo had helped him out of his hardship. These days, nobody does any of that. Santería is robbery. All is lost. There's no heart."

A *santera* in her fifties agrees: "The old ladies used to make sacrifices . . . Since I'm from the old school, I have to make sacrifices all the time. The *Santo* is there to help the needy."

In short, not a single branch or leaf is collected without depositing at least three symbolic grains of corn that El Monte—Osain or Gurufinda—will accept.

Since it is not the *santero* who pockets the *derecho*, this form of payment— which does not prevent indigent people from finding salvation—is very common. The needy person thereby avoids committing a crime (theft) that the Owner of the plants would otherwise punish by purging the magical or medicinal properties from plants they have gathered.

"Every plant has an owner that is watching. They all have their mysteries and their hangups," and Black people imbue all of them with supernatural qualities. The *osainista* or herbalist should know the peculiarities and "vagaries" of plants, the "personality" or manner of each one. Their ... psychology. (Just as they should know the "muninfuise or soyanga," the critters and animals that work with plants and the *nganga*.) Some plants and trees are more sensitive, "touchier" and more difficult than others.

For example, the Don Chaicho will stab anyone who does not salute it with exaggerated courtesy. Others need certain specific prayers and a minimum payment of a *real* and a half. The Palo Tocino becomes strangely agitated when someone goes near it, "grumbling" and arousing intense fear. If its branches incline toward a man who has come to cut off a splinter of wood or a few leaves, the man should stay still. The tree will embrace them. But when it "releases its arms"—that is, when the branches of the Palo Tocino move away—it is imperative to run away ... Other plants should never be mentioned out loud. They escape, slipping away, "making a run for it," or they become invisible. "Some plants enjoy mocking you." One herbalist lamented an indiscretion that made him come back from the country empty-handed. He innocently told his wife that he was going out to collect *baría*, a plant for Changó. He knew where it was growing abundantly, but on that occasion, he did not see any. Finally, tired from looking for the plant and about to return home, he found one and pulled it. On the way back to his house, he realized that "the plant had tricked him." The plant in his hands was not the *baría* that he needed so much. "It was bothered by hearing its name spoken, so it punished him." And the punishment was severe: the *baría* did not show itself to him in any "monte" or allow itself to be pulled for a long time.

Palo guachinango (which is named that way because it is so deceptive) and *cuaba* are two excellent trees for protective amulets, and we will need to discuss them further below. They need to be tricked and seized, practically by surprise, after much contemplation and pampering. Of course, they should not be named beforehand, not even by the slightest allusion ...

Palo jurubana, whose powers make it very precious, "looks like a human body," and it is very easily frightened. The sorcerer needs to win it over with loving care. With it, you can get anything you want. If a woman rejects the amorous advances of a man, he will overcome her resistance by soliciting the help of the *jurubana*, "los Siete Vicios" [the Seven Vices]. A person, who had previously flatly refused to give what was asked of them, will spontaneously give much more than was asked, without even needing to repeat the original request. A woman who had rejected a suitor will suddenly feel the most violent, unexpected passion. A businessman will gain every advantage he desires.

Bejuco Madrina—Vichichi Nfinda, or *Traba Camino*—is a small vine, and "it's one of the first things you need to put in a *nganga*." It is fearsome if it is stepped on absentmindedly. It enchants people, making them get lost in *el monte*, preventing the herbalist from finding their way out easily, and keeping them in an unexpected labyrinth for hours.

Every *palero* has been the victim of this mischievous vine, or some other plant's ill-disposed mockery.

Every tree and plant has its own prayer and its own propitious time of day. Some are cut in the morning or in the afternoon, others at night, and they are not all collected in the same way. Some very sacred plants need to be approached in the nude, and when it is time to walk away, you should walk backward so as to not turn your back on them. Others cannot be cut without the *palero* first making an incision in their own skin and letting a few drops of their blood fall on the roots. Some cannot be touched by women, while others require that even the smallest branch be removed exclusively by the hands of a virgin.

In short, the *Monte*—like the cemetery—must be paid. Without this payment, one cannot make a *nganga* or an Osain.

Felipe says, "The man who knows the laws of *el monte* can cut a tree in the middle of the darkest night. They feel their way along, dragging themselves through the dark, and the *palo* lights their way."

5

HOW TO PREPARE
A NGANGA

HOW TO PREPARE A NGANGA. THE BOUMBA.

HOW TO PREPARE A ZARABANDA. LA SANTÍSIMA PIEDRA

IMÁN [THE SACRED LODESTONE]. LA PIEDRA INDIA.

᠅

"Creoles inherited a trick from Angola that lets us take control of a dead person and make them our partner," Baró says.

"The *muerto* makes a pact with the living and follows all the living person's orders." "*Nganga* means *muerto*, spirit." "*Nganga* is the same thing as *Nkiso*, *Briyumba*, a spirit from the other world." "Mystery." "And for a man to be a real sorcerer, whether good or bad, Nganga Nsambi or Nganga Ndoki, and do the things that sorcerers do, they need to go to *el monte* and the cemetery. They need to be the owner of a *nganga*, a *muerto*." And they should—above all else—"know how to call them," invoke them. The remains are in the cemetery, and the spirit of the person who has become disembodied (as the spiritists say) goes to *el monte*, to the trees. The cemetery and *el monte* are equivalent and complimentary: in one and the other, you find the *fumbis* and forces that will act as invisible executors of the work— good or bad—undertaken by sorcerers. The *nganga* can be inherited or received from a godfather after a neophyte has been "scratched" (initiated) following several years of apprenticeship. It is constructed, "mounted" or "loaded" by a sorcerer, "with *muerto*, *kiyumba*, sticks from *el monte*, *nfita* (vines) or *bikanda* (herbs), earth, and animals." By association, the names *nganga*, *nkisi*, or *nkiso* are given to receptacles containing the supernatural forces they serve, "concentrated" in the bones, wood, plants, earth, stones, and animals. "The spirit comes as soon as it is called" into this jumble of diverse materials. "It's alive, right there!" Every *nganga* also contains a *matari* (stone)—preferably a thunder stone—which is given a blood offering separately, then "drinks blood again with all the rest of it."

Let us listen to Baró, owner of the *nganga* Palo Monte Siete Campanas Vira Mundo Camposanto a la Medianoche, who tells us how to "make a *nganga*." The procedure—"what's done in *el monte*"—should take place during a new moon or a full moon. Certainly not during a waning moon, "when everything tends toward death" in nature and vital energies are fundamentally diminished "while the moon is declining." "When the moon is dying, all of us are also in mortal danger." For the sake of my own well-being, Adriana Y. warns me that one should never cross a river that is illuminated by the light of a waning moon. And Oddedei said, "Ochukwa, the moon, has power, and one should proceed with caution during certain particular moments. When it's drying out. The moon shares tendencies with the *muertos*. The moon is a very powerful being. She won a dispute with the sun: it's because of her that the sun has no children." (The stars are the moon's children.) "The Congo said the Earth was the wife of the Sun, Tángu. The Moon, Ngunda, made a pact with the Earth to save her children, since the Sun would burn them during the day. The Moon gave her dew. When night fell, while the Sun slept, the Earth was refreshed. That way, its fruit stopped withering."

And according to the Lucumí: Pura says,

The sun and the moon were married, and they had many children. When the males started growing up, they said to each other, "Let's go see where father goes every day." And they followed him.

But when the sun looked back and saw a crowd of little suns following him, all of them shining so beautifully, he got angry. He was jealous, like a rooster, and he wanted to punish them. The boys ran away and, since they didn't know the way back, they stumbled over each other, fell in the ocean, and drowned.

Because the females—Irawo—never went out without their mother, they were fine. The stars accompany the moon as it moves around the sky at night. The sun, who had lost his sons in that fit of rage, always travels alone . . .

But one should not be so scared of all moons, because not all of them are as harmful as the waning moon, Ochukwa Aro. "That's where the Creoles' fear comes from, because they're confused, and they attribute all evil to it. The bad one, the one that is with Ikú, is the waning moon. The waxing moon, Osure, and the full moon, Ochukwaguamuko, are good. You salute the new moon by making the sign of the cross, greeting it like the sun who has awakened, and you ask for her blessing."

My old informant Omi-Tomi invariably salutes the new moon by making the sign of the cross and uttering this prayer, which she teaches to her grandchildren and close family:

"New moon, I salute you. Give me health and give the world peace. Let there be no war, no blood, and no illness." She shows it a one cent coin and closes by saying, "May I, my family, my friends, and my enemies never be without bread." She recites an Our Father, three Hail Marys, and a Glory Be to the Father (Gloria Padre).

Many are content telling the new moon, "Good evening, Nene, or Nana."

But in Matanzas, where traditions are conserved in a purer form than Havana, she is still saluted with this song:

Ochukwa, madeni, Ochukwa made rawo
Ochukwa, madeni, Ochukwa made rawo
Solode guinyi guinyi eko eko.

Or, the way the Yobas taught it:[1]

Ochukwa, imabere imawo
Imawo ima were.

After forty or forty-one days, newborn children were presented to the new moon. And they would bounce them around, tossing the baby up in the air a few times. It's also a custom in my family, the way they taught us, to take the child out of the house for the first time after forty days. The person carrying them should be educated and proper, so the child picks up good manners that day, the good qualities of that person.

Mercedes, one of my aunts, wanted to take my first son outside, but my grandmother forbade it, because Mercedes had a very bad temper and she wasn't refined. I took him out myself.

---

1   DF-N: Yoba is an analog of Yoruba; in this context, it is most likely synonymous with the Ọ̀yọ́ Empire.

The elders, accompanied by a group of small children, relatives, and neighbors, sing to the new moon: "Barachu mambela." And the children respond: "Ochukwa, Ochukwa."

While the children salute Ochukwa, they also salute Bara—Elegua Bara Eshu—and Oshun with the very same words. "The moon deserves a great deal of respect, and we ask for its blessing, like we ask for the sun's blessing. Many beseech it by offering it a plate full of milk, which is left outside so she can drink it. But the milk is drunk by a snake, which has a very close relationship to the moon." ("And with the twins.")

"The moon is the godmother of sorcerers."

For her part, Amalia B. adds, "You can see clearly that everything gets weaker when the moon gets empty and shrinks. Children born during the waxing moon grow a lot. They'll be tall. The ones born during a full moon are strong, like those born in a leap year, and they never suffer from any epidemic. Births during the waning moon are slow: the child is delayed in being born, and they'll be a small thing, short in stature, and sickly."[2] "That's why Congo *de nación* [from the nation, from Africa] used to say the moon is death according to its stages: *muna lunguva nfuiri yu pati mani patinguei musi-kuenda ntoto nani kinanfuiri munalungo kuna nsambia nsambianpungo*. When the moon dies, they would try to cure themselves by relying on the grace of the sun, which illuminates." "When it is red, it is bad. It is bloody. It takes over people's heads. If a man catches that cold fire in his sleep, he's liable to commit a crime."

Felipe explains, "The moon, which we call *gunda* in Congo, is a primary celestial body for the *mayombero*, who needs it for his *nganga* like he needs the power of the sun and the stars. In some, like the one known as Reflejo-Luna, the power of the moon is concentrated, like it would be during the new moon. They work with the moon, the snake, and the river."

Others harness the power of a *lucero* [star].

For example, in Siete Estrellas:

It's Madre de Agua, and it's so strong that, when it mounts, it makes the eyes of their *caballo* (horse, possession mount) roll back in their head. You can't see their pupils, and they walk around from one side to the other like that, without stumbling. Maybe that's why Siete Estrellas and Siete Sayas have few *caballos* [horses]. They only come every once in a while. It is a *prenda* from Mumboma and from Luanda. When it is fed, the *padre* and *mayordomo* distance themselves twenty-four paces away to recite their

2   LC: Emaciated, weak, small.

prayers. It is not given a *fiesta* at home, but rather in *el monte*. It wants the sky as its ceiling . . . because stars come down to this *prenda*.[3]

There's a time of night when it's left alone, because the stars come down to it. When you see a bright splendor, it's the star going to the *nganga*. Then the *padre* and the *mayordomo* pick it up with a white cloth and seal the cauldron. It's so difficult for a Creole to control the stars!

Whoever sees this operation performed in the middle of *el monte* is stunned when the star comes down from the sky.

A sorcerer takes control of the spirit of a *muerto* by seizing their bones. The soul remains attached to the body: "They go looking for their own," as long as their remains exist. And the spiritual essence of the deceased—"their intelligence"—is found in the cranium, the *kiyumba*, which is most precious to a sorcerer. To enter into a relationship with a *muerto*, it is sufficient to possess a phalange from a little finger or any part of the skeleton, a fragment that represents and "holds the value" of the whole body. "That is enough to own them." "The bone is kept as a support for the spirit. (The *muerto* has a fondness for its remains.) And the *muerto* can also be embedded in the stone."

The *mayombero* who wants to construct a *nganga* for themselves or one of their godchildren goes to the cemetery with their *mayordomo* or assistant and the godchild in question, whom they themselves have already scratched. (It is called scratching because a neophyte in Palo-Monte—a future *ngangulero*, whether male or female, in the act of becoming part of the temple, becoming a child, "the body of the Nganga"—has small, shallow crosses drawn into their skin with a razor or knife on either side of their chest and on each of their shoulder blades.

Once they are in the cemetery, the *padre* spills aguardiente in the form of a cross over a grave. They will take—"if and when it's possible"—the head (the *kiyumba* of a cadaver, "with the brain, where *fumbi* thinks"), fingers and toes, ribs, and "shin bones, so they run." They wrap the remains in black cloth and return home to "make a pact with the *muerto*," because it is difficult to do so in the cemetery. There, at home, the *padre nganga* lays down on the floor. The *mayordomo* covers him with a sheet, and as the *padre* lies on the floor—along with the remains—between four lit candles, the *mayordomo* invokes the spirit to possess the *padre* and speak. They try to ask the *fumbi* if it is willing to stay with them: customarily, the spirit responds through gunpowder. The *mayordomo* places seven

---

3   DF-N: A few literal translations of the various *ngangas'* names in this passage: Reflejo-Luna (Moon-Reflection, Moon-Mirror, or Shining-Moon); Siete Estrellas (Seven Stars); Madre de Agua (Water Mother or Mother of Water); and Siete Sayas (Seven Scarves or Seven Whips).

small mounds of gunpowder—*fula*—on both the back of the *ngangulero*, the blade of a machete, or a wood board. If these mounds explode together, the *muerto* has definitely accepted the pact: they agree to everything the sorcerer has proposed. They are at their service. These pacts should not be entered into with more than one *muerto*. Nor, according to an experienced *mayordomo*, should they include earth from other graves, which leads to subsequent confusion and misfortune. "If there are various *muertos* in the cauldron, one wants to work, but the others don't. They argue, they have misunderstandings, and they cause trouble!"

The sorcerer writes the first and last name of the deceased on a piece of paper. Along with coins—the price of the bargain, because the *muerto* practically sells itself to the sorcerer—he puts the paper in the bottom of a cauldron or pot. If the sorcerer does not know how to write, it is sufficient to utter the *muerto*'s name loudly and clearly. They deposit the bones and the earth from the grave. Later, using a razor or knife that has a white handle, an incision is made in the arm, allowing drops of blood from the wound to fall into the cauldron, "so the spirit drinks." But this is dangerous: the *muerto* can develop a taste for human blood; they might not be satisfied with the blood administered by its owner—necessarily in small doses—and could one day kill them. It is therefore more prudent and common to sacrifice a rooster. Sandoval belongs to the Regla de Ocha by virtue of a family tradition, and he had "medio Santo hecho" (that is, "washed"), a ritual that sometimes precedes the *Asiento* and is explained elsewhere in these pages. But he was also a *mayombero*. He had his *inkiso* carefully separated from his Lucumí *santos*, which are theoretically irreconcilable with the forces of Mayombe: "If he had been a son of Obatala, Las Mercedes or Dudua, they would not have allowed him to have a Mayombe *prenda*, much less use it." He explained its composition: "The fundamental thing is going to the cemetery. Take the head and bones of a dead person who was wicked. You offer a cigar and spray the grave with aguardiente. You start calling them near their feet, and you keep calling them until you get to the head, so when they stand up, they rise all at once, and strong. You propose a deal . . . If the spirit of that man wants to make an arrangement with you, you'll see the earth split open where the aguardiente was spilled. Then you take the bones. The man will follow you. Once you're back home, it's not unusual for the *muerto* to introduce themselves and talk"—through a medium. "Without fear, you make the deal. Shake his hand!" "The sorcerer always pours aguardiente in the form of a cross over the grave. They take the bones, *kiyumba*, arms, and legs. And they take four handfuls of earth: one handful from each of the parts where these parts were laid to rest; in other words, from the north, south, east, and west of the grave."

And another *taita* enumerates the *palos* that accompany the *fumbi*—"the spirit that resides in those bones"—in the cauldron, along with the other materials that usually accompany it.

And here, according to him, is "how you substantiate a good *Prenda*." First, you use plaster or ashes to draw a cross in the bottom of a new cauldron or pot, then you place five silver coins (*reales españoles de plata*) on top of it—one at the center, and the other four at each end of the cross:

I add plaster powder, candle wax, a little bit of ashes, and the butt of a cigar. Next to it, I put a piece of *Caña Brava* that's filled with seawater, sand, and quicksilver and sealed with wax. That's so the *Prenda* is always alive like quicksilver, moving like the ocean, which never rests, and so the *fumbi* can jump over the sea and go far away. A small, black male dog—whole and very well dried out—is placed over these powders in the middle of the cauldron, so it can smell and track someone's path. Next to the dog, a thunder stone (*piedra de rayo* or *centella*) that drinks blood before being placed inside. The jawbone of the *muerto* is put inside the head of the dog, and the bones from their fingers and toes are placed around it, then the kneecaps and ribs.

The brain, which has become a hard black paste, is put next to the head of the dog and the jawbone, from the lower jaw . . . the top one is no good. It doesn't work! Then we pour dirt from an anthill on top of it. The little pieces of *palos* are placed around it: *ceiba, cuaba, ayúa, tengue, cocuyo, garayúa, laurel, zaza, jocuma, amansa-guapo, guamá, guachinango, macagua, pino de la tierra, dagame, moruro, jagüey, palma, doncella, yaya,* and *yagrumo.* And vines: *batalla, jimagua, cocúmpeba, legaña de aura, nfinda,* etc. And herbs: *krúbana* (*sensitiva*), *canutillo, grama, barba de indio, escoba india,* etc. And over the sticks, handfuls of dirt from a termite mound. Once this *fundamento* has been created, you add *ají, pimienta* [pepper] and *ajo, jengibre* [ginger], *cebolla blanca,* canela [cinnamon], a shoot of *ruda, piñon,* and *anamú,* and you put them all over. The work concludes with the heads of Antillean nighthawk and woodpecker, vulture, bat, hummingbird, and *arriero* [a small species of mouse]. And critters: *jubo* [a small Cuban boa snake], *mancaperro* [a poisonous type of centipede], chameleon, etc. And for the *nganga* to be *cristiana*—good—a stream of holy water from the church or gathered in *el monte* on Holy Saturday. Or it can be left mixed. Neutral. *Judía* and *cristiana,* depending on what you need. When it does good, it's *cristiana.* When it knocks people down, it'll be *judía.* The *nganga* has now been made. Then I go back to the *camposanto*—Nfinda Kalunga—so it can spend three Fridays there buried in the cemetery. And later, we take it to Nfinda Anabutu—*el monte*—so it can spend another three Fridays under a ceiba or a *jagüey.* When the *Prenda* is raised up (that is, when the *ngangulero* removes the *nkiso* from the place where they had kept it), I take it by walking backwards for quite a few steps; you shouldn't turn your back on the *palo*. And from there, we go home and feed it right away, giving it its rooster blood. And *jengibre*, canela, *mani, ajo*, aguardiente with *pimienta, nuez moscada*, dry wine, and Agua de Florida perfume.

An old man who lived his entire life in the countryside tells me about how the Congo would make a *Boumba*: "The spirit that lives in a cloth bundle is called Boumba. That was the first *nganga*. Later, the Creoles transferred the *nganga* over to a cauldron or pot."

A historian friend who is very knowledgeable about the Black people *de nación* and managed to have close relationships with them once went—during a difficult time in his youth—to consult with a very old Congo:

His room didn't have any furniture except for his bed. He lifted up a board under the bed, which was covering a hole where he had buried a box. Then he took a cloth bundle out of the box, and he started taking out pieces of *palos*, placing them in a circle on the floor. Then he took out a skull and placed it in the middle. He sat next to me, facing the skull and the sticks. He leaned over it, murmuring in his language. After a little while, I saw him get agitated, and he started frothing at the mouth. He started talking to me, but I couldn't understand him. He put the skull in the palm of my hand. Astonished, I felt the skull begin to speak for itself, responding to the old man. It was light—I could barely feel its weight at all—as it moved in my paralyzed hand. And that went on for the entire length of that strange dialogue: alive, endowed with voice and motion.

This friend recounts that the old man gave him a coin that served as an amulet, and the coin did indeed get him out of a dangerous situation. He was supposed to return it as soon as it completed its protective mission:

Now that I was calm, and I could confirm that I'd left that danger behind, I went to see the Congo, with the coin in the inside pocket of my coat.

He asked me, "And the coin?"

"I have it right here."

"No. Take a look, it's not there."

My hand went to my pocket. I looked for it, but the coin wasn't there. The thought that I'd lost it made me desperate. Then he calmly showed me that he was holding it in his hand.

"No, son. It's not there. It's right here." Damn! The coin had a life of its own!

(We are told that it is not unusual for some amulets and protective charms—because they are inhabited by spirits, or because they are in constant contact with the *nganga*, which impregnates them with its supernatural powers—to follow orders, and move or transfer from one place to another. Ta Julián from Las Cañas was able to stand in his pasture and summon an *mpaka*, which he kept in his hut six kilometers away, making it fly through the air to him.)

This old man, who might have been a skilled ventriloquist and illusionist, like many of his contemporaries, had a *Boumba* (a *muerto*) in the same style described by the *mayomberos* we have consulted: the cranium, the sticks, and the other ingredients bundled in a sack.

The *saco de rusia* (*sacú*) used to wrap the *boumba*[4]—which Black people purchase in shops and is sometimes still used in the countryside—is marked with white plaster: a small white cross is drawn at each corner, and a larger cross is contained by a circle in the middle. The sorcerer, who has already cut the pieces of wood necessary to "assemble" his *Prenda*, places them around this circle, which is called *mesa de nganga* ["the *nganga*'s table," or altar]. He puts dirt from the grave of the designated *muerto* and dirt from the four corners of the cemetery on top of it. This is the base, the "firm foundation." On this, the sorcerer then places the cranium and bones of a subject—chosen by the sorcerer because their life was distinguished by wickedness—which have been exposed to the sun and night dew for three days. In the afterlife, the spirit of a man continues behaving the same way they did in this one: a bad person will be just as bad or worse. That is why *kiyumba* from crazy people and, most especially, Chinese people—"mingóngas" who were very vindictive, often committed suicide in fits of rage, and were unable to suffer slavery during colonial times—were widely regarded as being ideal for *ngangas*. Yet Baró says the *kiyumba* of a woman is preferable, "because they really don't listen to reason. People who know a lot but aren't willful are useless for *nganga*." And he adds, "You don't want a sage *muerto*. They won't work. They don't get hot. Why would they? They let things happen. But the dumber the *kiyumba*, the better. They don't reflect, they act blindly, they drag themselves through anything, and they don't have any scruples."

Next to the bones, the sorcerer arranges the other "ingredients" of the *boumba*: legs, head, and hearts from a dog, a cat, a hutia, and a black goat; birds, including owl, bat, vulture, dove, woodpecker, Antillean nighthawk, Gray kingbird, tocoloro, arriero, kestrel, etc. And snake, *jubo*, lizard, frog, toad,

---

4 DF-N: A *saco de rusia* (more commonly known as *saco de rucia*) is a cloth sack woven from palm fronds.

tarantula, *mancaperro*, scorpion, macao, centipede, dragonfly, wasp, Spanish fly, ant, leaf-cutting ant, woodworm, termite, worms . . .

It is worth underscoring that the body of a *nganga* made this way and wrapped in a *saco de rusia* is a *boumba* (or *Sacu-Sacu*), "the one belonging to the Black people *de nación* and the old Creoles. They never put it in a clay pot or an iron cauldron; it was in a sack."

It was an enormous *kita* (bundle) that was hung from the *barbacoa*, a wooden platform inside Black people's huts. It was a floor without doors that was raised near the ceiling and used to store grains, corncobs, tubers, fruits . . . and fetishes.

The *bozales* used to call the *barbacoa* Chamalongo—that is, cemetery—because "those mysterious things from the cemetery, *ndoki* from *chamalongo*, or *inkisi*, were kept in the *barbacoa*."

"When I used to travel around the sugar mills like Intrépido (where I was born), San Joaquín, or Corto y Harmonía, all the *Prendas* were hidden by the *ngangankisi* in the *barbacoa*: the *ngangas*, the *muertos*, the dolls with *fumbi* inside that walked around at night. The Congo—the Musunde, Embaka, Bengwela, Ngola . . . Húm! Their *prendas* were covered up; they kept everything they did very secret. In the Congo cabildo, there were no religious ceremonies. None. You couldn't see any signs of *ngangueria* there. It wasn't like the Lucumí cabildo, where the pots and tureens and bowls belonging to the *Santos* were in plain view. And in a little stone tank full of water in front of this big altar, set up like white people's altars, they put the stones belonging to the water *santos*."

"I visited that Lucumí cabildo at the Intrépido mill often. The boss—the Padre de los *Santos*, the most senior *babalawo* there—was Ta Cecilio. His Lucumí name was Laugue. Ta Rafael and his assistant, Ta Roque, Odyo Kule. The Godmother of the Cabildo was Ma Quintina. And they did the *Asientos* there. They had Bata and Bembe openly, not behind closed doors. But the *mayombero* kept the *nganga* in his own house: they played *palo* behind closed doors and very quietly. *Nganga* was bad stuff. Sometimes, it was the custom in a lot of the houses of *Padres* that whoever went to play had to identify themselves by singing at the door so a doorman and the others inside would let them enter. I remember some of the songs that the children would sing to make themselves known,[5] like this one:

> *Ay, lembe lembe*
> *Malembe Yaya*
> *Endale Siete Leguas que yo vengo,*

---

5   DF-N: In context, this indicates ritual rather than biological children (*hijos*), who are not necessarily younger.

Cuando llegué aquí lembe
mi caballito tá estropiao
Lembe lembe malembe
Siete leguas que yo vengo,
Gurubana de licencia
Jacinto Congo tá la loma . . . etc.

Ay, good day, good day
I greet you gently, Mother
Endale Seven Leagues I traveled
When I arrived, I greeted you
My little horse is dead tired
Lembe lemba malembe [greetings]
Gurubana, give your blessing
Jacinto Congo is on the hill . . . etc.

"For that same reason, they called the *barbacoa* Chamalongo like *camposanto*," Nino from Cárdenas explains; "you hear that the *ngangas* are called *makuto*, even if they're in a clay pot, a cooking pot, or a cauldron. And the same is true for all of the *Prendas*, even the little charms that fit in your pocket: a necklace, a little chain, *makuto sanga mbele*. Because the *nganga* was put inside the *makuto* and hung from the ceiling. The sorcery was hidden in a *makuto*. *Nkuto-pangabilongo*. In Congo, *kutu* means ear, pocket, sack: a container." (We will recall that *makuto* is a long, narrow sack woven from *guano* fibers, which is very common in our country: it also means "package" or "bundle.")

Bringing down the *makuto*—the *Boumba*—was a laborious, delicate operation: "It was next to the ceiling, it was big, and it weighed a ton." Juan O'Farril recalls clearly all of the songs that accompanied the descent of the sacred bundle—"the Sacú-Sacú"—on the days that the Padre "worked." Along with his *mayordomo* and the godmother, he would sing as they swept the floor. Because the mambos—the songs, the repetition of words, the rhythmic phrases—are the indispensable basis for the "juego" (the magical ritual) that is going to be celebrated and, of course, for the occurrence of trance.[6]

Bare bare, bare basuras,
Bare bare, bare basura,
¡Simbiko!

---

6   DF-N: A *mambo* is a chant or song. In *Vocabulario Congo* (Cabrera [1984] 2001, 220), *mambo* is translated simply as "canto" ("song"). More specifically, it refers to a ritual chant in Congo-inspired Cuban traditions and/or a mid-twentieth-century musical genre. See Waxer (1994).

Sweep sweep, sweep the garbage,
Sweep sweep, sweep the garbage,
Simbiko!

They sang until they had left the floor perfectly clean to receive the *boumba*. The Padre asked for *mpemba* (plaster chalk) and drew the "firma" (the circle and cross) where the *makuto* would be placed.

Pati pati pati
Mpemba, Simbiko!
Pati pati pati
Mpemba, Simbiko!

Then they intoned the *mambo*, the song for bringing it down:

Como Padre te mandó
Bájalo, bajo mi Mamá
Bájalo, baja mi Mamá.
Abako minganga . . .
Bájalo como Padre te manda . . .
Trailo, trailo minganga
trai nganga como paso lingüeña.

As Father commanded you
Bring it down, down my Mother.
Bring it down, down my Mother.
Bring down my *nganga* . . .
Bring it down, down my Mother.
Bring it, bring my *nganga*
bring *nganga* down, like the chameleon.

(Slowly, the way the chameleon walks.)
If the *makuto* was stored in a corner, they said:

Traila traila mi Mamá
Cucha, cucha, como Padre ti manda.

Bring her, Mother
Listen, as Father commands.

Once it was on the earth, after its slow descent enveloped by a thousand precautions, the chief of the temple exclaimed:

¡Mambe! ¡Mambe! Dio
¡Cosa buena tá lo mundo!

¡Mambe! ¡Mambe! Dio
A good thing is here on earth!

"And they saluted, and they kissed . . . Mamá." That *nganga* was called María or Mamá Lola. The elders untied the bundle:

Zafa inzafa, inzafa Mamá Lola
Zafa canastico. Yo zafa Gurubana,
Ndundu Karire dá licencia . . .
María Grubana tá la loma
Tiembla tierra nunca cae . . .
Zafa inzafa Mamá Lola . . . etc.[7]

The pieces of *palos* that the movement of the bundle have dislodged from the dark, a heavy jumble of diverse sacred, magical materials, whose contents look indefinable, are erected again and rearranged.

Páralo páralo mi Mamá
Como Padre te manda.
Páralo páralo, simbiko
Pa que yo jura, mi Mamá,
Simbiko, páralo.

Stand it up, my Mother
As Father commands you
Stand it up, stand it up, *simbiko*
So I can swear an oath, my Mother
Simbiko, stand it up.

And while they are rearranging, they say:

Ya e yá patimpolo
Yá yá yá patimpolo
Que vamos a ver
Goya ya que patimpolo
Pa to lo mundo, simbiko

---

7   DF-N: Here they are untying the bundle while praising various *prendas*.

Ya ya ya, María Nganga
Lo simbiko, que patimpolo.
Mambé mambé ¡Dio!

Once the "little basket" has been rearranged, everyone follows the Padre and *mayordomo* in spraying aguardiente and blowing cigar smoke over it.

Sála minganga sálalaló
Nsunga da vuelta l'ingenio
Arriba munda tó moana,
Súnga, vamo nsunga . . .

And later . . . "Yimbila, vamo un poco yimbila." The Nganga is summoned, invoked.

The Padre starts another prayer by singing:

Mayombe fué bueno en Guinea
¿Cuando viene?
Yo tá puntando la Nganga
Mamá Lola da licencia:
Mayombe va Gurubana.
¡Mayombe fué bueno en Guinea!
¡Sinbiko!
Con lonyáya, longoyaya
Vamo a vé Susundamba
Mayombe bueno en Guinea,
Abre camino
En to lo lao
¡Mayombero abre camino!
¡Simbiko! etc.

Mayombe was good in Guinea
When is it coming?
I'm pointing to the Nganga
Mamá Lola gives her blessing:
Mayombe goes to Gurubana.
Mayombe was good in Guinea!
Sinbiko!
With lonyáya, longoyaya
We're going to see Susundamba [Owl]
Good Mayombe in Guinea,

Open the way
Everywhere
The Mayombero opens the way!
Simbiko! etc.

At the end of the "juego," they would sing:

Chikirongoma recogé
Chikiringoma, a recogé
Vamos recogé.

Chikirongoa, let's clean up
Chikiringoma, let's clean it up
Let's clean it up.

And the *nganga* would be bundled up again, then raised up to the *barbacoa*.

We accept the chronology of those old informants, all of whom agree on this point and lived with *gente de nación* (African-born people). According to them, the *boumba*, the *makuto*, *sacú-sacú*, the bundle, the sack, and the *jolongo* ("the old timers also had *ngangas* in big and small gourds")—all of them precede the *kimbisa* and *briyumba*,[8] which are lighter than "the way Creoles work, with a *nganga* inside a pot or cauldron." "The Creoles simplified the business of the *Prenda*. Raising and bringing down the *makuto* and working with it was a very complicated affair, and it meant carrying a heavy burden of responsibility."

Lastly, in order to test the power of the *boumba*, it is buried next to a leafy plant and warned categorically: "When I come back to get you, I'd better not see a single green leaf on this plant."

After the deadline, the owner of the *boumba* should find the plant completely stripped of foliage. The *boumba* should have obeyed, demonstrating its ability by drying out all the leaves and not sparing a single one.

It should be asked to demonstrate its power in a number of ways. For example, by pulling a hair from the mane of a horse. It is ordered: "May the *kombo*"—the horse—"which is healthy and whole, break a leg." The animal, which was healthy and running around the pasture, will fall and—in effect—become useless after breaking its leg.

If one does not wish to sacrifice a horse, a dog is submitted to the same test: "Make this dog rabid." The dog will die of rabies. Indeed, the "moana mboa ntu kiyumba"—the head of a rabid dog—is highly regarded as an ingredient

---

8   DF-N: Cabrera's original has *vriyumba*.

in a *makuto*, "so it will attack" the victim selected by the *ngangulero* and make them rabid.

Once the *mayombero* is convinced that "his *Prenda* works," he unburies it, takes it home, and rewards it with an outpouring of blood.

Ngangas learn to fight by being buried in an anthill of *bibijagüa*, leaf-cutting ants. Our Black informants attribute supernatural intelligence and wisdom to these dangerous, hardworking, and tireless ants. "This ant never rests. It treats the night like day: it works at all hours. They don't have Sundays or holidays." The diligent leaf-cutting ant—*ntiawo*—gives the *nganga* that same extraordinary aptitude for work, absorbing the ants' industriousness and perseverance. It learns to demolish and to build—to demolish someone else's in order to build their own. That is why soil from an anthill of leaf-cutting ants is obligatory in a *nganga*. The boss (the Queen) of these ants has mysterious knowledge and relationships: "It knows everything that happens underground, and they should be gathered when they're carrying something back to their home."

Likewise, maggots from human or animal carrion should be included: "The worm we call Mandundu, the one that eats the *muertos*, it eats the flesh and leaves the bones. It's brown; when the air touches it, it dies too. We sing to it: *Mandundun wanterere kisondiko*. And there's another black-and-white worm that also dies in air," as well as those which are not found in cemetery graves, but rather in furrows made by plows.

Termites, woodworms, and "kimbonkila"—an insect, although I do not know which one my sorcerer informant was referring to, which "looks like a big fly and works in a crazy hive, making holes in the ground." Another, "which works opening holes in the corners of houses and is called Gandu-Cueva or *pocero* [well digger]."[9] "And all of that *ntiti*"—garbage, sorcery—"is very valuable."

In short, *ngangas*, *nkisos*, *kimbisas*, *viyumbas*, *makutos*, and *boumbas* are prepared with human bones, soil, sticks, roots, and animals. A "Bola-Mundo" is added: "the sacred green ball of herbs found in a cow's stomach. It's a very sacred relic, miraculous." Once it is inside the cauldron, "it gives life to the concoctions the Padre uses for his cures."

A learned *mfumo*, the eldest Padre and chief of a temple, tells us, "The power of the Congo is based on the virtues of the *palos* in *el monte*, *muertos*, and animals. In other words, spirits of humans,[10] spirits of trees, and spirits

---

9   DF-N: It is unclear which specific species of insects are mentioned here. Gandu-Cueva could be a Congo Spanish term meaning "guard of the cave," while *pocero* is a Spanish term for "well cleaner."

10   DF-N: The original Spanish refers to "espíritu de cristiano"; in context, *cristiano* is a some-what antiquated, generic synonym for "man," "person" or "human being." While *cristiano* does

of animals. Spirits that work in cemeteries, at intersections, on hilltops, in rivers, in the ocean, and in the wilderness, which is the home of all the spirits."

The spirit of a *muerto* commands the spirits of the trees and animals. The combination of all these powers that fulfill the sorcerer's orders and carry them out—"I'm the one in charge, and I'll command you until the end of the world"—is what is understood as *nganga* or *nkiso*. Therefore, a *nganga* is a maleficent or beneficent spirit. It does good or harm in the service of those who know how to control it with magical powers.

The spirit of a scorpion acts because the body of the scorpion—dried out in the cauldron—"attracts it." It will drive its venomous stinger whenever the *ngangulero* commands. Mayimbe, the vulture, will provide the wisdom of the unknown, prodigious sight, and its wings' phenomenal endurance. The dog—its *kiyumba*, bones from all four legs, eyelashes, and hair from its tail— will sniff out a scent, latch onto a trail, and make good spiritual use of its fangs. All of these animals, each by virtue of their nature, form "squads" of slaves ("sometimes they revolt") and aid the spirit in its work. "The *ngangulero*, the master, commands the *muerto*; the *muerto*, who is an overseer, commands the *palos* and animals, which are the cadre." "The *fumbi* is the general of the army."

A *kimbisa* explains: "A *Prenda* is like the whole world in miniature, and you use it to control and dominate it. That's why the *ngangulero* puts all of those spirits in his cauldron: inside there, he has the cemetery, *el monte*, the river, the ocean, lightning, tornados, the sun, the moon, and the stars." "It is a concentration of forces."

The spirit or *nganga*, "once it sold itself, it agreed to be a slave. The *fumbi* of a *mayombero* will not move from the container. It's always there, waiting to receive its orders."

An old man, who always spoke to me sincerely, without reservations, thinks it was much easier to obtain a *nganga* back in his day. By that, he means a venerable "nganga de confianza."[11]

("At the sugar mills, the *taitas* themselves would leave their own *kiyumba* to their godchildren. That was a *kiyumba* that commanded respect.")[12]

---

not necessarily denote religious affiliation, the distinction between *cristiano* and *judío* is deeply significant, especially in passages describing "Congo-inspired" traditions. See the Translator's Notes; MacGaffey (1983, 1991, 2000); MacGaffey and Harris (1993); Martínez-Ruiz (2013); Ochoa (2010); and Thompson (1981, 1983).

11 DF-N: The term *de confianza* translates variously as "legitimate," "well-known," "trustworthy," "reliable," "orthodox," "real," "spirited," etc.

12 DF-N: The *taita* (godparent or ritual mentor) in this passage wills their physical skull—and, thereby, their spiritual existence, "afterlife," or "soul"—to their child, offering a perspective on inheritance that shrinks materialistic squabbles over property to a microscopic level of pettiness.

Cemeteries used to be watched over less than they are now, or even completely abandoned. They had no guards, and the cemeteries in the countryside and at sugar mills were not looked after.

That is how one of his companions—like many others who "took very good *muertos*"—was able to make himself a dreadful *nganga*. It earned him great fame in that region, and it "did away with a lot of people."

He once unearthed the adolescent daughter of a *sitiero* [ranch owner]. She had been furious and insane when she died. "He carried her away when she was still soft." He was able to remove her heart, "which is the best part, but it's so difficult to get one that nobody has a human *tima* in their *sanda*."[13]

Kivú insists that some *ntu-kiyumba* were selected while they were still alive. "People would keep their eyes on them," intending to use them to make a future *boumba*.

One invalid *palero*, who is almost one hundred years old, can no longer roam around by himself. He tells me about curses the sorcerers of his day could effect. He also says that he left his *nganga* buried in the countryside, under a *jagüey*. "He sent it on its way," since he is no longer involved in that line of work, and his *nganga* could not stand to live in a room with a tile floor. That said, cemeteries remain accessible to the sorcerers, who still go there continuously—like they did in colonial times—to stock up, not just on dirt, but on *kiyumbas* "that still have a little brains, and *mioka* [fingers],"[14] as well as jawbones to "load their *mpakas*" [horns], make their *mpolos* (powders), and their cursed, malevolent ova. In a word, to do their "work." A watchful visitor to any of the municipal cemeteries in the region surrounding Havana—like the ones in La Lisa, Regla, or Guanabacoa, with their outdoor ossuaries—will observe a grave no more than seventy centimeters deep at high noon, already dug to receive a certain cadaver at five o'clock . . . Very interesting. Even the capital's own cemetery will undoubtedly make a demanding old sorcerer much less pessimistic—especially the section where they bury poor people. The *mayombero* always finds a collaborator on the other side of the wall: a guard or gravedigger who is also a *mayombero*, who supplies their needs. In this regard, we are reassured, "There's never a lack of *muertos*." Tá Julián D. says, "You can get a *muerto* for two *pesos*. Can't you see? The gravediggers do a lot of business. They take it out of the ground themselves, and you pay them whatever. Madam, almost all *mayomberos* are involved in that! Of course, you can't do that in the mausoleums. That's the only part of the Casa Grande that's well

---

13   DF-N: The word *sanda* remains obscure, although it probably refers to a ceiba tree (also known as *sande*); in context, the tree where most *ngangas* are buried. *Tima* clearly means "heart." See Cabrera ([1984] 2001, 282).

14   DF-N: In *Vocabulario Congo*, Cabrera translates *mioca* as "finger" ([1984] 2001, 228).

looked after. Go figure. Who's going to go there? . . . But X. has remains—a little bone—from a big *mundele*. Someone snatched it when they were putting him in the ossuary. It cost him dearly."

The kiyumba of a *mundele*! (The skull of a white person.) Excellent brains. The best. "The intelligence of a *blanco*," which had become a dry paste—hard and blackened—cost Pancho Tomás five pesos. Now, the intelligence of white people is placed in *ngangas*. "That little bit of brain inside a hollowed-out piece of burnt charcoal—there's no better *nganga*!"

My reliable informant L. explains the matter patiently:

> In the old days, Black people's sorcery didn't necessarily reach white people. You needed to put a little piece of *mundele* in the cauldron. These days we put the two brains together: the one from the white person right next to the black one. Now, they're equal under the constitution. And the *Prenda* kills white people just as well as it kills Black people. The young lady understands that, if I ask a white person to take down another white person, to shake them up hard, he'll play dumb; the white person won't do it. But if he has the Black one next to him, Watch out! The Black one forces him to do it. He pulls him along! And the white one will do the same thing whenever the Black one doesn't want to harm someone who's like himself. The white one will attack a Black person, and the Black one is forced to go along. Two *kiyumbas*, two *chocozuelas* . . . Some *mayomberos* only have *mundeles*, and their *ngangas* never catch *mundeles*.

Finally, when the owner of a *nganga* dies after having expressed his wish for the *nganga* to accompany him on his journey to the other world, or when—for whatever reason—they find themselves unable to have the *nganga* with them, or if they feel it is best to get rid of it permanently, "the *nganga* is sent on its way. It's released and bid farewell." It is paid one final *derecho*, then it is buried. In the first and second instances, this is done under the shade of a *jagüey*, ceiba, or laurel tree. Those who need to merely separate themselves from the *nganga* temporarily, with the intention of taking it back when the time is right, keep their *fundamento* under a palm, yaya, or ceiba tree.[15] *Ngangas* sometimes remain buried for several long years. Everything rots, of course, but that does not matter. The spirit remains, "settled" there in the stone—the "matari" that we have seen placed in the receptacle. Because it is indestructible, it does not disintegrate like the *palos* and the *mensi* (bones), and the *muerto* will not abandon it. As a spiritual instrument that can be used for good or ill, they can also

---

15 DF-N: The ceiba is effective in either scenario, underscoring its immense power and significance. See chapter 7.

be imbued with the energy of an *mpungu*, a deity: *mpungu* Mama Wanga, Kisimbi Masa, Choya Wenge,[16] Dibudi, Tonda, etc. The *matari* will continue functioning as the foundation of the power of the *fumbi*—the enslaved *muerto* "who sleeps" during that time—until the sorcerer recovers and reanimates it. Then it goes back to serving him again, with the *palos* and other components that are restored periodically.

To definitively destroy a *nganga*, it is buried in an anthill of leaf-cutting ants. It is given a sacrificial rooster, a libation of aguardiente, and a cigar one last time: "The ones that are bid farewell, they're gone forever." Many *ngangas*, upon the death of their owner, spontaneously "want to go back to their *palo*." But because they are "keys to the world" and "they can't die," they are generally inherited by a son of the Godfather, as we will see in more detail below.

While they are alive, they produce "children," limbs, offshoots . . . New *ngangas* are made by taking elements from old ones. In this way, those from earlier times that have disappeared, "the ones that have left," have left descendants—a great many of them.

How to Prepare a Zarabanda

In theoretical terms, some old *paleros* (especially those from Matanzas, with the sage Baró foremost among them) refuse to accept the notion that Zarabanda is a genuine *prenda* in Palo Monte, even if their magic—in practical terms—employs all of the powers at their disposal. They consider Zarabanda, for lack of a better word, a "mixture," a Havana Creole heresy. "Zarabanda is an *asiento* from Havana," where a very effective *prenda* is given this name. The *mpungo* Zarabanda—the main force that acts through it—is equivalent to the orisha Ogun (and Gu from Dahomey). It is another deity from *el monte*, and it is the owner of iron. As we know, he is Christianized as San Pedro, the gatekeeper to heaven. Likewise, Zarabanda, "like Elegua, defends the doors of those under his protection."

The Congo Zarabanda—or Ogun, or San Pedro—presents us with a typical example of what we understand as "*Santo* mixed with Palo Monte: *muerto* and *santo*, a spirit of a human and a *santo*." This is Congo-Lucumí syncretism.

Baró, in his own way, labels some sorcerers as forgers. ("Listening to these kids that mix up and confuse everything, you end up like the woman who says, 'Now I'm really confused! I don't know whether the cat eats the hutia, or the hutia eats the cat.'") One of these sorcerers tells us, "To mix it with

16   DF-N: Choya Wenge is much more commonly known as Chola, Mama Chola, Chola Wenge, etc.

nganga, you put San Lázaro or Obatala in a stone. Or Oshun and Yemaya, who are very witchy. Or San Pedro, or any *santo.*" (The old man Herrera exclaims, "For the love of God! *Sambi tuke! Santos* can't be mixed up with *kiyumba: basura lo nganga no tronca con santo.*" "In legitimate Palo Monte, the Congo bury it in the cemetery to send them on the path of the *muerto,* so the spirit of a *muerto*—rather than the spirit of a *santo*—goes to the stone. The *muerto* is put together with Palo, but *nganga* shouldn't be put together with *Santo.*")

But others protest that Zarabanda is an influential, very old, and respectable *prenda* that is "as Congo as the king Melchor himself." "Or like San Antonio, who is known as Bakuende Bamban di Angola, Kabanga Tengue Yaya, and Madioma. And Mpungu Kikoroto . . . San Francisco. And Pandilanga, Our Father Jesus Christ, who was very well known in Congo." "Zarabanda is, strictly speaking, the Congo Ogun. Like the Lucumí one, he is iron and the head of a black dog." This might be one of many exchanges between different groups of Africans imported to Cuba. ("Don't the Arará give Agroniga—San Lázaro—to the Lucumí?" "Excuse me, but the Lucumí San Lázaro—the oldest is called Agroniga Omobitasa and the youngest is called Asoyi—is transmitted in a stone. The Arará one, which does not have a stone, is in a clay vessel that is hermetically sealed.")

Recently, a young *villumbero* told me that he had made a Zarabanda for a godson from Asturias. "You know," he explains, "that the important part is catching the *muerto.* Imagine that we're sitting here with another person whom we trust completely. You think of some deceased person you knew and say, 'I would choose X.'" Meaning, the spirit and—if possible—the remains of X. "And I say, 'Well, I think Y. would be better, because he was a very reckless kid, a troublemaker.' And the third person with us suggests that Z., who was a woman with hair on her chest, would yield better results . . .'"

"In other words, it's a discussion, and an agreement is reached. If possible, we gather the remains we've chosen as we see fit. If we cannot get the remains, we summon the spirit, we attract them and make a deal with them. At midnight on the most appropriate day, we go to an isolated place. Ideally, we go to the foot of a ceiba or *jagüey.* We take a cauldron to make a Zarabanda. Zarabanda needs a cauldron. And we put all of the necessary ingredients next to the cauldron: the bones, the head of a black dog, the dirt, a horseshoe, a chain, and a ball of iron. Two candles, a bottle of aguardiente, white wine to spray, tobacco, and gunpowder. We start our songs, calling God and Mayimbe." (Mayimbe is the spirit of the vulture, messenger of death.)

Dió, Dió, Dió! Mayimbe, Mayimbe, Mayimbe! We prepare an egg with powder from the Júcaro and other ingredients. One of the three of us is in charge of taking that egg to *el monte*. And it's guaranteed that we'll find an Ogun-Matari as soon as we enter the bush: Zarabanda's stone, which is black with grayish veins. The spirit of Ogun—San Pedro, which is called Zarabanda in Palo—will leave *el monte* with you in that *matari*. You take Ogun in the stone, because you won them over with the egg; they were there waiting for you, summoned by the egg. Then we prepare a brazier and wrap the *matari* in black thread. We put it inside the fire to test it, to know if the spirit is inside it. And after calling *Dió, Dió, Dió*, and *nfumbi, nfumbi, nfumbi*, one of us will repeat three times: "Ya cortamos luwanda, tu kuenda mensu, mambo que yo boba Kindin Nsasi. ¡Mal rayo parta lo ngangulero! Candela qu'indica yo boba Congo kunambansa. Si de verdad, verdad, usted es viyumba que mandi Sambiampunga Nsarire, candela que yo quema, a usté no lo puede quemar; este mismo nganga que ngando-guerra, ya van fuiri, pero mboba luwenya va Nsasi; Nguiriko Mayimbe no leka hasta que uira Nkumba y uria Nsusu."

The *matari* is in the brazier, and we're filling the cauldron with every-thing that belongs to an Ogun, a true Zarabanda. Zarabanda contains *palos*: Jiquí, Quiebra-Hacha, Palo-Hueso, Malambo, Yaya. Around the cauldron, it has an iron chain, an iron ball, and a horseshoe, a knife, a magnet, a *real* coin's worth of quicksilver. Finally, the last thing we put on top is the stone—the *matari* that we have removed from the fire without the thread burning—which crowns the entire work. Because, if the thread did not burn or singe, it means the spirit is really in the stone, and that's the proof it gives us. As soon as it came out of the brazier, before putting it in the cauldron, we put it on a white plate for a while so it can drink aguardiente and white wine. Later, once it's in the cauldron, we kill a hutia for it, a rooster, and, if there's enough money for a pig, we also kill a pig for it. Zarabanda has eaten, so we cover it with black-and-white cloth and leave it buried under the ceiba.

We leave it there twenty-one days and come back at the end of that pe-riod. We pay *el monte* its tribute in both directions. And you already know that this business of paying *el monte* is just as important as paying the cemetery, because we can't do anything without paying. Once we're back at the foot of the ceiba, we call Sambia. With his favor, we remove the cauldron. That's when the person among us who will receive it says: "Yo mismo cheche, que kuenda ntoto. Tu kuenda la finda, tu kuenda kunan-bansa, ndoki que yo boba, tu mimo son mi pare, tu mimo son mi mare, tu mimo talankan moko kunansen kiyumba." And we grab the cauldron and present it to the one who will be its owner, and it's possible Zarabanda might knock them down and work them over.

Comparing this explanation with the one given by another owner of Zarabanda, G.F. objects emphatically that it is not *matari* (the stone) that should top the magical construction. First, one should take great care to spread palm oil on the receptacle that will receive Zarabanda—which, as readers will remember, should invariably consist of an iron cauldron. Palm oil pleases Ogun and all of the African deities with Ogun's temperament. Then they will draw the "firma" or emblem of Zarabanda: a cross formed by two arrows that divide the space into four sections, and small crosses in the middle of each of the four sections (figure 1). ("The roundness is the earth and the crosses are the winds. All *ngangas* are installed in the center of a cross, on a 'foundation of strength.'") The *viyumbero*, as is customary, sprays the lines of the drawing with aguardiente, then places seven, fourteen, or twenty-one small mounds of gunpowder along the main line, which they will make explode. (According to Juan Lara, the word *fula*—aside from meaning "gunpowder"— also means "to open.") Then they start to make their *prenda*, starting with the "fundamento" before all else: in this case, the *matari* in which Ogun, San Pedro is installed; "the stone where Ogun is already present." The different soils are placed around the stone, then the *kiyumba*, which will work with Zarabanda, is installed over it. It is not always a human skull: "Well, the spirit of the *muerto* will come, even if you don't have their skull." Then, next to the cranium: the bones, the *palos* (for obvious reasons, in small segments), and Ogun's iron implements (a key, a horseshoe, a magnet, an iron ball, a hammer, and a chain around the cauldron). And on top, as a final step: a knife or machete belonging to Ogun. Salako affirms, "The machete is Ogun himself!" We recall that this god is the owner of the machete, just as the hunter Ochosi is the owner of the arrow (or is the arrow itself). "Wherever there's iron, Ogun is there. A horseshoe? That's him right there."

Finally, the cauldron is decorated with feathers from *mayimbe* (vulture), kestrel, rooster, parrot, woodpecker, *arriero* mouse, or *tocoloro* bird, depending on the *mayombero's* preference. But the woodpecker's feathers are highly recommended, and a Zarabanda should have a beautiful, varied assemblage of feathers.

"Mundele quiere bundanga"—the white person wants to know, *bundanga* (mysteries)—is a common refrain among Black sorcerers faced with white people's curiosity. It is not unusual for a Black informant—never without a certain resentment—to believe that it is prudent to slightly distort what they teach white people. For example, if the *matari* is placed in the bottom of a cauldron, they judge it to be more prudent to say that it is placed on top, or vice versa. Another of my informants, a *viyumbero*, is usually very explicit, but he sometimes suddenly mistrusts the hidden intentions of his student

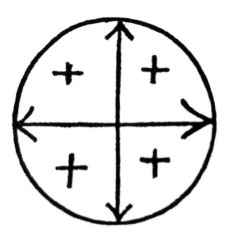

Figure 1.

and—as a precaution—insists on omitting or changing a small detail that he deems to be very important. Therefore, the white person that wants *bundanga*—to know "without swearing an oath" to any temple or making any commitments—should ask a lot of questions, register all of the answers, and consult with all of the authorities. The authorities will appear to be very reserved. As my old friend Calazán says, "The truth is scattered all over the place, and you have to walk a long road to gather it one small bit at a time." He adds that if a liar—Adakadeke, or *fon fon, iron*, or someone who appears to be a fool—"tells you they tossed a needle into the ocean to stick it in the eye of a big grouper fish, then you should answer yes, you heard the sound it made when it went in the water. Because there is some truth in everything, even in lies . . . and it could be that you're being told the truth within a lie. And what if the needle was 'worked' (bewitched)? And what if it pierced the grouper's eye, because it was meant to be his?" This is what happened to one woman, whose husband was brazenly cheating on her, when she heard her neighbor's insistent, singsong nonsense: "The fried fish has its eyes open, but it doesn't see."

When she finally discovered the betrayal, she complained at the top of her voice: "I was blind! And nobody warned me about what was happening!"

The old neighbor responded, "What?! Haven't I been telling you? Didn't I tell you—many, many times, my neighbor—that the fried fish had its eyes open but didn't see anything? You were the fried fish!"

As a sort of inventory, we will add how—according to the same *viyumbero*—to construct a good Infierno Ndoki. It is another *prenda* that is "substantiated" using a cat—a black cat, sent into a rage by cruel torture before being killed. Aside from trees, *ngangas* are sometimes composed of a single animal: *mayimbe* (vulture), *ngembo* (bat), or *tualango* (cat). Or *mbua*, a dog that had been rabid or intelligent and fierce, which is the animal used for Zarabanda.

A cat is boiled and buried. It is unburied after twenty-four hours, and one of the bones is chosen to make the *prenda*. In fact, it is not the *ngangulero* who chooses it; rather, their magical mirror indicates which bone will give their object the most virtue.

A candle is lit, and the bone is placed in front of the mirror. If the mirror does not become foggy, the sorcerer should get rid of the bone because it is useless. Every time the mirror gets foggy and stops being reflective, so nothing at all can be seen on its surface, the sorcerer will select the bone whose image mysteriously disappeared, setting it aside as precious. The *gangulero* stocks up on the good ones, then he goes to the cemetery to look for seven phalanges from little fingers—highly prized by sorcerers—and dirt from seven graves or "seven cemeteries." He places everything in a pot and covers it with a string of garlic cloves. He blows huge mouthfuls of dense tobacco smoke over it, sprays it with aguardiente, then wraps the pot in a black cloth and makes seven knots in the cloth. He takes it to a Ceiba, but he does not bury it. He places it among the roots, so it receives the magical emissions from the "nfumo tree," and it becomes saturated with the tree's invigorating shade until the following day, when he will take it to a savanna or a pasture, where he finds a gorgeous young bull. He will show the bull the pot: he must get the bull's attention so the bull looks at it—even if it is only for an instant. It should also be left out in a field where vultures are circling overhead and perched nearby on a dried-out tree, sniffing animal carrion, so *mayimbe* will "play with it."

Although the cat is an estimable animal in the lineage of Kadiampemba or Lungambe, the Ndoki Infierno is not. The *prenda* known by that name is exclusively maleficent, and it will be discussed in another book about the *ndokis* that drink human blood, "inherently evil spirits."

But *ndoki* is a generic name for all of the fetishes made under the protection of Evil.

The Sacred Lodestone

"It is not an African *matari*. It came to earth when Jesus was born, which is why everyone—black and white—worships it and uses it to attract good luck."

It is written: "Our Father and Lord Jesus Christ came down from heaven to earth at Mount Sinai together with the Lodestone."

The Stone, "which traveled with the Samaritan woman," is sold in markets, and in certain very specialized stores that sell religious objects. One of these stores is located next to a church, and it supplies—with abundant profits for its owners—initiates of either or both *reglas*, along with devotees of all the cults. There we find merchandise ranging from a portrait of the Sumo Pontí-fice to *tomate del mar* used to cure hemorrhoids.[17]

Anyone can "baptize" a Lodestone without any need to rely on someone trained to do so, nor is there any need to pay a *derecho*. Simply follow the instructions noted on the printed prayer cards, which include La Oración a la Piedra Imán, circulate profusely throughout the island, and are sold for five centavos:

> Procure a small amount of salt and mix it with water. At home, kneel in front of a portrait of the Redeemer and light two candles. During the ceremony, you will do the following: place a small amount of salt on the Lodestone as you pour out a small quantity of the saltwater over it. You will say, "Lodestone, I baptize you. In the name of God the Father, God the Son, I baptize you. You are Lodestone, and you will be Lodestone. For my good fortune and good luck, you will be called . . . (Recite the Apostles' Creed. Perform all of this with great devotion.)" Or, instead, put it in Benjuí, powdered canela, and powdered myrrh for five days.
>
> Then recite the Pater Noster three times and spray it with holy water.
>
> There are those who take the Stone with them to mass so it receives the virtues of the prayers and blessings from the priest, then they bathe it in holy water and—with that and nothing more—they consider it baptized. This is an excellent method that is used to consecrate many protective charms and small *Prendas*. Likewise, one can also "take the blessing and virtue of the mass by surprise, in one of those old Spanish silver *real* coins—the small ones. Then you give it to a child whom you love very much, so they're protected for the rest of their life."

But the Lodestone should be prepared and consecrated by a *babalawo* or *iyalocha*, a *mayombero* or Madre de Nganga. Whoever needs the protection of "this marvel of nature" can obtain it from one or the other: "It works in both Reglas, and it is given by both Congo and Lucumí rituals."

Apart from all of this, some *santeras* consider it to be the property of Oya.

We might also presume, as Sandoval suggests, that the Lucumí were and remain the most suitable for consecrating this stone: "The stone is *santa* by birth, and it is blessed by Jesus himself, who sat on it next to the well, and he baptized it with water given to him by the Samaritan woman. It has more affinity with Ocha than *nganga*."

But nobody could object to us also giving credit to an elderly *palero* who has always worshipped the Stone and "helped and hurt a lot of people with

17 DF-N: The "Sumo Pontiface" is the Catholic pope.

his Lodestone and needles." He assures us, "The Lodestone is a Lucumí thing because of its relationship to the *santos*, but nobody prepares it better than a *palero*"—letting me know, whether out of modesty or pride, that nobody prepares it like him.

Mayomberos call it Songe, and Baró calls it Fumandandanda-Kinpesa.

In any case, the most holy Lodestone is never absent from the *mayombero's prenda* or the *babalawo's* orishas:

> It's black and hard. It can be found in the savannas, especially on hot summer days, when the sun burns hot. The Stone is fed iron and steel filings. And you need to replenish the metal filings to make up for what it eats. There are male Lodestones and female Lodestones. The female one is round, and it's immediately recognizable because it eats less; it's less greedy. The male one eats all of the metal filings. The female Stone is given to men, and the male one is given to women. Its virtue is so strong that it can help you get anything you want.

It goes without saying that this is on the condition that it has been attended to properly. It shares the same psychology of all *prendas*: it is jealous and sensitive. "If it gives birth and its young one is not cared for, if its little child dies, every animal in its owner's house—dogs, cats, birds—will die. The stone will kill them."

The offshoot to which the Lodestone gives birth—and which requires the same care bestowed on its mother—is a fragment that breaks off of her.

A *mayombero* tells us,

> Like any *prenda* that receives the direct emanation of the Most Holy Sacrament on the Altar in the church and drinks holy water, it is necessarily a very prestigious *prenda*. But we prepare it like this: We wrap it in a white handkerchief and bury it in the cemetery for seven or twenty-one days. After seven or twenty-one days, I go get it, take it home, sacrifice a white rooster to it, and bathe it in the blood, so it drinks. The bones of the rooster are wrapped up in the same handkerchief we used to bury the stone, and I take them to the cemetery to bury them in the same place I buried her. Later, I wash the stone with holy water and *yerba mora*, and I give it sweet wine or dry wine with canela. Then I put her in a little clay pot or a cup, and I cover her in metal filings. I sprinkle little bits of gold, silver, and brass on it, nails from a horseshoe, pins and needles, and a magnet: a horseshoe magnet and quicksilver. We *mayomberos* also give it a small piece of Palo Cuaba and another of Palo Verraco—two wise trees—and a branch of canela, edible clove, and pepper.

When we want the stone to have *camino judío* [a malicious nature], so it works to do harm, we don't bury it in *campo santo*, but in a *bibijagua* anthill instead. And it'll eat all the ants!

A *kimbisa* will leave it in holy water and the blood of a (white) rooster for a whole day, then bury it next to a Plátano Morado (Red Banana) tree. "There's also a *Santo* of metal filings, a Nkita, who works in the cemetery."

In order to prepare a Lodestone for us, a *babalawo* will require coral, silver, an *escudo* coin, and a small gold female figurine.

He makes an *omiero*: he fills a wash basin with water and herbs belonging to all the orishas. This *omiero* includes orange blossom water, holy water (from the church), *agua de las dos vidas*, aguardiente, an egg white, cascarilla, snail, *efa* (powders), and smoked fish and hutia. A small gold key, a silver one, and a brass one. After praying and singing to Osain and all the *santos*, the Lodestone and the other aforementioned objects are washed with this water, then placed in a small pot. The prayer for the Stone is recited. Then it is cleansed with incense—"magical incense"—and entrusted to its owner who accepts the duty of praying to it every Holy Thursday.

Another *santero* prepares it this way: he submerges it in an *omiero* made with *albahaca, mejorana, prodigiosa, romero, álamo,* and *yamao,* along with aguardiente, honey, dry wine, river water, holy water, and Orula's *efa*. Incense made from *benjuí* [benzoin gum]. They cover the Stone with metal filings, as well as gold, silver, and brass, and they light a candle. The person receiving it will take care to pour holy water on it and recite La Oración del Viernes.

Another *iyalocha*, a daughter of Oshun, prepares it with an *omiero* consisting of five types of water: rain, river, ocean, holy water, and *agua de las dos Vidas*. Sweet wine, *oñi* (honey), canela, and five egg yolks. She prays in Lucumí to all of the *Orisa*, and once it is consecrated, she puts it in a small pot where it is kept with metal filings, small pieces of gold, silver, and brass, the birdseed, and a key with a yellow ribbon tied to it.

For another informant, it is sufficient to baptize the Stone and place it next to three iron nails, an egg, dry wine, and parsley.

Once every year—the morning of the feast day of San Juan is an excellent day for this—the Lodestone should be washed with *yerba mora* that has been gathered before sunrise. It drinks every week and gladly welcomes milk or egg yolk with dry wine. The one prepared by a *mayombero* does not object to aguardiente with *pimienta* and *ají guaoguao* [chili pepper].

A Lodestone prepared for good fortune is submerged in the blood of a dove ("never give it goat's blood, which is the devils' work") and washed with holy water and herbs belonging to El Santísimo.

The ideal thing is to own a pair of them: one male and the other female:

Since the females attract men and the males attract women, sorcerers or *santeras* will use one or the other, depending on whatever needs come up. For some work, there's nothing better than a needle or a pin from the Lodestone. You put needles of all sizes and kinds next to the Lodestone. For a romantic conquest, to tie somebody up, for self-defense—there's nothing better. If the *santero* has enough knowledge and ability, their needles never fail. Nor the hooks prepared to fish for a husband.

A woman who wants to attract the man she likes should offer *clavo* [clove], dry wine, and *pimienta*.

For good luck: Wine and Canela (cinnamon).

To separate a married couple or a pair of lovers, you separate one stone from the other.

C. performs all sorts of spells and curses with his Stone. "If I desire a woman, I steal a pin from her house, if I can't ask her for one, because a sensible woman won't give anyone a pin or a hook without a certain amount of wariness. I take it to my Stone and leave it there, sitting inside the pot with its needles. Then, I take a hat pin from the woman I like, and I nail it in my door. Then I take a needle from my Stone, and I leave it at her house. That woman will surrender and come to my house to seduce me."

To harm: The dry wine belonging to the Stone is spilled in the doorway of the hated person. If they step in it, they will feel pain and get sick.

For "binding" (*nkange*): Again, the wine belonging to the Stone is spilled in the doorway of the person who will be bound magically. But it is first necessary to pick up their trail (dirt they have walked over). This handful of earth or dust and white or red thread soaked in dry wine are used to wrap one of the stone's needles. The person performing the binding touches their needle to their head, then rubs it under their armpits and along the back of their legs. After "talking," pleading and praying to the Lodestone, they place it in the pot or vessel and cover it in canela. A talisman made with powdered fragments from the Stone and a little bit of powder made from the herb *sabe-lección* (*mastuerzo, chini chini*) will give a shy man a high probability of success to seduce any woman.

"The Stone is related to the Holy Spirit. If a person who owns a Stone to solve their problems is short on money, experience proves they should offer the Stone two white doves and let them wander free around the house. They'll be able to confirm that, just as the doves multiply, their business will prosper."

The Lodestone should always be very clean and covered with a white cloth. Immaculate. If possible, in a very fine handkerchief made from pure silk. According to Baró, it is fed every fifteen days, because it is important that it does not become weak or "die." "The Stone has a soul, a life, and thought." It listens, understands, feels, and suffers, and "it eats and drinks." Death occurs when the metal filings fall off or no longer stick to it: "When the little iron strings fall off, that's when the lady is losing her gift, and you need to reinforce her in a hurry."

When this happens, Baró revives her by burying her for seven or twenty-one days near the stump of a *plátano* [plantain] tree. Then he gives her the same sort of attention again—"giving affection, heating it up" with dry wine, blood, etc. The stone is revived—that is, "it grabs its metal filings again and gets thorny like an urchin."

According to F., it becomes much stronger with *jengibre* and three cloves of *ajo* [garlic]. In short, the most important point is that the stone be satisfied in the hands of its owner, "because its mission is to attract whatever is good for them."

"It is very good for all women in general, and it is especially helpful for those who, with more or less decency, sell their bodies. The ones common people refer to as *fleteras*, or—in Congo—*mbisi la Habana* and *ndumbas pikanana*. And others, less sordid and less scandalous, society girls, but . . . ¡*muedda mi yo papió lóbbi!*" If we recall its reported benefits, we have already seen that the devotion offered to the Lodestone is very simple, since—like the *cintaradna india*—it endeavors to fulfill all of one's desires. In sum: small libations of sweet or dry wine, and prayers and candles every Friday. A certain honorable woman insists she owes her happiness to it, and she makes her appeals to it by always reciting the following prayer:

> Oh most blessed Lodestone, whom I adore and venerate in this moment, you are my happiness, my luck, my money. Stone, you are my protector and you bewitch men. You who walked with the Samaritan woman, you gave her fortune and honor. Give me, the one who is giving you food and drink, good luck.
>
> Silver for my home, gold for my [144] treasure, brass for the poor, and health to enjoy it all.

And she always has this prayer of praise for her protective stone on the tip of her tongue: "Blessed be! Oh Stone, whom I honor and respect. I expect all good things from you, because touching you makes me happy. Nothing in this world intimidates me when I carry you with me. Because I believe in you, Lodestone, and I praise you and bless you." Amen.

After reciting the prayer every Friday, one should offer it a few drops of pure alcohol and steel or iron filings, since that is its only food, without which the stone would lose its efficacy and die.

After giving it food and drink, the Apostles' Creed should be recited. And on this day, like any other on which the prayer is recited, one should give centavo coins as alms to several poor people.

The old man Sandoval, an enthusiastic member of the cult of the Lodestone, provided me with these other Prayers which can be purchased from markets and street vendors.

THE SAMARITAN WOMAN'S CONVERSION

DEPRECATION · Oh great sinner, converted by the Savior when he asked you for a drink of the water you drew from the well! You, surprised by the revelations of the son of God, you embraced Religion. Your ears never stopped hearing, "Whoever drinks the water I give will never go thirsty." You, who with the Water of love, out of Christian charity offered by Jesus, have washed away all your offenses. We beg that you intercede with him, so you will grant what I ask of you, if it is for my own good. Amen.

ANOTHER DEPRECATION · Oh Samaritan woman! You who drew water from the well and spilled it over the stone on which Our Lord Jesus was sitting, at your feet. You gave him water from the spring to drink, in exchange for the holy water he gave you, filling your heart with Christian love, converting yourself from a sinner to a virtuous woman and a repentant devotee, accepting Christ's Gospels and faith. By the stone that received the water, I beg you to grant me what I ask, if I am worthy of it. Amen.

PRAYER · Stone, I see the number 1 and I remember the one and only true God. I see the number 2 and I remember the Holy Wooden Cross. I see the number 3 and I picture the three nails of the Christ. I see the number 4 and I am presented with the four Gospels. I see the number 5 and my mind recalls the five virgins who light the way forward for almighty God. I see the number 6 and I remember that God made the heavens and the Earth in six days— the trees, plants, and flowers.[18] I see the number 7 and I remember Sunday is the seventh day of the week, when God prohibited people from working and fishing. I see the number 8 and I am reminded of the eight people who were spared from the great flood. I see the number 9, remembering the nine monks. I see the number 10 and I remember the Ten Commandments. I see the number 11 and I remember the 11,000 virgins in the Holy Book. Finally, I see the number 12 and I feel the presence of the twelve apostles. Remembering all of this, I know very well that all of these things and more are absolutely real and true. I think and believe that this marvelous Lodestone has been granted all the virtues and wonders. With this Lodestone, I can do anything I want. I will

---

18 DF-N: The prayer suggests that plants are the essence and pinnacle of God's earthly creation.

escape from prison easily, without anyone seeing me. I will gain money and recognition. I will get whatever *p* . . . I want to love me,[19] and I will be spared worldly justice. I will be saved from my enemies without them even noticing. I will be spared from lightning, illness, and any and all fatal accidents. I believe this as firmly as if I were seeing it with my own eyes, and I know that this will be fulfilled by your unfathomable virtues. Amen Jesus.

ANOTHER PRAYER · Oh high King, my God, you who give the darkness light. Let your fall, when you carried the cross and your excellent crown, enliven you. My devotion makes me cry over the anguish of your passion. Oh my Lord and God! Do not allow this soul you gave me to die in sadness. You redeemed me with your most precious blood. Oh Virgin Mary! My mirror, my light. Widowed and alone, you found yourself at the foot of the Cross. You called out of profound desolation. I beg you, sacred Virgin and Mother of God, today, on this day, at this time. If some judgment should befall me in the heavens or on earth, in the name of God, the Holy Virgin, and the Holy Spirit, let me be forgiven.

Sweet Jesus, sad in the garden, covered with iron in the cold night, agony itself embodied on the earth. Mercy, Lord! Deliver me from those who speak to me but bear me ill will, from a bad neighbor, from curses and witchcraft. Lodestone, just as you carry our divine Lord's Cross, let my sins be forgiven, Lord Jesus. Salomé from Burgos, and the one from Rome, save my soul, my body, and me. Amen Jesus.

An Our Father and a Hail Mary for Jesus of Nazareth.

La Piedra India

It belongs to a type of wonderful stone that "comes up from the earth's belly, or down from heaven, with Holy Virtues." Macario says, "They arrive fully prepared, and all you need to do is baptize them and give them the name you like best. Like my Lodestone, which I call Chichi- Wanga."

Blue in color, the Piedra India is "hotter, more dangerous, than the Lodestone. It works to do whatever you ask, to play any game and win: horse racing, stealing, killing . . . It's very strong and dangerous. It's important to know how to work with it. It's not buried. It should always be covered in Ungüento de Soldado (Soldier's Ointment), which is sold in pharmacies, and you give it a little bit of fresh water to drink. It certainly likes tobacco and dry wine or aguardiente.

19 DF-N: Presumably, the *p* . . . stands for *puta* (whore, prostitute) or *pinga* (cock).

"With this stone, you can send a lightning bolt anyone's way. That's why, when you hear thunder, nobody except the owner should be next to it. You can't forget to pour water out in the street when the sky's overcast and full of lightning. It starts shaking in its pot when you can hear thunder. Always have some *guano bendito* (blessed palm fronds). The stone shoots sparks.

Nowadays, they're hard to find because they come from India. It's more demanding, more jealous than the Lodestone. We *mayomberos* give it rooster blood. And sometimes we put it in our cauldrons next to the *nganga*." "They are *prendas* that aren't made. Nature provides them. And, for those who know how to work with them, they're as good as a *nganga*."

6

....

THE MAGICAL AND MEDICINAL TREASURE OF OSAIN AND TATA NFINDO

Let us now take a small journey through the magical world of plants, "el monte," where Cuban *santeros* from the Regla de Ocha and *paleros, mayomberos,* or *nganguleros* stock up for the ritual needs of their cults and devotions. We will be guided by a few of the devotees who carry on the Lucumí or Yoruba and Congo traditions. They offer their experience and knowledge as *osainistas,* veterans of the bush, pointing out the curative virtues of *ewe* and *iki*.[1] The descendants of Congos or Bantus will tell us about their *palos,* "strong Congo palos" (belonging to *mayombe* or "monte raso"), and it is not necessarily a question of plant species being imported from the African continent. The centenarian José del Rosario tells us the history, and he is not wrong when he says that Black people from this nation arrived in Cuba very early, "since the days when the first slave ship dropped anchor, back in the days of Nana Sire, the first Congo who stepped on Cuban soil. He cut *palos,* disinterred *muerto* [the dead], and started doing his work and teaching his children."

---

1   DF-N: Generic Lucumí terms for leaves (*ewe*) and trees (*iki, igi*).

At the entrance to *el monte*, where we have ideally paid our tribute, accompanied by a few grains of corn and the light of a candle—or, to be even more truthful, in front of the stacks of index cards on which I wrote information gathered from those who know how to attain the favor of the god Osain, effectively buying the intelligent volition of plants—the grandson of a Lucumí tells me gravely, "When a godfather realizes that his godson is able to call the plants by their proper names without confusing one with the other, then he starts sending the godson out into the world alone."

For his part, a descendent of a Congo Musunde tells me, in a fatherly way: "Learn. Learn to recognize the *nkunia*, the *mufitoto*, the trunks of the trees, the roots, *bukele nkunia*, all of the *nfita nkanda* . . . Don't overlook any of them, because they're all born with their own gift and mystery from the *munganga*, and all of them will be useful for either good or ill. For their own good and the good of others, if they really, truly wish them no harm."

In all times and places, plants are first and foremost among the magical agents employed to incite and drive the gods, spirits, and forces of nature—visible and invisible—so they will act as aggressive or protective energies. Both the *alafoche* and *gangatare* warn me: knowing their secrets, it is possible that my altruistic feelings toward someone might waver in some particular instance; both agree that, if one wishes, even "the best plant" might, in my hands, become an instrument of harm—a covert weapon that is extremely useful for attacks—without needing to go back to them or rely on their help.

We constantly hear these informants repeat themselves, after dictating the names and properties of so many plants and trees that are "full of life" and can be bribed to go around and fulfill our desires, if we know how to perform the appropriate magical action: the plants are all, by and large, effective at producing both the best and the most disastrous effects. We already know that the orishas, *mpungus*, "santos," and the spirits that influence the plants are essentially neither good nor bad. In the end, good and bad are the same thing. Like nature: "A breeze is good and refreshing. But what about a hurricane? They're both wind."

We—"people, white or Black"—are a mix of good and bad. Both principles coexist inseparably, and they become manifest, alternating in all things, "in every heart." And this is what my informants insist on making clear, in response to any of my objections or surprise regarding their ethics. The circumstantial morality of *paleros*, *santeros*, and their numerous clientele is a reflection of a natural concept of life that our Black people have not lost.

It is advisable to always keep this in mind, in order to judge the amorality that is so characteristic of Afro-Cuban priesthood. And let's not go from the Afro-Cuban priesthood to the rest of society in all spheres. Period. *Dake!*

7

....

THE CEIBA

LEGENDS. CULT. IMPORTANCE IN THE MAGIC AND SUPERSTITION
OF THE CUBAN PEOPLE. THE EVIL EYE. MAYOMBEROS AND THE
CEIBA. HOLY THURSDAY, GOOD FRIDAY, AND EASTER SATURDAY.
THE SACRED TREE PAR EXCELLENCE.

LUCUMÍ: IGI OLORUN.

CONGO: MADRE NGANGA, MUSINA NSAMBIA.

"CEIBA, YOU ARE MY MOTHER. PROTECT ME WITH YOUR SHADE."

The ceiba, like the royal palm, is Cuba's most iconic and most sacred tree. This truth is so undeniable that it would be worth asking whether the ceiba is the object of an independent cult—"a cult of the ceiba, in which Black and white people commune with equal fervor." But we already know that all of the *muertos*, all of the ancestors, all of the African "santos" from all the nations brought to Cuba, and all of the Catholic saints go to her and reside in her permanently.

For the Chinese who were imported during colonial times and their descendants today, it was also "the throne of Sanfán Kón, the very same Santa Bárbara in China."[1]

---

1   DF-N: Clearly, the euphemistic word "imported" ("los chinos que se importaron") does not do justice to the brutality of colonial-era human trafficking, slavery, and indentured servitude in Cuba.

If we ask a white peasant, a "güajiro," about the mysticism surrounding the ceiba throughout the nation, they will invariably say that "it is blessed" and that elders taught them to adore her because she is "the most sacred and the greatest in this world." And everyone will repeat exactly the same thing: "The ceiba is *santa!*" "It is the tree of the Virgin Mary." "It is the tree of the Santísimo [Almighty]," "The Power of God," and a tree of "mysteries." As proof of this, even unleashed natural elements respect her: they do not bring her down; the fiercest hurricane does not split her, and lighting does not strike her.

"Lightning respects only the ceiba, and no one else."

Cut down a ceiba? What an atrocity! The ceiba should not be cut or burned. These imposing trees, which dry out as centenarians, are universally adored and feared in our countryside, and nobody would dare to knock one down without first making "ebo," consulting *orissas*, and taking precautions. The majority of our Black people and peasants—living in close proximity to each other and responding purely to an atavistic, millenarian religious instinct common to the entire human race—see a tree of such proportions and such a solemn majestic beauty as the materialization of a powerful divinity. The ceiba's divinity simply imposes itself.

"The ceiba is a saint: Iroko." "It is the Purísima Concepción [Immaculate Conception]." "Aremu, the Virgen de las Mercedes (Our Lady of Mercy) of the Arará, is inside her." And Yemu.

In this regard, the explanations of my elderly informants sometimes become confusing. The ceiba is "the seat of Iroko, who lives there," and of the Immaculate Conception, "who comes to the ceiba" and resides in her. Others assure me that "Iroko is the very ceiba." Also, "Baba is in the ceiba." "The ceiba belongs to Ogun and Orichaoko." Or "Obbá and Changó." "Agayu is the ceiba." It is called Iroko when it is ritually consecrated.

My centenarian friend from Matanzas, Addié, entrusts herself to the ceiba every morning "because you need the favor of the almighty mother ceiba to live." An Ocha chant includes the prayer, "Whether you like it or not, you must reckon with Iroko." And the ceiba is also a place to salute the *okus*—the dead, because the *okus* are in the ceiba.

Congo descendents call her *nkunia casa Sambi* (the tree which is the home of God); *nkunia* Lembán, *nkunia mabungu*, Ñangue, Gundu, (Mama Ungundu) Naribe, Sandam Fiame, Nfumba y Fumbe (*muerto*), Mama Fumbe. Those who claim Lucumí heritage call her Araba, Iroko, Eluwere, Asaba. (Igi-Araba) Iggi-Olorun. (Tree of God.)

Various elders agree that the Iroko tree—a species of African mahogany— did not exist in Cuba. The Lucumí referred to the Goma Francesa tree as Araba; Sandoval knew it as *gogo*. But the ceiba reminded them of Iroko, so they named it and "consecrated" it with the African name given to the immense and very similar tree which was venerated along the entire Guinea coast. The same thing occurred with many other trees.

"Although the Ceiba is not the original Iroko, it is known as Iroko. And it's sometimes known as Iroko, other times as Araba." "Here, the ceiba is like Obaburo: an African tree where the celebration takes place."

"Iroko belongs to the *santo* Odua, who lives up in the top of the tree." "Iroko is a tree that belongs to Olofi; it is the most sacred and mysterious tree." Aside from being known as Iroko or Iroke ("pure Oyo Lucumí"), it is also "named Loko in Dahomey," where it is an orisha considered to be the owner of the ceiba. The ceiba itself is given the common name Iroko, "an old, male *santo*. He has a spouse named Aboman who also lives in the ceiba, as well as a sister named Ondo."

Iroko is danced with a beautiful staff covered in strands of beads and a broom decorated with red and white beads. This *santo*, which is worshipped at the ceiba, belongs to the branch of Nana Buruku and Ayanu, San Lázaro. It is Lucumí and Arará. "And Iroko does not come down, like Oro, the one that roars." A young bull is led around the tree by *santeros* and sacrificed to it, with candles lit, before slitting its throat. Meanwhile, they also sacrifice roosters, hens, blue-winged teals,[2] and white turkeys. White chickens are sacrificed to it every month. Others believe the ceiba does not actually belong to Abanla (La Virgen Purísima), but rather to Agayu ("the Strong Arm"). Yet it is agreed that all the orishas "go" to the ceiba, and Agayusola, Changó, Nana—all of them are worshipped at the ceiba, along with Dada Awuru Magala—Hebioso, the Senior Changó of the Arará.

The *mayomberos* in the countryside call her "Fortuna-Mundo" or "Niña-Linda," "affectionately, to flatter her," and it is understood that "because she is *santa* and blessed, she is never used for anything evil." "The ceiba cries tears when they ask her to do something bad." That is to say, the tree warns the sorcerer when sap oozes from its trunk: "Don't do this wicked thing, it's bad for your soul." But . . . God can grant permission for anything. "God says, 'The affairs of men don't affect me one way or another. Let them sort it out. I'm not getting mixed up in any of it.'" In this way, the ceiba "can either kill or give life." Its power brings anything within reach, and—as we know—everything depends on paying its tribute.

One particular offering appears to decisively grant us the goodwill and assistance of Mother Ceiba. Sixteen eggs are boiled, then, at the base of the tree on the side facing the sunrise, a cross is drawn on the ground with cocoa butter. The eggs are removed from their shells and placed over the cross while

---

2   DF-N: The blue-winged teal (*Anas discors*) is known in Cuba as the *pato de Florida*, *cerceta ala azul*, and *pato media luna*, among other names.

repeating the same request every time an egg is offered. Finally, it is told, "I wish that in so many days you grant what I ask" ("because it's prudent to the terms"). The request is even more efficacious, and its results more fully satisfactory, if an old centavo coin is placed next to each egg. "In order to pacify an enemy and prevent them from doing any more harm, we boil four or eight eggs; coat them in cocoa butter, almond oil, and *bálsamo tranquilo* [balsam]; then cover them with cotton. As the sun is setting, we place the eggs among the roots of the ceiba and call the person we want to pacify. We speak with Obatalá, who is right there on her throne, and she—the one who soothes and calms—takes care of calming and deflecting the enemy."

"A sister of Oyá, who is very delicate and who is kept in a clay pot and represented by two curved shells made from mother-of-pearl, lives at the foot of Iroko, and she receives sacrifices on top of a table."

"The mother of all the *prendas*, she gives shade to the whole world and protects those who implore her. Without Sanda-Naribé, there is no *nganga*."

Aside from all the ancestors who perch in its foliage, all the orishas, *moungus*, *inkisos*, or *nkitas* and *nfumbis*, "a very powerful *fodu* (*vodu*) named Boku exists inside her" (Arará). We also find it in the royal palm. "Iroko, Boku, Loko . . . they are all *santos* who reside in the ceiba."

Whenever I accompanied one octogenarian at a sugar mill in Matanzas, I heard her salute a ceiba in a clear voice as she made the sign of the cross over herself: "Good afternoon, Mother Ceiba. Bless me." She told me that she approached the ceiba "as Our Lady, the Mother of God."

One should address her by saying, "With your permission, I'm going to step in your shadow." One should never pass alongside a ceiba before abiding by this formality. "Never turn your back! Show Iroko great respect, great courtesy!" The sacred shadow of Iroko is never walked over or stepped on without excusing oneself and asking respectfully for permission. A.Z. laid down to rest blithely under a young ceiba. "I didn't ask for permission, and I wasn't going around believing in old Black people's fairy tales," he said. The spirit of the tree let him know it was a "fumbe." For more than two hours, A.Z. was "simbao"—that is, unconscious—and ever since . . .

The more important a man is on earth, the higher he is in the hierarchy, the more quickly his spirit will seek refuge in this tree upon expiring. The spirits of the most illustrious—"the greats, the big heads," the *moana mutamba*—take shelter in her. Moreover, the ancestors come to her from Guinea, unknown grandparents who end up among her vigorous branches. "Iroko is the meeting place for souls." "Dead Africans and Creoles, all the deceased meet in Iroko." "Iroko is always an assembly of spirits" . . . "Munanso of the Fumbe."

"The spirits of the dead are always together with the spirits of *el monte*, *nfindo*, *cunánfindo*, and the trees."

As we have seen, *mayomberos* refer to the ceiba as Fumbe.

In this vein, a young woman was being tormented by the soul of her late mother who would make her sleepless, appearing to her in agitated dreams. Every Monday the young woman would fill a new cooking pot (offerings to the *muertos* always use a new vessel) with black beans, a boiled plantain, and beef jerky. Since her mother had been buried far away in a distant neighborhood of Havana, she did not take the offering to the cemetery, but rather to the ceiba. It is important to make sure the cooking pot does not break along the way: it is held safely with the left hand and carried in a straight line.

Generally, families in the countryside will feed their *muertos* at ceibas

because a *santa* sits at the top of the tree and calls the spirits, all the souls. The souls of the deceased go to the tree. A line is drawn on the earth, then offerings are placed along that line—depending on preferences, in a gourd or on a new white plate. The offerings consist of the food that the deceased enjoyed most when they were alive, but the food is cooked without *iyo* (salt), because the dead should not taste salt. They are also offered water, coffee, alcohol (if it was to their liking), or tobacco. Then four candles are lit. There, the deceased is called, and the deceased comes.

Iroko or *nkunia* Sambi protects everyone equally, "without making distinctions between rich or poor. It is like the sun." "In the time of the great flood, it was the only tree respected by the water." "It was a shelf for the heavens." A pillar. The water stopped advancing some distance away, and the men and animals taking refuge in her were saved from drowning. That is how the human race avoided extinction. "Men climbed down her to come to the earth." When a global drought threatened to exterminate all living things, this role of savior of the species was performed by the vulture, which is revered just as much: *ikolé, kolé-kolé, egú lugú* or *kaná-kaná* for the Lucumí, which is a road or avatar, and an inseparable companion, of the goddess Oshun. For the Congo, it is *nsuso mayimbe*—the *mayimbe* bird. On one occasion, "the sky and the earth fought, and the sky punished the earth by not raining." The vulture carried the offering that the humans and animals of the earth, the victims of the quarrel, had sent to Olodumare, requesting and, finally, receiving his forgiveness. Ever since, this nauseating bird, which all Black people rightly consider sacred and semidivine, has earned a blessing from Olofi—that is the reason it has no feathers on its head—and a guarantee that it would find sustenance for all eternity. He named it, moreover, "messenger of men and God."

"Kaná-kaná is the animal that always finds something to eat, even when the rest of the world is starving to death." And we already know what this bird eats, devouring carrion and waste. "But everyone needs to feed her, because she is *santa*, and as Elegua eats, on the day of a drumming, the innards of the sacrificial animals are placed on the roof. All *santeros* need to feed her."

A grandchild of the Congo tells me about one *nsuso mayimbe* that always complains, perched at the top of tall old ceibas who have lost their foliage, trees consumed from the inside out by the passage of time, raising their gigantic, twisted arms to the sky. "When lángo-lángo mámba Sambiánpungo, Mayimbe guari-guari . . ." In other words, when God makes it rain, Mayimbe grumbles and feels bad. Mayimbe has no *nso*. She has no home of her own. She lives wherever she can. When it rains, she complains, "I can't go on like this, without a roof over my head! I need to build a house so I can stop getting wet." When the downpour stops, the sun shines again and Mayimbe sits on the stump of a ceiba, spreading her wet wings. "She makes the shape of a cross," as they say, so that Tango (the sun) will dry her. But then the whole world mocks her, making jokes and insinuations about her and insulting her.

Then Mayimbe says, "Insambirirá! Ntoto luweña musimusi . . ." And while she complains under her breath, she sees everything from above, sitting at the top of the ceiba. "Ingiriko kuenda mensu vititi Ngombe que nfüire yo úrria kiá mbisi kiá kiá luweña musi-musi, Insambirirá." She sees a dying ox. Mayimbe says, "I have no home . . . but the sun has already dried me. After I eat the ox (*ngombe*), I'll crap on everyone!" And, at least until the next downpour, she forgets about her plan to make a roof that would shelter her from the rain.

Aside from vultures, owls—Susundamba—are also associated with ceibas because of their kinship with death. Like the deceased, owls go to the ceiba.

> *Susundamba, pone huevo en la ceiba con Mayombe*
> *Huevo en la Ceiba, con Mayombe.*[3]

The fugitive Virgin Mary hid in the hollow of a ceiba with the baby Jesus. The ceiba "opened itself" to shelter her and hide her from those who were chasing them. The trunk covered itself in thorns to protect the Mother and Divine Child. Since then, "ceibas open once every year, and the Virgin appears." Many have had the good fortune to see her. "Naturally, her wood is sacrosanct, since it not only received the blessing of the Virgin Mary, but it was also in contact with the divine bodies of the Mother and the Son. For the *güajiro*, the tree's cleanliness is another indication of its holiness. It does not produce rubbish; the ground that surrounds it and receives its divine emanations is always clear of dry leaves. When it flowers, the soft, nearly invisible

---

3 DF-N: The *mambo* (song or chant) quoted here is difficult to interpret, much less translate. One version would be "Susundamba [Owl] lays its eggs in the Ceiba with Mayombe [Magic] / Eggs in the ceiba, with Mayombe."

fleece from its flowers, which are used in cushions and pillows, scatter far and wide, "in order to avoid sullying herself, because she is so scrupulous."

Like other trees (such as the palm, the *jagüey*, *padre de palos*, and *caña brava*), the ceiba speaks to the sorcerer who is prepared to converse with her. The individual "swears an oath to *nganga*" at the ceiba, striking their head against the trunk violently—and, miraculously, without injury.

It is well known that ceibas converse at night, walk and move around from one place to another. Regarding this nocturnal roaming by ceibas around *oda*, the savanna, Juan O'Farril tells us the story of a man who had the good fortune to surprise the ceibas in the midst of their dialogue.

But first, he sings the *mambo* sung to them at midnight in *juegos de palo*.[4]

> *Sanda Naribe*
> *Sanda Nkunia Naribe*
> *Sanda fumandanga*
> *Dinga ngwei*
> *Ndinga mundo*
> *Pangalan boko.*
> *Medio tango*
> *Bobela Ngungu*
> *Medio tango . . .*

He was a very poor man who had a bunch of kids. He lost track of time, and found himself far from home when night fell, out in the countryside. He was tired, but he didn't want to go back home without taking them something to eat, so he curled up at the base of a ceiba. He fell asleep. Around midnight, that time of night when ceibas walk around, a noise woke him up. The noise was a huge black lump that was moving toward him. He realized it was another ceiba approaching, so he stayed very still, right where he was.

The ceibas greet one another: "Malembe Nguei, Malembe Mpolo."

"Kindiambo, kilienso guatuka nguei?" (What's new?)

"What's happening? Well, I live in front of the mayor's palace," says the ceiba who just walked up, while the first ceiba begins to move its roots around so it can go on its own walk. "And the mayor does nothing but cry and cry, like a woman, because his daughter—*buta ndumba* (beautiful

---

4 This *mambo* sets the tone for Cabrera's "transposition" of a long story told by Juan O'Farril. O'Farril is pictured in a photo portrait by María Teresa de Rojas at the end of this volume.

girl)!—is dying from a sickness that nobody knows how to cure, and it only has one remedy."

The first ceiba asks, "What?"

"They need to wrap her in a new sheet and keep her over a vat full of boiling milk, canela (cinnamon), and honey for three hours. As she is bathed by the steam from that milk, they should pray 'sakula musakula munbansa musu kuenda sanga ntiba karidi fuyande . . .' Then that girl would be saved."

"It's true," said the first ceiba. "That's the remedy. And now? Where are you going?"

"I'm going to see my aunt."

"And I'm going to see my sister."

"Buen lumbo . . ."[5]

The ceiba didn't realize the man was hidden among its roots, because the tree had been sleeping when the man arrived. The man left very quietly, without making a sound, but he'd heard enough . . .

Ceibas wake up around midnight, then they go out to visit acquaintances, have their get-togethers, and amuse themselves. Those two ceibas had stayed up late chatting, and the poor man—*kiangana, kiangana, kiangana*—arrived at the mayor's palace, then he waited at the door until daybreak. He said he was a doctor who only cured the gravely ill, so the mayor ordered him to come inside.

"If you cure my daughter, I'll make you rich. If she dies, I'll order them to cut off your head."

The man saw the girl, recited the prayers, and did everything the ceiba had said. The young girl was sweltering over that pail of boiling milk! After three hours, he carried her to bed, keeping her wrapped up, so she wouldn't catch a cold. With every breath she took, she got better. The man ordered that the windows be opened after they'd been kept shut for days and days. Rays of sunlight poured into the room, and the sick girl opened her eyes. She was cured. The mayor said to the poor man, "I want you to be our family doctor."

"Mister Mayor, I don't know how to cure anyone except those who can't be cured."

They put him in a carriage, filled it with money, and took him back home. Now . . . He can buy whatever he wants!

These strange situations can make a poor man rich from one day to the next.

---

5   DF-N: "Buen lumbo" is Congo Spanish for "Good day." See Cabrera ([1984] 2001, 212).

Home of the All-Powerful, Babade, and all the Obatalás, female and male, whomever entrust themselves to the ceiba should be very strict about how they fulfill their pledge. In one legend, Mother Iroko mercilessly punishes someone for forgetting about the gift they had been granted, neglecting their pledge, and dangerously delaying payment of their debt.[6] Here, one of these stories accompanies a well-known and amusing song in which the narrator imitates the movements of the great tree with their arms (the branches) and legs (the roots):

> Eruba, the fruit vendor, passed by an *iroko* every day on her way to the market, carrying her basket of fruit on her head. Every day she left a small offering to the tree, asking for the blessing of a child to accompany her and, later, to help her with her work. As payment for that favor, Eruba promised to sacrifice a ram to the tree. Mother Ceiba answered her prayer and "Eruba . . . Achu kwan." *Iya obi omo*: she gave birth to a daughter. But she forgot about the offerings. She stopped visiting Iroko. That is the way of the world. As Changó says, unless he thunders, almost nobody remembers to greet him:
>
> > *Kawuo Kabie Si*
> > *Ogana maya maya hunto*
> > *Dede mitone*

Or to pour water at their doorway, or burn *guano bendito*.

The girl grew up, and one day Eruba passed under Iroko's shadow with her daughter. Eruba greeted Iroko, but then simply kept walking along, carrying her basket of fruits on her head. The girl stopped next to the tree to which she owed her life. She picked up a little plant that caught her attention, paying no attention to her mother, who had kept moving along a little faster than usual, like a debtor avoiding an explanation when they stumble upon their creditor. When she reached a sensible distance, Eruba turned to call her daughter and saw Iroko dancing:

> *Iyon, yon, kuan, omo layon Kuán!*

The immense Iroko danced. The roots opened a hole in the earth, and the daughter sank into the hole. Eruba ran to rescue her daughter, but the girl was already buried in the earth, which had closed around her body. Only her head remained above ground.

6 DF-N: For "Mother Iroko," the original reads "Madre Iroko-Oko."

"Forgive me, Iroko," the woman groaned. "I'll pay you what I owe you."
And she began to offer:

> Kurukaruku yeye eure oguta
> Omole ambio oumole
> Omole ambio oumole
> Yan Yan Iroko.

The unyielding ceiba kept dancing and singing:

> Yon-Yon-Kua mi
> Omolorayon kuan
> Komo layon kua mi.

And she swallowed the daughter of Eruba.

To have a child, you need to pray at the foot of Iroko and ask for it. If the prayer is answered, offer it a ram every year as payment.

(It is not Iroko, but rather Boma who gives women children.)

Great things have always happened at ceibas. María Kinga—Yaya-lande—flew back to her homeland from a ceiba in the forest of the Valladares plantation.

María Kinga was her name in Cuba. They say María Kinga was named Eyande Laue in Africa. She was the daughter of a sorcerer chief, a Nfumo. She was born in a cave of snakes and raised playing with the *iñokas* (snakes). Traffickers stole her. She came to Cuba, and they sold her to the Santa Ana del Limonar plantation. The overseer fell in love with this Black woman, but she didn't want him, so the overseer ordered them to beat her. María Kinga fled the barracks, and she hid in one of the ovens used to prepare lime. When they found her, they surrounded the oven, but the woman escaped by flying away, and she landed at the foot of a huge ceiba in Alacranes. The ranchers found her sitting on one of the roots. María Kinga saw them approaching with their dogs, and she climbed to the top of the ceiba.

They started chopping down the tree. Suddenly, a storm cloud shaped like an eagle swooped down on the ceiba. María Kinga disappeared with it, and she flew back to her homeland. Her father was *mfumo-Sánga*, even greater than Kintoala. How could the most sacred ceiba, the mother of the *nkitas*, not protect her?

A *tata nkisi* tells me the story of the encounter between Tubisi Insambi and Mpungu Nsambi—the Great Gods of the Sky and the Earth—that took place at the beginning of the world, in the shadow of these trees.

Both had stiff, rigid legs, and

They couldn't bend their knees. They were solid. Tubisi Nsambi was God and Mpungu Nsambi was a Saint. They were born apart from one another, each at a different end of the world. They didn't know each other, and they met by chance next to the ceiba, the tree of Tubisi Nsambi and Mpúngu Nsambi, the tree of God and the Saints. They were brave and aggressive. They didn't kill, but they hit hard, and they were invincible. Bored of beating everyone who fought them, each left their respective territories in search of a more worthy rival. They roamed far and wide, and they encountered each other at the center of the world.

As night fell, they arrived at the ceiba at the center of the earth, each by a different path. Tubisisián Nsambi arrived first and lay down to rest. A little later, Mpungu Nsambi arrived and stretched out on the ground in front of another ceiba, which was covered by a *jagüey* tree. At the break of dawn, they both woke up. Tubisi Nsambi opened his eyes and saw Mpungu under the ceiba-*jagüey*, yawning and stretching.

He said, "Good morning, friend. What brings you here?"

Mpungu answered, "I don't like questions." Then he jumped at Tubisia Nsambi.

As they fought, Tubisia threw Mpungu up in the air, and Mpungu landed on his legs. In the end, both of them broke their legs. Tubisia Nsambi-Nsambi said, "From now on, no one will be born with straight legs."

Another *mfumo-ngánga* assures me that everyone who approaches the ceiba to ask for help receives the protection of the Virgin Mary. He illustrates his assertion with this story:

Ngana Santa María, Ceiba, Fortuna Ngongo, is merciful. The story I'm going to tell you, a miracle of the ceiba, happened like this.

A woman gave birth to a daughter who was afflicted with mange. It disgusted the mother so much that she said, "I don't want a child covered in sores!" And she left her in a rubbish heap at the foot of a *guásima* tree. You know, the *guásima* is a tree with no sense of responsibility: you can hang a man from that tree and it's no big deal. Justice doesn't investigate or ask any questions.

A bird, *nsuso*, arrived and saw her. The bird said, "Look at this little child of God. And she's alive! I was going to eat her, but . . . I'm a mother too." She wrapped the child in cotton and placed her at the foot of a ceiba. The next day, she was found by a *tiye tiye*, who picked up the child, put her up in the branches of the ceiba, and said, "With your permission, I'm going to take her up to heaven." The ceiba gave her strength, and, holding the girl wrapped up in cotton, she flew to heaven singing.

> *Yen yen yegwere mayem*
> *Kiva mio*
> *Pruu!*
> *Kwa mio Kwamio*

And she knocked on the door, and the Virgin herself opened the door.
"Who is it?"
"It's me, Tiye Tiye."
The Virgin said, "Goodness! We're so far away, and even here you're chasing us . . ."
"No, dear Mother. Look what I've brought you."
"Who gave birth to this child? Give her to me! Poor thing . . ."
She bathed the child with herbs and removed the sores from her body. She was a very beautiful girl.
"Well, well, Tomeguín."[7]
The Virgin wrote a letter.
"Give this letter to the Hawk (the king of the birds). It tells him that no other bird will bother Tiye Tiye in *el monte*, and that he must issue a proclamation ordering everyone to assist you." Yes, the Tomeguín has many virtues.

Like the Zun Zun,[8] it is a very important element in the preparation of many potions, powders, and amulets.

That's why the other birds help it make its nest.
Up in heaven, the girl was adopted by the Virgin Mary, and she was healthy and pretty. Down on earth, the woman who had thrown her in the garbage for having mange gave birth to another girl, who was born without any sores.
The woman forced the younger girl to work from a very tender age, and mistreated her. One day, the woman sent the younger girl to pound rice. The sister in heaven saw the girl pounding, peeling, and winnowing the rice, then picking it up and storing it in a pot. And, with the Virgin's

---

7 DF-N: The tomeguín (*Tiaris canorus*) is a small tanager known in English as the Cuban grassquit.
8 DF-N: "Zun Zun" is the Cuban emerald hummingbird (*Riccordia ricordii*).

permission, the girl in heaven climbed down a chain with a gold mortar, a gold pestle, and a winnowing fork.

She said to her sister, "Rest. Lay down in the straw and I'll do the work for you." And she told her sister who she was and where she lived. She told her about how their mother had left her to die in the trash, as if she were garbage.

"Oh! I want to be a daughter of the Virgin too! Is she very pretty?"

"You must be joking! Is she pretty? She's the most beautiful thing ever . . . And well dressed . . . She's very fancy! But . . . How much rice did mother order you to winnow?"

"A dozen *mancuernas*."[9]

"Rest."

And the older sister sang as she pounded the mortar:

> *Amo goro baraga*
> *Amo goro baraga*
> *Abongo fanga*
> *Fanga fanga*

She finished very quickly, and the younger sister said to her in astonishment, "How am I supposed to carry so much rice?"

The sister carried it to the house for her, because the rice paddy was a long distance away from the house.

The mother kept ordering more and more work from her daughter, who seemed to do the work of four people. She [the mother] was a very mean-spirited woman.

The woman prospered. She did not work, but she grew an abundance of rice and had her daughter do everything for her, and she began to host feasts. And while the mother gave parties, the little girl kept working, always finishing her work in no time at all.

Now, the mother had prepared a great banquet for all her friends and family, so an enormous amount of rice had to be prepared. She took her daughter to the rice paddy and left her there, then—just as soon as the mother had turned her back—the older sister came down. The sisters kissed each other . . . (That's why, ever since then, women kiss each other.) And that day, the older sister brought chocolate from heaven, along with cakes and a bottle of sweet wine, none of which her younger sister had ever tasted on earth.

---

9   DF-N: Although *mancuernas* presumably refers to a measure of weight or volume, the term remains obscure.

An hour later, so much rice was delivered to the house that the mother began to suspect something strange was going on.

"You did this all by yourself? You winnowed all this rice by yourself? No one helped you?"

"Just me by myself . . . Who would help me?"

And the woman said to her husband in secret: "She couldn't have done that by herself. No matter how much the guests eat, rice will be left over. Go to the village and sell half of it."

And she said to the daughter, "Tomorrow, prepare another batch."

The daughter obeyed. She went to the rice paddy early in the morning, but the parents had woken up even earlier and hidden themselves to spy on her.

The little girl looked up to the sky and called her sister.

"*Ngo! Let's see . . .*"

And the sister quickly came down the chain.

The parents saw the young lady who came down from heaven on a chain. She hugged and kissed their daughter, and then said to her, "There's no rush. Have a seat and I'll brush your hair." She brushed her hair and dressed her in a sky-blue dress. Then the parents heard what the girl from heaven had to say. Indeed, she spoke loudly, so they could hear her.

"My mother threw me in the trash. Our mother is evil. Mayimbe rescued me from the trash and took me to the roots of Mamá Ungunda. Since that's the Virgin's domain, thanks to Ngunda, the *tié tié* took me up to heaven. And in heaven, I'm with my Godmother, the Holy Virgin. She gave me a gold mortar and pestle."

The father did not know what the woman had done with his first daughter. This man was not so bad, and the news hurt him . . . The mother heard this and, being greedy, she was filled with a desire to steal the gold mortar and pestle.

"Today we're not working, and Mary Magdalene and the Virgen de la Caridad del Cobre are hosting guests, so I'm going to heaven to prepare rice for the *santos*." And she started dancing, doing a pantomime of pounding and preparing the rice.

> *Yen yen Ngo*
> *Mandarin fangara*
> *Ko marangen*
> *Ke aboborin*

The woman thought, "Now she's going to escape to heaven, and she'll take the gold mortar and pestle with her!" The idea sent her into a rage, so she rushed to grab the mortar and pestle, and her daughters too. But the older sister grabbed the little sister and grabbed the chain, then both sisters climbed up the chain (without leaving the mortar and pestle behind), disappearing from sight as they rose up into a cloud.

The husband killed the woman like a dog. To this day, the girls live the good life with the Virgin Mary, who is called Kenge in Congo.

Money doesn't keep quiet in anyone's pocket, and nobody avoids punishment for the harm they inflict in this life.

A young *babalawo* tells me a Patakin from Odi-Meyi:[10]

A long time ago, "at the beginning of the world," cadavers were not buried. They were taken to *el monte* and placed at the feet of ceiba trees. It was a betrayed husband named Mofa who put an end to this custom. He dug the first grave to punish his wife, whom he buried alive . . . This Mofa from the legend was in love with his wife, but she did not love him or their son. She had an *ale*, a lover, who was not nearly as good as Mofa, and he did not love her nearly as much as Mofa did. Nonetheless, the woman told Mofa that she could not live without her lover, and she told her lover that she could no longer suffer Mofa's company. One day the lover asked the woman if she was willing to be rid of her husband. He had devised a plan by which she would fake being dead. After they left her under a ceiba, he would go to her at daybreak, then take her home with him. It was said and done: the woman died that same night. Mofa's despair was beyond measure, but the moment came when there was no choice but to abandon her cadaver to Iroko. And just as they had agreed, the lover took her from *el monte* at daybreak—just as alive as she had been at both the hour of her death and after her sudden death.

Some time went by. The lover of Mofa's wife sold okra at the market, and it occurred to him that she should be the one selling okra so he could stay home and do nothing. And the woman took his place at the market. One day at the market, her son approached her, but she did not recognize him. Without knowing it, the son was in the habit of buying okra from his mother's lover. The son recognized his mother, and he threw his arms around her neck, but the woman rejected him, protesting with utter callousness that she was not his mother nor anyone else's. But the boy had no doubt whatsoever: he returned home, assuring Mofa that his mother was alive and selling okra in the market.

---

10   DF-N: Odi is one of the sixteen cardinal signs in Ifa divination, and the proverbial husband's name—Mofa—can be translated most simply as a contraction/elision of *omo Ifa*, "child of Ifa." Mofa is the only person named in this story.

"Unfortunately, my son, your *iya* is dead. She was dead when we left her under the ceiba." Three days later, finally giving in to the boy's desperate insistence, Mofa went to the market. He immediately recognized the woman he had adored, and he, too, tried to embrace her, but she shouted, protesting with all the strength in her lungs. Yet poor Mofa shouted even louder, and soon a crowd gathered around them to witness the strange scene.

Mofa's son arrived. He had followed his father's footsteps, thereby revealing the betrayal of that terrible woman who had made death an accomplice to her crime. The crowd demanded she be punished. Fearing another betrayal, Mofa proposed digging a very deep hole in the earth and leaving her there, buried like a seed.

"It wasn't part of those people's customs," the *babalawo* specified, "for women to be unfaithful to their husbands." And ever since that incident, cadavers are no longer taken to Iroko, as was the custom, but rather buried four meters under the earth.

The great god, the Diviner Orula or Orumila—San Francisco (Saint Francis), or Padre Tiempo (Father Time) for the Congos—spent long years buried up to his shoulders at a ceiba. According to one version, he was born after Obatala made an oath to not father male children anymore. The terrible disappointment that led Obatala to formulate such an oath is understandable: his son Ogun had committed incest with his own mother Yemu. But Changó, Obatala's favorite son and constant confidant, had heard the story of that family tragedy from his father's own lips. He hated his brother Ogun, who had been cursed by the Father ever since, eternally condemned to work forging iron.

In a way, Changó had already avenged his father when he stole Ogun's wife, Oya. Now he wanted to save his brother, Orula. He made use of a distressful and difficult situation Obatala faced as a king and which, perhaps due to his age, he could not conquer. On an occasion when Obatala—while in the company of his wife Yemu and Elegua, the youngest of the orishas—lamented the adversity that plagued him, contributing to his aging, hardship, and sorrow, Changó took advantage of the situation by insinuating that the source of those misfortunes was, without a doubt, the burial of Orula.

Obatala asked, "What can I do about that now? Orula is in the hands of Olofi. I, myself, buried him alive under a cciba. Orula is in the hands of Olofi!"

Obatala did not know that Elegua had followed him and seen where Obatala had buried Orula, under an immense and solemn ceiba whose branches rose up to the sky. The elderly and forgetful god Obatala did not remember that he had left Orula's head and shoulders sticking out of the ground. Orula's mother Yemu sent him food daily with Elegua, and the ceiba protected him from inclement weather. In short, Orula was alive. He was, more than anything, a prisoner of the oath, the word (*oro*) of his father.

"Orula is still alive," said Elegua. "Passing by a ceiba, I saw a reddish Black man buried up to his shoulders. And ever since I found him, I've kept going to the ceiba to feed him."

Obatala remembered and exclaimed, "That man, thanks to the mercy of the ceiba, is Orula!"

"Babami," Changó said, "Orula has the gift of Olofi on his tongue and in his eyes, and he can put an end to our misfortunes." Obatala immediately prepared himself to go in search of the ceiba that sheltered Orula. The legend adds that Obatala was losing his memory and could not remember the way back to the ceiba, so Elegua—in order to guide the Old Man without his realizing it and avoid hurting his feelings—appeared at every fork in the road, assuming a different form every time, until he arrived at the ceiba. At every turn, Obatala encountered a different person and offered each a little bit of food from his cooking pot. "Iberu, Babami," said Orula when he saw him. "Ibosise, Orumbila!" Obatala responded and unearthed him. Obatala cut a piece of the tree's trunk, using the wood to carve a divination board, which is sacred to all *babalawos* and which he entrusted to his son, making him the owner of Ifa and the divination board. Orula began to perform divination right away, and—as Changó had said—found a way to overcome all of the troubles that burdened Obala and the other orishas in those days.[11]

On another occasion, Obatala ordered three of his slaves—Aruma, Adima-Adima, and Achama—to cut *guano* fronds (*marigwo*) to make himself a new house.[12] Adima-Adima took the precaution of making *ebo* before entering *el monte*. In order to make the *ebo*, Orula had asked Adima-Adima for the machete he was carrying, which was not his own; it belonged to Obatala. When he met up with Aruma and Achama, they saw he did not have the machete, and they laughed at him, telling him that he should cut the *guano* fronds with his teeth. Then they left him alone.

Adima-Adima was ready, not to cut the *guano* fronds with his teeth, but to rip them with his bare hands, so he entered *el monte* looking for the lowest palms. A ceiba immediately caught his attention. A strange bundle was tied to its trunk and hanging down. Adima-Adima grabbed a stick and managed

---

11   DF-N: Obala is an alternate name for the orisha Obatala, also referred to in this section variously as Obanla, Orishanla, and/or simply Orisha.

12   DF-N: Like the preceding story of Mofa, the story of Adima is often associated with the divination sign Odi in the oratures of both Ifa and *dilogún* divination systems. See Bascom ([1969] 1991, [1980] 1993).

to detach the bundle, making it fall to the ground. Inside, he found a large collection of parrot feathers. The discovery had incalculable importance . . . In secret, Obatala had been searching eagerly for parrot feathers, but they had been oddly difficult to find for some time. Nothing was more valuable to the great Orisha, the sculptor and king of humankind, than those feathers he needed so urgently. Adima-Adima knew how to weave, and he quickly wove a basket of *mariguano*, beautifully arranging the coveted feathers inside. He had not yet finished wrapping up the precious basket when he saw *ayanaku*, a dead elephant, near the ceiba. He ripped out its two magnificent white tusks and wrapped them with the feathers.

Achama and Aruma arrived at Obatala's *ile* long before Adima-Adima. Orishanla asked about Adima-Adima. "We don't know. He didn't go with us. He told us that he gave your machete to Orula." Obatala thundered, "My machete? The machete I gave him so he could serve me?" He called Ogun and said to him, "Adima-Adima lost my machete. As soon as he gets here, cut off his head and drink his blood." And Ogun—*unlo olo ada okuta*—sharpened his machete, then he sat down to wait for Adima-Adima. But when Adima-Adima arrived, the first thing Obatala immediately saw was the parrot feathers and the splendid *enhinrin*, the tusks that the young man—quite pleased with himself—had brought. Obatala gestured to stop Ogun, who was already rising to his feet to comply with his orders.

Adima-Adima placed the feathers and ivory before Obatala, who ordered that a goat be offered to Ogun. "Take the goat, cut off its head, drink its blood, and go." In his joy, Obatala blessed Adima-Adima "for seeing what he needed" and covered him in riches. And for being *ifoyue* and *igo*, blind and stupid, he punished Aruma and Achama.

(N. says, "Adima-Adima is Changó, but many younger *santeras* don't know that anymore.")

At the ceiba, or by means of the ceiba, "mother of all the trees and humans," "Mother of the World," the most impossible things can be obtained. The magical spells cast at a ceiba—with her consent, "con licencia Mama Ungundu"— are considered infallible and indestructible. Her spirit is so powerful that many supplicants feel a weight on the back of their neck when they approach her. They do not necessarily lose consciousness, but they lack the strength to resist. "You need to be brave to face Mama Ungundu at night, alone."

"The ceiba is the altar of the *ganguleros*." Under her, the *ngangas* and *prendas* are "mounted," constructed, and animated. They are deposited under a ceiba so they incorporate the virtues of her shadow and become stronger. Or they are buried, as we already know, so they "learn her mysteries," absorb the energies that are in the roots, "and become consecrated." To the same end, they bury the mirror, *vititi mensu*, which shows them that which is occult. In

Ocha ceremonies, invocations to Iroko—the god of the Ceiba—are indispensable: "Terewama Iroko-Iroko, fumi arere terewama Iroko arere iyaguo." (The Akoire-iyaguo, the initiate in Ocha, should always pray to Iroko.)

Someone once said that, wherever you go, most sorcerers' clientele is driven by evil passions. Although we have seen that the ceiba is a benefactor, "merciful and holy," the invocation of its great power "can also be responsible for a person's misfortune or death." "She does all kinds of work." In this instance, the ceiba is also the mother of Hell. "Indoki is a sorcerer tree, fearsome and merciless, with a huge clientele." Anyone who wants to get rid of a person they hate will go to this tree at midnight or high noon. Entirely naked, they walk around the tree a few times, grazing the trunk with their hand and expressing their desires out loud. Every magical action is carried out by speaking and singing. Everything depends on the word, the prayer, the chant. "The *mambos*"—the chants—"give the orders." "A song can raise a house made of stone." When he was a child, Conguito once saw the great *gangulero* from his hometown of Alquízar make an immense cloud form in the sky, then make a torrential rain fall at the time he had decreed it would. "His *mambos* brought the rain." The rivalries between the *mayomberos* in that town's Black neighborhoods—Paloma and Catalina—were powered by their *mambos*, and they gave rise to the most astounding events on both sides. "Just like that, speaking sweetly to the ceiba, singing to it and pleading with it, you're able to touch her feelings and get her to do your bidding. All your most wicked desires . . ." The person who goes to solicit support for a wicked act will position themselves upside down under the tree, "like a *guembo*" (bat). In that posture, they will feel the effect of a spirit that will lift them off the ground. The person reiterates their desire and purpose to this spirit: "They say all the wickedness in their heart." Then, a drink of aguardiente is offered at the roots, tobacco smoke is offered, and a few coins are deposited as payment. Then they grab a new *cabiblanco* [white-handled] knife and wound the tree, saying, "Mamá Nfumbe, just as I am wounding you, wound So-and-So in the middle of their chest." They should make four slashes "on its *cuatro vientos*" [four winds]: one on each side of the trunk; North, South, East, and West. A lit candle is left as a final offering.

The wounds received by the ceiba are quickly received by the body—"the physical health"—of the subject one intends to annihilate.

"To take a fellow's life? There are so many ways to do it! First, one uses gunpowder to ask if it's possible, because if Sambia wants to take them himself, they can't be killed. If I have permission to do it, I'll go to the graveyard with a silver *real* to buy the life of the man or woman that bothers me. I open a hole in the ground, put the coin inside, and pay the earth. That's the person's grave. That man now has an open grave. I light the tail end of a blessed candle that I swiped from a church, and I take with me, wrapped in a clean rag, a little bit of the dirt from the hole . . . that's waiting for them. I work with that dirt in my *nganga*. I go to *el monte*, to the ceiba. I heat up a nail. When it's red hot, I nail it and curse it. I take a piece of the small cloth that I used to carry the dirt and put it in the Prenda. Then, every day, cursing, I hit it with an *escoba judía*.[13] And as I'm hitting the Prenda, the Prenda is also cursing that man, and the man will die."

"When you collect a *nganga* from the ceiba where it's been buried after it's committed so much wickedness, you need to burn a black cat. Or abuse it, to make it furious. And when it's desperate and enraged from the pain, you cut its head off and pour the blood over the roots and trunk of the tree."

A good woman confesses her regrets to me: more than thirty years ago, desperate from having been mistreated by her husband, she exacted revenge on him. The sorcerer in charge of freeing her from that man was possessed by the spirit Téngue Malo. He wrapped a black cloth over his head and tied another to his waist (as he does whenever he performs a curse). He skewered a scorpion—alive, furious, and wrapped in black thread—with a needle, then he started to call the husband by his first and last names. He took a little bit of grass, a human canine tooth, and a piece of fabric from one of the husband's sweaty shirts. And putting that all together—"wrapped up tight and prayed over"—he took it to a ceiba. There, he asked for the perdition of that man once again, then he nailed the scorpion to the trunk of the tree. He kept calling the man's name repeatedly—"calling him and cursing him, calling him and cursing him"—until the scorpion was left lifeless, nailed to the ceiba.

That very same night, the spirit of the scorpion stung the bewitched husband in a dream, and that was the beginning of an illness that sent him to his grave a few months later.

The same witchcraft can be done with a frog, *chula*. It consists of filling the animal's mouth with a bit of salt and a piece of paper with the victim's name written on it. Or the name is said out loud and blown into the frog's mouth, which will be sewn shut with a piece of fabric from an outfit or handkerchief that belonged to the person being bewitched. The frog is kept in a pot and taken to a ceiba so it dies there, desperate, cursing the person who is to blame for inflicting that torment on them. And one says, "Die, rage, and suffer, So-and-So, like this frog is suffering!"

If, as an act of vengeance, one wishes to ruin an unborn child in its mother's belly, a steel needle is run through the belly of a spider that is about to give birth. A little bit of bone from a *kiyumba*, or skull, is scraped from the *nganga*,

---

13 DF-N: An *escoba judía*—literally, "a Jewish broom"—is a broom made from *palmiche* (royal palm).

as well as bone from a phalange in the foot. This is mixed with the bones of a chameleon or a bat, which are also reduced to powder. Together with the live spider, these powders are wrapped up and bound with black thread. One says, "This is how I drive a nail into the belly of So-and-So. This is how I pierce the child in the belly of So-and-So. Just as this spider dies, the child of So-and-So will die." And so on. But it is recommended that this witchcraft be nailed to the trunk of a ceiba so the "muerto" takes care of the rest. And if it is not taken to a ceiba, it should be left in a cemetery.

In order to protect children from the evil eye (to which they are always exposed), a thorn from the *ceibón* tree—"a male ceiba"—works as a powerful talisman that is often carried by the children of peasants, hanging from a safety pin, or tied on a string around their neck or wrist. Such an archaic belief, which is both universal and permanent, keeps the mothers among our people—both black and white—continually on edge. Regardless of social class, maternal love succumbs easily to this tenacious superstition whose origins are lost in the darkest night of the past. More than a few women, who are strong in spirit and boast of their skepticism, will take care—"just in case"— to protect their children with a pagan coral charm, or a little hand made from jet or ebony, the *figa*, which dispels or absorbs evil in order to protect the child.

"One must believe in the evil eye!" "The woman who does not realize there could be evil eyes that sicken and bewitch the little ones might lose a child due to carelessness."

In a clinical tone, one midwife tells me, "I'm an educated person, and I laugh at all the fairy tales that ignorant people believe. But not the evil eye. The evil eye is real."

I cannot help but agree . . .

Did the authors and the fathers of the Church during the Middle Ages not recognize it? Did the Church not accept the existence of the Devil— complete with horns, a tail, spurs, and the scent of sulfur—with whom the *aojadores* (purveyors of the evil eye) share kinship?

It is midwives who believe most firmly—based on their own experience—in the power of this abominable talent, which is possessed by so many human eyes. Without hesitation, they know how to attribute the causes of certain physical defects whose malignance might not have been suspected— particularly cross-eyed children who had been watched by "some evil eyes" while they slept.

(Regarding cross-eyed people, Teofila says, "They're not good. My mother used to tell us that in Congo de Ntotila, being cross-eyed was a big disgrace. Her elders told her that newborns who were cross-eyed came with bad spirits inside them, so they killed them right away so they wouldn't do any harm.")

Like the thorn of the *ceibón*, which is used as a protective charm for children ("it pricks whoever gives them a bad look"), a white plate with an eye painted on it that is fixed behind the door of a house will also protect adults living there from evil looks.

There is no doubt that those who fear these eyes are correct. It is understood that many people can do harm involuntarily, and that any person—sometimes very much in spite of themselves—might be *aradye, oyuofo, oyunika, oyuburu, aojadora.*[14]

Sagacious, superstitious people, Black and white, all fear the evil eye, which is sometimes treacherously concealed in courtesy or flattery. When they are asked about their health—even if it is superb—they carefully avoid answering resolutely. Instead they stammer a prudent and vague "So-so, nothing special." The old Lucumí would limit their answer to the dangerous question, "Are you well?" "More or less: *vira virando.*" And they would never say, "I'm very well, thank you." Of course, one should never boast about their good luck, or anything else enviable: if a feeling of envy is awakened in the soul, the eyes—the mirrors of the soul—suddenly become evil, "unintentionally." They can break an object (they broke my neighbor Nena V.'s fancy comb), dry out a plant, or break the string on a coveted necklace. One song declares, "There are eyes that can knock coconuts out of trees and kill a turtle under the water." The eyes act as truly maleficent spirits. They are capable—unconsciously, as we have said—of causing convulsions or high fevers in children. Or even sudden death.

Cape reminds us that a Black man known as Gregorio Cinco Minutos killed the son of P.L., another man who was very beloved in the town of Alquízar:[15]

Mister P.L. was a very good person, and very well respected in Alquízar. He married a young woman when he was quite mature, and the heavens gave him a son that was truly his own. The old man was crazy about his son.

One day after school, the boy approached Gregorio, who was sitting on the sidewalk with a little display set up to sell peanuts. The boy saw the display, and he was curious, so he asked, "What are you selling?"

"That's the last time you ask something that's none of your business."

---

14 DF-N: These are Lucumí terms for evil-doer, several of which refer literally to eyes (*oyu*); except *aojadora*, which is a Spanish idiom referring to the owner or purveyor of an "evil eye."
15 DF-N: Alquízar, located southwest of Havana in the present-day province of Artemisa, was the hometown of Cape, one of Cabrera's most notable informants, and she may have conducted research there. Meanwhile, we can only speculate about the origins of Gregorio's nickname, which translates literally as Gregory Five Minutes.

A short time later, Don Pedro's son was thrashing around in pain, dying. By the time the doctor arrived, the boy was already cold. But the nanny had overheard what happened, so we all looked for Gregorio, as if he were a gold coin. The townspeople wanted to kill him, but Gregorio disappeared. He left Alquízar.[16]

One of my childhood friends could write a fascinating book about the intimate details of life during colonial times in Cuba. She told me the story of how her mother nearly died as a little girl, a victim of the evil eye, and how she was saved by the shrewdness of her African nanny.

The woman belonged to one of the most distinguished and wealthy families in Cuba. They were distinguished in many respects: one of its illustrious members—largely forgotten and possibly unknown to the present generation, which only nourishes itself on the military glories of the war of Independence—was one of the most noble and generous characters in the history of nineteenth-century Cuba.

On her deathbed, my friend's grandmother had asked her husband to never deprive the two children she was leaving behind of the care and protection of a particular slave from the Lucumí nation. The slave had earned the grandmother's complete confidence after many years of service, during which she proved her absolute loyalty.

In fact, the Black woman, Yeye, served those orphans with a poignant devotion until the end of her days:[17]

My grandfather bought a shipment of slaves for the sugar mill, and he reserved some of them for service in the house. My mother was a healthy child, but, without exhibiting any other signs of illness, she started getting thinner and paler. Nobody noticed the slightest change in her until a friend who hadn't seen her for a long time visited the mill and alerted the family. They called the doctor—a cousin and very close friend of my grandfather's—to examine her. But Yeye, for her part, went to consult the old man Kubi from Sabanilla del Comendador.[18] This diviner, a compatriot

---

16 DF-N: If we set accusations of witchcraft aside, this is plainly the story of an attempted lynching.

17 DF-N: The Lucumí names in this passage might be symbolic and/or literal. Yeye is an honorific Lucumí name for Mother, which is layered on the story of Cabrera's friend's mother, and Kubi might be a contraction of Ikúbíyìí (meaning Death Gave Birth to This One).

18 DF-N: Sabanilla del Encomendador (misspelled as Sabanilla del Comendador) is the historical name of present-day Juan Gualberto Gómez, a town in the municipality of Union de Reyes, in the province of Matanzas. Located just south of Cidra, it was founded in 1879, then renamed in 1934 in honor of Gómez, a hero in the Cuban War of Independence.

of Yeye, assured her that there was a Black woman among the new slaves who had evil eyes, and she was the sole cause of Mother's illness.

Later, Yeye said that one of the other slaves found out what was happening and offered to enact a curse with an enchanted arrow: she said that by pointing the arrow at a leaf and piercing it, the other slave would be blinded and never look at anyone else with an evil eye. Yeye was a very good person, and when she heard all of this, she pleaded with her master to send away the woman and the other slave. He never refused her anything: both of the other slaves were sold off, and the girl recovered as soon as those evil eyes stopped looking at her.

Teresa M., Omi-Tomi, recalls the case—one among several others—of a seven-year-old *mulata* girl who was the victim of the evil eyes of a pair of civil guards during the Spanish colonial era. The girl was sitting in the window. (It is true that she had no protective charm: no amber or coral beads, no jet pendant, no dog's fang around her neck or hanging from a bracelet.) The Spaniard said, "What a beautiful girl!" And the two of them gave her a *real* coin so she could buy some sweets. As soon as the guards left, the poor thing began trembling. "I understood immediately: they put the evil eye on her!" "She was ruined by those Orden Público [Public Order] soldiers." And Omi-Tomi, expanding on her memories, adds, "Her mother was a little crazy. She'd already lost a little boy that she adored because he was white, and she didn't want to give birth to *mulatos*. When the little boy died, she dressed him in Turkish costume, and there was a *rumba* at the house.[19] They sang, going around the coffin, accompanied by drumming on the box: 'Pitiminí is gone, Pitiminí is gone, Pitiminí, ay! Pitiminí, Pitiminí.'" That was the custom among the people, to celebrate the death of children, and some of it endures. In the countryside, the wake would keep going until the stench of the cadaver became unbearable. But Teresa buried her, and she prohibited "songs, *rumba*, or costumes."

"Wakes for children were like a *rumba*. It was a lot of dancing around the coffin. Especially if the little dead child was a son, nephew, or godchild of a *clave* or *rumba* musician, or one of the people from the *comparsa* troupes who go out during Carnival. They would dress the cadaver with the outfit and colors of the group. Colleagues from other *clave* or *comparsa* groups would come and dress them up in their own colors. That way, the little dead child was dressed and undressed constantly."

---

19 DF-N: Here, *rumba* refers generically to a party with singing, dancing, and drumming, not necessarily to a specific musical form or style.

A child should not be praised casually without accompanying the compliment with "May God protect them." "If anything happens to the child, if they get sick or cry in a difficult way, then the parents think someone has put an evil eye on them." In the countryside, a *güajiro* trembles if anyone compliments an animal. The evil eye can kill offspring. How many yearlings have succumbed to a look, or perhaps an ill-intentioned or even naively reckless compliment!

The use of *azabache* [jet] is common and necessary: it breaks at the appropriate time, acting as a harbinger of the danger caused by those powerful, harmful looks. Along with a jet charm, the child should also have a coral bead (the red color distracts or weakens the owner of the evil eye's sight) and an amber bead, which has a preventive quality, as well as an attractive red bow.

Additionally, it is prudent to carry a clove of garlic and a small piece of camphor hidden in a small bag, although many believe that the most efficacious method is to carry the well-known, tried-and-true prayer of San Luis Beltrán folded in a cloth pocket as a scapular. That classic prayer: "Save all the little angels and animals from the evil eye."

In any case, a vigilant mother who hears her child being praised will pinch the child or discreetly find some other pretext to make them cry. Their crying "breaks the spell of the evil eye."

In short, we will find that adults—though they may be stronger and more resilient—are no less susceptible to *oyu ofo*.

The thirtysomething niece of a *santera* friend of mine was a very good dancer. She danced so well that she was the object of so much admiration and had people's eyes on her: because *oyu kokoroi* [big eyes] were fixed on her feet, she was run over by a car coming out of a party, and her injuries left her lame . . . And I should confess that I am guilty of directing "great envy of the dangerous sort, the kind that rises up to the eyes," in the direction of a poor old lady when I went to visit her with the gift of a pair of shoes. The day she wore them for the first time, a neighbor watched her with "eyes that turned evil," and she suffered a fall getting off the trolley. But this tree resists all the fury of nature's elements; it is invulnerable to fire and hurricanes. A small piece of it works as a protective charm for whoever carries it, whether they are a child or an elder—not only from the evil eye, but from any possible harm. (From the wickedness of the living or the dead.) The *villumbero* C. assures us: there is no "guard" more dependable than a small branch from a ceiba to prevent wandering spirits from entering homes. A cross made from pieces of ceiba is fixed behind a door to calm homes in which creaking and inexplicable mysterious noises are heard: the ceiba clears out and keeps away intrusive, disturbed spirits that do not dare return. (The Ariku-Bambaya also performs this delicate function of impeding the entry of disturbing or harmful spirits into the house: it is a protective charm consisting of a stick dressed in a *faldeta* [a ruffled, layered, and colorful apron] that is fed like Elegua and placed behind the door.)

Another herbalist explains to me that there are seven possible ways to "work" with the ceiba, as indicated by the tree's own leaves.[20] Every part of this prodigious tree serves the sorcerer in his work: its trunk, for tying down and binding; its shade, to attract and call the spirits and bathe *ngangas* and all manner of protective objects—amulets and talismans made by sorcerers, which G.S. describes as "little *santos*, guardians who defend their owner"— in its powerful spiritual emanations; and the colossal roots ("we call them the stirrups of Mamá Ungundu"), which sink into the earth and walk along underground for very long distances. Among these stirrups or roots, they deposit their *wembas*, invoking and conjuring. The earth surrounding the tree "is full of the power of Odua and Agayu, who is also the owner of the river and is saluted and 'praised' at the ceiba: 'Oba Agayu sola okuo e wikini sogu iya loro ti bako mana mana olodumare kawo kabie si. Oluo mi, eku fedyu tana.'"

The leaves—seven are taken—provoke the manifestation of the spirit in the initiations of Palo Monte. "The *muerto* goes to look for Sanda." The initiate or "rayado" [the one who has been scratched or cut]—the new "*gando*," "head, *moana ntu*" of the *nganga*, "the novice"—sometimes takes a while to become possessed by the spirit. Jesús Santos recalls, "The *palo* doesn't always mount right at the beginning, or the same day a child is sworn. Sometimes the *fumbi*, before grabbing them, starts disturbing their heads. I lost my hearing. I couldn't open my eyes, and my heart kept racing from fear. When I woke up in the morning, my body felt like it was made of lead. It was as if I had pepper in my eyes, and I carried a weight that I couldn't bear. I was dazed. But all of that stops when the *palo* knocks you down." (The spirit in Regla Congo mounts—physically—astride the shoulders of the medium, who carries it on his back. In order for the spirit to depart and not punish the medium too much, it is sometimes necessary to burn *fula* directly on their back. The "yimbi" does not see with his own eyes, which remain closed during the entirety of the possession: "He sees from behind, from the back of the neck, where the *ndoki* is seated." That is why a mirror is held to the base of the cranium, so the spirit sees the images that appear in it and gives an account of what it sees.)

During the period of their initiation into Palo Monte, neophytes generally find themselves in an intermittent state of mental confusion. In some cases, as José Santos describes them to us, this can be permanent. After twenty-one days, they unearth a set of clothes that should have been buried in the cemetery

---

20 DF-N: The Ceiba's leaf has seven points.

during three Fridays in order to saturate them with the energy of the *muerto*. Then they are dressed in those clothes "so that their bodies are like that of a cadaver" and taken to a ceiba where the *palero*—their godfather—has his *nganga*, since many *mayomberos* in the countryside keep their *prendas* under ceibas, and these initiations are celebrated in *el monte*.

There they are made to kneel down, then the first *mambo* is sung: *Bangarake mamboya pangiame*. With this chant, the sorcerer, his assistant, and the *tikán-tikán* (godmother) invoke their deceased predecessors and the *palo*, the spirit of the *muerto* who serves the godfather and *nfumo*.

The spirit should acknowledge the initiate as a *gandó*, a *nkómbo* or *ngómbe*—yet another body he will enter from then on to become manifest, "a body the spirit enters, transforming the body into a spirit."[21] The forehead of the new *moana ntu nganga*—who should become the vehicle for such powerful spirits as Lucero-Mundo, Centella Monte Oscuro, Siete Rayos, Rumba Loma, Tumbirona Batalla, Vira Mundo, and Mamá Viviana—is crowned with ceiba leaves. Irresistibly attracted by the leaves, the "*muerto*"—according to the figures of speech used by *nganguleros*—"crowns the head of the new dog." A white plate with a lit candle is placed in his hands, then he is given the *kisenge* or Aguanta Mano del Muerto—the magical scepter of the sorcerer in trance, which consists of a tibia, earth from a grave, and other substances used to make a *nganga*, all of which are covered in black cloth and grass. This personifies the spirit and puts the "dog" or medium in communication with the world of shadows, *kalunga* or *kaluanga*.

Channeled by the tibia, the soul of the *muerto* penetrates into the living body, and, in total possession of its instrument, the spirit promptly identifies itself. It responds to the *mambos* that are directed toward it, engages in conversation with the father, the assistant, the godmother, and the other "children" who are present.

It declares that it is satisfied, that it is pleased with the medium, the "*yákara moana mpanguian lukámba nfíndo ntoto*, that person who's been buried in the cemetery."

The old man Baró recalls, "That's what they told me Centellita said when she knocked me out."

> *Ahora sí me voy con él*
> *Hueso cambia, no hay agravio,*
> *Hasta la púngun sáwo.*
> *Me voy con él hasta púngun sáwo,*

---

21 DF-N: Cabrera's original used the term "(*sic*)" to indicate an error in this statement, but her reason—presumably theological in nature—remains unclear.

Me voy con él pa la Casa Grande
Me voy con él pa medio Nfinda!

Now I'm really going with him
The bone is exchanged, there's no offense
All the way to the cemetery
I'm going with him all the way to the cemetery
I'm going with him to the Big House
I'm going to the middle of *el monte* with him.

As he departs, the *yimbi* tends to sing a farewell:

Má ceiba recoge tu sombra,
Abre tu puerta yo voy a entrá
Casa Grande, yo me voy,
Má ceiba coge tu sombra,
Abre tu puerta . . .

Mother ceiba, gather your shade,
Open your door, I'm going in
Mother ceiba, catch your shade
Big House, I'm coming,
Open your door . . .

"The leaves of the ceiba are the best cleansing for the head of a novice *yimbi*, so long as they are not crowned or mounted by Zarabanda or Madre-Agua." In cases where "the spirit is delayed," the leaves are applied with a little earth from the four corners of the cemetery. The head—which, according to Baró, is not fed in the manner of the Lucumí—and chest of the initiate are covered with the sign of the cross and bathed with ceiba bark, leaves from *yaya*, *guara*, *palo caja*, *téngue*, and *rompezaragüey*, all ripped up in water with aguardiente, ashes, wine, and melted candle wax.

It should go without saying that water has a sacred value in Palo Monte initiations. "Sin Mamba Ntoto fwá. ¡Ñan fuiri!" (Without water, the earth dies: water, *mamba*, *lango*, *masa*; it is inseparable from life itself, an element that generates life.) An ablution to dissolve all impurities precedes every religious act in Regla Congo, as in Regla de Ocha—indeed, as in all religions, always and forever.

The initiate in Palo Monte is "prepared," purified, by cleansing their body of any stain with baths that—like *omiero*—can provide complete regeneration.

To that end, a trough or some other large receptacle, such as a large clay pot—or, in earlier times, clay vessels imported from Seville, which are no longer to be found in Cuba—is filled with leaves (*nkanda-lele-nkunia* or *difue*) from *ceiba, guara, yaya, tengue,* and *caja.* These constitute the *mamba nsambia "pa' jurán nganga"*—the sacred water of Congo initiatory rites and sacred oaths.

The first step in the consecration in the Regla de Mayombe or Palo consists of drinking and bathing in an infusion of leaves from the ceiba and the other "strong trees" we have mentioned; their powerful properties are absorbed by the future *ngombe* in three long swallows that are administered while he is being bathed. Then the obligatory, indispensable visit to the cemetery: *campo simba, plaza liri, casa grande* or *quita peso, kariempemba, kabalonga, kumanso fumbi, malón, bansa lombahasadieto, pungun sawa, chamalongo, nso fuiri, kumangongo, sokinakue, kambonfinda, ntoto nfinda,* etc.

Paleros like Baró, who are children of Camposanto, do not go to the river. They do not purify themselves, like the Lucumí adepts, by immersing themselves completely in the current of running water, a cleansing that precedes the baths in *omiero* in a tub at the house of an *orisa.*

"The ceiba attracts *muertos* like a magnet," Baró insists. "It gives the *yimbi* clarity if they have the spirit of Lucero Mundo, Tiembla-Tiembla, or Acaba Mundo, which are all related energies. But one does not put its leaves on the *ntu* ("head," or medium) of Baluande, Mamá Fungue, Mamá Choya, or Kisimba, which are Madre de Agua."

"In Palo, Nkundia Lemban Sao pulls *muerto,* nothing else."

For his part, a *kimbisa* adds, "And you don't put ceiba in a Zarabanda."

The "swearing of the oath"—the initiation ceremony in Mayombe—should take place in *el monte* proper, underneath a ceiba or another *nkita* tree.

One of my old informants, although he is a *mayombero judío,* was nevertheless sworn "properly, as God commands," in the countryside. "Under the tree, not locked up in a room." During his seclusion, the sky, the sun, the moon, the clouds, and the tall, immense branches of Sanda Nkunia were the roof over his head. His feet stepped on *ntoto,* the earth—contact that gives life. Generally, a ceiba is the location for encounters by which sorcerers establish a personal and continuous communication with an otherworldly being who advises them on the most effective instruments of attack and defense, makes and animates the instruments, and works through his *wembas* and *bilongos.* In the countryside, the would-be *mayombero* sleeps under the ceiba for seven nights.

"When an evil (*judío*) sorcerer is in *el monte* and feels like it's high noon or midnight, he takes off his clothes, and—completely naked—kicks the ground three times, spits on the tree trunk three times, and calls Lungambe." (The hour is intuited by the *palero,* since one cannot take a wristwatch into *el monte:* "*El monte* has its own time, and time is not the same inside *el monte* as outside *el monte.* Spirits don't use watches. The light and dark are their clocks.")

But when you're there and whatever is coming finally presents itself, you need a lot of courage, and then you need to be ready to follow the orders you're given.

If the spirit that was called says that someone needs to go get a *muerto* at the cemetery, then they go. And they come back with the remains in a black bag and leave them at the foot of the tree. Then they come back again the next day and light a candle. The deceased shows up, and that is the very dangerous moment when the agreement is sealed with words; the moment to weigh the cost of one's word, and the final word on the price to be paid.

This is the time to stipulate, accept, or reject the demands of the *muerto* that will become enslaved to the sorcerer—"to make the agreement and the commitment." In short, this applies to *nganga* for pure Mayombe ("*muerto* and *palo*"), Villumba or Kimbisa ("crossed with *santo*," as in the case of the sect founded by Andrés Petit), or another sort of *nganga* in which the spirit of a *muerto* is the agent of a terrestrial, igneous, or aquatic deity that moves and directs it. "But allow me to explain it clearly. A *matari* (a stone) is kept in the cauldron where Fumandanda Kinpeso comes . . . who, in Congo, is like Oba, Saint Rita. Or Pungu Iyá Ñaba, La Mercedes. You understand? Another *kimbisa* might put the old man Tata Funde Cuatro Vientos in their cauldron, or Tondo, who is—in the Congo path—Orunla, Saint Francis. Or they have Gran Mama Lola."

("It's Yola, damn it!" a centenarian rectifies emphatically. "Yolá or Mama Sambia, not just any Lola or Lolita . . . Damn! That's the mother of God. She's the first thing the *ngangulero* salutes.")

"Another one that comes into a *prenda* and works is Cheche Wanga Furibimutambo. With her, you can't kill anyone and—go figure—you might kill a lot of people . . . And another *santo*, Mama Kalunga, La Virgen de Regla, the ocean of the Congo."

Kalunga, Juan Lara tells us, can mean many things. "Because *muerto* is Kalunga. A strange thing is Kalunga. The cemetery is Kalunga, and hell, and the other world. And a king is Kalunga. And the ocean is Kalunga."

"When you hear that song that says, 'By one foot, Kalunga carries me away, by one foot,' it's not talking about the ocean. It's the *muerto*." "Kalunga is *santo*, death."

"Some people also mix Palo with Ocha, which brings in Oya Kariempemba, Centella, Zarabanda, Ogun, Tata Legua, and Santa Bárbara, which is Nsasi."

Whether a *nganga* is *cristiana* or *judía*, the "dog" or "servant"—the medium—is nothing more than a spokesperson for the *muerto*, the *nkita*, or the *mpungu* that takes control of their body, speaks through their mouth, and carries out actions with their hands. In case of illness, they are always consulted by their godchildren and the believers who frequent the house of a Padre Mayombe, Kimbisa, or Villumba, and we very often see the *yimbi* employ the power of the ceiba, obtaining radical healing through her, particularly in treatments for "the viper's bite," syphilis.

In the magical and folk medicine of Cuba, the ceiba always enjoys a traditional prestige as an excellent and specific means to combat venereal diseases and urinary tract disorders.

A small piece of its root, cut on Holy Saturday or on the feast day of San Juan, is mixed with the roots from *palo ateje* (which should be from the side of the tree facing the rising sun), *piñon lechoso*, Palm, and *bejuco ahorca-perro*, which together are prescribed as an infusion to treat kidney disease and kidney stones. These tisanes are a specialty of *paleros*. Made with leaves and roots from strong trees, vines, and plants from *el monte*, they are given to patients to drink like regular water. They cure all illness, and they are very popular, especially for venereal and renal illness.

A *güajiro* boils leaves from the ceiba and makes his cow drink the decoction if it has become a little anemic after giving birth, or a calf, or his own child if it is pale or rickety. The cow, heifer, or child quickly gain strength at very little cost.

However it is used, the ceiba is a powerful purifying and restorative tonic that is guaranteed by faith.

Oriol is the youngest child of a well-known *mayombero* in my folkloric neighborhood. He is also a son of Agayu—San Cristóbal, one of the residents and principal owners of the ceiba, as we know. (Niní clarifies: "Yes, the children of Agayu should go to the ceiba because Iroko is a child of Agayu. His mother gave him to the ceiba to heal him. The mother couldn't repay the ceiba, so the ceiba kept Iroko, the *santo* that lives in its trunk. The children of Agayu find remedies at the ceiba.")

As soon as the child shows the slightest discomfort, his father will pick some leaves from a ceiba, which he has kept planted in a pot from the time the child was born. He puts them in boiled water and administers the cure: the youngster already knows the virtues of the concoction and how it works wonders; recently, it cured him of some rather mysterious bouts of fever.

Indeed, for the sake of a person's protection, one follows the instructions of a *santero* and plants a tree that has a relationship or belongs to their Angel or orisha, then cares for it religiously in order to prosper and maintain their health.

It is the plants—the *ewe*—of an individual's Patron Saint that are sympathetic and beneficial to him; other plants with which he does not share an affinity might harm him. That is why the herbalist should be very careful about prescribing plants: they do not have the same effect on everyone, and those which serve one person well might be toxic for another. In general terms, everything that disagrees with the temperament of the deity that rules a person's destiny should be avoided: foods, colors, places, occupations, etc.

A sensible *iyalocha*, a good *babalocha*, first determines the identity of the tutelary orisha of a head before launching into a recommendation for a simple cleansing. A *mayombero* should proceed in the same way when they prepare an amulet.

They made a protective charm for the *chino* [Chinese man] S. After a short time, this "prenda" started shaking his bed, lifting the frame and dropping it suddenly, and blowing in its ears. But it was not satisfied with these pranks, which were followed by more unpleasant manifestations.

The *chino* S. did not know how to control the power contained in that "prenda" *mayombera*. It ended up driving him mad. One night, the man's wife called two of his friends at one thirty in the morning. They found S. huddled on the floor, trembling, with his eyes bulging out of their sockets. These two friends were *paleros*. One of them was a "strong palero" who went into action with the utmost energy and speed. At that early hour, he carried the "prenda" and the *chino*—who was now completely out of his mind—on foot, heading to a farm that had a cesspit.

(These cesspits, which are so fearsome and full of mystery, are used to dispose of witchcraft. When we come to one of them, we should remember to always pass on their left side.) One of the story's protagonists tells me, "When we took the *makuto* to the cesspit, we could hear children crying all over *el monte*. We didn't turn our heads, even when they called out to us. We kept moving forward, but I won't deny it: all three of us were shaking in terror. We were praying in Congo: 'Sakula musakula mumbansa musukundenda . . . batuka Sambe barukurunda bingarakange!' Our teeth were chattering like castanets. We did what we had to do, and as soon as the pit swallowed the *prenda, el monte* went quiet." And the good *chino* S. was freed from that energy that was too violent for him.

The kind and dependable M.H. planted a ceiba in our garden with the generous intention that it would protect us until the end of our days . . .

Indeed, planting a ceiba is not a trivial matter. It is not a simple, profane act. It is more consequential than simply germinating a seed and growing another tree, which nevertheless always remains a miraculous thing in itself. Whoever plants a ceiba knowingly enters a religious commitment of major significance: "The ceiba is used to make sacraments." A mysterious thread will tie them to the sacred tree, which will dispense its protection and obligate them to pay certain tributes.

Generally, four people in a very close friendship, four "compadres"—*bakuyulas ngangas*—ritual brethren in *nganga* (of different sexes)—get together to plant and baptize a ceiba. The important thing is that these religious siblings get along and share an absolute mutual trust. "With a godfather, a godmother, and holy water, ceibas are baptized." Each one of these four individuals will bring earth from four different places: North, South, East, and West. (Daqui, Dumosi de Mensu, was the name of the gorgeous ceiba belonging to the sorcerer named Lincheta at the Marañón sugar mill; next to her, he had also planted Centella, "a matari," which was the *santo* that worked with his *nganga*.)

"It is baptized with prayers and by soaking the earth with the blood of a heifer, a male pig, or—more simply, when there's no *owo* (money)—a rooster. Then it's offered twelve boiled eggs covered in palm oil and cocoa butter, crackers, and other tidbits."

According to C., the most auspicious day to plant a ceiba for religious purposes is November 16, Agayu's day. The planting and ritual should be completed before twelve noon. Like "a newborn child" who has just been given a name, a party is thrown, and its baptism is celebrated with drumming and dancing.

"In the end, we swear an oath to adore her for the rest of our lives and nourish her every year. Planting a ceiba and consecrating it is the same as making an *nganga* and forming an alliance with her. Our health and luck will depend on her."

Every time a child is born to a *palero* or the godfather or godmother of a ceiba, they take the child and offer it to the protector tree so the tree will bless them, bathing the child in its shade and imbuing it with its strength.

This child will quickly learn to venerate the ceiba, to love and fear it: they will understand that they depend on it, like their parents and siblings.

"The baptism of a ceiba creates new generations"—spiritual kinships—"and descendants of the tree."

When a member of the brotherhood dies, a funeral ceremony is celebrated under the ceiba: the belongings of the deceased are placed in its shade and the remainder of the candles from the wake are burned, consumed alongside Mother Ceiba, so the soul of the deceased can be illuminated there. "The deceased sees the lights and finds peace at the ceiba, so they don't suffer in loneliness and darkness."

Apart from the construction of a *nganga*, a devotee who wants to feel protected by Iroko or Sanda can plant a ceiba himself by simply pouring holy water and tossing some coins and grains of corn into the open hole in the earth. It does not matter if they do not know how to pray in Congo or

Lucumí: they can say an Our Father and a Hail Mary in Spanish, because these ceibas—which our Black people, always in deep communion with nature and the earth, call Mother—"receive and understand people's prayers in every language, since they're all her children." To convey reverence and salute her at twelve noon or ten o'clock at night, anyone can "greet her in their own way, with whatever words come from their heart." (As Oddedei says, "Everyone speaks to God however they're able. In the end, Olofi only hears words that come from the heart.")

One *kimbisa*—a Mayordomo Nganga from Santo Cristo del Buen Viaje—shares a prayer he recites to the ceiba that he planted on his patio. Holding a crucifix in his left hand and kneeling, he says:

"Nikisi, Most Holy Sacrament of the Altar. Father, Son, Holy Spirit. Three persons in one and only one true essence. Virgin Mary and Mother Mary that cover Sambi. Ba Ceiba. *Con licencia* Nsambi and my Tatandi and Gandi *mi bisi*. With your permission, Mother Ceiba, at this moment I *mbobo* (speak) with all my *nchila* (heart) to call on your divine influence. And you are here before me, venerable example of motherly tenderness, flower of all children, form of all forms, soul and spirit and harmony. Ceiba, keep me, protect me, and guide me. Free me from evil spirits that continually besiege us, without us knowing it . . ." etc. (He then asks for what he wants.) Having finished the prayer, he kisses the root and trunk, spills three drops of water on the earth, strikes the ground three times with his hand, and moves away without turning his back to the sacred tree, Mabirinso Sambi . . . "altar of Nkisi, of the Holy Spirit," Mamé (Mother).

Whenever a tree is planted for religious purposes, one puts money, holy water, and blood in the hole that will receive the seed.

The spirit of the ceiba is eminently maternal. R.H. advises us,

Iroko is female . . . A lot of people go around believing Iroko is the Holy Spirit, male. But that is a huge misunderstanding.

That's why all the *santos* and spirits take shelter in her, because she is Mother.

Mother that doesn't abandon her children in hard times.

Did she save Desiderio Lima, the slave of Don Juan Lima? Yes, that really happened. That man Desiderio had an attractive wife, another slave, at the sugar mill, named Felipa. The assistant Overseer—Yito—fell in love with her. One day Yito went and shouted at Felipa:

"Come here, Black woman!"

"Sir?"

"Go sleep in my house tonight. I need you."

Felipa understood the assistant Overseer's order. But at six o'clock, she did not go. She disobeyed because, once everyone had scattered after work, her husband Desiderio told her, "Don't go. Go sleep in our *bohío* as usual."

The next morning, Felipa lined up to work at six o'clock, and Yito called her.

"Stand there, Black woman!" And he said to Leandro, the second assistant Overseer, "Send me four Black men." And Desiderio was one of the four men selected.

"Beat that Black woman."

Desiderio, the husband, jumped up:

"Go ahead and try! I'm the one who's going to beat you!"

"Desiderio! How dare you? I told you to beat that Black woman!" But none of the slaves stepped forward.

Then Yito called over a drover who was overhearing all of this. Without coming any closer, the drover warned him: "Listen, Yito. Don't hit her, unless you want to see your own blood spilled. Just walk away."

When those Black men got worked up, the best thing to do was to let their rage settle down. Later, things would get worked out. Those situations weren't always so easy for the owners. They had to tread carefully with a furious Black man. Desiderio had a machete in his fist, and he was ready for anything. At that moment, Juan Lima—Desiderio's owner— arrived at the mill.

"What's happening?"

The Overseer said, "Desiderio threatened me with the machete!"

"Yes, master. Because he wants my wife, and he was going to beat her."

"That's not true, Don Juan!"

Felipa said, "Yes, sir, it is true. And I had to tell my husband about it."

"Everybody get back to work! And you, Desiderio, get moving!"

But Don Juan was as hard as a *jiquí* tree. He wasn't like his wife, Doña Juanita Alfonso.

Desiderio sat down in the doorway of the house.

Sometimes, when he saw Doña Juanita Alfonso, he'd say to her, "Mamita, I have no coffee." And the lady would laugh and order someone to give him some.

Desiderio knew his master, and he knew this would end very badly. After Miss Juanita had ordered someone to give the enraged Black man a sip of coffee, Desiderio left the residence and went to his *bohío*. He prepared himself, sharpened his machete, and took off down the path to *el monte*.

"Where is Desiderio, gentlemen? What? He's a runaway! How could such a conscientious Black man become a *cimarrón* [maroon]?"

Juan Lima ordered Adolfo, the coach driver, to gather the *rancheadores*.[22] They brought six dogs and showed them the footprints to set them on Desiderio's trail.

The first thing Desiderio did was to hide in a ceiba that was in a cane field. He slept at the roots. Well, he didn't sleep: he was handing himself over to the ceiba, receiving its strength, doing what he needed to do. From there, Desiderio went into *el monte*. He was under another ceiba when the small hunting dogs arrived. The *rancheadores* were paid two ounces of gold for every Black man they captured—broken or whole. Desiderio had cleared the brush around the tree to fight the dogs. He could already hear them barking nearby. He waited for them with a stick and a machete. They surrounded him, and he cut one of the dogs in two. The *rancheador* said, "Black man, put down the machete and turn yourself in!"

Desiderio looked like the devil himself. With the stick and machete, he killed all the dogs, which was no small feat! I think that's why we're so afraid of dogs! Because they hunted us Black people with dogs for so many years, and I think fear—like everything else—can be inherited.

Desiderio was a *cimarrón* for a long time. In *el monte*, there were a lot of runaways. But he managed to escape thanks to the ceiba, which gave him the strength and courage he needed to defeat the dogs.

The narrator concludes:

A *puya* song says the peacock lives at the top of the ceiba,[23] at the top of the tallest tree:

> *Pavo Real, tá bucán palo*
> *Pá pará bien, bien, bien.*
> *Yá pará rriba jagüey.*
> *Dice jagüey tá chiquito*
> *Pá pará bien, bien, bien.*
> *Pavo Real tá bucán palo . . .*
>
> *Yá pará rriba téngue,*
> *Dice téngue tá chiquito*
> *Pá para bien, bien, bien.*

THE CEIBA

---

22   DF-N: *Rancheadores* were bounty hunters hired to hunt down fugitive slaves, usually on horseback and accompanied by dogs.

23   DF-N: A *puya* is, literally, a barb or sharp stick; idiomatically, it is a verbal jab or dig, including satirical poetry and songs.

Ya pará rriba Nángüe,
Nángüe ta bueno . . .
Pá para bien, bien, bien.

Peacock's looking for a *palo*
To stand there well, well, well.
He gets on top of a *jagüey*
And says *jagüey's* too small
To stand there well, well, well.
Peacock's looking for a *palo* . . .

He gets on top of a téngue,
And says téngue's too small
To stand there well, well, well.
He gets on top of Nángüe,
And Nángüe's good . . .
To stand there well, well, well.

It says there's no other tree like Nangüe, and Desiderio stood up on top of it very, very well![24]

"Even touching the ceiba with your hand gives you strength." Everything about her is beneficial: Enriqueta Herrera tells us that simply contemplating her—and, in the rain, watching the water slide down her trunk—"refreshes the heart."

This tree, which is believed to be everlasting and whose "gifts seem to help any situation," is the epitome of plants' mystical power. It is also understood—as we have mentioned—that it can make sterile women fertile. In order to realize her wish, a woman that wants to conceive will consult with an *alase* or a *palero* and drink—for the entire duration of three lunar cycles—a decoction made with bark taken from the east side of a female ceiba (the side facing the sunrise). On the other hand, a woman who does not want to give birth uses bark from the west side of a male ceiba (the side facing the sunset).

I recall a mother gesturing to her only child and saying to me, "The ceiba gave me this."

Many insist that it is actually Boma—the divine sister of Iroko—who accords this gift to the ceiba. "Boma has given children to women who'd spent ten years married and yearning for one."

---

24 DF-N: The fate of Desiderio's wife goes unmentioned.

"Its sap and emanations give life."

Therefore, it is perfectly logical for people to be cured of their madness at the ceiba. Is it not the trunk and mansion of Odua, the Obatala of the Oyo and the Bini Lucumí, the creator of the species and owner of heads, who cures the dying and helps women have a good birth?

Cape challenges the best psychiatrists—"shrinks"—in Havana, promising to take the craziest crazy person they have hidden in their asylums and make them sane.

They take the lunatic to the ceiba just before twelve noon, bound and dragged or kicking and screaming, if necessary. The precise time of day is so important that the success of this "work" depends on it.

Their eyes are covered with a *frontil* (blindfold) so they cannot see the least bit of light. The patient should be completely unable to see. If the patient is a man, the *mayombero* passes a black hen—also carefully blindfolded—over their body. If the patient is a woman, they are "cleansed" with a black rooster.

Three eggs are immediately required. A basin had been prepared before-hand with water and the following plants: *anamú*, *piñón botijo*, *alacrancillo*, and *rompezaragüey*. The crazy person is bent over the basin, then two of the eggs are broken over their head. Their head is washed with the water and they are asked (precisely at twelve noon), "What do you see?"

If the crazy person responds that they cannot see anything, the blindfold (a *mayombero* would call it a *frontil*) is removed immediately. The crazy person leaves sane, while the blindfolded rooster or hen that picked up the illness will remain crazy. The third egg is buried next to the trunk of a ceiba with the name of the patient written on the shell.

For a long time, that person cannot go near the ceiba because they would be exposed to the danger of a relapse. "The illness they left there might see them and attack their head again."

"The mounted Mambi-Mambi itself bathes the sick person seven times with ceiba and Yaya. Along with the other things you do to them, that cures their madness."

"You can also cure madness using a decoction made with seven ceiba sprouts."

A pillow stuffed with the soft fleece from a flowering ceiba produces strange and sometimes prophetic dreams. To explain: the person sleeping, in contact with the tree of the spirits, enters into a confusing exchange with be-ings and forces from beyond.

"Obatala, who rules over dreams, takes over the head of the person sleep-ing on a pillow or cushion containing flowers from his tree." (That is why F.G.

claims that the real "cotton" used to wrap the stone of Obatala is not from a cotton plant, but rather the fleece from a ceiba tree.)

In some *ile orisa*, a branch from a ceiba is placed next to the *iyawo* of Obatala as they sleep on the straw mat during the seven days of the *Asiento*.

The water that seeps from the trunk—"the sweat of the ceiba"—or collects in cavities among the roots has healing properties that are understood to be miraculous.

It works for both good and ill. This water is also used to bathe the person who will swear an oath and wash a magical mirror.[25] There, among the humidity of the roots, it is not unusual to find a *mancaperro* ("Ngúnguru"), a magical vermin that—most significantly—should not be absent from a *nganga*. Contact with this creature increases the virtues of this water, which is already blessed.

> *Agua Ngunguru*
> *Buena pa remedio*
> *Agua Ngunguru Bonanfila*
> *buena pa remedio.*
>
> Water of Ngunguru
> Good for remedies
> Water of Ngunguru Bonanfila
> Good for remedies.

The roots of the ceiba are always full of offerings and coins, which no one dares to take for themselves, given as promises and for requests that have been granted. According to one rather sanctimonious elder who says she "works better with Our Fathers and Hail Marys than anything else," the ceiba is where one should make vows to the Virgen del Carmen, Agome, Santa Teresa, Oya, and Jesús Nazareno [Jesus of Nazareth], Obalufon, wearing special garments— "dressing for the vows"—during the appointed time, or perhaps for the rest of their lives, as was so common in bygone days.

These vows, which now seem so antiquated, are still fulfilled by our Black people with devotion and manifest pleasure. Nkisos Fathers and *babalawos*, interpreters of the divinities, frequently advise them.

Notice the considerable proportion of people of color that still wear the Catholic habits of San Lázaro and Jesús Nazareno. This does not even

---

25 DF-N: A "person who will swear an oath" refers to someone who will be initiated, while "the magical mirror" is referred to elsewhere as Vititi Mensu.

include the vows to Nuestra Señora de Regla, La Caridad del Cobre, and Nuestra Señora de las Mercedes. (Blue, yellow, white.)

Iroko is given a sacrifice and a drumming celebration, which in Matanzas take on great solemnity. On this occasion, the *bobo kaleno* (faithful) each contribute one scarf. The ceiba is decorated with these scarves, folded by their corners and hanging from a belt that is covered in green and wrapped around the trunk.

In the patios of many *santeros* like my friends Marcos (*omó finlandi, olorin*) and Dolores Ibáñez (daughter of Agayu), a couple of *olochas* who brag about following the tradition zealously, a castle made from stone masonry encloses the base of a ceiba, which extends its young branches over it.

According to *mayomberos cristianos*, "When God returns on Holy Saturday, we sacrifice a rooster or a goat on that great day." The bones of the bird or animal are buried next to the tree trunk, and not a single bone can be missing or even broken.

The spirits managed by *paleros* always let them consume the meat of the sacrificial animals. They never complain about it. ("All they need is blood and liquor.") The Lucumí orishas are different, often depriving *santeros* when they most desire to commune with them by tasting a beautiful hen. After all, the birds and animals offered should please the orishas, and the best are chosen "so they're beautiful when they're given to the *santo*." Sacrificing animals that are in poor health, blind or lame, sick or skinny, would be an offense to the god. In this regard, one needs to be very careful.

For our Black people, who still scrupulously observe the precepts of Semana Santa (Holy Week), Holy Saturday was and remains a great and very important day. It is the best day of all to cut trees, pull herbs, and salute the ceiba. On Holy Thursday and Good Friday, *olochas, yalochas,* and *babalawos* abstain from performing their ritual functions or making food offerings to their *orichas*: they empty the water that bathes the stones of their cult, then cover them with black cloth. They do not light candles for them, nor do they ring bells, *agogo.* "They don't even give them anything to drink." "The orishas are rigorous in their mourning. And the *ngangas cristianas* too. The *kimbisas* visit churches and cemeteries from six in the morning until late at night. The *ñáñigos* cover Akanaran. Not a single leaf is pulled. But in the dark, before the sun rises on Holy Saturday, *iyalochas, babalawos,* and *paleros* all go out to the country to salute the ceiba and stock up on *ewe* or *vititi,* the herbs and plants they take back home, still dripping with that miraculous, sacred dew (*ororo*) of the dawn (*oyuma*) or *oloni* (of this day). The Father, Baba-Olorun, resurrects." Life defeats death and continues.

Let an elderly *iyalocha* explain the reason for this custom: "Because God, who has been dead, resurrects at sunrise on that day, the plants have much more *ache*, more life, and they cure and strengthen more than the ones gathered any other, regular day." Another *iyalocha* tells me,

> It's always been done that way. By ten in the morning on Holy Saturday, there's no *yerbero* [herbalist] or *santero* who hasn't brought back plants from *el monte*. Plants and well water. No, I don't know if my elders in Africa, before they were sold and brought to Cuba, went to gather them in the bush on that same day. But in Cuba, nobody misses the opportunity of the special occasion, and it's considered an obligation. When I was little, a gang of *negras santeras* would get together at my grandmother's house on Friday night. They would have themselves a party, and the racket they made! They had a great time, but always with respect. And before daybreak, they dressed themselves by candlelight, because it was still dark. They went out to the countryside to pull leaves, just as the sun began to break through the clouds, very wet with dew. By nine thirty or ten o'clock at the latest, they had all gone back home with their sacks and baskets full of *ewe* of all the *santos*.
>
> How the plants from Holy Saturday cure! My mother made a special point of picking up *santo piñón botijo*, tamarind root, *ateje*, cedar bark, palm root, *tábano* for the swelling in her legs, *malva, bejuco ñatero, tortuga, yerba de la niña* and *yerba de la vieja*, and *yerba fina, serpentina, caña santa, grama de castilla* and *grama blanca, siguaraya, guisaso*, and *palo caballero*. And later, with water from the first rain in May—which makes you youthful and clears blemishes, because it is sacred water—all of those plants would be boiled and stored in a jug. She was not an *iyalocha*, but she cured the whole town with that brew. They were cured by the *ache* of the plants and the *ache* of the water.

The same thing is still done today, although Black people are very fond of setting stories in a past that is not necessarily so remote.

Plants should also be collected—then used to bathe (otherwise "bugs come out of your skin")—on June 24, the feast day of San Juan. In Havana, Ogun—the owner of *el monte*—is celebrated on that day. "But the *ache* of the resurrection is much more powerful. There's no comparison!" That is because "God has been dead and he resurrects." Holy Saturday, the day of his rebirth, is the most sacred of the year, because it is about the renewal of universal life, the miraculous regeneration of life in the world of plants. "Everything is more potent" by virtue of all the energies generated by the Father, "who dies and resurrects every year." The new force of life is concentrated in the plants, in the trees, and in the water. ("We are without God on Thursday and Friday. If Jesus Christ didn't resurrect on Saturday, the world would end.") When

God "resurrects" on Saturday, the moment the sun comes out, he "blesses the earth," "he gives the *ewe* his *ache*," and he increases the curative and magical value of the plants that the *santero*—the adherent of the Regla de Ocha, the Lucumí—will employ exclusively for beneficial purposes.

The complete opposite occurs on Holy Thursday and Good Friday, as we know. The devil is set loose: "On those days, he does as he pleases," and the *mayomberos judíos* make the most of the opportunity to inflict harm. "They give *el monte* blood from black cats and dogs. Then Eshu, Lungambe, Lukankansa, Kachika, Karire, and Kadianpemba have no adversaries." ("Chakuana gets so happy then!")

God is absent and unable to oppose the devil's devilish deeds. It is advisable to guard against evil sorcerers who, during the hours of that great cosmic event, engage in hideous activities. They all go into *el monte* when the sun is at its zenith, or at midnight, "since there are no better days to cut the devil's trees and vines." They capture maleficent spirits, put together their fatal *wembas*, give blood to their *ndokis*, and traffic in all that is evil . . . "Eshu, king of wickedness, is reigning alone." And they go to wells to stock up on "the devil's water" for the year. Because Holy Thursday and Good Friday are the best times to talk with Satan, who is in the dismal bottom of the well. Whoever would like to speak with Lugambe on these days, as sorcerers do, should place a mirror on the parapet of an old well; the mirror blackens completely, and the evil spirit manifests itself. Address yourself to him: choose the most sonorous and ignoble curse words in the entire language (there is, necessarily, no creature more foul-mouthed than the *mayombero judío*) and ask them for what you want.

The Congo would take pride in performing a spell that uses a vat filled with water and offers those separated from a loved one—either by absence or by death—the consolation of contemplating their loved one's reflection in the water.

The water gathered from a well on that day and stored at the sorcerer's home has a terrible stench. The taste is foul, rotten. The *nganguleros judíos* administer it to their own in case of illness ("because the devil cures his own people"), to incorporate its infernal powers, or to make them invulnerable against the attacks of other diabolical adversaries. The *jigües* and the *güijes*, the elves of the rivers, rise to the surface of the water and show themselves on these days.

By contrast, the water of God—"the water of Holy Saturday," the resurrection—is collected from wells by the Congo and Lucumí on that Saturday and Sunday to drink it themselves and to be drunk by their godchildren and close family. It releases them from sorcery and keeps them in good health—unharmed by *bilongos*. It will not reek or spoil.

"The sorcery done by *kimbiseros judíos* on Holy Thursday cannot be undone. If somebody has their shadow stolen in the light of day, and they hear someone calling them by their name but can't see anyone, then they should prepare their funeral shroud, because they're lost." "So many graves are opened on Holy Thursday and Good Friday, the days for stealing shadows and voices!"

The solemnity of Holy Thursday and Good Friday, during which Black people abstain from all activity, is only profaned by sorcerers who have made pacts with exclusively maleficent forces. On those days, all things secretly suffer the death of Our Redeemer, "the master of the world and life," as Salako says. "Christ's corpse is in the church, in *el monte*, and everywhere." Trees and plants should be left untouched until the supreme owner is born again, when he "returns to rule the world" and blesses them.

All of my informants understand that "in the absence of God, the plants are not strong." "*El monte* observes a period of mourning and loses its essence." Its curative and preventive qualities, along with all the rest of nature's beneficial energies, are inevitably and greatly diminished: "Everything on earth is diminished while God is laid down to rest."

The old man R. explains: "Since I first opened my eyes, I've been living in the bush, like a deer, and all of that *ewe* from Holy Saturday is most sacred." He tells us how, during his childhood, the Black people at Mr. Pedro Lamberto Fernández's La Unión sugar mill would dress the *cepa* [stock] from a plantain tree,[26] which represented Olorún, light four candles for it, then hold a funerary wake for it. "Olodumare *okuo* (dead God). All the *ocha* are covered. The sight of their overseer's corpse makes them sad. Friday at ten, the funeral procession for the dead Jesus starts." (The Black people would bury the *cepa* from the plantain, which represented Christ.) "Saturday, God rises up. We go out to look for plants which are sanctified. They get that juice from Olodumare, fresh, from God, who is renewed. Now, that *ewe*, all those trees, are consecrated. They're strong, and they blow away all the *ñura ñura*—the filth. They clean everything, they cure, and they're blessed by God himself. Now, after we collect plants on Holy Saturday, we go salute Ocha. We go feed him and we have a party for him. We *siré*—play—because the Ocha is happy."[27]

---

26 DF-N: The *cepa*, or stock, of the tree is the underground portion of its trunk.

27 DF-N: Cabrera attributes the original to an elder referred to simply as R.:

> Denque yo abrí sojo mundo, yo son manigüero, yo tá viviendo como venao la manigua, y todo ese ewe de la Gloria son santísimo … Oloddumare okuó tó lo ocha tapao, triste sintiendo que capatá tá ahí su cuerpo presente. Vierne a lan dié sale entiero Jesucristo difunto … Sábado, dió levanta. Vamo bucá yebba que viene santificao, y coge ese zumo de Oloddumare, freco, de Dió que ta nuevo. Ahora ese ewe, to ese palo ta sacramentao, ta fuete y ese ranca con tó ñura ñura—porquería—, limpia tó, ese cura, tá bindito po mimo Dió. Hora, dipué que nelle coge yebba la gloria, vamo saludá Ocha, vamo en dále pa comé, vamo asé lo fiesta, vamo siré—a jugar—Ocha tá contento.

Here, Olorun and Obatala became Jesus Christ for Africans and their descendants. And these men and their dark-skinned divinities rejoice in celebrating the resurrection of . . ."the overseer," the God of white men.

In order to fully convince ourselves of the extent to which everything in nature resents the death of Christ, that trees and plants truly experience great pain, we have the *piñón botijo*. In Lucumí, it is known as *ado, olobotuyo, ole iyetebe*. In Congo, it is known as *masarosi*. It is a shrub similar to the European fig. The piñon contains an abundance of thick sap, which is white like milk. But if its trunk is cut on Good Friday, "the piñón spills blood, not milk." The sap turns into blood.

There are many mysteries and wonders that occur in the countryside during Holy Week, and only the *agugu* and the *muloyi* penetrate *el monte* to take advantage of the maleficent influence of Eshu or Kadiempemba. During that time, he is its uncontested owner, and he increases the power of wicked trees and vines, which he uses to make or reinforce his *prendas*.

Then, *el monte* becomes a theater for the strangest and most horrendous apparitions.

In Alquízar, it was common knowledge what went on in Monte Encueros [the Naked Forest], so called because a Congo *cimarrón* lived hidden there, and he went around naked. Certainly no woman who dared to traverse that *monte* on Good Friday would emerge unharmed. The *cimarrón* would cut their breasts to feed his *nganga*, or Kindoki, or to drink the blood himself.

The guards searched for him in vain: the Black man—whether he was dead or alive (because no one actually knew whether he was a *muerto* or still alive)—would call out to the guards. They distinctly heard his movements and his voice very close by, but they could never capture him.

To this day, Cape claims that this *cimarrón* slave appears—in half-animal, half-human form—to the *mayomberos* from that town whenever they cut trees in Monte Encueros during a new moon.

Even the Black man who is most arrogant about their beliefs and most removed from Catholic practices will observe great modesty during these days: they consider any entertainment or noisy expression of joy dangerous.

("It's not good to show your teeth during that day—to laugh, go out on the town, or put liquor in your body—just in case you get too happy and end up acting disrespectfully.") There is no cursing: that is how the foul-mouthed Beleña got a malignant sore on her tongue, for cursing on Holy Thursday.

"They'd put a piece of raw meat over the *ñáñara* (sore), to trick it, so it wouldn't eat the tongue." This is equivalent to the eminent doctor Tronchin putting veal tenderloins on the cancer of his patient, the elegant Duke of Villars—a palliative remedy that some indulgent doctors in Cuba employed to treat such cases, even in the second half of the nineteenth century. ("Cancer is like an insect which eats away at the person.")

"But God didn't want to forgive her." Because just as there are evil eyes whose wickedness runs through us, there are evil tongues that make curses effective. "Although, luckily, unjust curses don't always work."

During Holy Week, nobody should become upset: "You shouldn't even scold children." They are days of absolute abstinence, strictly observed in Santería.

"Married couples are very careful." If the woman sins and conceives on Holy Thursday or Good Friday, then "what they bring into the world will not be good. The devil will get inside it."

("And they say those who get together cannot separate themselves from each other.")

And, above all else, one does not work: "God punishes whatever is done that day, unless it is out of pure necessity."

In colonial times, some sugar mills were swallowed up by the earth for milling on Good Friday.

Out of consideration for the Father who is lying on his deathbed, there is no sweeping or washing at home, no ironing or sewing. "Sweeping the floor is sweeping over the face of Christ."

"No bathing either. The water turns to blood." "There's no cutting of anything, because it is cutting the body of the Father."

Making noise offends him.

Ogun Arere severed the hand of Abelardo, the carpenter who shut himself away in his workshop on Good Friday to finish a commission. And Choiadó "was killed by Boko with an embolism as a punishment for having gladly accepted a cash payment to carry a trunk for an American." Because "carrying anything heavy over your head is an atrocity."

One legend, adapted by slaves to the customs of their new homeland, tells the story of an only son who was spoiled and adored blindly by his parents. He ignored his mother's advice and pleading. When she finally consented to her son's whim, he grabbed a rifle—*nkele*—on Good Friday and went out to hunt in *el monte*. There he came face-to-face with the king of the monkeys, who confronted him with his heresy and devoured him.

Anyone who has lived in Cuba knows just how difficult it is to knock down one of these prodigious trees. They are eminently saintly and bewitching, and our people venerate them with a faith that completely rejects all doubt regarding their divinity. An obscure terror prevents a peasant from striking its sacred trunk with his axe, regardless of the tempting wages someone might be willing to pay him. Only a reckless, irresponsible man would agree to cut a ceiba.

In his eyes, it embodies—more than symbolizes—the terrible omnipotence of God. In her he feels the mysterious presence of a world of spirits. Its occult force scares him. It is an invisible and supernatural being that would turn its implacable hunger for vengeance against him. The majority emphatically refuse to commit this indisputably impious act ("it's the only thing nobody messes around with"). Sooner or later, it always brings misfortune. Cutting them down is a sin, with all the aggravating circumstances of a mortal sin. The ceibas take revenge. The ceibas do not forgive. Instilled from their earliest days with a reverential fear of these trees, which are loaded with legends and shrouded in mystery, it is rare for a *guajiro*—regardless of skin color—to have the courage to bring them down. The belief in their holiness is transmitted from one generation to the next, and it is stronger than self-interest. It is much stronger than the need—sometimes tragic—to collect a generous reward. "I'd rather go broke, let my kids go hungry . . . I'd sooner die of hunger than knock down a ceiba!" Invariably, this is the exclamation of a rustic man regarding the destruction of "the tree of the Virgin Mary," the Santísimo, Odudua, or Agayu, the tree of the spirits.

In any case, in Havana, no worker will ever commit themselves to this task—unanimously regarded as a sacrilege that entails the most terrible consequences for whoever carries it out—without first ensuring the consent of the sacred tree and the great spirits who live there. (In the countryside, it is an even more grievous matter.) If this indispensable ritual is not performed, experience provides ample evidence that a ceiba will never fail to punish its killers. Almost invariably, if the axe blade does not suddenly turn against the aggressor, they will soon suffer a severe and unforeseeable misfortune. How many people have watched each of their loved ones fall, one by one, after lending a hand in this heresy!

Not far from my neighborhood, everyone still remembers the cutting down of a very sacred, centenarian ceiba, which cost two men their lives and mutilated a third. Another ceiba was "willing to dispose of anyone who made an attempt against her" in a crew of workers led by an incredulous white man. After causing various misfortunes, the ceiba finally consented to perishing by fire. (Obatala, the male or female owner of the ceiba—Agemo-Yeme—agreed to let the ceiba be consumed by Changó, who is the fire and favorite son.) But everyone involved had to make *ebo*—that is, to spend the money they had made in order to appease the angry spirit and earn its forgiveness.

In the province of Matanzas, the splendid ceiba at the Central Socorro is very well known. In that area, they say the former owner of that plantation would offer his finest young bull to the Black people every November 16 so they would sacrifice it to Agayu.

They simply insist that, when he sold his plantation to an American company, he "specified" that he was selling it on the condition that "neither the ceiba nor the Black people who adored her should be disturbed." Because, my informant assures me, that owner "didn't ever want Iroko, who had protected him so well, to go without his bull and his *bembé*." But the Yankees, completely lacking knowledge of the facts, decided to bring her down as soon as they got there.

Nobody agreed to carry out the order, which caused grief and terror among the older Black people. They had revered that ceiba since the time of their African grandparents—and a previous owner, "who played Palo with her slaves and hung out with the Black folks a lot, although she was very wicked." Only one Black man—who was not from Socorro, but from Santa Isabel de Lajas, "a showoff"—showed up with his axe and his machete to tear down Iroko:

Ah! He didn't even get to the shadow of Iroko! He never even got to show God his fist! A wasp came out of the trunk of the tree and stung him on the pupil of his eye. That Black man had been boasting that Iroko wouldn't do anything to him because he was from Santa Isabel de Lajas. You see! He started crying out softly, "The wasp stung my eye! The wasp stung my eye!" And he got louder and louder every time, until his screams could be heard for miles. And he was still shouting—"The wasp stung my eye!"—when they took him away to the insane asylum, where he died, with his legs stretched out and stiff, and the wasp stuck in his brain.

The *osainista* assures me that the Americans were spooked and abandoned their plan. And since he has not been back to the Central Socorro, he supposes the ceiba—a centenarian twice over—will still be there, as always and forever. And it is indeed still there.

In Cimarrones, a day laborer "started to saw the trunk of a ceiba. And because the body of a man is a tree, he started feeling pain in his own body— at the same height—so intense it forced him to put down his saw. The ceiba was hurt by his saw, but he was hurt much worse. His wound became swollen. Then the gangrene said, 'I'm here now.' And then it sent him to his grave."

At dangerous curves along busy roads (like the one in Perico called Muerte), frequent and sometimes fatal accidents are quite often caused by the disastrous effects of spirits who have been made persistently, tenaciously furious by the chopping down of ceibas to make travel easier. The spirits retain a desire to go back to the spot where a ceiba once stood.

Havana's Parque de la Fraternidad has its own legend. It is claimed that certain prominent men once buried their "macutos" under this ceiba. "There will be no peace or order in this country until the *nganga* that General Machado buried there twenty-five years ago is removed and destroyed.[28] That *Prenda* is so strong and so wounded that it is making a mess, even if it doesn't seem like it. And it will require a lot of blood." Others insist that this *prenda* will avenge its owner for the ingratitude of the Cuban people. (It should consider itself sufficiently avenged.)

For all believers, both esoteric and exoteric, the official acts celebrated during the inauguration of the Plaza de la Fraternidad in Havana, which transformed the majestic former Campo de Marte, were characterized by a manifestly magical quality. And with good reason! The iron arrows decorating the fence around the ceiba in the middle of the Plaza belong to Ogun, Elegua, Ochosi, Ayaguna, and Changó. They are signs of Palo Monte, Nkuyo, Nsasi, and Siete Rayos. The earth to plant it was brought from twenty-one locations. Gold coins were deposited in the hole. It was purportedly supervised by Sotomayor, a famous *mayombero* who was friends with some of the influential politicians of that era. These are very eloquent indications that "there is something there." Something quite powerful: "a very strong *mañunga.*"

A folklorist would fill hundreds of index cards with the stories told about ceibas, venerated and feared from one end of the island to the other.

Whoever has had the patience to follow us through the explanations and digressions of our guides will retain the name of the ceiba as the perfect archetype of a sacred tree: Igi Olorun, Iroko, Nsanda Nkunia Sambi, the "Most Holy Ceiba." In the mystical consciousness of our people, it is, categorically, not simply a tree of God, but the God Tree.

---

28 DF-N: This refers to Gerardo Machado y Morales (1869–1939), president of Cuba between 1925 and 1933, whose regime is generally regarded as brutally repressive.

8

UKANO BEKONSI

THE CEIBA AND THE SECRET OF THE

ABAKUÁ, OR ÑÁÑIGOS.

The ceiba—*ukano bekonsi*—is equally sacred for the *ñánigos*, or Abakuá, members of a secret society that, unfortunately, became infamous in the nineteenth century. The society was founded by slaves and freed Apapas from Calabar in the town of Regla, on the opposite side of Havana Bay.

Human merchandise—"products" or "goods"—came to Cuba from Calabar in large quantities: Abayas, Suamas, Eluyos, Okankuas, Isiekes, Efis, Apapas, big Apapas and small Apapas, Bibis ("who were as troublesome as the devil himself"), Brinches, and Brikamos—all of them included in the generic name Carabalí.[1]

Among the many Anglo-Saxons who visited the island during the era of the slave trade and wrote their impressions, one writer offered the same account given today by many of the Black informants who knew them: "Very industrious and avaricious; also, choleric and hasty in temper. Most of the free negroes in the island who are rich belong to this tribe."

---

1   DF-N: The original Spanish spelling of the term Carabalí is maintained (not transliterated) because it is a widely used proper name in Caribbean and Cuban literature, making an English phonetic version (Karabali) unnecessary or counterproductive.

"They all had their own clay pitcher.[2] Carabalí people saved money. They were stingy. Tight-fisted! A lot of them were rich. They were more resentful and ill tempered than anyone else. You've never heard it said that the Carabalí eat people?"

Others claim they were among the most noble and docile of those brought by slave merchants.[3]

Docile or untamed, active or lazy: the reputation they enjoyed during the colonial era for being brave, arrogant, avaricious, thrifty, and wealthy persists—corrected and augmented—in the memories of Black informants. "When a Carabalí got paid, they saved it, while other Black people would spend it right away. And the Carabalí would always collect. They didn't forgive offenses!"

Catalino claims there were more free Black people among the Carabalí than among other nations, "because they were more hardworking than the others, and very united." This does not concur with the writing of Frederika Bremer, who dedicates many pages full of sympathy for slaves. She documents the plantation owner Chartrand, owner of the famous Ariadna mill: he is very knowledgeable about Africans, whom he drives mercilessly ("but feeds them well and takes good care of them, and they do the work cheerfully and quickly," according to the Rev. Abbott, a guest of the Laberinto mill). Bremer says, "The *callavalis* or *caraballis* are also a good people, although more lazy and careless" [1853, 314].

Regardless of their defects or virtues, to these Carabalí we owe the introduction of *ñañiguismo* in Cuba, especially the aforementioned Apapas, "who used to play in their former cabildo Abakuá Efo, with no desire to admit Creoles into their society, until the Creoles—who were their own children—insisted so adamantly on being sworn in that the African Taitas taught them and authorized the first group of Creoles, which was established on Calle Perdomo in Regla, during the time of Tacón.[4] But those Black Creoles didn't let *mulatos* into their groups, much less white people."

The secret fraternity residing in Regla was officially authorized. It was reminiscent of those that existed in West Africa during the slave trade and still exist, widespread and in countless numbers, throughout the Black continent.

---

2   LC: Money was stored in clay pitchers. They served as safes in colonial times. These pitchers were used to bring oil from Spain. They were also used in construction, placed under the flooring of houses to prevent humidity.

3   DF-N: Cabrera uses the euphemism *traficantes de ébano* (literally, "ebony merchants").

4   DF-N: This is a reference to Miguel Tacón y Rosique, the infamous Spanish governor of Cuba between 1834 and 1852. See Miller (2009, 68, 88).

A *ñáñigo* elder traces the genealogy of the societies—*potencias, tierras, partidos*, or *"juegos"*—that arose in the first third of the nineteenth century: Apapa (Efo), the foundation of Abakuá in Cuba, which authorized Efik Ebuton, which then authorized Efik Kondo, Efik Nyumane, Efik Akamaro, Efik Kunanakua, Efik Efigeremo, and Efik Enyemiya; then, Efori Isun, Efori Kondo, Efori Ororo, Efori Mukero, Efori Buma, Efori Araokon. These are the seven families or branches of the two original *potencias*, Efi and Efo."

The Enrikamo from an Efor *potencia* tells me, "When Abakuá grew, white people thought they could be *ñáñigos* too, and they started pestering and trying to get into *plantes* by force. Andrés Petit—the same one who founded the Regla de Santo Cristo del Buen Viaje, *Quien vence, vence batalla, Tiembla-tiembla nunca cae, El día que tesia mundo acabá*—was the sorcerer, the Nasako of the juego Bakoko."[5] (According to other *ñáñigos*, he was the Isue of Efo Guana [Wana].) "And this Andrés Petit negotiated with the white men, and sold them the secret for five hundred pesos. Because of his betrayal, white men were able to become *ñáñigos* and form their own *potencia*, which was called Akanaran Efo. Petit said that white people had to be admitted because of their *moropo* (head), so that *ñaniguismo* would endure in Cuba." Another informant comments, "This *potencia*, Akanaran Efo, gave birth to all the other mixed *partidos* of white and Black people. Among the white *ñáñigos* sworn in by Andrés Petit, there were people from high society, just like today. Military people and gentlemen in frock coats. Yes, ma'am, people with ranks and titles from the aristocracy of those days, the sons of counts and marquises. But the truth is that from then on, the rivalries and killing started, and *ñaniguismo* got ugly. Now it's calmed down. Today everything's mixed up, although once in a while a dispute arises, as is well stated by a *ñáñigo* refrain: we love each other like brothers and we're always fighting like roosters. Somebody gets slapped or fires a shot, then the police show up right away with their cage. In the past, there were huge brawls to the death! The *ñáñigos* from the neighborhood of San Lázaro would face off and come to blows with those from Jesús María. They would open their razor blades. That went on until the government of Gómez.[6] If a *ñáñigo* from Colón stabbed one from Jesús María? All of the ones from Jesús María would retaliate. Naturally, they needed to avenge their

---

5   DF-N: *Quien vence, vence batalla* is a reference to Sarabanda/Zarabanda. *Tiembla-tiembla* is the name of a *prenda*, or shrine, as is *mundo acabá*; see Cabrera ([1984] 2001, 126). *Tesia* (*parar*, "to stop") means that when the *prenda* stops working, the world will end—in other words, the *prenda* is immortal. Petit was Isué of the lodge Bakóko Efó, also known as Awana Mokóko Efó. See also Cabrera ([1977] 1986, [1979] 1986).

6   DF-N: This is a reference to José Miguel Gómez y Gómez, president of Cuba between 1909 and 1913.

brother. And beside revenge, there were rivalries and resentments over non-sense: in a dance hall, or because—as an example of something that was much more serious—someone who was going to be sworn into Ekoriofo was sworn into Ebion instead . . . and they were bloody battles between neighborhoods."[7]

A high dignitary from an Efo *partido* lists the following as the oldest *potencias* in Havana: Efik Abakuá, Efik Ibonda, Efik Abarako, Efik Ubane, Efik Uriabon, Efik Enklentati, Ekerewa Moni, Ekerewa Kamfioro, Guman Efo, Efori Komon, Ibiabanga Efo, Muñanga Efo, Efori Betongo, Efori Barando, Efori Bakoko (the ones who initiated *blancos*), Oru Apapa, Oru Abakuá, Abakuá Oru, Oru Bibi, and Ekorio Etan Oru.

The neighborhood of Jesús María, celebrated in the annals of the *ñáñigo* society (as well as Mayombe and the underworld of all colors), belongs to the following *partidos*: Ibonda (Efi and Efo branches), Efo Kondondibo, Ekerewa Memi Efo, Anandiba Efo, Amiabon, the illustrious Ekoriofo, and the equally illustrious Ibiabanga; Enyemiya Efi, Barondo, and Oru Apapa. In the neighborhood of Carraguao, Efori Guma. In Los Barracones (Carlos III), Efori Enkomo. "In the neighborhood of Pueblo Nuevo, we had Muñanga Efo, Betongo Efo, Apapa Umoni, and Urianabon Efi, a very strong *partido* located in Colón. Kerewa Ikanfioro Efi, which had many members, in the neighborhood of Belén. Usagare Mutanga, Sangrimoto, and Usagare Munankere in Sitios. Isun Efo in Atarés. Ebion Efo—which was very quarrelsome, and now includes representatives, senators, and councilmen among its ranks—in San Lázaro. Embe Moro, previously in Colón and now in Vedado, is wealthy; it prospered a great deal. On the other hand, two old *juegos* or *partidos* have disappeared: Odani Efo and Odani Efio."

Some of these "tierras" (groups)—such as Efori Guma, Ibonda, Kondondibo, Amiabon, Apapa Umoni, and Urianiabon—are constituted exclusively by Black people. Others—Ebion, Kerewa, Ikanfioro, Usagare Mutanga, Akamamoro, Ekueñon, Efori Onandiba Masongo, Otan Efo, Muñon Tete, Endibo Abasi Irionga—by Black and white people.

In Regla, we have Enyegueye Efo, Abakuá Efo, Irionda Efo, Obon Tanse Efo, Abarako Efi (First and Second), Efik Nurobia, and Efik Abakuá. "All are mixed," which is to say, with members belonging to both races.

Currently the majority of leaders of *potencias* are white people, although there are *partidos* in which only white people are initiated—or, at least, "those who look white."

---

7   DF-N: According to Ivor Miller, "Ekoriofo" refers to the Abakuá lodge Okóbio Efó, which is no longer extant, and belongs to the same lineage as Ebión Efó lodge of Pogolotti (personal communication, 2019).

This information should suffice to convey an idea of the importance of this secret brotherhood, which includes thousands of sworn members under its protection, even though the "tierras" extend no farther east than Matanzas. Ñáñigos can only be found in Havana and Matanzas. For unknown reasons, the rest of the island was less suitable for the germination of the Abakuá seed.

The terms *brujo* and *ñáñigo* are often confused by laypeople. This is, relatively speaking, equivalent to confusing a Freemason—a member of an esoteric order—with a sorcerer.

Others imagine that *ñañiguismo* is a name that encompasses all of the religious practices and beliefs of African origin still followed by our Black people. This ignores the fact that the subreligion or unofficial religion of Cuba—at the margins of Catholicism and in friendly communion with it—is that of Ocha, the Lucumí religion that is solidly established and constitutes a fairly homogeneous group in the provinces of Pinar del Río, Havana, Matanzas, and Santa Clara. This group includes members of the Regla Arará, Dahomeyans, and it should not be confused with Mayombe, which is magic with Congo origins. "Religion is not witchcraft. Ocha is religion, and *ñáñigo* is separate."

A devotee of the orishas can be admitted to the Abakuá fraternity without renouncing or distancing himself from his orishas. And more than a few Catholics can be found among them . . . and a great many *mayomberos*. What, in sum, is the great society of *ñáñigos*, according to an upright *ñáñigo*? We are told by an elder who was the Enkamina of his *potencia*. The Enkamina is a very sensitive position because they are responsible for "cleansing" all of the members of the *ekobio*, thereby becoming exposed to physical and spiritual contamination from others—like a doctor in contact with contagious people, or the "messenger" in an Ocha temple or Mayombe house.

"Abakuá is a society of mutual aid and fraternal support, of brotherly love for one another, who guard the secrets of the society and adore their secret the way our elders adored it in Africa. The *ñáñigos* are the Freemasons of Africa, and we Cubans are their descendants. *Ñañiguismo* is not what people think it is." Alluding to slander that was accepted in earlier times, which also upsets other elder and retired Abakuá, who, if we believe them, fought many battles in the illustrious barrio of Jesús María or Carraguao, "Ñañiguismo is not what it used to be in those days. They charged up to five pesos for the swearing-in ceremony! Now anyone can be a *ñáñigo* without confirming that they're a real man." This elder says, "It's not true that an Abakuá had to kill the first person they ran into after being sworn in. Yes, that's what they used to say. They called us murderers. Such lies! What we swore was to love each other, to help each other and respect each other as brothers. What is sworn, what we would swear beyond a doubt, was to not reveal our secret. To not spill the blood of a friend. As a matter of fact, we're prohibited from using bladed weapons, and

that is so true that we even kill the roosters and goats"—for the sacrifices—
"by striking them with blows, and we butcher them with our teeth and bare
hands."

"It's true that some *ñáñigos* would have disputes with others from different *potencias*, who are also their brothers, claiming they did or didn't do this
or that to me and I'm going to make them pay for it, taking out their razor
blade and starting brawls. And if blood ran, that's another matter altogether.
Naturally, people always quarrel, and there are rivalries in any religion. But
that doesn't mean that our faith obliges us to kill anybody or be a criminal. A
ñáñigo had to be a good man. The one that disgraced *ñañiguismo* was a chief
of police named Rocha, who was a *ñáñigo* himself.[8] And before him, a Spanish
governor who was also a *ñáñigo* in Regla." (He is referring to Rodriguez Ba-
tista.) "He was sent to Spain as a boy and returned to Cuba as governor. You
know that white people—and not just poor, ragtag white people—coveted
the secret of the Carabalí, and the Black Creoles sold it to them at a high
price. That's how *ñañiguismo* was spoiled . . . and saved! Yes, but it was disgraced, if you'll forgive me for saying so. To be sworn in, you had to earn
your merit. When I was sworn in in 1897, which was a very long time ago, the
potencia followed my tracks for two years. When someone was proposed as an
amanison [neophyte], they had to demonstrate that they were a decent, serious,
and proper person: a good son, a good godson, a good brother, a good husband . . . that they weren't a pimp, that they wouldn't let themselves get beaten
up or roughed up by a woman. That they weren't *un brazo roto, yankuni*"—
homosexual[9]—"or a thief, or a liar, or had their hands stained with blood.
And the initiation didn't cost two pesetas. What is true, and bad, is that we
downed so much aguardiente that any little spark would set us off and make
us explode. It was the same as it is today: a *plante* is no good without a fight.
There were some big ones! And you have no idea how scared people were of
us. Mentioning a *ñáñigo* was like mentioning the devil. Ah, Abakuá was truly
great! In good conscience, nobody who knows the depth of Abakuá can say
that *ñañiguismo* is bad simply because it makes a bad impression. It's humanity that is bad, that's all. Haven't I told you what they require from you if
they're going to initiate you? You can't be a murderer or a snitch, and you need
to be a hard worker, and trustworthy! In earlier times, a *ñáñigo* who committed a crime couldn't aspire to an important position in the *potencia*: after
they were sworn in, they had to continue displaying good conduct and obey
the commandments. If they have a peso in their pocket and their brother in

---

8   DF-N: See Miller (2009); and Roche y Monteagudo (1925).
9   DF-N: Cabrera's simple translation misses the nuance of the idiomatic expressions *brazo roto*
and *yankuni*, flattening them into a generic homophobia.

Fundamento has nothing, they should share it with them and be happy. And give, even if you're unhappy about it! What our conscience demands isn't the same as what we want.

"The *partidos* had funds to cope with tragedy—illnesses, accidents, and burials—like the cabildos of the other nations, but the Carabalí were the most serious about helping their brethren. They took care of the widows who didn't take any other man, and the fathers who lost children that had taken care of them. Is *ñañiguismo* bad? It's true that Black people were more united when their circumstances were more desperate. They were less shameless, and they had more heart—*enchila*, as the Congos say. And now, more than in the old days, a *monina* [brother] who has a peso won't give five *reales* to the *monina* who is broke. But sometimes they'll share, saying to themselves, 'Damn! I'm a *ñáñigo*, and my laws demand it.' And even if they swore they wouldn't steal and they stole, and swore they wouldn't snitch and they sang like Saint Peter's rooster, one day, the *potencia* will punish them. They get hit with four lashes, and they're mourned like a *ñampe*"—a dead person. "You know how terrifying that is? To be given a burial mass while you're still alive! So, we end up at a point where the man might straighten out and put himself on a good path. In the end, Abakuá is good, and it's the *abanekues* that are bad."

But due to ignorance regarding all of these details, the frightening *ñáñigos* and their strange *diablitos* [little devils] or Iremes (*ñañas*)—which have a very important symbolic function in the order, along with the "poupón," their astonishing masks—filled the childhoods of our parents' generation with terror. Likewise, in the Republican era, we were told that *los negros brujos* would take advantage of the slightest carelessness on the part of our mothers or nannies, by kidnapping white children to steal their hearts, thus troubling our childhood dreams.

"The sorcerer's going to snatch you!" That was the cry of the "handlers," the nannies looking after children who wandered off, distracted, as they played along the old Paseo del Prado, in the days before it was lined with bronze lions like colossal paperweights. "And he'll do the same to you that he did to La Niña Zoila!"[10]

For my part, I once felt that a black hand might appear suddenly, even in broad daylight, to take out my heart and run away with it. Frightened like a startled bird at the mention of La Niña Zoila, I imagined my heart was shaped like a pointy paper cutout, just as I imagined all hearts.

10 DF-N: See Chávez-Álvarez (1991).

As the aforementioned Enkamina tells us, it was widely believed that one needed to commit a crime to become an Abakuá, Abanekue, Obon, Obonekue, Ekison or Ekiñon, Monina, or Okobio. In the end, without the mystery, which was jealously guarded at the beginning of the society and surrounded its rituals ("Ñaitua") in the "Famba," "Ekufon," or "Batamu"—the room of their impenetrable secrets and bloody oaths, where the consecrations were performed, where the Ekue roared as an incarnation of the mystical fish worshipped by the brothers—*ñañiguismo*, seriously threatened and persecuted by the authorities for some time, now has a greater number of members. They employ a more transparent hermeticism, and their fights and rivalries are less turbulent and fearsome than they were in the nineteenth century.

What *ñañiguismo* lost in mystery and people's fantasies, it gained in electoral strength.[11]

Juan Urrutia—a great Ireme, and a most prominent dancer from the Usagare branch, one of the most respected and prestigious "juegos" in the tradition—tells us, "When the *ñáñigos* went out into the streets on Three Kings Day in the colonial era, they'd honor the *baroko*, which was housed on Calle Sitios." In those days, it included musicians, tailors, cigar makers: people who were relatively comfortable and had some education. "A *potencia ñáñiga* is just that: a government of a republic, a miniature state, which should be a model. That's why we impose order in our *baroko*. And for the sake of maintaining order, we only admit men that are serious and worthy. Worthy of being *ñáñigos!*"

Although Urrutia witnessed the last Auténtico campaign and the terrible political and moral collapse of Cuba,[12] he did not live through the amazing last years of the ideal, immaculate, and triumphant revolution, which converted the nation into a great *potencia ñáñiga*, but without the ethics this Usagare member had envisaged. According to him, his *baroko* was distinguished in the history of *ñañiguismo* for its honor.

These *ekobios* or *potencias*, "branches" of the Efik or Efo trunk that Urrutia compared to "a miniature state," are governed by four great chiefs.

The highest rank is that of Iyamba—king—among the Efo *ekobios*, and of Efimeremo Mokongo Obon among the Efik.

---

11 DF-N: See Sosa Rodríguez (1982), which includes reproductions of advertisements for political candidates using Abakuá language.

12 DF-N: "Auténtico" refers to Partido Revolucionario Cubana-Auténtico, a Cuban political party whose members included presidents Ramón Grau (1944–48) and Carlos Prío Socarrás (1948–54).

These positions are referred to as "plazas," and they include the Iyamba, the Mokongo (representing military power), the Isue (ecclesiastical power), and the Empego ("Royal Scribe or legislative power").

The Iyamba and the other dignitaries who form the *baroko* are given different names that allude to the successive actions they take in ceremonies.[13]

Iyamba receives the following: Iyamba Kekere Kuora Kaike Bongo, Iyamba Mosongo, Iyamba Nandokie, Iyamba Ña Morua, Iyamba Kurrukie, Iyamba Efori Sese Iyamba, Iyamba Manterero, Iyamba Tie-Tie, Iyamba Keremi, Iyamba Beko-beko, Iyamba Sankue Iyamba, etc.

Mokongo: Mokongo Yabutame, Mokongo Yabuyabuya, Mokongo Masausa, Mokongo Bekonsi, Makongo Makoiko, Makongo Guna Kambori, Mokongo Mauyo-Uyo, Chabiaka Mokongo Machabere, etc.

Isue, the Bishop: Isue Eribo Engomo, Isue Yunterere, Isue Nansese, Isue Sukuru Ekuan Tiyen, etc.

Empego, the Scribe, "the institution's most serious man, the trusted confidante of the Iyamba and Efimeremo (Mokongo): Empego Mongobion, Emepego Akaribongo, Empego Ekue Areniyo, Empego Embara Nasabio, Empego Ekue Iyamba, Empego Unasora, Empego Ten Kombante, etc.

After them, these "plazas" or ranks follow in importance: Nasako, who is the doctor ("he represents the authority of medicine"), the sorcerer, and the diviner of the society. Nasako receives the titles of Nasako Nageremba, Nasako Enribetan, Nasako Kundimaye, Nasako Tori Muñon, Nasako Saku-Saku, Nasako Namboroka, Nasako Entieroro, Nasako Tekombre Oroso, Nasako Sanga Enkanima, Nasako Endimefan, Nasako Beko-Beko, Nasako Sume-Sume, Nasako Ekumba Sorori, etc.

The assistant to the Iyamba: Isunekue. Isunekue Eribo, Isunekue Bongo, Isunekue Eran Eurabe, Isunekue Enkiko Guanemoto [Wanemoto], etc.

Enkrikamo, "the hunter," the character we see at the head of the *ñáñigo* procession attracting the *diablito*—the Enkoboro—with a small drum. Enkrikamo Akua Mañongo, Enkrikamo Guariniampo, Enkrikamo Kotoba

---

13   DF-N: In other words, the sequences of titles and names function as ritual narratives, and a person who understands the language and memorizes (or writes down) the sequence would be able to discern a road map for Abakuá mythology and ritual. During the process of translation, I asked several Abakuá friends whether they regarded the material in *El Monte* as being appropriate for publication in the twenty-first century. They all either laughed or shrugged at the question, acknowledging that the question of secrecy was moot, since the text had been in circulation for decades, and many other publications revealed much more sensitive ritual information in more explicit ways. Cf. the descriptions, diagrams, and photographs of Abakuá ritual in Ortiz (1952–55). Yet several supported Cabrera's interpretation, anecdotally and somewhat obliquely, by explaining that their unease with the text was not due to any particular "secret" ritual details, but rather to the revelation of "deep," "philosophical" logics and elements underlying their rituals.

Mañon, Enrikamo Afonkoro, Enrikamo Erumi, Enrikamo Igwandocha, Enrikamo Obon.

The assistant of the Mokongo, chief of the forces: Mosongo, "who guards the secret of the Abakuá in his staff." Mosongo Gwana Moto, Mosongo Guanaribo, Mosongo Okambomba, Mosongo Bakueri, Mosongo Basoraka, etc.

The assistant to the military chief's assistant: Abasonga Barinde, Abasonga Afiemene, Abasonga Muna Mukatene, Abasonga Namoringi, etc.

The *cantor* [lead singer, chanter] of the *potencia*, "the cantor of kings, the one who calls the spirits": Morua, Morua Tinde, Morua Eribo, Engonso Morua, Yansa Morua Empego, Moru Entoti, Morua Mochete, Morua Nangopobio, Morua Erikundi, Morua Fusante, etc.

The "Executioner," the killer responsible for the sacrifices and implanting the soul of Sikan in the bongo: Ekueñon, Ekueñon Tankuebo, Ekueñon Arafambe, Ekueñon Sakara Erikundi, Ekueñon Changanake Famba, Ekueñon Sanga Kanima, Ekueñon Arokobo, Ekueñon Nasako Iyamba, Ekueñon Sanga Kerobian, Ekueñon Enkanima, Enkueñon Efion Favorikondo, Ekueñon Tine-Tine, Ekueñon Biakonsi, Ekueñon Yagasigama, etc.

The assistant to the Isue, the one who bears witness to the consecrations, "Guardian of the altar and the Sese": Enkoboro, Enkoboro Navarakua Kisongo, Enokoboro Bongo, etc.

The assistant to the Nasako, the administrator of the temple, the Famba room: Ekoumbre. The Cook of the *Potencia*: Enkandemo, Enkandemo Mituta, Enkandemo Napige.

The porter of the Famba: Moni Famba.

The bookkeeper of the *Potencia*: Kundiabon. He was formerly responsible for collecting money for the *aguinaldo*—Christmas offering—on the famous Three Kings Day, "when the Carabalí Cabildo members dressed as *diablitos* and went to the Palace." Koifan and Kofumbre: the tailor and the one who guards the "outfits" or costumes of the masquerades, the *diablitos* or Iremes.

Moni Bonko: the guardian of the Fundamento or Ekue. In the absence of the Iyamba, Isunekue, and Ekueñon, he can "fragayar" with it—that is, "make it speak."[14] This *plaza* [title], like that of Isun Eribo, "captain of the Abanekue," was created in Cuba. Moni Bonko "was King in Efik land. He was a drum maker." He is the chief of the drums in the *baroko*. He plays the Enchemi. Whoever performs these duties should be a consummate drummer.

14   DF-N: In the original, Cabrera does not elaborate further on this sonic cipher ("fragayar ... make it speak") until twelve pages later.

The "plazas" of Iremes or *diablitos*, which represent spirits, are as follows: Anamangi, the one who officiates funerary ceremonies, "el muertero."[15]

Enkanima: the one who carries away all the "cleansings" of the *Potencia's* members and deposits them in *el monte*.

Aberiñan: also goes to *el monte* to deposit the remains. He is "the one who holds the goat" at the moment of sacrifice. He does not enter the Famba.

Aberisun, the one who kills the goat. He strikes it on the head with a stick. Aberisun kills it, then Ekueñon removes its head. But before killing the goat, Aberisun kneels down, looks up at the sky, makes the sign of the cross, prays silently, performs a gesture of supplication with his hands, and jumps over the animal twice. Aberisun does not enter the Famba either. After killing the goat, he knocks on the door. They do not let him in. He kneels, makes the sign of the cross, and leaves.[16]

Emboko, the policeman, guards the Ekue and the Eribo. "Ireme Emboko Fembe." We see him next to Ekueñon in the *ñáñigo* processions.

Miraba. This Ireme is only represented in the *potencia* Jurianabo. It is "Guardian of the sea" and remains in the Famba.

Embema. This position, like the previous one, has disappeared from the "juegos" or *partidos*. In earlier times, it belonged to Ero Enta Efi. "It danced with three horns, one of them in the middle of its forehead. It used a turtle shell as a *sombrereta*." This is the Etan Muson Afomiremo, the flat hat that adorns the hood covering the back of the neck and head of those who officiate the Iremes.

Embakara, the Judge. The one who passes sentences and pronounces punishments.

Mosoko: this *plaza* exists in the juegos Oru Apapa, Oru Abakuá, Abakuá Oru, Oru Bibi, and Okobio Etan Oru. Others as honorable as that of Abasi (Jesus of Nazareth) were created by *abanekues*—that is, Creoles, "*ñáñigos* from Havana"—and are prominent in all of the *juegos*. Yet that of Obon-Obonekue was totally suppressed. "An Obon Obonekue had a level of authority high enough to fulfill any of the high-ranking functions in the *potencia*. They needed to have enormous knowledge of Abakuá, and only very capable, wise individuals fit the bill. But that *plaza* always created rivalry and controversy among the Okobios themselves, so it was annulled . . . And, for the sake of caution, to avoid violence and conflict, the Obon-Obonekue was finished,

---

15   DF-N: In this context, *muertero* can be understood as "custodian of the dead" and/or "undertaker."

16   DF-N: According to Miller, the gesture indicates that Aberisun is pleading forgiveness for the crime he is going to commit (personal communication, 2019).

because they wanted to win every argument. They became very conceited, like all know-it-alls."

Only one *plaza* for women—the one representing Sikan—existed in Oru Apapa, and it should be filled by an elderly woman. "In that *juego*, the elderly woman, the Ñata, would bear witness to the oath-taking ceremonies, and she could carry the clay pot on her head."

At present, it is a man who enacts the role of Sikan in the "juegos" of Matanzas. And in one Havana *juego*, they have Kasikanekua, Sikan, or Akanabionke, the mystical mother of the *ñáñigos*. She was chosen by Abasi to be the originator of the secret fraternity, and she is symbolized in the Famba by a doll.

"All of us in the *baroko* reenact the roles of ancestors. It is a sort of representation of what our deceased Abakuá forebears did in Africa, and the spirits." Let us retain this definition. Every *plaza* or position in the various *potencias* has a very specific authority and responsibility. New "tierras" or groups, affiliates of one of the two original Efik or Efo branches, are founded by means of an application that is signed by thirteen *obonekues* who sponsor and recognize the new *Potencia*. Once the new society has been constituted, it should be accepted by all the other existing Efik and Efo "tierras."

But the *ñáñigos* do not celebrate their mysteries without first paying homage to the ceiba, "the representation of the Omnipotent, the Divine Majesty"—Abasi.

At midnight, under its protection, they offer this prayer to the holy tree: "Entomiñan afoma sere ebion endafion umbriyo atrgo boko makaire nanumbre achene ebion asere ukano bekonsi entomiñan sanga Abakuá." They ask for permission from the sun, the moon, the stars, the spirit of the wind, the clouds, and space. Then they begin the rites of initiation, which will finish at six in the evening of the following day.

Before they "commence a *plante*," or *ñáñigo* celebration, an Indiobon—one of the high dignitaries of the *potencia*, such as Mosongo, Abasonga, Enkrikamo, or Morua Engomo—will lead the Indisme (neophyte, "new child") to a ceiba, naked above their waist, barefoot, and blindfolded.

During years that were truly difficult for Ñaitua, it was necessary to mock the authorities' surveillance and persecution as they chased down any trace of African savagery or fetishism. In order to "plantar" or "jugar" (celebrate the rites and ceremonies of the society), a small room in a tenement or boarding house in Havana would sometimes be used, and even the *diablito's* telltale cowbells would be filled with paper to muffle their sound and avoid alerting the police. The ceiba and palm trees were symbolically drawn using chalk, and the Odan River—or Oldán, as many *abaekues* pronounce it—was reduced to a basin or trough filled with water. Today, *ñáñigos* are able to house their *potencias* wherever they see fit according to the needs of their rituals, and real ceiba and palm trees are never absent from their courtyards, or the empty fields and plots often found next to the *potencia*.

The *indiseme* is "readied" next to a ceiba. This is the first step of the initiation. Morua Engomo, the "administrator" of Empego, kneels next to the sacred tree, salutes the sky and the stars, fills his mouth with aguardiente, and sprays the tree trunk generously. Then he sprays it again with white wine, and—lastly—with a bunch of albahaca leaves (the Abakuá hyssop) soaked in Umon Abasi, holy water from Kufon Abasi (the church). Following these aspersions, which are constant during Abakuá rituals, incense is burned in a concave roof tile that serves as an incense burner, and he draws symbols on the tree. The dignitary Ekoumbre presents a rooster—*enkiko*—to the stars, and the Enkrikamo (or sometimes the Morua Yansa) calls the *diablito*, the Ireme Eribangando, who uses the rooster to "cleanse" or purify the neophytes who are in a row on all fours before the ceiba, as is common to all African rituals. Following this process, Eribangando or Enkanima hangs the live bird from their waist as evidence that the *indisemes* have been properly purified. The roosters used to cleanse future Abakuá members of impurities are later set free, which—according to the good judgment of many onlookers who regularly attend *ñáñigo* celebrations—constitutes a danger: the bird, like a sponge, picks up the filth, "the dark shadows"—*nasawana*—of those taking the oath, thereby becoming a medium for the transmission of God only knows what bad influences that should be avoided and which the rooster, free to go wherever it pleases, disperses. Following a "plante" or "juego," some heartless bastard always takes this undesirable rooster and tries to sell it cheap.

Once the *indisimes* have been purified at the foot of the ceiba (without having their conduct monitored closely for two years, as was done in earlier times), they are once again "cleansed" by the Ekoumbre with a handful of herbs and, finally, they all are made to stand up. Morua-Engomo "cuts" them by drawing on them with yellow chalk, the color symbolizing life: a cross on their forehead, on their head, chest, hands, and the insteps of their feet, and rubbing them gently with white plaster chalk, which symbolizes death.

Then they begin to chant a march that is well known among the people:

Indisime Emparawao Kende Yo

All in a row, they are led to the Famba room where everything is prepared for the ceremony: the four corners have been purified, the sacred attributes are cleansed, the head of the sacrificed rooster has been placed over the Ekue and its body underneath. (Before beginning this initiation ritual, Ekueñon Tankeo presents a rooster to the sun and the stars. He then gives the rooster to Nasako, who uses it to cleanse everyone officiating the ceremony inside the

Famba. They wash their hands in a basin containing water, a bone, albahaca leaves, ash, charcoal, Anamú, and Abrojo.) Iyamba calls Ekueñon Tankeo to sacrifice the rooster. (*In illo tempore*, this Ekueñon once lacked a sacrificial rooster for Ekue and offered his own blood instead.) He kills the bird with his teeth, and after presenting all the ritual fees (the offerings of fruit and food), he spills the blood over the drum. The rooster is used to cleanse all of the attributes. The head is placed on top of the Eribo. Ekueñon, accompanied by an *ekon*, an *obonekue* carrying a bell, and another carrying a candle, leaves the Famba to search for the voice of the spirit—Akanaran—and guide it to the secret. When Ekueñon returns, he strikes the drum three times while saying, "Ekueñon besun kan suabasi! Ya yo, ya yo!" Uttering the last word, Ekue begins to sound, the *plante* begins, and the first procession goes out. Each time a procession goes out, they display the head of the rooster, or the head of a goat if a goat has also been sacrificed. Two clay pots contain rooster blood: one for the Ekue, another for the initiates—made brothers through the blood—to drink.

The *indisime* kneel in front of the door and the Morua Engomo draws another sign or *firma* on the floor. Incense is burned again, and the initiates are again sprayed with mouthfuls of aguardiente and white wine, then they are sprinkled with the indispensable bunch of albahaca leaves soaked in holy water. Nasako—the sorcerer—or his assistant Ekoumbre explodes gunpowder, which they keep in a horn and distribute along the drawing on the ground, "opening," "clearing" the neophytes' path, "and carrying away all the negativity."

After turning them around in circles to their right several times, they are taken inside the Sanctum Sanctorum, the premises of the impenetrable Abakuá mysteries.

Nobody asks about what happens in the celebrated Famba or Batamu, which is guarded by Famba-Moni, the gatekeeper, who opens the door for the Amanison, where the high dignitaries of the *potencia* wait to administer the oath: Mokongo, Mosongo, and Abasonga, along with the Ireme Enkoboro who bears witness to the oath, and the Isue who will perform the baptism.

Meanwhile, Iyamba, in the Efe-Ekue, continually makes the Secret—the sacred object for which *obonekues* are willing to die—"talk."

The woman, Sikan, paid for her sin of indiscretion with her life. She had found the fish Tanze in the River Odan (these days, some white *ñáñigos* say it was the River Jordan) in the land of Efo. The fish was "the secret," a materialization of the Almighty which had taken the form of a fish. Although the divine discovery made by Sikan gave rise to the Abakuá society ("the Carabalí African Freemasonry") and "her spirit is embodied in the Ekue" in which she is worshipped, women cannot participate in these rituals in any way. Sikan's father took possession of Tanze, just as we will see below that the Sese

Eribo—after the Ekue, the most sacred attribute of the Order—was taken from another woman who owned it: Arumiga from the land of Oru. King Lenimota dispatched the guardian of his Fambayin, Temen Kava, so he could forcibly take control of Sese. A *ñáñigo* chant recalls Arumiga's sadness when her drum was snatched away from her: "Arumiga Sese Eribo, mi Sese Eribo." Arumiga of Oru met with the same fate as Sikan.

Therefore, women must content themselves with being distant spectators at *ñáñigo* celebrations, which—following the secret ceremonies—unfold publicly in courtyards or empty lots. Once, thanks to the deference of an understanding and kind Abasi and a Mokongo, I was able to witness an "eñoro" or "llanto," a burial lament, in the courtyard of the house where the ceremony took place. Women were prohibited there, in that space where a gorgeous ceiba had stood years earlier, where they performed the "tribute" for the deceased. A dead rooster—stretched out on a roof tile, with an ineffable human quality that was strangely pathetic—represented the deceased Abakuá (the "ñampe") in the funerary rites. In this sense, it would be absolutely impossible for a woman to penetrate the mysterious Famba and once again divulge the secrets of the Order, if these had not ceased to be secrets a long time ago as a result of investigations and reports by the zealous Trujillo Monagas—Havana's second chief of police—which were published in the Havana press in 1882. The skills of this functionary were so great, so famous among Black elders that Calazán Herrera, recalling his days as an *obonekue*, said, "Trujillo was a *mayombero* and a sworn *abanekue*. He was a sorcerer. He could see with *vititi* and that's why nothing could escape him . . . But he was fair. A great policeman! He kept all the *chénenes* in check—the most formidable Mokongos, Embokos, and Ekueñons in the neighborhood of Jesús María." (Calazán had unpleasant memories of Rocha [sic],[17] who hounded *ñáñigos* and *mayomberos* in more recent times.)

Returning to the room of the mysteries, the Famba: its impenetrable threshold is protected by the same conservative, millenarian principle common to every magico-religious group. This consists of the uninitiated remaining ignorant of the foundation and location of the seat of supernatural power, which is only known by initiates, owners, and members by virtue of consecration and shared mysteries and marvels—like Ekue among our *ñáñigo* informants, members of the fraternity who are known as "monina" or "ñaito." That is why the Famba can only be entered by those who have been initiated, those who will be initiated, and dignitaries from other *potencias* who have been invited to bear witness. But I do not believe that anyone who has felt a little bit of curiosity

---

17   DF-N: This is almost certainly a reference to Rafael Roche y Monteagudo, author of *La policía y sus misterios en Cuba* (1925).

and made the effort to ask people can remain ignorant about the fundamental rituals that take place there, nor about what is involved in the marvelous, shocking secret hidden inside. The obsessive, haunting Ekue, Ekue, Ekue!

The indiscretion of the *abanekues* themselves after leaving the Famba has left nothing—or very little—hidden of these mysteries that were undoubtedly inscrutable in the beginning, "until the *criollos rellollos* and *blanquitos* got into *ñañiguismo* to disgrace it."[18]

The Famba, at the home of an Abasi friend who is now deceased and who provided me with sacred texts, in his home—which cannot be read by a layperson and are most often illegible—consists of a table that serves as an altar and is fixed to the middle of the wall at the back wall of the room, facing the only door. That is where the Abasi keeps some of the sacred objects of his *potencia*: the Iton (scepter staffs associated with the authority of the Obones or chiefs of the *potencia*), and the costumes of the Iremes or *diablitos* that dance in public during ceremonies and cannot be touched by women.

On the day new members swear their oaths, "plazas" of high-ranking dignitaries are consecrated, or new *potencias* or "tierras" are created, a colored cloth is hung on the wall behind the altar.

During the ceremony of the "llanto"[19]—the funerary tribute to the *okobio*, or deceased member of the society, regardless of his position with the hierarchy—this cloth is replaced with a black cloth featuring the image of a skull between two tibia and surrounded by four painted circles, embroidered or decorated with white fabric. The *firmas* (*gando*) of the fraternity's kings—

---

18   DF-N: *Criollos rellollos* refers to people whose families have been Creoles for several generations—that is, "hyper-Creole," "super-Creole," or "ultra-Cuban"—and *blanquitos* might be translated as "white boys" or "little white boys."

19   LC: In the *eñoro* or Ñampe ceremony, the position of the altar varies. Behind the table, the wall is covered with a black fabric displaying the *gando* for mourning, known as Ebakurero, like a coat of arms. Another black cloth covers the table. The Empego's drum—Kankomo Abasi, which stands in for the Sese Eribo—is on the table, along with a crucifix, the Palo Mokongo, the Palo Mosongo, the Palo Abasonga, and a candle, *la vela del alma*. A clay pot lays upside down on the floor. In the room, they will find an Ireme and a Morua.

In another room connected to the Famba, one finds the *firma* Yebenben (a skull and four circles) on a black cloth, along with the *firma* corresponding to the deceased *abanekue*—that is, the one corresponding to the position he filled in the Okobio when he was alive. A *bonko* is on the floor, an Ireme that weeps on his knees, and a *ñáñigo* guard. And in the third room, the cloth wall hanging is white and has the *firmas* of Mokongo, Iyamba, and Isue on it. On the table, next to a crucifix, one finds the sacred attributes, with the *plumeros* [plumed rods] covered as a sign of mourning. The Sese Eribo is placed upon an overturned clay pot, and plantain leaves cover the Eribo. On the floor is a *bonko*, and all of the "derechos" (the same ritual offerings the deceased offered when he was initiated). Another *obonekue* serves as a sentinel. During the funeral procession, only the scepters belonging to the Mokongo and Abasonga are taken outside.

the chiefs or Obons—are drawn over this cloth with yellow plaster chalk, representing the founding chiefs of the various tribes or "tierras" [lands, regions] in Africa: Efo, Oru, Efi, and Bibi. On the left, Mokongo (Efi). At the center, Isue (Oru). On the right, Iyamba (Efo). Under the *firma* of Iyamba, we find the one for Empego (according to the *abanekue* historians, the king of the land of Mukando Efo who was appointed scribe of the Obones at the first consecration).

Under that signature, we find the one for Mosongo, the shepherd king, guardian of the Ubane. Next is the one for Abasonga, king of the distant land of Oru. And, lastly, the one for Abasi, a position—as mentioned earlier—created in Cuba "because they wanted to incorporate Jesus into Abakuá, and they looked for someone to represent him." It is a reputable position with no responsibilities, and it confers elders in the *baroko* with the role of . . . Our Lord Jesus Christ.

The *firma* for Mosongo is drawn on the left side of the tabletop or altar. In the middle, the one for the *potencia* or the one for Nasako (palm, ceiba, or dove),[20] and the one for Absonga on the right. The Sese Eribo is placed in the middle of the table: it is a goblet-shaped drum "that is not played"; it is adorned with four plumes of feathers from roosters or peacocks that symbolize the Four Heads, the four chiefs and four territories. This object—the Sese, "which is the secret of Oru land"—is used to consecrate the other sacred objects or attributes. Everything is consecrated through contact with the Sese Eribo, and only the Isue—the bishop—handles it. Sacrifices cannot be performed in his presence. He cannot bear witness to the punishment of *okobios* found guilty of a crime with lashes from a cane administered, with more or less exuberance, by the stern Ireme or *diablito* Aberisun or Embokoro, who are responsible for administering such punishments.

---

20   LC: The Dove. When all the great men of Efi were gathered to begin the *baroko*, they realized they were missing the *bonko*, and they entrusted the king of Efi Kunakua with the mission to travel to Enyemiya—the land of drums—and bring back a *bonko*. He accomplished his mission and offered it to Efimeremo. (Mokongo.) They began the celebrations, then, at the moment of the consecration, Mokongo saw a dove and wondered whether it might be a spirit that came to join their celebration. Ekueñon ordered Nasako to divine what this apparition might be, and Nasako said, "Anamieto, viaña irua akuaramina." No, it was not a phantom. It was a dove, the grace and image of the Holy Spirit. Ekueñon took it and presented it to Ekue, murmuring, "My mother, I offer you this dove, which is from the land of Oru, and which has been sent here by God and the Holy Spirit. Then Ekue sounded quietly three times, and Ekueñon set her free, letting her fly away. Everyone saw the Holy Spirit's white dove on the road to the palace of the king of the land of Besundi as the procession marched along with the princes from the lands of Efo, Yambeke, and Enyegueye carrying the *Fundamento*.

Christian elements have been superimposed on the Black foundation of the Abakuá fraternity with rejoicing solemnity, bizarre parodies of the Catholic cult that Creoles (and, later, white people) accentuate more every day. In this way, we see Sese Eribo—which is similar to El Santísimo—paraded under a canopy in processions accompanying ñáñigo rituals, especially in Matanzas and Cárdenas. It is carried by the Isue, who wears a purple chasuble over his pants, ties a sash of the same color around his waist, dons a bishop's miter, and wears sandals in the style of Franciscan monks on his feet. (The disconcerting elegance and luxuriousness exhibited by these Isues can fuel rivalries, which sometimes result in open violence among "juegos" in Matanzas.)

The Sese Eribo is decorated according to the economic means of the *potencia* or *partido*. It is wrapped in a tiger pelt, signifying—as in all the "Reglas"— strength, power, and royalty. It is circled with a silver hoop, or simply covered with beads and cowrie shells.

The chalice used in a Catholic mass can serve as a substitute for the Sese Eribo: "The chalice—*akarawaso*—is the Sese itself; both represent El Santísimo."

On the altar, behind the Sese, a crucifix can be seen representing Abasi, the Supreme Being. On the left, leaning against the wall, the scepter of Mokongo, the military chief: Manyene Iton, "I order and command." To its right, next to the Sese, is placed another small drum just as sacred as the Ekue, decorated by a single plume of feathers, belonging to Empego: the Kankomo Abasi. To the right of the Sese Eribo, we find a staff or scepter of Mosongo—Aprosemi Iton. And next to it, Besoko Iton or Sanga Mañon, the staff of Iyamba. This staff, which is also known as "Judge and Jury," represents the ultimate authority of the Abakuá society, the supreme leadership in every Okobio Efor.[21]

With the scepter known as Sanga Mañon in hand, Obon Iyamba issues orders, commands, and decisions. The Iyamba is the owner and guardian of Ekue, "which he took into his possession"—according to the sacred history of the secret fraternity—"by the express will of heaven, and made it sound for the first time, on a rock in the middle of the river."

To make the first staff, the Iton of the Iyamba, the sorcerer Ña Nasako "registró" [consulted, divined] using his magic mirror and saw that the Besoko tree was in *el monte* of Apapa Tarume. This tree would provide the proper wood for the scepter of the Iyamba of Efo (who was also a renowned sorcerer), so Iyamba and Mokongo went to the forest together to cut a branch.

The staff of Abasonga, the assistant of Mosongo—Enua Iton—is known as Embakaradibo. It is covered in goatskin and capped with a crown made of

---

21 DF-N: *Okobio* generally means "brother," but Cabrera uses it here to mean an Abakuá *potencia*, or lodge.

silver or another metal. It symbolizes justice: it imposes respect for the law; in instances when the commandments of the society are broken, it orders the just punishment. Infractions regarding any of the moral obligations demanded of adepts are subject to the consideration of an assembly, which pronounces judgments and sentences according to the magnitude of the offense.

A wood goblet—Ñangaipe—is also placed on the table altar. It is sometimes capriciously adorned with encrusted pieces of mother-of-pearl—like one in my possession—and contains holy water and the bunch of albahaca leaves for the never-ending sprinkling required by the ritual, as well as two candles when a *plante* is being celebrated—or, in a funerary "llanto," four candles.

Depending on a given *potencia's* degree of syncretism, the altar is adorned with metal candlesticks and vases of flowers of the same kind that decorated colonial churches in earlier times. The *ñáñigos* anticipated Yankee antique dealers and bought the furnishings from priests who were eager to renovate their temples.

The "derechos" or tributes paid by the *indisime* during their initiation (the same offerings made upon their death) are arranged on the floor in front of the altar. These include green plantain (*plátano verde, atereñon*), yam (*ñame, embia*), sugarcane (*caña, emboko*), sesame (*ajonjolí, mekrekre*), salt (*agreso*), peanut (*maní, embachan*), ginger (*genjibre, moto*), pepper (*pimienta, dochan*), smoked fish (*kondondo*), hutia (*enkuko*), a bottle of aguardiente (*okoro nimba*), another bottle of dry wine (*okoro besua*), charcoal (*ebionon*), three bundles of firewood (*iton*), basil (*albahaca, kaememeru*), Santa Maria feverfew (*escoba amarga, ifan*), thistle (*abrojo, mendiba*), plaster chalk (*engomo sarako*), gunpowder (*ekun*), and three stones.

In the corner of the room, to the left of the altar, one finds the Fambayin or Fekue, where the *fundamento*, or secret—Akanaran, mother of the Abakuá, the ineffable Ekue—is hidden behind a curtain boasting the *gando* or *firma* of Isunekue, son of Iyamba and king of Ekuendube. A small drum. Like the Iyamba, the Isunekue is able to play and "feed" it.

The clay pot in which the miracle occurred is placed in front of the "secret." Inside the pot, the supernatural fish that was "a manifestation of Abasi," flapping its tail, shining like a comet that became a fish, and emitted that first frightening sound. In other words, it literally "bellowed," and it made Sikan tremble with fear.

Directly across from the clay pot guarded by the Ireme Mariba Kankemo, the "outfits" (*afomiremos* or *kofombres*) of the Iremes or *diablitos* hang from the wall on the right side of the room. They "are the *muertos*, the spirits of the ancestors who are in *el monte*" and can be seen dancing in all of the Abakuá celebrations.

The *mokuba* or small pot is placed next to the Ekue. It contains blood from the sacrifice and small bits from all of the aforementioned offerings. The blood is absolutely indispensable for the Iyamba or Isunekue, who have the authority to make the secret speak throughout the duration of the initiation. And here we reach the bottom of the great Abakuá mystery that the old *ñáñigos* kept hermetically silent and which—even more painfully to a worthy *ñaito*— has become known to the public: How is the mysterious bellowing—which was, for many years, the impenetrable secret of the *ñáñigos*—produced? Simply put, "Fragayando." "Fragayando yin . . ." That is, using the thumb and index finger to rub up and down on a *gwin—yin* or *saekue*, caña de Castilla—which is held against the middle of the drum skin. (In the "llanto," the *yin* is held against the wooden edge of the drum, not in the middle of the skin.) Thanks to this *gwin*, we hear the voice of the spirit of Sikanekua, which Ekueñon goes to find in *el monte* and brings back to the Famba. Sikanekua takes possession and "speaks" in the Ekue, which is its materialization.

The fingers need to be wet for the *yin* to sound, and the Iyamba and Isunekue constantly wet them in the rooster blood collected in the *mokuba*. (Of course, the blood increases the power concentrated in the sacred and secret object, which is heard but not seen by the uninitiated.)

A curtain hides the interior of the Famba from the gaze of curious onlookers. In earlier times, a drum—the Enkamao—was placed next to the entrance, which an *okobio* would strike to request permission to enter the Famba, then announcing his name and credentials. In its place, we now find a small wooden bowl containing the Anamabo, the holy water in which seven sacred herbs are mixed: *incienso de costa, lino de río, pimienta de costa, paraíso, escoba amarga, abrojo, anamú*, and the quintessential *ñáñigo* albahaca.

Finally, the *indisimes* enter the Famba in a single file, always blindfolded, each one accompanied by an *okobio* who functions as their godparent. There they find Empego and Enkrikamo, another younger son of Iyamba, and Ireme Enkoboro, the spirit that appeared when the first consecration of the attributes and plazas was carried out, and who—as we have mentioned—is supposed to bear witness and authenticate all oaths.

When Enkoboro enters the secret room, the Enkrikamo says, "Ireme Enkoboro yumba sunaga arasande." Enkrikamo went to find Enkoboro and bring him to the Famba, and he will remain standing next to the Sese Eribo throughout the ceremony, guarding it. Naturally, the chiefs of the *Potencia* to which the *indisime* belong are present: Iyamba, Mokongo, Mosongo, Isue, and Embakara. Embakara holds the staff of justice. He watched over the sacred drum skins used in the first transmission of the Divine Voice, he presides over tribunals that decide on punishments, and he can substitute the Isue. Ekueñon, another king from Efik land, was Iyamba's faithful slave and guide because

Iyamba was blind and "it was Ekueñon himself who took out Iyamba's eyes." Nasako (the sorcerer) and his administrator Ekoumbre (who, as we know, gathers the ritual herbs and carries gunpowder in a cattle horn). The Old God, "the creole Christ" (*sic*) Abasi Okampo.[22] Abasonga and the Ireme Emboko (*Ireme Emboko enkabuyo fembe*) is the policeman of the *potencia*; like Embokoro, he is a guardian of the Ekue and Eribo who only leaves the Famba to march in processions alongside Ekueñon.

The *indisime* kneel in front of the altar and salute the *obons* gathered, as well as the *obons* from other *potencias* who have been invited to bear witness to the oaths of the new members. The godfathers stand behind the *indisime*. Then it is Mokongo, staff in hand, who recites the law, "the articles of faith" of the society, and asks them if they swear to answer his questions sincerely—not in *ñáñigo* slang, but in Spanish.

The neophyte should respond firmly: "Yes, sir."

"Why do you want to belong to this *Partido*?"

"To defend it to the death, to be a good brother," etc.

The godfathers repeat the Mokongo's words; he then offers his staff for the neophytes to kiss it. Following Mokongo's interrogation, Mosongo and Abasonga also present their staffs—the Enyua Iton and Aprosemi Iton—to be kissed.

And every time, the *indisime*—who, as we have said, are ritually naked above the waist—are sprayed with aguardiente and dry wine, then struck with a bunch of albahaca soaked in holy water.

Then Isue baptizes them with the Sese Eribo, resting the sacrosanct drum on each of the *idisimes*' heads and praying in Abakuá for a long time. At the end, he recites the Abakuá Our Father, which is well known by all streetwise Black boys, children of *ñáñigos*: *Atarabo guaso, makara guaso, mutasio chekedeke Mosongo, Obon Iyamba abairemo enkaura enkiko bagarofia ata Efimeremo bakongo Abakuá.* And the Credo: *Obon, Obon Abakuá komo Ireme Yanusa Ireme Sanga Kondo komo niene aberitan afoo tenten maseri okambo kambo yagasi Gabon.*

Isue—His Eminence—deliberately takes his time at this point in the ceremony: if an *indisime* regrets his oath, he has time to retract and confess that he will desist from entering the society. Isue begins to put the Sese in their hands: the *indisime* or *amanison* seem to not know what it is.

"What are you holding in your hands?"

---

22 DF-N: As in several other passages in *El Monte*, Cabrera seems to use the editorial interjection "(*sic*)" to indicate a conceptual or theological error rather than a misspelling or grammatical error. Here, she is presumably clarifying that Abasi Okampo is not—strictly speaking—"the creole Christ."

"I don't know."

"Sese Eribo."

Upon hearing that it is the Sese, they kiss it fervently, then they kiss the crucifix and drink the blood of the rooster collected in the *mokuba*. Then the knots in the blindfolds covering the eyes of the new *abanekues* are undone. These days, they are no longer frightened during their initiations by the terrifying pranks of earlier times, back in the glorious days when the knives and daggers of Ebion and Ekoriofo—the two great rival *potencias*—were painted bright red. At most, they allow a few drops of candle wax to fall on their backs, or they are pinched.

Immediately following the initiation, they exit the Famba to receive congratulations from their friends and "moninas" and to be paraded around in the procession. On the days of the solemn festivities, following this ceremony, the sacrifice of the goat is conducted on the patio; it is not done inside the Famba. In initiation ceremonies, only roosters are sacrificed, as long as there are less than twelve neophytes taking their oaths.

Enkandemo, the cook of the *potencia*, prepares a communion meal, reproducing the first *baroko*—Iriate Akamanyene Efik—that was celebrated "then" in Efik land. The ingredients were gathered at a place known as Aguanañongo Ekombre, and the meal was offered by Obune Efike Kiñongo Endiagame (from Ubane).

This ceremony—like all *ñáñigo* ceremonies, updating a page out of the mystical history of the society—proceeds in the following way: When Enkandemo, the cook, has prepared the food, he sends for Ña Nasako, the sorcerer and diviner, so that he can "see" and confirm the meal is not poisonous. "In those days," a young *abanekue* explains to me, "Agwan Enkare and Enkare Afrakaume were two characters that took care of this ritual. They were always with Batanga Baronga, who drew his *firma* at the moment of eating as a representation of Efo."

Nasako examines the pot of food, then he carries it over and places it on the floor over a "gando" or *firma* drawn by Empego. The *firma* combines the signatures or symbolic signs of Mokongo, Eribangando, Enkamina, Nasako (who authorizes this ritual), and Ekoumbre. In the exact words of my instructor, these *firmas* or *gandos*—Abakuá ideograms that validate every ritual—represent "emblems, commemorations, and reaffirmations of that which was done in Africa when the *Potencias* were founded. They are sacred evocations and authorizations which give strength to what is done here. The *firma* authorizes, consecrates, and certifies."[23]

23 DF-N: See Cabrera (1975).

Some of this food—which, incidentally, is not appetizing at all and consists of the remains of the sacrificial rooster, yams, plantains, sugarcane, fish, etc.—is separated into two portions. These small portions are placed in two small clay pots and taken as offerings to *el monte* and the river, "because Sikan was an earthly being, and Tanze was a water being," and because that is how it was done on that memorable occasion, "when the Bibi tribe from Efi united with the Usagare from Efo."

After placing the large clay pot over the *gando* drawn on the floor with plaster chalk, Ña Nasako summons Isue who, in turn, summons the *obones* and *obonekues* to share the meal. The *obones* chant to the clay pot—"Banbako Mama Nagarike"—and dance around it with the *obonekues* and the Ireme Eribangando, who takes small bits from the wing of the rooster, a yam, and a plantain in order to scatter them as an offering to Los Cuatro Vientos [The Four Winds]. Morua Yansa—"the Master of songs," the one with the pretty voice—leads a series of chants and dances next to the pot for approximately one hour.

At the moment they are about to eat, they chant "Eribe makaterere" to the *obons*. They move continuously around the pot, like the adepts of Ocha doing *ñangale* at daybreak, or the Kimbisas' meal for the *muertos* at midnight, in the dark, which is daytime for the dead. The food is offered by the Isue from a *jícara* and received with bare hands. "Amana amana empaira" are the words that should be uttered by the Isue as he distributes the communion food to the *okobios* and the new *okobios*.

At midnight, when the *plante* begins in advance of the hidden oath ceremony in the Ekufon or Famba, the officiants leave in a procession—except for Iyamba and Isunekue, who remain in order to guard Ekue—and each "plaza," each of the dignitaries, marches with their corresponding attribute and drum.

The door to the mystery room is opened, and Ireme Eribangando, Ña Nasako, and Morua stick their heads out. Nasako burns a handful of gunpowder in his hand to ward off bad spirits and "open" the way.

The Isue places himself in the center, holding the Sese Eribo between Ekueñon and Empego, the Royal Scribe. Each one holds their respective drums. Mokongo, Mosongo, and Abasonga follow behind them, each holding their respective scepters, then the other "plazas" carrying lit candles, and one *obonekue* bearing the cup of holy water—Ñangaipe—and the bunch of albahaca leaves used to spray, purify, and bless the participants. Behind them, the Moni Bonko, the chief of the drums, holds the Bonko Encheme and three *obonekues* hold the three small drums—the Biapa, Tete Ndoga, and Kuchiyerema, which enliven the *ñáñigo* celebration or *plante*; although they are "marked with chalk, baptized, and consecrated"—a drum is always a sacred object—they do not enter the Famba. They are accompanied by an *okobio* who plays Ekon, the bell, and Erikundi, the rattles. Yet another *ñáñigo* strikes the side of the Bonko Encheme with Iton—sticks or a *clave*.

These processions of Abakuá liturgy move around the more or less reduced space of a courtyard or gallery in the home occupied by the *potencia*, or inside its rooms, if the house does not have a courtyard.

In the towns of Regla and Guanabacoa, in Pocito or Pogolotti in Marianao, and in some neighborhoods in the city of Matanzas or Cárdenas, where there are many *ñáñigos* and the *obons* enjoy influence in the municipal government (especially on the eve of elections), the procession parades through the streets and the masses join them. They are easily aroused by the drums, and they march along, moving to the rhythm and singing along with the choruses of the chants.

For many who consider *ñañiguismo* a national disgrace, it is an incredible, disconcerting, and lamentable spectacle: parades of shirtless white and Black men bringing together African drums, Christ in agony on the cross, the pagan severed head of a goat, and an archaic clay pot. For the observer, their primitive and barbaric character is precisely what produces an extraordinary interest that does not need to be underscored.

As they move, the rigorously stylized gestures—every gesture is a phrase—of the *okobios* dressed as *diablitos* represent ancestors initiated in the distant past. The eternal masks play a religious role whose significance transforms them into abstractions, unreal and sacred beings. Seen in the light of Cuba's magical nights, their mimicry and dance are a strangely beautiful spectacle so timeless, so remote and mysterious, that it cannot fail to leave a strong impression on anyone who beholds it.

I have not forgotten the terror that the Iremes, with their white Cyclops eyes, aroused in Federico García Lorca, nor the delirious poetic description he shared with me the day after witnessing a *plante*.

If Diaghilev had been born on this island, there is no doubt he would have made these *ñáñigo diablitos* parade across Europe's stages.

After the swearing-in ceremony, the duration of which depends on the number of neophytes who will be admitted into the fraternity, the same procession is repeated the following morning with the new *obonekues*. They are presented to the rising sun at dawn with these words: "Abasi kesonga obonekue embremeri amana korobe Efike"—or "Efo"—"baroko." They are also presented to the ceiba, "the image of El Santísimo." And at nightfall, when the "*juego*" is concluding, the procession goes out from the Famba for a third and final time with all of the moninas or brothers, to render one last tribute to the divine Ukano Bekonsi.

Nasako is essentially like a sorcerer or *mayombero*, and he is responsible for all of the sorcery performed in the *potencia*. He "ties down" the four corners every time a *baroko* is celebrated. The technique is the same: "nkanges" made with corn straw and "guardian nails" buried at the corners of the house that ward off police (Enkabuyo) and insure the "plante" against any possible accident. Thus, one day prior or on the same morning of a *baroko*, Nasako will "ask for the ceiba's *licencia* [permission, blessing, and authority]" to work in its shadow as he makes the binding and protective ritual objects that he will bury at the four cardinal points along the edge of the house-temple where the *ñaitua* will be celebrated.

As we have mentioned, every ritual involves the officiants drawing the *gando* or ideogram that corresponds to their position. The "firma" of Nasako is drawn on the roots and trunk of the ceiba, "because all the sorcery is done under the ceiba, and Nasako is the one who does it and authorizes it with his *gando*."

In the oath-taking ceremonies of the *obons*—positions that are lifetime appointments—the great Mokongo swears his oath at the foot of a ceiba. His mythical ancestor, the first Mokongo from Efi land, was consecrated under a ceiba in Erube, where he later consecrated Iyamba and Isue. And he was the first to spill the blood of a goat over the Ekue. Mokongo was the husband of Sikan and one of the founding chiefs of Abakuá. According to the Efi, Sikan gave Mokongo the title of Masause before she was sacrificed, because he received the secret. And it was Mokongo who verified the sound of Tanze in the clay pot, the incarnation of the Supreme Being—all of this according to the tangled history of the *ñaitos*, which might be better understood in the following chapter dealing with the royal palm tree.

Empego, the scribe, drew the symbol of the *baroko* on the roots and trunk of the ceiba. When Mokongo was consecrated, he leaned his back against its trunk. That ceiba on which Mokongo leaned and rested on before going to his consecration is called Ekoi-Meson. When a Mokongo is "made," their scepter—the sacrosanct Palo Mokongo—is taken to a ceiba. It was Nasako who "authorized" the staff's "load" or "charge"—that is, the magic contents of the scepter—and prepared it with the help of his administrator Ekoumbre in the presence of Isue, king of Afiama.[24]

("Nasako loaded Mokongo's staff with water that he ordered to be collected on the shore of Yorabia with the Ireme Erume, and he consecrated the water.")

Along with the staff, the celebration of this ceremony involves taking two ritual candles "which illuminate the man in life and death" (in other words, when they enter the society and when they die in its bosom), yellow chalk

---

24 DF-N: The original Spanish grammar of this passage shifts from present tense to past tense, suggesting the synthesis of mythological precedent and (in a passive voice) contemporary ritual.

"used to inscribe that which is never erased" (the initiatory marks on the skin of adepts), white chalk symbolizing death, aguardiente, dry wine, holy water, albahaca, and incense.

At that time—the ceremony, like all the others, repeats the original ceremony performed at the dawn of Abakuá—Empego, in order to "scratch" [mark signs] on Mokongo, was authorized by Nasako to make the chalk for the consecration with the yellow clay from the hill named Itiamo Kanda and water from the lagoon named Hei, both in Mokonda land.

Then, as now, in the immutable time of Abakuá ritual, Empego draws the everlasting sign of the *baroko* with chalk as he chants: "Asubuo aramiñon endora anye . . ."

At the ceiba, the goat for the consecration of Mokongo waits to be sacrificed. Both sides of the goat are also marked with yellow plaster chalk. Horizontal lines run along both sides of its spine, grazing the backbone. In the middle, a vertical line descends down to its belly, with two circles on the right and left side of this line. These are the eyes of Tanzen or Sikan—the two zeroes, as *ñáñigos* refer to these circles which are inscribed—simply or in more complex designs—on all Abakuá liturgical objects (Arakasuaka). The circles are given the name Iboko Iro when they are found on the left, and Iboko Eroko Nimi on the right. "The circle, Chiabaka, symbolizes the union of all *obonekues*."

The horns are inscribed with the crosses of Efik land or the ovals of Efo land, along with a stylized image of a palm tree frond. Each leg of the goat represents a nation or tribe that constituted the society's origins: Efo, Oru, Efi, and Bibi.

Mokongo, the pastor king of goats, took this goat—Embori Sorobia—to his initiation, and he sacrificed it, with Ekueñon and Iyamba, in the presence of Mosongo. Together they "united their heads"—an attitude expressing that they would share the same thought from then on and remain united forever. "They saw the ghost of Sikan and swore to never reveal the secrets of the religion."

Then Mokongo said what he still says now: "Awana Embori Mokongo Ibañon." And, mounted on the goat, holding his scepter—Mokaiten—which was baptized by Isue with sacred river water, he chants, "Biwi biwi ponponte mi yao." Then he enters the *baroko*, where the three *obons* welcomed him, exclaiming, "Mokongo bariba kondo sere kondo unon enton ñaña kua kerefe."

During the act of his initiation, Mokongo is known as Mokongo Ura Kambori. He is called Mokongo Arikua Arikua when he goes to *el monte* to gather his staff. When he enters the Famba, he is known as Mokongo Forifa Arita. Before the altar, he is Mokongo Chabiaka Yabutame.

When he parades in a procession, he is Mokongo Machevere. When he goes to war, he is Mokongo Muchangana. Among his numerous other titles, many of which we have noted, he is also known as Efimeremo Bihuraka Embori.

Using his magic, Ña Nasako lured the spirit of a Congo man to a ceiba in Oru land. The Congo was sacrificed by Aberiñan in Enchemiya, then flayed, and his skin was used as the drum head of the bongo (the Ekue).

In the end, the woman Sikan is sentenced to death by Embakara under a ceiba tree. That is where she hears her sentence, tied to its sturdy, venerable trunk.

Ukano Bekonsi and Ukano Mambre, as we will see later, are the two most sacred trees in Abakuá Freemasonry. "They authorize our work, and everyone who swears an oath to Abakuá kneels before the ceiba and salutes her before entering the Famba. The ceiba belongs to Abasi." Embori, the goat that is killed by Aberisun with a single blow to the forehead, used to be consecrated at the foot of a ceiba.

The man that swears an oath to be a *ñáñigo* first offers a tribute to Ukano Bekonsi ("Asere ukano entomiñon bekonsi sansa abakuá") before offering one to the Great Ones of the Potencia at the altar ("Asere itia obon idiobon etenye nefon abakuá bakankubia").

THE ROYAL PALM

ITS RELATIONSHIP TO THE GREAT ORISHA CHANGÓ, WITH OYA
AND AGAYU. CHANGÓ'S STORY. INCEST. CHANGÓ AND OGUN. NSASI.
THE THUNDER STONE. CHANGÓ, OYA, AND MAYOMBEROS. CURSES.
THE PALM TREE AND THE OMO CHANGÓ. AN OMO-CHANGÓ:
CALAZÁN. RITES. GUANO BENDITO. ASHES. THE PALM IN MEDICINE.
THE DESMOCHADOR.

LUCUMÍ: ILE CHANGÓ ORISSA. IGI OPPWE. OPE. ALABI. SEFIDIYE.
ELUWERE. OLUWEKON. CONGO: LALA. MABA. DIBA. DUNKENDE.

ॐ

The most popular orisha—Changó, "Alafi-Alafi, king of Oyo,
king of kings," Changó, Santa Bárbara—is inseparable from Cuba's most beautiful and evocative tree. As we have seen, Changó
Olufina lives in ceiba trees. But the incomparable *palma real*—
the royal palm, which adorns the island's landscape with its
lofty grace, refinement, and melancholy—enjoys the honor of
being "the true home of Alafi," his favorite dwelling. "It is his
throne and lookout." There he tends to manifest in his most terrible aspect, Changó Obaye. He is the owner of other trees: the
melodious *álamo*, the *jobo* [hog plum], the incandescent *framboyán* [flamboyant, or royal poinciana], the *cedro* [cedar], the
pino [pine]. But the palm is the most symbolic of his divinity.
"The king of the world who dresses in palm fronds, the beautiful dark-skinned Black man that eats fire." From the palm tree's
slender stalk, which trembles and rises up to the sky, the god of
fire shoots his arrows down at the earth.

"Wherever you find a palm tree, there's Changó standing out on the branch, like he stands in the tower of his *ile olodin*" (castle).

The shoot that rises above the opulent plume formed by its branches is a true lightning rod that attracts electrical discharges. Changó, the thunder, "the artilleryman of the sky," "always goes to the palm tree," "falls on the royal palm." The association with the great orisha becomes inevitable. Because lightning bolts strike a considerable number of these trees every year, especially during the rainy season, Alabi (the palm) is—roughly speaking—as sacred and important as the ceiba in the religious economy of our people.

("The ceiba belongs to El Santísimo, the royal palm to Santa Bárbara.")

"The palm tree receives the lightning bolt and holds it inside." "It has the authority to restrain the lightning." According to G.S., "that tree is family of the true fire of Changó Obakoso." It is the "pedestal of Obakoso," which devotees often confuse with the orisha himself: Felix D. affirms that "the royal palm is Obakoso himself."

Naturally, because of its relationship and affinity with Changó, other orishas participate in the cult that worships him at royal palms, such as Oya or Yansa, Mama-Oya-ferekun, the Virgen de la Candelaria, "Owner of the lightning," Changó's inseparable and faithful concubine, who follows him everywhere and fights beside him in all of his battles.

"Oya Obinidodo"—one "omo" of the goddess tells us—"is Changó's right hand. She is the woman he loves and respects the most. When Changó goes out to fight, she leads the way. She always fights beside him with two swords. Without Oya's help, Changó would have been defeated many times, like in his first war with Ogun."

Oya—Oya of Tapa is from the same territory as Changó. She jumped from Ilorin to Cuba. She is the daughter of the land of Ota, where my grandmother was from, just as she declared in this *soroyi* (song):

> *Oma do omo ota*
> *Oma do omo ota*
> *Re bi iwa Oya*
> *Mala eleya . . .*

But she followed Changó to Takua. "Oya, hekua hei yo ro obini dodo! Oya wolenile ira!"

The Yesas say she is Yesa. The Takuas say she is Takua. The Minapopos say she is Mina. But believe me, she is Takua.

All of the orishas hated Changó. They schemed to wage an all-out war against him. He knew all about it and said, "Come on, all of you! I'll fight to the death!" Oya sat down to watch the battle. Changó fought with an axe and a machete, day after day, alone against everyone. The battle dragged on and Changó couldn't take any more. Oya watched. When he started to lose heart, Oya jumped into the battle furiously, and it was thanks to her that Changó triumphed.

Oya's loyalty, her fidelity and constant abnegation, were never absent for a single moment of Changó's hazardous life.

"Changó experienced many hardships. He was a gambler, *un tropa*. He was troublesome . . . He was a man and a king, Alafin, before he become a *santo* and went up to heaven. All the kings of the other tribes chased him and declared war against him to finish him once and for all. Changó spent his life misbehaving, fleeing and fighting. And Oya was firmly by his side. Oya, Dada, and Obañeñe, his foster sister, who had been nursed by Changó's mother (*hermana de leche*). Changó went into the earth with Oya and Obañeñe, then the three of them went to heaven . . ." "Changó was a king who became Ocha."

Sometimes Oya—who is also the "Bad Wind," the tornado, the hurricane, or devastating gust of wind—precedes Changó, bringing the storm in her skirts, while the orisha fights by hurling lightning bolts and stones and breathing fire. (And although Oya is "very revolutionary, just as brave in a fight and even more fierce than Changó, she's also very womanly, very loving of her home. She'll spend years without going out, holed up in her hideout.")

"Obakoso, Santa Bárbara, when he lived in this world, was a king of all the Lucumí. But he was as bad as a devil, and they couldn't stand him. He was a roaming king who had to flee all the time. He committed atrocities in Oyo, then he went to Nupe with Oya. That's where his mother Yemaya lived. When they thought they were rid of him, because he'd pretended to be dead, he came after all of them, shooting fire from inside a storm, and killed them all."

"Changó Eyeo," Bangoché tells us, "fought by breathing smoke and fire from his mouth and launching lightning bolts. He also fought with a club, an axe, a machete, and a knife shaped like a half moon. Wherever he went on the warpath, he reduced towns to piles of ashes. *Aina yole omoba!* He was more violent than anybody else, and he destroyed whatever they put in front of him . . . That's why a statue dressed up like Changó should never have its sword arm raised. He'll definitely cause a commotion."

"There's a Changó that's more serious and rides on horseback, and another one that is on foot and runs away. The most boisterous and combative is the one from Takua. Eshu and Osain, his godfather, were always with him. And he's in lockstep with Oya-Yansa, who was the wife of Ogun, a rival of Changó."

(Ogun treated her badly. Oya and Changó were made for each other and understand each other perfectly, so Changó took her from Ogun.)

"Oya was queen of Koso. She is a *santa* with a crown, *boloya*—good-looking, like Obatala, Oshun, and Yemaya. She would go in *el monte* and hunt animals like a man. She had a sister, Ayao, who is a young lady who is praised, but not consecrated. When Oya comes down, she sings to her sister:

Abeokuta mo fi Ayao
Abeokuta lu sange

This is danced like a march. Ayao forbids marriage, like Yewa. She is like Yewa. The Gangá respected her very much."

"Changó did whatever he wanted. Obatala received complaints about him from every quarter. 'The problem is that he was raised far away from me,' the old man said. 'But he will feel the weight of my authority.' And so it was. One day Changó tied his horse at a woman's door.

"Obatala and Odua walked by and took the horse. When Changó asked about his horse, they told him two old people walking by had taken it.

"Changó ran out like a shot. Obatala saw him coming and shouted: 'Kunle, foribale!' And Changó felt the weight of his authority: he threw himself on the ground. Changó was wearing his *eleke* (necklace) made entirely of red beads. Obatala mixed them with white beads. 'That way, they will know you are my son.'

"Obatala lived in a palace with sixteen windows. Oba, who was in love with Changó, told Obatala, 'Tell him I love him.' She brought him a black horse as a gift and left it in the courtyard of the palace.

"'Changó, look at what Oba has brought you.'

"Changó replied, 'That's a very nice horse, but Oya is the woman I like best.'"

The legitimate wife of Changó is Oba. Like him, she is a native of Takua territory, Oba Yuru, Oba Girielu, Saint Catherine of Sienna or our Lady of Carmen.

Manuela clarifies: "As my late father would say, Changó actually has three women: Oba, Oshun, and Oya."

Oba is the first of the three women, "the primary one, the lady, a respectable woman." Her own jealousy, along with deceitful advice from Oshun (according to some) or Oya (according to others), condemned her to live apart from her husband.

He holds her in high esteem but stopped having marital relations with her after she fed him her ear.

Oba would pretend Changó was faithful. One day, she complained to Oshun that he didn't spend very much time with her. Oshun asked her, "Do you want Changó to live peacefully at home?"

Oba answered, "How could I not!"

"Well, then. Cut off one of your ears, make a *kararu* (soup) with *amala* and your ear, then feed it to Changó. As he swallows it, you'll be inside him, and he'll love you much more." And Oba cut off one of her ears, made *kararu*, and called Changó.

> *Amala mala kararu*
> *Amala Oni Sago*[1]
> *Mala mala kararu!*

Changó was with Oya.

"You hear that? Oba is calling me. Un loni!" (I'm leaving!)

Annoyed, Oya says, "She's your favorite!"

"She's my wife. I respect her."

Oba had set the table and served the food. "Eat," she said. Oba had covered her head with a white cloth.

"What's wrong, Oba? Why are you not eating?"

"I don't have an appetite."

"Why are you sad?"

"Mibinoyi, mi sukun sukun . . . I never see you!"

Changó finished and left. He went to see Oshun, who told him, "Eluwekon, how is it that a man as elegant as you seems to feel no shame about living with a deformed woman?"

"What woman?"

"Oba! Changó oba o mague alado yina!" And everything was revealed. Changó ripped off the cloth covering her head and saw that she was missing an ear.

"What have you done, Oba! Oba ode-eti! I won't leave you, and you'll be my senior wife. But since you've mutilated yourself, I won't live in your house anymore!"

Oba made a legal claim against Changó. The presiding judge for the hearing is Ocha-Oko, San Isidro Labrador, who settles disputes between the *santos*, and Changó explains why he abandoned Oba. Changó took her to heaven. She doesn't come down into anybody's head.[2] If Oba Yuru comes down, it is only to take one of her children from this world. She is

---

1   DF-N: The original reads "Sagó."

2   DF-N: In other words, Oba does not possess devotees, like some other orishas.

Changó's legitimate wife: we sing "Oba sere Changó Iloro" to her, and she is just as fierce as he is. And Changó always consults with her. She is in the cemetery, at the edge of the graves.

When Oba is danced, whoever is dancing puts their hands to their head to hide their ears.

Gaitán, a nephew of the well-known Tata Gaitán, says,

They told me that Yemaya talked with Oba and told her about what a glutton Changó was, and about how much cornmeal and okra had to be cooked for him. That once they were married, he would leave her. He'd go away and spend days and days away from home.

Changó only wanted *bata* drumming and feasts. During one of his absences, Elegua told Oba that she should throw a party. He found Changó and took him to the *bata* drumming party Oba had prepared.

Oya went looking for Changó to take him away from the party, but he was enjoying himself. He showed her the head of the ram they'd sacrificed for the feast, and she got scared and left. As a form of sacrifice, a way to bind Changó to her, Oba cut off her ear and put it in the okra. But Changó saw the cut ear floating in the stew and left. Then Obatala covered Oba's head with a white cloth that she never takes off.

These goddesses are enemies ever since. "Oba adores Changó, who is called Obalube when he is with her, and Obadimeyi when he is in the land of her father-in-law Obatala. She has never forgiven Oya for giving her that little piece of advice about the ear. She lives isolated, hiding the scar from her ear. She is deeply respected, and she takes good care of her husband's *ile*."

But the lover, the "official" concubine of the god of thunder, is just as jealous as his wife Oba.

Changó is an incorrigible womanizer. One legend explains why palm trees are a target for lightning more than other trees.

Changó climbed a palm tree, and from there he used signals to communicate with the women with whom he had very secret relations. Without a doubt, this was to avoid the suspicions and fearsome anger of the goddess Oya. Because Changó fears Oya, and he takes a thousand precautions before he plays with her head [deceives her].

Nonetheless, Oya knew about Changó's strange manipulations. She began spying on him and saw him climbing up the palm tree too often, so she decided to find out for herself what he was doing there, hiding in the palm fronds.

Changó knew immediately that Oya had climbed to the top of a tree. He deduced that the goddess was watching him, keeping a close eye on him, and perhaps about to discover his secret liaisons. But he did not summon her. Instead, he filled the tree with lizards, which Oya fears.

When she returned to the palm and began climbing, countless lizards, black and green, slid around in every direction along the tree trunk. In her shock, she killed them by burning the palm tree down with a bolt of lightning.

Since then, these trees are the victims of Oya's jealousy. She was deceived by the obvious collusion of the lizards, accomplices who prevented her from advancing her investigations.

Another version of this legend exists in which Oya does not intervene. The lizard—Agema (which Adyai called *aloma*), messenger of Changó—failed to deliver a small, valuable gift to a woman that Changó had promised to a girl he was courting, trying to overcome her feigned, calculated resistance to his advances. The lizard put the gift in his mouth and took off immediately in search of the lady. But in a moment of carelessness, he swallowed it, and the gift never reached the hands of the very eager, coquettish woman awaiting it. She blamed the oversight on the proverbial inconsistency of her turbulent suitor.

The lizard had been restless for some time, struggling to rid himself of that object stuck in his throat, but he could not expel it no matter what he tried. (Since then, he still has it embedded in his gullet.) The woman's reproaches alerted Changó to *aloma*'s reprehensible failure. Furious, Changó demanded an explanation, asking in his thunderous voice what he had done with the gift, branding him a thief, and threatening to kill him unless he immediately returned what he had stolen. Return it! That was the impossible problem that had been facing the lizard every day.

With every word, flames bubbled out of the furious orisha's mouth. Changó listened to the lizard for a moment, but the object stuck in his throat—now pulsing and stretched out like a red flag as he strained mightily—and his fear of Changó's explosive fury prevented the lizard from explaining himself. He fled, climbing back up the smooth trunk of the royal palm and hiding in its fronds. Changó, now completely indignant, fired a lightning bolt at him. Instead of reaching the tongue-tied messenger, he mortally wounded the palm tree.

The conclusion of the old man who shared this story with us: Changó has still not forgiven the lizard. The lizard constantly meanders on palm trees, and when he reaches the shoot at the top very quickly, the god angrily remembers the details of those events. Alafin, half-cocked and impulsive, invariably misses his target because the lizard is too slippery and quick, but he believes he is punishing the lizard whenever he fires at the crest of the palm tree.

"When the weather gets bad and you hear thunder far off in the distance, the lizards raise one of their little hands to the sky like they're asking for forgiveness. At twelve noon on the dot, they climb down and kiss the earth. They make the sign of the cross with their mouths, then immediately climb back up to the highest part of the tree."

Over time, the *ganguleros*, "who love the palm tree madly," have come to tell this story, which is of Lucumí origin. Sometimes, when they need Changó—Nsasi—to kill someone, they take a lizard, open its mouth, and stuff its throat with a piece of paper, on which the name of the victim has been written to attract the overpowering rage of Changó.

Once the lizard's mouth has been sewn shut, it is left at the palm tree, suffering and hanging from a red string, which is tied to a nail with a square head—the old-fashioned ones—fixed firmly in the trunk. It is expected that the lizard will attract the lightning, "since the stone Changó throws is meant to kill the lizard." This object is collected and "sworn in" (that is, consecrated by an oath), then kept alive and tied up in the *Prenda*. "If there's trouble, it calls lightning, and the lightning will kill anybody you want."

Changó is the great dancer and Owner of the Drum, *olu bata*—"by being the best dancer in the world, he went everywhere." In another legend, he was invited to dance *meta*, which is a dance that is different from *bakoso*. In *meta*, all of the movements are accompanied by hand gestures. At that moment, he was in Mina territory, and he went to dance in Takua territory.[3] He was, as we have been told so many times, a diviner and a healer, and he left his *ate*—the divination board on which he marks the signs of the omens—next to the trunk of a palm tree where he lived. Changó had confidence in her: he had no doubt the palm tree would take good care of it in his absence. But shortly after he left, she took a nap and fell into a deep sleep. (There is no tree that is more distracted, no tree that gives one a stronger sensation of wanting to give oneself over to sleep, than the palm tree.)

Orula walked by and took the board "to use it to crown himself."

When Changó returned from the feast, upon reaching *eba odo*, the shore of a river next to his palm tree, he encountered Osain, who signaled to the tree. When Changó found that his board was missing, he understood. He shot a lightning bolt at it, and since then, he punishes the palm tree because it did

3   DF-N: This anecdote contains siginificant historical references to musical instruments, genres, and dances associated with specific regions of West Africa. According to the mythology of *bata* drums, the instruments are widely understood as having been introduced to Ọyọ from Nupe/Takua land, then adopted by Changó as his favorite music and dance (Marcuzzi 2005). In contemporary Cuban Lucumí liturgy, *meta* refers to a *bata* drum rhythm, while *bakosó* refers to styles of *bembé* drumming; both repertoires are explicitly associated with Changó.

not know how to protect the divination board, nor how to stop Orula from appropriating it.

There might be a great deal of truth in what these fables tell us: the essence is that the lightning "chooses" palm trees, and this clear preference is an obvious sign of an extremely sacred, mysterious connection. "It jumps from the sky to the palm tree."[4] "The lightning sanctifies her."

In Africa, Changó's tree is a very hard wood called *Aya*. "I saw an *oche* that a Lucumí brought from his land that was made from that tree," Sandoval says. "But here, all the nations did *moforivale* at the palm tree for Oni Changó, Eluwekon, Obaluba, Alaye, Obadimeye, a king twice over, first head of the Lucumí race."

This *oche*, the scepter of Changó, is made from the wood of a palm tree, and when the god comes down to the *wemileres*, he holds it in his fist as he dances.

The Congo call the god of thunder Nsasi and Nkita, and "they also invoked him at the royal palm."

The Arará give him the name Hebioso. Akadó is more specific: "Hebioso, Anama, Ahokei, Akrifodu, Luwuru, Dada, Akoda, Awuru Magala, Tadade, Boko, Bori, Olelebioke, Ograda Año, Ekun, Fedyu, Okundayo, Tana Omogodo, Alabaloke, Hanu Yemoru, Oba-Agayu, Santo Cristoba. Changó Jebioso is the boss of all of those I just named. Dada Aworu Magala, that's a senior Olofi, the war chief of all the Changós. We greet him at the palm tree. And with Dada, we salute the Candelaria that sets the palm tree on fire. We say, Agabini bitioke, Oriri ata masi adyana dekalu Obanka ekwahen!"

The peoples he punished most severely praised and venerated him. "When all the different people came—Popos, Egbas, Iyechas, Egwados, Binis, Oyos— all of them, all the Lucumí, they all recognized Changó in the palm tree. They saw the palm, and they saw the sword of Obakoso."

We listen to Alipreté tell us the story of his *orissa*:

Changó was born in Takua. He went from Takua to Sabalu, and from there to Dahomey and later to Congo. In Dahomey, they call him Hebioso. In Congo, Changó Agayu, Gangá Zumbá is Siete Rayo, Tronco Batalla, and they call him Nsasi. Changó Agayu is the same, Nsasi-Nsasi.

Changó camina pé la pamma, brinca pá güin. And he's the King of Cuba!

"King of the world. Because every nation has Changó, who swings a machete in heaven: *chack!*"

---

4   DF-N: The original reads, "Salta del cielo para meterse en la palma." The subject of the quotation is ambiguous: lightning ("it") lands on the tree, but it also embodies Changó ("him") landing on the tree. The phrase might also refer directly to Changó (as in "él salta," meaning "he jumps").

"Changó walks across all of the skies over the earth, and Oya walks with him." One particular devotee of Palo Monte and a spiritist—very decisive in their affirmations, since much of their knowledge was revealed by African spirits—refers us to the true history of their Father Changó which, in this instance, was not narrated by a spirit, but rather by an old Congo woman. (Others tell us a Lucumí version: "He rose up from the earth to the sky to become Orissa and reign eternally.") Changó, who comes from the sky, "lands in Africa. He lands in Congo-Real, where he is welcomed by Madre de Agua, who raises him. Madre de Agua, Kalunga, she never gave birth, but she also raised the Jimaguas [Twins], Nsamba and Ntala, who are the children of Centella, Kariempemba, and the thunder. Together with Kalunga, his adoptive mother, Changó became a very rebellious, mischievous young man. He was responsible for many outrageous misdeeds and created so much disorder that Madre Agua Kalunga tossed him out of the Congo."

Changó took up the divination board, the castle, and the mortar he had brought from heaven, and set out on the road as an exile.

"He was," this enlightened person tell us,

a handsome Black man, strong and red. He put his mortar on the top of the palm tree and stood very straight on top of the mortar. He had a castle on his head, an axe in one hand, a drill in the other hand, because he had been a borer, and a machete at his waist, because he had been a *desmochador de palmas* [a palm tree lumberjack].

When he was out, walking and walking, he encountered Orula (Ifa) and gave him the divination board. He knew that Orula was an elder, a serious man who had the gift of vision, so he would take good care of the board and respect it. Divining with cowrie shells and coconuts, singing and dancing, starting fights and parties, Changó arrived in Yesa territory. The people embraced him and praised him. There in Yesa land, a miracle happened. The people received a mortar that arrived flying through the air; they took it to Changó, and he recognized the mortar as his own. But the castle never appeared.

Other tribes recognized him as a sovereign. "He was hailed by every single Lucumí."

When I ask why Yoruba are called Lucumí, Sandoval and Lara explain. "The name Lucumí comes from saying *akumi, akumi*. When they greeted each other, they would say *akumi*. They were Aku. The tongue preferred pronouncing Lucumí to Akumi. When they were asked who they were, they themselves would say Akumi Lucumí."

There is a story about this:

Two civil guards [Spanish colonial soldiers] came across *los nazarenos* (Nazarenes), two *negros de nación* [African-born Black people], *brutos y bozalones* [brutes who spoke "broken" or "Africanized" Spanish], which a neighborhood family had bought recently. The guards didn't know them, and they seemed suspicious. When they asked for the names of their owners, where they lived, and who they were, one of them answered:

"Yo . . . lo kangá."

And the other insisted, "Y yo l'Akumi."

The guards said, "What are you saying? Filthy swine!"

"Yo lo kangá."

"Yo l'Akumi."

One was saying he was Gangá, and the other that he was Lucumí!

"In one of those lands," a story from F. tells us, "he was consecrated Oni-Changó, king. They put a cap decorated with a two-headed axe on his head. He's a great sorcerer, a great diviner, and the old man Orula confirms his words. Orula recognized Changó's authority in that land and everywhere else they asked him to perform divination. Changó was king of Koso, Moba, Owo, Ebini, Oso, Ima, Tulempe, and Ado. That's why he has so many names and titles. He's the one with the most paths (avatars), because he went all over the world. He never gets tired of fighting. He was cruel, and because of his wars and abuses, he flees from one country after another with a slave who follows his every step and doesn't leave him alone for a single moment." Others refer to "an old man who follows invisibly and cares for him."

"All of his friends banded together and became strong—the Apostle Martí said that unity creates strength—and they chased him and hounded him.[5] But in the end, Changó annihilated them. When he gets carried away, Yemaya tries to calm him. Olofi intercedes. Otherwise, he'd burn the world down to ashes! Don't you see? The atomic bomb belongs to Changó."

An image of Our Lady of Mercy, the Catholic equivalent of Obatala, should always be placed next to Changó to continually calm him.

"Once," F. continues, "when Changó was divining in public, a lame leper that heard his words asked him, 'Why aren't you saying anything to me? Don't you want to divine for me?'

"'I will tell you,' Changó replied. 'My father told me that I have a brother and a half-brother in this land, both older than me. You are my half-brother. Listen now. I couldn't live where I was born. Now I'm called Oni Changó, but

---

5   DF-N: This passage juxtaposes José Martí (iconic hero of Cuban independence) and Ogunda Osa (Ifa and *dilogún* divination orature) in the proverbial phrase *la unión hace la fuerza* (unity creates strength).

I live in a foreign land. Your future and fortune are far away from here. Turn your back on this place and leave. Cross *el monte*, then you'll find where you will rule.'

"'How can I walk the earth in this condition?'

"That man was Babalu Ayé, San Lázaro. Then Changó addressed himself to another man there: his other brother, Ogun, who was accompanied by two big dogs. Changó took the dogs and gave them to Ayé.

"Ogun complained to Changó, demanding he be paid for the dogs." (Ogun has a lot of dogs and Changó has a lot of horses.)

"This led to a war between the two of them. They're rivals. Both are very powerful, and they're always quarreling and fighting for no good reason.

"On that occasion, Changó tried to settle the matter by launching a lightning bolt at Ogun, who deflected it with a small piece of iron he was holding in his hand (which is probably the origin of the lightning rod). Changó threw the lightning bolt at Ogun's forge—Ogun is a smith—filling the forge with smoke. Even though Ogun is as brave as Changó, he was caught by surprise, and was scared. Meanwhile, Babalu Ayé was crossing the jungle in the direction indicated by Oni Changó. Protected by the two dogs, he reached the land of the Arará, then he lay down to sleep at the door of a house. He spent the night and early morning there, then a young man woke him up. The body of the adolescent, like his own body, was completely covered in sores. The young man said, 'You must suffer so much with those sores! You suffer like I do.'

"Hearing this, Baba asked him, 'Do you want me to cure you?' With a great deal of faith, the young man answered, 'Cure me!' Babalu Ayé asked him for flour, palm oil, and a sack made from cotton or burlap. He made bread with the flour, dipped it in palm oil, and he rubbed the young man's whole body with the bread. He burned the clothes the young leper had been wearing, and he dressed him in the sack.

"'Take this bread,' he said when he finished the cleansing. 'Go home, nail it behind your door, then take off your clothes in front of your mother.' When the mother saw her son's body, completely clean and healthy, she ran around town proclaiming the miracle, and they were all able to see the magical cure for themselves. San Lázaro, just as Changó had predicted, reigned in Dahomey, where he exalted his brother with the name Hebioso."

Yet, another *olocha* tells us,

In those days, Changó was a vagabond. He didn't have a roof over his head, but he had women all over the place, and he was wooing Oya. He was on the road one evening when nightfall caught him by surprise. He looked for shelter, and the first house he found was a castle. That castle belonged to Babalu Ayé. He asked for hospitality, and the old man granted it. When he

woke up—because Changó was like that, sometimes treacherous and . . .
a thief—he said to Babalu, "Go away and leave this castle to me. This is
my home now."

"That's impossible. It'll be war. If you want my castle, you need to take
it by force."

Changó had no weapons. He went to see Oya.

"I'm going to war against Babaye to take his castle."

"But Alafin, who's going to fight with you against Baba? He's stronger
than you, and he has a big army."

"I'm relying on you. We'll fight together, you and I."

The truth of the matter is that Changó's fire belongs to Oya. The next
morning, the two of them showed up at the door to the castle.

Changó shouted, "I'm ready now!"

Babalu Ayé wrapped himself in a cloak and opened the window to
look at the morning light. Then one of Oya's flames went into the castle
and lit everything on fire. Baba and his soldiers, without ever having
fought a battle, had to leave the castle to Changó.

"They fight with fire and gales of wind." "That's why, in my time, Changó
didn't let us smoke inside the cabildo. He says nobody except him breathes
smoke from his mouth and nose."

Oya granted Changó her service countless times during the course of his
nomadic life, in the fights to the death and wars that everyone ended up declaring against him!

One of the times he had to hide from his enemies, because they would cut
his head off if they captured him and they would kill him by any means
necessary, he went inside Oya's house. They surrounded the house and
there was no way to escape. Changó hesitated that day. Then Oya cut
off her braids and put them on Changó. She dressed him in her clothes,
adorned him with her jewelry, her necklaces, earrings, and bracelets, and
she spread the word that she was going out for a walk.

Changó and Oya had the same body type. Looking just like her, Changó
went out dressed like a woman. He walked like Oya, haughty like she is, and
greeted people by nodding his head—very formal, and without speaking
to anyone. Oya is not a *Santa rumbanzunga*.[6] She is very serious. Because
of the long hair, the clothes, and the movements, nobody suspected that it

---

6   DF-N: *Santa rumbanzunga* is a neologism that can be loosely translated as "a saint who likes
to party, dance, and drink."

wasn't Oya Ayaba herself in person. Believing it was the *Santa*, Changó's enemies were very respectful, and they made way for him to escape.

When the danger had passed, the real Oya went out and the soldiers said, "Wait, what's this? Changó slipped through our fingers wearing Oya's braids and dress!"[7]

Another time, Changó went from Mina to Takua to kill a fierce creature that was killing all the men there. Nobody could defeat it.

They asked Changó, "Why have you come? To end your own life?"

When that dragon roared, the whole earth would tremble. He ate the women. Changó didn't want soldiers to help him defeat the creature. Alone in hand to hand combat, he fought it and won.

> *Kaui Kaui Maforile*
> *Ke eñi Alado, titila eye*

Changó sang this and spit fire from his mouth.

The people of Takua and Tulempe celebrated feasts in Changó's honor hypocritically: the women loved him madly, but the men hated him. At one party, they arrested him and locked him in a dungeon with seven locks on the door. Changó had left his mortar at Oya's house.

Several days went by, and Changó hadn't returned, so Oya moved the mortar: she looked, then saw that he was imprisoned.

In prison, Changó felt that someone was moving his mortar around, and he said to himself, "Nobody except Oya knows how to calm it down." And he spewed thunder and more thunder. Oya lit her fire and started to *ochiche* (cast a spell).

"Oya samaterere, Oya samatere! . . ." But the chant didn't work for her, it didn't take hold. The fire burned her. When she saw the fire was burning her, she changed the chant:

> *Centella que bá bané*
> *Yo sumarela sube,*
> *Centella que bá bané*
> *Yo sube arriba palo . . .*

She says nothing more than these words, makes the sign of the cross, then the number seven appears in the sky. The lightning bolt bursts open the prison and Changó walks out. He sees Oya advancing, riding in on a tornado in the sky, and she takes him away from Takua land. Until

7 LC: "The Santa Bárbara that is adored in the church is Changó dressed as a woman."

that day, Changó didn't know Oya had power over lightning. That's when he started to respect her.

In Cuba, according to Calazán, Changó "is born in the palm tree" (like Brahma in Vedic India is born in the lotus). Altars in working class homes often include a small palm tree growing in a tin can; a little lead soldier representing Changó sits in its branches. Toy palm trees are invariably found on these altars as a traditional symbol of the god of fire and war.

Aside from Oya, the royal palm also has a close relationship to the great orisha Agayu, Brazo-Fuerte, La Bola del Mundo, Agayu Sola, Agayu Lari, San Cristobal, Babadina. He is the owner of the earth and the river. For Sandoval and other elders, he is the older brother of Changó.

According to others (and this is the most common version now), he is Changó's father (or Changó himself). "Changó did not know his father, who was Agayu." Agayu was so fearsome and respected that he left the door to his house wide open. Nobody dared to go inside. Agayu's house was always full of fruits, since the river, the land, and the great savanna belong to him.

Changó went inside Agayu's house, ate everything, stuffed himself, then lay down to sleep very peacefully on his own straw mat. When Agayu returned from the countryside, he found that Black man resting there, so insolent and relaxed. Oh my . . . He grabbed him. "Iki busi sian!" He gathered firewood, lit the fire, and threw Changó into it. But Changó didn't burn. Isn't he the fire? How could he be burned? So Agayu carried him over his shoulder to the seashore to drown him. Yemaya—Yemaya Konla, the mother of Changó—appeared in the ocean.

"What are you doing, Agayu? You can't kill our son!" Then Agayu said, "I'm the fiercest man in the world, and you, Changó, are as fierce as I am. You are truly my son." Nonetheless, many elders insist that, although Changó is often thought to be Agayu's son, he is actually his brother: they are both children of Obatala.

Changó respects Agayu very much. Changó is liable to be "foolish, inclined to commit one of his *barrabasadas*" [outrageous acts] at a feast or wherever he manifests, since it is his nature to become furious quickly and easily, and he "doesn't see straight when he gets carried away." But if Agayu is present and intervenes, Changó bows his head. It is enough for the orisha, who is as big as the pillars of the firmament, to stand next to Changó and give him a stern look. "With one look, the father controls the son."

"What belongs to the father also belongs to the son," a *santera* named Dolores Ibañez tells us. "And although the royal palm is acknowledged to be the throne of Changó Lubeo, the rightful and universal heir of Obatala, it belongs to Agayu. Oke, the mountain, is the staff of Olofin, and the palm tree is the staff of Agayu." (The ceiba is also the staff of Agayu.)

"Agayu and Changó are two in one: by worshipping Changó, you worship Agayu. When a child of Changó is despondent, one pleads with Agayu. Agayu transfers the ownership of the palm tree to him, and they both rule from the palm. They dress alike. They're both kings."

They both have the same temperamental personalities, angry and combative. Especially Agari, "a very ancient Agayu."

"They are two inseparable Santos, and they eat the same things. The *iyawo* initiated to Changó as their primary Angel also receives Agayu, either at the same time or later, just as anyone who is initiated to Yemaya must also receive Olokun.

"Someone who is a child of Oshun and Changó must receive Agayu.

"When someone is initiated as a child of Changó or Yemaya, the stone of Agayu is not held over their head, but only placed on their shoulder."

The tureen destined to contain Agayu has two horns, four stones, and sixteen maté seeds. Since he is the owner of the river, his *otan* remains tied up and submerged in water for nine days. A daughter of Oshun takes the neophyte to find it at the river, where offerings are made to him during those nine days.

Regarding the paternity of Agayu, the following is said:

The owner of the river, Agayu, had amorous relations with Yemaya. Changó was born from Agayu and Yemaya, but Yemaya abandoned him and Obatala picked him up and raised him. When he recognized him as his son, he placed a white beaded necklace around his neck. He said that he would be king of the world, then built him a castle.

Changó did not know that his real mother was Yemaya and his father was Agayu. Without realizing she was his mother, he wanted her to be his wife. A slave who followed Changó everywhere warned Yemaya, who— before committing the sin—said, "Omo mi!" Changó replied, "I have no mother." Then Yemaya said, "Lubeo!" And she offered him her breast, and Changó, recognizing her as his mother, wept.

Oshun was also unaware that Changó was her nephew, and she became his wife. This was considered unacceptable; it was *ire* for a nephew to lay down with his aunt.[8]

8   DF-N: For a discussion of the Lucumí word *ire*, see the Translator's Notes.

Although Yemaya is not considered Changó's mother by blood, she adores him as a mother. Other authorities maintain that Obatala (*achupa* Changó) gave birth to Changó and had to abandon him because he was the fruit of a sinful union. Yemaya took on the responsibility of raising him. "She is his wet nurse."

"Yemaya birthed the sixteen *ocha*. Yemaya is the mother of Alafi."

"And there are mysteries in the religion that should not be spoken.[9] Yemaya loved her son so much that she initiated him herself. She was his lover. She taught him to dance, and she didn't want him to dance with any other woman. Orula, who was her husband, was jealous of the preference she displayed—in all things—for Changó. Later, when Ogun was Yemaya's husband, the same thing happened, and it started a war."

In another story from the land of the Mina, Yemaya does not commit incest, but teaches her son a valuable lesson instead:

Alafi arrived in the land of Yemaya. Without knowing she was his mother, he tried to seduce her at a *fiesta*. Yemaya said she wanted him too, and she told him to go see her at her home.

"That big blue thing in the distance, that's my home." She pointed to the sea.

"Do we have to go there? I don't know how to swim, but I'll go if you take me."

They walked to the shore.

"We have to go farther."

"I don't know how to swim," Changó said again.

Yemaya jumped in her boat, made Changó get in, and rowed out to the open sea. They went so far out that they could no longer see the shore. Yemaya jumped in the water and swam down to the bottom. A huge wave rose up behind her, and it capsized the boat, tossing Changó in the water. He grabbed the edge of the boat and struggled to keep from drowning. Yemaya, who had returned to the surface of the water, saw Changó's desperation as he shouted and asked to be saved. But she stayed still and laughed at him, not saving him.

Meanwhile, Obatala arrived, standing on a snake, and he said, "Yemaya, don't let your son die!"

"Ayagua e omodukue Orisago."

Yemaya answered, "Alakata One feba Orisa Nigwa."

9   DF-N: This is a paradox at the heart of *El Monte* and the traditions it enshrines: Cabrera's informants warn us that "there are mysteries in the religion that should not be spoken," but then they immediately proceed to speak some of those mysteries, which Cabrera writes down.

And when Changó couldn't hold on any longer, Yemaya propped him up on the surface of the water.

"I'm going to save you, but from now on, respect your Iya."

"Kofiedeno, Iya mi! I didn't know you were my mother."

Yemaya righted the boat and helped him get in. Then, sitting in front of the two reunited *santas*, asked them, "Which one of you brought me into the world?"

"Yemaya," said Our Lady of Mercy. "I raised you, but she gave birth to you."[10]

Changó and Yemaya embrace in the sea, and when these two *ochas* come down at a *bata* drumming, Changó—who says that after God, there is no bigger *santo* than him, *laye laye mi saguo*—will shrink in the presence of his mothers. He respects both of them, and they both pacify him when he gets furious.

My elders do not like discussing such scabrous topics as this one regarding incest among the orishas, and almost all of them evade it. I tried, unsuccessfully, to loosen Gabino's tongue on the matter. His Egwado ancestors knew the sea and were very devoted to that goddess. One day, perhaps to rehabilitate Changó, or out of respect for the truth, he addressed the topic spontaneously:

It's time to tell you, so that you're clear on the truth of the matter, that Changó did not sleep with his mother, even if his natural mother was Yemaya. The wife of the old man Obatala Obaibo, Iyemu, was the mother of Changó and Ogun. And the degenerate was Ogun, not Changó. The old man had been observing that the affections and care Iyemu showed for her son were beyond all proportion. Iyemu saved everything for Ogun, and nothing was good enough for her favorite son. She dressed him better than anyone else, and he received more of her attentions than her husband. Baba began to harbor suspicions. It was a very odd kind of affection . . . an affection that seemed wrong. Not that of a mother's, but of a woman in love.

One day, Baba went out to take a stroll around the countryside. He had a five-year-old white rooster that would call him back home if it seemed prudent; otherwise, the rooster would simply tell him everything that had happened during his absence.

---

10 DF-N: This section uses numerous different names and transliterations for individual orishas (Obatala, Obaibo, Ibaibo, Baba, Olofin, Las Mercedes, Yemu, Iyemmu, etc).

Baba's house only had one door. As soon as he left, Ogun arrived. They closed up the house, and Yemu went to bed with Ogun.

Far off in the distance, Olofi heard his rooster shouting, "Ogundadie!" And he flapped his wings, "ta-ta-ta!"

When the old man returned home, he saw the door closed and the rooster rushing around flapping its wings.

Hearing the racket the rooster was making, Iyemu said to Ogun, "Leave me. Obaibo is coming. Enough."

When Baba entered the house, he saw that the straw mat where he slept was rumpled. He saw Yemu's eyes.

In the evening, he said to her, "Prepare my *jolongo* (sack with food provisions). I need to go on a long journey tomorrow . . ."

That night, Yemu was very attentive with Olofi. She was so eager for him to leave!

She prepared the *jalongo* right away and, later, at daybreak, she went out to say goodbye to him.

No, Olofi didn't go far from home. He went back after a short time and hid behind a bush near his house.

Ogun arrived. (Olofi was listening.)

"And Baba?"

"He won't be back all day!"

"Let's take advantage."

Olofi waited a short while. The rooster started singing, "Ogundadei! Ogundadei! Ogundadei!" He kept singing his song, faster and faster, and Baba came out from behind the bushes. One small step at a time, he came to the door and knocked. And knocked and knocked.

Finally, Ogun answered in an ill-tempered way: "Who is it? Go away and let me sleep!"

But the rooster was flapping its wings so much, *jo-to-to-to*, and making such a scene—"Ogundadei!"—that Iyemu said to him, "Go take a look."

Ogun got up, unlatched the door, and opened the door halfway. The face of his father! He threw himself on the floor. "Forgive me, my *taita-señor*! Punish me day and night."

Baba answered, "You have condemned yourself. Until the end of the world, you will not be able to rest during the night or the day."

And Yemu said to him, "Forgive me as well, Olofi."

"It's all right, child. It doesn't matter. I know I'm old."

And in the home of the old Obatala, one must always prepare three places at the table: his, hers, and one for Ogun as a reminder of his offense.

When Ogun offended his father, Obatala made Changó leave the house. Even though Changó was still just a boy, Obatala wanted to avoid having him follow that bad example. He turned Changó over to Obañeñe. But she would take Changó to visit to the old man every day. He always kissed his father, and sometimes he would not kiss Yemu. Obañe would ask, "Alafin, why don't you kiss your mother?" And Obaibo would grumble, "It's enough for him to give me a kiss."

"Baba, don't spoil him so much!"

Changó observed that Ibaibo and Yemu were together, but they were not close. Sometimes he asked Obañeñe, "What is going on with Baba and Iya? They barely speak to each other."

"That's none of your business, foolish boy! That's between grown-ups."

The silence and distance between his parents was striking to him. One day he asked Baba himself.

"Etie aro? Are you sick?"

"No, son. When you grow up, I'll tell you about the pain in my heart."

And finally, when Changó became a young man, his father told him everything.

"That's why. Because of what happened with your brother Ogun, I sent you away from home to live with your sister Obañeñe."

"Tani kinche die Ore Ogun?" (Who is Ogun's wife?)

"Oya."

"Wait, Baba!"

At eighteen years of age, Changó went out every afternoon. Because he was *lubeo* (prince), he would dress up and go out with an entourage, a parasol, and drummers.

And Ogun was condemned to work day and night. When does iron rest? His time had come. Because Oya fell in love with Changó, who had resolved to avenge his father. He arrived at Oya's door, called to her, and she crossed the threshold. He stepped back a little farther away, and she followed him. He kept walking, and Oya kept following. And that's how they arrived at Changó's *ile*. At the door of the house, Changó pushed her into his *ile*.

Obañeñe said to him, "What have you done, Changó? You've stolen Ogun's wife!"

"If Ogun is a man, let him come and get her."

Now you'll understand why, if someone says publicly that Obatala Yemu abandoned her son, they don't explain the reasons why. There are things about the *santos* that should not be spoken. Those who know about them know, and those who know keep quiet.

When you hear someone say that Changó rested in the cedar tree, for example, understand what's really going on. Because ... (*kofiyedenu, kawo kabiesi*), you can't really say that Changó ... rested.[11]

"You mean, he died?"

"Don't say it ..."

Now you'll also understand why Changó and Ogun are two *santos* that are always ready to fight. And when they encounter each other in the cabildo, Ogun drinks moonshine liquor to forget. If he spills it on the floor, it can end up becoming big trouble, because whenever he's drunk, he always challenges Changó. It's an obsession ...

The wars, the resentments, all of those problems between them happened because Changó won't forgive his brother for betraying their father, and Ogun won't forgive Changó for taking his *obini*.

Obañeñe or Bayoni, the sister of Changó, is a very elevated *santa*. She does not come down to possess devotees, and she remains always very devoted and loyal to her brother.

In another version of the same story, Obatala lives with his wife and children—Ogun, Ochosi, and Elegua—and he has a guard, Osun.[12] Ogun was the favorite son of Obatala and Yemu. He was the most hardworking, and his brothers were obliged to do as he said. Ogun fell in love with his mother, and he was on the verge of raping her many times, but the little one—Elegua—kept watch and warned Osun, who would then arrive unexpectedly and summon Ogun:

Ogun understood that Elegua, who was always snooping around, had told Osu what he intended to do.[13] Ogun made up a pretext and sent

---

11   DF-N: Here is a restatement of the theme ("things that should not be spoken") that Cabrera established several pages earlier, lending Gabino Sandoval's story an authoritative, sensational quality that recurs throughout the book. (In the original: "Ya es hora de que yo le diga, para que esté en lo cierto...") Clearly, Cabrera's retelling of the story transfers some of Sandoval's authority to her: the elder seems to be leaning in close—first to Cabrera, then to her readers—to tell a little-known truth, letting us in on a deeper, more intimate sort of "insider" knowledge. In that sense, the anecdote from Sandoval—like his private, handwritten *libretas* (notebooks), which he shared with Cabrera—is an example of deliberate ambiguity and encoding; the exchange, which includes the reader, suggests an exceedingly subtle relationship between ritual authority and discretion.

12   DF-N: These four orishas are often referred to collectively as *los guerreros* (literally, "the warriors"), *orisha ode* ("orishas of the outside" or "hunter orishas"), etc.

13   DF-N: Osu (as in Osun) should not be confused with Oshun (as in Ochún, etc.).

Elegua out into the street. Elegua hung around at the corner. He went all around the house without going inside, never taking his eyes off Ogun, who had started pouring mounds of corn on Osun to keep him from informing on Ogun. While Osu ate, he [Ogun] took advantage of the opportunity to abuse his own mother, who went along with it. And so, every day at the same time, Ogun would close the door of the house, leaving Osun outside so he could gorge himself on corn and . . . well, you know.

Elegua waited for Obatala and told him, "Babami, I haven't eaten for many days. Ogun has punished me by leaving me out in the street to keep me from seeing his wicked deeds, and Osu hasn't warned you because Ogun gives him a lot of corn to make him fall asleep."

"But Osun can never fall asleep!"

The next morning, Obatala got up early and returned home earlier than usual, then he lay down and hid in the grass behind a tree. From there he saw Osun fall asleep, and he saw Ogun close the door. Obatala wept with so much sorrow and shame that his legs trembled. He cut a branch from the tree to lean on, and he knocked on the door with that cane . . . Yemu understood it was Obatala who had come to surprise them, and she hastened to open the door. But Ogun, knowing his mother was not the guilty one, said, "No, mother. Don't open the door. I'm a man, and I'm the guilty one!"

Obatala had his hand raised to curse him when Ogun opened the door.

"Don't curse me, Baba. I curse myself! I, Ogun Agwanile, Ogun Onile Koba Kobu, Ogun Tokumbi, will work day and night, until the end of the world."

Then Obatala went inside the house. Ogun gestured to Yemu, saying, "My mother is innocent."

Obatala said to Ogun, "Get out! You cannot live in this house." And Ogun, ashamed, left and shut himself up in his forge, Ogun Alagwede.

To Osun, Obatala said, "I trusted you, and you sold yourself for *agwado* (corn)." And to Elegua, he said, "You'll be my sentinel." And to Yemu, he said, "I do not curse you, but if we give birth to another baby boy, I will kill him." Orula was born to them, and Obatala ordered that he be buried under a ceiba tree. Changó was born next, and in spite of his oath, Obatala saw how funny the boy was and felt compassion for him, so he turned the boy over to his older sister, Dada. Four years went by, and Dada dressed him in red and took him to visit his parents' house. Obatala was very happy to see his son and showered him with affection. Meanwhile, Yemu contemplated him with tears in her eyes because she was thinking of Orula. Obatala sat him on his knees. Seeing Yemu's tears, Changó Mokoken asked why she was crying.

"Someday, I will tell you."

He ordered Dada to bring him his son every day from then on. And every day, Obatala narrated a different episode of his life to Changó. Every day, he told him about what Ogun had done.

That's how Changó—known as Olufina Koke when he was a child—grew up: cultivating hatred and resentment for Ogun in his heart. When he became a handsome and fun-loving man—*Ayala Yeo!*—he dressed himself as a warrior and mounted his horse, Esinla. He headed for Ogun's domain to steal his wife, Oya. When she saw Changó, she was immediately turned on by his beauty. Ogun worked like a slave, and the only thing he thought about was drinking like a sponge.

He was a brutish man, despotic and heavy-handed, and Oya was delighted to let herself be stolen away by Changó.

This abduction was the origin of the great war between Changó and Ogun. Changó did not emerge victorious—at first.

For reasons of kinship, the Ibeyi—the twins, adored by all Lucumí, Taebo and Kainde, associated with the Catholic San Cosme and San Damián, children of Oya and Changó—reside in the palm tree:

The female Ibeyi, Santa Rufina and Santa Justa, recline against palm trees, appearing next to the trunk of the tree.[14]

The Ibeyi are allies of Changó. Changó loves them madly, just as they love Changó. They protect the children of Obakoso a great deal, and the children of Obakoso need to pamper them. Offerings and petitions are made to them for money. Here is an *ebo* to have them do for us what they did for Changó, once upon a time, when the orishas were stealing all of Obatala's money.

Wherever he hid it, they found it and took it. When Obatala needed *owo* and went to look for it, there was nothing left. He would ask what happened, and everyone would answer, "It wasn't me!" Nobody knew anything about it. Finally, he called Ochosi and asked him to make a sack and a ladder. When Ochosi brought them, Obatala filled the sack with money. He used the ladder to climb up a very tall tree in the middle of the savanna, and he hung the sack from the highest branch. He then filled

---

14 DF-N: The informant quoted here equates the Ibeji—the divine twins, Taiwo and Kainde (Kehinde, etc.)—with Santa Justa and Santa Rufina, a pair of Catholic saints who were said to have been sisters born in Seville in the third century.

the entire area with all kinds of dangerous animals—hunting dogs, lions, tigers, panthers, big venomous snakes—so they would protect his treasure. Whoever tried to rob him would be devoured by those fierce beasts.

Meanwhile, the Ibeyi happened to be playing near the tree, and they saw Obatala's schemes without him noticing them. Since they hang around the savanna and know a lot, Changó would take them fruit—that is what they love most, fruits, sweets, and pigeons. And he also made an offering to Yewa, so they would tell him where the money was hidden. In exchange for the sweets, the twins told him everything. Changó walked happily toward the tree, but the fierce beasts started chasing him. He escaped, but he was badly wounded, so he went to sit down far away from the tree. He wondered, "How am I going to steal from Obanla?"

He went home and cooked everything he had. He cooked a portion of each food, and he left another portion uncooked. He filled the sack with all of that food. He also took water, sugar, and liquor. He went along, scattering the food in the savanna and all around the tree. While the animals ate the food, he went up the ladder, grabbed the sack full of money, and left his own empty sack in its place. He distributed the *owo* among his people.

Changó, in the end, is "just as much Congo as Lucumí. *Niktan, kita, santo grande Kongo!* He stayed in Takua because he liked the food. He's more Congo than Lucumí, in his roots, from birth." And who dares to argue about this with Nino when he declares it so categorically? All my creole informants of Congo descent insist passionately that their own homeland is the god of thunder's point of origin. Later, he chose the Lucumí territory (Nigeria) as the setting for his exploits, and he acquired a crown in Oyo, "but he was already crowned by Olorun himself, his father, when he came into the world. He was already powerful in heaven before coming down to earth." "Of course, among the Congo, he had a different name," they explain. "Nsasi. He was the son of Sambi and Kalunga." From the sky and the ocean. "And the Gangá Congos call him Wafi-tiembla-mundo."

Other informants will tell us, to the contrary, about Changó Nipa. "Alafia Kisieko! He was a very beautiful Black man. He was raised in a stream, and he was disobedient and wicked. He would throw rocks, and he committed so many offenses, he killed so many people wherever he went, that he ended up in Congo, fleeing from justice. There he performed more miracles than anywhere else. There, they gave him the name Nkita. The African-born *Congos de nación* also called him Pungun Sasi and el Torito de la Loma (the Little Bull on the Hill)."

He's the only *santo* recognized by the *mayombero*. When a Ndoki says,

> *Abukekia, yo no juega con lo Sambi*
> *Yo no va casa lo Santo*
> *Ogun son mi zapato*
> *Elegua son mi camisa . . .*

> Abukekia, I don't play with Sambi
> I don't go to the Santo's house
> Ogun is my shoe, and Elegua is my shirt

they'll show him respect right away:

> *Santa Bárbara son bendito!*

Santa Bárbara [Changó] is sacred!

"All *nganguleros* respect him and praise him." "And even if they say that he doesn't go to Campo Santo,[15] or anywhere there are sick people, before we open the *nganga* to play Palo, the first thing we do is salute him. And they even do this in the *juegos de mayombe judío*, which have nothing to do with *santos*. When the Congo name and salute Nsasi, they've already mentioned all the *kimpúngulu*.[16] It's got nothing to do with the rest of them. And he's always together with Santa Bárbara. And you already know that *ganguleros* love the *fuiri* (the dead), but Changó doesn't like the *fuiri* or black cloth!"

"Changó was going around *arakisa*, filthy and ragged, when he fought death. It was death who'd put him in that condition. He had to go down into the middle of the earth with her, and when he came back, he said that he'd never go back there again, and he didn't want to keep company with *muertos* [the dead]. When his children are going to die, Changó asks for his *otan* to be taken away." "Changó died and resurrected," says José del Rosario. "The day Oya stole his secret, he kicked the ground three times and buried himself. The end of a chain remained, coming out of the earth, where he went down." "He doesn't like the dead, and it turns out his legitimate wife Oba is the queen of the cemetery! And that his lover Oya works in the cemetery! And that his other concubine Oshun also walks with death from time to time!"

"But how can he not be a Congo? Changó was the king of the *mayomberos*, the most powerful sorcerer the world ever knew." His curses were terrifying.

---

15 DF-N: Campo Santo (or *camposanto*): the cemetery, and, in a more abstract and more literal vein, the land or country of the dead, saints, and/or spirits.

16 DF-N: In *Vocabulario Congo*, Cabrera defines kumpúngulu (i.e., kimpúngulu) as as "todos los santos," meaning an entire collective of deities and spirits ([1984] 2001, 153).

"They would say, 'Here comes Changó!' And everybody, all the chiefs, would throw down their weapons and run away."

Then, I ask, why is he so afraid of the dead?

"Because on one occasion," Bangoché answers me, "he performed sorcery so formidable that he incinerated his own people, all of his children, everyone he loved.[17] The impact of that stayed inside him . . ."

"His *prenda* drew lightning. His own *olodi* burned him, and it burned up his beloved children. In his distress, he went into a tree."[18]

Tolá does not accept the notion, which appears in more than one story, that the omnipotent orisha is terrified of the *ikus*. He respects Oya, one of whose paths makes her the owner of the cemetery. "I would say that she is more like an associate than an owner, since several *santas* are in the cemetery." Although they have fought many times, he only scared her once, by showing her a decapitated head of a ram.[19] Ultimately, he respects her because "he respects himself, and as a king, he honors a queen." Changó Kawo Kabiesi—afraid! That sort of conjecture offends the old man.

"No, child. Changó is not afraid of anything. He doesn't run away from *muertos*." And in his eccentric and perplexing language, another old man weighs in by telling me that Changó "doesn't like to play around with cold skeletons, because he's so alive and so hot, *tá buriri*," overflowing with life. From this, I think that what he wants to point out to me is a fundamental incompatibility between the god and death—the cold skeleton. Incompatibility, never fear.

The following story, which Salako rejects as a falsehood never countenanced by his elders, is conveyed to me by another devotee of this orisha: "Changó and Oya, up there in the sky, got into a heated argument. Changó lost control of himself, grabbed and shook Oya, and shoved her backside, sending her plunging down from heaven to earth. Oya, rippling down, ended up falling in a cemetery. Changó followed her to ask her to forgive him, but

---

17   DF-N: Here *brujería* is not used with the moralistic stigma that often relegates the term to superstition or heresy; rather, in context, it invokes a notion closer to an ethics of magical power.

18   DF-N: The phrase "se metió en un arbol" can be understood to mean that Changó went in, went up into, or went inside, a tree. The idea that he went inside a tree implies that he became the tree, which helps us understand the worship of that particular spirit of Changó—as a tragic sorcerer king who burned his own people alive—both in that tree and through that tree. The inherent violence and potential danger of fire and war are never far removed from the veneration of Changó, and this passage refers obliquely to stories in which Changó hangs himself in a tree after his army rebelled against him, providing one interpretation of the epithet Obakoso (the king did not hang).

19   DF-N: This is a reference to the story, outlined several pages earlier, in which Changó scared off Oya with the head of a sacrificial ram in order to keep enjoying himself at a drumming feast.

when he saw her there, standing among the dead, surrounded by skeletons, he didn't dare to go in the cemetery."

"I know that when Changó came back to the world after burying himself at the foot of his tree, he heard Oya grumbling inside a hole." (Oya often lives in caves.) "She had followed him, sneaking around to spy on his sorcery. And that offended him, so he rushed at her, to punish her. She got scared, and before he could sink his claws into her, she flew away, scattering *aina* (fire). She ended up at Olokun's house, in the middle of the sea. There, Olokun defended her."

In other stories that are unfamiliar to Salako, the thunder god is frightened of death.

"The Ikú make Changó tremble. Once, Oya was talking to him and distracted him, leading him into a cemetery. She stopped him at the edge of a grave and said, 'Changó, look down . . .' When Changó saw a dead person laying down in that open tomb right next to his feet, he ran away like a shot." Ogun—who, in another version of this same story, is still married to Oya and witnesses the scene—yells at Changó: "Changó huye! [Run away!] Alakamade, Kawo!"

On another occasion, Changó danced to drumming music in a cemetery without realizing where he was: "A white figure appeared to him, a spirit in the form of woman who asked him, 'Why are you drumming and dancing in this place?'

"Changó replied, 'I drum and dance wherever I please.'"

(It is true that he has license from Olofi and Agayu to do that and much more.)

"Then the woman painted white said, 'Here, I rule.' And she vanished.

"Terrified, Changó picked up his drums and ran to the house of Orula. Orula told him, 'That apparition was Yewa, the owner of the cemetery. The place where you were dancing is the home of the dead.' And because Changó, for all his bravery, is horrified by Ikú, he never went inside another cemetery again."

"Oya wanted Changó for herself," R.A.M. tells us, and

She suffered when he went out. To keep him from leaving her side, she called the dead, surrounding the house with Ikús. That's how she kept Changó prisoner. Every time Changó opened the door and tried to go out, the *muertos* rushed at him, shrieking, "Fuii!" He would go back inside and close the door. One day, Oshun went to visit him while Oya was out, and Changó was able to talk to her. He complained about the situation in which he found himself. Oshun went to get a bottle containing *oti* [aguardiente], *oñi* (honey), and *efun* (*cascarilla*, chalk made from egg shells). She painted Changó with the chalk, then she got the *muerto* guarding the door drunk with *oti* and sweetened him with *oñi*. Then Oshun started flirting with an *iku*, and the *iku* started trying to seduce Oshun, thinking he was going to win her over. Meanwhile, Changó—plastered in white—was able to free himself from the *muertos* because they didn't recognize him, and he fled from Oya.

After Oshun saved him by helping him escape from that fate, Changó always resented Oya, and everything the goddess did bothered him. It even caused them to "wage a war." Oya considered the best way to defeat Changó. She went to the cemetery and removed a skull. Oya initiated the combat, then she suddenly placed the face of the *muerto* right in front of Changó:

> *Ingio balele engerio*
> *Oya made kolaso*
> *Ingio balele*

Changó quickly abandoned the battlefield. As soon as he saw the skull—*Jerijekue!*—he ran away, terrified.

Matari Nsasi, *matari mukiama, matari mono yilo*, is "the package," "the stone in which Nkita or Nsasi *siempungu* falls from the sky. The same stone, called *oduara* by the Lucumí, is the one Changó (Muilo) fires—*busuban!*—from above. Nsasi is the thunder stone: Nsasi munansulu fula inoka muinda munansulu sakrila Nsasi kinfunla munantoto."[20]

"He comes down from *kain Sambi* (heaven) and everyone knows he, *Saulan bembo kongo* (the king of Africa), comes in his *matari*." Directly from the sky. He is the divine expression of the power that "makes the *mundele* and the *mufuita* (white and Black people) tremble when it *munan sulu bongan kele*, or *bobelan kele* (thunders in outer space).

Oya is of the same essence: *fula inoka* (tempest), *kitembo tembo* (whirlwind), *songe munalanga, pungun banso Yaya wanga, moana bango, bango, sasingili*. In the Congo "path," it is another powerful "fundamento" employed by *mayomberos*.

Oduara or *matari Nsasi*—this stone in which Changó or Nsasi are present, which is their materialization—is found next to a royal palm seven years after it falls to the earth. "It isn't gathered by a *bakoyula Nganga* (a child of the Nganga), but by the godfather, the Mambi- Mambi, the Elder of his branch, or the *mayordomo* who—above all else—feeds it. Upon removing it from the

20 LC: Nsasi is in the sky, explodes, and falls on the earth.

ground, he will give it an egg yolk and refresh it, so the lightning doesn't go looking for it again. Later, he will give it *menga* (blood) from a rooster or a ram." Once the stone is prepared, they give it to their godson, who will keep it in a little bit of water "so it doesn't get too hot."

Another *mayombero* tells us, "It doesn't fall precisely at the foot of the palm tree, but halfway up a hill. It hides in the earth for seven consecutive years."

"The stones of Changó and Oya fall and hide. After years, they come out of the ground. If an *aberikola* discovers it because it is destined for them, they need to notify someone with authority (an *olubocha*), because they need to do *oro* for that *otan*, praying and singing to collect it."[21]

A bit of controversy divides opinions on this point. Do *oduara* only fall in the vicinity of palm trees?

All of the information offered by my instructors is valuable, and I copy it faithfully:

"The children of Changó or another orisha, in one or another Regla, can gather their *oduara* or their *matari Nsasi* in the ground under a royal palm or an avocado tree, although the palm is preferable."

"Changó throws his stone. If it falls in black soil, the stone absorbs more darkness. That stone never loses its *ache* from outer space." And they add this sharp observation: "*Oduara* is found right there, where it fell."

Oya is also buried at the royal palm. *Oya Centella matari mbele.*

On this point, my Uluku informants seem to agree. As we know, Changó— "in the Lucumí path"—lived with his sister Dada, Obañeñe, or Bayoni, the orisha he loves and respects as if she were his mother. "You should know that Changó has a brother that is often confused with his sister. Changó salutes him by saying, 'Aburo mi Dada bako yi bale.' I salute my brother Dada. 'Dada-bodiun ori Dada omo lowo yo.' Obañeñe is the sister." Yet these stories constantly refer to Obañeñe as Dada.

Once upon a time, Changó refused to admit that he was the son of his real mother. He only dressed in red. This is because of the family matter we have already discussed, although this informant considers it indelicate to insist on discussing it: "He took defending his father to heart, ignoring his mother. This conflict resulted in Changó taking Oya back home with him, so Obañeñe, Oya, and Changó all lived in the same *ile*. Whoever finds three similar stones together in the savanna knows they are Changó, Oya, and Obañeñe.

---

21 DF-N: This passage, which in the original is packed with esoteric Lucumí vocabulary and references, might be further translated as follows: "If an uninitiated person discovers it because it's destined for them, then that person needs to notify someone with authority (an initiated priest), because they need to perform a liturgical ritual for that stone, praying and singing to collect it."

"This happened during the time when Changó was fighting a war against Ogun.

"Changó had an *osain* (a magical calabash) at home. Every day, as he was going out, he'd open the calabash, put his finger in the gourd, and make the sign of the cross on his tongue.

"Oya noticed that Changó never failed to perform this operation. She was curious, so she opened the calabash, which had fire inside. She stuck her finger in and did the same thing as him.

"Immediately, two flames came out of her mouth, dancing in the air. Oya was terrified and called Dada, who'd just started cleaning the house. Although she adored her brother and he loved her very much, she was frightened by his temper and careful to never upset him. Before Dada could go and see what was happening, Oya ran off to the royal palm and buried herself in the earth.

"Dada looked for Oya, but she could not find her. She saw that Changó's calabash wasn't in the same place where he'd left it, and, moreover, it was half open. Curiosity is too strong in women, and so Dada also put her finger in the Osain and tasted it. She called Oya and fire came out of her mouth.

"She thought, 'Changó's going to kill us!' And she ran off to bury herself under the royal palm next to his brother's wife. How could she explain this to him, especially since she was in charge of taking care of his *ile* and entrusted to make sure nobody went near his sorcery?

"When Changó returned, he called the women, but they didn't answer. He went to look at his calabash and found it open. He figured out what had happened, and he quickly made his way to the palm tree. He sank into the earth and found them inside.

"Changó scolded them, but Oya Obinidodo didn't get upset. Instead, she told him off. She incited him to wage war against Ogun once again, and they went off together to attack him. (Changó and Oya became stones.)[22] Since he fought without weapons, Osain—who is Changó's godfather—prepared the secret of the calabash for him: the ingredients. When he touched them with his finger and put it on his tongue, they produced the miracle of spitting fire from their mouth. With that fire, he defeated his enemies." For that reason, whenever he sounds upset, thundering and flashing, one says to him, "Kawo Changó, kawo si le yeye o afudere ma" or "Eluekon osi Osain."

Changó is adored by devotees—whether they are affiliated with Lucumí, Arará, or even Congo ancestry—in these celestial stones, polished axes that

---

22 DF-N: With a very succinct parenthetical commentary, Cabrera guides readers through literal and metaphorical dimensions of the story, making it clear that the stones are simultaneously (1) the result of going to war, (2) the tools of war, and (3) manifestations of the spiritual agents of war.

the masses call thunder stones and were carved in Cuba by Native peoples (*aborígenes indios*).[23]

The Congo Oya (if we can call her that), *pungo* Mama Wanga, Sansingila, who is a whirlwind in one of her manifestations—"Malongo Vira-Vira"—is harnessed by a sorcerer to put her in his *prenda* and take advantage of her energy. "Well, *Oya salanga munu impenso*, she works with the wind," and the whirlwind is used to make a very destructive *Boumba*.

When A.Z. was a boy, he saw Pelayo Jústiz, the *mayombero* "who lived with his grandmother, and another Black man who was the *mayordomo* of his *nganga*, capture the whirlwind as it was moving down the street. He used a candle in one hand and an *mpaka* in the other, singing a *mambo* softly. He had prepared an empty cauldron next to his *nganga-fundamento*, which was called Mala-Vianda. He hid them behind a red cloth. Pelayo Jústiz burned *fula* from the outside to the inside, and when the gunpowder exploded, I remember him yelling, 'Now we've got it!' The whirlwind disappeared because it had gone in the cauldron." The sorcerer takes control of the whirlwind, "or *nkanga*," following its movements in a very simple way, according to Jesús Santos's explanation of his technique: "As soon as you see it, you take off your hat. If the *mayombero* makes the sign of the cross, he won't be able to grab it. They say, 'If you're in hell, I want to be with you, and I'm calling you to accompany me and help me, so I'll pay you and help you.'"

Having pronounced these words, Jesús Santos, with his hat in hand, plunges into the middle of the cloud of dust that is being lifted up and spun around by the wind. "I hunt it. I cover the hat with a red kerchief and I take it, Oya-Ndoki, inside the hat, spinning around. Later, I put it in the *Prenda* and use it to destroy anything I want." Oya is inside the whirlwind: "It is also San Bilongongo, *nyunga nyunge*, the storm." Wherever it passes, the earth is impregnated with its strength "and its mysteries," which sorcerers use for the sole purpose of destroying or driving mad whomever they like. The dust, "lifted by the skirts of Rabo de Nube [the Cloud's Tail]"—another name of the *pungu Mama wanga*—is mixed with dust from the ground where two dogs or a dog and a cat fought. They are longtime enemies. ("Ever since the incident where Olofi granted the dog a certificate granting his freedom, which was stolen by the wife of the Mouse then lost, which finally resulted in the dog remaining a slave.") Finally, a wasp nest is ground and powdered together with guinea pepper and China pepper, then mixed with the rest to make one of the most reliable ways to sow discord.

---

23 DF-N: "Thunder stones" (*oduara, edun ara, matari*, etc.) are often indigenous artifacts repurposed and reinterpreted as divine meteors from the sky and/or outer space, and/or stones created by the impact of lightning bolts striking the earth. See also chapters 3 and 5.

The whirlwind—the dust storm—inspires a great deal of fear because "bad things come with it." It brings illnesses and epidemics, and one should keep a respectful distance, greeting it and "giving it the right of way."

The daughters of Oya, like one Iyesa descendent I met near the town of Pedro Betancourt, "cannot close the doors of their houses to the whirlwind."

This elder—like her Angel, a dynamic and agile warrior—was confronted by Oya herself in person one day when strong winds were blowing. Oya gave her a decisive order, which she follows to the letter. I can confirm this, because we experienced that sort of inclement weather on the day of our interview during the season of Lent. Her living room was wide open to the dust clouds stirred up by the stinging, turbulent wind that swirled over the unpaved road where she lived.

"Oya gave one hard knock on the door and stood there, in that doorway, very angry. And she told me, 'I need to come and go whenever I please. Do you think you can step on my tail? Take care to not get tangled up, stumble, and break your head open. This is my house, and you don't have the right to shut the door on me. From now on, I'd better not find this door closed again. Not on your life.'"

Everyone agrees that when Oya gets angry, she is even more impulsive and violent than Changó. "He is more boisterous. A tough guy. If she gets bored with all his grumbling, she launches a lightning bolt so he'll let her be in peace. He gets scared and shuts up."

When the sound of thunder is heard, children are told that Changó is scolding the kids. "Oya approaches to find out why Changó is upset. 'They'll never get any better by scolding them! This is how you punish them!' And she takes the whip from Changó. *Chisk!* You see the flash of light in the sky, then you hear the voice of Changó again, still grumbling and saying, 'No, Oya! That punishment is too rough.'" When they heard the sound of thunder, the elders would say "he's roaming around, partying with his women or riding around on his horse."

The *ngangas* and *nkutu dilangas* ("guides," talismans) in which work Changó and Oya, Siete Rayos or Remolino, Viento Malo or Centella, as well as the "fundamentos" (strictly speaking, a beginning and foundation) of any other magical structure with this same "tendency," are distinguished by their devastating effects. "They are the fastest and the most destructive."

For example, "Rayo vá caé" [Lightning will strike], as its name indicates, mandates an immediate explosion from a bolt of lightning. Oya works in it:

> *Oya Oya china bankere*
> *¿quien manda aquí? ¡Oya!*[24]

24　The expression *¿quien manda aquí?* can be translated as "Who's the boss here?" "Who's in charge here?" or "Who gives the orders here?"

If the owner of this *Prenda* pours water on the sweltering ground at high noon, calling Nsasi and Oya at the moment the sun burns hottest, they will cause lightning to strike.

These *ngangas* live out in the sun, under a palm tree. To cover the receptacle containing such a fearsome power, a face is drawn on a half gourd which is used as a lid.

"The heads of the animals sacrificed to it are left to rot on top of that mask. The spirit of that *nganga* is formidable. You can't delay in giving it blood, because it might take its owner's instead."

"Remolino Campo Santo is the sister of Campo Santo Buenas Noches," and

some of them leave no choice but to feed them with women's blood. They're wrapped in a rag that is soaked in menstrual blood. Careless women expose themselves to that danger, because that blood is stolen and, most of the time, the woman whose blood they stole will die of anemia.

The owner of these *ngangas* cannot sleep in a bed; instead, they sleep on the floor, next to it. They are priceless as a means to kill, but only in exchange for so many sacrifices! For nine days of the month, the *gangulero* cannot have contact with his wife. And they need to humor that *nganga's* every whim—for example, taking them for a stroll in the cemetery, even in plain view of the police!

One son of Ogun claims that the thunder stone belongs to Ogun. "Ogun, who smokes as much as Elegua and Osain, lights his tobacco with it, and Changó stole it in *el monte*, along with his clothes. He left him naked, so Ogun had to cover himself with *mariwo*."

But this claim's only merit lies in the devotion of an *omo* who wants to exalt his divine Father at every possible opportunity. He even goes as far as declaring that Oya's flame came from the forge of her husband Ogun.

In the countryside, the *iguoro* or *iyawo* in the Arará and Lucumí Reglas sits on a mortar under a palm tree, and the Mayombe neophyte "swears an oath" to Nsasi there.

In the Palo Monte-Cruzado temple to which Cape belonged, they initiate members at a palm tree of short stature which they decorate with seven flags of different colors, excluding black. "Red, blue for Mama Kalunga, white for Mama Tenge, yellow for Mama Choya, purple for Sarabanda." (Red and white, another informant tells me.) At the moment when they attach the flags to the palm tree, the *bakuyula* lies down on the ground with their forehead touching the tree trunk. Their half-naked body is rubbed down with *mungoa d'inkisi* (holy water), dry wine, leaves, three kinds of pepper, liquor, and earth. When the neophyte gets up, an egg is run over their body then buried at the same spot where they had rested their head. This initiation should take place at the beginning of the rainy season in May, or in June, when "the lightning looks for the palm trees." And Cape assures us that when they go back to the spot where the egg was buried, they will find a *matari-Nsasi*.

At palm trees, "the *Santo* can resolve, respond to, and work through anything." The faithful from all the Reglas invoke him and make offerings of *amala* and *alila*, or fruits, including the obligatory bunch of *plátanos verdes* or *manzanos* (green plantains or bananas) tied with a red ribbon, *mamey*, or *marañón*, all of which this orisha enjoys. "It is the ideal place to leave him *ebo*," which means that all of the *ebos* prescribed by the *santo* end up at his most symbolic tree.

Due to the number of offerings it received daily, one particular miraculous palm tree, where the *santo* appeared and was seen by many people, was cut down by the municipal government of Marianao. This was seen as the only possible way to suppress the never-ending deposits of putrefying materials, which produced an unbearable stench and an alarming plague of flies, mosquitoes, cockroaches, and rats. But these impious sanitation measures—which oblige whoever carries them out to "perform a ritual of atonement beforehand," a sacrifice to Changó—also bother another *santo*: Okada, who, according to an old street sweeper, lives in trash heaps, just as Osesu lives in the gutters and latrines, nourished by waste. "Trash is also sacred."

Without resorting to a *babalawo* or *olocha*, an *omo Changó* who smells danger, suspecting that someone is "working" against them with witchcraft, might employ the following method, which is among the most common. They buy a beautiful bunch of plantains and a large plate with a red edge. When the first plantain falls off the bunch, they rub it with palm oil and say, "Changó, my father, they're doing witchcraft on me. I want this and that . . ." And they wrap the plantain with a red ribbon.

They repeat the same procedure with three more plantains, "pleading" every time they make a knot. They use four plantains because four is Changó's number, and they place them on the plate. They light a candle and pour a little water on the ground. "Santa Bárbara, I'm leaving the evil that is being done against me here in front of you. Let's see if they dare to go against you!" When the plantains are completely rotten, they remove them from the plate, wrap them in paper, and take them to a palm tree. "Alafi Obakoso, I'm leaving the evil they wish for me here with you. This is your business now." And because Changó has already eaten the plantains, "he takes on the responsibility of defending" the man, leaving him carefree. Alafi Obakoso will punish his enemies.

Once the plantains have been left at the palm tree, he should go back home immediately. On the same white plate, he places three pieces of green coconut and a pound of cocoa butter. Three times each day, he will rub the coconut and cocoa butter over his entire body. After that, he will bathe for four or eight consecutive days with leaves belonging to Changó and Obatala, with castile soap and a new washcloth. He will dry himself with a towel that no one else should use. In each bath, he will add four or eight drops of seven different essential oils, and holy water from the church. While he is cleansing himself, he will have a lit five-peso candle next to him. He will say, "Alafi, Father, this cleansing is in your hands." He should comb his hair with a new comb and dress in white. Once the baths are concluded, he will leave the comb, soap, and towel at the palm tree after reciting three Our Fathers and three Hail Marys.

L. is a humble state employee and a son of Changó. He carries out the following procedure to secure his position in these "treacherous" times. Judging by the good results he has always obtained with this "amarre" [binding spell], it should be recommended for anyone who has the fortune or misfortune of belonging to the "emplomanía," the official name for the entire coterie of government employees in Cuba. L. writes the full name of a brand-new minister, usually an impatient politician eager to put his entourage in place. He enchants the name, "pleading," inside his *santo's* tureen. He places the piece of paper under a vessel into which he pours bee honey, molasses, and *ewe orosu*, a plant that belongs to Ochun and has a sweet taste. During four days, he leaves a nail submerged in this syrup, then he removes it and wraps it in the paper along with quicksilver and the extremely efficacious powder from an Amansa Guapo. He wraps it in seven different colors of ribbons and makes the magical pronouncement, saying the name of the new boss with every knot. It is very important to do the wrapping motion toward yourself. Once the nail has been worked over, L. takes this "consolidation charm" to the foot of a palm tree. There he calls Changó, talks to him, and hands over the man, properly wrapped up. He steps on the nail three times with his left foot and buries it under the palm tree.

In the flower beds and gardens surrounding the capitol building in Havana, hidden in the earth, more than one "amarre" keeps an employee in their position as they grow old and grey, calmly fulfilling their duties.

"We make good money from employees," a *santera* confesses to me. One specialized *palero* says, "I always do pretty well for myself making *nkangito* to help people hang on to jobs, and *guaguankisi* to find them."

Malevolent sorcerers summon Kadiempembe or Lugambe at the trunks of the palm trees, since the devil frequents them assiduously. He buries the *balongo* or cauldron next to it, and creates deadly curses under its protection. In particular, the mysterious and feared *palmas jimaguas*—twin palms with a double trunk or growing right next to each other—tend to bear witness to cruel torture and sacrifice of animals, fierce spells, and terrifying apparitions.

They are the home of beings like Elufama, "the son of bad reputation," Eshu. Although his name is from a Lucumí lineage, it is also used by the [Congo] *ngangulero* to refer to the Evil Spirit and Kolofofo. At the twin palm tree, the sorcerer invokes him in these terms:

> *Elufama hijo de mala fama,*
> *Gallina come maíz entero*
> *Y ensucia maíz molido*
> *Remolino da vuelta*
> *No puede llegar a Nsulu.*
> *Bika dioko, bika ndiambo*
> *Tú, hijo de mala fama.*
> *Candela infierno no te quema*
> *Que tú mismo son Infierno.*

> Elufama, child of ill repute
> Hen eats whole kernels of corn
> And poops cornmeal
> The whirlwind goes around
> It can't reach Nsulu.
> Bika dioko, bika ndiambo
> You, child of ill-repute.
> The fire from hell doesn't burn you
> because you're Hell itself.

"Maríam Boumba, may lightning split the twin palm where you live.[25] María Boumba, *tripa quemá* [burnt entrails], you wretch. Come out of there, *Ndoki malongo*. I'm calling you."

Tata Lubuisa, the demon, is there—"*bafungu ba kongo gadia bando*, always ready to destroy the world."

"It's the house of Ndoki, it's Kuikimafinda. In the twin palms, Nkombo Akino (the devil's little horse, or Nsusu Muteka) grabs the Spider (Yaga or Nansi) and buries it down there, next to the trunk. And there—*sapunta!*—a bramble mysteriously emerges."

These twin palms—Majumbu Mpungu Mpungu, twin *santos*, Nino calls them—tend to be inhabited by awful forces. One of my informants is active "on both sides," in both Regla de Ocha and Mayombe. Were it not for his enormous vitality and blind faith in Changó, who always helped him in the

---

25 DF-N: The Cuban Spanish idiom *mal rayo (te) parta*, "may lightning strike you," is a generic, old-fashioned curse, but in this unusual context, it also carries a literal meaning.

midst of the most difficult moments of his life, certain festivities he organized there might have ended in mourning for many mothers.

A very famous set of twin palms grew on the Manuelita farm next to Alquízar. After a *fandango* [party],[26] he decided to return to town by way of a shortcut that crossed the farm.

One of the fainthearted guests confessed to feeling a sense of dread in the presence of those two diabolical palms at midnight. "Everything in nature that grows as twins is a frightening mystery." Another guest was cocky, bragging about how brave he was. Backing up my informant, he declared that he was willing to challenge the Eshu they said appeared between the trunks of the *meyi* trees.

"I'll eat Eshu!"

It was also well known that a very feared *mayombero* had his Nkuyo (*prenda*) "planted" there, which offered a serious explanation for why so many credible people had seen a *fwa-ka-fwa* (a ghost, a *muerto*) swirling around the trees.

The moon was bright, and the gang of kids followed them. They were going along singing and joking around to make themselves seem brave. Then, as they approached the palms, one of them suddenly shouted, "Alosi!" (devils!). As the siren from a sugar mill announced the midnight hour, all of them saw a black smoke rise from the earth, up to the double crests of the trees. The smoke took the shape of an enormous ball. Buzzing like a hornet, it plunged down toward them. Many of their companions fell to the ground, crying and begging for mercy at the top of their lungs.

Others, more numerous, suffered the same symptoms of terror as the Condes de Carrión in Quevedo's romance.[27] Ah! But the one who recounted this event to me, arming himself with courage even though he was trembling, called Changó, invoking his name and showing that infernal force his *sanga*, his protective necklace, just before it would have attacked and destroyed them. He swears on his children's lives that the immense ball, whose blackness made the blue of the night sky seem even deeper, stopped instantly, obeying Changó's authority. It went backward, shrinking slowly until it disappeared over the ground behind the two palm trees.

---

26 DF-N: The word *fandango*—much like *rumba* and *mambo*—carries multiple, closely related meanings. In this context, it refers generically to a party. In other settings throughout the Iberian Peninsula and the Americas, *fandango* also refers to various genres of music and dance.

27 DF-N: The reference to "symptoms of terror" means they soiled themselves. See De Ley and Crosby (1969).

Fortunately, there was also a *desmochador de palmas*—a trade that Changó performed on the earth—among the group of friends who was very fond of Santa Bárbara.

When these *taita ngangangulas* want one of their enemies (or anyone they hate for no good reason) to perish in a fire, they summon and sentence them at a palm tree, unleashing one of these exterminating forces—Siete Rayos, Nsasi, Ma Wanga, Karire, Lauisa.

And here is one of the typical curses—the *nkange* of death—that is carried out at royal palm trees: Using a knife, they open the craw of a chicken that is entirely black, then spray it with plenty of liquor. Pepper and guinea pepper—indispensable ingredients in all witchcraft—mixed with sulfur and dust from a cemetery are put inside the wound, then the chicken is wrapped up in a black cloth. While this operation is being carried out, the subject is cursed incessantly, and the spirit that lives in the palm tree is ordered to make them die in the bloodiest way possible. The chicken is buried under the roots, wounded but still alive, with its head sticking out of the ground. A *kamba*—a new broom made with fronds from a royal palm—is used to beat the tree's trunk to make Nsasi or Siete Rayos furious so they will act quickly and severely.

A *kimbisa* elder, stirring and sifting through the ashes of his memories, confided in me that he had avenged himself with impunity in his youth. Without having to go to Nso-Sarabanda (the jail), he took revenge on a bad woman, a *contoria*, a prostitute, who robbed him of his money and his health. "For a long time, she had turned him into an idiot with a Ndiambo that she had sent after him. It turned him into a drunk who would collapse on the sidewalk and in doorways, unable to make a living for himself."

A symptomatic profile of the bewitched: mental confusion, "doesn't know what's happening to them"; lassitude, indolence, or a worsening of the allergic reaction to disciplined work common to Black people;[28] and, in many cases, an irresistible need to drink aguardiente. This is the most common situation: the vice of drinking tends to be the effect of magical "work," and the desired consequence of that sort of *nsalala* is destitution, the hospital, and death. That is the intended goal. The victims of these *morubas* lose their willpower and become unable to fight against them. But thanks to the strength of a good *compadre* who was able to overcome the woman's witchcraft, this *kimbisa* was pulled out of the physical and moral misery he had fallen into. The *kimbisa's* buddy kept fighting until he removed the curse. Once he was free from the situation that he recalled with horror, and particularly his inability to reason,

28 DF-N: This blatantly racist sterotype is translated literally. See the Translator's Notes.

he was overcome by a desire for vengeance. He let time pass. He made himself a strong *prenda*. And when the woman thought she had incapacitated him forever, or that he might be dead, he went out at midnight and knocked on the door of that *ndumba pikanana*, reciting a prayer with each knock. He was carrying an empty bottle, which had been prepared to steal her voice and take it to a royal palm, shut up in the bottle. "Empty bottles! Never leave them open, because the souls of *muertos* go inside them." It is a piece of advice that the *taitas* give everybody, but especially to the children of Oya, who should not keep broken bottles, plates, or glasses.

The unsuspecting woman answered three times. It is well known that the voice is stolen for "bilongo," which amounts to taking someone's life, "which is their breath." So it is rare for a Black person to answer a call at midnight, since they are always afraid of a "moruba" from some unknown enemy who might take control of their voice, bottling it up or holding it captive symbolically in a trap that has been prepared beforehand.

("It is not good to open your mouth or yawn without making the sign of the cross.") Now, next to the palm tree, our confidant took a black chicken out of a black sack, lit four candles, and began invoking Nsasi and vigorously calling the woman. He recited the necessary prayers and nailed the bird to the tree trunk, alive, so it would suffer a slow agony. And, having captured it in the "entumbo" (bottle), he buried the breath, the life, the voice, the soul of the woman.

The following day, according to the old man, the victim of this curse got it in her head to pour a liter of alcohol over herself and light herself on fire with the flame of a candle—a method of suicide employed by working-class people when they cannot resort to a strong drink of "salfumán" (hydrochloric acid).

Other sorcerers make this *nsalanga* not with a chicken but with a fierce dog, by tying it to the trunk of a palm tree and leaving it there to starve to death.

Sometimes *mambos* and prayers are used to remove *ngangas* and *mpangas* that have been buried in the earth. Similarly, "guides" or "branches" can be created by taking substances from a primary *nganga* "fundamento" and burying them next to a palm or some other strong tree in *el monte*—ceiba, *jagüey*, *cuaba*, laurel, etc. Occasionally, the spirit is opposed to being taken by the sorcerer. In order to pacify the spirit, the sorcerer leaves three fierce, strong dogs there, as a gift, with the intention that they destroy each other, letting the spirit "drink the blood little by little."

Another way to "knock down" an enemy: a *bilongo* is placed in their path so the *diambo* grabs hold of them. The *bilongo* consists of pulverized bark from a palm tree mixed with soil from a grave and "muninfuisi"—bugs, scorpions, and *manca perros*—from the *nganga*, which are also reduced to powder.

A temperamental affinity with Changó is the most eloquent indication of the orisha's paternity. A woman who is headstrong, determined, and domineering is always considered to be an *omo Changó*. Or a man who thinks himself courageous; a braggart; "a dog"; arrogant; impulsive; quarrelsome; wasteful; a partier; "chévere";[29] with an insatiable passion for women, drumming, and dancing; or someone born under circumstances in which a reflection of the god's actions can be discerned. They will brag about being *omo Changó* or *bakuyula moana Nkita Siete Rayos*.

This spiritual parentage is revealed, before or during a child's birth, by the *santo* themselves, mounted in possession of a devotee, the *dilogún*, or Ifa. But a child of Changó will provide unmistakable signals confirming their pedigree. ("The sons of Santa Bárbara aren't always hooligans or belligerent, though, just like not all the daughters of Oshun are shameless.")

When he was four years old, F.—a son of Changó—would raise his hands up to the sky every time it thundered, yelling with all of his strength, "Santa Bárbara, take me!"

The grandson of a friend of mine—who, incidentally, is prone to frequent and inexplicable temper tantrums, very arrogant, "sassy, and only his grandmother can control him, because she's a daughter of Oya"—has stuck his hands in fire several times.

"Wherever you have a flame, there you have the boy looking for his father. With every day that goes by, they show more of the tendencies and insolence that belong to the Orisha."

"A real child of Changó puts their hand in the fire and doesn't get burned. Like Ma Dionisia Arará, who would come down with Jebioso and dance holding a cooking pot full of hot coals on her head without feeling the least bit of heat."

Cape was born in the middle of a lightning and thunder storm. And, just so there would be no room for doubt about his descent, he was born Ibeyi, a twin. He tells us that the "midwife and a doctor, the kind that would visit and prescribe on horseback," struggled to save his mother, but the situation was hopeless. Moreover, without the means to perform an operation in the middle of the countryside, the only possible outcomes were a fatal end or a miracle:

But in those days, a relative of ours was staying at the house. They had sent her to the kitchen to heat water, and she was possessed by Yansa.[30]

---

29 DF-N: The word *chévere* is a clear example of Abakuá language becoming part of colloquial Spanish and—most significantly—maintaining its essentially positive valence in the process.

30 DF-N: The name Yansa is an abbreviated epithet of Oya (Iyansa, Iyansan, etc.), often translated as "mother of nine."

She made a few turns like a tornado and went straight to the bed where my mother was lying, too weak to even complain anymore. The people who saw this and the midwife, Chicha Godínez, all say my mother was more dead than alive. Chicha told everybody this story until the day she died. The *santo* put her hand on her belly, on her hips, and that was it. Right away, Oya pulled me out, half dead from asphyxiation. And as I was being born, a lightning bolt struck a palm tree fifty meters from the house, and through the door came a Santa Bárbara mounted on the body of a Black lady that lived nearby.

The failed doctor and the midwife sat and watched the *santos* work: Yansa and Changó, who revived me, since I was half dead. Changó said to my father, "I'll take care of this one. You take care of the other one." And he "closed me up" right there and then. The "other one" was my sister. My father was careless, and he neglected to take precautions: he didn't close her up quickly enough, and she left this world quickly. I was held captive and stayed.

Because the threat of a premature death always hangs over them, the Ibeyi are "closed up," or bound up symbolically, by welding a chain with a small key around their wrist or ankle. (Female keys with a small perforation for girls, and "male" keys, *sin calado*, for boys.)

"I'm *mulato* and I was born Black, like I was burned, marked by Changó. I was born in the middle of thunder and lightning, like the turtle and the boa. A bolt of lightning lopped off the fronds of the first palm on the path to our farm, and Changó, as I've told you, gave me my life."

The bang of thunder, the electrical discharge, provokes mediumship in the children of Changó and Oya. The first time Baró was possessed by Changó was at the "banfuko" La Diana, the sugar mill, under a twin *jagüey*, when lightning struck. He regained consciousness at the home of an *iyalocha* consecrated to this god.

It was imperative to immediately place the ritual necklaces on him as protection. He bought a ram to offer it to the orisha. On the day of the ceremony, the ram ate the *jobo* leaf it was given resolutely, thereby demonstrating that Changó accepted the sacrifice. At the moment when the ritual dictates that he put his forehead against the ram's, the animal butted his head so hard they thought his skull had cracked. Then, when the *babalawo* cut the beast's throat, Baró collapsed "with *santo*," falling over the tureen full of blood. In those days, he was already well known as a *mayombero*. Even though Changó claimed him "by every which way," he asked the old Lucumí—who washed the *Santo* and placed the necklaces on him in a ceremony that is equivalent to a half *Asiento*—to not mark "*eye*" on his face, the tribal cuts, tattoos also flaunted by

Creoles. Nowadays, the markings in the *Asiento* are drawn with paint, but in those days, they were carved in the skin with a knife.

"In the days of the intervention,[31] the elders would mark little lines on the skin of their children and godchildren. And they would file their teeth into points. A lot of them worked filing teeth in the sugar mills, and right here in Havana." (And more than a few white *guajiros* followed the example of Black people.)

Since then, Baró—who still does not frequent the *ile-Orisha*—sacrifices a ram for Changó on the *otan* of a *santera* friend whenever it is within his means, and he wears a red sash as a belt or armband under his clothes. This is normal for children of the orisha and Agayu. Their *iyalochas* wear red pants, often with small bells sewn on them to scare away the spirits of the dead. The faithful constantly flaunt scarves of the various colors associated symbolically with the *santo* to which they are devoted. They are protective, and it is believed they have a purifying effect.

"People get fixated on the color, which draws the eye. If the woman showing off the scarf is not a *santera*, it stands out even more, and people make comments. The people talking about her will inadvertently pick up whatever bad energy that person might have, and the person cleanses themselves."

The children of Changó are almost always born diviners, spontaneously seeing things in the great beyond, and they don't necessarily need anyone to "prepare their eyes" by washing them with specific substances in order to develop clairvoyance. In Baró's *Rama*,[32] they use the rheum from turkey vultures and other animals who possess penetrating sight.

"El Moro," Calazán, appears before us as a great specimen, physically and morally, of an *omo Changó*. How could he not be? He was the best dancer of his time, the instigator of so many magical brawls and wars. A Black man so handsome, "*chévere*," a heartbreaker, *rumboso*, a bully and a killer! Everywhere he went, in the cigar factory, in the docks, in the sugar mill, wherever he worked, anywhere Calazán went, his personality and genius prevailed, and he was invariably considered to be a leader, an *olu*: Bangoché. Let us listen to him:

"When my mother gave birth to me—on the floor, the way they did it in those days, even though women give birth differently these days—as soon as I showed my face, I started sucking my thumbs." Changó's gluttony is proverbial, and many elders allude to a saying: "Losing the crown over food, like Obakoso."

---

31 DF-N: Cabrera's informant refers to "la intervención," the period between 1898 and 1902 when the United States took over the government of the island after the Spanish-American War (i.e., the Cuban War for Independence).

32 DF-N: The term *Rama* (literally, "Branch") refers to ritual lineage.

"With the edge of a glass bottle, my grandmother—who was African like my mother—cut my umbilical cord, and she put the Lucumí marks on me herself.

"The elders used to call the belly button *yesca*. It's a sacred part of the body, the root that contains the secret of life. When it's cut, you don't throw it away. That root is kept safe to help make the child strong as they grow. You cook it and feed to them in small pieces. Using their own umbilical cord, they can be cured of all the children's diseases: croup, scarlet fever, dysentery, rickets, fever from teething. And it cancels out drunkenness. If you put a little bit in your drink, I think it's a better remedy for drunks than all the other ones people like to recommend: sweat from a bay horse, pig's milk, or those little newborn mice they put in bottles of aguardiente, still alive, so they release their juice, which they say is so good.

"Later, when the child is grown, so they can't harm him, the umbilical cord is buried in *el monte*, at the foot of a tree that belongs to their angel."

(In Trinidad, it is thrown in the river on the feast day of San Juan.)

"The first thing they did when a woman was going into labor was to call their *santo*, so they could help to get through the danger. Sometimes, a family member would get mounted and the *santo* themselves would deliver the baby. Later, when they had to cut the baby's umbilical cord, the *santo* would remove it with their teeth. But even without being possessed by the *santo*, the African women would cut it with their teeth.

"When I started crawling, my grandfather said, 'Don't ever let him show anybody the roof of his mouth! And don't let them touch this child's head!'" (A *zahorí* or clairvoyant is born with a cross on their tongue.) "And that's why—back then, when people gave a lot of thought to the things they did— they didn't cut my hair until I was six years old. A few days before that, I had stuck my hand in the fire, but the fire didn't burn me. My aunt Panchita Baribá, my mother, my father, my grandmother, all of them cried that day: 'Bangoché, Bangoché, oh my, big head, true son of Alafi!' When they cut my hair, they made *ebo* with my braids, and it was another son of Changó who cut my locks. If someone who wasn't a child of Changó had cut my hair, they would have ruined me. They learned that the messenger who took the *ebo* to *el monte* kept a braid of my hair to make a talisman for himself. But he died three days later." This is a very common custom among both races, and we still see it among *guajiros*: the offering of a vow that condemns boys to keep their hair long and braided almost until puberty.

Not long ago, at an old sugar mill owned by the Jorrín family, my attention was drawn to a young adolescent girl. She threw rocks with considerable skill, leading a group of little kids of all different colors who called her Jorge. Well, Jorge—they explained to me later—was a turbulent young man of thirteen years who was not supposed to cut his blonde curls until he turned fifteen, when he would offer them as thanks to his patron *santa*, La Caridad del Cobre.

"The first trade I learned was as a shoemaker, in the workshop of an Arará Mahino. One day, my teacher scolded me and hit me in the head with his shoemaker's stirrup. I just stared at him, but I didn't say a word. In those days, we respected our elders. And the elders hit us! When they spoke to us in a serious tone, we lowered our heads. Six days after that, Martín Arará, my teacher, was sick in bed. Everyone was running around saying, 'He's dying!' They made offerings, *cambio de vida* . . . [33] And my mother, who helped him, said to him, 'Martín, you've lost your mind! How did it occur to you to hit him in the head? You should have hit him somewhere else!' My dear mother was right: it's a strange notion, because by hitting my head, it's not that he mistreated me, but my Angel. He should've remembered that God created butt cheeks so they could absorb blows. We can't lower our heads. Our *santo* greets others by putting his hand on their shoulder or embracing them. He's very proud. Later, when I was going around being a ladies' man, I had a beautiful Black girlfriend. What did she want?

"'Oh, Calazá, let me see the roof of your mouth! Come on, my love, that's what I want. Even if it's just once, let me see the top of your mouth. Open up.'

"It seems she'd heard something about me, and she wanted to know whether I was clairvoyant or not. These women! She was really brazen, and . . . well, those are weaknesses we men have. Yes, she finally saw it. But both of us got sick. And for that, four children of Changó, each holding *pácha-chucho-punzó*, they hit me four times, hard.

"We never learn our lesson. Two years later, I showed the roof of my mouth again. My grandmother would say to me, 'Black man, you're stubborn! Ah, Calazán! Changó is going to leave you lying on your back, with your face looking up like a dead cockroach!' But I haven't done it again. The thing is, the story got around, and all the women wanted to see the cross, that mark of a prodigy that I have . . .

"One season, when it was fashionable to cut your hair short, I almost shaved it off. The woman I was with at the time insisted that I follow the trend. I forgot about the other thing, and she kept going on and on: 'You're so handsome and stylish, Bangoché.' So I went to the Malaysian barber.

"'Malayo, cut my hair in the new style.'

"'You, Bangoché? I'm not going to cut your hair!'

33 DF-N: A *cambio de vida* is a ritual exchange of lives, indicating a proverbial "scapegoat" ritual.

"I insisted, but the Malaysian knew better, and he really didn't want to do it. You know, back then, the children of Changó, the old *santeros*, would leave a small, long braid in their hair like the Chinese. He starts cutting my hair, and when he gets to the middle of my head, to the crown: *Cataplún!* I lost consciousness, right there in the barber's chair. An offering with *Ayakua tiroko* (turtle) . . . Remind me to tell you a story about Ayakua that my grandmother used to tell me in her language. It starts, 'Okutan si! Inyamu ilu bogbo koiri unyeun . . .' Later? Well!

"I couldn't get my hair cut like that, so short.

"I was a live wire in those days. Oh, my goodness, I was fire when I was young! And the truth is that I would go from one woman to another. Back then, I was living with Clementina. Clementina, Clementina! She went through a lot with me . . .

"'You have no choice,' she told me. 'You have to wear your hair long.' The fashion had changed.

"I said, 'But so much hair? It's too much! Like an old Jesus?'

"'No, it's a very nice-looking hair style, with little rows between the buns.' Honestly, I needed to have plenty of hair on my head, but not that much!

"That poor woman. I was in love with her, so I indulged her. She would braid my hair and comb it. One day, I woke up late and had to rush out to work at the factory. I showed up there with my hair in little braids. My co-workers at the cigar factory burst out laughing at me. And all of us working at the factory were full of jokes! But I didn't get it. Not until later, when I went to a café and saw myself in a mirror. Oh my God, Bangoché! I almost killed Clementina!"

It was Calazán's custom to "menearle el guarapo" ("stir the sugar cane juice")—that is, to hit his numerous women.

Moniquín, an old *santera* contemporary of his who loathed white people (starting with me), never forgave Calazán for the beatings he administered liberally to her sister, the very same Clementina who braided his hair, all under the banner of being a "true son" of Changó (and Calazán was also a son of Yemaya).[34] This was in the days when Clementina was among the favorites in his harem. Nonetheless, Moniquín respected him. El Moro's wanton lifestyle made him a sort of human replica of that divine archetype: his triumphs, his almost always reprehensible behavior toward the fairer sex, his self-indulgence (since he earned good money at the cigar factory and as a stevedore, even the way he alternated between squandering his money and destitution underscored the resemblance).

THE ROYAL PALM

---

34 DF-N: For more on Changó, Calazán, and Moniquín, see also the entry for CALABAZA in this edition's botanical encyclopedia.

And in order to complete his profile, he had royal blood in his veins, and he was among the most wicked sorcerers. "Wise" and "erudite"—he was a very professorial Black man when he got excited or wanted to make an impression on his audience—he also had the enviable gift of eloquence. The embittered Moniquín concluded: "There's no denying he's his father's son." In him, all of Changó's peculiarities were genuine and natural, while other children of his only simulate them with effort.

"Changó was a man from the gutter who lived defending himself with cunning and tricks. When he can't support a woman, he lives off her and hits her. When he can, he's *rumboso* [lavish, generous] and keeps her in fine clothes."

Therefore, let us not judge Calazán too severely.

Moniquín hates him, but—objectively—she admires him, because deep down, his terrible flaws are . . . divine, the product of a divine transmission. Calazán was "a son who resembled his father," and she cannot help recognizing him as such. She condemns his behavior and the nature of his witchcraft: "Changó's witchcraft! Doesn't he burn down his victim's houses from a distance?" But she understands and respects not the man Calazán but the orisha who inspires him and is reflected in everything he does in life. "You only need to see him show his teeth. The child of a cat will hunt mice." In this sense, the reactions of El Moro, including some of his more gratuitous misdeeds—the death of Rufino, a skull from the Cabildo—can be analyzed to seem justifiable, or at least explainable, and they undoubtedly increase his prestige as Alafi's chosen.

The royal palm exerts a special attraction on all of the children of Changó, and it is especially strong among Changó's most beloved children.

Calazán said, "In colonial times, I used to climb up the palm tree to cut down *palmiche* [palm nuts] to feed the pigs. I felt like I had wings."

Baró, for example, "loses his mind at the palm tree, and Santa Bárbara always grabs him there."

It is well known that those who belong to this deity—"whether Congo, Lucumí, or Arará"—hear him by pressing their forehead to the trunk of this tree. Changó lets them hear his voice from inside the tree. "The Padre Nganga who is mounted by Nsasi, Siete Rayos, or Batalla will hit their heads against the trunk without hurting themselves at all or even getting any bumps or bruises." The same thing happens when the orisha "eats fire" and their mount—I have witnessed this—buries their mouth in a handful of hot coals held in their hands. His children, in a state of trance, are numb and invulnerable to fire.

In an *nkombo* [horse] belonging to Nsasi, the presence of Nsasi is often substantiated by their taking the *muinda* (the candle burning next to the

Nganga's cauldron) and applying it spectacularly to their own eyelashes without burning their eyelashes or eyebrows. They slide the flame over their chest and sides, then show that their skin has not been blistered.

It is sometimes necessary to defend the horses from Nsasi's violence. He mistreats their bodies savagely during trance, his fury surpassing human limits.

The *Mayombero* finds himself obligated to send away the *mpungu* who has taken control of the medium by delivering hard blows to their back. When the *mpungu* leaves after violent convulsions that leave the medium exhausted, the medium is helped to regain consciousness with massages and rubbing.

The feast days in honor of Changó are officially celebrated all over Cuba on the fourth of December with vigils at altars, sacrifices, and drumming celebrations. In the countryside, the *babalocha* or *mayombero* at Kuna-Kuan-Kuna (cabildos) that have a royal palm growing on their land are obligated to keep a watchful eye on the devotees, children, and mounts, regardless of their sex. Frequently, an *aberikula*, *aleyo*, or some unknown guest among the attendees is possessed by Changó, climbs to the crest of the palm tree and emphatically refuses to come down, making it necessary to sacrifice a ram to the god very quickly and perform an *ita* [divination].[35]

It is completely logical for Changó to guide his children to his preferred dwelling. This happened to a cousin of Nino's at a *bembe*. "He escaped from the *santera* and climbed up to the very top." It was necessary to inform his parents and perform *Oro* to make them come down, which placed a considerable burden on the poor parents due to the cost of these unavoidable offerings and sacrifices.

Certain rituals for rainfall are performed next to a palm tree, where Changó and Yemaya are beseeched to make it rain. "The Oduara is put in the *bangaña*," the small cedarwood container where the stone is kept, "and coated with plenty of honey. It is offered coconut, then Changó is called by shaking the *achere* [shaker, rattle, maraca] and singing until—through the strength of playing the maraca and praying—the sky will darken, and it will rain. When it rains too much, they need to be asked to make it stop. In that case, a rooster is killed for Changó, and another for Yemaya."

Lighting twelve cotton wicks soaked in a mixture of palm oil and olive oil will incite thunder and a downpour.

---

35 DF-N: The order of the two steps—sacrifice, followed by *ita* divination—is reversed here from Cabrera's original. The change reflects a consensus regarding ritual logic and norms among Lucumí priests, and it corrects a small but significant error in the original text.

The famous sorcerer Lincheta—about whom we will have a great deal to say[36]—would make it rain with one of those Ngangas that has Nsasi as its *fundamento*. It was "so powerful that it would go off with a bang if you bothered it even a little bit. I have seen that old man talk to his *Prenda*, then ask the late Petrona Pulido to pour out a *jícara* (gourd bowl) of water on the dry ground. Immediately, the lightning would snake down, the bolt would shoot out of the palm tree, and within five minutes, there would be a deluge."

"Under a palm tree, you draw a cross on the ground, then put a mound of soil on top of the cross. On top of that, you place the offerings to Changó, with Pitahaya and fruits for the Ibeyi. You light two candles, kill a rooster, then start singing. Before the songs are finished, Changó will respond, and it will rain."

"To call him and make it rain, go to the foot of the palm tree. Offer him a ram. Or quail, since he'll grant anything you ask in exchange for quail."

Chant and *achere*:

> *Chororó baki chororó*
> *Va llorobé llorobé*
> *Mira hijo tuyo como tán*
> *Tó lo labranza secá*
> *Chororó* etc.

> *Chororó baki chororó*
> It's going to cry rain, cry rain
> Look, see your children, how they suffer
> All the fields are dry
> *Chororó* etc.

One of my old friends "calls the rain" through Changó—since the thunder brings Oyouro—and Oke, the owner of the mountains.

Under the palm tree, she simulates a hill with a mound of dirt, surrounds it with plantains, places four *obi kola* seeds on the peak. She kills a rooster and spills its blood. She dances and sings until it starts raining.

---

36 DF-N: Lincheta is only named in one other passage of *El Monte*, in a parenthetical note in chapter 7:

> Daqui, Dumosi de Mensu, was the name of the gorgeous ceiba belonging to the sorcerer named Lincheta at the Marañón sugar mill; next to her, he had also planted Centella, "a matari," which was the *santo* that worked with his *nganga*.

> However, Cabrera also describes Lincheta much more vividly in *Reglas de Congo* ([1979] 1986, 204–6), and he is likely an important source of information for *Vocabulario Congo* ([1984] 2001).

The old man Baró recalls that during great droughts, his African grand-father, who was a rice farmer, would take his *matari* Mamba, his *santo*—a stone he had brought with him from Africa—to a royal palm, "so the water in the sky would decide to come down." (Mamba is the owner of waters.)

There, next to the palm tree, he would sing in chorus with his *munangeyes* (companions):

> *Mamba umbe yamambe*
> *Omi nao omo mambamba*
> *Umbe ya Mambe.*

"Mamba . . . danced all by herself. Yes, Mamba's stone would dance when they sang to it." (Many *olochas* make their sacred stones dance without touch-ing them.)

Baró became pensive, then added:

Ngulo, the pig, sniffs and roots around the earth to eat, because he can't look up. He was cursed by the wife of Nsambi. The yam was his food, and *palmiche* was the food of Sao, the elephant, who can reach up high and eat the fruit from young palm trees.

One day, they crossed paths, and Ngulo said to Sao, "I like *palmiche*."

"And I like yam."

And they both said, "Let's trade."

The pig performed a ceremony, because he was a sorcerer. He dug up *yambuco* (yams) and gave them to the elephant, who stuffed himself until he couldn't eat anymore. But he didn't keep his end of the deal with the pig. He didn't give him *palmiche*. Then Ngulo went to the foot of the palm tree with his Nkise, recited his incantations, and sent a Tie-Tie— Mbaka Tie Tie, a little bird similar to the *bijirita* that flies very high[37]— with a message for the Cloud, asking it to swell and fill the elephant's house with water as if it were a *wata* (*jícara*). And it fell *lango lango*, flooding Nsao's home.

When the elephant found himself up to his neck in water, swimming with his ears, he thought he was going to drown. Then he remembered Ngulo and asked for his forgiveness.

When Ngulo got tired of keeping Nsao in the water with his trunk sticking up in the air, he went back to the palm tree to perform his cer-emony, and it stopped raining. That's when the elephant came to bring

---

37 DF-N: *Bijirita* is a word for warbler (*Sylviidae*).

him *palmiche*. But the pig said he didn't need it, since the *palmiche* would ripen and fall, then he could pick it up from the ground.

Using a *matari* Cheche Wanga or Centella, or a Nsasi, others "unleash the rain." It can also be made to rain by preparing a magical needle with the prodigious Piedra Imán, then nailing it into the trunk of the palm tree.

Sometimes, at the beginning of a downpour, "You can hear Changó running around behind the clouds. And Ogun can be heard moving his iron around to fight him, so we say to him: *wo ti soro yo*." And if he gets carried away—Oya accompanies him, setting off the gunpowder, and making lightning bolts explode, profuse and terrifying—then one should do what Má Francisquilla Ibáñez does and advises (along with other elders in her circle):

"I present La Merced to him." (The Obatala who is Changó's mother, so she pacifies her son.) "I open the door and I say, *Kawo Kabie si, oganya maya maya juto. Dede, dede mi to e* (Be calm, be calm, settle down)." Others put the thunder stone, the axe, or a symbol of the orisha in a vessel full of milk. "If you sang a war chant to him in a thunderstorm, his fire would annihilate the universe."

"The Changó with the booming thunder and lightning bolts is the Changó de Ima, or the one from Isu."

The Takua Ogodo, *kulenke ayala* and *akatayeri jekua*, is the one who thunders the most. ("But all of them thunder. *Dada Oworu Magala, yanun yemoro Alafi ya boko bori . . .*") In these instances, "when Changó goes wild," although the same *Matari* that unleashes a storm can bind it up again, both white and Black people burn a little *guano bendito*, the leaves from young palm trees distributed to the faithful at church on Palm Sunday. A handful of those ashes offer protection from lightning, and many use them to draw a cross on their foreheads during a storm. Or they blow them into the air, praying to Santa Bárbara and lighting a candle, which is also blessed. To deflect lightning from a home, a palm frond is stuck between the iron bars or arabesques in the bars of a window. Additionally, some consider tying the main rib from a palm frond snugly around their neck to be the most reliable method.

The superstitions of white people have always run parallel in many ways with those of Black people, who adopted and adapted all of their owners' superstitions according to their own criteria and convenience, including the use of blessed palm leaves as a deterrent or protection from lightning. These leaves are always found in the homes of *santeros*. You can find them next to both the *nganga* and the orisha. They appear in many offerings and *ebos* for the sick. And who doesn't know that a sorcerer can use seven branches of *guano bendito* to force death to leave a house in which it is hiding?

The scene that would unfold in old Cuban houses—among all social class—on stormy days was very odd. The same precautions were taken in big homes and small ones, as well as the humble boardinghouses. And warding off the electrical discharge by burning *guano bendito* and covering mirrors is not merely a thing of the past.

My friend Dr. E.S.Z. recalls,

My mother kept pairs of silk ankle booties in one of those massive, old-fashioned wardrobes. The booties were made especially for dressing her children on stormy days. The servants also had similar garments. As soon as it started thundering, she would dress us all in those outfits. She would let her hair down, to relieve herself of the danger from metal hairpins, and the other women in the house would imitate her. The Black people would join in, circumspect and dressed in the same sort of outfits. We would suffocate in the heat, because the house was hermetically sealed! Most important, all of the mirrors were covered very carefully, and needles, scissors, and hand mirrors would be put away. Surrounded by all of the Black servants—arranged according to status, the elders very ceremonious and full of importance, and the children sitting very still by their side—my mother would light some candles, burn the *guano bendito*, and start reciting her prayers loudly, to which the Black people would offer replies. Only my father and grandfather, who mocked her, would resist attending the spectacle. If the squall coincided with a mealtime, nobody sat down at the table until the danger had passed. All activity in the house came to a halt.

Guano bendito, mariwo, was a miraculous article and a basic necessity in the home, regardless of race, and the people keep burning it.

In the countryside of Santa Clara, to curb the "fury" of Santa Bárbara, protect oneself from her, and divert a storm, they burn an ox horn instead of *guano*. On evenings when a rainstorm seems imminent, the horn is burned as a protective measure before going to sleep. "And if the weather is unsettled, Changó is not mentioned, to avoid making it worse." Uttering his name attracts lightning. It is a precaution—and a matter of courtesy—to lift oneself from one's seat when thunder is heard, place the palm of the hand on the ground, kiss the fingers, and salute him with the customary formula: *Jekua, Baba, Kawo Kabie si.* Or: *O bakoso Kisieko, Alado Olufino, Nikoke o oluweko asasain.* This reverence should be performed every time a *Santo* is mentioned.[38]

---

38 DF-N: The symbolic gesture of rising from one's seat is an act of reverence performed specifically for Changó.

"Whenever there's a tornado, Oya"—the whirlwind—"far away, in the distance, the people who have the power to do it will grab a sheet of paper and a pair of scissors and fix their sights on the tornado while praying. They face the tornado and cut the paper, or they simulate cutting the tornado with the scissors. And the cloud disappears." But it is the daughters of Oya who are able to ward off the whirlwind. If they have the magical power to do so, they cut it with a machete that has been "worked"—enchanted—after drawing three crosses on the ground. Many will "scare it away" from their roofs or patios by drawing a cross with ashes on the blade of a machete and hanging a rosary from it. Regarding mirrors: quicksilver—due to its excessive vitality, its mobility, and its cold, sparkling brilliance—irritates Oya, who cannot tolerate having anything else shine as brightly as her. To avoid the catastrophe that would result from an encounter between lightning and quicksilver, mirrors are carefully covered, just as the lady mentioned earlier would do. On stormy days, women take care to avoid combing themselves in front of mirrors. Only Yemaya incarnate, who enjoys them so much, or Oshun, could do so.

"Therefore, not a single mirror can be hung in the *cuarto de los santos*, and her daughters should never dare to have anything on their head that shines too brightly, in order to avoid perturbing the *Santa*."

(Her contemporaries recall that Casimira, shortly before independence, was the queen of a Chinese *comparsa*. Her head was adorned with a brilliant crown of small, lively pieces of mirror. Parading majestically on her carnival float, sitting on an equally dazzling throne among maids of honor, paper dragons, metallic paint, and *escarchilla*, she collapsed suddenly. She remained unconscious for seventy-two hours, this queen. Since the doctor was unable to bring her back to her senses, they assembled a conclave of *babalawos*.[39] They mandated *kari Ocha*: making her *Santo*. She recovered consciousness during the ceremony, when the goddess Oya took possession of her head. Something similar happened with Pastoriza, President of the Bando Azul de la Unión Fraternal.[40] Because she wore dazzling, ostentatious jewelry to one of that honorable society's lavish functions, Oya knocked her off the platform in front of the entire audience.)

---

39 DF-N: While Cabrera seems to confuse *babalawos* (Ifa diviners) with *babalochas* and *iyalochas* (*dilogún* diviners), it is not difficult to imagine a conclave of Ifa diviners gathering to discern a remedy to such a dire situation.

40 DF-N: According to Abakuá elder Alfredo Sánchez Osuna (quoted in Miller 2020, 3), the Abakuá lodge Fokondó Efó formed the Unión Fraternal in the 1950s as a mutual aid group based in the Havana neighborhood of Jesús María. He recounts, "These unions helped each other: a sick member received a stipend. They also organized dance events, because in the great clubs like Tropicana, Havana Yacht Club, Casino Deportivo, Vedado Tennis Club, El Carmelo and others, blacks and mulattos could not enter."

In case one of these lapses—unintentional or imprudent—occurs when there is no *guano bendito* available to protect the person's home and life from the rage of Changó or Yansa, one should remember that ashes from charcoal or firewood found in any kitchen have the same power as those from *guano* and horns.

Ignacio Vergara from Trinidad and the old man Baró silence thunder by blowing ashes into the air and singing this *mambo*:

> *In cielo tronando*
> *¿I por qué?*
> *In cielo tronando . . .*

Many "scare away" the rain by simply drawing a cross with ashes. But that sort of thing is not recommended, "because it makes the elements fight each other, and, in the end, they turn against the person that tries to restrain them."

Ash—ordinary ash from the stove or fireplace in a home—has many virtues and magical applications, and it is a precious substance to the *ngangulero* and the *alase*.[41]

An *ngangulero* will purify himself before manipulating his *ikiso*. If he has had sexual contact, he always purifies himself with ashes, which will dissolve even the worst stains and impurities.

Whenever a woman who is menstruating recklessly enters the vicinity of the *nganga* in a *juego de palo* [*palo* ceremony], the Yimbi quickly intones a *mambo de puya* [musical jab, gibe, cutting remark], warning the *ngangulero* of the impure and dangerous presence of that woman, who should leave immediately:

> *Ié mi casa oler mancaperro, síe, síe.*

The *mfumo* rushes to spill ashes to purify the space and ground of his befouled temple. The *oluo* and *babalocha* will do exactly the same thing. Menstruation is taboo in all religions, and women cannot come close to anything sacred during their period—much less enter the *igbodu* or *nso nganga*.[42]

Ashes—*mpolo banso menfuru*—are used to draw the "sign of strength and resolve." The magical consolidation of *nkiso* or *sungu* are performed over this sign so that none of the sorcerer's "works" slip or waver. And ashes are used to undo witchcraft that might have been deposited, discreetly, in their path.

---

41 DF-N: This rendering of the word *alasé* (a Lucumí term for medicine man, sorcerer, etc.) includes a noteworthy use of an *s* (rather than *sh* or *ch*).

42 DF-N: See Baumgartner (2002); and Jay (1992).

Ashes from a kitchen are the primary ingredient in curses whose goal is to make a specific person starve to death. Whoever suspects a neighbor of harboring ill will toward them should keep a close watch on them; they will always try to find their way to the humble stove where they cook. Everyone knows that ashes are stolen in order to make food scarce in the house where they were taken, and the destructive power of ashes is so strong that no one dares to step on them.

Stepping on ashes or retracing one's steps—going out on an errand and returning along the same route—"cuts off" good luck. That is why *santeros*—courtesy notwithstanding—will preclude being put in the difficult position of retracing their steps when someone calls on them.

The sin committed by an *iyawo*, *baba*, or *iyalocha* by violating an *ewo*—a prohibition against eating a food from which they must abstain for their own well-being, from their "birth" in the orisha religion until the end of their life—can be removed by drawing a cross on their tongue with ashes.

A sin can only be committed knowingly. Therefore, whenever this happens in a *Santo* feast, devotees are careful to avoid saying the name of the taboo food being eaten in front of the *iyalocha* or *baba*, thereby dodging a grave offense. As we can see, there are an infinite number of ways to fool the *Santos* and jump over the barriers of an *Ire* or *Ewo*.

A *mayombero* uses ashes to produce all sorts of calamities. "The ones from tobacco are the worst." In the city of Trinidad and its environs, "the witches—not the black butterflies that predict death and have the winning lottery numbers written on their wings, but the flesh and bone witches who fly at night—can be trapped with ashes."

We know for a fact that Rosita, the one from Los Periquitos, would fly. Uncle Lión caught her in a mamoncillo tree by drawing a cross backward with ashes, reciting the Oración de la Santa Cruzada prayer, and scattering mustard seeds around the tree.[43]

The witch begged Uncle Lión to let her go before the sun came up, to avoid a commotion, and she gave him many, many gold coins.

The old man hid the gold and kept the secret of the capture until the witch finally flew far away and stayed, permanently, in the land from which no one returns.

Another dark-skinned man from Trinidad did not have the same luck as Uncle Lión. That man was walking by himself, after midnight, along a lonely trail. He was carrying a little drum, and he ran into two witches . . .

---

43 DF-N: The mamoncillo (*Melicoccus bijugatus*) is also known as *guenep, quenepa, mamón, mamones,* limoncillo, and Spanish lime.

They asked him, "Want to fly, *taita?*"

"Oh, yes." And because men are absolutely incapable of flying by themselves, those two witches grabbed him by his elbows, a witch on either side of him, lifted him up, and carried him around on a pleasant flight up in the sky.

He was playing his little drum, feeling very happy and safe, but they, out of malice, ended up dropping him in a cactus patch, so the poor man got cactus thorns stuck all over his body.

This happened "in another time, when everything was possible." Yet today, in the deserted blue hills of Trinidad, "there are still some who fly. The Oración de la Santa Cruzada has not put an end to the witches."

The following is another effective way to capture a *ndoki*—a male witch that flies to inflict harm—and prevent them from flying:

> Get a shirt that the witch has used recently, so it's alive with his emanations. You take it to *el monte*, to a remote spot. There, you open the shirt, and you use ashes to draw a cross in the middle of its back. Then you bury a knife in the center of the cross.
>
> "The witch will fall, together with their shirt."
>
> "Why?"
>
> "Because they're attracted to their own emanations. Just like a *muerto* is called by the earth from their grave or anything else that belonged to them—their hair, nails, bones, anything that really hangs on to their *vaho* [vapors, odor]" (*sic*).[44]

On the other hand, ashes from a cooking stove have beneficial and curative properties, and "secas"—swollen lymph nodes—sometimes disappear after a single application of cool ashes.

To reduce a *seca*, it is not necessary to pay the fees charged by a *gangatare* or a *mamalocha*.

A.M. assures me that she cures her husband with this old method "every time he gets a *seca*," to which his body seems particularly inclined. This way, she saves them from both the cost of the consultation with a pharmacist and the medicine that goes with it.

---

44 DF-N: Again, Cabrera's diverse use of "(*sic*)" seems to mark an objection to an error made by the anonymous speaker vis-à-vis theology rather than grammar or spelling. In this instance, the parenthetical interjection seems to caution readers that a *muerto* does not necessarily behave according to the conceptual framework outlined in the quotation.

She wraps very hot ashes in white linen and makes a doll from them. She prays over them, lays her patient down, and makes seven signs of the cross over the swollen lymph node. Seven times, she asks, "What do I remove?"

"A *seca*."

The strictest impartiality obliges us to recognize that the stars in the sky, when they are moved by love of their own, make *secas* disappear just as quickly as ashes and without anyone's intervention.

One stares firmly at a star, contemplating it and saying to it,

> *Estrellita reluciente*
> *Tengo una seca.*
> *Que se seque ella*
> *Para que brilles tú.*

> Little shining star
> I have a seca.
> Let it dry out
> So you can shine.

Or one delivers this flattering and effective little speech:

> *¡Estrellita reluciente!*
> *Yo tengo una seca*
> *La seca dice que se seca*
> *Y tú relumbres para siempre.*
> *Amén, Jesus.*
> *La seca dice que brilla*
> *Más que tú, estrella.*
> *Estrella, seca la seca,*
> *Y brilla tú más que ella.*

> Little shining star!
> I have a *seca.*
> The seca says it will dry out
> And you will shine forever.
> Amen, Jesus.
> The *seca* says it shines
> More than you, my star.
> My star, dry out the *seca*
> And shine brighter than her.

Of course, "the little eyes of Olofi" can cure!

The Palm Tree gives people their *orile* (the roof of a *bohío* or a Cuban peasant's home), their walls, the "blanket" for their Mulunda (head, a hat), and even their *ogungu* or *egboyi* (medicines).

An infusion prepared using the roots cures kidney disease, "because there is water with special virtues in the roots of the palm tree." Boiling it with milk sugar gets the kidneys back to work, eliminating and cleansing the body again. The old-timers prepare a beverage they call an "Amedoal," which they consider an excellent remedy for asthma and bronchitis: start with the boiled roots of a palm tree, then add a *marpacífico moñudo*,[45] unrefined sugar, and honey. "If the sick person is a woman, it is advisable to drink it with a little bit of a boy's urine; if the patient is a man, then with a girl's."

This tree's very useful fruit, the *palmiche*, is known as *mekeye* in Lucumí and *Yonyo kuamo* or *karondo* in Congo. It is also known as "wealth of the fields," since it constitutes an unbeatable food for pigs. It also has enormous magical virtues. The round seeds, about as thick as garbanzo beans, were used—like corn—as a substitute for money in the homes of *santeros* and sorcerers if a client was too *onukoju* (poor) and had nothing else with which to pay.

Both of them use *palmiche* according to their circumstances. Sorcerers disperse it as a very fine powder, mixed with various animal materials and dirt from a *fuiri* (*muerto*), to promote discord and disputes. To force a subject or a whole family to move out of a house: *palmiche* is burned, and the ashes are "prayed over" in the *nganga*, then put inside an egg, along with shavings from the *kiyumba*, salt, and vinegar; the egg is then smashed on the door of the house at midnight on a Monday or Friday. We will not belabor how much "harm" can be caused with *palmiche*; its roots and sprigs are also used to cure, when the tree flowers. The sorcerer bottles the juice from *palmiche*, exposing it to the sunlight and dew for forty days and nights, then employs it to humanitarian ends by administering it to patients suffering from arthritis. They are cured or relieved of their pain by massaging themselves with this liquid, which also soothes liver disease and burning pain from insect bites, as well as helping to strengthen patients convalescing from infectious diseases.

Additionally, an invaluable oil is extracted from the young *palmiche* for hair care. It cleans the scalp, refreshing and nourishing the hair's roots.

If the oil—which remains unknown to innumerable brunette and redhead beauties in the autumn of their lives—is extracted from the purple *palmiche*, it significantly stimulates hair growth, making it smooth and shiny. At the point just before they dry up, the seeds start turning black, and the oily juice they contain will darken the color of hair. One healer declares that it even prevents

---

45 DF-N: The *marpacífico moñudo* is a double-petaled, tufted variety of hibiscus.

gray hair! An old, rather simple riddle suggests the different aspects offered by the decorative bunches of fruit from the palm tree:

Blanco fué mi nacimiento
Morada fué mi niñez
Verde fué mi juventud
Negra fué mi vejez.

My birth was white
My childhood red
My youth was green
My old age black.

When the *palmiche* is dry, old, and black, the branches break off and fall, thereby providing the sorcerer with a broom—*bale, nmonsi, moana kamba*—that is endowed with the trees' considerable virtues. "Worked" with garlic in Cuba, it becomes the broom that witches from the Canary Islands ride when they fly through the air.

This *moana kamba karondo* is used to beat *Prendas* and the Yimbi if they manifest themselves in a way that is "*plana, muruanda*, troublesome," or bellicose. Many use it to hit the Abikus, settling scores with those twisted spirits that incarnate in children, although it is more common, from one end of the island to the other, to use *escoba amarga* branches for that purpose.

While a *yembu* or *osu* [leather strap] or a stick can also be used, brooms made with *palmiche* are the preferred way to punish stubborn trees that refuse to bear fruit.

In the company of another person and armed with a *palmiche* branch, the owner of the tree begins by striking the trunk of the tree with all his strength. Then the assistant, whose role is limited to that of a spectator who asks questions, intervenes.

"Why are you hitting the tamarind (or the mango, orange, *mamey*, etc.)?"

The owner, out of his wits, should respond, "Why am I hitting it, you ask? Because it's a lazy, despicable bum! Because it's cheating me and doesn't want to give me fruit!" And he continues hurling curses, breathlessly hitting the tree and threatening to cutting it down with an axe or burn it down unless the tree shapes up. He should seem furious, so the tree is made to feel, in equal measure, scared and ashamed at having been beaten and insulted—with good reason—in front of a witness.

Whoever executes this punishment—sometimes a good and mild-mannered housewife—walks away confident that they will not wait long to savor fruits the tree had hitherto refused to bear.

These beatings administered to trees that refuse to bear fruit "give excellent results," and they take place in many old, enchanting, provincial courtyards.

In short, the green fronds of the royal palm are used to represent *el monte* in the temple or *casa de santo*, and they are used to make the hut in which an *iyawo* of Ogun receives congratulations and homage after their consecration. Ogun, Ochosi, and Elegua should necessarily be "consecrated" ("asentarse") under an open sky, in the bush. Branches from royal palms and other trees and plants create the leafy, mystical atmosphere of the sacred jungle on any patio or corner of the *igbodu*.

Santeras use the dry palm fronds to make the skirts worn by the daughters of Oya on the day of their "birth" in Ocha, and they use them to make the fringes—*malipo*—with which they adorn their altars or the threshold of the door of the *igbodu*.

Marigwo [dry palm fronds] is also used in the ritual clothing of an Ogun.

The silent palm groves are habitually full of mysteries. Like the one in the Angeles mill, which hides a treasure guarded by a small, headless Black man who descends from the top of a palm tree and makes anyone who sees him lose consciousness, as well as a yellow cow that has spoken to Juan Montero there in a human voice. And we would be remiss not to mention the interest and personality, at times no less mysterious, of the *desmochador*, the man who climbs to the top of these trees to cut the fronds and the *palmiche*. He is permeated by the tree's magic because, in his solitude, he rubs shoulders with the gods and spirits who own the palm's vibrant stasis.

Invariably, the *desmochador* is a son of Changó. The orisha himself was a *desmochador*, and one of his tools or attributes—aside from the machete, sword, scimitar, the club (*kumabondo*), the jimmy, and the sledgehammer—is the axe: one with a single blade and another with a double blade, like the one associated with the cults of Crete.

Countless stories are told about the machete-wielding *desmochador* throughout our countryside, like the stories of harvesters of sugar cane, which is another plant belonging to Changó. In these stories, the *desmochador*—astonishingly—accomplishes work in a few hours that would normally take a man several days.

To cite a specific and . . . historic example (let us accept it on those terms), Antonio Díaz would prune an entire palm grove in a single day. His companions would see him at the top of the trees, talking to himself and roaring with laughter.

Remolino, a short Black man who was raised among palm trees, had a shy, retiring personality. "He looked like a Changó sculpted from wood," and he did the same thing. But he was also seen cooking enormous quantities of food in his shack—much more rice, jerky, and cornmeal than he could eat by himself, just like he was able to prune and harvest more palm trees by himself than seemed possible. "Nobody ever saw who Remolino gave that food . . . What would you deduce? Remolino, who was always among the palm trees, had special powers. He had profound knowledge. He had an affinity, *concumitancia* (*sic*),[46] with the spirits, and he had a crew of spirits that worked for him." Once he went to the Poleas mill, behind Ceballos, looking for work cutting sugarcane.

They asked him, "Don't you have a partner?"

"No, I take care of things by myself."

They tried him out. By nine o'clock, the overseer was frightened: Remolino was already finished, and he asked them to send him a cart. The driver was amazed too. He asked, "Don't you have a partner to help you put all that sugar cane in the cart?"

"He's on the way. But I'll put a few in while I wait for him." Remolino rubbed his hands together and spit on them. He said, "Here you go, driver!"

And the driver saw bundles of sugarcane raining down on the cart from every direction.

There are a lot of stories to tell about that man Remolino. Speaking in the language of sorcery: the *ada* (machete) cleared the ground by itself, or the *egungun* did it for him. He climbed the palm trees like a monkey; he would reach the top in one second. All *desmochadores* are—out of necessity—sorcerers. We would not dare to refute the informant who assures us that "whoever spends their time among palm trees will learn a great many mysteries without needing a teacher." This is understood, beyond a shadow of a doubt, by anyone who has experienced the fascination and enchantment of a palm grove, or felt the living presence that a royal palm can call forth.

46　DF-N: Cabrera's use of "(*sic*)" indicates a misspelling of the Spanish word *concomitancia* (concomitance), which she attributes to the anonymous teller of Remolino's tale.

UKANO MAMBRE

THE ROYAL PALM AND THE ABAKUÁ.

The spirit worshipped by the *ñáñigos* or Abakuá first appeared under a palm tree, on the shores of a river in Calabar.[1]

"Our religion was organized at the foot of the palm tree. That is why we worship it. That is why it is our symbol. The apparition happened in the palm. The palm was eyewitness to the mystery. Sikan was buried under the palm tree . . ."

The chosen tribe, the Apapas, first owners of Ekue, who brought these mysteries to Cuba, were also witnesses and trustees of the secret, as we mentioned earlier.

Sikan is often called Sikanekua Jembe Apapa, on account of the revelation she received. "But," an Akabuá tells me, "Akanabionke is her real name." She was the daughter of a king of Efo, the Iyamba Suwo Manatieroro. But Eroko Sisi appears as Sikan's father in some of the *ñáñigos'* manuscripts, while others assert that Eroko Sisi is the successor of Suwo Manantieroro . . . One Isue assures me that Eroko Sisi is the name given to Iyamba Suwo Manantieroro "after the miracle."

Based on brief interviews with the *ñáñigos* who were deported from Cuba and jailed in Ceuta, Rafael Salillas notes the name Akaureña Apapa, which the *ñáñigos* I have consulted seem to be unaware of.

---

1   DF-N: For more on the Abakuá, see Cabrera (2020); and Miller (2009).

Isunbenke was the mother of Sikan. Her brother was Ebion Benke. Her husband, an Efimeremo chief from the neighboring land of Efi, was named Mokongo, the son of Chabiaka. All of the confusion regarding the genealogy of Sikan can be easily avoided by merely remembering that the Iyamba—king of Efo—was her father, and Mokongo, Efimeremo of Efi, was her husband.[2]

One Abakuá identifies Sikan with a *nasakola*, who is a virgin and a witch from Ntacho, Kurinamakua. She predicted wars and illnesses, and all of the tribes of Efor were under her protection. In any case, Sikan went to the river daily to fill a clay vessel with water from the river that separated the lands of Efo and Efi, "because the peoples of Efi and Efo look at one another from opposite shores of the same river, and they drink the same water."

This river, sacred to the Abakuá: Afokando Odane Efi, Odane Efo Yenemumio, "which is nourished by ocean water," flows throughout the entire Carabali territory, according to the geography of another *abanekue*.

"Its waters bathe some thirty-four lands." Among these are Osamanga, Omariogo, Oromeke, Goyuma Iyan Obamaon, Okomona, Ibuguame, etc.

The place where the river divides the lands of the Efi and Efo is called "Otan Otara fiana Ubane" (or Obane). ("They call it the River of the Cross because its tributaries form the shape of a cross.")[3]

Sikan filled her clay vessel, and she was going along with it on her head when she began to feel as if the water inside was boiling, and shortly thereafter, she heard a terrible voice that said, precisely, "Ekue!"

A palm tree grew there, on the shore of the river. Next to the palm tree and near the riverbank, Sikan—horrified by the mysterious voice booming inside the clay vessel—dropped it.

Meanwhile, a Spirit—the Ireme Eribangando, which we already know—was purifying the road, and it killed a crocodile. As the sound of the mysterious entity rang out, an enormous snake—Erukuruben Nangobio, another sacred symbol of the *ñáñigo* society, the *majá*, which is venerated in all Reglas—wrapped itself around Sikan's feet.

2   DF-N: According to Ivor Miller, multiple and conflicting versions of this myth are documented in Abakuá treatises consisting of long phrases in ritual language that Abakuá members share, discuss, and debate among themselves; in rare instances they discuss their myths and liturgy with noninitiates like Cabrera (personal communication, 2019).

3   DF-N: The River of the Cross starts in the mountainous Southwest Cameroon, and runs into southeast Nigeria, emptying into the Atlantic Ocean in the port city of Calabar, Cross River State, Nigeria.

The Ireme Eribangando quickly freed her from the reptile, and the daughter of the Iyamba said these words: "Abasi Bomi Eribangando mutu Chekendeke." (My God, Eribangando is great.)[4]

Iyamba immediately learned of his daughter's miraculous discovery and said, "I'm going to speak with Eso." He went to the palm tree next to the river and grabbed the clay vessel. It contained a fish—Tanse, a supernatural fish, which was an incarnation of Abasi.

He hid the clay vessel in a nearby cave whose entrance was hidden by a crag, placed it on three stones, and ordered Sikan to keep as a grave secret everything that had happened .

When Akanabionke, the Sikanekua, terrified by the otherworldly voice in the clay vessel, dropped it and shouted "Dibo makara mofe!," the fish jumped and fell at the foot of the palm tree, landing in its ethereal shadow at the edge of the river.

Sikan's father, Iyamba Manatie Eroro, made the first *fundamento* with wood from the palm tree and the voice of Tanse—that is, the skin of the fish. Let us remember that the *fundamento* or secret is a drum, the *ekue*, a small "bongo."

(Ekue should—according to the religious canon—be constructed with wood from a palm tree, but it is substituted with mahogany or cedar.)

According to the version in some manuscripts, with which one of my informants agrees, Iyamba "heard Tanse screeching in the Clay Vessel," received his instructions directly, and "consecrated himself." In the river, "alone, with the palm tree bearing witness, Iyamba lifted the clay vessel to his own head." Later he gathered all of his tribe's elders and shared the secret, on the condition they swear a solemn oath to remain unbreakably united in the future, and he created the first Efo Partido or Potencia [lodge].

"The chief of the Efor people demanded that his men guard that sublime secret deep in the back of their minds." "And he swore that he would impose the death penalty on whoever divulged the most minute detail." The Efor lodge of the Apapas grew quickly. "The chief of the Efor was the most respected leader of all the tribes."

But Sikan entrusted her husband with the great secret of Efo, and he told his father Chabiaka . . .

"A short while later, Sikan went to the Efik tribe and married the son of Chabiaka, Mokongo Efimeremo. She told her husband that she had heard the Voice of Abasi, and that her father Iyamba was the greatest man because

---

4 DF-N: According to Miller, the phrase can be translated more literally as "Great God! Eribangando has a lot of heart [is brave]" (personal communication, 2019).

he knew the secret of God. And Chabiaka, her father-in-law, was envious of Iyamba's power."

After several secret meetings with the powerful men of the Efi tribe, Mokongo and his father Chabiaka decided to cross the river and demand—by hook or by crook—that the Efo tribe allow them to share in their mysteries. "The Efi wanted to have Ekue too." With Ekue's favor, the Efo had prospered noticeably, despite the fact that "they had no clothing, or music, or money." "They had God"... And it was clear that God protected them. Even though Sikan had sworn to keep quiet, "she let her tongue run away from her" in front of the powerful men of Efi, revealing the mystery possessed by Iyamba.

The men of Efik advanced resolutely upriver, some in canoes and others on land, making a lot of noise with voices and drums. Apparently they were willing to fight to obtain the Secret.

Some texts refer to a war between the Efi and the Efo because the latter refused to admit them into their society, let alone "give them" Ekue. Yet it seems that the two tribes or nations, later united by a common faith, made a pact before the fighting started. "In exchange for the secret, Efi gave Efo music and garments they did not have, and the means to season their food." The most complicated passages of these texts (which are nearly indecipherable due to the writers' poor penmanship and unconventional grammar) are clarified by some *abanekues*, either in their own words or while slowly moving an index finger, the nail broken and blackened like Monipodio's, over the passages.

When the men of Efo found out the Efi were advancing on them from the other side of the river, they arrested Sikan. Or—before the attack—they suspected that their neighbors coveted the mystery, and they kidnapped Sikan in Efi.

"Sikan went to the place where the lands of the Efi and Efo were clearly divided, and the Efike kidnapped her there. From that moment, the Efi assembled their expedition with help from Sikan, who provided them with all the details they would need to easily recognize the Great Power. The Efikes faced off with the Efo. The protest took place on the Afokando River, next to the palm tree. The Efori remained in a small boat. They agreed to give them the secret. Then the Efi kneeled, and the Efo baptized them in the river. The war ended, and they signed an alliance on the pelt of a tiger, using the hide as a flag, and paraded under it together, the Efi and the Efo, after paying homage to Ekue." The transaction took place under the palm tree.

"But not everyone in Efor agreed to give their secret to Efik. After they had acquired Ekue, a prince of Efo went to Obane to steal it." He went to Obane Kende Enyuao, but the guards blocked his way.

"Koifan, prince of Efo, snatched the Fundamento in Itanga, on the right branch of the Obane River."

"The first Efí ñaitua [initiate] was celebrated with blood from Obantue and Iyanga . . . [5] The population of Itanga consisted of men from Barondo and Oron-Oron."

Koifan took the "secret" to a sacred river—Neri, Odane Neri—and washed it in the presence of a spirit, the Ireme Tenkama. On that occasion, Koifan said, "Umon Neri mi akanara akuaramina." (Mother, I am washing with you in the waters of this river Neri to rid you of bad spirits.) Later Koifan sacrificed a rooster and, in the great silence of night, spilled the blood over the *fundamento* under a palm tree. Koifan said, "Embara enkiko Ireme Tenkama efion sarori." (I take the body of the bleeding rooster and give it to the Ireme, so the blood will also run through the river.)

The sacred books of the Ñaitua make it clear that when the people of Efik went to the river chanting battle cries, "Nasako ordered Ekueñon to hide the *fundamento* in a cave named Akuaberoñe, and to cover the entrance with a rock known as Asoga Itiaba. Near Akuaberoñe, there was a palm tree named Iguaroñe. Nasako sat at the entrance of the cave and said, 'Enebion efiana kamaroro itamo bafende.'"

A guard watched over the secret. But the people of Efi did not attack the people of Efo. Nor did the Efo attack the Efi.

If the Efo people did not attack the Efi, it was because the Efi were stronger and more numerous. And the people of Efi, who were stronger and more numerous, did not attack the Efo . . . because they did not have Ekue. And instead of resorting to violence, they negotiated in a parley. Thus, when the two armies confronted each other, after a string of questions and answers from one side to the other (from one riverbank to the other), which every learned Abakuá knows by memory and recites in the "*plantes*," the matter was resolved peacefully, with exemplary religiosity, when the Efik, at the end, responded to Iyamba's question:

> *Efi fokando agoropa?* (Do you agree?)
> *Mo mi afokando agoropa.* (We agree.)
> *Efi Efo abakuá abomiga!*

And Iyamba spoke under the palm tree. The men of Efi and Efo gathered beside the palm: the seven Efori chiefs: Iyamba, Isunekue, Isue, Enkrikamo, Nasako, Empego, and Abasonga. And the seven Efi Efimeremo chiefs: Chabiaka (father-in-law of Iyamba's daughter), Moni-Bonko, Ekueñon, Morua-Yuansa, Mosongo, Mokongo, and Enkandemo. They adored the Clay Vessel that was

---

5 DF-N: See Miller (2009, 273n134).

solemnly presented by Efori Kondo Iyamba Apapa. Iyamba leaned over the river, caught a fish with the clay vessel, and took it to the congregation gathered next to the palm tree.

There the chiefs washed their faces and feet in the river. (And whenever *obons* are initiated, they continue to wash their faces and feet with river water.)

"Iyamba washed the sacred clay vessel and repeated seven times, 'Dibo Barakandibo.'" And then, under the palm tree, next to the river, the chiefs of the Efi and the Efo together established the great accords of the Abakuá founded by the Efo-Apapa.

Following the union of the Efi and the Efo, Akanabionke Sikan Efori was sentenced to death. "To give her blood to the *fundamento*." It does not follow, either from the difficult manuscripts I have been able to consult nor the anecdotes I have been told, that this woman—adored equally by both the Efik and the Efo—was punished exclusively for the crime of treason, for "not guarding the secret of the apparition of Tanse."

Tanse, the wondrous fish, had died, and it was essential that his voice be heard again. "The voice of Tanse had to be brought to the *fundamento*." That is, to the drum: let us not forget that the terms *secreto, misterio, fundamento* all refer to the drum or *bongo* in which that mystery resides. The sound made by "fragayando yin"—rubbing fingers wet with blood on a giant cane stick which is pressed against the drum's skin[6]—"is the voice of the Spirit that comes to the drum."

"Immediately after leaping out of the clay vessel, Tanze was marked by Empego [with chalk], but she died soon afterward."

"When the fish that Iyamba had hidden in the cave died in the clay vessel, Iyamba called Ña Nasako, who was a one-eyed Congo"—like Enkrikamo, who lost an eye in the Efi territory—"and remained in Efo territory working as a sorcerer."

Nasako's "prenda" is called Mañongo-Empabia. Nasako "kept his sorcery inside a gourd, guarded by the snake Amiñange. His messenger and assistant, his *mayordomo-nganga*, was Akoumbre."

Nasako consulted the oracle with his seven *mate* seeds after saying these words: "Akaibeto enirome akaibeto." He would cure and "work," preparing his spells with seven plants.

In his zeal to revive Tanse, Nasako demanded the blood of Sikan because he believed that he could use it to revive Tanse. He condemned Sikan to die—"to die in order to resurrect in the drum." Embakara sentenced her, as we have already seen, under the ceiba.

---

6   DF-N: The "giant cane stick" refers to the giant reed (*Arundo donax*), also known as *caña brava.*

The execution took place under the palm. "At the foot of the palm tree, they performed the sorcery on Ekue, then they killed her"—Sikanekue—"so the voice, the spirit, would transfer into Ekue with her blood."

Ekuenyon—who was present at the first consecration, when Nasako recognized Ekue—decapitated her with a knife on orders from Mokongo.

Since then, a knife is never used to kill in the Ñaitua [Abakuá rites]. And since then, Ekueñon has the role of performing ritual sacrifices—as executioner—within the Order. He is the one who rips the heads from roosters, and he kills and butchers goats.

The blood of Embori [the goat] is offered to Ekue. The animal's legs symbolize the Four Heads, the four chiefs of the fraternity: the front right leg, Iyamba; the front left leg, Isue; the rear right, Mokongo; and the rear left, which symbolizes Mosongo, is offered to Cuatro Vientos [the Four Winds]. The entrails are offered to the Vulture. In remembrance of the first *baroko*, "when Iyamba swore his life to Ekue in the presence of Isue, Mokongo, and Isunekue," the Moropo (head) is given to Embakara, the *ireme* that guards all of the drum skins, "the transmissions of the Voice," so he can present it to Iyamba.

In one episode of the story, this Ekueñon—who became Iyamba's slave in the course of war, sacrificed Sikan, and served as Iyamba's guide—hides the Secret under some rocks, then sits the blind Iyamba on top of them, keeping him unaware of Ekue's location.

Ekueñon decapitates Sikan, then he carves her up. Her intestines, as we have seen, were taken by Mokongo to decorate his walking stick. The bones were reduced to powder and burned as incense. The head ... is taken by Nasako, and the eyes are stamped on top of Ekue. The martyrdom of Sikan under the palm tree was witnessed by the bird named Enkerepe Endobio, "a bird who talked when Sikan died," and a woman named Nahebia, who picked up Sikan's blood and head in her skirt. (This dress later became the banner, *sukubakarion*.) They say that a man, the Obon Akanapo, also saw Sikan die.

But the sacrificial blood of Sikan did not revive Tanse ...

The annals of Abakuá—convoluted, fragmented, and disconcerting for the layperson—say that, when Tanse died, Nasako used the skin of that supernatural fish to make a skin for the drum, "to make Ekue speak." But the fish skin did not have the right consistency, so the voice, naturally, sounded too soft: "As Tanse dies and the Voice fades, the voice of Morua—the enchanting singer who calls the Spirits to the *baroko*—"starts fading too."[7] Although

---

7   LC: When Morua—who fulfills the same role as the Apwon in the rites of Ocha—leads the singing with a fresh and sonorous voice, he is called Morua Yansa. He is called Morua Tinde when his voice is hoarse, and Morua Erikundi when he loses his voice completely and finds himself

Ña Nasako gave it the blood of Sikan, put her eyes on top of it, and covered it in the victim's warm mesentery to give it more strength, Tanse only emitted a weak sound . . . The transmission of the voice—fully, from the Spirit to the Drum—was unsuccessful this time.

It is not explained clearly, nor do my *abanekues* explain clearly whether it was the spirit of the woman Sikan they were trying to "take to Ekue," or whether it is the spirit of Tanse together with that of Sikan that Nasako insists on luring to the drum.

This first drum—in Efo—was called Ekue-muna-tanza, "when the transmission of the fish was performed" (by using the fish skin as a drum head). But "the transmission of the fish," as we mentioned, was a failure. They headed to the land of Eron Enta, where the king raised rams, and they sacrificed a ram—*eron*—and used its hide to cover the *"fundamento." Eron* did not work. It was too greasy. The spirit did not allow itself to be heard. So Nasako "looked" again, and he said that it was necessary to sacrifice a Congo—or, according to other sources, a Carabali Brikamo or a Bibi. "The first bongo"—"tambor de fundamento"—"that was made with a fish skin in Guanabecurabendo didn't work, and they used the skin of a Carabali Bibi for the consecration of the Fundamento. It was done in Ubane land, and the Baroko was named Baroko Beba."

In Enchemiya, there were many drum makers; "it was a land of drummers." A Congo fugitive heard the sound of the *ekon*, and he headed toward it. When he arrived, he found Morua Engomo and Aberiñan. They overpowered the Congo and took him to Nasako, who was working on the transmission of the voice. Morua Engomo *lo rayó* [marked him] and Aberiñan killed him.

(In low voices, many *ñáñigos* affirm that "here in Havana, the blood of a Congo was once given to Ekue.")

The spirit of that Congo, sacrificed by Morua and Aberiñan, left his image imprinted on a rock and became the Ireme Anamangi.

This Ireme Anamangi, "which appeared when the first Abakuá died" after the order was founded, officiates in the *ñampes* (funerary ceremonies). His mission consists of finding the spirit of the deceased Abakuá—"Anamagui besua sanga buke"—and guiding it to the "Fundamento."

But human skin—like fish skin and ram hide—muted the Voice. The last transmission was performed with the hide of a goat, and "Nasako heard the voice of Ekue," the voice of the spirit embodied in the Fundamento.

"Then Nasako said, 'Efori meta eremi neyo Ekue Sangari Tongo.' And he asked Iyamba for a rooster, to sacrifice it and spill its blood over Ekue."

---

obligated to play the *marugas* [shakers, rattles]. Morua Yansa sings in all the ceremonies, and his voice enchants the spirits of the dead, attracting them to the *baroko*.

"The spirit of Sikan told Nasako that the four *obons* should take an offering to the river; make a *mokuba* [ritual drink], and put it in the river to attract the spirit of Tanse."

In the end, Nasako managed to use his magic to take the Spirit to the Fundamento, the bongo. He said to Iyamba, "Abasi un keno yambumbe Ekue efo bongo mofe Abasi efori Sisi Iyamba." Previously the fish skin itself had told Nasako that the Empego drum—Kankomo Abasi—would substitute him, and that the goat skin "was just as sacred as the fish skin." This is why its owner received the following title during the consecration of Guanabekuramendo: "Munarosa embabia itakua yumba asere yumba Kufon endabo añeneru."

These first consecrations of "fundamento" are discussed in *ñáñigo* texts with an exhaustiveness that is as tangled as it is meticulous . . .

"In the first consecration, the Obons put the *fundamento* on Iyamba's head." (We can recall that Iyamba had already put the clay vessel onto his own head in the river.) "The *fundamento* was given blood, and they gave Iyamba a peacock feather and a feather from the rooster they had sacrificed. He gave this plume of feathers to Abasonga, who was then initiated by Ekueñon and gave thanks to God in the presence of the other *obons*."

"In Sangrimoto—the place in Usagare where the first consecration was performed—the king of Mutanga land watched the consecration of the Fundamento, and he recounted that the four chiefs brought their heads together over the Fundamento. Nasako 'looked,' and he said they needed to kill a goat and a hutia, then pay tribute to the river, so the divine Voice would come to the *fundamento*."

"After they successfully transmuted the Spirit of Sikan into Ekue in Guanabekura Mendo, an old king from Efo land told the three Heads assembled there (the three Abakuá) that none would be greater than the other because they were of one mind. And the king Efori Isun was given the title of Isun Efo; the king from Bakoko, the title of Situ Guanabakoko; the king from Usagare, the title of Ibonda Usagare." "Nasako performed the first transmission at Guanabekura, on the banks of the river" ("and next to the palm tree"). "He cleansed the sacred objects with leaves, and the Ireme Enkoboro attended the ceremony." (Guanabekura Mendo was the primordial theater for the great ceremonies celebrated by the society.)

Sacred historical precedents of the fraternity; prayers, discourses in esoteric ritual language (*lengua*), *enkames* that the *ñáñigo*—every *monina fitumbariyen* ("properly baptized")—should memorize in order to recite them when they are completely immersed in their role within the "plantes" or "juegos" of their Potencia), and which describe the original episodes of the Abakuá society, appear in disorganized fashion in these dirty notebooks, the *okobios'* manuals, worn with use and written with the most earnest lack of concern for syntax, sometimes in two different colors of ink. They have been placed in my hands by various *ñaitos* [initiates] as luminous ciphers to guide me through the dark labyrinth of their traditions.

The current Iyamba, Isunekue, or Mokongo—all the Abakuá dignitaries and *okobios*—"must study a great deal in order to carry out their respective duties."

A good memory is an essential requirement: the *ñáñigo* "juego" is an imitation, a repetition of situations, a copy or reproduction of the actions that took place at the origins of the society, and "nothing is done without being grounded in the knowledge of what was done at the beginning." That is, in the *illo tempore* of all myth . . . [8]

When Abakuá "play," everything reverts to ancient times [the foundation myth]. When the Ireme Aberiñan holds the leg of the sacred sacrificial goat, he is carrying out the same actions of the first Aberiñan who accompanied the first Mokongo to the first consecration. If Eribangando takes an offering to the river at sunrise, it is because he initially took it in Pete Yegasi Gabon.

Likewise, when he goes to gather river water in a *jícara* and presents it—as he did then—to Nasako for his sorcery. Or when the Isue of Usagare receives his attribute—the Sese Eribo—and exclaims, "Efimeremo Ñongo Abasi Kiñongo nnairan Sese Abasi," "and then he presented it to the moon, Embaran, in the presence of the other *obons*," to offer only a few examples.

"If an Iyamba doesn't know, in each and every moment, how to speak the way Iyamba spoke, if he's not fluent in *la lengua* [the tongue], he cannot be Iyamba, who is a great man wherever he goes . . ."

The foundational events in the sacred Abakuá history always take place near a palm tree, the witness to its mysteries, next to a river and a hill.

Abasonga (Otoguañe), a king from Oru, "was frightened" and fled into *el monte* when war broke out between the Efi and Efo tribes. He got lost in the forest when night fell. Morua looked for him by shaking the *marugas*: *Cha kacha kacha kacha*.[9] After a long time—seven years had gone by—Biabanga called him with a whistle, and Abasonga finally appeared, holding the scepter that shares his name, and the plume of feathers for Iyamba.[10] (Another mystery: Biabanga's whistle sounds exactly like: *tu tu tu . . . tu ti tu ta*.) He crossed

---

8   DF-N: The Latin term *illo tempore* is a phrase used in the Catholic liturgy to mean "in that time" or "in those days," suggesting primordial myth (akin to "time immemorial").

9   DF-N: Cabrera transliterates an iconic rhythmic pattern (*clave*) played by the shakers (*marugas*) in Abakuá music.

10   DF-N: Regarding Abakuá ritual communication through whistles and shells, see Miller (2009, 130).

a path to get to the river's edge and found all of the "derechos" [ritual offerings, fees] for his initiation under a palm tree.

Abasonga was consecrated. Iyamba and Isue entrusted him with the Ekue and the Eribo so he would guard it. Mokongo was a witness. "Abansonga stopped next to an old palm tree, killed a rooster, and fed the roots . . ."

In the land of Efi, Abasonga bore witness to "the covering of a gourd with a fish skin, which they used to make a sound with a *cañamo* [cane reed]. He heard the bongos, and he knew that they called the bongo Nglon in Kuna Mariba." And he witnessed other major events: "He saw the ceremony they celebrated on the oldest hill, in which the first bongo was sworn" (consecrated). Abasonga "swore an oath before the altar—*Abasi kankubio*—next to the palm tree." He killed a rooster and a goat, and he gave the blood and head of the goat to the Secret; he buried the legs and testicles; he kept the skin for the Enkrikamo and Ekueñon drums . . . "Ekueñon, whose duty—*Ekueñon sanga Abakuá akua ye bengo*—is to go hunt tigers in *el monte*."

But let us not tire the reader's attention any longer.

Ukano Mambre raises its incomparably slender trunk, sways its languid crest in the Abakuá sky, and anchors an eternal mythical present. For *abanekues*, it evokes the seminal episodes of their history: the revelation of Ekue "jumping out of the clay vessel and falling at the foot of a palm tree"; the sacrifice of Sikan, the heroine and victim of the Abakuá drama, the Sikanekue that dies—*okwa moropo!*—executed at the palm, her blood bathing, sanctifying the roots; and the birth of Abakuá, since the first *obons* gathered at the venerable tree and organized their society.

· BOTANICAL ·
ENCYCLOPEDIA

"Osain agweniyi owaloye iya mi
koye mi agroniga oni gwagwado
olo malu guda guda."

A

ABA

LUCUMÍ: ABA CONGO: FINLI.

OWNER: ELEGUA.

In the absence of swelling, the Owner of the Road lends his gifts to the leaves and roots. Boiled well, they are used in a bath to refresh and relieve a traveler's sore feet.

Its leaves are applied as a remedy for paralysis.

ABEY MACHO

Jacaranda sangreana D.C.

ENGLISH: JACARANDA.

A *PALERO* TELLS ME HE KNOWS IT AS ABANKE.

OWNER: INLE.

Its leaves and roots are used in a decoction to bathe the legs at the onset of lymphangitis.

It is also used for vaginal washes and treatments for skin rashes.

A glassful of this decoction during a fast will relieve constipation.[1]

ABRAN DE COSTA

Bunchosia media D.C.

ENGLISH: BUNCHOSIA.

OWNER: INLE.

For cleansing rituals.

A branch is used to make the sign of the cross over children to protect them from the evil eye, or to relieve them of pain. (*See also* ALBAHACA.)

---

1   DF-N: The original Spanish (*corrige el estreñimiento*) puns on the verb *corregir*, which means both "to correct" (i.e., fix, provide a remedy) and, idiomatically, "to defecate."

Its sap is used to make an ointment to reduce navels that protrude excessively in some children.

ABROJO

ENGLISH: THISTLE.

LUCUMÍ: EGBELEGUN, IGILEGUN.

OWNER: INLE.

For cleansing rituals.

Used in baths to counteract swelling. It is one of the ritual herbs of the Abakuá secret society, in which it is given the name *mendiba*.

ABROJO AMARILLO

Tribulus cistides L.

LUCUMÍ: BERI OGUN.

CONGO: FUGWE.

OWNER: OGUN; ALSO ATTRIBUTED TO INLE.

It is administered as a drink in spoonfuls to expel the placenta.

ABROJO TERRESTRE

ENGLISH: THISTLE.

LUCUMÍ: EWE CHORO, IGBELEGUN.

CONGO: NGUNGO.

THE *ÑÁÑIGOS* CALL IT MENDIBA.

It is used for cleansing rituals and to do harm. ("It is an *ewe* for *olugo*," to perform witchcraft.)

"Just as Christ's path was filled with thistles," one herbalist tells us, "it is very good for doing harm." Nonetheless, some unfortunate women—with whom nature has been too generous by giving them facial hair that is black and thick enough to merit the name "mustache," thereby exposing them to people's admiration in ways that are not always subtle—are definitely unaware that they can apply the sap of this plant to impede their hair becoming thicker and preventing the possible sprouting of an accompanying beard. With the patient, constant application of *abrojo* sap, Cape also assures us that it weakens the roots of hair follicles until it does away with these unusual mustaches.

Many *curanderos* [folk healers] recommend it for asthma. It is good for washing the eyes. It also works well in a poultice to ripen recalcitrant tumors, "those lazy ones that take a long time to burst."

ACACIA

Gliricidia sepium Kuth.

LUCUMÍ: SIDE, BONI.

CONGO: TOPIA.

OWNER: OBATALA.

A decoction made with its leaves and roots is used to combat dizziness and fatigue.

ACANA

Bassia albescens Griseb.

LUCUMÍ: IGI YAITA, TOBI, TAIMAN, AGAYU IGBO.

CONGO: ANKANA NTOLA.

OWNERS: CHANGÓ AND OGUN.

It is strong like the *guayacán* tree, and it is used for *ngangas* and protective amulets. Crosses made with *acana* ward off evil influences and curses, and they divert the evil eye.

Individuals who are clairvoyant and are frightened because they see ghosts at night can carry a small cross made with *acana* around their neck to avoid seeing them. The cross makes them run away.

Pimples are cured by boiling its leaves, bark, and roots, then using the liquid in baths.

It is "antibubero"—that is, it cures skin diseases. It disinfects wounds, and its resin is reduced to a powder and inhaled to contain nosebleeds. A decoction made from its leaves is taken several times a day to contain bouts of diarrhea.

ACEBO DE SIERRA (or DE TIERRA)

Ilex montana Griseb.

ENGLISH: MOUNTAIN WINTERBERRY.

LUCUMÍ: SUKUL.

CONGO: ABAYO.

OWNER: OBATALA.

For cleansing baths.

The leaves and roots in water (without boiling) are good for purifying the liver and to facilitate digestion.

Its bark, cooked with dry leaves and a few fresh ones, is administered very hot to sweat out fever.

ACEITERO

LUCUMÍ: TUKIO, EPAIRO, EBOIN.

CONGO: NKI.

OWNER: BABALUAYE; SOME *OSAINISTAS* ATTRIBUTE IT TO ELEGUA.

Its branches and leaves are crushed and prepared to make a rubbing oil with alcohol, aguardiente made from sugarcane, or aromatic wine to relieve rheumatic pain, improving and "even curing rheumatism."

It is used to treat numbness and muscle strain.

ACEITUNILLO

Hufelandia pendula Sw.

LUCUMÍ: IGIRORO.

CONGO: ANKAYO.

OWNER: ORUMILA.

A decoction made with the leaves is used to wash the hair. It leaves hair shiny and silky.

The roots are used to prepare an amulet for intellectuals who are impatient to gain renown.

ACHICORA

Leptilon pusillum (Nutt.) Britton

LUCUMÍ: AMUYO.

CONGO: GE.

OWNER: OBATALA.

Its leaves and roots are used in regular water (without boiling) for the stomach. It is also used to treat dropsy, bleeding, and "intestinal trouble." It is a diuretic. (Other herbalists praise its laxative qualities.)

ACHIOTE or ACHIOLE

Sloanea curatellifolia Grisb.[2]

LUCUMÍ: BABA IYE, ANUYO, ACHIOLE.

CONGO: GUE.[3]

OWNER: OBATALA.

The sap from its leaves and bark are drunk often to calm asthma. "It opens congestion in the chest."

ADORMIDERA

ENGLISH: OPIUM POPPY.

LUCUMÍ: ERUNKUMI.

Papaver somniferum is sold in pharmacies, but the wild poppy from the savanna (*Desmantus veigatus* Willd.) "puts

---

2   DF-N: This species is particular to Cuba. *See also* BIJA, the plant more commonly known as achiote (*Bixa orellana* L.).

3   DF-N: Pronounced in Spanish as "geh" (as in "get"). The Lucumí and Congo names are practically identical to those in the previous entry.

a toothache to sleep."[4] A decoction made with it is used to gargle. It can also be smoked in cigarettes made from clippings from this herb mixed with *mpolo Sambia* (incense from the church); "the critter causing the pain goes out with smoke." It is recommended in enemas as a treatment for dysentery.

To strike someone dumb and neutralize their willpower, the poppy from the pharmacy is mixed with Caraguá (a parasite in cedar and *guásima* woods, which some call *Guinda-vela*), nails from the feet of the person one wishes to enchant, and hair from the front or the nape of their head and their armpits. All of this is reduced to a powder and administered in a dark beverage: coffee, chocolate, or sweet wine (taking care to add cinnamon to the wine).

"*Adormidera* can be female or male," one Madre de Palo tells us, and it is the best herb on earth for swindling someone. To dominate someone, you take a nose ring and rope from an ox. The rope is powdered, then mixed with powder from *adormidera* and two branches from any tree, which have been worked and entwined and rub against each other constantly. All of this is mixed into coffee and given to drink."

In Matanzas, they call it Vergonzosa.

AGALLA DE COSTA

Randia aculeata L.

ENGLISH: WHITE INDIGOBERRY.

LUCUMÍ: BIEN.

CONGO: KLE-KUKUMENGA.

OWNER: ELEGUA.

When its leaves and roots are prepared in infusions, it is a great purifier of the blood. Its seeds are used in vaginal baths to contain hemorrhages, and as a treatment for leukorrhea.

AGAPANTO

LUCUMÍ: EBBLEH (?) OR WEBBLEH.

CONGO: NFEI.

OWNER: OBATALA.

"Its sap is used in bandages as a very good treatment for tumors that form in the head." For cleansing baths, it is used either boiled or without boiling.

AGRACEJO

Gossypiospermum eriophorus (Sw.) Urb.

LUCUMÍ: YAN.

CONGO: DOUKI.

OWNER: OBATALA.

It is used in the *omiero* for the *Asiento*. In the Regla de Mayombe, it is used for harm or good. "It works well powdered and mixed with *yaya* and a maiden's blood."

Some Mayombe *prendas* are prepared with *agracejo*.

Prepared in a decoction and drunk like regular water, it combats dropsy. It is also used to treat malaria. "It is very good for the stomach." The roots are used to treat gonorrhea.

AGUACATE

Persea gratissima Gaert.

ENGLISH: AVOCADO.

LUCUMÍ: ITOBI, ODOFRE, BIMA, AKATARA.

CONGO: AKUN, NFLU.

OWNERS: CHANGÓ, ELEGUA, AND OGUN.

---

4   DF-N: A play on words on the plant's common Spanish name (literally, "puts one to sleep"). Note also that the name given to the plant in Matanzas means "shameful" or "ashamed."

The purple fruit of *aguacate* belongs to Oya. That is why, in Matanzas, an *iyawo* of Oya is often initiated under a purple *aguacate*.

A decoction made with its buds is used to expel the gas produced by its fruit, and to treat a cough. The bud of the purple *aguacate* is used to induce menstruation. It is abortive. In a vaginal wash, it used to combat "flores blancas" [leukorrhea].

The seed is ground and boiled to remove wrinkles on the face. In a decoction, it helps loose teeth. And to combat bedbugs, it is used to wash furniture or bedding that has been invaded by this insect, which is as prolific as it is hungry for human blood.

AGUEDITA

Picramnia pentandra Sw.

LUCUMÍ: AIYA.

This is the Wakibanga in the Regla de Mayombe: Bulan Kane, Kabanga, Bemberiko.

It is very magical. It goes inside the *Nkiso*. "It is a highly respected Palo." It is also known as *Rompe Hueso* (Bone Breaker), because it knocks down and agitates its medium when it "mounts" them with such force that it is liable to break their bones.

Among its many virtues, it is able to ward off sickness. Using its roots, Baró cures the worst fevers and all of the secret illnesses of men.[5]

AGUINALDO BLANCO

Rivea corymbosa (L.) Hall.

LUCUMÍ: EWE BERE, FUN EWE NILE.

CONGO: TUANSO.

---

5   DF-N: Probably a reference to venereal disease.

OWNER: OBATALA.

It is used to cleanse evil influences, in cleansing baths, and in purifying washes for the home.

A decoction made with its flowers is used to control heart palpitations.

Using its flowers, leaves, and roots, a healer prepares a nutritious syrup that is very good for children. Its roots, boiled and used in a vaginal bath, cure leukorrhea. A decoction made with its stalks, leaves, and roots activates delayed childbirth. Its fresh leaves are placed over sores to heal them, although care must be taken to refresh them regularly.

AGUINALDO MORADO

Ipomoea crassocaulis Benth.

LUCUMÍ: EWE BEBERI, KOGGIKAN.

CONGO: NBUEMBO.

OWNERS: ORUMBILA, OGUN, AND YEWA.

With Ifa's blessing, its flowers, branches, and roots are boiled to calm whooping cough. Some include it among the *ewe* for *omiero*.

AJI AGUJETA (a variety of AJI GUAGUAO)

LUCUMÍ: TAULI, ATA.

CONGO: DUNGA.

OWNER: OSAIN.

The sap from the roots and leaves purifies the kidneys. "Take it in spoonfuls dissolved in soup or any other food. If the sap from the leaves and roots is mixed with the sap from its fruit, it creates a tonic that fortifies the tissues of the testicles."

AJI CHILE (also known as AJI CHILENO)

A variety of *Capsicum annuum*, Linn.

LUCUMÍ: KAYUEDIN, TWAULI, ATA.

CONGO: KUALAU, INKAKO, OR KINDUNGO.

OWNER: ELEGUA. (IT IS ALSO ATTRIBUTED TO OGUN AND OSAIN, THOUGH IT SHOULD BE KEPT IN MIND THAT THE LATTER IS "THE OWNER OF ALL PLANTS AND WORKS WITH ALL OF THEM.")

The sap from its roots, leaves, and fruit is used to combat the onset of typhus.

AJI DE CHINA

Salanum havanense Jacq.

LUCUMÍ: ATA, GUARU, ATA FINLANDI.

CONGO: DOMBE, NKAFO KIBULO.

OWNERS: ELEGUA, OGUN, AND OSAIN.

The sap from its fruit is excellent to clear one's eyesight. A single drop in each eye twice per week will be sufficient.

The juice from the roots and leaves combats tapeworm.

AJI DULCE

LUCUMÍ: GUARO, ATA YEYE.

CONGO: MOWNGO, INKAKDO MUNGUA.

OWNER: YEMAYA.

It fortifies the bones.

It is used to sauté some of the food for the *Santos*.

It is good to chew on to treat a toothache.

In a decoction, it is gargled as a treatment for tonsillitis or a sore throat.

AJI GUAGUAO

Capsicum baccatum L.

LUCUMÍ: ATA, GUAO-GUAO.

CONGO: YUMBE, INKAKO KINDUNGO.

OWNERS: ELEGUA, OGUN, AND OSAIN.

"A food used to restore a *nganga*."

Chamba—the aguardiente sprayed by *Padres* and *Mayordomos* over the pots, cauldrons, and amulets of Mayombe, and spilled over the neck of the sacrificial rooster or animal whose blood has been poured over the *nganga*—is loaded with *ají guaguao* to make it more potent. Spraying it among the participants of a "juego" always provokes a veritable explosion of sneezing.

This *ají*, reduced to a powder, is an important ingredient in all strong, harmful sorcery.

The sap is atomized in a spray to treat hoarseness.

To abort a pregnancy: "Three roots of *ají guaguao* are put in a jar with five cups of water until they are reduced down to three cups. But if the woman is six months pregnant, seven roots should be boiled in the same amount of water. Three days after drinking this decoction, the woman is given saffron oiled with a good dry Jerez sherry, and it's done."

Ripe *ají guaoguao* is ingested as a pill to combat hemorrhoids.

In massage oil, it is used to combat rheumatism. For fever caused by a cold, it is cut into tiny pieces and mixed into a very hot decoction made with orange.

AJO

Allium sativum L.

ENGLISH: GARLIC.

LUCUMÍ: JOKOJO, EWEKO.

CONGO: KUALANGO DIANPUTO, NIASA KUMPIRIKUNANSIETO FIALONGONDO, NDUNDO, DUNDUNGONFIALA.

It is not used to season the food of Lucumí *Santos*.

To counter the evil eye, carry it on your head, held in place with a pin.

"The people from the Canary Islands taught us that a string of garlic has the ability to neutralize any evil. That's why it helps to add a clove of garlic to the incense, *mirra*, *benjuí*, laurel, and brown sugar, when you purify the inside of houses. To ensure that money is never lacking, garlic skin is burned in the kitchen fireplace."

It provides sustenance for strong *ngangas* and *prendas*. It gives them strength. But some *prendas* can be killed by garlic. They are weak and cannot withstand it.

Garlic domesticates the snakes who "guard" the *nganga*.

"In Trinidad, witches would put garlic under their arm to fly. They would go to the mountains, where they would meet up and have their *bembés*, flying through the air and playing a little drum."

"Garlic is a cure-all."

We know that, ground and applied as a rub, it is the usual antidote against scorpion, spider, and wasp bites.

It dissolves bladder stones, and it improves rheumatism, gout, and syphilis. "It disinfects the lungs from tuberculosis and alleviates lumbago. It cures pain in the feminine or masculine sexual organs, and indigestion; mange and ringworm. And its sap softens stubborn calluses."

Some claim it is good for losing weight.

The *mal de madre* is "a ball that forms and spreads around the belly. If it goes under the rib cage, it can be deadly. That ball is principally the result of unhappiness, and poor eating. If not from sadness, it is due to a lack of appetite, but garlic cures it." The patient is treated, on an empty stomach, by massaging her belly with cooking oil.

The hand should slide smoothly, always in the direction of the navel. Meanwhile, two cloves of garlic are placed in the patient's nasal cavities. Following the massage,

she is given three roasted garlic cloves, followed immediately by a spoonful of *aguardiente de Isla*, another of *agua de la Vida de las mujeres*, and finally a spoonful of orange blossom water. After two or three more minutes, she is given a decoction made with *ruda* or marjoram. During the three days of treatment, their food will consist solely of garlic soup overloaded with oil. To finish the cure before administering the decoction during the final treatment, a poultice made with *galván macho* is placed over the navel.

The treatment for *mal de madre* only involves *santeras*, and it is accompanied by a prayer with which I am unfamiliar.

Empacho is a condition in which "food stays in the stomach and does harm, causing pain and sometimes fever." Massages like the one used to treat *mal de madre* can be employed to treat it, adding a little salt to the oil. One starts with the belly of the patient (generally a child, as children are most commonly afflicted by *empacho*), then moves to their back, rubbing their spinal column by going down from the back of their neck to their waist. The rubbing and pressing become more forceful over the skin covering the spine until a pop is heard (women from the Canary Islands call this *opilado*), indicating that the *empacho* has been removed. This procedure is performed before breakfast on three consecutive mornings.

Along with the pushing and pulling, a decoction made with garlic root, skin from white onion, egg shell, the membrane of a chicken gizzard, cumin, and three *anón* buds. During the treatment, they will eat a light diet: orange juice, broth, and hot sugar water. On the third and final day, they take a powerful purgative made from castor oil or Erba brand milk of magnesia.

A crushed clove of garlic and *nkanda* (leaves) from the *yerba de aura* plant are

A

prepared as a decoction to cure *el padrejón*. (Regarding *el padrejón*, see *Reflexiones Histórico Físico Naturales Médico Quirúrgicas* by Lic. Francisco Barrera y Domingo. Ed. C.R. Havana.)[6]

For treating intestinal worms, three large cloves of garlic are peeled and boiled in three cups of cow's milk until they are reduced to one and a half cups, then given lukewarm as a drink to the child, so they expel the worms.

A highly recommended and well-known protective charm: a clove of garlic, *yerba buena*, and parsley are carried in a small white cloth bag. Before using it, it is advisable to take it to seven churches and wet it in the holy water from each of these temples. At the moment the bag is to be wet, one says, "Free me from my enemy, whoever wishes to do me harm, and give me health and good fortune."

AJONJOLI

Sesamun indicum L.

ENGLISH: SESAME.

LUCUMÍ: AMATI.

CONGO: NDEBA, GUANIYILA, GUANGILA, KOLELE BATAMA PIMPI.

OWNER: SAN LÁZARO.

It is taboo in the houses of this Orisha.

If a child of San Lázaro eats sesame, they become ill. They might even die. "They can't even look at it."

It is true that they are strictly prohibited from eating *iru*, grains: beans, lentils, pigeon peas, etc. Especially lentils, "which

are the very sores of the Leper" (Orisa Adete).

Neither can they be eaten by the *iworos* who are children of Obatala. Nor can they be eaten by *nganguleros*. Naturally, it does not mix with the *nganga*. Only the *Santos* eat it without danger.

If sesame is scattered, it provokes an epidemic.

It wards off evil when it is mixed with the bark of the *corojo* tree, quicksilver, and guinea pepper. "And it also attracts evil" . . . Babalu Ayé works *bilongo* using sesame.

Its seeds are used in a decoction to alleviate asthma, administered immediately at the onset of an attack. It strengthens the heart.

Powdered and drunk in coffee, the seeds are an aphrodisiac.

It is also drunk by women nursing children to increase their milk production.

ALACRANCILLO

Heliotropium indicum L.

ENGLISH: INDIAN HELIOTROPE, INDIAN TURNSOLE.

LUCUMÍ: AGUEYI.

CONGO: BIWOTO.

OWNER: OBATALA; SOME *SANTEROS* ATTRIBUTE IT TO OSHUN, AND OTHERS TO OKE.

It is used for cleansing baths. In a decoction, it is drunk like regular water to calm internal irritation or irritation of the skin. The roots, branches, and leaves reduce hemorrhoids.

ALAMBRILLA

OWNERS: YEMAYA, OSHUN, AND INLE.

Look for it in artesian wells. It does not belong in the *omiero*.

6   DF-N: Cabrera and María Teresa de Rojas edited and republished *Reflexiones* under the same Ediciones C.R. imprint as *El Monte*. The name C.R. is an acronym combining the initials of their surnames, Cabrera and Rojas.

ALAMO

Ficus religiosa L.

ENGLISH: SACRED FIG.

LUCUMÍ: OFA, ABAILA, OGOLE IKIYENYO.

CONGO: MANLOFO.

OWNER: CHANGÓ.

It is one of the principal trees consecrated to this orisha. It is included in the *omiero* for the *Asiento*, as well as the *omiero* used to consecrate and wash his attributes.

When Changó is angry, he is soothed with *álamo* leaves, along with *rompe zaragüey* and *culantrillo*.

"The first time they played drums for this *Santo*, they did so in the shade of the *alamo* tree. It is Changó's cloak." His stone is covered with *álamo* leaves and stored in a small container made from cedarwood, painted red and white. The leaves are also used to decorate the altars and thrones of his chosen ones.

Changó "likes to eat at the *álamo* tree," and that is where his usual offerings are deposited, tied with red ribbons.

The ram, which is always offered to him, is offered *álamo* leaves before being taken to the room where it will be sacrificed—symbolically, by Ogun himself—at the *otán* that houses the orisha.

If the "messenger" animal, which has already been prepared for the sacrifice by the *santeros*, eats the leaves, it is a sign that the god has accepted it gladly. Otherwise, the ram's throat will not be cut.

To purify his children and protégés, Changó orders them to bathe with a decoction made with *álamo* leaves.

Cleansings using the sap of the *álamo* tree rid the body of all negative influences. "The *álamo* picks up all the evil and takes it away."

To dissolve even the worst witchcraft and ward off evil spirits from a home, use it in washes.

It is often also used in powders that are dried out and sifted, mixed with plantain, and—after being prayed over—used for good or harm.

To radically destroy a *bilongo*, *álamo* leaves are mixed with *salvadera*, *yerba buena*, *prodigiosa*, *abre camino*, and a piece of camphor. Some people add a teaspoonful of ammonia to this, along with smoked fish and hutia.

Mayomberos do not use the *álamo* tree.

Changó used the *álamo* to close the road to Orula's house:

"The aleyos couldn't find their way because the road was hidden by the alamo trees, so Orula found himself without work.

"He had offered Changó a ram, but he kept delaying in giving it to him. The *apestevi* reminded him of the debt."[7]

Orula kept his promise, the *álamo* trees blocking the road disappeared, and the *aleyos* returned to the diviner's home.

It is used in medicinal baths to fortify the person, to reduce swelling in the legs, and to cure rashes.

It is used in a decoction to fortify the nervous system. The seeds are used to prepare a liquid that is not very oily and helps grow and darken hair.

It is also used against albumin in pregnant women, in which case it should be drunk in great quantities. Midwives administer it in vaginal washes.

---

7   DF-N: Commonly written as *apetebí*, the term *apestevi* is a very unusual rendering of an epithet for female godchildren, companions, and wives of Ifa priests. See Elebiubon (1994).

A

The small fig, or *ori*, is mashed into a paste and applied to reduce hemorrhoids.

J.A.C. has approached me to ask permission to cut a branch from one of the old, lush *álamo* trees that offer shade on one side of our house.

For what? When we talk, smoking a cigarette and drinking a cup of coffee, this *iworo* of Changó tells me what he intends to do with the branches. Although spiritism attracts him very much, and he has "the prayer card of Alán" (Kardec), this son of Chinese and cinnamon-colored ancestors is a great devotee of the orishas. When "the rope tightens around his neck," he seeks the orishas' protection and prefers them to *los hermanos del espacio* ["the otherworldly brethren"] who are contacted in spiritist ceremonies.

J.A.C. consulted a *babalawo*. He wanted to know the cause of certain disturbances and difficulties he had been experiencing lately. And the "sign" that appeared was Dariko.

(Gaitán says, "Kukufe kuku adifa fun Ogun Ochosi Yekunsa Karere fun Oya.")[8]

The reading of this *odu* or "sign" is more or less as follows: The subject of the consultation—in this case, J.A.C. himself—has offered something to a person who will visit them soon and complain that they have not kept their word.

"Yes," J.A.C. says. "It's true. I promised one of my cousins a few lottery tickets."

In fact, he needs some money for a project he has in the works. ("A little loan sharking," in fact.) He needs to give thanks, because this time his wife is

pregnant, and it is a child of Ogun in her belly.

"I already knew that, because Mercé the *santera* had said it to my wife. But, because a long time ago—well, that's what happens, you start neglecting things and the next thing you know, they've started making trouble." Now all the *santos* are upset with him. He sees *babalawos* and does not greet them with the proper respect. ("Because, setting everything else aside, *babalawos* are something else, and I go through long spells when I don't want anything to do with those people.") That is the source of his setbacks, as well as the reason for often feeling irritable, annoyed, "bored with work and everything else." Ifa warns that this irritable state could lead to a sudden spilling of blood in his workplace. In short, in order to reconcile himself with the *santos* and to keep his situation from deteriorating, he should cover the stone or image of Changó with *álamo* leaves. For this purpose, he wants to choose a beautiful branch. But this is not the only thing J.A.C. needs to do. During nine days, he will need to play the *achere*—maraca—for him.

And if he happens upon a funeral in the street, he should cover his eyes and face if the deceased is female, or remove his hat if the deceased is male.

He has a son in *aratako*, in the countryside. At that moment, J.A.C. was speaking with me confidentially. He was not sure, but he believed that he had a son near Sagua de Tánamo, although he had never accepted any responsibility in that regard. Nor does he intend to take care of the boy: the boy has a mother, and the mother has another husband. He is warned that his older brother is very jealous of him, and another "new" one—whose whereabouts are unknown—is destitute.

---

8   DF-N: Dariko (or Darico) is an epithet or nickname for the Ifa divination sign Oyekun Osa, and Gaitán's recitation ("Kukufe kuku adifa fun …") is a prayer or musical verse (*suyere*) associated with it.

It is true that J.A.C. is considering going away to the countryside. But he should not leave without first making offerings, because, under the current conditions, he cannot cross rivers or oceans, or ride locomotives. Doing so would be very dangerous.

A daughter of Changó ("he was already certain of it, and he knows who she is") has cursed him . . . and if he neglects himself, it will catch up with him. "That damn . . ." But he should not curse. He will be told of the death of someone living under his own roof.

("It's an old neighbor who's awfully *matunga* [elderly] and falls down all the time.")

J.A.C. should not eat *quimbombó*, nor should he split paying a bill with anyone. In the end, the "sign" advises him to be very cautious and work fast, because they want to kill him on a street corner. J.A.C. will follow all of this advice down to the last letter; his peace depends on it. There he goes, on his way with his *álamo* branch and a friendly contribution to the *ebo*, which—fortunately—will "contain" the harm predicted by Dariko. This consists of a rooster, three ears of corn, a black hen, a fish, and $12.60.[9] (If this *odu* appeared for me or anyone else in a consultation with Okuele, we would be told the same thing.)[10]

---

9   DF-N: Throughout, monetary amounts should be understood in historical terms; they refer to Cuban pesos in the early and mid-twentieth century, not US dollars.

10   DF-N: *Okuele* (*opele, okpele, opuele,* etc.) refers to a divination chain used by Ifa priests. In this passage, Cabrera and/or her informants regard Ifa priests (*babalawos*) with particularly high esteem; in the following paragraph, however, Cabrera offers a counterpoint by way of a nostalgic critique of mid-twentieth-century Ifa diviners.

I later learned that the *ebo*, which works to "uproot" the evil and attract goodness, can be performed with the tail or excrement of a horse, a *güiro*, a rooster, two small chickens, and $16.80. Although, nowadays, most *babalawos* forget—unadvisedly—to illustrate matters with an example from the orature of the *odun*, I also learned that the *babalawo* could have told J.A.C. that Dariko, under similarly adverse circumstances, had gone to Orula's house, where Orula made *ebo* with all his belongings and ordered him to whitewash the walls of his house. The example—a *pataki*, or historical narrative—is the following: Obatala, the Virgen de la Mercedes, was surprised by a sudden storm out in the street, so she took shelter in the recently whitewashed house of Dariko. A short time later, Dariko showed up at the *ile* of Obatala, in the middle of another stormy night. His clothes were soaked by rain, and the Santísima Virgen de las Mercedes gratefully made the most of the occasion to return the hospitality she had previously received in Dariko's house. She gave Dariko new clothes to replace those that had been wet and splattered with mud. And, most important, she gave him luck; she gave him "Aché." Sometime later, Dariko had amassed a considerable fortune and became very self-important and conceited, like everyone who prospers quickly. Riding on his horse, Dariko passed by Orula, who was walking on foot, and greeted him in a distracted way, without coming down from his horse; instead Dariko quickened his pace. Orula was hurt by this treatment, which he considered an insult to his dignity, and he entrusted Eshu with punishing Dariko for his arrogance and stupid ingratitude.

Eshu reduced him to a state of misery and hardship, surrounding with the dangers that had threatened him before he had made *ebo* . . .

A

ALBAHACA

Ocimum basilicum L.

ENGLISH: BASIL.

LUCUMÍ: ORORO.

CONGO: MECHUSO.

It is used in cleansing baths, for good luck, to sanctify and cleanse bad influences, and against the evil eye. Burned with incense, it wards off evil spirits. It is crushed and used in a poultice to treat swelling. In decoctions, it is used to treat the stomach. They say that an infusion of its leaves and flowers soothes headaches. To cure an illness that is suspected to be the product of the evil eye, one gathers three boughs of basil, a glass of water, a candle, and the prayer to San Luis Beltrán, which is indispensable in these cases. If the patient—usually a child—is not too weak to sit up, the ritual specialist performing the cleansing makes the patient hold the candle and glass of water. A crucifix is also necessary, which is to be placed inside the glass with the basil. At the beginning of the recitation of the prayer, the *santiguador* takes a bough of basil in one hand and a crucifix in the other. If they do not know the prayer by memory, they will read it from a prayer card held in one hand while holding both the basil and crucifix in the other hand.

As they recite the prayer, from memory or by reading it, they make the sign of the cross over the patient with the basil—first over their forehead, then their chest, belly, knees, and feet.

Afterward, they recite three Our Fathers, three Apostles' Creeds, and three Hail Marys. The candle remains lit—for San Luis Beltrán—until it burns out. Strictly speaking, this should be done three times by three different people, each of whom will clean the person who is being afflicted by the evil eye, without each knowing the identity of the others.

In order for the operation to be effective, these three people should not cross paths; ideally, they will not know each other.

Sometimes, three people cannot be found—or, as often happens, people will excuse themselves from the requests of the cursed child's parents or close kin because they believe the cleansing involves a risk of picking up the "harm" themselves. In this case, one person can execute the operation by reciting the Prayer to San Luis Beltrán three times and lighting three candles. Even if they are not prone to picking up "the harm," either because they possess a protective charm or because their "body has been prepared," they should take care to purify themselves afterward by striking their body with nine boughs of basil, or by taking a cleansing bath.

In the Regla Kimbisa del Santo Cristo del Buen Viaje, which is distinguished by the marked syncretism of its practices, basil—*mechuso*—is the chosen herb for "cleansing," and San Luis Beltrán and Zarabanda are the principal "influences" in this Catholic-Congo-Lucumí spiritist sect. The "brothers" cross themselves on Fridays, which is the most suitable day, although it is always beneficial to cross oneself, "because it removes curses and bad luck."

For followers of the Lucumí tradition, it is not one of the ritually essential herbs, and old Baró claims that those scratched in Mundo Campo Santo and other branches of Mayombe do not use it.

Nonetheless, basil baths are very popular. The *ñáñigos* or Abakuá use it like a hyssop, and they use this fresh, fragrant herb a great deal.

Their famous "diablitos" or "íremes" represent the African (Carabali) spirits of the secret society's founders in the "plantes," or oath-taking ceremonies—which we might describe as their mysteries—on the occasion of inducting new members into their fold through a secret ceremony that is inaccessible to noninitiates. Later, during various other ceremonies, they dance in front of the lay public while carrying a bough of basil, which they use to constantly purify themselves and everyone in attendance at these celebrations. Ñáñigos call basil by the name *akamaruru. Abanekue Abasi akamareru.* (Ñáñigos are baptized with basil.) *Emboko ses monifamba! Emboko sese agwyaka nairion obonekue masenisen!* (*Diablito*, strike this man who has just taken the vows of an *abanekue* in the *fambá* room and is now your brother.)

Three baths with all different species of basil, white roses, and *azucena* (Madonna lilies) are enough to saturate oneself with their prophylactic virtues and attract positive influences. For seven days, the basil plants should be in an isolated place, where no one sets foot. Meanwhile, an egg yolk with honey should be kept next to the subject's bed, as close as possible to their pillow, for five consecutive days, then tossed into a tall, dense pasture. Seven corn balls are cooked without seasoning, then left at seven street corners; the person performing this ritual should calculate the locations so that their house is located at the center of those seven street corners.

Moreover, when a neophyte falls into a trance in some "cruzado" Kimbisa temples and the Padre knows which *palo* (spirit) is taking possession of them, they spray their body and the *nganga* or cauldron with *chamba*, the ritual aguardiente. Once the new *ngombe* (medium) is possessed, their eyes are immediately washed with *mamba* (water) that has been prepared with basil, *grama* [grass], dry wine, and other ingredients, in order for them to see things in the other world.

In some Mayombe temples (though not all), basil is used. Sixto, an *osainista* from Perico, confirms that the Lucumí "only use it for rheumatism, and the real fanatics of the basil plant are the Congos *cruzados* de San Cabruya."

"We use basil to resolve those cases of delayed marriages, when the man drags his feet and says, 'We need to be patient. I don't know when we'll be able to get married.' The basil is prepared with a perfume that has led many women to the altar: basil juice, toasted hay, holy water, and orange blossom extract, along with water from Oshun's clay vessel and dry wine or *aguardiente de Isla*."

ALBAHACA ANISADA

Ocimum basilicum, var. *anisatum*, Hort.

LUCUMÍ: TONOMIYO, ORORO, NISE.

CONGO: MECHUSO.

OWNER: OBATALA.

Boiled or not, it is used to purify or "cleanse" the body.

Its aroma is embedded in colored handkerchiefs—the color depending on each person's guardian Angel—and used to counteract the evil eye.

A decoction made with its branches and roots is used to treat pain from colic and gas.

ALBAHACA CIMARRONA

Ocimun sanctum L.[11]

ENGLISH: HOLY BASIL, TULSI.

LUCUMÍ: ORORO.

CONGO: MECHUSO.

OWNER: OSUN, THE MESSENGER OF ORULA AND OLOFI.

BOTANICAL ENCYCLOPEDIA

A

11   DF-N: Also known as *Ocimum tenifluorum*.

Pure sap from the roots and leaves of this plant is heated and applied to body parts where *nigua* (chiggers) are found.[12] The old man J. from R., who suffered from chiggers, says this remedy is just as effective as the one that involves applying very hot, caustic ashes from tobacco leaves.

ALBAHACA DE CLAVO

Ocimum micranthum Willd.

LUCUMÍ: BERENRE, ORORO.

CONGO: GWANGAS, MECHUSO.

It used for cleansing the body.

Its sap is poured into the ear to stop buzzing or pain, "clearing away the wind" that can enter the ear and produce an uncomfortable noise.

With a decoction made with its sprouts, Odua relieves the pain of menstrual cramps. The juice from its leaves, which is extracted by pressing the leaf between the thumb and index finger, is applied to the eyes to cure a stye.

ALBAHACA MONDONGUERA

LUCUMÍ: ANGAITO, ORORO.

CONGO: MEDALO, MECHUSO.

OWNER: OGE.

Boiled, it is used in "cleansings" of the body.

The sap is used to treat hives when they first appear.

Mondongo (tripe) is cleaned with this species of basil to give it a pleasant odor.

ALBAHACA MORADA

Ocimum basilicum L.

LUCUMÍ: ORORO.

CONGO: MECHUSO.

OWNERS: OGUN AND YEMAYA.

It is included in the *omiero* for the *Asiento*.

In decoctions, it is used to treat the stomach.

ALBAHAQUILLA (also known as ALBAHACA DE SABANA or ALBAHACA TRAVERSERA)

Eupatorium villosum Sw.[13]

LUCUMÍ: SINBIA.

CONGO: ORUTA.

OWNER: BABA[14] OR OCHOSI.

It is used in regular water to treat dry or bloody straining when defecating. It is also used to treat fevers and malaria.

---

12 LC:

> *El que tiene nigua no puede caminar*
> *no puede caminar y si la saca,*
> *se vá pasmar se vá pasmar.*

The person with chiggers can't walk they can't walk, and if they take it out, they'll be lame, they'll be lame.

Regarding chiggers, an eighteenth-century dictionary cites a remedy employing hot ashes and provides the following description: "A type of very small flea from the West Indies. Like the crab louse, it attaches itself, especially to the feet, irritating the area where it buries itself between the skin and flesh. There it makes a nest and produces its larva in a small sack. Therefore, great subtlety and caution are necessary to remove it. If it bursts, its larva multiply incredibly quickly, thereby making a cure almost impossible."

---

13 DF-N: *See also* TRAVESERA.
14 DF-N: Here, Baba—which translates literally and generically from Lucumí as Father—most likely refers to Obatala, not (as in numerous other instances) Babaluaye.

ALCANFOR

Cinnamommum camphora T.Nees & Eberm.

ENGLISH: CAMPHOR.

LUCUMÍ: TEEMI.

CONGO: GOUGORO.

OWNERS: CHANGÓ AND ELEGUA. (CALAZÁN ASSERTS, "NO. IT BELONGS TO OBATALA.")

The sprouts and roots are boiled for cleansing baths which, if taken in time, will prevent an illness predicted by the diviner.

Solid camphor resin found in pharmacies is also used as a preventive measure during epidemics. All of the orishas recommend it.

When one visits a hospital or has a contagious sick person in their home, a small piece of it should be mixed with toasted corn kernels and carried in a small bag made from canvas or red cloth (hidden in one's clothes or bosom).

It has the power to ward of illness. It is an anaphrodisiac.

"Because camphor melts, women who betray their husbands will work them with camphor, so the husbands become indifferent and stop bothering them."

Its leaves and boughs, soaked in alcohol, are used frequently to massage rheumatic patients. The same preparation is used to treat blows, contusions, and sore muscles. And ". . . it helps soothe those women who are on fire with the uterine fury (*sic*): to calm them down, you cover their private parts with compresses made with alcohol and camphor root."

ALGARROBO

Pithecolobium saman (Jacq.) Benth.

ENGLISH: CAROB TREE, LOCUST TREE.

LUCUMÍ: AFOMA, GUINANDE, KIEREDAN.

CONGO: FLECHEO, NKUNIA KUYA.

OWNERS: OGUN, CHANGÓ, AND BOKU.

A decoction prepared with its leaves, sassafras, and limoncillo is good for treating cough. It must be included in the *omiero* of an *Asiento*.

It is highly venerated. Its leaves can also be used to cover Changó.

Its roots are used for *prendas* and protective amulets. It feeds the *ngangas*.

"You bury the Prenda under an *Algarrobo* tree. You offer it a rooster there, and when you unbury it . . . what comes out of there is a frisky bronco."

At midnight, the foliage of the *algarrobo* is filled with souls: "You can hear the *muertos* murmuring; the tree moves the earth, and the branches burst out." The *mayombero* that "works" under an *algarrobo* at that hour will "feel an avalanche of spirits descend on them."

It is included in an amulet that should accompany cowards and those who lack tenacity and determination to accomplish an objective.

Mayomberos use its sap to prepare a mild poison. But administered prudently, in drops, it strengthens the brain.

> *Pluma pavo yán vuela,*
> *Yán vuela . . . la kangarobo*
> *Ya caen la kangarobo . . .*

In this *mambo*, the *nkisi*, through its medium's mouth, says its spell has already taken effect: the turkey is already flying, and it has already come down from the *algarrobo*.

The pulverized resin is used to treat sores. Its leaves are shredded to reduce hernias.

ALGODON

Gossypium barbadense L.; *Gossypium herbaceum* L.; and *Gossypium arborum* L.[15]

ENGLISH: COTTON.

LUCUMÍ: ORU, ORO.

CONGO: NDUAMBO.

OWNERS: OBATALA BABADE, OCHANLA, BABALUBO, AND ALAMORERE.

Creator of the human race. Father and Mother of all the orishas. King and Queen. "From a pair of Obatalas, all the rest are born." "They are couples." "There are sixteen Obatalas." (The number sixteen is sacred for the Lucumí.) (There are sixteen orishas and sixteen signs in *dilogun* and Ifa divination.)[16]

"Obatala is the same thing as Santísimo, as God. Our Lord. And Obanla, a female Obatala, is the same thing as Nuestra Señora la Virgen." ("Obanla is Our Lady of Mercy, La Virgen de las Mercedes.")

"Olorun sent Obatala to the earth to do good, to be the king of the planet and rule in his name. Obatala is Father and Son and Holy Spirit. And *oeko-bo* (a hermaphrodite). Yemu and Baba descended trembling. They were afraid. They said, 'Eruba mil!'"

"Obatala is the Father, and the *santos* are the kids. His children."

"He has white sideburns."

"From one couple, all of the rest were born, beginning with Odua, Oduaro, and Iyemu, his lady—here in Cuba, Santa Ana. Odua's necklace has sixteen white beads and eight red beads. He rides a horse, carrying his *Obe* (a machete) at his waist and going out to fight. For the ancients, Odua is the same as Olofi, the root of the other Obatalas."

"The wife of Odudua is named Oduaremu."

"God in person: Iba Ibo, who represents the Eye of Divine Providence, the idea of the Divine."

"My child, don't say it that way, Iba Ibo. He is called Oba Ibo. This is the Obatala that blinds. Very old. It's the mystery of the gourd. Although he is the true one, he doesn't allow anyone to see him, and whoever sees him loses their sight."

"They say the female Odua, known here as Santa Ana, is called Oduaremu? I disagree! She is called Oño oro." ("Ena oro," Manuela, a Changó mount, corrects.)

"According to both Lucumí and Arará paths, Nana Buruku is a truly primary Obatala. It is two in one: female and male, Nana and Buruku."

"And in the Arará path, you also have Akkado, adored by the people of Vuelta Abajo (from the province of Pinar del Río), a San Joaquín."

"Agemo or Alagema, an old female Obatala, la Santísima." (Ageme or Agama is also the lizard, which belongs to Obatala and serves as their messenger.)

---

15   DF-N: A few long entries in the botanical encyclopedia (e.g., ALGODON, COCO, LAUREL) are similar in scope and approach to the essayistic chapters in the first part of *El Monte*. The most robust entries among these can be read as microcosms of *El Monte*—that is, smaller-scale iterations of the book's overall structure—that contain its main elements: elaborate mythological stories, ritual formulas, vivid quotations (some attributed, others anonymous), and philosophical precepts. Likewise, longer entries' narratives and data—that is, images, themes, and ritual formulas—recur in fractal-like iterations whose various scales effectively mirror the bifurcating, organic quality of plants' physical structures.

16   DF-N: *Dilogun* (also *dilogún*, *dinloggún*, *dinlogun*, *merindilogun*, *mérindínlógún*, etc.) refers to cowrie shell divination. See Bascom ([1980] 1993).

"Obamoro is another Obatala that dresses like Jesus of Nazareth here, an old *Santo*. He really disfigures his mount when he descends. And Baba Fururu, also San Joaquín, is the one that sits and commands instructions to the juniors."

"Ocha Olufon, all dressed in white, very old, with a very, very white head of hair, like a cotton ball. It is sometimes called Obalufon. Sometimes a king, sometimes a *santo*. As you already know: Ocha, Oba, Olu, *oluo* mean *Santo*, king, and owner. And *fon*? Or *fun fun*? White. Yes! Ochalufon trembles all the time, but since he is a warrior, he trembles more from rage than from cold, and he always wins the battle. When he descends, hunched over and trembling, he is saluted with this chant: *Ara dide o didena, ana fu no tolo o odidena*."

"In Palo Monte *cruzado*, Tiembla Tierra is Obatala. It is very risky to have him. You cannot bother him, much less hit him. Mamá Kengue is Obatala by the Congo path."

"Obalufon was the first one who spoke, and he gave humans the power of speech and the right to be human, to couple. *Foko!* He governs: *Obalufon oba lolu*. He is more peaceful than Agiriñan, not to mention Yaguna, the one who started all the wars."

"Ochagriñan, Aginiñan—*Obatala Agiriñan, jekua Baba!*—is the oldest of all the Obatalas. He is hunched over, weak, and tremulous. He trembles so much that he's unable to take off his cape. He hides from the cold breeze. He walks with crutches, but Oh! When he gets upset, he tosses them aside and charges with a machete. That old man Agiriñan is fierce. He does not descend often. 'Agiriñan Koluko.'"

"Eyuaro, Eruadye is the pampered, only daughter of Olofi and Iya. She married Ayaguna, San José. She does absolutely nothing. The beloved daughter of Olofi, light of his eyes! He never allowed her to make the slightest effort; her hands never knew work. She does not move— not because she is *oyu-yeru*, lazy, but because she is too divine and *odaradara*, precious, to be bothered. She is always seated: still, *yoko*, *chole*. Just the way she looks in the church, on the golden throne.

"Ayaguna married her because he was able to take sixteen human heads to Olofi, who had asked for them. Thanks to Orula, he did not have to cut off the heads himself: another suitor was bringing them back from *el monte* in a sack; Ayaguna surprised him and took the sack."

Eruadye is a static figure. "She is a Santa that is never upset. She does not move. For Obamoro to intercede, she needs to be addressed first."

Ayaguna, on the other hand, "is the one that lit the gunpowder. He is *edyila*. Wherever he goes, he's armed. He spread war in the world and took it everywhere. He fought his way all the way to Asia. He works with gunpowder because he's the king of war. Olutuipon. This one does not tremble. He dresses in white like all the Obatalas, males and females. When he arrives, his *omo* are dressed in a white outfit with a red stripe on his chest. This Obatala fights on horseback, and a big toy horse is always included in his regalia."

As they do with Changó, *santeros* place a wooden horse in their *igbodus* to honor this bellicose god. If the dimensions of the horse allow it, he sits on top of it and simulates riding it when he possesses his *omo*.

Ajaguna is the youngest Obatala.

One of his selected devotees repeats to us what his elderly godfather told him about his Patron Saint:

A

When Olofi divided up the world, he distributed duties among his children. Ajaguna was chosen as the Creator of Fights. He revolutionizes everything. Wherever he goes, it's war. He governed a large part of Africa, and he fought with all his neighbors. His nature is revolutionary. Olofi called him to task, "Why are you governing in such a quarrelsome way? I want peace. *Alafia* for everyone!" He answered, "Baba, you sit there, but the blood does not run through your veins." Everyone complained to Olofi about the constant fighting. Ajaguna was always looking for fights. Then Olofi removed him from power in Africa and sent him to Asia. There, Ajaguna found peaceful, calm people. They never challenged one another or argued. "This place is too calm. I can't stand being here!" He asked one of the men, "How can you live here, resting all the time?" "Yes, sir. We all live in peace." "You never fight?" "Never." "Well, now you're going to need to fight. I am the warrior, the chief, and there's no calming me down." Ajaguna marched off. He went to visit a neighboring tribe and said to them, "Go and dominate those people. They're dumb." He went back to the first town and rallied them: "Here come the invaders. You must defeat them! You have no choice but to defend yourselves, to become the vanquished or the victors." And in that way he did not leave anyone in peace. He started war here, there, and everywhere, sowing discord until war blazed over the whole world. And the people went back to complain to Olofi again.

"Ajaguna, my son, please! I want peace. I am peace, Alamorere, the white flag. Prima chincha boré!"

"Without discord there is no progress."

"And discord advances the world?"

"By making one who has two want four and making the most able triumph, the world advances."

"Very well," Olofi said, "if that's how it is, the world will go on until the day you turn your back on war and lay down to rest."

That day has not arrived.

Africans themselves were quarrelsome. They were the most beloved children of Olofi, the elders. It was Ajaguna who brought white people with their rifles to Africa, and they took cloths, drink, jewels, and—of course—like a blind person seeing for the first time, everything they saw astounded them. That is how white people dazzled African natives with their baubles, colored bits, fake jewelry . . . Rubbish! There was gold and ivory there worth more than anything brought in, and the Arará waged war against the other people, to take Black people and sell them to the white people in exchange for gunpowder, rifles, and wine. Black people themselves are to blame for slavery, maybe even more than white people. (Oh, Ajaguna, my father! *Ajaguna ori maro ekun ile Olodumare ewe kabe ayuru olo iwafe olo afi oyagu yanu ota fachorro eguo.*)

"Among the Obatalas, there's one called Ekenike. It was the *Santo* of Leonor Jorrín. He is also a warrior, elderly, and trembling. He doesn't come down very often, but when he does visit, you need to cover the whole Ocha room in white cloth, all the way to where the drums are outside. Then the mount is dressed in white and given a toy rifle. To make him go outside to dance in front of the *bata*,

A

you detonate a cap of explosive. (This is what was done to Leonor when he was possessed by Ekenike.) The *Santo* is surprised, jumps up, and decides to start his dance."

"In the land of my elders, they worship an Obatala Bebenike Olu mio."

"What was the land of your elders, Irene?" (Irene is a man.)

"Iyebu. Fierce Lucumí, known for being brutes. They were *onigo ara oko*,[17] *montunos* (countryfolk). Here, they couldn't do it, but over there, among themselves, they ate people, like the Bibi. At least that's what they said. There were many of them at the sugar plantations. They had *eya* (tattoos) on their bodies." Baró says something similar about them. And according to Serapio:

> Although one of my grandmothers was Yebu ... The truth is, they were considered evil savages here! But the Musulungos were even more brutish! When they said a Black person came from Musulungo, it was understood they were an animal.
>
> That old lady was big and strong. She looked like a man. The way she talked was more mixed up than the devil himself, she could cut and pull more sugarcane than three men, and she gave birth to more kids than a guinea pig. She baptized the kids herself. An African baptism. Yebu. She put a handful of salt in her mouth and spit it on the kids' head. I saw her do it.

"Strange," says a *santera* when I asked her if she knew this practice,

> because Obatala doesn't eat salt. Why? It's Babalu Ayé's fault ...

Baba lived in *el monte*, and he arrived at Obatala's house after everyone had already eaten. There was only one plate of food left, and Obatala gave him his own plate. When Obatala went to cook for himself, there was no salt left. So if Obatala doesn't eat salt, then it doesn't seem appropriate to put salt on the child's head—which, like all our heads, belongs to Obatala. Washing with Obatala's herbs, that makes sense. What I know about African baptism is that when the child was born, they would give them a name, then they would cry for them, because whoever is born comes to work and suffer, to carry out a sentence. They would cry for a newborn, and they would celebrate a person when they died, because they were leaving this life, becoming free after completing their sentence. That's what the Lucumí and Congo did. That's why, when I was child—even though it was prohibited by the police—they would dance the *muerto* around in the coffin, carrying it on their shoulders on the way to the burial. Four pallbearers carried them singing and marking the rhythm with their steps, so the coffin looked like a boat bouncing on waves ...

Guayabito con botas
Tu no quieres, tu vas pá'allá!

Mouse in boots
You don't want to go, but you're going!

And in another verse, they would sing,

Remando pa boboya.

Rowing to the other side.

---

17   LC: This [*onigo ara oko*] is the name given to *guajiros*, those who live in the country.

The custom of "dancing the *muerto*" was so deep-seated that the authorities ordered that the burials of Black people be attended two by two, and no more than that, and "wearing their ordinary clothing, not *diablito* costumes or anything else." Back when my old friend Calazán was still a child, although the costumes had already disappeared long ago, and despite the Bando (which also prohibited mourners and companions to stop at taverns and cafes during funerals), there was often lots of alcohol as the coffin was carried on shoulders, strutting around and showing off the beautiful cadaver, their "carabela" [companion], all the way to the final resting place, pouring out aguardiente along the way.

This *sonsonete* [little song] comes from the funeral of Guayabito con Botas, a small, chubby Black woman who sold buns, pork rinds, and tortillas. She was knock-kneed, her feet were notably small, and she wore booties and enormous shoes.

Her unique footwear earned her the nickname, which made her furious, and which men and little kids shouted at her to torment her. The vendor would then put her merchandise down, leave it on the sidewalk, and unleash a string of cuss words. But even when nobody bothered her, she would stand with hands on hips and ask, "Who's going to call me Guayabito con Botas? I dare you!" That nickname proved fatal. Singing to Yemaya at a *bata* drumming—that is, Yemaya herself "in the head" of the *iyalocha* Yeye Menocal—pulled her aside, "Guayabito Quita Medio," made her stagger and fall down. Guayabito received a hard blow to the chest. She complained, "Yemaya, Yeyá Menocal has killed me." And Yeyá Menocal, the famous *santera*, was accused by Guayabito's old employers, important people who loved her very much. Menocal was forced to defend herself before a judge, but she was able to prove her innocence. They say that Guayabito con Botas died as a result of that divine blow. She was famous for her boots, her insults, and her rich vocabulary of improprieties and insolence, and for her buns, her fried beef, and her tortillas. She was one of the comical popular figures of the Havana of 1880, and the very same people who tormented her mourned her. "She was given a grand burial, and we carried her to *ile yansa* singing,

> Guayabito con Botas
> Tu no quieres, tu vá pá llá.
>
> Guayabito con Botas
> You don't want to, but you're going there."

Following this digression, my informant continued,

> Talabi is an Obatala that pretends to be deaf.
> Yeku-Yeku, Humility and Patience, the Divine Trinity, or the Face of the Divine. With this one, like Ochagriñan, you have to ask for everything backward.
> You want money? Ask for poverty. You want health? Ask for illness! That way, you ask for the opposite of what you desire, so they grant it. You can't look at Yeku-Yeku directly, because he can blind us suddenly. His *sopera* [tureen, vessel] needs to be opened little by little while averting one's gaze. He can't be in bright light. It can't be loud around him. He's bothered by noise, as well as light and air currents. (The *soperas* of all the Obatalas are only opened to feed them. Obatalas are particular that way; they are all very delicate/sensitive.)

Obatala, as Our Lady of Mercy, "takes the prize in adoration."

"Obatala is merciful. *Kofiedeno!* She takes pity on us. She is the world's refuge and dries all of our tears. When Olokun flooded the earth, the people were saved, thanks to Obatala. She made a ladder so everyone could go up to where she was. She submits her children to many trials, making them struggle and suffer, but they never die of hunger."

To summarize, we have the following "roads," avatars, manifestations, or names of male Obatalas:

Son of Olofi, sometimes confused with Olofi the creator, or the creator himself, Odua: Oba or Igba Ibo ("Fodu Daa, for the Arará"). Baba Fururu. Ochagriñan or Akiriña (as old as Odua). Obalufon. Obamoro. Ayaguna, "the most refined." Male (from the land of the Arará).

Females: Yemu, or Oduaremu, Oremu, Agueme. Obanla. Yeku-Yeku-Oño or oro. Eruadye, Nana.

(Salako, a devotee of the Regla Arará whose name identifies him as a child of Obatala, mentions the following: Odua-Oduaremu; Odua-Yomu-Yemu; Yeku-Yeku; Oba; Ocha Lufon; Ocha Griñan; Ocha Orolu; Oba Ibo; Obamoro; Ayaguna, Acholo; Akeyabiamo; Katioke; and Talabi. He also specifies: Mabu is an Obatala. Frekete is Yemaya, but also enters the category of an Arará Obatala. Nanabuluku is also "a very elevated Obatala.")

Some *iyalochas* identify Odua-Yomu with Mary Magdalene: "She is Takua and also lives with the Arará."

"The Obatala who followed Olofi and came down when the world was created is Edegu, the one belonging to Efuche."[18]

In the end, "there is one Obatala, no matter how many names we want to use. Female Obatala, Iyala, or male Obatala, they are all one," without excluding the intrepid and combative Ayaguna. This one, because of its character, is sometimes identified with Changó, though he came before Obakoso:

Well, the first generation of *santos* in Oyo—where all the great ones came from, the *odaradara*— are the Obatalas that formed the family of Ocha, which is demonstrated by placing their *sopera* in the highest position on the altar, so that Obatalas are always above the other *santos*, because they are the Fathers—Mother, elder, youth—and owners of the world. Obatala lives on Oke, on a hill, and they are all refined and sensitive to cold. They're always *tutu*, cold.

And they are supremely meticulous; anything dirty offends them. They can't touch anything that isn't white and clean.

Ou, Ododo, the flower of the cotton plant, has the enviable privilege of being the cloak and blanket of Obatala, covering him perennially, "living" next to Orishanla.

This honor provoked a terrible jealousy among the *Eiye*, the birds. They conferred with the sun and the moon. They defamed poor cotton, asking the one to burn him with fire, and the other to dry it with its coldness. But the innocence of the naive Ou triumphed: at the edge of death, he made *ebore*, and the birds were revealed to be despicable and wicked schemers. Then Obatala ordered that the birds would poke their eyes when they attacked the cotton plant,

---

18 DF-N: Efuche was a seminal, African-born *olorisha* in Cuba during the late nineteenth and early twentieth centuries. See Brown (2003a, 330); Mason (1996, 18); and Ramos (2003).

which he equipped with small defensive thorns.

All of the Obatalas, Bibinike—the greatest ones, which are most delicate and extremely sensitive—are wrapped in cotton, as are the objects and symbols that belong to them.

The *sopera* contains the white stone—*oke*, the materialization of the great Orisha ("Obatala is supported by her and eats through her")—and four other smaller stones, all of which are covered in cotton, adorned with necklaces of white beads, and sixteen parrot feathers. These stones are placed inside the *sopera* along with "tools of the santo," its symbols: a serpent made of silver or white metal, the sun, the moon, the *paoye* (a silver hand holding a royal scepter in its fist), four silver bracelets, two ivory eggs, eight or sixteen *okoto* (snails), a piece of cocoa butter, and a piece of *cascarilla* [chalk made from egg shells], all of which is covered with cotton.

("Yeku-Yeku is not embodied in a stone: it consists of cowrie shells and is accompanied by a ball taken from a cow's stomach.") A ladder is another tool of Obatala, signifying salvation, as well as a chair, "because he does not sit on the floor."

Obamoro, "because he is Jesus of Nazareth, can be given all the tools of the Passion, if one likes." A globe of the earth is a symbol of Odua, who made the ball of the world. We find among these attributes two identical dolls—a pair of *ibeyes*. Plants, as we know, have the virtue of firing up or soothing the orishas that are its owners. Cotton soothes Obatala "when he is *iroro*," and it soothes all of them.

Obatala, Our Lady of Mercy, La Virgen de la Mercedes, "is the one that brings peace to all the disputes and fights of the *Santos*. In her presence, all of them

control themselves. She subdues them with her *ori*. In a *bata*, if Ogun arrives furious, watch Las Mercedes come down, place her hand on him, and calm Ogun. If he has behaved badly, Ogun says *etie mi ikano*, I am sorry, and he cools off. Las Mercedes is his mother, but he was conceived as the result of a misstep by his mother; to conceal the error of her ways, she abandoned him in *el monte*. Nobody knew she was his mother. There, in *odayare* (the savanna), she left him with his complete *aché* (all of his powers). Elegua was nearby, cutting *garabatos*; cutting and singing, he overheard a baby crying. Running over, he saw the baby and picked him up. Elegua raised him in the bush, and as Ogun grew powerful, the world recognized his merits. Ogun marries Yemaya. He wages war and more war, and the war never ends. At the height of the fighting, Yemaya said to him, 'No more war, Ogun!' The *ochas* all met to try to end the war, and Yemaya said to them: 'I will end it!'

"She created the deluge. She stirred up the bottom of the ocean. The warriors were forced to flee to *oke*. Obatala sheltered them and planted his white flag on the earth. Ogun went to *el monte*, ashamed of his defeat, *ofo*, that a woman had forced him to flee. Las Mercedes intervened with Yemaya Olokun, so the water returned to run its normal course." ("Obatala had to tie Olokun down with chains!")

"He forgives many errors on the part of his children—at least the first time they're committed. She intercedes so that the other *Santos* forgive their own children. She almost always serves as a godmother and defender. She is sweet and composed. That's why her dance is *lile*, gentle and serene."

That is different from the warlike, agitated nature of the unruly Ayaguna's dance. All of the Obatalas dance when they visit us, peacefully and—like Oya—hold a whisk made from the tail of an ox or cow, its handle covered in white beads. (The beads decorating Oya's are red.)

"That's why, whenever we have revolution, disruptions, war, *iña, kuruma, ika,* or epidemics—*tianka*—here on earth, we put white flags inside our houses, up high on the spot where there is most movement; for example, on the wall that divides the living and dining rooms, or behind the front door to the street. Everyone—children, the elderly—clean themselves with cocoa butter, coconut, popcorn, and *cascarilla* chalk.

"In a small bag made of white cloth, you place four or eight pieces of cocoa butter, then an equal number of popcorn kernels, small pieces of coconut, and a little bit of *cascarilla*. Then, beginning with the forehead and the head, you rub it all over your whole body, asking Obatala for peace and health. After the cleansing, you dispose of the bag in an open field or in the bush."

Obatala always performs this calming action with cocoa butter and *cascarilla*, "which softens, refreshes, and clarifies."

"The trouble is when Obatala gets upset! Then all of the *Santos* intervene. They rub a lot of cocoa butter on him. And it's difficult to calm him! When he is ill-tempered, I wrap his *sopera* in four pounds of cotton, and I make offerings to him for eight days. I start by offering him a big serving plate of white rice, and I spread rice on the floor of the whole room. The second day, a tower of meringue decorated with silver dragees. The third day, a milk custard. The fourth day, four liters of milk in a white cup sitting on a white plate. On the fifth day, *arroz con leche* (rice pudding) on eight white plates. On the sixth day, *arroz con leche* without salt, and cocoa butter. The seventh day, white pumpkins. On the

eighth day, a jug of *champola*,[19] and—if they're in season—sixteen *anón* fruits [custard apples]."

All of these offerings are deposited on a hill, or in the shade, in *el monte*.

"Since cotton is *kamae irori*, or *irosi ilori ilori* (a pillow) for Obatala, it's the base and covering for all rogations." Along with *obi* (coconut), *ofun* (chalk), and *ori* (cocoa butter), it is an indispensable element in rituals for the *Santo*, owner of all white things. On one occasion, in order to save someone from death, Oya requested nine *iye eiye para kodi* (parrot feathers), nine *bollos* (buns), nine *olele*, nine *eko*, nine cobs of corn, nine yards of printed cotton cloth, nine needles, nine pesos and ninety centavos, and nine cotton buds, among other items.

When Iku is in the house (which old *santeros* tirelessly say can be avoided by covering all the holes on the floor, cracks in the walls and bottles, and turning empty vessels upside down so death finds no cavities in which to hide), Obatala makes her come out of her hiding place and frees the sick person of her menace through another *rogacion*, which will require a white sheet, four white doves, plenty of cocoa butter and palm oil (*manteca de corojo*), a basket with snails, a *jícara* (gourd bowl) with *sara eco* (*dengue*), and sixteen pesos with eighty centavos.

A subject threatened by that most undesirable of guests will also dress in white.

Often, when death delays in departing from a household, or when it resolves to not leave alone, but rather in the company of a gravely ill person languishing in their bed, in spite of the *ebos* or the *ebo iparo ori* that have surely been

---

19   DF-N: *Champola* is a drink made with soursop pulp, sugar, and milk, usually served with crushed ice.

performed for them, then the harm can be transferred to a doll representing them, or a stick the same length as the person.

> *Cuando Dios no determina*
> *O no remedia los males*
> *No le valen los cordiales*
> *Ni los caldos de gallina,*
> *Ni le valen los collares*
> *Que le puso su madrina*

> When God does not resolve
> or remedy a sickness
> tonics are no use
> and neither is chicken soup
> and even the beaded necklaces
> their godmother put on them are
> worthless.

It is advisable to hang an *odo* (or *edun*) from the headrest of the bed, or at the threshold of the bedroom. Or a stuffed animal of a monkey, a toy—although it stands to reason that, under such circumstances, a real monkey would be ideal—"to distract death." Or to entertain death with its monkeying around and calm death's impatience. Or perhaps the monkey imposes respect, because it is a very sacred animal—like Ayanaku, the Elephant—with a close relationship to Obatala (the monkey is Obatala's secretary), so his presence protects and extends the life of the sick person.

"Along with coconut and cocoa butter, which soften hearts, and chalk, cotton is fundamental. Obatala is never without cotton."

"If we can't perform a rogation for someone's head without cotton," as we shall see below, "then neither can we make an offering to Obatala without cotton. Everything that is offered to Obatala on the head (of his devotee)—coconut, the blood of a pigeon, meat, fish, fruits—is covered with cotton. The last thing placed on the head is always the crushed

egg shell (*cascarilla*), which cannot be stained by blood."

Naturally, the cotton fleece is brought close to the mouth to speak to Obatala. "We implore him to illuminate and strengthen a mind that has been exhausted by an excess of intellectual work, or to calm and clarify a mind tortured by passions or bitter worries, a mind that is *daru*, confused by tangled and dark ideas." *Olochas* advise these rogations to Obatala, owner of all heads, to all those who use their own heads more than they should. "The effects on thinkers are marvelous: writers, doctors, professors, financiers, bankers. Everyone who heats their brains should perform a rogation with cotton often."[20]

In short, a discussion of all of its applications in magic would make this note too long. "We use cotton balls to cover the sight of an enemy, so they cannot see us undoing their work, or to do what we want without raising suspicion."

Healers take advantage of the therapeutic qualities of this shrub, which grows wild in Cuba to a height of approximately two meters. Made aware of its size, the "foreign" (*aleyo*) reader will not confuse it with the gigantic silk cotton tree, which throughout western Africa is an object of devotion analogous to that inspired by the ceiba tree here. These two, along with other colossal trees on the continent, were likened by Black slaves—in terms of veneration, cults, and magic—as being equally inhabited and protected by deities and powerful spirits.

To soothe earaches, green buds of cotton are submerged in lukewarm water, then squeezed slowly to allow several drops to fall inside the ear.

---

20 DF-N: This particular prescription would be well suited to Cabrera and her circle of intellectuals and artists. *See also* ACEITUNILLO.

Ground seeds mixed with mutton tallow are used to make a poultice that dries tumors quickly. A decoction made with the seeds is taken in cases of bronchitis or asthma. Another, made with its roots, is used to regulate menstruation; in a strong concentration, this decoction works as an abortifacient.

The flower is used in concoctions to eliminate impurities that keep people in ill health, and—by moral extension—help individuals who have not purified themselves completely.

The leaves of the cotton plant are employed in the *omiero* of the *Asiento*.

Like *obi*, *coco* [coconut], cotton cannot be dissociated from Obatala; therefore, we will return to speaking of the eldest orisha when we explain the importance of that fruit in the divination and ritual of the Regla Lucumí.

Regarding cotton and the morphology of the ear, we add this account from Calazán:

> Well, then. You should know, Miss Lydia, that at the very beginning of the world, heads only had one eye. A Congo told me that at a funeral wake, where everybody told little stories to keep ourselves entertained the whole night after singing and praying to the *muerto*. But those stories the elders told, they said they were true. And why wouldn't it be true (it was such a long time ago!) that heads didn't have two eyes? The thing was that back then, both ears were exactly alike, both of them the same size—not like today, when one turns out to be longer than the other.

This afternoon Calazán is feeling, as he puts it, "the need to speechify, *soro-soro*." Many *pataki* come to his mind:

The reason ears are not the same is because of a thieving bird named *eiye ole bole*, the so-called Wom . . .

My father, may he rest in peace, would tell me about a man in ancient times, one of the first humans, who was *ara-tako*. He had a grown son, and he was so strict that everybody trembled whenever he opened his mouth to speak. He had planted fruit groves, but somebody was stealing the fruit. "The day I catch whoever's doing this, I'll kill them!" But the *ole* (thief) was a black bird with a white collar.[21] The man set a trap in his trees, and he caught the bird with its feet stuck to a branch. He took the bird to his house and warned his oldest son that if he let the bird escape, he'd rip off the son's ears.

They put the bird in a cage. When the man left to attend to his fruit trees, the bird spoke to the son and his younger sisters:

"If you open the door to the cage just a little, I'll give you a bunch of fine beads from my own body." And he defecated a mound of little balls of coral. *Iyon, iyon, iyon!* . . .[22]

The young man in charge of the bird and his sisters grabbed some thread and strung the beads.

"If you open the door a little more, so I can see the open sky, I'll shit jet black beads. *Iwayu, wayu, wayu!*"[23]

---

21   DF-N: The image of the bird evokes Catholic priests' white collars and black garb.
22   DF-N: *Iyon, iyon, iyon!* is onomatopoeia (akin to "Yum, yum, yum!"). Cf. the story of Eruba in chapter 7.
23   DF-N: In Lucumí and Yoruba, *wayu* (*waju*, *iwaju*, etc.) suggests facing or moving forward,

He kept his promise. Then the bird told them that if they opened the door more, there would be no trouble if they opened the door all the way, and he would pour out beads of every color.

He left a mess of *elekes*: yellow, green, blue, and the little painted ones. There were enough beads to make necklaces for the entire celestial family. But the bird got away. And when the father returned, as the oldest son sat silently with his head down, the little girls showed the father the beads.

"The bird shit all of this, then escaped."

The father ripped off a liana vine, gave his son a good beating with it, and then he ripped off one of his ears.

The young man was honorable. When he recovered and his *eti* (ear) had scarred over, he asked for his father's blessing, because he was going to *el monte* to look for the thief bird, and he wouldn't return until he found him.

He took a sack full of corn, a little drum, and an *apoti* (a little chair). There, in the middle of *el monte*, he sat down and started to play his little drum very early, when the sun and the birds come out. He surrounded the drum with grains of corn and all the birds came closer to dance—except one, which sat at a distance watching.

The young man realized the suspicious bird was the thief who defecated the coral and jet beads. And the bird, who'd seen the young man since he entered

el monte, did not want to come down from the branch.

Gúom, gúom, kuru gúom, gúom, gúom, kuru gúom . . .

They all danced, overjoyed, pecking at the corn. And the thief didn't know what to do with himself. He liked music. And corn. He felt desire. And fear. The young man pretends to be distracted, not even looking at the bird. And since the dance is so contagious, and that need to dance that gets inside you when the drums ring out is so irresistible, the bird takes a little step, a turn, and dances . . . He eats a little grain of corn very carefully, then he keeps dancing. He gets confident, and when he least expects it, the young man grabs him.

He took the bird to his father. "Here's Gúom. Take him. I kept my word, and now sir, keep your word with me. I'm missing an ear. I give you the bird, and you put my ear back on me."

His father made him an ear from cotton silk and stuck it on him, but . . . it was smaller than the other ear. And since then, we all have one ear that's bigger than the other. Look. Everyone born since then has kept the shape of that ear made from cotton silk.

ALMACIGO

Elaphrium simaruba (L.) Rose[24]

ENGLISH: GUMBO LIMBO, COPPERWOOD, CHACA, TURPENTINE TREE.

LUCUMÍ: IGI ADAMA, MOYE, ILUKI (?).

CONGO: IMBI IYE.

on the front, facing forward, leading, etc. In *Anagó*, Cabrera defines *wayú* as "the face" (*la cara*) ([1957] 1986, 316).

24   DF-N: It is better known as *Bursera simaruba*.

Decoctions made with its shoots stop stomach flu. Those made from its roots, bark, and shoots are prescribed for bloody diarrhea. Its resin is applied on patches used to cover wounds caused by nails, cans, or other metal objects. "There's no need to fear tetanus if you have an *almácigo* tree nearby" . . . and God's help.

To relieve gas: Apply a poultice made from its leaves behind the ear.

To treat a cold: Drink a decoction at bedtime and place four or five leaves in the shape of a cross under your pillow.

To treat a child's cold: Wrap their feet with warm *almácigo* leaves. For the belly, diarrhea, colic, and gas, a "fix" or poultice made with *almácigo* is at least as highly recommended as a "fix" using *panetela* (sponge cake) and white wine. Fresh leaves are stretched over the patient's bed.

Above all, it is highly regarded for "its God-given ability to cure children's hernias and navels on Good Friday" or on any other day of the year. The child is taken to the tree. Their foot is placed on the trunk of the tree, and a knife is used to carve the shape around their foot into the trunk of the tree. We can be sure that the child's umbilical hernia will be reduced by the time the lines disappear from the bark of the tree.

("Old people's hernias and kids' herniated navels are cured that way, by leaving the illness at the Almácigo. It scars over and the hernias go away.") Other wounds are healed in the same way. This procedure is performed early in the morning. The shoots of the tree are heated next to the stove, then placed over the belly. In the treatment of both stomach and respiratory flu, it is important that the leaves are placed in the form of a cross over the chest or belly of the sick person. For colds, decoctions made with

Almácigo are mixed with *canela* [cinnamon]. Its bark, mixed with *paraíso*, cures diabetes.

For a sore throat, the patient is administered decoctions and, simultaneously, massaged with lard from a pig's navel on their chest—from a female pig for a male patient, or a male pig for a female patient. Its resin, mixed with alcohol, will "absolutely kill all lice and crabs."

Let us remember that the *almácigo* tree—like other medicinal plants—is more powerful on Good Friday. "God isn't offended by cutting that tree for the sake of curing and healing people, because that's its mission. And, above all else, it's important to know that this *palo* cannot be used to do anything bad. It's a medicinal tree, nothing else." It is also used for "warding off witchcraft" and purification. In baths for "cleansing" and good luck, it is mixed with *cuaba, aguedita,* and *yagrumo.* The smoke produced by burning its resin with a clove of garlic will dispel negative influences.

"Fire does not attack it. The shrubs and trees all around it might burn, but flames won't go anywhere near him. The fire respects him, no matter where he may be."

ALMENDRILLO

LUCUMÍ: DENDEN, EKUSI, ORENDE.

CONGO: BONDEI.

OWNERS: OBATALA AND ODUA (BABALUAYE?).

Shavings from its trunk, roots, and leaves are used to prepare decoctions, sitz baths for relaxation, and to treat hernias (*quebradura*).

ALMENDRO

Terminalia catappa L.

ENGLISH: INDIAN ALMOND.

A

"Almácigo." Index card with Cabrera's handwritten notes. Lydia Cabrera Papers. Courtesy of the Cuban Heritage Collection at the University of Miami.

LUCUMÍ: IGI URE, EKUKI.

CONGO: TUANSO.

OWNERS: OBATALA AND IFA.

The leaves are used to wash the hair (to refresh Eleda) and for "spiritual cleansings," baths, and washes to purify a home. For good luck.

Folk healers recommend a decoction made with its bark, roots, and leaves for vaginal washes. This can also be drunk like regular water to refresh the body. The sap is mixed with oil extracted from its fruit and applied to the skin to keep it tight and fresh.

Decoctions made with its bark, drunk on an empty stomach, are considered an effective treatment for worms.

Little sticks made from its wood are very good for cleaning one's teeth. ("They're the old-timers' toothbrushes.")

Its leaves are included in *omiero*.

Almendra oil is used in the lamps lit for Obatala.

It is a good laxative, and it is given to newborns in the Apreparo de los Cuatro Compuestos [Preparation of the Four Compounds], gently massaging their bellies during the first year of their lives.

ALMOREJO

LUCUMÍ: IGOYO OR IGONGO.

CONGO: DUN ORO?

OWNER: ORULA.

A decoction made with its leaves and roots is used to regulate menstruation.

ALTEA

Hibiscus syriacus L.

LUCUMÍ: LUKUARI ERE.

OWNERS: OBATALA AND ORUMILA.

Its roots are boiled to make a liquid used to gargle, and as an intestinal and vaginal wash.

AMANSA GUAPO

LUCUMÍ: KUNINO.

It is used to subdue, soften brusqueness, reconcile, and control others.[25]

This is a classic binding (the work of an *Iyalocha* in Villa Clara): "*amansa guapo* and corn straw, along with the sole of

---

25 DF-N: The plant's Spanish name, *amansa guapo*, can be translated literally as "tames tough guys," "subdues fierce people," etc.

a shoe, an undershirt, and some hair from the person that you wish to bind. You tie up the hair with thread of the color associated with the *Santo* who's blessing your work, along with hair from the person who asked you to do the binding."

Using *amansa guapo* "entisado" (wrapped) with white and black thread, aguardiente, dry wine, honey, and *canela*, one can obtain whatever one desires.

AMBARINA

Hibiscus abelmoschus L.

LUCUMÍ: IYEYE-TANAEKO.

OWNER: OSHUN.

It is used in a decoction to sweat out a fever and treat chest colds.

AMOR SECO

Meiboma barbata L.

LUCUMÍ: KOKODI.

OWNER: OSHUN.

It is difficult to find. It is used for magical "work" dealing with love. It is also very good in decoctions to treat tenesmus and colic. An herbalist praises its efficacy in the treatment of severe dysentery. Additionally, it is mixed with *palo caja*, boiled very well, and served hot as a drink for sick people who are vomiting blood.

The leaves are mashed well to rub onto irritated or itchy skin.

ANAMU

Petiveria alliacea L.

LUCUMÍ: YENA, ANAMÚ, OCHISAN.

It is one of the most common and easily obtained herbs, but it is only gathered when necessary.

It is not included in the herbs for the *omiero* of the *Asiento*.

It is an abortive, which is the reason it is sometimes called "saca muchacho" (remove child). J. from R. calls it *Ochisan*.

If cows eat it, they miscarry.

The roots are ground into a paste and mixed with tallow from oxen to relieve toothache and to seal cavities.

It is maleficent during October, November, and December. It is possible to use this herb to kill. The rest of the year, it is beneficial.

It cures madness, and baths with *anamú* will rid the body of dark spirits of the sort *mayomberos* often send out to attach themselves to their victims and torment them.

If *fula* (gunpowder) is also used in the course of this cleansing, it should be done with a great deal of caution, because the body can be damaged by the shock to both the spirit and the flesh.

"Not all spirits can be removed with *fula*."

As a protective amulet placed behind doors, seven boughs of *anamú* are tied together with red ribbon, especially when there are people in the house who are being pursued by spirits.

"When someone is really jinxed," it is used in a cleansing bath together with *apasote* and *albahaca de anís*.

Powders made from *anamú*, guinea pepper, peony, and *maní* shells are blown in order to instigate continuous arguments and fights among people that live together in the same house.

It is boiled with *piñon botija* and *caisimón* to wash feet that are covered in sores, as well as swollen or injured feet that have picked up witchcraft. (*Mputawanga nsila yari yari*.)

That is why many prudent people place two *anamú* leaves inside their shoes in the shape of a cross, in case they step on a *malembo mpolo*, which cannot take effect in the presence of *anamú*. It stuns even the worst witchcraft, and it is called "mata brujo" (witchcraft killer) and "espanta brujo" (witchcraft repellant).

In order to cast a spell on someone, it is boiled with *yerba fina* and *yerba sanguinaria*, dry wine, and *agua de Florida*, then administered as a drink.

"To fight *kimbamba* (witchcraft), one should always have this preparation on hand: *anamú*, *ruda*, and very rotten urine."

"Obatala uses anamú to obliterate witchcraft."

Witchcraft can be touched with impunity by using the left hand, then washing the hand with *anamú*, urine, ashes, and a centavo coin. This will destroy the witchcraft. Some authorities maintain that it is sufficient to urinate on any witchcraft in order to nullify its effects. That makes it possible for many, both young and old, to pick up money that accompanies *ebos* and offerings without experiencing any harm at all. "That's one of the first things mothers teach their children: to urinate on anything that might be witchcraft."

As a precaution, sorcerers always keep a vessel containing water—if possible, water in which turtles live—mixed with urine, ashes, *anamú*, and a cigar butt, to throw in the doorway of their house when they suspect that another sorcerer is attacking them, but it is necessary for this renowned and infallible preparation to rot for several days before it is used.

In the Regla de Ocha, however, neither the children of Obatala nor those of Yemaya can use this plant. A bath with *anamú* will be extremely harmful to an *omo Yemaya* who might use it, out of sheer ignorance, often in search of relief from rheumatic pain. "This *ewe* is prohibited in Lucumí houses."

ANIS

Pimpinella anisum L.

ENGLISH: ANISE.

LUCUMÍ: EWEISE.

OWNER: OSHUN.

In a decoction, it is used to combat all abdominal pain and digestive problems, especially to expel gas. It is also used to treat hypochondria, bouts of "hysterical sobbing," and exhaustion brought on by partying.

ANON

Annona squamosa L.

ENGLISH: SUGAR APPLE, SWEETSOP.

LUCUMÍ: IRABIRI.

OWNER: OBATALA.

Its leaves are used in a decoction to calm a person's nerves. ("Who calms and soothes? Obatala.") The bark and roots are used after massages to cure *mal de madre* and *el padrejón*. (See also AJO.)

The leaves are toasted and ground with oil to combat parasites on the head. "*Anón* seeds kill lice."

The *anón* is also renowned for its ability to cure acidosis by mixing its leaves with leaves from *mari lópez* in an infusion. It is considered an excellent ingredient for magical medicine.

According to the person supplying me with this information, it is an excellent treatment for cystitis and all disorders of the bladder.

AÑIL

Indigonfera suffruticosa Mill.

ENGLISH: INDIGO.

LUCUMÍ: YINIYA, EWE NYI.

CONGO: FIRIO.

OWNERS: YEMAYA AND OSHUN.

By the grace of Yemaya, decoctions made with this plant have the power to destroy tumors as they take form in the body, whose unsuspected presence is always opportunely found by the diviner.

A decoction made with its leaves and roots is used to treat epilepsy, *ipa*. A decoction made with its roots is drunk like regular water to treat gonorrhea.

APASOTE

Chenopodium ambrosioides L.

ENGLISH: MEXICAN TEA, EPAZOTE.

LUCUMÍ: OLINE.

CONGO: KOSIKU (?).[26]

OWNER: BABALUAYE.

Its leaves are used to season the food offered to the orisha.

In a decoction, it is used to expel gas. Juice extracted from its roots and leaves is used to cure children of worms and parasites.

In houses purified with *apasote*, the seeds are left out in the open for twenty-four hours. The walls are whipped with its branches to punish and scare away the *malambo*.

Following this cleansing, the floors are washed with egg whites.

It can substitute the "agisa" made from *escoba amarga* or *palmiche*, which are used to flog the *abiku*. (*See also* ESCOBA AMARGA.)

---

26   DF-N: The question mark in Cabrera's original text likely indicates a sense of confusion because *kosiku* is a common Lucumí phrase, roughly meaning "may there be no death." She might have wondered if this was a confusion on the part of her informant, or perhaps a new bit of Congo vocabulary.

To firmly bind the tongue of an indiscreet person, it is sufficient to have roots from two *apasote* plants, a lizard's tongue, a yard of white cloth, a half bottle of aguardiente, an object belonging to the person being bound, and their name written on a piece of paper. Divination with cowrie shells or coconut will indicate where this binding charm should be placed and where the sacrifice accompanying this *chiche*—"work"—should be deposited.

ARABO

Erythroxylum havanense Jack.

LUCUMÍ: BENKEYE.

OWNERS: ORULA AND OSHUN.

The roots are boiled together with its leaves and branches, and the vapor is inhaled, to combat the earliest stages of flu. It will suppress fever, relieve throat and muscle pain, and counteract lack of appetite and other kinds of discomfort caused by the flu. It is also used in incense.

ARABO COLORADO

Erythroxylum affine A.Rich.

LUCUMÍ: GIMBO (?).

OWNERS: CHANGÓ AND ORUMILA.

The leaves are pulverized and scattered in the house of a family one wishes to harm. This *afoche* will create an unhappy atmosphere that will keep escalating and eventually provoke arguments that become scandalous quarrels precisely when visitors are in the house.

ARABO DE PIEDRA

Erythroxylum minutiflorum Griseb.

LUCUMÍ: BUNDA.

CONGO: FIKO.

OWNER: OGUN.

A

The roots are used to work at the feet of Ogun in order to safeguard a business or enterprise that is unstable and seems liable to fail.

ARARA

LUCUMÍ: BIOSE.

CONGO: GRO'O.[27]

OWNERS: SAN LÁZARO AND ORULA.

A decoction made with its flowers is good for reducing fever.

The healer prepares cigarettes with clippings from *arará* leaves for maritime journeys. Smoking them will prevent the discomfort of seasickness and nausea.

ARBICUAJER or ARBICUA

LUCUMÍ: AFILAYO.

CONGO: MBENTUN.

OWNER: ODUA.

To calm pain in the ears or constant buzzing, small branches and green leaves from this tree are chewed and placed in the person's auricle.

ARBOL BONITO

LUCUMÍ: KUKUNDUKU, IKI, ODARA YEYE.

CONGO: BUKUA.

OWNERS: OSHUN AND OYA.

To attract success in business, gambling, and love, a propitiatory ritual is performed with its branches under the auspices of Oshun.

ARBOL DE LA BIBIJAGUA or CAMPANA

LUCUMÍ: AGOGO, BALANKE.

CONGO: BUKUN, MUSI NGENGA, NKUNIA DUNDU MUNANTOTO.

OWNERS: OBATALA, ORISAOKO, AND YEWA.

The sap—*ore*—is applied to *culebrilla* [shingles], "an outbreak that is definitely shingles." Shingles appears on the neck and waist, and it should be attacked immediately, because it is believed the imaginary reptile will kill the person suffering from this illness if its head meets its tail.

According to Capé, the root is used in certain "work." *Garabatos* [hooked staffs] made from this plant are good for attracting and uniting people who have been separated for any reason.

ARBOL DE LA CERA

LUCUMÍ: AKI YEMBU.

CONGO: MASERE.

OWNER: OBATALA.

An infusion made with its leaves and roots is used in baths to neutralize bad smells caused by sweaty feet. (*See also* ARBOL DEL SEBO.)

ARBOL DE LA VIDA

(ONE OLD MAN CALLS IT ANÑÚA, ALTHOUGH HE DOES NOT TELL ME WHETHER IT IS A LUCUMÍ OR BANTU NAME.)

OWNERS: OBATALA-ODUA.

It is employed in infusions to treat neuralgic pain. During Holy Week, its sap is extracted then left outside, in the sun and night dew for forty days and nights, to make a great tonic that regenerates the whole body.

See also TUYA.[28]

---

27   DF-N: Cabrera's spelling is *gróo*.

28   DF-N: However, there is no entry for TUYA in the encyclopedia.

ARBOL DEL CUERNO

Acacia cornigera Willd.

ENGLISH: BULLHORN ACACIA.

LUCUMÍ: MAERI.

CONGO: GWANGANGO.

OWNERS: OGUN, OSHUN, ODUA, AND OBATALA.

The roots are boiled and given as a daily drink to combat impotence. (*Onilagbara.*)

This *palo* is used to prepare a good amulet for recovering virility.

Its leaves are used to wash one's hair and give it shine.

ARBOL DEL SEBO

Stillingia sebifera Minch.

LUCUMÍ: SAINDE.

CONGO: KOUSU.

OWNER: BABALUAYE.

A maceration of its roots and branches is used to massage the joints of the crippled. Constant application of these massages and the favor of San Lázaro will prevent the limbs of those who are prostrated from becoming rigid, thereby reducing pain.

ARCEDIANA or ACEDIANA

Celosia cristata L.

ENGLISH: COCKSCOMB.

LUCUMÍ: BIOLE.

CONGO: SIGUA.

OWNERS: ORULA AND AGAYU.

It is pulverized and used to make a great amulet that facilitates speech and stimulates courage when it tends to decrease.

A few drops of its juice are diluted in water to calm the nerves, but it is worth noting that, if consumed in excess, it can also be quite poisonous.

ARETILLO

Savia sessilliflora Will.

GUANKE (ACCORDING TO ONE HERBALIST, THIS IS WHAT LUCUMÍ SANTEROS AND PALEROS CALL IT).

OWNER: ELEGUA.

Its small branches and green leaves are chewed to whiten and polish teeth and strengthen gums.

AROMA AMARILLA or OLOROSA

Acacia farnesiana (L.) Willd.

LUCUMÍ: ERITE, EREN.

CONGO: SUNSUMIE.

OWNERS: OSHUN AND ELEGUA.

Its seeds are used to make *mpolo* and to work Mayombe charms and spells.

"By throwing a branch during a party, it can end in blows" [*como la del Guatao o el rosario de la aurora, armándose la de Pancho Alday, o la de Manita y Cañamazo*], as so often happens at dances in the countryside.[29]

A decoction made with its branches and roots is recommended in baths for people who suffer from an indefinable discomfort during the day, or those suffering from scabies or gangrene. An infusion made with its flowers is used to treat palpitations and nervousness, "hysterical little jumps of the stomach."

The roots soaked in alcohol are used in massages to treat rheumatism.

Its sap is applied with castor oil to make eyelashes grow.

---

29 LC: The dances at Guatao, a town near Havana, invariably ended in blows. Likewise, brawls in the middle of the nineteenth century between two *ñáñigo* chiefs (*ako ko meremo*), "Manita en el suelo" y "Cañamazo," became famous for their bloodiness.

A

AROMA BLANCA

Leucaena glauca (L.) Benth.

LUCUMÍ: RIANI.

OWNER: OBATALA.

The aroma of its flowers is inhaled from a handkerchief to control sneezing in difficult cases of rhinitis.

AROMA UÑA DE GATO

LUCUMÍ: MADE.

CONGO: BERIKOLAE.

OWNERS: ELEGUA AND OGUN.

For work in Mayombe *judío* and *cristiano*. It breaks apart marriages, makes people enemies, distances fiancés, makes friends fight among themselves, and engenders discord in families. Therefore, it is often used in ritual work "de desbarate" (to destroy, break apart, spoil).

For good, it is used to treat sporadic fevers.

ARRIERO

Didymopanax morototoni (Aubl.) Decne. & Planch.[30]

LUCUMÍ: PIKOTO.

CONGO: KUAKARI.

It is used in cleansing baths to remove negative influences.

"When someone is hysterical, when they're not clear-headed and their nerves get out of control, after the sorcerer has done what they need to do to remove whatever they had on them, you give them a drink made with the leaves and roots boiled, then bathe their body in the virtues of this *palo*."

ARROZ

Oriza sativa L.

ENGLISH: RICE.

LUCUMÍ: EWO, SINKOFA, IRASI.

CONGO: LOSO.

OWNER: OBATALA.

Water used to wash rice annihilates witchcraft. It is used to wash the doorways where witchcraft has been sent.

In a decoction, it is used to treat diarrhea. It is also mixed with flour to treat erysipelas on the face and, more generally, any skin rash, as well as to beautify the skin.

Kamanakú is an ambrosia made from ground rice. It is soaked until the grains swell, then it is peeled, sifted, and powdered. It is pounded in a cooking pot and cooked slowly over low heat.

It is mixed with milk and offered to Obatala.

The "levantamiento de plato" [lifting of the plate] is a costly ceremony that takes place in the morning at least one year after the death of an *olocha*.[31] Following an overnight vigil in which *bata* drums play exclusively for the *muerto*, everyone who participates in this ritual also attends the funerary *honras* [honors, tribute], which should also be offered at the church. Returning from the mass, rice is cooked without salt and scattered throughout the entire house, along with the meat left over from the pig sacrificed in honor of the deceased on this occasion.

White rice with *guéngueré* is a traditional offering for Oya.

ARTEMISA or ALTAMISA

Ambrosia artemisfolia L.

ENGLISH: RAGWEED.

A

338

30   DF-N: Also known as *yagrumo macho. See also* YAGRUMA.

31   DF-N: Literally, "the lifting of the (ancestor's) plate." *See also* MAIZ.

LUCUMÍ: LINIDI.

CONGO: DIOKE.

OWNERS: OSAIN (AND OBATALA OR SAN LÁZARO).

It is used for "cleansing rituals" and baths.

Its roots and branches are used to make a poultice used in rubs to treat contagious fevers. To combat rheumatism, it is mixed with camphor, alcohol, and *incienso*, or with *romero, canelilla de costa, carquesa, salvia marina*, and *incienso*.

It is used in a decoction which is drunk like regular water to reduce the inflammation caused by appendicitis.

This plant, which is also said to be an abortive, is used a great deal in poultices.

"To cure cancerous hemorrhoids, the kind that turn into sores and fester constantly, you get the *artemisa* plant, paying it its *derecho* [ritual fee, honorarium, or tribute]. You boil the leaves, and the sick person uses the liquid for nine sitz baths or vaginal washes: one when they wake up in the morning and another at bedtime. After the treatment with Artemisa, they'll start washing and applying a poultice made with boiled *guajaca*. Combining these two treatments, they'll be cured." Certainly! It also combats mange. The juice from its roots is mixed with good wine and administered to people with heart disease. When someone needs to perform a duty that is risky or terrifies them, such as dressing a cadaver or simply walking among lonely tombstones in a cemetery at night, they should place a few *artemisa* leaves over their chest. These will give the person courage.

This prayer is used to petition it:

Alta tu eres,
Y como alta eres
Dame de tus poderes.
Misa se dice,
Y como misa se dice

Te tengo ante mi altar
Para que me libres de todo mal.
Altamisa.

You are tall
And because you are tall
Give me your powers.
Mass is said
And because mass is said
I have you on my altar
So that you may deliver me from all
evil.
Altamisa.[32]

ARTEMISILLA

Parthenium hysterophorus L.

ENGLISH: SANTA MARIA FEVERFEW, WHITETOP WEED, FAMINE WEED.

LUCUMÍ: EWE IRII.

CONGO: LUANGA.

OWNER: OBATALA.

It is also attributed to San Lázaro.

It is used for spiritual purification. It provides happiness and helps one obtain material, moral, and intellectual wealth.

"A cleansing with *artemisilla* leaves you with a happy feeling, and then you seem happy to everyone."

ASTRONOMIA

Lagerstroemia indica L.

ENGLISH: CREPE MYRTLE.

LUCUMÍ: TAKE.

CONGO: DUANHE.

OWNER: ORUMILA.

It is used for cleansing baths.

---

32 DF-N: This is a play on words on *alta* (tall or high) and *misa* (mass), as in the Catholic High Mass.

A

The roots are used to make "resguardos" [protective charms] for maritime workers.

ATEJE AMARILLO

Cordia alba (Jacq.) Roen & Sch.[33]

LUCUMÍ: MBOTA.

OWNERS: OSAIN AND OSHUN.

It is also attributed to San Lázaro.

It should not be used during a waning moon.

Decoctions made with its roots and leaves are used to bathe the legs of those who suffer from frequent cramps. The roots alone are used in a decoction to treat dropsy. Its pulp is used to make a poultice that causes tumors to burst quickly.

ATEJE COMUN

Cordia collococca L.

LUCUMÍ: LACHEO.

CONGO: LANGWE.

OWNER: OSAIN.

The leaves and roots are inhaled to combat a harmful draught ("aire pasmoso").

Its roots are used in an infusion to treat leukorrhea.

ATEJE HEMBRA

Cordia valenzuela A.Rich.

LUCUMÍ: BEMBERE.

CONGO: CHUNUE.

OWNER: OSAIN.

It is used to remove blemishes and bruises from men's skin.

It should be cut before sunrise. And it must be paid its *derecho* to work properly.

ATEJE HERMOSO

LUCUMÍ: MALAU, IREDAN.

CONGO: BIYAKA.

OWNER: OSAIN.

The sap from its leaves and stalks fades skin blemishes caused by burns. It also makes superficial scars disappear.

ATEJE MACHO

Cordia sulcata D.C. (*Cordia macrophylia* Roen & Sch.)

LUCUMÍ: SAYI.

CONGO: PANGUA.

OWNERS: AGRONIGA AND BABA[LUAYE] (SAN LÁZARO).

The sap clears skin blemishes, and it is applied on women's skin with this intention. But one should not wash their face with it.

If *ateje macho* is applied to a man, it is ineffective. Likewise, if the *ateje hembra* is applied to a woman, the result will be equally ineffective. (It should be gathered before sunrise.)

In all magical procedures and plant remedies, "the sexes should always face each other. Female for male; male for female. Female and female doesn't work, and male with male doesn't work."

Ateje "works"—*nsaranda*—with the *bejuco leñatero*, *nfinda*, and *campana*.

ATIPOLA

ENGLISH: BOERHAVIA.

LUCUMÍ: ACHIBATA, ATIKUANLA.[34]

---

33 DF-N: This section includes five different types of *ateje* (genus *Cordia*), one of which (*ateje hermoso*) is missing a botanical name.

34 DF-N: Also commonly known as *atiponla*. *Atipola* is one of the few plants identified

CONGO: MAIKE.

OWNERS: OBATALA AND ELEGUA.

It is used in a decoction to be drunk like regular water to help the urinary tract. It is also used for cleansings and to "refresh the head." It is used—the *atikuanla*—in the *omiero* of the *Asiento*.

Baths for good luck are prepared with *atipola*, common basil, and *albahaca menuda*.

AVELLANO DE COSTA

Omphalea trichotoma Muell., Arg.

LUCUMÍ: MUYALE, RUERI.

OWNERS: OSAIN, OBA, AND OSHUN.

The roots are mixed with other plants to make a purifying tonic for bad blood.[35]

Its leaves are applied to the soles of the feet to combat the cold chills experienced by many people.

AYUA

Zanthoxylum martinicanse (L.) D.C.

ENGLISH: MARTINIQUE PRICKLY ASH, WHITE PRICKLY ASH.

LUCUMÍ: ELEGUN.

CONGO: LUNGA KUMA.

It is used for protective charms.

For an effective "desbarate,"[36] it is mixed with black *cuaba*, woodworms, and wasps.

Its thorns protect one against the evil eye. The *ayúa hembra* (female) has thorns growing on the top half of its trunk and it is prepared for boys, while the *ayúa macho* (male) is prepared for girls. "The *ayúa* is used to stick and puncture ill-intentioned looks that make people sick or jinx them, just like the Espina de Cristo, which is so difficult to find."

A decoction made with its leaves is used to wash sores.

Its bark is bottled with aguardiente for several days and then prescribed as a treatment for asthma.

It is very effective as a purifying tonic for the blood, and as a treatment for syphilis and rheumatism.

In the countryside, its bark is chewed as a treatment for toothache.

It appears among a great many remedies employed to cure drunks of their vice. In that case, a highly concentrated decoction made with its bark is administered on an empty stomach.

It is very astringent.

AZAFRAN

Carthamus tinctorius L.

ENGLISH: SAFFLOWER.

LUCUMÍ: EWE PUPO.

CONGO: MAYANDA.

OWNER: OBATALA.

"There's a plant called *azafrán del país*, but the one used to bring on menstruation is the *azafrán* sold in the market. If the interruption was caused by some

in the botanical encyclopedia primarily by a Lucumí name. Different correspondences between these names (*atipola* and *achibata*) and various plants are sometimes disputed among herbalists.

35   DF-N: It is unclear whether this refers to toxicity in the blood and/or metaphorical "bad blood" (festering resentments and conflicts), both of which can be written in Spanish as *mala sangre*.

36   DF-N: *Desbarate* translates literally to "breaking apart," "wrecking," or "destroying."

foolishness, like taking a cold bath or sleeping under the moonlight, the remedy will be a *peseta* coin worth of *azafrán de hebra* strands, a bottle of pure honey, three very small coconuts split in half, and a liter of water.

"The coconuts are boiled in water with the azafrán and a half bottle of honey, then left on the fire until the liquid is reduced to three cups. These should be drunk very hot three times a day."

The medicine woman affirms menstruation can present itself with hemorrhaging the day after this remedy is administered, so they boil three coconuts and drink three decoctions.

Healers also use an infusion made with *azafrán* to treat spasms. The plant contains an oil that is very beneficial for those suffering from paralysis and cramps ("engarrotados").

AZUCENA

Polianthes tuberosa L.

ENGLISH: POLYANTHUS LILY, TUBEROSE.

LUCUMÍ: ODODO FUN, PEREGUN, ETAFUNFUN, YENYEI, AYUME.

CONGO: TOUHE.

OWNERS: OBATALA-ODUA.

The flowers are boiled to make a decoction that should be drunk regularly as a treatment for a weak heart.

Like all white flowers, they calm the environment, attracting good and sweet influences.

"To get something you desire, you make a bouquet of *azucenas* and take it to the altar of the Santísimo Sacramento.[37] Then you take the flowers and let them dry out in the shade. You grind them down to a fine powder. You spill the blood of two white pigeons on the powder. You remove the hearts from the pigeons and reduce them to powder. Then you go and find a *corojo* palm, and you take a piece of the root from its east side and pulverize it. Everything gets reduced to *eri*, then you put it in front of a ceiba with holy water from seven churches, recite the Apostles' Creed seven times, seven Our Fathers, and seven Hail Marys. And the person receiving the talisman will bathe with *ewe* Oshun, *guacamaya*, *colonia*, *laurel*, *jaboncillo*, and *mataperro*."

For good luck: eight baths with *azucenas*, *campanas*, fresh *sauco blanco*, rose water, and orange blossom water.

B

BAGA ("THAT IS CHONA.")

Annona glabra L.

ENGLISH: POND APPLE.

A *Mayombero* "nsaranda"—conjures—with an excrescence from bark he removes from the trunk of this tree. Like all the *musi*, it is ambivalent. For a harmful *uemba*, the bark is taken from the side of the tree that faces the sunset. To do good, it is taken from the opposite side, which faces the east. That is the rule. The sun and day are good, the moon and night are evil. We have already been told that sorcery is performed at specific times: "*Ngangas* should absorb the power of the stars. We call the moon and stars so they come down into the *nganga*. That's why some *prendas*, because of their nature, work at twelve noon, and others work at midnight (evil hours), and others at six in the morning." "'Levanta-cuerpo,' a very small *prenda* that is kept in the horn of a suckling goat (the right horn), is very dangerous;

---

37   DF-N: The Holy Sacrament, meaning an altar in a Catholic church.

it works and is fed at sunrise." Indeed, since it spends all of its time working and stalking prey, it is necessary to feed it very well. It is a talisman for thieves, gamblers, smugglers, and other men who risk their lives in unspeakable ventures. These lines of work are much less risky now than they used to be, and, with a little luck, can become honorable. A thief carries the *prenda* in his pocket, and it moves around in his pocket to warn him of impending danger.

The *mayombero* cuts his *palos* at daybreak. A wicked one will do so between six in the evening and midnight or before sunrise. After that time, the darkness is weaker, the shadows less dangerous.

For certain sorcery, *palos* are cut during the waning moon. Earth is also gathered from *camposanto* during the waning moon. We should recall that the propitious time to cut them is during the waxing or full moon, "when their sap still has the energy of the stars," and on Holy Saturday and June 24.

In sum, it is possible to do great good and great harm with the *bagá*. But more harm than good. Since it lives in swamps, the person who is subjected to an "nkange" [a binding spell] performed at the trunk of this tree "will sink down into the mud."

"When you want to set someone back, you call them by their name and bind them with *espartillo* or black thread at a *bagá* or *palo bobo* (*guaeco*) tree on a Tuesday or Friday at twelve noon or six in the evening. Turn a candle upside down and light the bottom to turn their fortunes upside down, and curse them, saying, 'Let So-and-So's life be like a swamp, like yours, so they can never get out of the mud.'"

Meanwhile, the *bagá* tree "has the ability to calm the spirit when it is used in the right way." (*See also* PALO BOBO.)

BAGUEY

When a fish is bewitched, you put a splinter from this *palo* in it.

BARIA

Cordia gerascanthus L.

OWNERS: CHANGÓ, OYA, AND ELEGUA.

It is used for offerings and cleansings.

"It's mischievous. It hides from herbalists. Don't call its name when you're going to look for it." Baths with *baría* are recommended for individuals who need to establish control over a situation, attract good luck, or enchant someone. Work intended to overcome and dominate needs include the irresistible virtues of this *ewe*, along with the powers of *paramí*, *amansa guapo*, *no me olvides*, *alamo*, marjoram, *tuátuá*, orange blossom water, rainwater, holy water, and *precipitado blanco*.

An infusion made with its leaves purifies the blood. An infusion made with its flowers and roots, honey, *bejuco caraguala*, and *marpacífico* will cure colds and aphonia. In baths and poultices, *baría* is a tonic. It is used to treat cases of insanity. ("In spiritualist cleansings, the Beings prescribe it.") Its sprouts are used to combat insomnia.

BASTON DE SAN FRANCISCO

Leonotis nepetaefolia L.

LUCUMÍ: MOBORO.

CONGO: TONGO.

OWNER: ORULA.

Its leaves are used in rituals and "worked" by *babalawos*.

It is used in a decoction to regulate blood pressure.

Its flowers are used to prepare a liquid that cures herpes.

B

In a tea, its leaves are used to treat malaria, cholitis, and anemia.

BAYATE

OWNER: OBATALA.

It is excellent for preventing, once and for all, bothersome visits from those dumb, boring, mean-spirited, and bitter people who take pleasure in slandering and denigrating others and whose conversation consists of nothing more than a string of rumors.

As soon as they leave, a branch is used to strike the ground of the path they traveled. This is equivalent to beating their shadow or flogging their spirit. Later, the branch is thrown out into the street, violently, and accompanied by a malediction.

If what the *mpambia* tells me about the virtues of the *bayate* is true, then this is the most estimable plant in Cuba.

BAYONETA or PEREGUN

Yucca gloriosa L.

LUCUMÍ: PEREGUN, DENDERE.

CONGO: NGOOTO.

OWNER: OBATALA.

It is one of the most important *ewes* for carrying out the *Asiento* ceremony: it is the first of the sixteen essential plants for each orisha placed on the head of the *iyawo*.

BEJUCOS

ENGLISH: LIANAS, VINES, CLIMBING PLANTS.[38]

LUCUMÍ: IYE, IRE.

CONGO: KUNAYANGA NFITA.

Among the large collection of pieces and roots from trees and bushes—*nkunia*—that sorcerers require for their white or black magic, *bejucos*—sarmentose plants with long, thin, twisted stalks that crawl or climb, sometimes as parasites—have a seminal importance. The mystical power in some of them is as significant as that of the *palo* itself, and they cannot be absent from cauldrons or pots, the abode of the spirits and focal point for all of nature's magical powers. "In the pot, you not only have the spirit of a human man, woman, or child. You also have the spirits of animals, *palos*, and *bejucos*. And the energies of the stars."

> This is the story of the ancient people. My godfather told it to me once, when we went to *el monte* looking for a *bejuco* to make a *nkange* for a white man from Cienfuegos.
> Sambia made the first man and woman on earth. Naturally, the new couple—he made them so beautiful!—got married and had a son. They showed the baby to Sambia. He told them that, if the baby died after seven days, they should not bury him. Instead, they should put the baby in the middle of *bejucos* and cover it, so the earth wouldn't take it. It turned out that their son died after seven days and, instead of leaving him in the middle of the *bejucos* like he'd told them to, they made a hole in the ground and buried him like a seed.
> They waited a few days, then they went to tell Sambia that the boy had died and couldn't be

---

38 DF-N: In this entry, *bejucos* refers to a generic type of plant—vines, lianas, or climbing plants—rather than a specific species, followed by forty-three entries for specific types

---

of *bejucos*. The distinction is analogous to referring to trees as *palos* and herbs as *yerbas*.

revived. But Sambia sees everything. He'd already seen them disobey him.

"Didn't I tell you what you needed to do?"

"*Antela bila bulu wambo yayendale! Ignorant fools!*"

"Now, everyone who is born will die. Not a single person will be revived . . . Because you didn't listen to me."

We're all descendants of that couple, and nobody comes back to life after they die.

"*Bejucos* are very magical, and they're among the first things that go to work in a *nganga*."

BEJUCO ALCANFOR

Aristolochia trilobata L.

ENGLISH: DUTCHMAN'S PIPEVINE, BIRTHWORT, BEJUCO DE SANTIAGO.

LUCUMÍ: EWE TUKO.

CONGO: EMBI.

OWNER: OYA.

It is used in a decoction for cleansings, and it fortifies the brain.

BEJUCO AMARGO

LUCUMÍ: IYE KORO.

OWNER: YEMAYA.

"I have been told it's called Ebule in Lucumí and Biínsa in Congo. What I know from experience is that this *bejuco* cures drunkenness when you drink it like regular water."

BEJUCO ANGARILLA

Serjania diversifolia (Jacq.) Radlk.

LUCUMÍ: YENKEMI.

CONGO: SERIKON.

OWNER: BABALUAYE.

Drunk in a decoction or used in sitz baths, it reduces hemorrhoids.

BEJUCO BATALLA

CONGO: WANGARA.

"It's the one with the hard leaves that look like they're made of glass, and it's the principal *bejuco* for a *prenda*."[39]

This name can be used to refer to any *bejuco* that is good for fighting.

"Orula was born in Ayalaigbo . . . a deep jungle in Africa. A little *bejuco* is worthless. But everybody has to crawl before they walk. And if they don't stand up after crawling, they can't take a step. And if a man walks without knowing where he's going, he gets lost. With a little *bejuco*, someone who knows what they're doing can do quite a lot. And if they know a lot, even if they don't have that little *bejuco*, but they have a little piece of mirror—which is cheap, too— then they can kill whomever they want." (By projecting light from a small mirror that has been prepared magically on a person.)[40]

BEJUCO BOROCOCO

Thunbergia fragrans Roxb.

LUCUMÍ: YILA.

CONGO: WANIKO.

OWNER: OGUN.

In a decoction, it is used to soothe insomnia.

---

39 DF-N: This entry describes a category of plant based on its functional qualities rather than a particular botanical species.

40 DF-N: Beyond the particulars of this ritual formula, the principle at work here is noteworthy: humble but extraordinary materials are capable of the most formidable mystical and psychic effects. See Doris (2011).

B

"It's called Borococo because its buds make noise when they open."[41]

BEJUCO CARABALI

"It's Vence Batalla," and very *mayombero*.

BEJUCO CAREY

Tetracera volubilis L.

LUCUMÍ: UNYUARE, KAWON.

CONGO: NDUKORA.

OWNERS: CHANGÓ AND OSHUN.

The leaves are burned to alleviate shortness of breath. The sick person should inhale the smoke deeply.

"According to some *osainistas*, it's wrong to say that the *carey* belongs to Changó. *Carey* is at the top of the list of plants that 'agitate' Oshun, so it makes sense that the owner of the *carey* tree—Oshun—owns the *carey* vine too."[42]

BEJUCO COLORADO

Serjania diversifolia (Jacq.) Radlk.

LUCUMÍ: OBOLO.

OWNERS: CHANGÓ, ORISAOKO, AND ELEGUA.

It is used to treat tightness in the chest and dry cough. In a decoction, it is a depurative, diuretic, and sudorific.

(One informant calls it *guánniyo*.)

---

41 DF-N: In other words, the name Borococo is onomatopoeia.

42 DF-N: The original Spanish quotation is complex and ambiguous: "Entre las plantas que 'embravecen' a Oshún figura en primer lugar el carey, por lo que su atribución a Changó es acaso errónea en concepto de algunos osainistas, y que la dueña del árbol de carey—Oshun—lo sea también del bejuco."

BEJUCO DE CONCHITA or LAINTO

OWNERS: OSHUN AND ORISAOKO.

Boiled, left in the sun and night dew, and drunk on an empty stomach, it is a laxative or purgative.

See also PAPO.

BEJUCO DE CORRALES

Serjania diversifolia (Jacq.) Radlk.

LUCUMÍ: WANIRI.

CONGO: TWONFI.

OWNER: YEMAYA.

In a decoction, it is used to harden the gums. It is held in the mouth as long as possible. Its sap is used to massage the gums.

BEJUCO DE CRUZ

Hippocratea volubilis L.

ENGLISH: MEDICINE VINE.

LUCUMÍ: ANMELE, SARAUNDERE.

CONGO: NPOTI.

OWNERS: OBATALA, ODUA.

It is used in offerings to help people who are sick or find themselves in terrible economic conditions.

BEJUCO DE CUBA

Gouania polygama (Jacq.) Urb.

LACUMI: IDAYA.

CONGO: NYOUYOLE.

OWNER: OSAIN.

Boiled thoroughly and strained very carefully, it cures sinus infections. It is administered with a syringe, "or, more commonly, inhaled from the palm of the hand."

BEJUCO DE FIDEOS

Cuscuta americana L.

LUCUMÍ: UTI.

CONGO: MUNTO.

OWNER: ORUMILA.

The sap is used in bandages to treat swollen lymph nodes.

In decoctions, it acts as a purgative, and it is used to treat the liver (jaundice).

BEJUCO DE INDIO

Ipomoea tubersa L.

LUCUMÍ: CHINYO.

CONGO: ADEI.

This *bejuco* is used to make a liquor whose properties were not disclosed by the *osainista*. The *bejuco* is normally found among *algarrobo* trees. It is yellow, and it blooms flowers of different colors that hang down toward the ground. An *iyalocha* assures us, "The root is boiled with five centavos' worth of *ruibarbo* [rhubarb] and an equivalent amount of bee's honey. If a person has a curse on them, I give them a small cup of it at bedtime, then another cup when they wake up in the morning. Every time they sneeze, they'll blow out that nasty stuff, even critters. That person who'd been suffering from a *bilongo* gets completely cleaned out! They drink that for a week, and they're all set."

Calazán regards an infusion made with its roots to be an excellent treatment for gonorrhea.

Its sap is frothy, and it refreshes irritated eyes. It is used to clean teeth because it stops cavities and combats pyorrhea.

See also BEJUCO LEÑATERO.

BEJUCO DE JAIBA

OWNER: YEMAYA.

It is used to treat hemorrhaging.

BEJUCO DE LA VIRGEN

Cassia chrysocarpa Desv.

LUCUMÍ: ALAI.

CONGO: NFITA NGANA MARÍA, IRDO.[43]

"Babaluaye works with this *bejuco*."

Its juice is used in ear drops in cases of tumors or infections.

BEJUCO DE PURGACION

Commicarpus scandens (L.) Standley

LUCUMÍ: OGETIYO ARO.

OWNER: BABALUAYE.

A decoction made with its roots is used—like *siguaraya*, *nsimba dian finda*, *yerba del Monte*—to treat gonococcal illnesses.

It has no other applications.

BEJUCO GARAÑON

OWNER: OGUN.

Decoctions made from the whole plant are used by healers as a treatment for impotence.

BEJUCO GUACO

Mikania cordifolia (L.) Willd.

OWNERS: OGUN AND OSAIN.

It is used as an abortive.

"The roots of the *bejuco guaco* are mixed with the thorny *bledo bejuco*. You boil them together with their roots and all. You strain out the liquid and you add five centavos' worth of honey to it, an equivalent amount of aguardiente, and grains of roasted and burnt corn. Then you bottle it, seal it, and put it away. When it's fermented, it'll blow

---

43   DF-N: Note the name María (Mary) in the Congo name for this plant, whose name, *bejuco de la Virgen*, translates literally as "the Virgin's vine."

B

the top off. That means the concoction's ready, so you take a cup of it at bedtime and another in the morning."

"It's a salvation! And very bitter. You should put some in aguardiente and always keep some on hand at home for rheumatism. Three cups a day are good for women's troubles."

It is used to treat skin ulcers and insect bites. It is also used to treat . . . morbid cholera, bloody tenesmus, and bile. It is powdered and ingested to counteract harm, to stop a *bilongo* from thriving inside the person.

BEJUCO GUARANA

Davilla rugosa Poir.

LUCUMÍ: KENSA.

CONGO: DISOTO.

OWNERS: ORISAOKO AND INLE.

"Since it grows in lagoons, it has the grace of Oshun and Yemaya."

As an *egboyi* (medicine), it is used in decoctions to treat scarlet fever. It is used as a gargle for singers and orators.

BEJUCO GUAURO

LUCUMÍ: EGWA.

CONGO: TABI, TAOI.

OWNERS: ELEGUA AND OKE.

Its sap is used in emetics.

In an infusion, it is used for sitz baths to treat hemorrhoids, and as a drink to treat tetanus.

BEJUCO JICOTEA

"That *bejuco* belongs to *echora*, (the devil) *ebora*. It's for working with Ikutu."

It is placed inside the *Nganga*, like bejuco tortuga. It is also used in *Nkanges*.

BEJUCO JIMAGUA or PARRA CIMARRONA

LUCUMÍ: EWE LOPAMO, AJARA MEYI.

OWNER: ELEGUA.

"It's used for mothers who have just given birth, and to wash newborn babies. Although Elegua doesn't have a wife, Lopamo is his."

"This *bejuco* complains. You can hear it grumbling in *el monte*. Don't talk or make any noise when you approach it. You leave seven centavos and three grains of corn."

Some people "entertain it, sing to it, and, when it's eating and distracted, they take it. Because a lot of them will attack you. You'd better believe it! You need to proceed with extreme caution!"

BEJUCO LECHERO

Ipomea ramoni Choisy

OWNER: ORISAOKO.

Its sap is applied to infected wounds and bites from poisonous insects.

BEJUCO LEÑATERO

Gouania polygama (L.) Radlk.

LUCUMÍ: YEMAYA.

CONGO: ETUN.

Its sap stops wounds bleeding. Regularly chewing the small stems, which make a froth, will prevent pyorrhea.

It whitens teeth. It is also used to treat dropsy and gonorrhea.

(It is also known as *bejuco de indias* and *bejuco jaboncillo*.)

BEJUCO LOMBRIZ

Philodendron wrigtü Gris.

LUCUMÍ: OMISU.

CONGO: SEKUSE.

OWNERS: ELEGUA, BABALUAYE.

Boiled and drunk like regular water, it cures jaundice.

An infusion drunk at breakfast and followed by a castor oil purgative is used to expel intestinal worms.

BEJUCO LONGANIZA

It smells like very well-seasoned stewed meat if it is rubbed.[44]

It is good for making *masangos* over the *nganga*.

BEJUCO MADRINA

LUCUMÍ: VICHICHI NFINDA.

"That tiny little *bejuco* is very magical. It's the first one you need to put inside the cauldron for the *nganga*. If a *palero* names it or steps on it, it'll hide in the *nfinda*. The *bejuco* will wrap itself around them, and they won't be able to get out of *el monte* until the plant feels like letting them go." For this reason, it is also called Pierde Camino.[45]

It is one of the *nfita* most often used in Mayombe.

See also PIERDE RASTRO.

BEJUCO MARRULLERO

Vigna vexillata (L.) A.Rich.

ENGLISH: ZOMBI PEA, WILD COW PEA.

LUCUMÍ: FLOIDO.

In an infusion or "tea" made with various plants, this *bejuco* is a stabilizer that prevents the other plants from becoming agitated when they are mixed together.[46]

BEJUCO PARRA

LUCUMÍ: ONGWE, IYARARE.

CONGO: MASANI.

OWNER: YEMAYA.

It is used to treat the stomach.

The leaves are used in stews and foods offered to the orishas.

See also BEJUCO JIMAGUA.

BEJUCO PELADOR

CONGO: BUANYA, BUARE.

OWNERS: ORISAOKO AND OBATALA.

"I don't think it belongs to Orisaoko or Obatala, but to Agroniga" (San Lázaro).

The sap is applied to smallpox rashes. ("Since they're not around anymore, nobody remembers its name: *chapano*.")[47]

In a decoction, it is used to bathe people convalescing from this illness. It will make the pock marks and blemishes caused by smallpox disappear or become less visible.

BEJUCO PENDOLA

Securidaca volubilis L.

LUCUMÍ: LEREMI.

---

44 DF-N: *Longaniza* is a Spanish name for a type of sausage, and the plant's informal name is derived from its similar smell.

45 DF-N: The Spanish "Pierde Camino" can be translated as "Lose(s) the Way" or "Get(s) Lost on the Path."

46 DF-N: The plant's function as a "stabilizer" might entail biochemistry, perhaps by virtue of reactive, alkaline, or acidic qualities.

47 DF-N: The name offered by an anonymous informant in the quotation (*chapano*) is analogous to Ṣọ̀pọ̀na, an epithet or avatar (path, *camino*) of orisha/*fodun* who are—like Babaluaye, Agroniga, Afimaye, et al.—intimately associated with smallpox.

CONGO: ARETO.

OWNERS: OSHUN AND OBA.

It is used to make an infusion that is good for the liver and for reuniting—at the feet of the *Santos*—a married couple or lovers who have been separated by the effects of a curse.

BEJUCO PERDIZ

Bignonia unguis L.

LUCUMÍ: DUELA.

CONGO: MANSAGRO.

OWNERS: ORISHAOKO AND OCHOSI.

It is used to do harm: to cause conflict and make enemies.

Mayomberos subject it to a process of putrefaction and use this *bejuco*, "working" with the *nganga*, to separate marriages. The spell is done on a handkerchief stolen from either of the spouses for this purpose.

The handkerchief should be returned or placed back in the home to have the desired effect.

See also UÑA DE GATO.

BEJUCO PRIETO

LUCUMÍ: RUYE.

CONGO: BROSE.

OWNER: ESHU.

The sap from this plant cures ringworm.

BEJUCO SABANERO

LUCUMÍ: OGUMONA.

OWNERS: ESHU, OGUN, AND ORISHAOKO.

In Mayombe, this *nfita* is used to cause trouble and compromise a person, leading them to run afoul of the law and be convicted of a crime.

BEJUCO SAN PEDRO

Stigmaphillum lineare Wr.

LUCUMÍ: HISOYO.

CONGO: BEJUCO SARABANDA YAYANKE.

OWNERS: OGUN AND ELEGUA.

It is used in *afoche* (powders). These are prepared in order to be blown into the air at political or family meetings that one wishes to break up.

"You find it on curujey trees, and you gather it the feast day of San Pedro. You keep a piece of it in a bottle of aguardiente for forty-two days, praying and calling San Pedro, Sarabanda. It's a great amulet that can save troublemakers or anybody else from a lot of misadventures. If a fight breaks out and someone fires a gun, the bullet won't come out. If someone's going to use a blade, it falls out of their hands. But for that to happen, you need to pray to the *bejuco* a lot, and saturate it with the energy of the *Santo*."

It is carried in one's pocket and acts as protection. "It wards off danger and accidental death. But you need to pray and invoke Ogun forcefully."

BEJUCO TORTUGA

Bauhinia heterophylla Kth.

OWNERS: CHANGÓ AND YEMAYA.

During an outbreak of measles, a decoction made with its roots will dry out the lesions and prevent the complications of convalescence (bed sores).

It is highly recommended as a purifying tonic; a decoction made from a handful of it is drunk like regular water to treat chronic chest conditions.

BEJUCO UVI (with five leaves)

Cissus sicyoides L.

OWNER: YEMAYA.

Drops of its sap are used as drops in the ears when they fester, or in cases of deafness caused by a buildup of earwax. A decoction is used to wash out the ears, and as a treatment for colds and flu.

BEJUCO UVI (with wide leaves)

Cissus sicyoides L.

LUCUMÍ: EGWELE KERI.

OWNER: YEMAYA.

It is used to wash the *otan*, implements, attributes, etc., of this orisha (and to cure glanders in horses).

It is an abortive. Its juice disinfects the bladder.

BEJUCO UVI MACHO

Cissus trifoliata L.

LUCUMÍ: LEKERI.

OWNER: YEMAYA.

"If the opportunity presents itself," a strong caustic can be prepared using *uvi macho* as the principal ingredient, along with other plants and ingredients.

BEJUCO VERDAJO

Banisteria laurifolia L.

LUCUMÍ: FALILA, ATIRE.

CONGO: NSONTORI.

OWNER: ORISAOKO.

It is a *nfita* used by *mayomberos* for binding spells, as well as business enterprises, love, gambling, and luck.

BEJUCO VERRACO

Chiococca alba (L.) Hitchc.

LUCUMÍ: AREBO.

CONGO: FUMASI, KUENYE.

OWNER: ELEGUA.

A decoction made with the whole plant is an unbeatable purgative. It is used to treat kidney ailments and it dissolves kidney stones. Swigs of it will soothe toothaches. It will revive and blacken hair.

It is called *Verraco*, or pig, because it has the distinctive feature of smelling like this animal.

"Its roots poke out of the ground at exactly twelve noon, then it hides. You need to pray to it and grab it quickly."

It is poisonous for livestock. "Yes. And, from time to time, for two-legged animals too."

BEJUCO ZARZUELA

OWNER: OSAIN.

(According to some, it belongs to Orisaoko.)

"It's called Bauba, and its roots and leaves are used to *nsaranda*, to work over the cauldron and bind a child in its mother's belly, so it can't be born. This is revenge work. Parents' vengeance and quarrels are the downfall of many innocent little angels."

BIBONA

CONGO: KINKUA.

OWNER: ESHU.

It is used for conjuring in Mayombe. Its roots and leaves are pulverized and used in a curse that is intended to deprive its subject of a position or job they hold.

BIJA

Bixa orellana L.

ENGLISH: ACHIOTE.

LUCUMÍ: OEN.

OWNERS: CHANGÓ AND ELEGUA.

It is used in offerings to Changó. *Bija*, not *azafrán* [saffron], is used to color the food of certain orishas.

Its roots and leaves are used in a decoction to treat the kidneys. The leaves are used to treat headaches.

The seeds are used in a decoction that cures poisoning from *yuca agria*.

Its oil is rubbed on burns to heal them. Also, it is often used with honey to treat "sapillo" in children.[48]

See also ACHIOTE.

BIJAGUA or BIJAGUARA

Colubrina colubrina Jacq.

Palo Mayombe. The very powerful spirit of the Bijagua disrupts a person's sanity. "When it mounts them, it weighs heavy on the shoulders of the *ngombe*. It stupefies their brain, and it leaves them exhausted when it departs."

It is good for everything. It is placed in the cauldron or pot of the *nganga*.

"It contains many dangerous secrets that shouldn't be circulated. One story says the Virgin encountered the Jews, who wanted to kill her child under its shade. She left, and the Jews who wanted to capture her were blinded and unable to follow her. It has *bereke*, thorns on its leaves, and the sorcery is done with its leaves."

But these leaves, which can be used to perform so many enchantments and curses, can also be applied medicinally for good, and a *ngangatare* or Madre Nganga will recommend it in a decoction to suspend menstruation. The bark is used in decoctions to cure malaria. Its roots are known for their virtues as a purifying tonic.

BLEDO

Amaranthus viridis L.

ENGLISH: AMARANTH.

LUCUMÍ: LOBE, TETE (CHAURE KUE-KUE-WEIKO).

OWNER: OBATALA.

("There are several types of bledo that are included in *omiero* for the *Asiento*.")

It is used for cleansings. To refresh or cleanse, in aspersions.

Its shoots are used in the orishas' food.

Its roots are boiled "to purify the body internally."

The leaves are cooked in poultices to treat tumors and "nacidos" (furuncles).

The type of *bledo* known as *carbonero* "is the most medicinal of them all, because it's good for constipation and syphilis, and they say it prevents malignant tumors."

For sluicing down places: *bledo blanco*, *añil*, and *rompezaragüey*. Then scatter cornmeal and honey in all of the corners.

BONIATO (BATATA)

[Batatas] edulis Choisy

ENGLISH: SWEET POTATO.

LUCUMÍ: UNDUKUMDUKU, KUANDUKU, ODUKO.

CONGO: MBALA, ONSO.

OWNERS: ORISHAOKO AND OSHUN.

Osain eats it, and when someone wants to speak to him, they take a *boniato* covered in palm oil to the savanna and call him.

It is an offering enjoyed by all of the orishas except Obatala and Oya.

B

48 DF-N: "Sapillo" are small white sores on a child's tongue or mouth, especially while lactating.

A decoction made with its shoots increases milk production in women who breastfeed their children.

Boiled and used in baths, it prevents blemishes and spots on the skin, making it shiny and smooth.

The sap of the boniato is drunk diluted in milk or in other foods to fortify the bones and brain, and it enriches the blood.

On the day of *ita*, the third day of consecration in the Regla de Ocha, the *Asentado* listens to the recitation of their future, and their various *ewos*—prohibitions related to their destiny—are revealed, which should be followed throughout their life. These might include prohibitions against going to certain places, such as shops, markets, hospitals, or cemeteries; crossing train tracks; approaching or bathing in the ocean or river; particular colors; types of clothing; certain substances; and, rather decisively, foods.

Most *iyalochas* are prohibited from eating *boniato* (*batata*). But, as we have already heard, none deprives themselves of this food when the opportunity presents itself.

In that case, it is called—if it is mentioned by name at all—*papa dulce* [sweet potato]. Do not offer an *iyalocha* a *boniato*. They will refuse it. On the other hand, they will eat it very calmly and with great pleasure if it is offered, without insistence, as "sweet potato." Otherwise, she will be condemned, in public, to deprive herself of *boniato*, which always goes well with "ropa vieja," beef jerky, or cornmeal.

BRUJA

Sternergia lutea Ker-Gawl.

ENGLISH: WINTER DAFFODIL.

LUCUMÍ: ERERE.

CONGO: GENGE.

OWNER: OSHUN.

It is used to cure heartburn. It works as an emetic.

C

CABIMA

LUCUMÍ: KAIGE.

CONGO: KUENYE, KABINDA.

OWNERS: OGUN AND CHANGÓ.

It is used to cleanse and strengthen those convalescing from a grave illness. "A *chicha* [fermented beverage] made with *cabima* gets rid of sickness in the blood."

CABO DE HACHA

Trichila hirta L.

LUCUMÍ: ERE, IGI NIKA, AKUDIYIKA.

CONGO: NKUNIA BELELOASU.

OWNER: OYA.

It is a tree used by Oya for war.

"Leaves from *cabo de hacha* are used to infuriate and egg Oya on so she fights and wins a war" magically.

An *olocha* stimulates Oya's fury and bellicose passion against their enemy or that of their client. They always achieve victory, no matter how difficult and thorny the struggle.

It is one of Oya's most powerful ritual trees. It is also highly esteemed by *mayomberos*; it is a "strong *palo*" used to assemble *ngangas*.

As "medicine," its leaves, which have restorative virtues, are administered in an infusion to treat anemia, asthma, bronchitis, and pneumonia.

Its new leaves are scattered on the dirt of *bohíos* [thatched huts] to repel lice and fleas.

Baths with its boiled leaves purify and dissolve all wickedness.

Cleansings using *cabo de hacha* should be performed at twelve noon on the dot: some mix its leaves with *apasote* and albahaca, which are left out in the sun for a long time before the bath so they absorb the sun's power.

CAFE

Coffea arabica L.

ENGLISH: COFFEE.

LUCUMÍ: OBIMOTIGWA, IGI KAN, EKANCHACHAETE.

CONGO: TUFIOLO, KUANDIA.

"Coffee is a balm and a necessity that God gave poor people. You can stop eating, but you can't stop drinking coffee."

"Without coffee, life is no good . . ."

"Apart from being tasty, coffee is medicine. It is medicine for the heart and stomach. It makes them warm."

Mouthfuls of liquid made with its green leaves are used as a mouthwash to treat toothaches.

Its green beans are used as a laxative. The roots, cut into three pieces in a decoction, are used to reduce fever. In cases of very high fever, a paste made with coffee and fat is applied to the feet of the sick person, which will "absorb and relieve them of the fever."

Ground coffee is poured in a coffin over the most intimate parts of the cadaver to prevent them from decaying quickly, and it is sometimes mixed with *guayaba* leaves.

Offerings to the *muertos* never lack the cup of coffee they always enjoyed in life.

"It's the great intermediary for sorcery," and there are places where one should not drink it.

CAGADILLA DE GALLINA

Uncidium undulatum Sw.

LUCUMÍ: MUNUMI.

CONGO: PENTONGO.

OWNERS: THE IBEYI.

At midnight, and especially on very quiet nights, this plant can be used to perform spells from very long distances.

Mayomberos use it to "send maleficent messages."

CAGUAIRAN

Copaifera hymenaofolia Moric.

LUCUMÍ: BI.

CONGO: UYE.

OWNER: BABALUAYE.

"Pata-Llaga" or "Pata-Puri"—as the Regla Congo refers to San Lázaro, the owner of leprosy—disinfects and cures the unmanageable sores with this *palo*, which is the very same *quiebra hacha*, an unbeatable and "very hardworking" *palo* for *ngangas*.

When an owner of the *nganga* Coballende calls the spirit and it comes into "this plane of existence," manifesting itself, they need to hold a staff made from *caguairán* in their fist.

Its sap alleviates the pain from blood calluses.

See also QUIEBRA HACHA.

CAGUASO (also CAGUAZO or CAGUATE)

Paspalum virgatum L.

AN *OSAINISTA* FROM THE OLD PLAZA DEL POLVORÍN USED TO CALL IT ANDURE.

OWNER: OCHOSI.

It is burned, then its ashes are spread over the bed that had been occupied by an infectious sick person, and all over the rest of the room.

It is also shredded and scattered around barnyards and animal pens to prevent birds from becoming infected with pip.

CAIMITILLO

Chrysophylum oliviforme L.

LUCUMÍ: DIDERE.

OWNER: OYA.

It is used to encourage Oya to work on behalf of a particular person.

The fruit of the *caimitillo* reduces "glandular ruptures and hernias."

A decoction made with its roots and leaves is used to bathe the body and to combat obesity.

CAIMITO

Chrysophyllum cainito L.[49]

ENGLISH: TAR APPLE, STAR APPLE, GOLDEN LEAF TREE, MILK FRUIT, AGUAY.

LUCUMÍ: ASAN, AYEKOFOLE.

CONGO: ENUA, YERE.

OWNER: OYA.

It is among the strongest *palos* in Mayombe.

"It's a very magical *palo*," Calazán says. "And it grants us the miraculous ability to see what does not exist, and to prevent us from seeing what exists."

"Because it has two faces," Baró explains. That is, its leaves are green on one side and brown on the other. "It has two faces . . . and it changes its faces."

It is used to "work" with the *nganga*, to conceal or transform someone who needs to flee, allowing them to cross paths with the people with whom they consort as if they are perfect strangers. "Thanks to the *caimito*, anyone who knows them well, most especially the police, won't be able to recognize them. They'll look like a completely different person." Thanks to this miraculous work performed with the *caimito*, it is often impossible for accusers to identify the accused in legal trials; they retract, and the accused walks away without facing the true justice they deserve.

"The *caimito* is used to *linga* (bind) the police or whoever is on our trail. Whoever it is, you bury the name of the person chasing you in the roots, light a candle backward, spit on the *nkange* (binding amulet), and kick it three times. That will suffice. The person looking for you will encounter you, run into you and, even face-to-face, they will not see you."

And here is a *mambo* to perform sorcery with *caimito*:

Ayere yi Caimito, Ayeré yé.
—Ayeré yé Caimito
Si hueso cambia cambia
Unyeré yé Caimito
No hay agravio.
Makuto paga costudera.

Yo entierra vivo, yo lleva muerto.
Sacru mata son Cosa Mala
Yónguirigombo, Matende bana
Sanguijuela no pega hierro.
Borrico tonto arriero bobo
Unyéreyé Caimito
Caimito cambia coló
Unyere yé cocuyero cambia coló
Cabeza malo que tié tu amo.

Enyéreyé.
Pájaro que tu amarra
Po gusto no lo amarra
Yereyé, caimito
Basura que tu barre
Enyéreyé . . .

Agua que llueve, un dia campará
Ayerc ye caimito, Ayeré yé,

49 DF-N: It is also known as *cainito*.

Caballo cuenda Luna Nueva
Allá la loma Camarioca
Yo gana Ndoki
Yo saca fiesta, asi lo gano
Enyére yé caimito, yeré yé
Congo luwanda cambió coló, etc.

Ayere yi Caimito, Ayeré yé.
—*Ayeré yé Caimito*
If bone changes, it changes
Unyeré yé Caimito
There's no insult or harm done.
Makuto pays for the seamstress.

I was buried alive, I carry a *muerto*.
Sacru mata is a Bad Thing.
Yónguirigombo, Matende bana
Sanguijuela doesn't strike iron.
Dumb *borrico*, idiot *arriero* [bird],
  dumb *Unyéreyé Caimito*
Caimito changes color
Unyere yé cocuyero changes color
Your master has a Bad Head.

Enyéreyé.
Bird that you trap
You don't trap it for the hell of it
Yereyé, caimito
The garbage you sweep
Enyéreyé . . .

The rain falls, one day it will stop
Ayere ye Caimito, Ayeré yé,
Horse walks in the New Moon
Over there on the hill Camarioca
I win Ndoki
I have a fiesta, that's how I win
Enyére yé caimito, yeré yé
Congo Luanda changed color, etc.

A person who is two-faced, a hypocrite, a liar, and disloyal is compared to the *caimito*.

One of my elderly informants was spectacularly indignant when she left a gathering because one of her acquaintances, intending to bother her with a *puya* [jab or dig], sang under her breath:

En hoja de caimito
Tu tienes dos caras

Hoy sí, mañana no,
Caimito tu tienes dos caras.

A Caimito leaf
You have two faces
Today it's yes, tomorrow it's no
Caimito, you have two faces.

In the extensive repertoire of these satirical songs, a particular person is wounded in a veiled and indirect way. Black people have a great gift and flair for improvising them at opportune moments, like one elderly native of Matanzas who came to Havana and recounted that he had attended a *Santo* celebration. Once he realized that the *babaocha* was faking going into a trance in front of the drums, he unloaded, singing this *puya* to that fake Changó:

Lube lube
Pá los hijos de Changó
La bána no tiene Changó.
Yo busco y no veo caballo de Changó.
Lube lube pá lo hijo de Changó.

Lube lube
For the children of Changó
Havana doesn't have Changó.
I'm looking, but I don't see a horse
  for Changó.
Lube lube for the children of Changó.

Many songs that have become classics of the genre are repeated whenever they match the circumstances and intentions of the person launching them. Often these sung or spoken *puyas* are nothing more than witty, impersonal, and good-humored exercises meant to pass the time, since one should be answered rapidly by another. A few years ago, I attended a true tournament of sung *puyas* between two old men who attacked each other, happily and unceasingly, with exceptional exuberance, throughout an entire afternoon, sometimes in Lucumí and others in Congo. We understood little of it, but their laughter was contagious, and their attitudes, gestures, intonation, and back-and-forth exchanges were so funny that we laughed as if we followed every syllable. But the tone changed at the end. It seems the *puyas* turned bitter—as the proverb says, "first *puyas*, then insults"—and the two old men were visibly upset when they separated.

In Ocha fiestas and Palo *juegos*, *iyalochas* and *babaochas*, Padre Inkisis and Madre Ngangas, launch them at each other, sometimes witty, other times so violent that they end up making a person's blood boil. But the orishas and *fumbis* are no less adept at *puyas* than mortals, or perhaps they set the example for mortals. *Santos* often instruct or scold the *isayu*, devotees, in a formulaic way. Among the Lucumí, Elegua, Ogun and Changó are famous for their use of *puyas*. Among the Santas, Oshun, Yemaya, and Oya: the first is picaresque, cutting, and mocking; the second is arrogant, sarcastic, and severe; and the third is doubly so, violent, hurtful.

A *mayombero* and their *prenda* regularly talk to each other in terms of *puyas*. The *fumbi* only communicates figuratively, and *mambos de puya* come up constantly during *juegos*.

Returning to the Caimito: if the *fumbi* feels their sincerity or efficiency is being questioned, they respond:

> *No hay Palo, palo.*
> *Palo como yo.*
> *¡Ay! Palo, palo,*
> *Que no hay palo*
> *Como yo.*

> There's no *Palo*, palo.
> *Palo* like me.
> Ay! *Palo*, palo,
> There's no *palo*
> Like me.

In other words: Unlike the *caimito*, I only have one face; I only have one word, and I keep it.

In real quotidian life, *puyas*—especially in songs—are the cause of frequent and violent ruptures and hard feelings, the touchstone of brawls that land both those who throw and those who receive a *puya* in a police station.[50] One might say that women, even the peaceful ones, are more vulnerable to insinuation. The sensible attitude is to not respond to a *puya*, pretending to not hear it. Or instead, as someone I know does, retort with this personal adaptation of a *mambo*:

> *Taconé, taco sincero,*
> *Taconé, tu puya de acero*
> *Taconé, tu puya no hiere!*

> *Taconé*, taco sincerely,
> *Taconé*, you jab with a steel blade
> *Taconé*, your jab doesn't cut!

The *mambo* that inspired it says:

> *Taconé taco sincero, taconé*
> *Tu son tronco Yabá, taconé*
> *Tú son Palo Maruro, taconé,*
> *Taco sincero, voto va Dios soberano,*
>   *etc.*

> *Taconé taco* you're sincere, *Taconé*
> You're a Yabá tree, *Taconé*
> You're a Palo Maruro, *Taconé*,
> *Taco sincero, voto va* God almighty,
>   etc.

To request and obtain what one desires from another person:

The fruit of the *caimito* is covered generously in palm oil and honey. Nine pins and nine needles from a Piedra Imán are driven into it, piercing a piece of paper with the name of the person whose will one wishes to enchant by these means. A candle is kept lit for nine days, and at the end of the nine days, the remains of the candle wax are tossed at the corner of the street where the object of this spell lives.

---

50 DF-N: See "Satirical and Commercial Song" in Ortiz (2018, 236).

C

"Once you've done this work, you can ask the person for whatever you want."

Also, to acquire money, one opens a *caimito* and pours palm oil, sugar, cognac, and *bálsamo tranquilo* into it. After nine days, after nine candles have been consumed, it is deposited under a *framboyán* tree.

In folk medicine and home remedies— *ogunile*—the *caimito* leaves possess two curative gifts that are analogous to their colors. If the green, exterior side is placed on a sore, it makes the sore fester. On the contrary, if the dark, golden, silky side of the leaf is placed on a wound, it immediately contains hemorrhaging.

A decoction made with its bark is recommended for diarrhea and loss of blood.

It is unnecessary to praise its fruit.

CAIMITO BLANCO

It is used to load *prendas* and strengthen *mpakas* (horn talismans).

CAIREL

LUCUMÍ: INABI.

OWNER: CHANGÓ.

It is used for rogations "at the feet of the *Santo*" and to prepare valuable jewelry that will be transformed, in this way, into amulets that provide their owners with good luck in love, business, and gambling.

See also PICA-PICA.

CAISIMON

Pothomorphe peltata (L.) Miq.

LUCUMÍ: IGEDI EKUAA.

CONGO: TAGWAN.

OWNER: YEMAYA.

Others attribute it to Changó or Babalu Ayé.

A poultice made with its leaves is used to treat erysipelas and irritation of hernias, cysts, and the belly.

Warm leaves applied to the belly with palm oil and cocoa butter reduce swelling caused by orchitis.

A decoction made with its roots is used to treat cystitis and gonorrhea. And to cure

> *canchilas* [hernias] caused by witchcraft, the evil eye, or *eleseyo* (a curse), it is necessary, as in many other cures, to include the intervention of a man who is a twin, *meyi.*
>
> They will place two *caisimón de anís* leaves over the hernia in the form of a cross and say, "San Hermenegildo, Patron of Men's Crotches, because of the torture, the savage Solimán, sultan of the Saracens, made you suffer in your private parts, wrecking your urinary tract, you, in the midst of your horrific torment, promised to help anyone who would suffer from your malady, like . . . (say the name and surname of the sick person)."
>
> They make the sign of the cross over the hernia and pour out a little holy water.

One can also recite an Our Father and another prayer to San Hermenegildo. In general, *despojos* (cleansings), baths, and washes with the type of *caisimón* known as *caisimón de anís* are very common and often recommended by *santeros*.

CAJUELA

H[yeronima] alchorneoides Griseb.

OWNERS: OSAIN, CHANGÓ, AND OGUN.

C

Its sap is used to make an ointment that relieves pain from burns and prevents blisters.

CALABAZA

Cucurbita maxima Duchese.

ENGLISH: PUMPKIN.

LUCUMÍ: ELEGEDE.

CONGO: MALE, MALENGE, MAKONGE, MALUKA, MAKUKE, YUMURU.

OWNER: OSHUN.

Those *asentados* who receive the "letra" or sign Obara Meyi in *ita* (the reading of their future) should respect pumpkins; they are not allowed to eat them or give them away as gifts to anyone, because they are genuine daughters of the orisha Changó, who was Obara in one of his avatars. The *ebo*, or sacrifice, recommended by this sign to overcome any obstacle consists of a rooster, a basket of pumpkins, *ñame*, and plantains, and two or four pieces of firewood that are used in the *ebo* to burn clothing next to a royal palm. Afterward, they will dress themselves again with *acho fun fun* (white clothes).

This *ebo* reproduces what Obara did in the wilderness.

This is the story of Obara:

Olofi invited all of the orishas to a party. Obara—Changó—found himself in abject poverty. Dirty—*obo eleri*—and threadbare, he did not dare to attend. When all the orishas were gathered at the home of the *Arugbo*, he gave them all *elegede*—pumpkins—as gifts. They looked down their noses at such a common and insignificant gift, and they decided to take them to Obara as a way to mock him. Obara received them. Far from scorning them, he said, "Emiche o

elegede" (I cook pumpkins). But when Obara picked one up, it felt like it was full of bugs. Yet when he opened it and emptied it out, he discovered the pumpkin was full of gold. They all had gold inside. After some time, Olofi invited the orishas to another party. It had already started, and the drums were already ringing out, when they saw a man approach. He was dressed all in white, riding on a white horse.

"Who is that? He looks like a prince."

"Ago ile!"

"Come in!" Olofi shouted to him.

It was Obara, who now owned the wealth inside the pumpkins. He had come to give thanks to Olofi.

This story has many versions.

Monikin told it like this:[51]

Olufina was a liar. You couldn't believe a word he said, and every-

---

51   DF-N: The various elements of the mythology of Obara—characters, themes, and narrators—inform and reinforce each other, creating a densely layered metanarrative about truth, lies, and (in)gratitude. The narrator of this passage—Monikin—is undoubtedly Calazán's sister-in-law Moniquín, who is cited at length in chapter 9. Her telling interpretation of the stories reflects an intimate, firsthand relationship to the "characters": Obara, Changó, and Calazán emerge, like narratives of orishas more generally, as idiosyncratic composites of divination signs, gods, and/or humans (cf. Akiwowo and Font-Navarrete 2015). The stories of Obara, Changó, and Calazán are therefore necessarily both collective and personal, and they are effectively inseparable from the truth(s) of their narrator(s)—in this case, Monikin/Moniquín (via Cabrera).

C

body thought he was a phony. But he was going through very hard times. "Another one of Obara's lies! Not a single truth comes out of his mouth!" The other *santos* accused him of being a liar in Olofi's court. Olofi said to himself, "We'll see whether or not Obara *irori* (lies)."

He announced that he was having a party and invited all the *santos*, including Obara, who was flat broke. Olofi cut sixteen pumpkins, and he grabbed one of them—a very small one that was already wrinkled—and hung it from one of the beams in his *bohío*. The Ochas arrived. The old man asked, "Is everyone here?"

"Yes, sir, we're all here."

"No," Olofi told them. "One is missing."

"Obara is missing. He said he'd be here, and that's how you know he's not coming."

"Look! It's him! Over there in the distance, Obara's coming," said Olofi. "And he's riding a horse."

"It can't be!"

Indeed, it was Obara, and he was neither dirty nor ragged. He had huge, empty saddlebags on the horse. ("Where did he get that horse?") He dismounted, stepping down onto the ground. "Bless me."

"*Santo*, my son." Then Olofi turned to the others and said to them:

"You said he wouldn't come, and he's here. Now that we're all together, I want to give each of you a gift." And he gave each orisha one pumpkin. Obara received the smallest one. The others were upset by that gift. "This is why you've called us together, Olofi? That's how badly you wanted to ridicule us? Unbelievable!" And

when the party was over, each one picked up their pumpkin to avoid hurting Olofi's feelings, but they threw them away on their way home. Obara was the last to leave. He saw the pumpkins and picked them all up, filling his saddlebags until they were stuffed. He stored the pumpkins in his house. The next day, as he worked on his farm, his wife called to him: "Oko, etie mi ochiche mo yeun osi elegede!" (My husband, I'm going to cook and eat pumpkin.) She grabbed one, split it open, and many, many gold coins spilled out from the opening made by the *obe* (knife). "Ode, ode okomi, afefa pipwo elegede!"

Oba got scared and put the two halves of the pumpkin back together as well as she could.

When Obara came back home from work, Oba told him what had happened and showed him the pumpkin. Meanwhile, Olofi gathered the *santos* again. Obara dressed himself in white clothes, grabbed the little pumpkin Olofi had given him, got on his horse, and went to visit the Old Man. When he arrived, everyone had already gathered.

Olofi said, "I want to know what you have done with the gift I gave you last time you were with me."

They all looked at each other. One coughed, another cleared their throat and swallowed, and finally, there was no choice but to call out.

"I threw it in the bush."

"Me too."

"Carrying it felt like a burden."

"Mine was too heavy, and I had a long walk back home."

"And you, Obara, what did you do with your *elegede?*"

"Here's mine, Baba. I kept it. And when I found a bunch of pumpkins in the savanna after I left here, I thought to myself: Look how they scorn our father. And I picked them all up."

"You're the only one who appreciated my gift. And since they all say that you're such a liar, I now command that your word will shine over the earth. Both your truths and lies will be treated as true. The honor of the son is his father's honor."

Obara was not poor anymore. Capetillo says, "That's why, when the children of Changó suffer from bad luck, and they all go through highs and lows at different moments, they should sleep with a pumpkin under their pillow."

Why was Obara so famous for being a liar? According to another story:

Since he liked hunting so much, Ifa advised that he make *ebo* with a rooster, his shotgun, eight parrot feathers, and six silver peso coins before his next hunt. Obara went off to gather those things Orula had requested for the *ebo*, but he ran into Eshu, who asked where he was going in such a hurry.

"I need to make *ebo*!"

Eshu said to him, "Bah! You have more than enough power to do whatever you want. No doubt, Orula is trying to throw a party with your money . . ."

So Obara didn't make *ebo*, which is a mistake anyone could make. He went off hunting without any worries. As soon as he entered the forest, he saw an enormous *ayanaku* (elephant). He aimed at it, fired, and killed it, then he ran back to town to tell his father he'd killed an elephant. They rang a bell to call the people,

and they prepared to butcher and eat the elephant's meat. But when they arrived in *el monte*, instead of Ayanaku, they found a pile of firewood.

Oche asked Obara, "Where's the elephant?"

"There!"

"There? That's firewood!"

They looked everywhere, but they couldn't find a single trace of the animal. Obara felt shame. They complained to the king that his son was a liar who mocked the people, and that he hadn't killed anything.

Oba was ashamed of her son.

"Go away! I can't stand to see you, and I don't want anything more to do with you!"

And Obara withdrew to *el monte* with his wife. She saw that everything Obara did turned out badly, and she said to him: "Your luck has to change. This happened to you because you didn't follow Orula's advice. Go see him, and tell him about your situation." She insisted until, finally, Obara went to consult Ifa.

"Ah! If only you'd followed my advice! Look, the *ebo* is bigger now: bring me two roosters, six bundles of *oluigi* (firewood), two bottles of water, the clothes you're wearing (they were his only clothes), and twelve silver peso coins." Even though it was a hard struggle, Obara got all of those things together. He told him to do a cleansing in the middle of *el monte*, put the firewood (*ikibusi-aina*) together, then burn his *acho* [clothes] in that fire. He should pay close attention to the direction the smoke took as it drifted away in the air. Once his clothes turned to ash, he would need to put out the fire with the water

C

he brought in the bottles. Well, Obara had been hiding away in *el monte* for three months when a prince wandered nearby with his entourage, drummers, and treasure. The prince was lost, and he couldn't find his way out of the forest.

When the prince saw the smoke from that distant campfire, he ordered they go find the person who made the fire. Several emissaries approached Obara, who was completely naked. He hid behind some bushes as soon as he saw them.

"Halt! Stop right there!" Obara shouted to them. The prince's emissaries explained their situation and asked him to go with them, because the prince wanted to speak to him. But Obara refused to expose himself, naked, without a *bante* (apron), like an ordinary person.

The prince sent him *acho*, and Obara went to see him.

Obara said to the prince, "I am the son of Obalube."

"I am on my way to pay him tribute. I am bringing many slaves and gifts for Obalube. Guide me to him."

Obara and his wife set out on the road to the town, with the prince at the head of the army. When his father's subjects heard the drums, they went out to see who was advancing on them, and they saw Obara riding a white horse. The news spread all over town in a flash.

"Obara is coming with an army behind him, and I bet he's coming to fight!"

Oba climbed up to the lookout tower, peered out, and recognized his son, and his son pointed Oba out to the prince.

"That one, at the top of the tower, is Obalube. Wait here, so I can go ahead and announce the prince's arrival."

But Obara had barely greeted his father and explained the reason for his return when the father said:

"You're a liar! The prince you're talking about is you. What is it you want, Obara?"

"I'm not lying! Those people are coming to salute you."

"And what were you doing in *el monte, omo mi lakoti?*"

"Oh, Baba! Didn't you tell me to go away, where you wouldn't see me anymore?"

Then Oba gave him a ball.

"Toss it. Let it roll along on the ground. Stay, and live wherever the ball stops rolling, and receive everything the prince has brought for me."

That's what he did. At the spot where the ball stopped rolling, which was where it bumped into his horse, he made a home for himself, living with the army and the treasures they'd brought.

I think . . . the prince in this story, or maybe the horse that the prince gave Obara, was called Yebe Chintilu. I'm not sure. These days, my memory flickers sometimes, like the light from a candle.

Capé says, "After the great flood, the *babalawos* in Oyo performed divination to discern who would become the kings. Baba, under the name Asoyi, was given the kingdom of Dahomey. But there was no road there, only *eweyuko*, a desert of grass. They started farming, and the pumpkin was born, which signaled the path from Oyo to Dahomey. Following its direction, they founded the kingdom of Dahomey. They blessed and fed the land, and they made a city.

"Using a pumpkin, Oshun made the first lamp, and danced around carrying the pumpkin and the light on her head. The way she still does it. Oshun started performing miracles, curing women in the river with pumpkins and millet. She was the queen of the rivers. In one of her miracles, the twins showed up and did an *oro* for Oshun with prayers, songs, and small bells.[52] They sang until they arrived at a pumpkin patch.

"Babalu Ayé remained in Dahomey as a king: *Asoyi fe mayi agroniga mobitasa.* Everyone touched the earth with their hands. And the stalk of the *elegede* marked the way."

An *ewo*—prohibition—also condemns the children of Oshun to never eat pumpkin. Its origins lie in the shame ("*Oshun atelarago*") that Oshun experienced when her sister Yemaya surprised her inside a well, surrounded by pumpkins, *indoko*, committing a sinful act with Orumbila, who was Yemaya's husband at the time.

"All the *santos* heard about it, and she experienced terrible shame." Oshun keeps her witchcraft and her money inside a pumpkin, in the river.

The stalk or "guide" of a pumpkin symbolizes prosperity by virtue of its long length.

"After giving birth several times, Oshun saw that her body had become deformed. She went around the countryside crying and cleansing herself with different *ewes*. Her first rogation used a *güira*, but when the gourd dried out, its seeds made noise when they moved around inside—like the sound of a maraca—and it bothered her. She found a pumpkin in a field and took it. Rubbing it over her belly, she recovered her good figure."

Well, to "do the rogation," the deformed belly is measured with five silk ribbons, a pumpkin is rubbed with honey, and the ribbons are placed inside the pumpkin.

Omi Tomi feels obligated to clarify the matter for me: "The measurements taken with a ribbon, if they're from a belly, are meant to work on the belly itself. If it measures the whole body, it involves the whole person from top to bottom. That's why, for the peace of mind of the living, if someone dies in a family, they take a string or ribbon and measure the relatives and friends the deceased loved most, then they put the lengths of string in the coffin, to keep the *muerto* happy, so they believe their loved ones are there with them, so they don't feel alone. That way, they don't get sad or annoyed with those who remain."

Although this custom is maintained among families "that are part Lucumí," according to what they tell me everywhere I go, many white people, perhaps influenced by Black people, also practiced it.

Around 1870, the English writer Goodman observed a funeral vigil in Santiago de Cuba, a province with a plethora of African blood:

> On the morning of the second day of the *velorio* (wake) . . . certain strange ceremonies are observed.
> An undertaker's man is announced, and, apparently with no other object in view than to provide becoming robes of sable for the bereaved, proceeds to take the general dimensions of everybody present. But I observe that a separate length of white tape is employed in each case, and that when a sufficient number have been thus collected, the measures are consigned to the dead

52   DF-N: In this context, *oro* refers to a sequence of Lucumí liturgical music. See Cabrera ([1957] 1986, 275).

C

man's pockets, together with the mourners' white cambric handkerchiefs.[53]

The pumpkin, then, "is the belly. That's why people with problems in their belly shouldn't eat much pumpkin."

Many women, "the ones that know religion" (*omo abusaye ocha ano*, this religion that the Creoles have ruined") do not eat pumpkin for five to ten months after giving birth.

To cure a subject who complains of pain or poor digestion in their belly, Oshun uses a pumpkin to rub it over them, first in the form of a cross, then in circles.

These rogations are performed next to Oshun's *otan*. They measure the belly of the person who will be cured, then they put five sweet buns and five egg yolks—or *oñi* and palm oil—inside a pumpkin. That pumpkin is taken to the river and paid its *derecho*; a lit candle is put inside it, and the pumpkin is left to float away on the river's current.

Because the goddess is "the owner of bellies," a recent hernia can also be cured with three good, round pumpkins:

> The *santera*, standing next to the patient, removes the pumpkins' stems and searches for the hernia, near the groin, with her finger. She rubs it with the liquid from the inside of the pumpkins, and puts the tops of the pumpkins back on. The pumpkins are kept where no one can touch them. You'll see that, as the tops are put back on. the hernia will also close.
>
> A lot of good is done for humanity with *elegede*. When my Santa Madre wants to do it ... For example: to make someone prosperous, after their star has

stopped shining, you tie them to the stalk of a pumpkin and say, "Pumpkin, just as you grow and move forward, let So-and-So grow and advance." And, believe me, that person will be lucky in all their affairs. If they're ruined, they're not getting paid, or they're not given what they deserve? ... There's a very reliable and very old *trabajo* done with a pumpkin, to make a creditor pay what they owe, or to get money from a rich person.

(A spell is placed on a silver peso coin, symbolizing a creditor's capital, or a very rich person's total wealth. This peso is "bound" with a border woven from white thread—or red, or white and yellow, depending on which orisha endorses the work, with the silver belonging to Obatala. The center of the coin remains exposed. The pumpkin's stalk—its small, tender, twisted shoot—is placed over the coin to symbolize prosperity, then all of it is covered by a very heavy piece of bronze. In this way, they "crush" the person's fortunes, "blocking the path to money." They cannot free themselves from the weight immobilizing them until they pay up and deliver the amount demanded from them.)

To induce a person to return after they have left and gone far away, one does the following: Take a pumpkin, five *uñas de gallo* (rooster nails), an egg, *pimienta*, marjoram, *agua de Florida* perfume, the first and last name of the person written on a piece of paper, and the band lining their hat, or some other jewelry or object belonging to them.

All of this is placed inside a pumpkin. Then, one spits three times inside the pumpkin and leaves it for ten days beside Oshun's stone. At the end of this period of time, it is taken to the river.

53 DF-N: See Goodman (1873).

"But you can also do a lot of harm with the pumpkin. Because Oshun is very hard when she decides to say "ona!" and walk away—*obiobayadde!*—the way she does. In that case, using a pumpkin leaf and ash from three different fireplaces, you wrap the name of the person in a little piece of paper, together with something that belonged to them. Hair, if possible, or a picture of them, or nothing at all. Their name is plenty . . . Just as these ashes were consumed, let her be consumed! And the person will be consumed. If she's a pretty woman, soon enough, she'll wilt and wither.""

The pumpkin is also used to work in Palo Monte. It is filled with egg shells, heads of wasps, termites, herbs from the cemetery, dogs' fangs, and roots of *mazorquilla de la costa*, all of which is boiled together. Seven needles rolled together with black thread and soaked in *aceite de palo* that has already been soaked in urine from the person who is the object of this curse. The pumpkin is buried in an anthill, and that person is effectively sentenced to death.

Seven very dry pumpkin leaves ground with twenty-one grains of ground *pimienta de guinea* (guinea pepper) are able to "ruin" a home down to its very foundations.

"The first Congo cauldron was a pumpkin. Long before clay pots, the *nganga* was kept inside Nkandia, the pumpkin."

In the *onichogun's* or *nkisi's* medicine, it is used in poultices to soothe pain from burns. Its seeds are powdered and mixed with boiled milk, a well-known traditional treatment to expel tapeworms. Its sap is applied to treat eczema. It cures the irritation in the tocs (*la mazamorra*), which afflicts many campesinos or *guajiros*. Its flowers are boiled to alleviate whooping cough, which lasts seven lunar cycles, and common colds. Its in-sides are fried with oil and seeds from the red *mamey* as a hair treatment. It makes hair grow, making it shiny and bright.

CALAGUALA

Polypodium aureum L.

ENGLISH: CABBAGE PALM FERN, GOLDEN POLYPODY, GOLD FOOT FERN, HARE FOOT FERN, RABBIT'S FOOT FERN.

"THE LUCUMÍ USED TO CALL IT CALAGUALA, AND I HEARD OTHER OLD TIMERS CALL IT ENIN AND WANDO."

OWNER: OSHUN.

It is a last resort for those lacking beards. The leaves and roots are boiled for baths—*aluwala*—to help rapid hair growth over the whole body. Its sap is used to gently rub the skin, so a beard will sprout. "Because a man without a beard isn't quite right. It tends to provoke doubts." It is not recommended for the scalp, however.

In a decoction, it is also good for colic, rheumatism, bad bruises, and "women's problems when they miss their period." Drinking a decoction on an empty stomach, then taking a footbath, returns the menstrual cycle to normal.

Calaguala is also included in the composition of infusions specifically used to combat syphilis.

CALALU

ENGLISH: OKRA.

LUCUMÍ: KALALU.

CONGO: ANLANGUO.

OWNERS: CHANGÓ AND OGUN.

Its branches are used in a rogation on behalf of a child who will be born to ask that they come to the world "with a lucky star."

The Congo used to prepare a very tasty dish made with *calalú* and pork or shrimp.

CAMAGUA

Wallenia laurifolia (Jacq.) Sw.

CONGO: BISONTO.

OWNERS: CHANGÓ AND OGUN.

A decoction made with its leaves and roots is used to combat constipation.

CAMAGÜIRA

LUCUMÍ: KOKO YAKEBERE.

(ONE HERBALIST CALLS IT *NMURA*.)

OWNER: YEMAYA.

It is used to treat the lungs, lesions, and weakness due to pleurisy. A syrup is prepared with its roots and leaves.

It is another of the good trees—*cristianos*—in *el monte*. It allows the healer to overcome pleurisy, to cure tuberculosis—before the appearance of symptoms—and to soothe those who are terminally ill with consumption.

CAMARON

Acrostichum excelsum Maxon

LUCUMÍ: EWE DE.

CONGO: TOUFEN, INBRINDA.

OWNERS: YEMAYA AND OGUN.

It is used in a decoction for sitz baths, to treat pain in the waist, kidneys, hips, and *fogares de vientre* (flare-ups in the belly).

COMBUSTERA CIMARRONA

Manethia coccinea Griseb.

LUCUMÍ: ESUE.

CONGO: MOLUANGUO.

OWNERS: OYA AND CHANGÓ.

It is rubbed onto cows' udders when it is time for their calves to stop nursing.

Its bark is reduced to powder and used as an emetic.

CAMELOTE

Cyperus ariculares L.

LUCUMÍ: IBARU.

OWNER: OCHOSI.

It is burned, and its ashes are scattered into boiling water for healing gumboil or whitlow with moisture.

CAMPANA

Datura suaveoleus H.B.K.[54]

ENGLISH: BRAZIL'S WHITE ANGEL TRUMPET, ANGEL'S TEARS, SNOWY ANGEL'S TRUMPET.

LUCUMÍ: AGOGO.

CONGO: KUSUAMBO NGUNGA.

OWNER: OBATALA.

It is used for this orisha's *omiero*.

It is used in cleansing, to purify homes. "For *ibora omitutu*," bathing.

Its sap is used to treat bronchitis; it facilitates expectoration.

Its roots and bark are used to treat the effects of inebriation, but it should not be administered while someone is drunk.

Its flowers are used to make *achaike*, cigarettes that alleviate shortness of breath. (The flowers are dried and toasted in the sun, chopped up, then wrapped in cigarette paper, which can be purchased in pharmacies.)

54   DF-N: Also known as *Datura sauveolens* and *Brugmansia suaveolens*.

Its leaves are boiled and made into a paste, and they are used often by our people to treat swelling.

They say that *campana* is equally beneficial as a treatment for irritated, painful hemorrhoids and as a way to rid a person or a house of bad influences.

It has many magical applications.

It is used in baths to remove an *Ndiambo* [spirit, *prenda*]. *Campana, prodigiosa,* albahaca, and *algodón*. Four consecutive baths are sufficient "to cleanse ourselves of an evil look."

CANDELILLA

Tragia gracilis L.

LUCUMÍ: EWE TINABO, EWEIN, IÑA.

CONGO: BANSO, NFULA, FEINO.

OWNERS: CHANGÓ AND OKE.

It has no curative properties. It is only good for maleficent powders. An *agugu* or *mayombero* uses it with one common goal: to create conflicts and make people enemies. It is blown furtively over the person whom one wishes to harm, then they will lose control of themselves and insult the very last person they should aggrieve.

The asafetida resin sold in pharmacies is mixed with *candelilla*, and the results of this *mpolo-banso* are . . . atomic. They are harmful to the eyes. Much inexplicable aggression and gratuitous insults are caused by the effect of *candelilla*, which is as troublesome as *pimienta*.

"Highly recommended for *iña* (war, quarrels, fights)."

CANELA DEL MONTE

ENGLISH: CINNAMON.

LUCUMÍ: IGI EPO KAN, DEDE.

CONGO: MOKOKAGUANDO, MAMA CHOYA.

OWNERS: OSHUN YEYE KARI.

This is the quintessential tree of the Lucumí Venus. Cinnamon is used to prepare all of her teas, *afoches*, and love talismans. In issues regarding love, it resolves all of the problems a *palero* or *babalocha* might face. It has a great attractive power, and it is indispensable, we are told, "for all matters of love."

Powdered and mixed with aguardiente, it is a food for some Congo *prendas*. (The iron filings from a Piedra Imán [Lodestone] are always sprinkled with cinnamon and *pimienta de guinea*.)

Applying the same procedure used with *palo guachinango*, a splinter from this tree is carried inside one's mouth whenever a request of any sort is formulated—even the ones that are most difficult to obtain.

Calazán recalls, "When I was at my peak, whenever I seduced a woman, I had my little cinnamon splinter in my mouth, to sweeten my words. And, after I got old, I had even more reason to do so." (An amulet containing *canela, cuaba, caimito, guachinando, ciprés, palo román,* and *palo verraco* is "an invincible conjunction." To tame (seduce) someone, the following is one of the most common formulas for *mpolo* and *afoche,* employed by devotees at both Congo and Lucumí temples. Grate *palo canela, amansa guapo, parami,* and *bejuco congo* (which attaches itself and does not let go) and let it dry in the sun for three days. These are then mixed with powder used by the person whom you want to subjugate, then you visit the person after dusting yourself heavily with the powder.

Coquettish women and anyone else who wants to be fancied will mix cinnamon into their facial powders. "Some powder their whole body, because cinnamon attracts men like flies to honey, so they always have plenty of suitors."

A cinnamon toothpick in the mouth is used to cajole and seduce. Its essential oil is used in a bath, and the whole body can be powdered with cinnamon to arouse violent passions. These means are very well known and widely employed by our people, who are deeply devoted to Oshun Panchagara.

The curative arts practiced by *paleros* and *santeros* employ it in syrups to treat stomach flu, diarrhea, and bloody vomit. Recall that Oshun punishes with illnesses in the belly, and she also cures them.

CANUTILLO

Comelina elegans H.B.K.

ENGLISH: WHITE MOUTH DAYFLOWER, SLENDER DAYFLOWER, WIDOW'S TEARS.

LUCUMÍ: EWE KARODO, KOTONEMBO, KOTONLO, MINI.

CONGO: TOTOI.

OWNERS: THE WHITE VARIETY IS OWNED BY OBATALA AND YEMAYA; THE PURPLE ONE IS OWNED BY CHANGÓ.

It is used for purification. Canutillo is used to wash all of the female orishas.

The white variety is used to wash the eyes.

The purple variety is beneficial in baths.

For cleansing and good luck: "purple *canutillo*, white *campana*, albahaca, and *paraíso* are all boiled. Then they are mixed together in the pot with Espíritu Vencedor y Espíritu Tranquilo perfumes and *amansa guapo*."

CAÑA BRAVA

Bambusa vulgaris Schrad.

ENGLISH: BAMBOO.

LUCUMÍ: PAKI, IGISU, YENKEYE.

CONGO: MADIADIA, GUMA, YENKILA, ENDOSONGO.

OWNERS: NANABULUKU, SODYI, AND BABALU AYÉ.

Babalu Ayé blessed the *caña brava*, which is why lightning never harms it. There is no other plant or tree—not even *ateje*, *jocuma*, *cundiamor*, or *apasote*—where Baba receives offerings more gladly. It is consecrated to Nana, "Mother of the San Lázaros."

At the stroke of midnight, a light, an ephemeral flower like a twinkling star, appears at the top of the tallest *caña brava*. "It is like a flower of light that spins around for a few seconds, moving from one stalk to another."

Whoever sees this light will die. And if they do not die, they will suffer a terrible shock.

They should perform an offering immediately. "Not even people whose sight has been prepared" dare to gaze upon it. It only appears on Good Friday.

"The *caña brava* talks." It speaks like other prodigious trees.

The earth around it has many virtues.

It is *munanso mboma*, the home of the boa snake (which increases its prestige).[55]

A section of its stem is used as "the heart, *tima*, for *ngangas*"—that is, by sealing its open ends, it can be used as a container for quicksilver and ocean sand, "the spirit of the ocean and the quicksilver." This will confer their perpetual motion to the *nganga*, which translates

55 DF-N: The original passage refers to the *majá*, the Cuban boa (*Chilabothrus angulifer*).

into a sense of diligence to obey the *may-ombero*'s orders.

The earth surrounding it, which contains the Leaf-Cutting Ant and Termite Queens, can be used to "destroy" anything.

"In a decoction, the roots have properties that soothe asthma and shortness of breath, when one has the taste of blood in their mouth."

Otherwise it should not be drunk.

It is also employed in an infusion that is injected in vaginal washes.

It is also used to treat cystitis and purify the blood. And . . . it makes hair grow when it is used to wash the head.

Abakuá mythology tells us that, at the first *baroko*, "Eroko gave Iyamba the tip of a *caña brava* when they baptized him and gave him the title of Mosongo."

CAÑA CORO

LUCUMÍ: FUNKI (?).

CONGO: LIDE.

OWNERS: YEMAYA AND CHANGÓ.

In an infusion, the entire plant is used to cleanse the kidneys and bladder.

CAÑA DE AZUCAR

Saccharum officinarum L.

ENGLISH: SUGARCANE.

LUCUMÍ: IGERE, IREKE, OREKE, EREKE.

CONGO: MADIADIA, MUSENGA.

OWNER: CHANGÓ.

Sugar sweetens an Angel, an enemy, or anyone else that needs sweetening. In a glass of water mixed with two spoonfuls of sugar, you place a lit candle and a piece of paper with the name of the person who you want to sweeten written on it, until . . . they melt.

As an offering to Changó, sugarcane is cut into chunks and placed on a plate with its leaves.

A decoction made with its roots is a diuretic. Sugarcane syrup—*guarapo, omibosa*—is mixed with *naranja agria* to treat malarial fever.

It is very important in the Abakuá liturgy.

If two segments of sugarcane are placed on the ground in front of an *ireme* in the form of a cross, the *ireme* will remain motionless. They do not dare to proceed.

CAÑA DE CASTILLA

LUCUMÍ: IFEFE, IRE.

(CARABALI: YIN, SAEKUE.)

It is used to "fragayar"—to sound the *ekue*, object of *Ñáñigos*' devotion.

CAÑA FISTULA

Cassia fistula L.

ENGLISH: GOLDEN SHOWER, PURGING CASSIA, INDIAN LABURNUM, PUDDING-PIPE TREE.

LUCUMÍ: IREKE MOYE.

CONGO: MUSENGE, MONUAMBO.

"It has a great many virtues, and is among those most highly valued by *santeros* and *mayomberos*. They use it to cure a variety of diseases, including very delicate ones like heart disease, jaundice, kidney stones, and sexual impotence." It is an excellent restorative tonic, and it purifies the blood; an emulsion prepared with the pulp of its fruit stimulates the appetite of those suffering from anemia or a general lack of appetite.

The entire plant is a laxative.

C

CAÑA SANTA or CAÑUELA SANTA

Costus spicatus (Jacq.)

CONGO: NFITA, MADIADA.

OWNER: OGUN.

This plant is used to inflame and incite Ogun.

In a decoction, it is used to treat chest colds, and to suspend menstruation. In vaginal washes, it is also used to treat leukorrhea.

The roots are used to prepare a liquor, which has an exquisite flavor and warms the belly and lungs. It is also a good treatment for high blood pressure.

CAÑAMAZO AMARGO

Paspalum conjugatum Berg.

LUCUMÍ: OGBO, OKUTAKO.

OWNERS: YEMAYA AND BABALU AYÉ.

One informant knows it by the Lucumí names *fourole* and *benange*, as well as the Congo name *mbreanyi*.

Decoctions made with any part of the plant are used in baths for the *Asiento*. This decoction is also good for washing and spraying wood, shelves, wardrobes, etc., that have been infested by clothes moths and other insects.

CAÑAMAZO DULCE

Axonopus compressus Sw.

LUCUMÍ: OGBO; ONE HERBALIST CALLS IT *ANREO* AND *PANUI*.

OWNER: OSHUN.

It is burned and pulverized, then used to make a poultice to treat dislocated joints.

CAOBA

Swietenia mahogani (L.) Jacq.

ENGLISH: MAHOGANY.

LUCUMÍ: AYAN.

CONGO: YUKULA.

OWNERS: CHANGÓ AND OBA.

"One piece of its bark is cut from the side facing the sunset, and another is cut from the side facing the sunrise, along with three flowers said to belong to *muertos* and exactly three small drops of essential oil from its wood. All of this is blended together and administered daily in three small measuring cups to treat pneumonia. If the sick person is expelling coagulated black blood, there is no reason to be afraid; they will be given the sap of the grapevine with *la Trica y el nitradato hervido*.[56] They are given three spoonfuls and, if necessary, the first prescription is repeated.

"A decoction made entirely from its bark is used as a purgative and to treat *flores blancas* (leukorrhea, candida fungus).

"The sap from its leaves is used to contain bleeding from wounds."

(This is a recipe shared by an *iyalocha* from Cienfuegos.)

CAOBILLA

Swietenia mahogani (L.) Jacq.

ENGLISH: AMERICAN, CUBAN, AND WEST INDIAN MAHOGANY.

OWNERS: OBA AND OGUN ARERE.

The roots are employed in protective amulets for those who suffer from sleepwalking or distressing nightmares, and for neurotics who are at the edge of insanity.

Its leaves are used to "cleanse" insane people, or those whose judgment is impaired sporadically.

---

56   DF-N: Cabrera's reference to "*la Trica y el nitradato hervido*" remains obscure.

In baths, it soothes those who are already completely insane, and as part of treatments carried out at the home of a *Padre Nganga*.

CAOBILLA DE SABANA

Rondeletia stellata (Griseb.) C.Wright

LUCUMÍ: MOSEYO.

CONGO: ONGWAO.

OWNER: ESHU.

Its sap is used to treat dog bites, pricks from poisonous barbs, and insect bites.

In an infusion, tea, or *chicha*, its roots are used to purify the blood.

CAPULINA or CAPULI

Muntingia calabura L.

LUCUMÍ: YETU. (SOME HERBALISTS IN HAVANA CALL IT KUABO AND BABUAN.)

OWNER: ESHU.

Its sap is used to treat herpes.

Its sprouts and tender leaves are employed in cleansing baths.

A decoction made with its roots is used to treat chest pains. Its flowers are used in a decoction to treat nervous disorders, vertigo, and insomnia.

CARAGUARA (?)

It is used to make *ngangas* and to cure. It is born under *cedro* and *caoba* trees. "It's hairy," like *sasafrás*, and it has great virtue.

See also CALAGUALA.

CARAMBOLI

LUCUMÍ: OSIYEN.

CONGO: MOANYERE.

OWNER: CHANGÓ.

Its leaves are applied to swollen glands caused by the mumps. The roots and bark are used in a decoction to dissolve tumors and purify the blood.

CARBONERO

Cassia biflora L.

ENGLISH: DESERT CASSIA.

LUCUMÍ: ERU, GIFIDANA, EBINYUALE, YINGI.

CONGO: NAONU, PANKUNIA MATARI.

OWNERS: OGUN AND DADA.

Its leaves are boiled for a bath used to treat bunions. Its sap is also applied to bunions.

Three of its roots are prepared in a decoction to treat fever. Taken before a meal, it is an aperitif.

One can say the same thing about *carbonero* as the *palo caja*: its bark is excellent in combinations of those infusions that *paleros* prepare to recover strength or maintain a healthy body, which *guajiros* call *Cuatro Leños* (when the infusion is composed of four strong *palos*).

CARDO SANTO

Argemone mexicana L.

LUCUMÍ: IKA, AGOGO, IGBEELEGUN.

CONGO: CANDO ERE (?).

OWNER: OGUN.

Some attribute its *ache* to Obatala.

It is used to inflame Ogun. "To make Ogun take care of strong work, you place his cauldron among Cardo plants."

The sap is applied to cold sores and parts of the body where humidity and sweat make it difficult for wounds to scar over.

An infusion (using its seeds) is used to treat colic and fever.

In baths, it is used to treat erysipelas and skin diseases such as eczema and herpes.

Its flowers are boiled to treat colds, and its stalks are used to treat the urinary tract.

Its sap cures wounds, clears canker sores, and removes wrinkles.

On Good Friday, a stone is found among its roots that will become a powerful protective charm for whoever finds it.

CARDON

Euphorbia lactea Haw.

LUCUMÍ: IKA, AGOGO.

CONGO: DISA.

OWNER: OGUN.

Its sap is used to erase tattoos when it is advisable for them to disappear. ("Some people see them as being bad.")

It is a poor person's quinine when they suffer from malaria.

Its seeds are emetic. The sap from *cardón* blinds. But the blindness caused by *cardon* is cured by washing the eyes with the boiled fluff from inside the root of the prickly pear tree.

CAREY

Krugiodendron ferreum Vahl.

ENGLISH: BLACK IRONWOOD, LEADWOOD.

LUCUMÍ: AYAPAEKA.

OWNER: OSHUN.

It is not included in the *omiero* of the *Asiento*.

The goddess asks for *carey* when she goes to war, and its one and only function is to agitate her. There are many different types of *carey*, and they all belong to Oshun.

CARQUESA

Ambrosia hispida Pursh.

ENGLISH: COASTAL RAGWEED, BAY GERANIUM, SEASIDE AMBROSIA.

LUCUMÍ: MIREURE.

CONGO: UREKERE.

OWNER: YEMAYA.

One of the *ewe* used in the *omiero* for the *Asiento*.

It is used for cleansing and washing.

Its sap is abortive; if that is not effective, then the roots are crushed well and used instead.

It stops or provokes menstruation.

In alcohol, the whole plant is used to treat dislocated joints, muscle pains, and in daily rubs for those who are suffering from rheumatism or lameness.

CARRASPITA

Iberis odorata L.

LUCUMÍ: ARONYU, INA.[57]

OWNER: ESHU BI.

Powdered, it is used to do harm. It causes blindness and desperate itching.

CASCABELILLO

Crotalaria lotifolia L.

LUCUMÍ: LADE, EWE PARIWO.

CONGO: KORO, NKERI.

OWNER: OSHUN.

It is used in baths to treat mange, scabies, and itches that have no rash.

---

57 DF-N: Cabrera spells this Lucumí name *aronyú* (rather than *aroñú*).

CASTAÑO

Cupania americana L.

LUCUMÍ: ORUN.

CONGO: BOUE.

OWNER: OBA.

A decoction made from its root is employed in invigorating baths, as well as in a drink consumed like regular water when one is extremely fatigued.

CAUMAO

Wallenia laurifolia Jacq.

LUCUMÍ: PATIRE.

CONGO: BAUTENSO.

OWNER: ELEGUA.

"I don't know if it goes into making a *Prenda*, but when the rheumatism starts to hurt, the juice from the roots and the bark in very hot water really helps to ease the pain . . ."

The *Caumao*, C. says, "is the octopus of *el monte*: it wraps around all the trees and weeds near it, and the *mayombero* uses it to entangle people, to make traps and mischief. A *masango* made with *caumao* is a serious thing. You use it to work the *prenda* with *macao* and *bejuco tortuga*. In the days of slavery, *caumao* was used to make *musinga*"—whips—"to punish Black people."

CAYAJABO

Canavalia cubensis Griseb.

LUCUMÍ: IRU, ORIRE, IGI, IRUBI. (SOME CALL IT MINYORA.)

OWNER: ELEGUA. ("IT IS GIVEN BY YEMAYA.")

It is used in a great amulet that we see constantly, mounted in gold or silver, hanging from the wrists of *santeras* or devotees, and from chains around the necks or attached to the pocket watches of men—*babalochas*

or the uninitiated—for good luck and to ward off bad influences.

Its sap has the ability to gradually make warts disappear.

CAYAYA

Tournefortia bicolor Sw.

("I'VE HEARD IT CALLED ENYEO.")

OWNER: ELEGUA.

The branches and bark are fermented and sprinkled around the house to purify the environment when a person who is gravely ill and contagious endangers the lives of their family members.

Additionally, it is recommended during times of epidemics; in a decoction, it is an effective prophylactic when sprinkled on doorways and windows.

It is a good purifying tonic that renews and purifies tainted blood.

CAYUMBO

LUCUMÍ: ODO, OSA.

CONGO: IYANGA.

OWNERS: OGUN AND YEMAYA.

"Its properties and virtues are a secret. They are made known to experienced *Asentados* who have seniority in the hierarchy.

"You need to know how to find it. If you don't find it at three in the morning, it'll be difficult to track down.

"In Mayombe, it works together with Espuela de Caballero in *nkanges*."

CEBOLLA

Allium cepa L.

ENGLISH: ONION.

LUCUMÍ: ALUBOSA.

CONGO: MOLABO, FIALA, NFIALA.

It belongs to all of the *santos*.

The small one, crushed and powdered together with the strong *palos* and *soyanga* (critters) from the *nganga*, is given as a drink to make someone insane.

It is a diuretic that supposedly dissolves stones in the bladder. Raw, it prevents colds and influenza. Cooked and eaten at bedtime, it helps insomniacs sleep. Applied in a poultice with flaxseed, it destroys tumors and herpetic whitlows.

CEBOLLETA

Cyperus rotundus L.

LUCUMÍ: ALUBOSA.

CONGO: TENJE-TENJE, NFIALA.

OWNER: BABALU AYÉ.

(It is also attributed to Yemaya.)

It is used for rogations in cases of leprosy (*Adete*). It alleviates the itching experienced by those suffering from elephantiasis (*onidete*).[58]

Finely chopped up, it is mixed into incense and dispels bad influences.

CEDRO

Cedrela mexicana M.J.Roe.

ENGLISH: CEDAR.

LUCUMÍ: OPEPE, ROKO.

CONGO: NKUNIA MENGA TUALA.

OWNER: CHANGÓ.

"Ogun, Osain, and Ochosi agreed to make music together. Osain knew all the *palos* in *el monte*, and he knew which ones would work best. Ogun and Ochosi cut down the trunk of a *cedro* to make a drum. Ogun hollowed out the trunk and

killed a goat. Ochosi, the hunter, added the goatskin. Then Baloge—*Kawo kabiensile!*—snatched it away."

The *cedro* is one of the most sacred trees for the Lucumí because Changó rested in its shadow when he was a fugitive. Its sacred wood cannot be burned, and it is the most suitable to make relics, symbols of the orisha, statues (*ete*), and crosses (*iya*).

Its mysteries are numerous: "It is Awo."

Therefore, in order to prevent evil from entering homes in any form, a small cross made from *cedro* is tied with a red string behind the door.

Mayomberos use its wood to construct their *nkisi-malongo*, members of the same family as the statues—*ita, chichereku*—of the Lucumí, "which walk around at night and go out to misbehave at their owners' orders." It is one of the most noble *igi* in *el monte*, because it cures many maladies. The leaves in its decoctions and its resin in syrups are used to treat hemoptysis and strong colds, and it is a great tonic. As an abortive, its roots are mixed with those of a *palma real* and sweetened with bee honey. The sap extracted from the seeds of the female *cedro*—*pasia*—calm the burning sensation caused by infectious bites. Its roots, bark, and leaves cleanse and enrich the blood. This infusion is reinforced with roots from *perejil* and cures gonorrhea; in women, it treats the irregular menstrual discharge. During times of epidemic, a piece of *cedro* should be placed in drinking water. The female *cedro* should be used by men, the male for women.

Those suffering from hernias use a knife to cut the shape of the sole or outline of one of their feet in its trunk, and when the mark disappears from the tree, the hernia also disappears.

All sores (*yaya, oyuyu; yari-yari; yaola, nfuka, pati-polo*), including the most unmanageable, are cured in the countryside

---

58   DF-N: Curiously, while both Lucumí terms share a common root (*ete*), Cabrera capitalizes one affliction (*Adete*, or leprosy) as a proper name, but leaves another in lower case (*onideté*, or elephantiasis).

(Santa Clara) with this formula: "The underside of the shell of *ayapa* (Tortoise); you burn it and reduce it to a very fine powder, then sift it with a silk cloth or some other fine fabric. The same work is done with a piece of *cedro*.

"A seed from an *higuereta* is toasted and pulverized. You wash the sores with boiled *bejuco guaco*. The liquid should be as hot as the sick person can stand it, then you dust the sores with the mixed powders from the tortoise, *cedro*, and *higuereta*.

"To treat erysipelas that have burst, I have Ungüento del Soldado sent to me from Havana, which Changó recommends often, and I use it after the baths." (R.S., an *iyalocha* and, for many years before her *kariocha* initiation in Guanabacoa, *madre de palo* "Acaba-Mundo.")

CEIBON DE ARROYO or DRAGO

Bombax emarginatum Dene.

LUCUMÍ: GIDONDO.

CONGO: MABIRE. (ONE HERBALIST SAYS HE KNOWS IT EN *LENGUA* AS NAINSO AND AMBRA.)

OWNER: AGAYU.

Burned and reduced to a powder, it is employed to exterminate bedbugs in the home, ticks on animals, and mange on dogs.

CELOSA CIMARRONA

Curanta repens L.

CONGO: NAGANI.

OWNERS: OBATALA AND OSHUN.

Its sap is used to gargle as a treatment for all illness in the throat.

CENIZO

Pithecellobium obovale A.Rich.

LUCUMÍ: KUENIA. (AN *OSAINISTA* CLAIMS THAT IT ALSO HAS TWO

OTHER AFRICAN NAMES: BIYOMO AND KONLEME.)

OWNER: BABALU AYÉ.

It is very important for ritual work in Santeria.

See also ABEY MACHO.

CIPRES

Cupressus funebris Endl.

ENGLISH: CHINESE WEEPING CYPRESS.

LUCUMÍ: IGIKU, ORU, IKO, IGI KAN.

CONGO: NKUNIA LELE SAMBIANTUKA.

"The tree of the dead."

Mayomberos use a branch from a *ciprés* growing in a cemetery to "call the Devil and make arrangements with him." This is what San Ciprián tells us. A particular book of spells, *El libro de San Ciprián*, has exerted a considerable influence on our Black sorcerers. (It is a complete treatise of real magic—that is, the treasure of one sorcerer—written on ancient Hebrew parchments, revealed by the spirits to the German monk Jonás Sifurino, etc.) Before procuring a copy for me, several elders spoke to me about "San Ciprián, who learned from Africans and was the first white sorcerer."

("That book was brought by the Spaniards. But San Ciprián learned everything wicked he knew from Black people from the Congo.")

It makes perfect sense that a Black sorcerer should recognize his own magic in that of any other race, yellow or white. The differences are so slight and superficial that *El libro de San Ciprián* was destined to become a bible for Africans who knew how to read, as well as for Creoles. And it is absolutely certain that San Ciprián was an illustrious *mayombero*.

Some elders assure me that the cult of the Piedra Imán, which is so old and widespread throughout Cuba, "was brought here by San Ciprián himself, and everything his books says about the Piedra needs to be learned."

Repeated references to other magic books—which "people kept hidden back then," full of formulas and strange, disconcerting magical words, such as those of "Solomon," "Prince Albert," "La Quijada," and even Solomon's Clavicle?—sometimes slip into the notebooks and conversations of some *santeros*, thereby demonstrating how widely spell books circulated in colonial-era Cuba. They were owned by Black people, some of whom were unable to read them but knew them by ear.

Before I became acquainted with the well-used magical treatise of San Ciprián, one of my elderly informants shared an experience he had with the Devil:

> Thanks to a book my father kept hidden in his trunk, I knew how to call Lucifer. I already had a wife and child when I decided to talk with him. I was a little scared, but I went to the shore at midnight with my compadre José.
>
> We made a circle with ashes, and I suddenly had a strange feeling, so I left José alone and distanced myself from him to see what would happen. The moon was shining, and I squatted down to wait. We had brought *ciprés* wood and three shin bones from cadavers, to burn them. And we had a black cat, in a sack made of fine cloth, a stove, and a tin can full of water. When the water boiled, José put the cat in that boiling water and called Satan, and he covered himself with a white sheet. I didn't see any-

thing. But he saw a dragon with its mouth open flying through the air, and he started shouting, "Look out!" He says that the instant he shouted, the dragon was moving toward me, then it disappeared. Then he came across a crab he could use for *malembo*.

> But I didn't want to get myself into calling Satan like that anymore, because it seems like it's very complicated, and you have to wait too long.

Through another channel, I learned,

> Here, whoever wants to talk to the devil just needs to find a *ciprés* branch from a cemetery, and the shin bones from a skeleton. They draw a circle with white chalk, sit in the center of that ring, and plunge a black cat (a kitten) in a cauldron of boiling water. Every time the cat screeches, they shout, "Satan!" And Satan responds. He asks what they're going to feed him, because he takes whatever he is given and passes it along to the spirits who serve him. They say, "I'll give you a frog."
>
> "You have yourself a deal!" He laughs and signs the contract. But he doesn't sign with ink or pencil. The signatures of the agreement are written with blood, and whoever calls him has to write with ink from their own veins. Otherwise, there's no deal. That's how Conde Barreto did it.

In the Book of San Ciprián, we find this invocation to the Devil, along with other formulas for curses, as common among *mayomberos* across the island as nailing a black hen to a ceiba or palm tree.

The relationship between the *Ciprés* and "the one the *mayomberos judíos* call the Devil, and evil spirits," might have its origins and establishment in one popular treatise on magic, which is still being edited and sold because "the *conguería* worked with him a lot, and he's a guide for *mayomberos*."

Even if there is no romantic *ciprés* tree growing in a cemetery, every other tree, herb, and shrub within its walls is useful for black magic:

You can summon and work wickedness with any *eweko de ile-Iku* [plants from a graveyard].[59] Those plants should be ripped out of the ground in the cemetery, and then right there, you stick them with sixteen needles"—Babalu Ayé's number—"and say, 'I rip you out of the ground, *egbogbo*, so you'll rip So-and-So from wherever you want him removed. I'm taking you because I need you, and you're coming with me so you'll put me above So-and-So, so I can dominate her, and do this or that nastiness to her.' You explain to the plant what you intend to do to the person.

"When we get back home, we wrap whatever we have from that person in the plant—some clothing, hair, nails, a picture of them. Or, even if we don't have anything else, their name. And then we bind it seven times. Every time we tie a knot, we recite a credo."

Everything gathered at the cemetery exerts a deadly or wretched effect, because these plants are nourished by death's mysteries. It is also possible to project a terrible shadow of misfortune onto a man's destiny by saying their name and, ideally, binding them to the tree growing nearest to a grave. The power of death permeates everything in *campo santo*.

As we follow one elderly woman to the cemetery, she shares a detailed recollection of one example of innumerable, fateful magic ("work") she carried out under its auspices:

To go work in *ile-Yansa*, you need twenty-five centavos. It's even better if the coins are the old ones. You buy five centavos' worth of sweets. A small pack of cigarettes, a box of matches, and a five-centavo cigar. And you need some coffee and sugar. A bottle of water and a small half bottle of I. brand aguardiente.[60] Outside, at each corner of the cemetery, you toss a coin.

You visit seven graves. At the first one, you say, "I've asked for permission from God and the earth, and now I ask permission from Oya, Santa Teresa Bendita. As the queen of this house, may she grant me the request I came here to make. May the *muerto* that lies here, under her authority, obey my orders." Then you say to the *muerto* in that first grave, "If you have a good spirit, I want it to turn evil. I want you to devour So-and-So, like this sweet that I'm offering you. If you smoke tobacco, here you are, you've got it. If you smoke cigars, I'm giving you some, right here. If you drink coffee, here you are. If you're thirsty, drink this water. If you drink aguardiente, then drink up. And even if you have no vices, then here. With this, I'm paying you for the earth I'm taking."

Then you use your left hand to grab a fistful of earth, and you put it inside a sack, or you fold it up in a paper bundle. You do that same

---

59 DF-N: A literal translation: *eweko* (Lucumí: plants) *de* (Spanish: from, of, belonging to, in) *ile-Ikú* (Lucumí: the house of death, the cemetery).

---

60 DF-N: "I." is an abbreviation for an unidentified brand of aguardiente.

invocation at the other six graves, taking a fistful of earth from each one.

Now that you have the earth from the graves, you buy a new cauldron, and you draw the face of the person you want to ruin with white plaster chalk—that is, if you don't have a picture of them. All of the earth from the seven *muertos* is tossed inside, covering the drawing or picture. (So the seven *muertos* will finish them off.) You bring ten centavos' worth of kerosene, a clay bottle, and five centavos' worth of candlewick. You pour half the kerosene on the earth, and then put the bottle with the candlewick on that. You make a hole in a thick board and, on its four sides, you put the first and last names of the person. You cut a yard of black fabric in half, and you prepare twelve needles and a black rooster. If the harm is being done to a man, you need a black rooster, but if it involves a woman, you use a black hen.

At midnight, you go to the river. There, you summon that man or woman thirty-three times. Using a knife with a white handle, you open the bird's chest, take out its gizzard and heart, and, as you summon and curse the person, you pierce them with the twelve needles (invoking them every time you sink a needle). You place that on the black cloth, tie it in a bundle with three knots in the cloth while saying their name again, then quickly toss it in the river as you say, "Here, I'm tossing away the life of So-and-So." Then you put the knife all the way through the bird, leaving it impaled in the earth, and pronounce the name of the victim one last time. You light a lamp and let it float away with the current, but you keep cursing the person that you have bewitched as you contemplate the lamp's light, until you lose sight of it down the river.

Once she's back home, the *iyalocha* lights a lamp. She takes the clay bottle with kerosene, a prayer card for San Lázaro, and the full name of their victim written on a piece of paper, and she goes behind the outhouse. She puts the paper that has the person's name on it down on the ground, then she lays San Lázaro's prayer card facedown on top of it and says, "So-and-So is already dead, and this is where we light a candle for the *muertos*, not inside the house. And as for you, may you burn in hell."

A strand of sesame seeds is made for Babalu Ayé's stone. A lamp will burn for three days and nights straight. After three days, it's picked up, along with the prayer card. At that very same spot, a hole is dug in the earth. A mixed-color rooster, a bottle of aguardiente, as much as ten centavos' worth of toasted corn, palm oil, two dry coconuts, dried fish, smoked hutia, and *eko* or bread are required. The rooster is used to clean the body of the *iyalocha*, then she kills it and spills its blood and the aguardiente into the hole, followed by the corn. Totally nude, she cleanses herself by rubbing a half yard of yellow cloth over her entire body, followed by a blue cloth and a white cloth. Later, she will roast the rooster and offer it to San Lázaro's stone. The coconuts are broken open. She rubs palm oil on the rooster and puts it in the hole. She kneels down and asks three times for the

C

blessing of Afimaye.[61] The hole is covered up, then three small jars of water are poured over it. The sesame seeds are picked up, along with the earth and the rest of the materials, and a small bell is rung seven times for the *santo*. The person being "worked" is invoked once again, then it is all scattered at the doorway. San Lázaro takes care of doing away with them. The day this work is being done, San Lázaro is left outside until sunset, then put back inside the house.

CIRIO

Xylopia obtusifolia A.Rich.[62]

LUCUMÍ: ENE'EN OPA.[63]

CONGO: SONJUO, BOUMBA.

OWNER: YEWA.

For spells in Mayombe *judío* performed during Holy Week. (According to Sandoval, "*Cirio* and *Palo Bomba*, another strong *palo*, are the same thing.")

---

61 DF-N: Cabrera's original refers to "Afimaya," which is most likely a typo. Afimaye is a well-known epithet for a formidable avatar or "path" of the *fodun* (deity) of pestilence in the Arará tradition, which—as the passage makes clear—is analogous to San Lázaro and Babalu Aye.

62 DF-N: This species is only found in Cuba, but it is closely related to *Xylopia aethiopica*, a tree in the Annonaceae family found in the forest and savannah regions of West and Central Africa.

63 DF-N: The Lucumí name given in this entry is a notable exception to the orthography employed throughout the original and this translation: both Enéen Opa (in the Spanish original) and Ene'en Opa (here) suggest two consecutive "eh" sounds (not tonality).

CIRUELA

Spondias citronella Tussac.

ENGLISH: CITRONELLA.

LUCUMÍ: IGI YEYE, EROKOYASI, REWO, ESO AGIN.

OWNERS: OBA, OYA, AND BOKU.

It is Oya's favorite tree, her *palo* for War.

The saying goes "phony like the *ciruela* tree," because its wood breaks easily.

Three boughs of *ciruela* are used as a whip, and they are necessary in an *ebo* for a sick person. (*Marpacífico* is also used.)

Assuming it is Oya who takes responsibility for the healing (which, naturally, the *santera* determines by asking her cowrie shells), then the following are also required: the head of a he-goat, a sheet to cover the sick person, nine candles, nine *eko*, nine yards of different colors of cloth, *ofun* (*cascarilla*), different types of beans, a rooster, two hens, three pigeons, *eku*, *eya*, three *pitos*,[64] and nine coconuts.

"Oya controls men with the *ciruela*." They all belong to her.

CLAVOS DE SANTA ELENA

The plant oozes a sap—*Magonde*—that is harmful to eyesight, and which can be employed in equally damaging magical operations.

COCO

ENGLISH: COCONUT.[65]

---

64 DF-N: The Spanish term *pitos* might refer to either fruit from the *pito* tree or whistles, or it might be a eupemism.

65 DF-N: The entry does not offer a Latin botanical name for any single species of coconut. Rather, it discusses the coconut as a single category or type of plant, even if various species are recognizably distinct.

C

LUCUMÍ: OBI.

CONGO: SANDU, KUMULENGA, KANOMPUTO, NDUNGI.

OWNER: OBATALA.

The fruit of the coconut "is indispensable in the Regla de Ocha."

It is given to the Orishas in all circumstances, as an offering and ritual food for the gods and ancestors. All the rituals and ceremonies begin with an offering of coconut.

"When Obatala, the owner of the *obi*, gathered all the *santos* to give each of them their missions and jobs, this conclave to apportion power met under a coconut tree. Obatala gave each of them a broken coconut, placing it on the ground at their feet. That's why all the *santos* are entitled to the coconut—even if it is not peeled completely, inside and out, which is how it is offered to Obatala.

"The orishas sat around this tree to listen respectfully to Obatala's instructions. The only one who expressed reluctance and dissent was Babalu Ayé, but Obatala overpowered him and, in the end, he had to abide by the supreme chief's will."

Since then, it is impossible to conduct a single ritual without the well-known offering of a coconut to the *ikus* and the orishas.

An *Awo* named Biage had a son named Adiatoto,[66] and

the father gave the son his only secret: the art, which he had created, of divining by casting coconuts.

Biage had other children in his house, young men who obeyed him as their father and were considered his children, but Adiatoto was Biage's only child.

When the Awo died, those adoptive children stole everything he had, and his true son was left alone on earth to suffer hardships.

After some time, Oba, the king, wanted to know who owned a large landholding that Biage owned in *ile ilu*, the city, and he summoned the current owners to appear before him. Those who declared themselves to be owners of the land had no proof of their claims. Then the king's town crier called out the name of Adiatoto, who went to see the Oba and told him that the only proof he could offer was his coconuts, with which Biage had taught him to divine. Every time the king asked a question, Obi responded with the truth, and Adiatoto received the properties that belonged to him by natural rights but had been usurped by Biage's false children.

He was the first *awo* to perform divination with coconuts.

A coconut, broken into four pieces, is used continually to ask the *muertos* and the Orishas questions: where they want *ebos* delivered to them; whether they are satisfied with the sacrifice they have received (which is what matters most and the goal of every ceremony); whether a detail has been omitted or an error has been committed during the course of the work; whether the work that has been done will be efficacious; etc.

The coconut is employed in the most basic system available to an *olocha*. It provides a quick answer from an orisha, who answers all of their questions affirmatively or negatively.

---

66 DF-N: In the Spanish original, Cabrera refers to Biagué and Adiátótó. The latter is notable in its use of accents, which do not adhere to Spanish orthography at all, suggesting African orthography and tonality (and reminding readers that Cabrera's approach to language was often ambiguous, artful, playful, and/or inconsistent). See the Translator's Notes.

"The Coconut," Sandoval says, "is the ABC of Lucumí divination."

Generally, it is used to engage the *santo* regarding a single issue. Questions and answers are brief and laconic.

"The coconut only speaks with five words." That is, according to the positions that they represent when the four pieces of coconut fall to the ground after being cast by a *santero* (or a person interrogating the orishas without a *santero's* intervention). If they cast while kneeling down, they drop the pieces of coconut from the height of their solar plexus; if they cast while standing, which is the more common posture, they drop them from knee level.

Many claim that it is not necessary to go to an *iyalocha* in order to interrogate the *santos* by these means.

Before handling the coconut, three libations of water are offered to Elegua, saying: *Atanu, che oda li fu aro mo be ache, ache mi mo aro mo be omoi tutu, ana tutu tutu laroye.*

The fingers of the left hand are closed, and the right is used to touch the ground three times, saying: *Ile mo kuo kuele mu untori ku, untori, aro, untori eye, untori ofo, untori mo de li fu loni.*

Then the four pieces are picked up, saying: *Obi ku aro obi eyo obi ofu, obi.* The name of the *santo* being interrogated is mentioned, and those present answer: *Akaña.*

At the beginning of the consultation, while sprinkling the water, many recite this other prayer: *Omi tutu la ero pele ri la be keke koko laro peleri ke bo mo gan lori gan boye iga. Ibori bechiche*—here, one touches the ground with the tips of the fingers, then kisses them—*ile mo piko mo poleni untori iku, mo poleni untori ofo mo da ri mo poleni obi eyo arun obi ilue. Obi oyo Obi Eleguara.*

"Akkuaña."

The old man Sandoval used to say: *Omi tutu laro ero pesi pesi baleke kokolodo peleriki boma iga bori iga boye iga bochiche ile mo kue.*

And he would repeat four times: *Mo pelomi untori iku, mo pelomi untori arun, mo pelomi untori ofo mo da bi funle ni obi iku obi ofo, obi ele bareo.*

Akkuaña.

"Offering coconut" and asking questions by casting the four pieces to the ground is the first thing learned by the *iyawo* (and even all the *aberikola*, uninitiated devotees). Asking the *dilogun*—the cowrie shells—is a much more complicated matter, as we will see in another separate volume to follow.[67]

In order to help them understand the language of the coconut, *santeras* sometimes—"since, nowadays, they don't like to teach their godchildren, so they can take advantage of them better"—provide their disciples with this explanatory diagram of the different configurations in which the four pieces fall, their names, and their meanings.

In the first configuration or "sign," the four pieces fall with their bark facing down and display only their white flesh, representing Alafia, and Changó and Orula speak through them.[68]

---

67   DF-N: It is unclear what future publications Cabrera might have had in mind, but several of her later works include discussions of *dilogun* divination. See, for example, *Yemayá y Ochún* ([1974] 1980) and *Koeko iyawo* (1980).

68   DF-N: Curiously (and confoundingly), the figure in the original edition reversed the colors of the coconut pieces in the configurations: pieces "facing down" (with the dark testa side up) were illustrated by white circles,

C

When only one piece falls facedown in Otawo (the word *otawe* means facing frontward), Ogun, Yemaya, Changó, and Ochosi speak.

Eyife, two pieces facedown, reaffirms a positive response of Alafia. Three pieces facing down signify Okana Sode, in which the *ikus* or the orishas Yansa, Elegua, Yewa, Babalu Ayé, Changó, and Agayu speak. For some *santeros*, only Changó and Babalu Ayé speak in this sign.

In Oyekun, four pieces facing down, Changó and Yansa (Oya) speak.[69]

"If Alafia falls in response to a question, the question is repeated. If the *santo* is happy with what they have been given, if they will respond to us, they will answer with Eyife immediately: two upside down. That means the answer is really yes, without any doubt, and the question is not repeated.

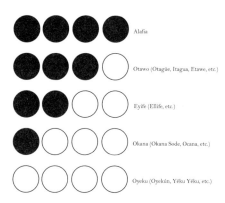

Alafia

Otawo (Otagüe, Itagua, Etawe, etc.)

Eyife (Ellife, etc.)

Okana (Okana Sode, Ocana, etc.)

Oyeku (Oyekún, Yéku Yéku, etc.)

"Alafia is a good sign or a bad sign. It is good when it is followed by Eyife or Otague.

"It is bad when, instead of Eyife or Otague, all of the coconuts fall facing down, in Oyekun. Then you need to ask the *santo* what should be done to kill that sign" (a sacrifice to prevent any sort of adversity, which is what Oyekun and Okana Sode always augur).

"When Otawo repeats itself, we can be certain. But if it only comes once, hmmm! You need to be careful with that: you ask again. Otawo meyi"—a single coconut facing down on two successive casts, one after the other—"is certainty, decisive affirmation."

When Oyekun falls, one asks immediately whether it is the *santo* who is speaking, because a deceased relative might be speaking; to warn us of someone's impending death (a candle is lit right away); and what *ebo* they want, in order to make the offering quickly and save the person in danger, because their salvation lies in the *ebo* and there is no time to lose.

If the *santo* marks Oyekun, the four pieces of coconut are collected and refreshed by putting them in a *jícara* filled with water and eight pieces of cocoa butter. One continues asking until reaching absolute certainty about what is being said.

---

while the pieces "facing up" (with the white meat or kernel side up) were illustrated by black circles. For example, Alafia (four pieces with the white sides "facing up") was illustrated by four black circles. The contradiction is made explicit below, where Cabrera writes, "If three whites and one black fall, that sign is called Itagua." Instead, the figure here follows the description in the text and ritual practice, and it is a more accurate visual representation of the *obi* configurations: the pieces "facing up" are illustrated by white circles, while the pieces "facing down" are illustrated by black circles, thereby correcting what might have been an error or a bit of artful obfuscation.

69   DF-N: The names of the five configurations vary in their pronunciation and spelling: (a) Alafia (Alaafia, Lafia, etc.); (b) Otawo (Otague, Itagua, Etawa, Etawe, etc.); (c) Eyife (Ellifé, Ejeife, Ejife, etc.); (d) Okana (Okana Sode, Okanran, etc.); (e) Oyekun (Oyeku, Yeku Yeku, Okana Yeku, etc.).

If Oyekun repeats itself by appearing twice in a row, Changó speaks of a person who is in a very bad situation and advises that an offering be performed for them to improve their luck. That person is cleansed with a black chicken in front of Elegua (Elegua's stone), so he may open the person's road, and Changó is given a rooster and corresponding turtle. It is certain that whoever performs this rogation will get better little by little; if they do not comply, they will get worse every day.

In Okana Sode, the *santo* responds with a very solemn no to the question they are being asked. Ah! Why do they answer with Okana, three coconuts facing down? This is a very delicate matter. It needs to be looked into thoroughly, because it might mean, for example, that ritual work being undertaken is being done poorly and its outcome will be detrimental.

Everyone who is present when Okana appears pulls on their ears.

Doubts are resolved by another sign. The sign Alafia, like Etawo and Eyife, indicates that an *aleyo* (someone to keep watch) be posted at the door to the house where they are casting the coconuts. And when this happens, the *jícaras* and pieces of obi are placed in the hands of the subject of the consultation, and coconut water is poured over them. Or they lie facedown and drink a drop of water that always remains on the coconut, then make the sign of the cross and say, "May whatever is for the best come to pass. Health."

Coconut divination is learned by practicing and paying very close attention. It is easy, and the more a *babalocha* knows, the more *obi* will speak to them.

The children of Inle do not make inquiries with *dilogun*, but rather with coconut.

"In sum, remember this: Alafia signifies goodness, tranquility, happiness. Yes: everything is fine, but one asks a second time to be safe."

Eyife: the senior sign of the coconut. Its word is firm and invariable. There is no need to ask again.

Otague says yes, but one needs to ask again because it is uncertain.

Okana says no and heralds something negative. That is why everyone pulls on their ears and opens their eyes wide.

Oyekun says no. It is a bad sign that announces death. When the coconuts fall in Oyekun,[70] a candle is lit for the *muertos*. Changó also speaks, and the person casting the coconut puts their hand on their chest and says, "Olufina." Then they touch the floor and repeat twice: *Mo fin kare mofin kare godo godo, da fa mo fin kare godo ba e. Alafi kisieko beke lo rie eña kan Ori mi afere asaka be ke ouani moyuba abe eba eba mi oma tun oma ese aba mi che fun omo omo ni mi . . .*

When the four pieces fall in Alafia, whoever is inquiring in good conscience mutters: *Eyionle Obatala oru aye.*

For Okana, one says: *Mo guaye, mogua Ogun, mo ri Yeye o Alafua Ogun Alafia omo Alafia ka marien kamarano kameri eye araye.*

In Otawo: *Itaura oko oko oko Obara ni bara Obara Koso tele rio aye kika te ala kamake araye. Kobo, Kobo sile Elueko. Ache Osain. Inle. Ogun Arere la boko.* And, because Otawo does not have the firmness of Eyife, the pieces of coconut are cast again. According to Inocenta, one continues: *Ire la koti re Olufina Elueko. Ache Osain. Osain atague heri heri ke heri*

---

70 DF-N: The original sentence mentions *okana* (rather than *Oyekun*), which is almost certainly a typo. Cf. the reference to *Oyekun* two sentences earlier.

C

beri akuana kosi Obaniye ala guo guo Obara oñareo okuni oma omi kabie kapotile Elueko Ache se Osain agua bere bara kawo kapotiele Ogun ala ka ke di re ati kunla, epa logwo ipa lo mio. Orumila ara raba Oregun peti le ri obe ago meko egueyi Olodumare bani lobo iku kamarano kari eye ala mo yerun ala mo yiyi, ala mo yibe dede la boru dede la bo che a ti ko leri ada ibo ibo le ti a la la patua akelesi ala bomife, jekua Obatala. Oru aye. Moguaye. Moguaye. Moguye.

Mogu aye Ogun. Mo ri Yeye Alafia. Omo Alafia. Omo kamariku kamarano.

> *Babagua mogu aye*
> *Babagua mogu aye*
> *Babagua mogou aye.*

Gabino Sandoval, like Calazán and all the elders, always has a coconut within reach to consult the orishas under any circumstances that might come up. He begins his interrogation with a long prayer to the ancestors. When Alafia responds, he prays: *Itague, ita bo ta ote ariku Baba o ariku Babaguo.*

For Eyife: *Eyife olowo eyite omo ariku babao ariku babagua.*[71]

For Okana and Okana Meyi (Yeku or Oyeku), he says: *Okana sode okua ti sode . . .*

Yewa hekua heri apu yan fu Oya ara orun.

Once Gabino has offered coconut and water to his gods and everyone accompanying him has responded "akuana," he continues with these prayers, which he repeats from memory and has carefully written down in a notebook. On the first page of this notebook, the old man has written the following words with firm, clear penmanship and rhapsodic, curving decorations:

> *Si esta libreta se perdiese*
> *Como suele suceder*
> *Suplico al que la encuentre*
> *Que la sepa devolver.*
> *Y si no sabe mi nombre*
> *Aqui lo voy a poner:*
> *Gabino Sandoval Herrera.*

If this notebook is lost
As often happens
I beg whoever finds it

---

71 DF-N: This passages offers a particularly rich example of the inherent challenges of transliterating and interpreting Lucumí. The original reads, *Ellifé, olówo ellité omó arikú babao arikú babaguá.* Cabrera writes the consonant *y* sound phonetically in Spanish as *ll.* As usual, she uses accents to indicate stress, not tonality. Yet it is worth clarifying that Spanish speakers in Cuba and elsewhere pronounce the consonant *ll* with varying degrees of fricative intensity; therefore, depending on a Spanish speaker's accent, *ll* might indicate sounds along a spectrum of pronunciation between English *y* and *j* sounds (as in *you* and *jump*, respectively). Therefore, in correlating the Lucumí liturgy transliterated by Cabrera with West African languages, the Spanish *ll* sound might be transcribed in English as *y* and/or *j.* Although *y* is generally substituted for the Spanish *ll* throughout this English translation, passages like this one might be reasonably and usefully rendered quite differently. In this instance, the *ll* sound in the invocation correlates much more neatly with the modern Yoruba *j* sound—as in *eji* (meaning "two"). Likewise, Cabrera's rendering of the word *babaguá* is somewhat misleading: in Spanish, it could have been written phonetically as *babagüa* in order to indicate either the *gu* or *gw* sound, but it might also correlate to West African languages more neatly with a *w* sound, which could also be rendered in Spanish as *gü.* Elsewhere, Cabrera cites José Isabel Salazar's recitation of the same phrase as "arikú babagwá" (1992, 387). Therefore, readers correlating this Lucumí prayer with modern Yoruba (and presumably applying tonal grammar to the text) are probably better served by this transliteration: "Eji fe olowo eji te omo ariku babawa."

To kindly return it.
And if you don't know my name,
I will write it here:
Gabino Sandoval Herrera.

He lends it to me, offering me even more evidence of his trust, so that I might learn these prayers by memory.[72]

Upon his death, the notebook ends up in my hands.

Let us copy:

For Elegua.
   Alaroye aki loyu bara baraba Eshu boru boru Eshu Bi Eshu boch-iche Eshu bara Barakikeño.[73]

---

72   DF-N: In this brief first-person note, Cabrera makes it clear that Sandoval's sharing of the text with her represented an intimate act of trust. This is reinforced in the next sentence by the fact that she inherited the notebook, which is now archived at the Lydia Cabrera Papers at the Cuban Heritage Collection. Even more meaningfully, Cabrera also makes it clear that Sandoval wrote, employed, and shared the text as an ancillary tool for the express purpose of Cabrera herself learning to recite the prayers from memory. In other words, the written text—like all writing, including *El Monte*—is a mnemonic device that is secondary and subservient to trust, memory, and the spoken word.

73   DF-N: Readers interested in the linguistic content of Lucumí prayers should consult the *Música de los cultos africanos en Cuba* (1956) collection of audio recordings, which was produced by Cabrera and Josefina Tarafa and published as a boxed set of fourteen LP discs (total 11.5 hours of audio) and twenty pages of liner notes (with text by Cabrera and photographs by Tarafa). The collection includes several examples of "spoken" Lucumí liturgy which, like the transliterated orature from Sandoval's notebook reproduced by Cabrera in this section, constitute a liturgical mode that is relatively distinct from musical performance. Excerpts from the *Música de los cultos* collection were curated by Morton Marks and published by Smithsonian Folkways as a set of three compact discs (Cabrera and Tarafa 2001a, 2001b, 2003). See Font-Navarrete (2022).

For Ogun.
Ogun chibiriki ala oluo kobu kobu Oke Baba mi siu biriki kualo to ni gua Osun du ro gago la bo sie.
For Ochosi.
Ochosi ode mata ata mata si du ro oru du ro mata.
For the Ibeyi.
Ibeyi oro omo mo kueo Orunla apestevi ayai aina alaba igue, Ideu, Kainde.
For Changó.
Elueko Asosain a kata heri heri. Kaguo Kabie sile aya tutan aya layi apende ure Alafia Kisieko tu ni Yeyeni ogan gele yuo okure ari kasagun.
For Yemaya.
Iya mio atara magua mio hoho o achere Ogun ayaba tigua odun; omio Yemaya asayabi olokun, aboyo aboyo yogun euo aya balo euo mi emi boche Iya olomi akara biaye Yemaya igere ekun asayabio Olokun ya bi elede omo ariku alalahara de yuoma kamariku kamari arun, kamari eyo. Kamari ofo kamari yen bipene.
For Oya.
Yansa Orire oma lelu Oya koye kofiedenu. Oya ayi lo da ayi me mo omi enti omo kue kue aye Orunla mio talembe mi lo hekua hei Yansa Iyansa oro iku heri obini dodo.
For Inle.
Inle makueo ara kabo aragua ni le aragua Inle araguaniye.
For Oshun.
Oshun igua Iya mio igua Iya mio. Iko bo si Iya mi guasi Iya mi mo. Yalode ogido abala abe de bu omi

C

male ado Elegueni kikirisokede to che ni kuele kuele Yeye moro.

For Obatala.

Obatala Oba tasi Obada bada badanera ye okulaba okuala ache olobo ache omo ache ku baba.

Obatala dibenigua binike ala lolaa ache afiyu Ocha ai lala abi koko ala ru mati le.

The more one prays, the better. And not only for offering coconut to the *ikus* and the orishas. Oddedei says, "Prayers make a ladder—*tekunileoro*—used to rise up to heaven." My elderly informants take pleasure in stretching out their prayers and litanies, while "little Creoles today" are satisfied with a brief prayer when they pour water and break off a little bit from each piece of coconut: *Obinu, iku obinu aro, obinu eyo, obinu ofo, ariku Babagua.*

Ile mo kueo (*Ile mo kueo Yemaya* or *Yansa* or *Changó*) is said when changing the pieces from one hand to the other and using the left hand to touch the ground, the receptacle of the orisha, or the gift being offered. After wetting their fingers in the water spilled on the floor, they use them to touch the other hand, which is holding the coconuts, then they quickly say *akue ye oguo* three times in a row. *Akue ye ariku Babagua.* Then they bring their hands together, raise them, and repeat: *Obi Elegua, obi Elegua.* And they cast them without any further ado.

In some temples, they respond with "apana" or "aseña" rather than "akuanna."

José Isabel Salazar is kind enough to teach me, with variations in the details, "the trustworthy, reliable method for asking questions with *obi*, according to the *orubo yoba* I grew up with."[74]

At the risk of indulging in exhaustive detail, we will reproduce this other guide to *obi*'s signs and write out their precepts.[75]

When you throw the four pieces of coconut, you say *obi ele bake.* When you take the little bits that you've chipped off from each piece and place them over the *orisa*, you say *obi osi ikuo run eyo ofe.*

(If the questions are being asked of Elegua, three small pieces of coconut are chipped off. If Oshun, five. Changó, four. Yemaya, seven. Because each *orisa* imposes its own mark, its number, the fragments are removed from the four larger pieces of coconut in numbers that correspond to the *orisa* who must respond.)

If two white coconuts and two black coconuts fall, that sign is called Eyife. Elegua, Ogun, Ochosi, and Osun speak in Eyife. This sign says that *lo que se sabe no se pregunta* [one does not ask what is already known].

If three whites and one black fall, that sign is called Itagua. Changó, Inle, Oshun, and Yemaya speak in Itagua. That sign speaks with doubt, so there's no certainty, and you ask again. Which path does that sign follow? The paths are death, *iku. Ano,* illness. *Eyo,* blood, war. *Ofo,* great loss. *Iña,* tragedy. *Ona,* punishment, blows dealt by the *santos.*

You say: *Iga soru, iga kocheche, Eshu kabie sile.* You put the coconuts in water. Later, you toss the water out into the street, holding the *jícara* or bowl with both hands. You hold the coconuts in your left hand. Then use your right hand to touch your left hand and the ground, one and then the other, quickly, four times, saying *mo fe loni unlo, tori aru, obori, efo, tori ore.*

74 DF-N: In the original this was *orubó yobbá,* an archaic Lucumí phrase analogous to "Yoruba elders."

75 DF-N: In other words, the following section is an edited reproduction of Salazar's notes and testimony.

If three blacks and one white fall, it's bad. You need to do the same thing again.

If four black pieces fall, in the sign called Oyekun,[76] Oya, Oba, Nana Buruku, and Yewa speak. When this sign appears, you pour out a little water four times.

If four whites fall, that sign is called Alafia, and Obatala, Orula, the Ibeyi, and Babalu Ayé speak. You kiss the ground and say *Alafia, alafia omo, alafia ago, alafia osi, alafia ariku babagwa.*

Now, let's see the *odu* of the coconuts and their "conversations."

Eyife

Elegua, Ochosi, Ogun, and Osun speak.

Elegua says the person needs to bring him into their home; otherwise, he will close all the doors. And the person should recall a dream they had. They should proceed with caution, because they might injure one of their feet by jumping from one spot to another. A deceased relative is calling to them. They should dress in white clothes. They cannot wear striped clothes. They cannot lend money. They need an operation, and their life is in danger. They need to make *ebo* with feathers (fowl).

When this sign appears, the pieces of coconut are pressed over the heart, and the following prayer is said: *Baba Elegua mo ri bale laroye to edun lo osun ni iya ago moyuba okokan laroye.*

They should offer a yam to Elegua, along with five *burro* bananas and bee's honey.

Ogun says others will entangle the person in gossip. Do not ask about it or get involved. When the person crosses an intersection, they should pay attention, because someone is following their tracks. A slender woman wants to steal the person's good fortune. Do not go out of town, on horseback or in a vehicle, without offering a rooster to Ogun and three small fish to Elegua.

Ochosi says the law wants to catch the person. The person should not visit a woman who is about to give birth, because it is not in their interest. They need to make *santo*. The person believes and does not believe in the *orisas*. If they do not believe, they should not have "dolls" or prayer cards in their home; no matter how much money they make, they will not have enough to cover the costs of doctors and pharmacies.

Osun says the person is a child of *santo*, not spirits. They should not get involved in spiritualism because the devil will get inside their home. They should not speak rudely to the elderly. They should always wear a beaded necklace for Obatala. They should not eat red beans, which are harmful to them.

The neighbors are listening to the person's conversations, pressing their ears against the wall, and looking at them through cracks and slits in the walls. The person needs to keep a hutia in their home. And they should not be hardheaded: they should listen, follow good advice, and recite a prayer every day, invoking their deceased father and godfather. Call to Obatala, saying *Obatala Baba mi ofe mi ele unlo Eshu totojun ara ina, kosi iku kosi ano.* Do not let me be without *unye,*[77] *chokoto kotobae, ke bofi ke boda.*

Itagua

Changó, Oshun, Inle, and Yemaya speak in this sign.

---

76 DF-N: The original refers to four black pieces as Okana, which—in context—is clearly an error. See Ramos (2012).

77 DF-N: Curiously, Cabrera's Spanish uses *ny* (rather than *ñ*) to indicate a nasalized consonant to transliterate *unye*, a Lucumí word for food. See Cabrera ([1957] 1986, 314).

C

Changó says he is the person's father, and the person needs to have Changó and take care of him, because the person has found Changó's stone, which they should feed. Otherwise, they will be set on fire.

The person needs to refresh their head and wash it with four of Changó's principal plants, along with *yagruma, uva caleta, curujey,* and *siempre viva.* Two coconuts, *oñi,* twelve candles, cocoa butter, *cascarilla,* a wooden sword, and $6.25.

They should keep a frond from a white prickly pear tree in their home, sprinkled with holy water, and a red ribbon. They should go to a palm tree and invoke Changó with this prayer: *Obatile baba mi Changó mo roko mi Eleda kabio sile hekua baba.*

Osun is telling the person who needs to wash *santo* (to have their stone consecrated), keep it in their home, and attend to it. They will give the person a winning lottery number.

If the person consulting is a woman, they should know that the daughters of Oshun cannot go to the hospital. They are warned that they must not sew for anyone for free, because their hands will become disabled. They need to place a miniature ladder with fifteen rungs made from *cedro* next to the door to their house. A white cushion embroidered with a yellow swan. They will not marry or overcome the obstacles they are facing until they make *santo,* and the person who needs to initiate them is a child of Oba or Obatala. One of their fiancé's relatives is against them, because they don't want them to be married. But they either believe with their heart or do not believe at all. Let them ask for proof, and the *santo* will give them a big one.

Inle advises they wear a necklace made of amber and *azabache* (three pieces of *aza-*

bache, jet). If the person is a man, they are told: Beware of a married woman.

They will find themselves in trouble with the woman's husband.

The subject of inquiry is being chased by a very dark shadow. They will have to deal with a wart or a boil that will become cancerous. They cannot eat hutia or crab. To avoid this illness, they should do a cleansing using three fresh fish, a white sheet, candles, and $3.75. They should give something (any offering) to Changó every Friday.

They should not wear red or blue clothes, nor should they eat from a scratched plate.[78] Nobody should touch their head. Do not curse anyone. They should leave the harm that is done to them in the hands of their guardian Angel and remain calm, because they will watch their enemy's cadaver pass on its way to the cemetery.

Yemaya tells the person to go to the church the first Monday of every month and recite three Salve Reginas and four Hail Marys.

They must dress in keeping with their promise. They should wear clothes with blue stripes, offer two statues or dolls consecrated by the grace of the *jimaguas* (twins), and dress them one in a red outfit, the other blue. The person should be very careful about where they relieve themselves, because someone wants to take what they defecate and use it to make the person's stomach sick. They will see a relative that lives far away, inland. They need to take seven baths with seawater and offer Yemaya seven *palanquetas* [pieces of candy] made with toasted cornmeal and sugarcane syrup.

---

78 DF-N: The original term *plato rayado* is translated literally here as "scratched plate," although it should also be understood more poetically and symbolically.

They should have a Piedra Imán in their home. And do not curse: they cannot allow anyone to speak ill of someone else in their home. They need to wash their hair every seven days, rinse with *agua de añil* [indigo water], and toss the water into the street. They must not allow arguments in their home. They must not threaten anyone.

Okana

Oba, Oya, Nana Buruku, and Yewa speak.

Oba says the person should offer a white basin full of water, *salvadera* leaves, and three pieces of cocoa butter. They should invoke Orula for their salvation, because the person is in a very serious predicament. They need to offer Yemaya pork and ram meat. They need to accept what is coming their way, and they must not attempt to harm themselves.

Oya says that one cannot live alone, but there are places the person should not go. They should not throw a party for a relative without first fixing their hair. Do not light any altars without feeding the *santo*. They should not discard what their dreams say, and they should not eat *ruda*, unless it is to treat stomach aches.

Nana Buruku says she wants the person to go the hospital to distribute whatever alms they can manage during twelve days. They should wear the necklace for the Ibeyi and worship them. The person's well-being depends on them. The person should not attend a celebration without dressing up first, because they (*los santos*) will embarrass him when they see him.

Yewa tells the person that they should not hit any child on the head, and children should not run inside their house. Nor should children whistle, because there will be tragedy. The person should not drink alcohol. Nor should

they extinguish fire with water. Nor should they give someone else a flame.[79]

The person will go to a fun, intimate party, but they should beware, because they are on the verge of acquiring a venereal disease.

Alafia

Babalu Ayé, the Ibeyi, Orula, and Obatala speak in this sign.

Babalu Ayé says they must move him from behind the door. That is not his place: he needs to be in a corner, and it is the Warriors—Elegua, Ogun, and Ochosi—that need to be behind the door. The person should not have doll or paper *santo* (*estampa*) in their home, because they will expect one thing and another will happen. Babalu Ayé should be offered a toasted corncob covered in palm oil and a small loaf of bread.

Ibeyi. They say the person needs to place the Ibeyi on a separate altar, and each of them must be given an equal offering of sweets. The person should dress one of the Ibeyi in red and the other in blue.

The person should not let anyone know they are a child of the Ibeyi, who are not keen to have other people know someone is their child. The person should be careful to avoid falling into a trap, and they should avoid roughhousing, which might be fatal to them.

Orula asks that the person stop wasting their time and money on gambling. The person will lose their money without advancing at all. He says there is a war between Oshun and Yemaya, and the person is to blame. He advises the person to control their impulses, avoid

---

79 DF-N: The phrase *darle candela*, translated literally here as "give someone else a flame," might also suggest "giving someone a light" (as in lighting a cigarette or cigar), or (in a more martial vein) "opening fire."

C

talking excessively, and avoid offending others, especially young ladies. If it is a woman that is inquiring, they should not mistrust their husband and stop causing him headaches with words that offend and wound him, because he loves her with all his heart. He simply has an abrupt and dry manner.

Obatala says he will be responsible for the person and help them. But the person needs to beg and adulate him a great deal. The person must not allow fighting or cooking with wood fires in their home. They should not keep cats or dogs as pets; they will require too much attention. The person should not eat white beans or pigeon. They should dress in white as much as possible and always wear a crucifix. When this sign appears, a lamp must be lit for Obatala with edible oil and six small pieces of cocoa butter. For six Thursdays, they should go to the church and recite Salve Reginas and four Hail Marys, then they will win their wars. The person should not worry about being disparaged by others, because those people are making an *ebo de lengua* for the person.[80]

"Eleda is that which thinks, *oni*. It sees, keeps a look out. It's always *kuni kuni*. It guides us and makes decisions about our life. What's in the head, the spirit, is a *santo*: the head is called Ori and Eri, both names are correct. All of us children of God have Eleda in our head. We all have an Angel, a Guardian Angel, which is each person's *eleda*.

"Refined white people like yourself don't take care of your heads like we do. They let elderly people casually handle their children's heads. They never feed their heads. They don't remember . . . or they don't know that it's the seat of their Angel, that's where their

Eleda lives. With the baptism, the sacrament and the blessing of the priest, the Ori is a very sacred part of the body. Of course it is, because Ori is a *santo!*"

Slightly concerned, an *alubata* gives me a sidelong glance and asks my dear Bangoché, "In that case, what about those machines at the hair salon, the ones that look like helmets, that women stick their heads inside to heat them up to curl their hair?"

"Ototo!" the old man, who does not like interruptions, answers.

It's never good to heat up your head. We'll talk about that, since we're going to discuss the coconut.

Listen here, child. The owner of the coconut is Obatala. The owner of the head is Obatala. The owner of brains, Obatala. The whole skeleton, the bones, *egugu*, which are white: Obatala.

Everything that is *efunfun*, white, in the body and the world, the whole world. That's why an *iyawo* and a *santero* who is a child of Obatala needs to dress in white . . . and if you really press them . . . To be honest, they should only eat white foods. The true children of Obatala are the *talako*, albinos, who are born from a Black woman and a Black man. They are wondrous, and they come to earth with white skin, kinky hair, discolored, and they have blue eyes, which they have to squint to see during the daytime. They see better at night, like the Owl, which also belongs to Obatala. They belong to the Iyesa Obatala Ochagriñan, the one who trembles so much. Old, very old, and very illtempered. I had an albino relative. They fed him at night, and they didn't add any salt to his food. When he was born, they wrapped

---

80 DF-N: The section reproducing Salazar's testimony ends here.

him in cotton. The ones who come into the world covered in a caul—the males are called Salako, the females Talabi—and those who are born deformed, hunchbacks, are children of Obatala, who is Jesus of Nazareth. Many of these *desencuadernados* [deformed or misshapen people] also belong to Baba. They come to purge the bad they did before.

Obatala is the son of Olorun, Olofi, Oloni. Olrait. He finished his father's work: the creation of human beings. When he finished the work, Olorun blew on the body, and the heart went *fuke-fuke*, and the first man moved. Olofi said, "Here is my *omo*, my heir, the world's *ologun*, so you must respect and obey him. Everyone must render *odubale* to him."[81]

Yes, for that same reason: Obatala is a sculptor, and he created human beings. At least the Lucumí. All the Lucumí, and there are a great many of them. As far as I know: Eguado, Iyesa, Yebu, Isaga, Usa, Oyo, Egwa, Odo, Takua. And the people from Ayase, Araefa, Komore, and Ekiti. And the people from Ketu, whose Elegua was a stone, not made with cement. And there are also many Obatalas, which are one and the same Obatala. And both sexes. The oldest is Odudua.[82]

The female Odudua, the other half of Obatala, is Yemu. They're the ones in the gourd. The other Ocha are born from this couple. Another old Obatala is Oba Lufon, who's from the Oyo, Yebu, and Egwado Lucumí. The people from different lands—"tribes, nations"—worked together. They came together in their devotion. As a result, the Ochas traveled to many lands, sometimes with the same name, other times with different ones. They'd change the name, but it was the same Ocha. That's why, for example, Olorun is known in Carabali lands as Abasi Bomo Ekwa, Kebasi. Changó was called Hebioso in Dahomey, San Fan Kon in China, and Santa Bárbara here. Ayaguna ran around half the world, and he came to be known here as San José.

According to Gabino's account of Odudua, who is always considered "the oldest Obatala" by my mythologist informants,

He was the one who made the heads. (And the one who distributed the coconut among the *santos*.) Olorun only made the body. The body walked around, but it didn't know where it was going. Olorun turned it over to Odudua and told him, "Okoni moves, but he has no direction! Finish my work." Then Oduduwa made the head. But that man still couldn't speak. Ibaibo came. He opened the head's mouth and

---

81 DF-N: The term *odubale* is archaic Lucumí, referring to the act of rendering referential respect by prostrating oneself before elders and royalty. Literally, it refers to bowing down toward the earth, and it is analogous to other Lucumí formulations, including *dobale*, *foribale*, *moforibale*, *aforibale*, etc.

82 DF-N: The description of Obatala in this passage outlines two notable paradoxes: (1) the ethnic and regional diversity contained

by the broad term Lucumí ("All the Lucumí, and there are a great many of them"), which is analogous to the modern use of the ethnonym Yoruba; and 2) a multifaceted, pluralistic concept of the orisha ("also many...which are one and the same").

gave it the word. *Oro*. Odudua had only given the head one eye. Ibaibo only has one eye, and that *odyu* blinds whoever it sees. To let the head see better, Ibaibo made another eye for it, on top of giving it *mokbo* (voice).

Bangoché accepts the veracity of this story, but his understanding is that it was Balufon who gave humans the word.

"In sum, Obatala rules all heads. Eleda and Obatala amount to the same thing."

In this sense, humans "must attend to their Ori above all else, not allowing it to heat up too much or get weak. From time to time, it needs to be refreshed."

"The head carries the body," Bangoché concludes sententiously. And during a brief silence, the old man lights the butt of his cigar and laughs.

> Now I'll tell you what happened to the head.
> Write this down. Since Ori thought he was the Oba, the Orifice said that even so, he was the King of the body, and he'd prove it. What did Oriolo do? He closed himself up!
> One day passed, and the head didn't feel anything. On the fourth day, the head was fine. Maybe a little heavy. But the stomach and *funo*, the intestines, they were quite uncomfortable. On the sixth day, *ilu* (the belly) was very fat, *wo wo*. The liver . . . *odosu*, it was as hard as wood, and the head started to feel bad. Very bad. *Elugo*, fever, made its appearance. They didn't know about the purgative Lerroá back then,[83] and

the situation got much worse after the tenth day. Nothing was working right. The head, arms, and legs couldn't move. What went in, the purgative made from Guaguasi, didn't come out . . . The head couldn't get up from its straw mat bed to carry the body. The head and all of the organs had to beg the Orifice to open up. He proved his own importance, even though nobody paid any attention to him where he was, in the dark and scorned by everyone.

Eleda, like all divinities, "eats."

In many cases, it should be fed. In others, it should be refreshed:

> The Angel can be stolen away with flattery. Your enemies can conquer you in many ways, including by leaving us without an Angel. It's enough for Eleda to stray a little or abandon the body for a moment to receive its favorite food, when someone else offers it with the intention of working us. When they distract our Angel, we're left defenseless.
> There are so many dangers, so Ori must be very clear. That way, it's more difficult to trick him.

Therefore, one must *Ibori Eleda* (offer a sacrifice, feed the spirit that resides in the head).

"When the Guardian Angel is hungry, it drinks the blood in the head of the

---

83 DF-N: "Lerroá" is Cabrera's transliteration of the brand name of a purgative (Les

rois). The phrase ("Lerroá purgante") is also a vivid example of ways *El Monte* has become absorbed, quoted, and plagiarized on the internet: like a snake biting its own tail, Google search results lead stubbornly and directly back to Cabrera's text, often without attribution.

person they protect. The person will experience a blow to their head, have an accident, and, right there, they drink the blood that spilled."

The first thing a *baba-ocha* or *babalawo* determines, using the *dilogun* or *okuele*, is the current state of the Eleda of the person who has come to consult the oracle. Generally, it is necessary to perform a "head rogation."

"A rogation to the head begins, like everything else, with coconut. *Obi* also means to pray, petition. *Obiocha*."

Many elders begin this ceremony (and all the others that take place in the Regla) by saying *Obi ori, Obi Eleda, Obi iku*, etc.

Ori is given blood from pigeons and white guinea hens, if it is requested or when it is necessary due to illness, or in order to escape punishment from the law. (These offerings are very delicate and very secret.) And if the head is simply "bona" (hot), you refresh it by offering coconut.

Offering coconut to Eleda is very common, and everyone needs to "refresh their Angel" from time to time.

"When the Angel is depressed and in need of blood, life, strength, then the rogation needs to be performed by a qualified *santero*. A person can refresh their own Angel at home without too much fuss. A lot of people have the good habit of washing their Ori with coconut and praying to it, and their intelligence is always clear and bright. Always avoid your Angel becoming stifled or exhausted. That's the source of missteps and mistakes." To perform a head rogation with coconut, "a simple, prudent rogation," *iyalochas* require: two new white plates, *akoto fun fun*; a white cloth, *acho fun fun*; cotton, *ou*; white chalk, *cascarilla, efun*; two candles, *atana*; and, as an

offering to Elegua, smoked fish, *eya*, and hutia, *ekun*. You can also add *eko, ekru*, and snail to this list. (The snail is inseparable from Obatala.)

All of these ingredients are placed on two white plates. Two candles are lit, then the *iyalocha*, holding one plate in each hand, recites a "moyuba" while facing the person—*aberikola* (uninitiated) or *omo orisa*—whose Angel needs to be fed or refreshed. The person is seated on a low seat (*apoti*) barefoot, as is customary in all religious ceremonies, with their hands resting with their palms up on their knees.

At the beginning of the procedure, if *bogbo kalenu* (various people) are present, three songs might be sung to each orisha, beginning with Elegua and ending with their orisha. The prayers are repeated four times.

In order for the head to receive the blessings of all the *santos* and *muertos*, the *iyalocha* usually says, *Ori ete asalaga elegue ohuani moyuba re ori hu hu ori etie ori alafia eba che huni.*

Akebo ake to, ake omo, ariku Babagua, Orio oguo ke oke to mi re. Or, perhaps: *Ori etie asaka le gue ohuani moyubare, Ori hu hu, Ori a me alafia eba tie Olorun okalerun Orun male Ori etie.*

(This means: Your Angel takes care of your head so nobody will mistreat you. May Ori be fresh so Olorun and all the Ocha protect them.)

Raising the plates, the *iyalocha* presents them to the devotee's forehead and the back of their neck. Then she places the plates lightly on the shoulders, both sides of the chest, the palms of the hands, the knees, and the feet.

Offering the coconuts to Ori, the *santera* also says, *Emi kobo Ori: kosi iku, kosi ano, kosi eyo, kosi ofo, ariku Babagua.* (This

C

formula is continually repeated, equivalent to "deliver us from evil": from death, from crime, from illness, from disgrace.)

Once they finish their prayer, they put both plates on the floor, wetting their index fingers in the water from the indispensable *jícara*. They make a small cross on the forehead of the *aberikula*, then wet the back of their neck, hands, and feet.

Some *santeras* also place cocoa butter on the points they have moistened and blessed. On the devotee's forehead and the palms of their hands, the *santera* uses *cascarilla* to draw two small vertical lines if the tutelary orisha of the devotee is male, or two horizontal lines if it is female. Immediately, the *santera* takes a small portion of each piece of coconut and a chunk of cocoa butter, which she puts in her mouth and chews until they become a paste, and then she applies it to the center of the devotee's head and sprinkles *cascarilla* over it. ("Saliva has *ache*.") They cover the paste with cotton and, finally, wrap the whole head with a new white cloth, because a used cloth should not be used under any circumstances.

The remaining pieces of coconut on the two plates are left under the bed and next to the headboard of the person who has "refreshed their Eleda." This ritual is practiced at sunset, the time of day Ñaná called *alele*. ("The times of day have their own names. Sunset is *akale*. Nighttime is *oru* or *okuku*, which should not be confused with the word for rooster, *akuko*. The morning is *ola*. Noon, the dangerous hour, is *osaga*.")

A head rogation is performed near sunset or at night, before going to bed. The person who has offered *obi* to their Ori sleeps with the poultice of coconut, saliva, cocoa butter, *cascarilla*, and cotton on their head. The following day, after removing the head wrap, they very softly and carefully move the precious goop from the back to the front, so that not even a single particle falls to the unclean floor, and they place it on one of the plates, together with the other pieces of coconut. They cover that first plate with the other one, then place it under the bed in the evening, when they take it to the home of the *iyalocha*, wrapped in another new white cloth or white paper. The *iyalocha* will send the "rogation" bundle "on its way"—which generally means taking it to the forest, where they will leave it in a shaded spot, hidden in thick tall grass, in a safe place, away from the sun's rays.

Once this ritual has been concluded, the *iyalocha* takes four other pieces of coconut in their left hand, removing a small piece from each one again, as we have seen, and repeats, *Obi nu iku, obinu ano*, etc. Then they hold the pieces in their fist and touch the forehead, the back of the neck, both sides of the chest, shoulders, hands, knees, and feet of the inalienable owner of the head, which has just been cleansed of whatever might be harmful to them. They put their hands back together, murmuring four times, *Ori mo kueo*. They toss the coconuts—*obi oriri*—to ask if the *ebo* is *odara*, *alafia*, whether or not the rogation has been done properly and the head is clear, and where they should deposit Obatala's rogation.

The head will not be exposed for eight days or, at a minimum, four days, and especially not to the inclemency of the sun, because Obatala cannot bear it, nor to the cold, dewy night air.

They will protect their head with another white cloth. Even if it is impossible for them to stay at home, above all else, they will avoid letting the sun shine directly down on their head. ("It heats up their crown.") The same procedure is followed for a "rogation to Eleda" with pigeon (*eyele*, a bird that is consecrated to Obatala and, "because it belongs to Santísimo, has no bile"), guinea hen, raw meat, fish (*pargo* or *guabina*),[84] or fruits (soursop, cherimoya, pear, grapefruit, pineapple, and other juicy fruits). The blood from the birds is poured over the middle of the head, "so it drinks it," and a few drops are allowed to spill on the back of the devotee's neck, *hoyuela* [jugular notch],[85] hands, knees, and feet. On a separate plate, apart from the one holding the four pieces of coconut chewed by the *iyalocha*, some of the blood from the birds is spilled over four other small pieces of coconut. The feathers and cotton are used to cover the head, which has been bathed in blood, and a few more of the feathers are placed on the back of the neck, jugular notch, knees, hands, and feet.

The *guabina* fish (*eya oro, eya la gisa*), which is offered in rogations to combat illness, is placed in a bowl with water. The *babalocha* or *iyalocha* raises it and presents it to the head, saying these words: *Eya Oro tuto mo fi oro lo mi lori, Olodumare mo fe oru mu Ala Echu maresa be se ori mi ke mo pada kori tuto ko dire awo ko di re Omo ai kiti cha legua.*

It should go without saying that a "head rogation" is the first ritual performed on a future *iyawo* before consecrating Ocha, given that "the head is where *santos* are installed," as we will see when we deal with this lengthy ceremony in another section.

During the seven days the *iyawo* remains in the temple after the "installation" and

marriage to the orisha, their breakfast consists of small coconut pieces whose number is equivalent to the "mark" of their orisha. If they are a child of Changó, the *oyubona*, or second Godparent of the *Asiento*, offers four pieces; if they are a child of Ogun or Yemaya, seven; Obatala, eight; etc. The *oyubona* carries the weight of all the responsibilities and tasks involved in an *asiento*, and they look after the *iyawo* at all hours. Their diligence might even extend to sleeping on the floor next to the *iyawo*.

In addition to coconut, the *oyubona* also feeds the *iyawo* a small piece of smoked fish and turtle meat, along with a small *jícara* of *omiero* during this first meal of the day of a new *santo*.

After the seven days of isolation in the *igbodu*, the *iyawo* is accompanied by the *oyubona* on a visit to the four corners of the marketplace (*oloya*). The first thing they buy there—or, more precisely, the first thing they are given as a gift—is coconut, along with the fruit, smoked fish, *eko*, and hutia they will need to offer the orisha when they return.

When the *iyawo* "lifts up the *santo*"— that is, when they move their *santos* from the temple to their own home— they should pay a tribute of $1.05 to their godparent or auxiliary priest in exchange for offering coconut to their Elegua, along with $10.05 for the sacrifice of a rooster.

The *iyawo* should give every *iyalocha* invited to attend the *Asiento* two coconuts and, if their means allow it, $1.05. This invitation is known as *achedin, icheyin*, or "levantar el *santo*" [lifting up the *santo*]. The amount fluctuates, "but paying tribute with coconut is sacred."

Immediately after "making the *santo*," the ceremony presenting the *iyawo* to the drums takes place, unless it took place during the second day of the *Asiento*, the

---

84   DF-N: *Pargo* refers to the northern red snapper (*Lutjanus campechanus*). *Guabina* refers to a type of catfish (*Rhamdia sebae*).

85   DF-N: The word *hoyuela* literally means "dimple"; idiomatically, it refers to the suprasternal or jugular notch, which is the dip between a person's clavicles at the juncture of the neck and chest.

C

"middle day." Otherwise, the ceremony is carried out at a celebration. Sometimes several *iyawos* are presented, paying homage to the drums.[86]

They are dressed in their "acho omorisha," the clothing for the consecration, which they will only wear once to inaugurate the full majesty and glory of their new status. From ten in the morning until six in the evening, they receive the congratulations of friends, relatives, and the numerous new relatives they now rely on inside the bosom of the religion. Their head, which is not painted on this occasion, is adorned with the *akoide*, a cap or tiara adorned with parrot feathers—theoretically, at least, parrot feathers, because the true *odide*, the parrots from Guinea, are scarce due to their high prices, or because they no longer come to Cuba like they did in the past, during the golden age of Santeria at the turn of the century.[87] The *iyawo* comes out of the *igbodu*, the sacred room, accompanied by their *oyubona* and godparent. They are preceded by the Llamadora de Santo,[88] the Apwon, who holds a *jícara* in her hand, delicately picking up drops of water from it with the thumb and index finger of her other hand,

and sprinkling them from one side to the other along the way, as if they were diamonds.

With their head slightly bowed and their eyes looking down—their steps very slow and sometimes halting, filled with religious devotion, humble in their striking attire and covered in beaded necklaces—the *iyawo* moves through the cramped, expectant group of *aborisas*, *eleyos*, *olorisas*, and *bobo kalenos* gathered there. On a white plate they reverently carry two coconuts, two candles, and $1.05 as an offering and tribute to the three sacred drums, the *Bata* (*Aña*).

They arrive in front of the drums in the living room of the home (*eya arala* or *yara-buyo*), which serves as the temple where the celebration is taking place: the Iya ("the mother"), the drum that sits between the other two; the Itotele, smaller than the Iya; and the Okonkolo, the smallest. When the *iyawo* reaches the drums, the drummers—the *olu bata*—stop playing. The *iyawo*, assisted by the *oyubona* and godparent, places the tribute on the floor in front of the Iya and salutes the drums as an orisha by prostrating for several seconds, their forehead resting on the floor,[89] their legs together, and their arms extended along the sides of their body. If the *iyawo* is a woman,[90] they also salute stretched out on the floor, but they support them-

---

86 DF-N: See Schweitzer (2013) and Vaughan (2012).

87 DF-N: This is a reference to the grey parrot (*Psittacus erithacus*), also known as the Congo parrot or African grey parrot. As its name suggests, its body is covered in gray feathers, but its tail feathers are a bright reddish orange. For ritual and symbolic use, the feathers are sometimes substituted with pigeon feathers, which are artificially dyed to mimic the natural color of the much rarer (and much more costly) grey parrot.

88 DF-N: The Spanish term *Llamadora de Santo* (analogous to the Lucumí term *apwon*, *akpon*, etc.) is gendered here as feminine, implying that the role was normally performed by women.

89 DF-N: The head of the *iyawo* normally rests on the offering, not directly on the floor.

90 DF-N: Normally, it is the orisha's gender (not the human initiate's) that determines the posture of the salute. For example, a female priest of the orisha Changó would salute in the male fashion by lying facedown, while a male priest of the orisha Oshun would salute in the female fashion by lying on one side leaning on his elbow, then turning

selves on one elbow, then the other, turning from one side to the other. The maracas (*achere*)—or bells (*agogo*) for a *iyawo* of Oshun, Yemaya, or Obatala—are rung next to the *iyawo*'s ears, calling the orisha. Then the *iyawo* is raised up, and they place a first kiss on the Iya, then the Itotele and the Okonkolo, facing the impassable dignity of the *olubata*. The *santeros* make a circle, the Apwon leads a chant in honor of their Orisha, and the *iyawo* dances in front of the *bata* until their *oyubona* takes them back to the *igbodu*, sometimes in trance, or on the verge of being "mounted by the *santo*."

The *iyawo* has saluted the drums and made *dodobale* (*aforibale*), and they are now authorized. They can dance in any *guemilere*.

Three months after *kari-Ocha*, their *Asiento* or mystical birth, when the *iyawo* celebrates their "three-month *ebo*," they will need to pay the drums a tribute of seven coconuts, a bunch of plantains for Changó, and seven pesos.

In fact, the drum is . . . but, why would we discuss its mysteries here, its sanctity, its authority, its seminal importance in the Regla de Ocha?

Without needing to repeat what my informants have told me, including an old Baloge whose drum sometimes "sounds on its own," everything regarding Aña and the sacred music of the Lucumí Creoles can be found in the exhaustive series by Fernando Ortiz, "Los instrumentos de Música Afrocubana."[91]

Returning to the subject of Ori: In these times of strange diseases, unprecedented phenomena, and odd happenings, Catalino Murillo recommends a very

---

and assuming the same position on the opposite side.

91   DF-N: See Ortiz (1952–55, 2018).

easy and pleasant "rogation" to keep the body in good shape and, most important, the mind lucid.

"You make a cross with *cascarilla* and cocoa butter on the forehead. During nine days, at twelve o'clock, you cut open a green coconut and use its water to wash your head, face, and feet. You toss the rest of the coconut in the street. You rub cocoa butter on your head, then use an *oyan efun*, a brand-new white comb, especially for this purpose, to comb your hair after the cleansing. In your house, you burn incense, *Benjuí*, and white sugar, and you toss little pieces of ice in all of the corners. This refreshes your spirit and vision. Ideas become clearer, and stifling bad influences dissipate. The heart is calmed. The home is purified, and the body's support—the feet—also feel fresh and light."

"The house is completely, divinely purified. It becomes clear, and the evil shadows that cause illness and quarrel are removed by sprinkling the corners and doorway with coconut water, holy water from three churches, and an herb belonging to Obatala."

A *santera* tells me, "Coconut water is sacred. Because it has the *ache* of Obatala, it's as valuable as the water from the church. I refresh my Eleda with coconut water, regular water, and river water, raw milk, and Valencia rice. I put the rice in water overnight, then I add milk to it the next day. I also leave the river water outside overnight in the night dew, then I add milk, coconut water, *cascarilla*, and cocoa butter to it the next day."

Olofin was very fond of Obi.

Obi was just and pure of heart, modest and unassuming like the righteous. Olofin made Obi's heart white. He made Obi's insides and his skin white, and he elevated him to a great height.

C

But up there in those lofty heights, Obi became vain. Elegua, another of Olofi's servants, was at Obi's service.

One day Obi threw a party and sent Elegua to invite his friends. Elegua knew all of Obi's innumerable friends. Everybody considered themselves Obi's friend. These included the great ones of the earth—the Okboko, Olorogu, Tobi-Tobi! Onisese, Ogbeni, Ayiyebaloguo—as well as the poor—the *aini, ochi, eburegua, aimo, alakisa, alegbo* . . . Ugly, miserable, dirty people covered in sores; beggars. The ugly, the deformed, and the beautiful. The clean and the dirty. They all loved Obi.

Elegua had observed the change in Obi. He developed surprising gestures of arrogance and pride that left invisible stains on his immaculate whiteness. Instead of inviting the wealthy exclusively, as Obi intended, Elegua invited only ragged, foul-smelling beggars and abnormal, revoltingly ugly men and women.

When Obi saw that ugly miserable mob of shabby cripples, he was beside himself, and he asked who had invited them.

They responded that it was Elegua, on Obi's behalf. Obi dismissed them, but not before scolding them harshly for showing up in such a filthy, neglected state. And so, the wretched of the earth left Obi's house ashamed, and Elegua went with them.

Sometime later, Olofin sent Elegua to the earth with a message for Obi. Elegua refused to deliver it. He told Olofi about the callous behavior of the pure, the just, the impeccable Obi.

Olofi disguised himself as a beggar and went out to look for Obi. When Obi saw that *okure* in his filthy rags, threatening to contaminate him, he chastised him for neglecting to bathe and dress in clean *acho* in his presence. Obi turned his back on him. Then Olofi, indignant, without dis-

guising his voice, uttered his name. Obi turned around, shocked. He recognized Olofi and threw himself at his feet.

"Forgive me."

And Olofi said to him:

"Obi, you are just. That is why I made your heart white, and I gave you a body worthy of your heart. You will keep your insides white. But, as punishment for your pride, you will fall down from your lofty heights, to roll around and soil yourself on the earth."

And the punishment consisted of falling from the branch and rolling around on the ground . . .

Since then, the coconut is used to "break illness." The one who has offended cripples and sick people covered in sores, refusing to let them into his party, rolls around in the poorest homes of sick people, and he cleanses them, on Obatala's behalf.

You scrape the shell of a dry coconut, whiten it with *cascarilla*, and leave it under the bed of a sick person.

As an instrument of the orishas, it also dispels harmful influences.

It is kept in the house for a certain number of days indicated by the orisha. Later, the *olochas* prescribed that it be smashed on a street corner, in a pasture, or tossed in the river, the ocean, or the trash.

The coconut works as an agent sent to "break apart" illness, but it works just as efficaciously as a way to destroy the happiness of a home, or a person's life. Normally, it is broken at a crossroads while saying, "Just as I break this coconut, may the sickness of X be broken." Or "As I break this coconut, may the life, home, fortunes, etc. of So-and-So be broken."[92]

---

92 DF-N: One of many ritual formulas in *El Monte* whose polarity can be inverted, from

(To break up lovers, a marriage, partners, *compadres*, or friends, "you go to the top of *oke*"—a hill—"and smash two coconuts together, then toss them in opposite directions," so they are destroyed as they roll down from the top. To disturb someone or "turn them around," a coconut is rolled around on the ground after it has been "pampered" and covered with oil. The coconut will contain the name of the person whom one is trying to "flip upside down," along with a prayer card, in order to torment the subject at all hours of the day and night.)

Coconuts painted white are instruments of Obatala's protection.

The ones belonging to Yemaya are painted blue (*obichadodo*). These are placed in a clay pot with water, or they are left out to roll around the house.

Oshun's coconut—*obi ako*—is painted yellow (ocher). Changó's is red and white.

Oya's is painted with all of the colors. This one is hung from the ceiling in a woven basket of nine colors. At the end of the period the coconut is supposed to remain in the home, the duration of which the goddess herself marks by "speaking" through her cowrie shells or her "horse," the basket and coconut are deposited in a forest. To ward off illness, the coconut is scraped until it is smooth and polished. Then it is rubbed with cocoa butter, caressed, and called upon. It is painted with *cascarilla* made from egg shell and allowed to roll around the home. Meanwhile, eight pieces of *ori* are placed in a cup of water. The water is replaced every two days. This cup—or a *jícara*, "which is the most appropriate"— should be placed near the headboard of

---

positive to negative, beneficial to harmful, generous to cruel, and vice versa. *See also* ESTROPAJO.

the bed "of the person whose health is shaky," fragile, sickly, or ill.

These coconuts, "which roll around according to their own will," are found constantly in the homes of our people: "People who are weak or threatened by disease, or those who the *babalocha* has warned will be attacked by witchcraft, should have a coconut painted white rolling around the house, or on a white plate."

"To cleanse the victim of an *ebora*, a harmful spell, you rub a coconut over the body, *ewe* (*ciguaraya, albahaca*, and *piñon*), and the bird corresponding to their Angel." ("If it's a cleansing under Obatala's auspices.")

"Coconut was Orumbila's wife. But she neglected him so much that he separated from her.

"Coconut managed to get many people to intercede on her behalf, and Orula finally forgave her. But on the condition that they live separately. Each one in their own *ile*. And he gave her a gift: *ebos*, cleansings, and rogations must be dressed in her clothing. That means *ebos* include coconuts, so they're well received."

Obi warns the *santero*—or any devoted and vigilant *aberikula*—in a very curious way when they are in danger of being betrayed. Quite simply, it causes them indigestion. Obi puts them on guard, alerting them that witchcraft is being sent their way, hidden in a sweet or some other confection using its pulp. By abstaining from tasting it in any form from then on, they avoid the witchcraft.

"Once," the invincible L.M. tells us, "they put something harmful for me in a coconut. I was going to drink the water from the coconut, but he gave me a signal. The coconut turned completely black. You think Mama Kengue would let them do that to me? To *me*?!"

A goat ("the lord of the four-legged animals") or a ram that is going to be sacrificed to an orisha carries a leaf associated with the god and a piece of coconut in its mouth.

Those attending the sacrifice are terribly afraid of being charged by the beast, who is going to be sent to meet the orisha, who is already sharing its divinity ("it's in a sanctified state") and is the messenger of everyone's prayers. When it passes alongside them, as it is guided by the *babalawo* to the place where it will be sacrificed, the *Igbodu*, or sanctuary, "the room of the *santos*," the women touch their foreheads and their breasts, the men their genitals.

Once inside the *Igbodu*, the person making the offering and all those assisting in the sacrifice chew a small piece of coconut and a grain of *pimienta de guinea*, then they spit it in each of the animal's eyes and ears. Then they speak into the animal's ear, each one expressing their wishes. The goat will transmit their requests to the *santo*. The person making the offering of the goat or ram is the last one to spray the bits of coconut, and—just before the sacrifice is carried out—they put their forehead up against the animal's.

Enumerating all of the coconut's uses would require us to describe each and every ritual practiced in the Regla de Ocha and Regla Arará, from the simple act of daily adoration by the *iyalocha* when saluting the heavens—*Olorun ka ko koi be re*—to the most complicated.

Together with Oddedei and Calazán, we repeat: "Everything we ask of God, we ask with *obi*. With *obi*, we address the *muertos* to ask for their permission. But before we mention the *muertos*, we need to say to them, '*Ibaye, ibaye tonu . . . Iba Baba ye ni iba, apete vi aya fa, iba kana ache le.*' And we avert our gaze when the *iworo* offers coconut to the *ikus*. All of us,

at that moment, turn our backs. We address everything that is *santo*, beginning with the father of all the *santos* and all of us: *Obatala birinigua alano sia buke.*"

. . . . . .

Some *Potencias* in the Abakuá society that intend to found a new *tierra*—that is, a new group or "juego" (lodge, chapter) issued from its own bosom—use a dry coconut to construct "an imaginary Ekue," which is called Bambito Eribo or Kambito.[93] It is an embodiment of the mystery and Spirit adored by the members of this society. To that end, three cuts are made in the base of the coconut so that it stands on three legs, like the Ekue. It is painted—in this case, using indelible yellow paint—with the emblematic symbols ("gandos") of the great fraternity: Iyamba, MoCongo, Isue, Empego, Nasako. It receives a sacrifice consisting of a rooster and the same tributes as Ekue: sugarcane, ginger, *maní*, sesame, dry coconut, *ñame*, charcoal, etc. A *marímbula*, which is put on display but not played, is placed next to the "sacks": *cofombres*, the *diablitos*, "because the *Juegos* had them in Africa, and it's the Africans' piano."

For similar historical reasons, this coconut is venerated. "It serves as Ekue, to honor the memory of the first *Potencia* that was founded in Cuba—Efike Buton—where the Divine voice was also heard in a coconut." (*Efike Buton ke nameruton Efike Buton eyego Efimeremo akuatoito akua embori mokuba feafe*. They made the *mokuba*, they killed *embori*—the goat—and they made the sound inside a coconut, which was the first *bonko*.)

Not all *ñáñigos* know or recognize this history ("tratado"), which is confirmed

93 LC: "Kambito Eribo is the son of Itiaroro, the earth, who is the daughter of Ekon Abasi, god, Nature."

by a well-known Abakuá authority, Ch. C. And, as we have mentioned, not all *Potencias* display it when they create a new *tierra*.[94]

With the Voice of the Spirit already introduced in the sanctum, once the procession of numerous dignitaries goes out with the *diablitos*, in bare feet and holding the sacred Abakuá attributes (except for the Ekue drum, which only allows its astonishing panting breath to be heard), a coconut is broken at the door of the *fambá*.

The initiation of Isunekue, the representative of the Bibi tribe, took place under a coconut tree, near a river. (And he sacrificed a deer to the Fundamento.)

......

Folk healers consider the water inside a coconut to be unrivaled as a diuretic.

Mixed with ginger, it cures gonorrhea. Its juice is a tonic for anemia, and a decoction made with its bark cleanses the blood.

The flesh of the dry coconut, which should be eaten on an empty stomach and grated so it is easier to digest, is regarded as an excellent way to expel tapeworms.

Coconut oil is an excellent purgative, and it is one of the Four Compounds in the laxative known by that name, which is still administered to nursing children: castor oil, coconut oil, almond oil—"because they are cool, so they mitigate the heat of castor oil"—and *miel rosada* [pink honey].

Coconut oil is consecrated to Obatala. In the slang of the *kimbisero—cruzado*—it is known as "a little piece of Obatala," and is also often referred to as

"Obatala." It is valued just as much for hair care. ("Since it belongs to Obatala, it's used a lot for combing your hair or rubbing on your head.") Nonetheless, it has the disadvantage of smelling rancid if the person using it does not wash their hair frequently, or if they fail to add a few drops of *bergamota* to the oil.

> *Como duende soy odioso*
> *y aunque a mi nadie me vió*
> *el que en dulce me comió*
> *siempre me encontró sabroso.*

> I am as odious as a pixie
> and though no one saw me
> everyone who eats me in a sweet
> always finds me tasty.

It is true. The flesh and milk of this tasty fruit are used to prepare the most delicious and most traditional Cuban desserts.

This includes from the popular and very humble "coco quemado" (burnt coconut):

> *Coquito quemado caliente!*
> *Pá la vieja que no tiene diente . . .*

> Hot burnt coconut!
> For the toothless old lady . . .

(Yemaya is very fond of it.) "La alegría del coco," made with cane molasses and sesame seeds, and "coco amelcochado," made with sweet potato, were among the coconut sweets sold in the streets by *pregoneros* [street vendors], including the most elaborate and exquisite ones.

COQUITO AFRICANO

Obi-Kola.

"It is used to make *santo*." "The secret of the *Santo*."

It is a very hard seed imported from Africa that is—along with two others, *eru* and *tuche*—indispensable in the *Asiento*. "Many heads" come out of a single seed of *obi-kola*, a type of palm nut. In other

---

94   DF-N: In this context, *tierra* (earth, land, or soil) refers to an Abakuá lodge or chapter.

C

words, a small fragment is enough to consecrate various neophytes.

Each *iyalocha* that bears witness in this ceremony places a small mound of mashed leaves on the center of the *iyawo*'s head. Lastly, the Madrina adds the *obi-kola*, along with *eru* and *tuche*.

Under the mortar, the throne that will be occupied by the *Asentado* "who is a new king," they place other bits of the sacred seeds.

Nowadays the seeds are very scarce, and *santeras* who have inherited them will guard them as priceless commodities.

Some claim that a palm tree that is similar to the African one can be found in Guantánamo, on the eastern part of the island, and that unscrupulous *santeras* and *santeros* use them as substitutes.

"That's criminal. It's a ruse that's just as pernicious as an *eri* (offering) to Changó that substitutes pigeon for the quail he loves so much."

According to what I have heard from elders, who complain about ingredients being unavailable for a lot of "work," it is possible that contact with Africa was maintained until after *la guerra del 14* [World War I], thanks to travelers from the Canary Islands. For example, the well-known Bernabé regularly imported these precious "little African coconuts," *eru, tuche, obiaya,* beads, and ornaments, along with certain liturgical objects. These included cowrie shells; stones; parrot feathers; monkeys; parrots; seeds; roots; "bere" (?) pieces of wood;[95] animal skins, fangs, and excrement (from lions, tigers, leopards, and hyenas); nails, hooves, hair, horns, and

bones of certain animals and birds; weeds; soils, and other substances and magical powders, both medicinal and aphrodisiac; *turari,* skins for drums; idols; stones; brass bracelets, *odani,* for Oshun. In short, everything needed by the cults and their magic.[96]

This trade, which was very profitable for those who engaged in it, survived during the colonial era until the 1890s. Once the republic was established, some of those who supplied Santeria resumed their activities. One particular Canary Islander made two trips to Guinea each year, fulfilling orders from *taitas* who were favored by numerous and wealthy clients. These merchants also visited the homes and annexes of devotees to offer their wares, which were bought and sold at very high prices, although a set of shells from Guinea (twenty-one cowries) used to cost half of what it costs today. An *apo dilogun,* a little sack filled with genuine cowries from Guinea, a handful of *obi kola,* a bunch of antique beads, or an *oche* made from Ayan wood are like gold to their owners.

COCUYO

Paralabatia dictyoneura Griseb.

LUCUMÍ: OFUNTANA.

CONGO: NKUNIA NTOKA, MUINDA.

OWNER: OSAIN.

It is eminently magical. It enlivens Mayombe *prendas.* Its wood is used to make *chicherekus.*

Its sap eases back pain.

---

95 DF-N: The term *bere* (Lucumí) refers to wooden sculptures, statues, and figures, and is analogous to the Yoruba term *èré*; see Crowther ([1854] 1913, 89).

---

96 DF-N: Cabrera suggests—implicitly, at least—that the transatlantic trade of imported African ritual objects described to her by "elders" was defunct during her years of research (roughly between the 1930s and 1950s).

COJATE or COLONIA

Alpinia aromatica Aubl.

LUCUMÍ: EWE ORU, DIDONA.

OWNER: OBATALA. (IN MATANZAS, OSHUN.)

The juice from its leaves is used to soak a cotton ball or a handkerchief, which is then stuffed into the mouth of a cadaver expelling bloody, fetid froth, and to plug the nose and ears and the other orifices.

Its fresh leaves are applied to the temples to treat headaches.

Placed over the navel, they prevent gas.

A decoction made with its roots is a diuretic.

It is used in cleansing baths for good luck. And to "destroy an evil," it is used with *piñón botijo* and *artemisa*.

It is frequently used with albahaca to ward off the Egun, free oneself from negative influences, and purify the home.

COMECARA

Eugenia aeruginea D.C.

LUCUMÍ: GERERE.

OWNERS: YEMAYA AND OGUN.

Following the corresponding *ebo*, its roots and bark are boiled to make a bath that is recommended to fortify the feet and legs of people who stagger and tend to fall down often.

When a person falls to the floor often for no apparent reason, they should realize that the earth has taken an interest in them. It is an unsettling sign that a desire to devour the person might have been awakened in our mother Aiye, the earth. It is not always a sick or feeble person who is called by the earth, letting them know that she is opening a hole in her bosom and taking swift action to receive them. The earth can be capri-cious, seizing the healthy, gorging itself on the strong, and relishing in the young. ("It swallows good ones too.")

Falls are invariably a very bad omen. "They are a sign that something is going to collapse: bad luck, failing business, declining health."

If it is a *santero* that falls down, the matter is much more grave. If a "horse" falls down possessed by a *santo*, if an *iyawo* falls from their *pilón* [mortar] on the day of their *Asiento*, or falls from their stone or throne,[97] if a sacred object slips from the hands of a *baba* or *iyalocha* during a ceremony, then Orula is consulted immediately and an expiatory ritual—an *ebo*, a purification and a sacrifice of animals—is performed straightaway to prevent their death.

Luckily, there are ways to mislead Iku or the earth when they demonstrate a premature appetite, "even if we're nothing more than their food." If a grave is open, it is generally fed a he-goat.

It is an extremely grave matter when Osu falls down. Osu, messenger of Olofi and Orula, is a rooster made of silver or white metal that the *iyawo* receives when they are given the stones of Elegua, Ogun, and Ochosi to worship, along with their respective iron symbols.

It is prepared by the *Babalawo*, and its function for the *iyawo* consists of "always remaining upright and strong." The Osu is only laid down—that is, placed horizontally on the floor—when the person dies. Some people are supposed to possess an Osu of the same height as its owner; in these cases, the Osu consists

---

97 DF-N: During several climactic portions of the Asiento ceremony, initiates are seated on an inverted mortar (*pilón, odo, odón*, etc.), a large stone, or a chair. See Brown (2003b, 193, 352) and Cabrera ([1957] 1986, 235). *See also* YERBA DE SANTA BARBARA.

C

of a tube supported by a wide base, and it is also made of metal and topped by a rooster. Osu "eats" with Elegua. If it falls, tragically, it is necessary to "work" and offer it the blood of a pigeon immediately. "When he falls, the *iyawo*, its owner, falls down, because Osu is the pillar for their life, their health, and their fate."

The same danger exists for the *mayombero* who falls down, or whose hands drop a *prenda*—an *mpaka* or horn filled with magical substances and animated by spiritual energy—on the ground.

It is likewise for a *ñáñigo* or *abakuá* on duty as a *diablo* or *ireme* who collapses while wearing their suit, which is magically "charged" and transformed into a spirit.

Surrounding the fallen *mayombero*, following the outline of a spiral that extends around the entire room, it is necessary to burn *fula* so the gunpowder—*tio, tio, mputo fula!*—carries away the evil that has provoked and predicted this accident.

The *ireme* needs to be "cleansed," post haste, with a rooster at the very spot where it fell, then taken to a ceiba so the cleansing can be repeated, followed by the sacrifice of a goat to the Secret. If, while inside the *Famba* or during a procession, a dignitary from the *Potencia* or a guest from another *Potencia* drops the Eribo—the sacred drum adorned with feathers—or any of the sacred attributes the public might see during these parades, the tremendous commotion this produces in everyone, actors and spectators alike, is a sight to behold. The *ñáñigo* who was carrying the object should remain motionless, as rigid as a statue, until the Isue or Ekueñon or other principal members of the *Potencia* arrive, showing signs of dismay as they lift the sacred object and purify the *obanekue* who unintentionally committed a sacrilege. Under such circumstances, the Mystery—Uyo,

the Ekue, always invisible—can be heard roaring frantically, relentlessly.

When an old *santera* suffers from repeated falls—"and it's not the *santos* knocking her down, demanding the payment of a debt"—it is clear that the earth is announcing that it is waiting for her. "The *santera* starts preparing to surrender herself."

When a person falls and hits themselves, it is customary to give them a little water mixed with earth in order to avoid the formation of tumors. "And to satisfy the earth."

COME-MOSCAS

"It's a tiny shrub, somewhat similar to a *plátano*, with thick, fleshy leaves. The Black people from the Ingenio La Esperanza in Sagua La Grande feared and esteemed it a great deal. When an insect like a fly settled on its leaves, the leaves would roll themselves up, and when they opened again, there was no trace of the insect.[98] Only a virgin girl could cut it with a machete to collect its blood, a red sap that looked like blood from an animal and flowed in great quantities from the trunk.

"The sorcerers would make what they would call *apreparos de salvamento*, or lethal witchcraft, with that blood and the piece of the trunk they'd cut off with the machete."

COPAIBA or COPALBA [or] Palo de Aceite

Copaifera officcinale L.

LUCUMÍ: ENENEN, KIORORO.

CONGO: MONCHUNTO.

---

98   DF-N: The name *come-moscas* translates literally as "fly-eater."

OWNERS: BABALU AYÉ AND ODUA.

It has many properties: its resin, leaves, roots, and bark are used to cure secret infectious diseases. "Babalu Ayé, the Syphilitic *Santo*, cures them."

COPAL

Protium cubense Rose

LUCUMÍ: BORU, FEFE.

CONGO: NYIMBO, GUARIA.

Its resin is used to remove coldness or "blocked gases."

During difficult or delayed births, midwives place patches on the soles of the feet of the woman giving birth, and they place her husband's hat over her belly.

It is the fennel of the Savanna.[99]

COPALILLO DE MONTE

Thouinia nervosa Griseb.

LUCUMÍ: BORU FEFE.

CONGO: NYIMBO.

OWNERS: YEMAYA AND OLOKUN.

"For medicine, you need the one from *el monte*, because the one that lives in gardens is nothing more than a dandy, and it's only good for decoration."

Its leaves are boiled for steam inhalations for those suffering from the effects of a harmful draught ("un aire pasmoso").

Its roots are mashed, shredded, or pulverized, then inhaled to soothe headaches caused by anxiety.

In an infusion, it is used to treat stomach aches. For good luck, baths with *copalillo* are highly regarded. Likewise, it is used in incense, mixed with *cuaba* or the in-

cense sold in pharmacies, to clear an atmosphere of evil spirits.

COPETUDA

Calendula officinalis

ENGLISH: POT MARIGOLD.

OWNER: OSHUN.

It is used to perform "sarayeye," cleansings, purifications, and rogations for people who are easily frightened and become pale or even lose consciousness at the slightest surprise.

These very sensitive subjects are liable to suffer cardiac arrest or an embolism, lose their mind, or suffer from amnesia.

In these cases, the *copetuda* is very useful to the *santero*.

It is used in efficacious poultices, and it is said that an infusion made from it soothes toothaches and earaches.

It regulates menstruation.

Its seeds are a vermifuge.

COPEY

Clusia rosea Jacq.

LUCUMÍ: INLANA (?), PAMO.

OWNER: ORULA.

Its sap and resin are used in a poultice to extract fluids from ulcers and sores, and to help them heal. Its roots, leaves, and bark are boiled and used in poultices.

According to Capé, it is used to make *prendas* (talismans), "because it's very powerful. Wherever it grows, it takes over the earth and doesn't let any other *palo* live there. That's why it's good, above all else, for winning fights and gaining possession of property."

Its seed is poisonous, and it is used to do harm. Its resin is used to disinfect the rooms of contagious sick people.

---

99   DF-N: Cabrera's original, *Hinojo de Sabana*, suggests that *copal* has similar qualities and uses as fennel. *See also* HINOJO.

CORALILLO BLANCO

Porana paniculata Roxb.

LUCUMÍ: KUEYEN.

CONGO: YUHE.

OWNERS: OBATALA AND OSHUN.

It is used in cleansing baths to attract good luck. In a decoction, it cures underarm abscesses that have become stubborn ("emperrados") or red: its sap dissolves or bursts them.

CORALILLO ROSADO

Antigonon leptopus Hook., Hook. & Arm.

ENGLISH: CORAL VINE, MEXICAN CREEPER, SAN MIGUELITO VINE.

LUCUMÍ: CHAUKO.

OWNERS: OYA AND AYAO.

A decoction using the entire plant, including its flowers, revives a person after a bout of drunkenness, neutralizing the effects of alcohol.

CORDOBAN

Rhoeo discolor L'Herit.

ENGLISH: BOATLILY, MOSES-IN-THE-CRADLE.

LUCUMÍ: PEREGUN, TUPA, DIELA.

CONGO: NRIO.

OWNER: CHANGÓ. OTHERS ATTRIBUTE IT TO OGUN AND YEMAYA.

In Matanzas, they consider Cordobán to be one of the principal *ewes* of Osain.

It is used for cleansings and baths.

In Omiero, it is used to wash the tools and relics of the orisha.

Its leaves are used in a decoction to treat asthma, colds, and hemoptysis. (It is an excellent treatment for whooping cough, as well as coughs caused by measles.) Its roots are used to prepare a syrup which is administered in cases of respiratory illness.

COROJO

Acrocomia crispa H.B.K.

ENGLISH: CUBAN BELLY PALM.

LUCUMÍ: EPO, LUFI.

CONGO: GESI, MABA, ANYETA, KARENDE. (*COROJO* PALM OIL: MASINGESE, MASI MABA, MASI MABA ANYETA.)

OWNER: CHANGÓ.

It also belongs to all of the other orishas except Obatala, Oshun, and Yemaya.

When Changó is mad at one of his children, his stone and accompanying cowrie shells are bathed in palm oil—the oil eaten by the orishas—and bee honey in order to make him calm and forgiving.

This rogation is performed over the course of six days. The first day, which begins with pleas that will be repeated during each of the six days: a bunch of plantains. The second day: six pitahayas. The third day: a *jícara* of cornmeal porridge (*amala*) with *quimbombó* (*lila* [okra]), bee honey, *corojo* palm oil, and six grains of *pimienta de guinea* (*ata*), all of it adorned with a red ribbon. The fourth day: six Calabazas (pumpkin, *elegude*), also adorned with ribbons. The fifth day: six *mameys* (*emi*). And, finally, two white roosters are sacrificed and a large batch of *quimbombó*, with its seeds removed, is cooked and offered. The *otan* is covered with a white cloth (*afo fun fun*). The offerings are distributed among three bundles that are delivered to a hill, a *palma real*, and a ceiba, respectively.

The cloth covering the *orisa* is removed and placed over the *omo* for whom the ritual is being performed, in order to indemnify them from Changó's displeasure. Palm oil is an extremely important substance in the cult of the orishas, who continually demand it for their cleaning and well-being. Elegua, Ogun, Ochosi, Changó, Babalu Ayé, and Oya are always coated with *corojo* palm oil. A little palm oil is always added to certain foods prepared as offerings: toasted corn and black-eyed pea fritters (*bollos de frijoles de carita*) for Elegua and Oya, and bread and roasted corncobs for Babalu Ayé.

In the Regla de Congo, it is only used to clean Zarabanda. (That is, the iron implements used to symbolize Zarabanda.) The *nkises*, cauldrons, are also rubbed with palm oil.

CORONA DE NOVIA

Pereskia pereskia (L.) Karst.

Three or more small flowers are prepared in an infusion as a purgative or laxative. (It was a favorite laxative among many ladies in Trinidad in the old days.)

CRESTA DE GALLO

Celosia argentea L.

LUCUMÍ: LIBE KUKO.[100]

It is used for "cleansings and rogations, performed under the auspices of Changó and Agayu, for men who are shy, timid, pusillanimous, irresolute, whose souls wander around their body."

Using *cresta de gallo*, Changó and Agayu will fill the person with their valiant and combative spirit, their energy, and what they lack most: courage.

---

[100] DF-N: The Lucumí and Spanish names of the plant are analogous; both refer literally to the crest of a rooster, and the ritual prescriptions in the entry make it clear that the plant embodies the combative, pugnacious spirit of roosters and formidable masculine orishas (Agayu and Changó).

CROTO

ENGLISH: CASTOR OIL PLANT, CASTOR BEAN.

"You can invoke Elegua and talk with him at the foot of a *croto*. After counting to seven, you dig a hole in the ground and fill it with sweet red wine, anisette, and some of the other trinkets he likes."

CUABA

Amyris balsamifera L.

LUCUMÍ: LOASO.

CONGO: INKITA,[101] NKUNIA BONDAN SUA, KISIABOLO.

A *palero* who goes looking for this tree in *el monte* must wound himself and offer it a few thick drops of his own blood. Otherwise, this tree removes its virtues from the parts of it that have been taken, and neither spells nor medicines prepared with it will take effect.

Cuaba is the same *palo* known as *guachinango* and *Cambia Voz*, which hides or makes itself invisible, and plays a great many tricks on those who do not know how to deal with it. We already know that it is the prankster of *el monte*, the one who sneaks away and is perfectly capable of fooling an *mfumo* or his *bakulu*, disappearing suddenly from under their noses. Once they have established a connection with this tree, many take a staff made from *cuaba* wood every time they go to *finda*, where they find everything they need.

It is not a tree of great stature or corpulence, but it is so prodigious that "no *nganga* works well without the *guachinango*."

The black variety of the tree is used to perform hexes, the white variety for

---

[101] DF-N: Cabrera uses *inkita* and *nkita* interchangeably.

good. In baths, they have the virtue of being able to cure people who suffer from constant tremors. And since its roots have extraordinary beneficial properties, they are burned, and the person being tormented by incessant twitching, obviously a victim of witchcraft, is made to inhale its smoke in the open air and will regain the equilibrium they had lost by breathing its virtue—slowly but surely—*sualo, sualo*. It is worth mentioning that if a person has suffered from tremors for more than seven years and the inhalation of white *cuaba* fails to provide relief, it becomes necessary to repeat the treatment using yellow *cuaba*.

One should always carry a splinter of *Nkita* wood for protection, or—when proposing a business venture, soliciting employment, or asking for favors—in one's mouth. It is ideal for lawyers and all those who defend a cause, right or wrong, since the *guachinango* in a speaker's mouth will enchant listeners, who will be subject to the willpower of the person talking. "In that case, the words are commanding by virtue of the *palo*."

A timid, ugly man will be able to declare his love to the most beautiful, carefree, and daring woman, without any fear of being rejected. She will find him to be an irresistible Don Juan, despite the fact that he is nothing more than a timid man, "un ombligo encogido" [a shrunken navel].

Absolute control over a person can be obtained by mixing powders—*cuaba, amansa guapo*, and *bejuco verraco (nkunia bondan Sambi y guanguangulo)*—into their food and drink, along with a drop of blood from the person who is administering the powders in order to dominate their subject.

But Baró, who holds the *guachinango* in exceedingly high esteem, insists that

"it's enough to have a prepared splinter in your mouth, and another from *canela*, to trick even the most clever person."[102]

Experience has proven the virtues of a very traditional protective charm made with *cuaba, canela, caimito, ciprés, palo Ramón, bejuco verraco*, and powder from the bones of a good *nganga*.

In the empirical medicine practiced by our folk healers, the *cuaba* is associated with many virtues. Its bark is used to cure venereal diseases, and its leaves are used in hot baths used to treat runaway fevers.

CUABARI or AMBIA

OWNERS: CHANGÓ AND OGUN.

In infusions, it is used to strengthen the nervous system.

CUAJANI

Prunus occidentalis S.W.[103]

ENGLISH: WESTERN CHERRY LAUREL.

LUCUMÍ: MADETEO.

CONGO: FAERE.

The entire plant is boiled in a decoction used to treat the flu, whooping cough, and asthma. It is also prepared as a syrup.

In strong decoctions, it is a good treatment for persistent itches and rashes.

CUCARACHA

Zebrina pendula Schnize

LUCUMÍ: AÑAI.[104]

---

102 DF-N: The original uses the idiomatic phrase "*el Pinto de la Paloma*."
103 DF-N: It is also known as *almendrón*.
104 DF-N: *Cucaracha* and *añai* are analogous Spanish and Lucumí words meaning

CONGO: KIENGENE BISA MAMBA.

OWNER: YEMAYA.

In an *omiero*, it is used to wash this orisha's objects.

In decoctions, it is used to treat internal irritation, crises caused by colitis, and to provoke menstruation.

Its leaves are boiled and mixed with a little sugar to break up kidney stones. Its leaves can also be applied to calluses to dissolve them.

It is also believed to ward off cockroaches, like the *reseda*.

CULANTRILLO DE POZO

Adiantum tenerum Sw.

ENGLISH: BRITTLE MAIDENHAIR FERN.

LUCUMÍ: KOTONLO, EWE OFI, NESENTEN.

CONGO: VITITI MASA, NGOSO.

OWNER: OSHUN.

It is used to make *omiero* for the orisha and to perform "head rogation" with *flor de agua, helecho de río (imo* or *omo omi), vinagrillo,* and *algodon.*

Ogboyi: *Culantrillo* is used to prepare a syrup that is efficacious for the bronchial tubes.

Its sap destroys tartar buildup on teeth. It is used in decoctions recommended for colds and hepatic, intestinal, and renal disorders.

Purifying qualities are attributed to it.

"cockroach." See Cabrera ([1957] 1986, 54). The plant is "believed to ward off cockroaches," and both the plant and insect are associated very closely with Yemaya, whose predilection for the insect is described in graphic detail in chapter 2. In *Vocabulario Congo* ([1984] 2001, 59), Cabrera identifies the Congo name for the *cucaracha* plant as *ningosa.*

CULANTRO

Eryngium foetidum L.

ENGLISH: CULANTRO.

LUCUMÍ: ICHORO.

CONGO: BIANKI.

OWNER: YEMAYA.

Its tender leaves are used to season the orisha's food.

Its juice is an abortive. In an infusion, it regulates the menstrual period.

Its roots are boiled with roots from *reseda, malva,* and *ruda* for poultices often used to treat hemorrhaging. (The *santera* who provides this recipe takes care to warn us that it is exclusively for women.)

CUPIDO LA UNA (the red one)

Ginoria americana L.

CONGO: MAMBOTI.

OWNER: CHANGÓ.

This flower is given this name—Cupid at one—because at one in the afternoon on the dot it "closes its eyes and goes to sleep."

It is good for purifying baths and cleansing the home.

CURUJEY

OWNER: ELEGUA.

"It's a parasite that's inclined to live perched on top of a tree. It's used to make protective charms and *afoche.*"

"It has a mission: it absorbs and dries out even the last harmful microbe. That's why we use its powder to cover sores, *ile aro.*"

The *mayombero,* who calls it *Akin,* uses the roots to reinforce his *Nganga.*

The *curujey* "cleans and strengthens the body," and it is a good tonic for the blood.

CURUMAGÜEY

Marsdenia clausa R.Br.[105]

LUCUMÍ: IWO.

According to some, its owners are Ogun or Eshu. According to *mayomberos*, it belongs to Kadianpembe.

In the middle of their search for the wicked *curumagüey*, the *palero* stops in *el monte*, pours aguardiente on the earth, lights a *muinda* (candle), removes their clothing, and *moana katuko kamulele* ("naked from head to toe"), they will find it without delay.

It is unequivocally bad, *ndoki*. Powdered and mixed with tiny bones from a chameleon (*ñoka pemba*) and the saliva from a toad (*echula pemba*) that was hung from its legs, we are assured that it is a very active poison which can be reliably concealed in any drink.

"We *prenderos* sing its praises:

Curumagüey Curumagüey
veneno que mata perro . . .

Curumagüey Curumagüey
poison that kills a dog . . .

"We say a dog, but we mean a man. And it kills fast. Its powder can be blown into the air, but the most appropriate way to do away with somebody is for them to drink it in their coffee. A single dose does them in. Sometimes one gulp is enough.

"It also has the advantage that it doesn't leave a trace, so doctors won't find it, even if they do an autopsy, and nothing can be proven. The best occasion to give it to somebody is at a party, a *chichiringoma*, when the person you want to eliminate is happy and off guard in *kus-*

ingila with the *moana nkento*—blabbing with the women. The best way is to put it in their coffee."

("Whenever there's a fierce *mulonga*—war—between *taitas*, *curumagüey* is always put to work.")

"The counter (antidote) is the San Piñón," the new shoot that sprouts from dry *palos*: "It's the only thing that can save someone who's been struck by a *kindambazo* that uses *curumagüey*. Apart from that, they need to have a good protective charm (*resguardo*) inside their belly, like the ones they used to make and put in our bodies before baptizing us."

Now that I know about the "virtues" of the *curumagüey*, it no longer seems strange that my elderly informant Gumi responded so dryly when I asked her what she could tell me about this liana: "Throw that out. It's the devil. The *olougo* mess with that! The Lucumí don't work with it." (*Olougo*, according to Sandoval, means evil sorcerer, like *Alau*.)

CHAMICO

Datura stramonium L.

LUCUMÍ: EWE OFO, EWE ECHENLA.

OWNER: ESHU.

Ndoki malongo. Very malevolent. *Mayomberos* use it to poison people and ruin their eyesight. "But at the same time, it has its good qualities. Its leaves are dried,

CH

---

105 DF-N: The *curumagüey* represents a nexus of Congo and Lucumí traditions, both of which are literally demonized in this entry.

106 DF-N: The consonant *ch* is sometimes treated as a separate letter in Spanish, and Cabrera grouped entries for plants whose proper names begin with *Ch* between *C* and *D* in the alphabetical order of the botanical encyclopedia.

burned, and inhaled to alleviate shortness of breath."

"It's good in hip baths and poultices for hemorrhoids. In a poultice, it's good. In rubbing oil, it's used to treat rheumatism."

CHAYOTE

Sechium edule Sw.

ENGLISH: CHAYOTE, MIRLITON SQUASH.

LUCUMÍ: WODEDO, MIONLO, TUTO, LALOYAGO.

CONGO: BENBANGUARIA, BORENKERI.

OWNERS: YEMAYA AND OSHUN.

"Chayote is used to make *dimbo* (syrup, honey) to treat pneumonia."

It is a diuretic, and it is used in a decoction recommended for kidney and bladder diseases. It helps expel kidney stones.

Its tender leaves are used in stews and food offered to the orishas. It is eaten by Oshun, Yemaya, and Inle.

CHICHARRON DE MONTE

Terminalia A.Rich.

ENGLISH: TROPICAL ALMOND.

LUCUMÍ: YENKE.

CONGO: MORONKI.

OWNER: OSAIN.

After hesitating for a moment, an old *palero* confesses, without his kind smile fading from his face, "It's good for drying people out." Consultations with other authorities spontaneously confirm the words of the kind old man, who is a relative of Cachica. It is recommended for anyone who wishes to desiccate one of their neighbors.

A *bilongo* using the yellow *chicharrón de monte* will destroy even the most robust body. Another *palero* writes to me regarding the yellow *chicharrón de monte*, which is known as *yerenyere* and *bonsomao*. It belongs to Oshun and Yemaya, and it has the same application as the previous recipe, but it "works" more slowly in powders meant to be ingested, diluted in coffee or chocolate.

CHICHICATE

Urera baccifera (L.) Gaud.

LUCUMÍ: EWE ÑINA.

Like the *guao* and a liana known as Manuelito, it belongs to the Devil. "They walk together to do harm."

Although many *mayomberos* insist that it is only used for harm, like the *guao* and *curumagüey*, and that "its essence is wicked," it offers very good results as a treatment for "female hemorrhaging, and there's nothing better for an *aro nigbe* (someone suffering from tuberculosis) than a decoction using the whole *eweko*," the entire plant.

It is also used to narrow the prostate, "but use with caution, because it can do a little damage."

CHINCHONA

Existema ellipticum Gris.

LUCUMÍ: MONBALAN.

CONGO: MONKORINA.

OWNER: YEMAYA.

Evil Things—*malembo, morubas,* invisible messengers sent by sorcerers, that take advantage of the hours during which men sleep to take possession of their bodies, introducing themselves into homes under the cover of night, and bringing misfortune with them—will find their path blocked if someone takes the following precaution: mash leaves from the *chinchona* or *palo vigueta* in a bucket of water, then pour out the water at the doorway.

CHIRIMOYA

Annona reticulata L.

LUCUMÍ: MEKERI.

CONGO: BILOKO.

OWNERS: OBATALA AND BABA.

It is used for cleansings. Its leaves are often included in the *omiero* of the *Asiento*.

It is used in stimulating decoctions to treat cases of weakness or momentary exhaustion, as well as to combat diarrhea and tenesmus.

D
....

DAGAME

Calycophyllum candidissimum D.C.

ENGLISH: LANCEWOOD, LEMONWOOD.

LUCUMÍ: LIONSE.

CONGO: BONDO, HINYAO.

It is used as the basis of a *nganga*. It is very powerful. "It has the virtue of being able to make women pregnant." "Bondo's life depended on the *dagame* tree, and he was the apple of every woman's eye. They ordered him to cut down his tree, and he died just as the *dagame* died. But the splinters flew through the air, and all of the women from Bondo's land became pregnant, because the splinters stuck in their bellies." That is why a decoction using *dagame* bark is recommended for sterile women who wish to have children.

A talisman made with its leaves will deliver seafaring travelers from danger and prevent them from getting sick on their journey. Naturally, in this case, the *dagame* is ineffective unless it is reinforced with other powerful, complementary ingredients.

"Women on their moon cannot walk under the branches of a *dagame* tree, because it will steal their menstruation. Under those conditions, the shade of the *dagame* is bad for women; it drives them insane."

It is used to purify the floors of homes by sluicing them.

DAGUILLA

Lagetta lintearea Lam.

ENGLISH: JAMAICAN LACEBARK TREE.

OWNER: OSU.

Those who are obligated to work outdoors protect their heads by covering them with *daguilla* leaves, which mitigates the sun's rays. "It extracts heat from the head."

Its bark is used to prepare an unguent for rashes and other skin outbreaks.

DIAMELA

Jasminum sambac (L.) Soland., var. *trifoliatum* (D.C.)

ENGLISH: ARABIAN JASMINE, SAMBAC JASMINE.

LUCUMÍ: ITANAKO FUNFUN.

CONGO: MUNDELA.[107]

---

107 DF-N: In *Vocabulario Congo*, Cabrera translates *mundela* as *estefanote*, a different variety of jasmine plant with its own entry here in the botanical encyclopedia. Meanwhile, *mundele* is translated as *blanco*—meaning "white person," not the color (2001, 237). The same page offers a pertinent phrase in translation:

Congo: *Mundele kualiukila nmukanda Bafiota Kualukila*

OWNER: OBATALA.

Its leaves and flowers are used for cleansing baths.

Its roots are used in a decoction to treat whooping cough. Its exquisite aroma, which women in bygone days would use to perfume their rice powder, is used in a love amulet.

E

EBANO CARBONERO

Maba crassinervis Krug & Urban.

LUCUMÍ: IGI LILE OR IGI DUDU.

OWNER: ELEGUA.

Its leaves are used in a decoction to blacken the skin beautifully. Its bark is boiled for the same purpose as a rub for the skin.

EMBELESO

LUCUMÍ: OYOYU.

Embeleso is used constantly in love magic.[108]

A powerful talisman to accompany professional womanizers is made with *embeleso* (because it is bewitching), eyes from

---

Spanish: *Blanco sabe con libro, el negro con yerbas (brujería)*

English: White people know with books, Black people with herbs (sorcery) (237)

Cabrera also offers a translation of the Congo term *bafiota*: "Una de las etnias del Congo. Negro 'mulato muy oscuro.'" (One of the ethnicities from the Congo. A Black person [or] "very dark-skinned mulato") (158).

108 DF-N: The Spanish word *embeleso* translates literally as "captivating" or "bewitching"; hence, "the captivating one" or "the bewitching tree."

---

a boa (*inioka, mboma*, because they also fascinate and bewitch), and the splinter from *palo paramí*.

ESCLABIOSA or ESCLAVIOSA

Capraria biflora L.

ENGLISH: GOATWEED.

OWNER: ODUA.

In his old notebook, one of the herbalists at the Plaza del Vapor has it written down that the Lucumí name for *Esclaviosa* is *Gauti*, and its Congo name is *Rakiongo*, a name which several of my informants reject.

Its leaves are mashed and used in poultices to dissolve abscesses in the armpits. It is also applied to "secas," swollen lymph nodes.

In a decoction, it is mixed with *guanábana* and flowers from *palo blanco* to soothe coughing.

The entire plant is used in an infusion to treat the kidneys; the same preparation, much more concentrated, is used to treat women's internal disorders. It is also applied to wounds as a poultice.

ESCOBA AMARGA

Partenium hysterophorus L.

ENGLISH: SANTA-MARIA, SANTA MARIA FEVERFEW, WHITETOP WEED, FAMINE WEED, CARROT GRASS, CONGRESS GRASS.

LUCUMÍ: EGWENIYE.

CONGO: BAOMBO. (CARABALI: IFAN.)

OWNERS: BABALU AYÉ AND AYANU.

Escoba amarga is used to cover the two *jícaras* that contain the orisha in the Regla Arará.

It is one of the favorite plants Baba uses to "cleanse" sick people. Any illness can be cleansed with *escoba amarga* and toasted corn. After passing them over the body, a chicken egg is taken to the road and smashed while saying, "Babalu Ayé, eat the flesh and leave the bone. Save So-and-So for me." As a cleansing, an egg will be passed over the body of the sick person for seven days.

Escoba amarga is also used constantly to purify homes. It works well with *rompe zaragüey*, and these two "elanga" are often mixed to wash the floors and spray the walls.

Escoba amarga is a prominent plant in the liturgy of the Abakuá secret society.

Its primary function is to whip *Abiku*, the "*aye*, the deceiver or impostor in a family." "*Abiku* is a child who dies as a newborn or as a very young child, then their spirit returns in another child that is born later. They die and are born, over and over. They leave and come back. When they die, in order to recognize them and not allow them to continue to deceive the family they're born into, a mark is made on the cadaver. They cut off a small piece of the ear, or a toe, or the tip of a finger. Then when they return to this world, it is already known who they are. Then they're bound, because that fledgling traveler won't be able to fool anyone."

"There's a heaven for children who have not been born yet. A heaven of *Abikus*. There, one of them says,

"'I'm going to the earth.'

"'For how long?'

"'This long.'

"They come, they're born, and when the time's up, they leave.

"They leave, and they come back whenever they feel like it."

"I had a little brother who died. My grandmother grabbed a pair of scissors and cut the tip of one of the little *muerto's*

ears.[109] Then another little brother was born. They told my grandmother and she recognized them. The baby was missing the little piece of its ear, and she said, "'Ah! You're a cat, and I'm going to give you a name from my country: You're Durokike.'

"In the old days, when a child died, they would make a cut on its body as a precaution. Not like today, when only families that have had an *abiku* born into them do that.

"When a first child dies, others are born afterward. Like the first one, they all die as children because the firstborn was an *abiku*, and it takes the others one by one. Or else, the firstborn doesn't die, but their siblings die in succession. That first child that stayed alive but doesn't let the others live, that's *abiku*." The child who survives their siblings, regardless of their ages, is widely suspected of being an *abiku*.

Emizún explains to me, "Ikube is the one that comes to destroy the whole family. It is a dissatisfied spirit. The *abiku* is a wretch. You shouldn't call anyone *abiku*. It's a curse. And an insult."

"An *abiku* is born and eats the family bit by bit. The *abiku* cries and cries. The home is backward and nothing good comes in, regardless of how much they feed the street. They ask.[110] Well, the

---

109 DF-N: In this context, *muerto* refers to a flesh-and-blood body more than a spirit or ghost, though the word can serve for both. For poetic and literary reflections on *abiku*, see Obuke (1978) and Okri ([1991] 1993).

110 DF-N: "Feeding the street" (*darle de comer a la calle*) refers to ritual offerings intended to attract good fortune to the home by appeasing the thoroughfare outside it. "They ask" (*preguntan*) refers to divination performed to determine the cause of the family's misfortune.

problem is that there's an *abiku* in the house! You take a little *palmiche* [palm frond] broom and tie a red, white, or blue ribbon on it, and you use it to whip the *abiku*.

"Every time they cry, you beat them. Or, even better, you hit them with branches of *escoba amarga*." "An *abiku* doesn't gain weight. It's miserable. The spirit inside eats everything given to the child, who can't absorb the food because there's nothing left of it. Along with that *abiku*, others come to eat the food too. Without hesitation, you need to hit them hard, threaten them, and scare them. Hit them with *escoba amarga*! You need to punish them. There's no other remedy. The blows hurt the other one, the *abiku*. Sometimes you get rid of them that way, but if the child dies, it's because the *abiku* dried them out. They need to be identified when they return, so you make a mark, a password, in their flesh."

They are insistent. "They take a liking to a belly."

"One was born and *simiku* (died) four times. Two of them had a piece of their ear removed. The other two, toes. The fourth time, they didn't die. After going away, when they came back, they'd spend the whole night crying. 'Get out of here! I'm going to beat you with *escoba amarga*!' Nothing made it shut up. The more they hit it, the more it cried."[111]

Abiku put up a strong fight. "One way or the other, one day of the week—Wednesday, I think—it's good to beat them, even if they didn't give you a reason to do it."

One *santera* tells me,

---

111 DF-N: It is impossible to ignore the unsettling impression that *abiku*, when held accountable for their mother's loss and suffering, might be invoked to justify abuse, neglect, torture, and infanticide.

I don't want anything to do with them, and I have never bound a child—*abiku*—for anyone. I want them to go away fast!

One of my sisters-in-law gave birth to a girl. She had a face like an *albarda de mal tiempo* [bad-weather packsaddle], and we saw her for what she was right away. She had an old woman's forehead. And she couldn't stand me. She died at five years of age. Her mother cried, mourning her. Three days after she died, Mañina, which is what they called her, appeared to her mother to ask her to not say her name anymore. One of my neighbors had a disgusting *abiku*, a ragamuffin, who yelled and shit himself constantly, and the mother was trying to just keep holding on, putting up with it. I told her straight: "Don't *nk-ange* that piece of trash anymore! Let it go!" That *abiku* went away quickly.

An *abiku* "tends to know a lot," behaving with an alarming gravity, and they even know how to maintain a terrifying silence. "They look like grown-up people." Sometimes their ears are cut long before they go away.

A friend tells me,

The mother of an *abiku* at our sugar mill was desperate, because all her little children kept dying, so she called a sorcerer from far away who was famous for binding *abiku*. The sorcerer went there, even though he was very old, and he showed up at the woman's hut with all of his gear.

He lit a candle, grabbed the child's ear lobe, and cut a piece of it off with scissors he had in his pocket. The little one was furious, but it didn't cry. It just stared at him with terrible eyes. "It's okay," the old man said to him. "This will be the last time I do this to you. Yes, sir! Because you're going to come back and stay."

The old man died, then the child died too. Later, that woman had a son who, positively, had a scar on the same ear they had cut on the other child, which everyone recognized as the cut from the sorcerer's scissors. That child didn't die. He was strong and healthy.

When an *abiku* is reborn, they are "locked down," tied with a symbolic chain on their ankle or wrist. They are captured, and they cannot go away.

"They're given an *abiku* name. They're called Bankoye, Yekiñe, Apara, Oku, Ibeyoku, Akuyi, Oñike, Ibekoyi, Tiyuko, Ekupine, etcetera."

For a small sum, an *abiku* can be paid off to not go away by "buying the belly" of a woman who is pregnant and previously gave birth to an *abiku*. With the proceeds from this purchase, the mother-to-be buys plantains that only she will eat. Only women who are single, virgins, or have no reason to fear an *abiku* visiting their own bellies can "buy a belly." ("When they become a mother, they will not give birth to *abikus*.") When that child is born, they will wrap them in a red, white, and blue fabric and say to it, "Olonu koko ibe omo kekere kani wa umbo kada." (Remember that you went away, but you've returned.) And they immediately strike it with *escoba amarga*.

"That way, buying a belly, *abiku*, a lot of children are saved." And many are also saved by blows delivered with *escoba amarga*.

It is understood that *abikus* are afraid of this plant, which is used to dominate and punish them, sometimes with bla-

tant cruelty. In some cases, simply seeing it will quiet and calm them down.

An *abiku* is an *aye*, a spirit that tends to spend a lot of time in *el monte*. There, it is not unusual for one of them to introduce itself into the belly of a careless woman, or that it "follows her home and sneaks in." The story of C., a neighbor from Corral Falso, is typical. "C. would make charcoal in *el monte*. She spent too much time in *el monte*. When she laid eyes on the child she bore, the old lady M.A. put her hands on her head. "It's *abiku*! How could you carry this in your belly, C. Look at what you brought back from the jungle, child! A run-down, beat-up *abiku*!' Because the girl was born with a cleft palate and sores all over her body."

This *abiku*, a true child of Iroko, still enjoys good health today. "Yemaya bound her, and she knows a lot."

Besides all of these magical prophylactic and punitive applications, Baba's *escoba amarga* is also a great "healer." Using three of its roots in a decoction, Capé breaks fevers.

The whole plant is used in an infusion to combat malaria. In poultices, it bursts tumors and cysts. In powders prepared as a paste, it cures ringworm, mange, scabies, eczema, and all "sores" on the skin.

Capé insists that it provides a great deal of relief to *adete* (lepers), or *bibiaye*, as J. del Rosario used to call them.

ESCOBA CIMARRONA

Abutilum trisulcatum Jacq.

LUCUMÍ: BELENDEKE.

CONGO: KORUNLA.

OWNER: ESHU.

To force a *muerto* to leave a home where they stubbornly insist on remaining, its branches are hung from the inside of the door.

ESPARTILLO

Sporobulos (L.) R.Br.

LUCUMÍ: ELENGA, IYE ERAN. "THIS ONE IS CALLED KIORO AND NBLELE."

OWNERS: ELEGUA AND OSHOSI.[112]

It is boiled for footbaths.

It is used to weaken Congo infusions (the ones prepared by *paleros*) a little bit when they are too strong.[113]

In cases where ownership of land is under dispute, a stalk of *espartillo*, which has been prepared beforehand in a *nganga*, is used to make a *nkange* on the trunk of a strong *palo*. The knot is tightened every day until, ideally, the adversary has been strangled. After winning the fight, the *espartillo* is given blood or eggs from a Sabanero bird, *nui nibaleke*.[114]

("Miss, that Sabanero bird, Nibaleke, is amazing. It says very clearly: '*Negro clavo tá joío*—This Black slave is screwed' . . . A drunk named Hilario thought the Sabanero was insulting him by reminding him of slavery. 'Listen to that damn Sabanero insulting me!' Anytime he saw one, he'd stone it to death.")

ESPIGELIS

Spigelia anthelmia L.

ENGLISH: WEST INDIAN PINKROOT.

LUCUMÍ: MINIRE.

---

112 DF-N: The original entry spells the name of the hunter orisha as Oshosi (rather than Ochosi).

113 DF-N: The phrase "too strong" reveals stereotypes regarding Congo people and their ritual traditions, which are regarded as being so formidable and effective that they tend to be dangerous.

114 DF-N: A subspecies of eastern meadowlark (*S. m. hippocrepis*). In *Vocabulario Congo*, Cabrera translates the Sabanero bird (*pájaro*) as Nibaleke susu ([1984] 2001, 250).

CONGO: GOMAGUA.

OWNER: OSHUN.

It is used for cleansing baths. It purifies and rejoins broken marriages.

ESPINACA

Spinacea oleracea L.

ENGLISH: SPINACH.

LUCUMÍ: OBEDO, EWE TUTU, EDE.

CONGO: MBI-MBI.

OWNER: OSHUN.

It is used to cover the receptacle of this goddess and refresh her.

ESPINILLO

Parkinsonia aculiata L.

LUCUMÍ: IKILEGUN, BIBOREI.

CONGO: NGOTO.

OWNERS: ESHU AND OCHOSI.

It is powdered and scattered to provoke heated rivalries in business or any contest involving various competitors.

ESPUELA DE CABALLERO

Jacquinia aculeata Mez.

LUCUMÍ: IÑAENERI.

CONGO: INBO.

OWNER: ELEGUA.

"This plant was born when the *kerekete* bird had its nest trampled by a hunter who stepped on its eggs. The *kerekete* cursed him. From then on, it lays its eggs on a rock, and this plant was born to protect them."

"Since it's born on rocks and covered in thorns, when it works in a *linga* (binding), the binding is strong!" It is excellent for making powders for *mayombe* and other magical preparations. It is used in offerings or "work with *santos*" to help people who have been bankrupt or ruined. It opens the way. This plant is used to make a fence around Elegua when it is advisable to rouse him. ("It's used to spur him on.")[115]

A little bit of its fresh bark is placed in cavities to soothe toothaches.

Juice from its leaves is used by breeders of fighting cocks to cure their roosters' injured eyes.

ESTEFANOTE

Stephanotis floribunda A. Brongu.

ENGLISH: MADAGASCAR JASMINE, WAXFLOWER, HAWAIIAN WEDDING FLOWER, BRIDAL WREATH.

OWNER: OBATALA.

It is *awo*, mystery. Although some *santeras* do not know the *estefanote's* secrets, one herbalist insists, "I couldn't divulge its deep mysteries to you unless you'd undergone the *Asiento* in *santo* and become a senior *iyalocha*."

ESTROPAJO

Luffa luffa (L.) Lyons

OWNER: OBATALA.

It is used for cleansing baths when luck abandons us. *Estropajo* "has the virtue of untangling luck" and bad situations. ("And it can make them more entangled too.")

Folk medicine considers infusions of *estropajo* administered as an enema to be an effective treatment against intestinal parasites and gonorrhea.

EXTRAÑA ROSA

Callistephus hortensis Cass.

LUCUMÍ: ODERERE.

CONGO: MONONLO, NKARDA FITITI.

OWNERS: OBATALA AND OSHU.

It is used for cleansing baths.

F

....

FLOR DE AGUA

Eichornia azucea Kunth.

ENGLISH: WATER HYACINTH.

LUCUMÍ: OYUORO, TANA FUN FUN, BODO.

CONGO: IRITUU.

OWNER: YEMAYA.

It is one of the principal plants for the *Asiento* and the *omiero* used to wash Yemaya's ritual objects.

FLOR DE MAYO

Laelia anceps L.

LUCUMÍ: WEGIGU?

OWNER: OBATALA.

It is used to wash this orisha's stone.

FRAILECILLO or CAIRECILLO DE MONTE

Adenosopium gossypifolum (L.) Pohl.

(AN *OSAINISTA* FROM THE PLAZA DEL VAPOR CALLS IT BASIGUE AND PAIME.)

OWNER: OSHUN.

"In the middle of *el monte*, the *Frailecillo* whistles. It likes scaring people, and it calls to the *ngangulero*."

"Oshun works a lot with *Frailecillo*, and she uses it when she goes to war."

Folk healers recommend drinking a decoction made with it, like regular water, to treat inflammation of the liver and the blotches [liver spots] produced when this organ malfunctions.

115   DF-N: This is a play on words based on the plant's Spanish name, which translates literally as "horseman's spur" or "gentleman's spur."

"It's cursed, and it works in a malevolent way ... I consider it a *palo* that belongs to Elegua, because it really does whistle like Eshu. It's used to make bad *prendas*."

FRAMBOYAN

Delonix regia (Bojer.) Raf.

ENGLISH: ROYAL POINCIANA.

LUCUMÍ: IGI TAMBINA, INAWEKO.

OWNERS: CHANGÓ AND OYA.

"It is *iginla* (a great tree) that belongs to Changó Onile."

"At a certain time of night, the *framboyán* burns as if it had a fire in its trunk.[116] If you go near it, if you sit on its roots, you'll hear it crackle. It lightens the weight of our burden. You know why? Because at that hour, Changó and Oya made a pact. Because Changó was stubborn, and because he ran around from one place to another, he was caught prisoner in enemy territory. Oya would often tell him, 'Let them come find you at home. Stay calm at home.' But he was a sorcerer and healer, so they came to get him whenever people got sick, and he would use his mortar to heal them. During one of those journeys away from home, they snatched him in another land. Oya got tired of waiting for him. She was sure he wasn't coming back, so she went to a *framboyán* tree, lit a bonfire under it, and lay down on the fire. Changó saw the fire from prison. The message was received. The fire signaled to him. Thunder came and went, but they did not melt the bars of his jail cell, so Changó couldn't leave. Oya understood that something else needed to be done.

This time, she tossed her machete in the fire. A lightning bolt burst out of the machete, Oya jumped up on the bolt of lightning, and she burned down the prison. Changó found her. He told her, 'Go put out your bonfire.' She took him to the *framboyán*. Changó stuck his hand in the fire and found Oya's machete, then he understood that she had saved him."

"On years when the *framboyán* produces a lot of seed pods or flowers early in the season, you should expect high infant mortality. It is necessary to take precautions and make offerings ...

"Prayers are made and its trunk is rubbed with cocoa butter. An *ebo* for children is made with fruits."

"Babalu Ayé wants to rest under its shade, and that's why he's at war with Changó, who knows the old man's sores prevent him from walking in mud, so he makes it rain and keeps the *framboyán* surrounded by mud. Baba gets angry, and he lets loose epidemics of disease, and that's when the children die."

The seed pods from the *framboyán* are painted red then used in ritual as shakers, or *achere*, to call Oya.

The *framboyán* is a good treatment for rheumatism. The following is a formula for a treatment that is very typical of Trinidad: it is mashed with *jengibre* and cane aguardiente in rubbing oil and simultaneously drunk in a decoction.

FRESCURA

ENGLISH: ARTILLERY PLANT.

LUCUMÍ: EWE RU MATAN, TUTU.

OWNERS: OSHUN AND YEMAYA.

This plant, which grows in humid soil, brings good luck to anyone who uses it to wash the floors of their home.

It is considered beneficial for the kidneys.

"When Ifa and Osain went to war, the children of Ifa took *frescura*, which

---

116 DF-N: It is also known as *framboyán de Madagascar, flamboyant*, etc.

grows on rocks in *el monte*, and the plant didn't dry out. It stayed alive for a whole month. When Ifa saw this miracle, he acknowledged that Osain was the greatest orisha of all."

"Really, whenever we talk about Osain—*difun Osain! (Osain agweniyi owaloye iyame ko yemi Agroniga oni gwagwado olo malu guda guda)*—we should raise ourselves partially up from our seat and touch our bellies."

"And not only when we mention Osain. If we name any of the sixteen Ocha when we're sitting down, we get up from the chair, or we make the gesture, and *fibale*, touching the floor with our hand."

"Oto bale, kofun bale." (Make the sign of the cross when you hear the Ocha mentioned.)

Frescura is very good for purifying homes, refreshing spirits, and clearing up a person's luck, and people suffering from kidney disease should drink a decoction made with it like regular water.

FRIJOL DE CARITA

Vigna unguiculata (L.) Walp.

ENGLISH: COWPEA.

LUCUMÍ: ERE-E PIPA, ERECHE.

CONGO: GUANDI.

All grains belong to Babalu Ayé.

The so-called *frijol de carita* is used to make a paste called *olele* for the goddess Oshun. Bija and a little salt is added to the lard used to fry *olele*. This same type of bean is mashed, unsalted, to make *ekru*, a delicacy offered to Obatala.

FRIJOLES NEGROS

Phaseolus vulgaris L.

ENGLISH: BLACK BEAN, COMMON BEAN.

LUCUMÍ: ERE IDUDU, ERERE, ERECHE DUDU, AGANDUDU.

CONGO: GUANDI.[117]

For good luck, frijoles, garbanzos, and *maíz* are wrapped separately in paper and scattered at different crossroads with three centavos in order to gain the favor of guardian spirits.

Black bean soup is often used to conceal a powerful love potion that unites lovers in an unbreakable bond. The *santera* R.S. explains its preparation: "You remove the hearts from two pigeons that have mated. When they're in heat, you rip them out. You toast them and reduce them down to a very fine powder, along with traces of the subjects and hair from their temples, the backs of their necks, the *cocorotina* (the top of the head), the *oroti*, and the armpits. All the hair and nails from the toes and fingers are powdered and mixed together with the powdered hearts and offered, 'traditionally,' in a black bean soup."

FRIJOLILLO

Lonchocarpas latifolus H.B.K.

OWNERS: CHANGÓ AND OGUN.

It is used to make amulets for police officers.

FRUTA BOMBA

Carica papaya L.

ENGLISH: PAPAYA.

LUCUMÍ: IDEFE, IBEKUE.

CONGO: MACHAFIO NSIKE MOANA NKENTO.

---

117 DF-N: *Guandi* (or *guando*) is the generic Congo word for bean. See Cabrera ([1984] 2001, 73).

"ITS NAME? WRITE DOWN OBO. AND,
IN CONGO, KISONDO!"[118]

OWNER: OYA.

It is used in rogations for the head, to
cure madness.

It has diuretic, digestive, and nutritious
qualities.

A *santero* consults their cowrie shells,
or whatever instrument they employ,
to divine "whether the madness is due
to syphilis or a spirit." They extract the
juice from the fruit and prepare a beverage by grating the core and mixing it
with *jalapa*.[119] Seven doses are administered during alternating days on an
empty stomach. Afterward, a strong
decoction made with its dried leaves is
given three times per day.

To refresh the Angel: Sleep with leaves
from *fruta bomba* and white *higuereta*
under your pillow for sixteen nights. The
leaves are gathered in installments and
kept in a paper bag. At the end of the
sixteen days, they are taken to the *santero*.

---

118 DF-N: Because Cubans use the word *papaya* as a euphemism to refer to female genitalia, *fruta bomba* is the preferred term for the
tree and fruit. Therefore, the Congo and Lucumí
names in this entry translate Havana slang into
archaic African vocabulary. In *Anagó*, Cabrera
translates the Lucumí term *ibekue* as "papaya"
(also known as *ibepé*; [1957] 1986, 147), while
obo is translated as "female sex organ" (*órgano
sexual femenino*) and "guanábana"—that is,
"soursop" (*Annona muricata*; 229). In *Vocabulario Congo* she translates the Congo term
Nsike muana nkento as "sex of a woman" (*sexo
de mujer*; [1984] 2001, 257), while *machafío*
is translated generically as "fruit" (*fruta*; 215).
Here the quotation from Cabrera's anonymous
informant ties all of this together by offering
two other Congo and Lucumí words for female
genitalia.

119 DF-N: *Jalapa* refers to caper spurge (*Euphorbia lathyris*).

FRUTA BOMBA MACHO

To treat pain in the side, a stalk approximately one meter long is boiled and used
in very hot hip baths to settle the person
on three days every month. Additionally,
it is drunk in a decoction to cure pain.

Mixed with coconut milk and drunk
in spoonfuls on an empty stomach—in
large or small doses, depending on the
patient's age—it is used to combat intestinal parasites.

The fruit, sap, and leaves (which should
be removed carefully by pulling them
down) are used to cure madness.

FULMINANTE

Ruella geminiflora H.B.K.[120]

LUCUMÍ: EWE NIRO, VEN-WEN,
PATOTO.

CONGO: ONCHAON.

This wild plant produces seed pods that
burst when they dry out, launching its
seeds like projectiles. The *ngangulero*
uses them to prepare a very efficacious
amulet for police officers and thugs who
expose their lives to other, more fearsome detonations.

(This plant is also known as *salta perico*.)

G
....

GALAN DE DIA

Cestrum diurnum L.

ENGLISH: DAY-BLOOMING CESTRUM,
DAY-BLOOMING JASMINE.

LUCUMÍ: ORUFIRIN, OTOIRO.

---

120 DF-N: The Spanish name *fulminante* translates literally as "instant," "sudden and fatal,"
and "detonator."

CONGO: MONTO'O.

OWNERS: OBATALA, ODUA.

It is used to purify the home, remove bad influences, attract good luck, and create an atmosphere of happiness and clarity. Its petals are scattered throughout the house.

GALAN DE NOCHE

Cestrum nocturnum L.

ENGLISH: NIGHT-BLOOMING CESTRUM, NIGHT-BLOOMING JASMINE.

LUCUMÍ: ORUFIRIN, ELUBE.

CONGO: DONDOKO.

OWNERS: OBATALA AND ORUNLA.

It is used for cleansing baths, and it is highly recommended for widows who wish to marry again.

A decoction made with its roots provides great flexibility and endurance in the muscles of the legs and feet. Acrobats, dancers, and athletes will benefit from these baths with *galán*.

It is said that its virtues as a treatment for nervous disorders, including epilepsy, are no less valuable.

GAMBUTE or GAMBUTERA

Brachiaria platyphylla, Grisb.

ENGLISH: BRACHARIA, SIGNALGRASS.

OWNER: ELEGUA.

Mazos [bundles] are made with its branches—"garrotes"—and placed next to Elegua in order to weaken an enemy's witchcraft and neutralize its effects.

GANDUL

Cajanus indicus, Spreng.

ENGLISH: PIGEON PEA.[121]

OWNER: BABALU AYÉ.

It is used in decoctions to treat the flu. These are very refreshing and nutritious. Loaded with sugar, they are fed to children.

In baths, it alleviates the itching caused by mange. The fruit is a type of edible pea that is seldom consumed in Havana.

GATEADO

Brossimun alicastrum Sw.

OWNER: ESHU.

It is pulverized and used in an *afoche* to "set back," "harm," and disturb a person.

GENCIANA DE LA TIERRA

Voyra aphylla Pers.

LUCUMÍ: IYENDERÉ.

CONGO: LONLÓ.

OWNERS: YEMAYA AND OGUN.

Soaked in alcohol, it is used as a rub for people with rheumatism. In a very hot tea, it is used to treat the stomach, and as an aperitif.

GENJIBRE

Zingiber (L.) Karst.

ENGLISH: GINGER.

LUCUMÍ: EWE ATALE.

OWNER: OGUN.

The fruit of the ginger plant, along with *caña santa*, agitates Ogun.

Its medicinal applications: in a tea, it is used to provoke menstruation and alleviate its pain; it is also used to treat shortness of breath and for the stomach.

121 DF-N: Other names for the plant are red gram; in South Asia, tur (or toor); and, in Jamaica, gungo pea, gunga pea, and gungu pea.

GERANIO

Pelargonium odoratissimum

ENGLISH: GERANIUM.

LUCUMÍ: PÚPAYO.

OWNERS: CHANGÓ AND OYA.

It is used in cleansing baths. It brings luck.

For the nerves, and for the heart, a tea is made from this mixed with lemon balm. "The strongest is the red one, *pupa*." For disruptions of the ovaries, it is taken daily with a good dry wine.

GIRASOL[122]

Helianthus annuus L.

ENGLISH: SUNFLOWER.

LUCUMÍ: KÉKUORO, ORÚNIFÉ, YENKEMI.

CONGO: YÓNGOSO, TÁNGO.

OWNER: OSHÚN.

This flower exerts a positive influence wherever it is kept.

It dispels "undeveloped" spirits. "Oshun likes to see these plants in her children's homes."

It softens chronic tumors.

In teas, it is used for vaginal baths.

GRAJO

Eugenia axillaris (Sw.) Wild.

ENGLISH: WHITE STOPPER.

("I CALL IT MBORÓ.")

OWNER: OGUN.

At night, all of the evil forces or spirits who wander freely at those hours try to penetrate poorly defended doorways.

Our sleep should be well looked after, and our body, which is left without its soul, should be well defended. Spreading crushed *grajo* at the entrances to the house before bedtime makes that access impossible, "blocking the path of depraved *muertos*, the ones who work in bad faith. Their mission is to do harm, and they hold an oil lamp in their hand as they approach."[123]

GRAMA

Cynodon dactylon (L.) Pers.

ENGLISH: BERMUDA GRASS.

LUCUMÍ: COTONEMBO, EWE ERAN, DENGO, ELUGGUE, TUMAYA, IYERAN.

CONGO: NFITA SOLANKI, GUANDI, INDONSO.

Like *Pata de Gallina* (*Kimbansa*), this is also a member of an extremely modest class of plants that grows in all terrains with the same obstinate will to live, and it has identical virtues.

Before beginning a *juego de palo*, it is used for the *nkangues* (*amarres*, binding charms) which are placed in the corners to protect the meeting of the sorcerer and his clients.

> *Ingrama ngrama Nene vamo nkanga mundele*
> *Vamo nkanga mundele. Barajo! Kanga mundele!*
> *No hay mundele que me bonda, no hay justicia que me isa (agarra)*
> *Si tiene mensu (ojo) no me mira,*
> *Si tiene nkuto (oido) no me oye. Si tiene lembo (brazo) no me coge*
> *Si tiene malo (pie) no me alcanza. Si tiene masuru (nariz) no me kamba (huele).*

---

122 DF-N: The plant's Spanish, Latin (botanical), Lucumí, and Congo names are all literally analogous.

123 DF-N: The oil lamp refers back to a description of Haitian and Jamaican sorcery in chapter 2.

G

Mundele que kuenda kiako (que huya el policía)
Ngrama vamo a mundele
Medio fuerte no hay cambio, Sube nsulu (cielo) cae Ntoto (tierra)
Sulu son mosquitero, kariempemba ta eperando.

Ingrama ngrama, child, let's go, *nkanga mundele*
Let's go *nkanga mundele*. Damn! *Kanga mundele!*
No *mundele* can *bonda* me, no police can capture me
They have eyes, but they can't see me. They have ears, but they can't hear me. They have arms, but they can't grab me. They have feet, but they can't catch me. They have noses, but they can't smell me.
Mundele who runs from the police
Ngrama, let's go after the *mundele*
Half-strength changes nothing, sky goes up, earth falls down
Sulu is a mosquito net, *kariempemba* is waiting.

With Grama, there are no surprises, and the *Mambi* sings with confidence:

Kimbisi kinsense, mi grama leri,
Mi nganga tara, kimbisi kinsense
Mi Nzarabanda . . . etc.

He sings as he works, binding and tying down the *mundeles* in his cauldron, so the authorities will not arrive.[124]

Without complicating matters too much, it is possible to seize any individual by simply leaning down to the ground, saying their name, and tying a stem into a knot. The subject named at the moment of tying the knot will remain virtually bound, a prisoner of the *grama*.

An elder I know employed this method to prevent his wife from going to get him at the café where he played dominos with his "conguakos" (good friends), spent more money than he should, and drank more *malafo mamputo* (liquor) than was good for her. The woman who knew she was tied down would not even try to go near that damned café.

Grama is "a very witchy plant," and it is used in many amulets, *nsarandas*, *bilongos*, and magical instruments: "it works very well," and it should be used with caution.

This is declared in a well-known *palo* song:

Eh! pie . . . yerba malo. Con pie no pisa yerba malo
Ngrama, un pie, ngrama ngrama, yerba mala.

Eh! foot . . . bad grass. Don't step on the bad grass with your foot . . .
Ngrama, a foot, *ngrama ngrama*, bad grass.

In the Regla de Mayombe del Santo Cristo de Buen Viaje, a handful (*manojillo*) of *grama* is put to the head of the person being initiated, along with a *kanga* of corn soaked in dry wine, cognac, and earth from the *nganga*. The initiate is then asked their name and surname three times. After touching their head with the *grama*, a tuft of their hair is cut off to be kept in the *nganga*, along with blood from the crosses made on the neophyte's forearms, both sides of their chest, and the insteps of their feet.

When a "*ngombe*," a recent initiate in a branch of Palo Monte, returns to collect the clothes they buried in the cemetery—because "when they become a *mayombero*, their body belongs

---

124 DF-N: *Mundeles* refers to white people generally; in this context, it refers more specifically to repressive "authorities" (overseers, police, military) who must be kept away from rituals.

to the *muertos*"—they are given the juice from *grama* that has been crushed and strained. They drink three sips. Along with a handful of the *grama*, they are presented with the *kisenge, kisengere,* or *kisenga*—the tibia of a skeleton that has been magically prepared. This is waved around their legs, around their waist, and over their head. With the blades of *grama* and the shinbone in their hands, they kneel in front of the *nganga*. The spirit does not delay in taking possession of their body: "it knocks them down and climbs on top of them."

"The *kinsenge* is like tube the spirit goes through to enter their *ngombo*."

Grama is also greatly appreciated for its curative properties. People consume it in teas for the stomach, and women insist that it is good for the uterus, the womb, and irritated ovaries.

GRANADA

Punica granatum L.

ENGLISH: POMEGRANATE.

LUCUMÍ: OROKO, MAYAKU, YAYEKU-KANSORE.

OWNERS: OYÁ AND CHANGÓ.

A branch from this tree will ward off ghosts and prevent them from disturbing our rest. The fruit is offered to Changó Orisha.

If one is consulting the cowrie shells and the sign Eyionle (which announces death) repeats three times, the diviner can frighten away ill fortune with leaves and seeds of the pomegranate. But in this case, it is not a bad idea to also sacrifice a dove and paint the entire house white. If the person for whom divination is being performed has not been initiated to *santo*, their arms should be painted with white chalk; if they are *Asentada* (initiated), it is necessary to paint the faces of all who are present.

"Sorcery that creates boils or sores on the body can be removed with pomegranate. Aside from the pomegranate, three nails are tied together with white and red string in the form of a cross, three lemons are cut, and all of this is boiled. You use this infusion to rub the part of the body that is cursed, and this gets rid of it."

The pomegranate's ability to blacken hair is well known, as are the benefits of a decoction made with pomegranate, which is accompanied by a castor oil purgative and used to expel pinworms and tapeworms.

GRANADILLO

Brya ebenus D.C.

ENGLISH: COCUSWOOD, JAMAICAN RAIN TREE.

LUCUMÍ: TOITON, OROKO, LILE.

CONGO: MÓNDUO.

OWNERS: CHANGÓ AND OGUN.

It is used to "work" with Ogun and to manufacture the "toletes" (billy clubs) used by the police.

("My *oye* for Changó"—also known as an *oche* or scepter—"was made from *granadillo*.")

GRENGUERE

Cochorus olitorius L.

LUCUMÍ: EFÓ.

OWNERS: YEMAYA, OSHUN, AND CHANGÓ.

It is food for these orishas.

It is like *quimbombó* [okra].

"Slippery like *quimbombó*; it's not used to work in Mayombe."

GROSELLA

Cicca desticha L.

ENGLISH: CURRANT.

G

LUCUMÍ: MEYELE, ESO, AKIVARE.

CONGO: MBUNDA, MIGUA.

OWNER: OSHUN.

A tea made with the roots and leaves is used for "cleansing" the digestive tract and for treating enteritis (intestinal swelling).

GUABICO

Xilopia glaba L.

LUCUMÍ: EWÚ.

OWNER: ELEGUA.

"When Mfumanbata (the law) or an enemy is chasing us, an *mpolo* that's been worked over with Guabico will protect us. If you spread it over the place where that person will pass, we'll be freed from their persecution."

GUACAMAYA AMARILLA

Poinciana pulcherrima L.

ENGLISH: PEACOCK FLOWER, BARBADOS PRIDE.

LUCUMÍ: ORUMAYA, PUPURUSA.

OWNER: OSHUN.

It is used in spiritual cleansings (which use a tea made with its flowers). The roots, branches, and leaves are used for swelling, and in rubs for rheumatic pain.

GUACAMAYA COLORADA

LUCUMÍ: ORUMAYA, EWE PON, KAMARERE, ERUNTOKO.

OWNERS: CHANGÓ AND OSHUN.

This one is "more finely tuned": it is "faster than the yellow one [described in the previous entry]; it has the virtue of connecting more quickly with the divine powers, which respond more quickly."

GUAGUASI

Zuelania guidonia (Sw.) Briton & Millsp.

LUCUMÍ: BESI.

OWNER: BABALÚ AYÉ.

Cures sores. It is one of Baba's genuine tonics. Every part of it is useful. The resin for syphilis; the bark for pustules; the leaves for the intestines, rashes, and rheumatism.

GUAIRAJE

Eugenia buxifolia (Sw.) Willd.

OWNER: YEMAYA.

The leaves of this plant cannot go near Yemaya unless one has the deliberate intention of infuriating her. In that case, an *omiero* is made for her using the leaves of the *guairaje*.

GUAJACA

Dendropogon usneoide (L.) Raf.

OWNER: ELEGUA.

In teas, it is used as a mouthwash to treat cases of gumboils or cracking skin on the tongue. For hemorrhoids, it is prepared in a cream with pork lard.

GUAMA DE COSTA

Lonchocarpia latifolius (Willd.) H.B.K.[125]

LUCUMÍ: YEREKETE, ADERE ODO.

CONGO: NKUNIA BONDÁ MABISAO.

OWNERS: YEMAYA AND OSHUN.

It grows along rivers. "Iki egbado"— from the edge of the river.

These goddesses receive offerings at the *guamá*, and some *ebos* should be

---

125 DF-N: Other species are *Loncocarpus latifolius* and *Loncocarpus heptaphyllus*.

performed in its shadow. Both goddesses work with it.

In the Regla de Palo Monte, it is considered one of the most powerful and magical trees, among the first and best to put together a *nganga* or a *Prenda* pot. "The spirit of the Guamá is one of those that crown the head of the *yimbi*."

"Not even the *jagüey*, who lives off the other trees, can beat it. What the guamá can do in the water, the *jagüey* can't. That's why the *mambo* says:

> Guamá bajo río
> Guamá Palo macho,
> Guamá bajo río
> Bajo río tiene fama.
> Guamá Palo macho
> Láo río, Guamá Palo Macho,
> Láo río tiene fama.

> Guamá in the river,
> Guamá, strong male *palo*,
> Guamá in the river,
> It's renowned in the river.
> Guamá, strong male *palo*
> At the edge of the river, *Guamá Palo Macho*,
> It's renowned by the river.

The Guamá tells you where there's water."

Its virtues are more magical than medicinal, and it serves all requests, both *cristiana* and *judía*.

The juice from its leaves, which one should take to avoid getting in their eyes, softens the skin on one's face and cures acne.

In a tea, it is often recommended as a treatment for afflictions of the urinary tract.

GUAMA HEDIONDO

Lonchocarpas blainii C.Wright.

OWNER: YEMAYA.

It is used with the mask representing Olokun ("Olokun has seven masks and seven chains") to pray when the *santero* "works" to save someone that is gravely ill, so "the stench of death which threatens them dissolves in the stench of the Guamá."

GUAMAO or GUAMARO

"If they have a lot of pain in their waistline, the leaves of the *ingüemo*—boiled and prepared in hip baths—will ease the pain. Snake oil is as good or better."

The roots mixed with those from other trees—*ateje*, *palma*, and *yerba fina* (*erenamo*)—break up kidney stones.

GUANABANA

Annona muricata L.

ENGLISH: SOURSOP.

LUCUMÍ: IGI OMÓ FÚNFÚN, GWÁNIYO, NICHULARAFÚN.[126]

CONGO: OMBÁNDINGA.

OWNER: OBATALA.

The leaves are used in a tea to treat colds. The roots and bark are boiled for poultices to treat cases of gangrene.

Many healers assure us that facial neuralgia is soothed immediately by washing the face with a decoction made from the leaves or the pulp; this is as effective or more effective than cinchona bark, which is used often in the province of Havana, or *salvia* [sage] with *nuez moscada* [nutmeg].

GUANABILLA

Curatea cubensis Urb.

LUCUMÍ: BOIYOKO, IGI OMO FUN.

CONGO: OMBÁNDINGA.

---

126 DF-N: In *Anagó*, Cabrera translates the Lucumí word as "guanábana" ([1957] 1986, 229). *See also* FRUTA BOMBA.

OWNER: OBATALA.

A decoction with the leaves: for heart disease.

The root and bark: to stimulate appetite.

GUANINA

Cassia tora. L.

LUCUMÍ: EWE HASISAN KROPOMU.[127]

It is used in decoctions for menstruation.

It is Abortive.

GUANO BLANCO

Copernica glabrescens H. Wendl.

LUCUMÍ: MARIGWO FUN.

CONGO: TOYIYEKÉ, MOLÚNSE.

OWNER: CHANGÓ.

The boiled root is prescribed on an empty stomach as a purgative.

GUANO PRIETO

Copernicia wrightii Gris., Wendl.

LUCUMÍ: MARIGWO IDUDU.

OWNER: CHANGÓ.

The offering of food and the *ebo* for Changó are deposited next to its trunk.

GUAO

Comocladia dentata Jacq.

LUCUMÍ: EWE INA, IPAPEYÉ, IGI BÉRU, ICHÓCHO, AKIMA, IKÁ.

CONGO: GUAO, MASOSI, MABIMBI.

"Its owner? Elufá! The Devil! And Ogun. Zarabanda."

This shrub is only useful for doing *iká*, harm. Touching it, its shade, its fluids, everything about it is malignant.

"There is no more awful plant in *el monte*. Nor is there any better for killing, breaking, exploding, and putting an end to everything."

"Wickedness is natural in the *guao*, and nobody dares touch it." The slightest contact with this shrub causes swelling and sometimes fever. The dirt around the spot where it emerges from the earth is just as harmful. The figures of speech "as bad as the *guao*" or "worse than the *guao*" are severe when applied to a person's nature. It exists, and, in fact, the *guao* is abundant all over the island, and it is good to know it, in order to avoid its unpleasant effects and immunize against possible future contact.

"If the *guao* stings you, come back right away with a whip or a stick. Insult it. Hit it hard, then spit on it. If your hand or another limb got swollen and itchy after touching the *guao*, you'll be cured immediately after the beating. And it will never harm you again, even if you touch it. This procedure should be done, as a precaution, wherever there is *guao*."

It is used in many curses to cause swelling in an enemy and—above all else—*falaiña*, to create tragedies, occasion the ruin of a household, sow discord in a family, or turn friends into enemies.

Here is the traditional formula for this *mpolo*: powder from the *guao* is mixed with powders from the *aromo*, the *picapica*, and bones from the head of a dog and a cat. *Pimienta china, pimienta de guinea,* and regular pepper from the shop. Tarantula, Macau monkey, a flint rock, quicksilver, salt, charcoal, and earth from a cemetery. Naturally, they are prepared, like all *mpolos*, at the foot of the *nganga* and under the direction of the spirit whose power works through them.

---

127 DF-N: In the original, Cabrera lists the botanical name as *Cassia torq.* (a typo) and transliterates the Lucumí name according to Spanish orthography as Ewe Jasisán Kropomu.

Because the essence of this tree is destructive, its very caustic resin can be used to destroy warts and other excrescences of the skin.

GUARA

Cupania cubensis Maza & Molt.

LUCUMÍ: GUARA, AGAGWAN.

CONGO: NYUKO (?).[128]

OWNER: OYA. (SOME *SANTEROS* ATTRIBUTE IT TO DADA.)

Oya rests in the shade of the *guara*.

It is among the magical trees with which a *mayombero* puts together their magical cauldron.

Together with Yaya and Rompezaragüey (*ntema*), it is used for cleansings preceding the *juramento* [oath-taking ceremony] of a *moana nganga*.

For *despojos* (cleansings).

The bark and roots are boiled and used in rubs to calm the nerves and reduce swelling.

The leaves, in a decoction, are used to treat bouts of hysteria and kidney conditions.

GUARACABUYA

Caesalpina coriaria Jacq.

OWNER: OSAIN.

Paleros use it more than the Lukumi. According to one informant, some call it Arámbana.

It is very valuable for *nsaranda*.

---

128 DF-N: Cabrera identifies the tree primarily by its Lucumí name (pronounced as *güara* or *gwara*, not *gara*), while a question mark indicates that "nyuko" is dubious as a Congo name.

GUASIMA

Guazuma guazuma L.

ENGLISH: WEST INDIAN ELM, BAY CEDAR.

OWNER: YEMAYA.

"Good for hanging yourself."

"Good for *oungué*." (?)

Mayomberos—like the owner of the *prenda* Vira-Mundo-Camposanto, and other elders—do not work with this plant because "it makes a slime like the one made by *quimbombó* [okra], and the *muerto* and the *murubba* slide off it, and the *masangos* [sorcery to tie someone down] get loose."

Meanwhile, other *paleros* observe that "when the work done with *guásima* doesn't become loose, it's extremely fast, because that tree is slippery."

Thus, the virtue of the *guásima* resides precisely in this slimy sap over which the *wángas* slide. That is why the crushed leaves are used to wash the doorframe of a home, combining these with *ciguaraya*, *cucaracha* leaves, and *guanina*—*ewes* belonging to Yemaya that destroy even the most "harmful" sorcery.

One young *kimbisa*, at odds with the above information, assures us that the *guásima* "has two faces"—meaning two opposing magical qualities—"because its sap can be used to kill with *Nfúmbi*, and that same sap can be used for good to cure someone's eyesight."

"The *guásima* is only used in Palo Monte for medicine. It's no good for anything else. The *Nkisi* orders that its slime be used to treat abscesses and ulcers on the feet and legs, which prevents sores from degenerating and becoming malignant."

Depending on the patient's commitment and the faith their *Ngangamune* (healer) can inspire in them, any ulceration can be healed with this mucus-like liquid. It

G

is also an antidote for burns and itching produced by the *guao.*

The *guásima cochinera* is used to wash the head and enhance hair.

A decoction made with its bark "refreshes the blood."

GUASIMILLA

Prockia crucis L.

"It causes swelling like the *guao.* But walking backward away from the tree makes the swelling go away immediately."

"Girl, who told you that? The *guasimilla* causes swelling? You can eat the fruit! Bring me that Black person or whoever told you that lie!"

Many call the *guásima* the *guasimilla.*

Its flowers, which the herbalist from Matanzas named Sixto calls *oyó koyé,* are used in a tea to calm the nerves.

GUAYABA

Psidium guajaba L.

ENGLISH: GUAVA.

OWNER: ELEGUA.

Its fruit is one of the offerings Elegua likes best. It works best with its *garabatos* [hooked sticks], *iwó* (*Lungoa*) and its leaves, and *koka* (*nkanda*).

"Good luck is drawn in with seven little *garabatos.* After they're used, they're set aside and stacked. They cook a sweet potato, rub it with palm oil, and bury it at a crossroads with powdered hutia, rice, and *ereché* (beans). The person cleanses themselves with the sweet potato before burying it, calling Elegua and offering it to him."

Later, cleansing baths with *ewes* belonging to Oya (*grama, grosella, albahaca morada, cucaracha morada, guacamaya,*

croto, ponasí, malanga amarilla) and ewe Oshun (*frailecillo,* laurel, *mastuerzo, angarilla, mata perro, platanillo de costa, jaboncillo, fruta bomba* leaves, and *caimito*).

It is used to treat hernias.

"If we take a string or a small ribbon to measure the hernia (*manungua*) and place it inside a slit made in the trunk (*musitoto*) of a *guayaba* tree, the hernia will close along with the slit in the tree."

GUAYABILLO

Pithecoloblum tortum Mart.

LUCUMÍ: KENKU, MOYÉ, ATELEWÓ.

OWNERS: OGUN, ELEGUA, AND CHANGÓ.

Its sap is used for hands that are calloused, cracked, and sore. To relieve cramps in the hands.

GUAYACAN

Gaicum officinale L.

ENGLISH: ROUGHBARK LIGNUM-VITAE, GUAIACWOOD.

CONGO: YUNKAGWA.

It is among the strongest trees in *el monte,* and very magical.

R.F. assures us that it is like the Holy Father of all the *nkuni* and, "if you burn its *nti,* its wood, it emits the same smell as the burning flesh of a human being."

Even if some of my consultants do not consider it as sacred as the ceiba or laurel, this does not devalue it, nor does it negate that "Yunkagwa, the Guayacán tree, has the authority of a chief."

"*Mambei!*"
"*Dio!*"
"*Quín Dió?*"
"*Guinda vela, Mayordomo. Primero Sambi que tó la coas.*"

"*Gó, Gó!*"

"*Guayakán son palo duro!*"

"*Go, gó.*"

"*No hay ndiambo sin guayakán. Palo duro guayacán.*"

"Silence!"

"Yes!"

"Who is it?"

"Guinda Vela, Mayordomo. God first, before all else."

"*Gó, Gó!*"

"*Guayakán is a strong palo!*"

"*Go, gó.*"

"There's no *ndiambo* without *guayakán*. The *guayacán* is a hard, strong tree."[129]

If a *guayacán* is destroyed in *el monte*: "What a profound mystery! All the trees in that *monte* dry up and die. One needs to know how to cut it down to avoid destruction."

A very powerful talisman or amulet is made with this strong tree, and it is carried in a small bag covered in leather and decorated with beads and a cowrie shell. It is made with *guayacán* and the pincers and tip of the tail of a scorpion, *nkutu tatikanga*. The head of a tarantula spider (*masúa*), a damselfly (*nsusu muteka* or *nkombo muteka*), a centipede (*bondán*) on which you count seven rings, the head and heart of a vulture (*mayimbe*) and owl (*susudialonga*), heart and claws of a hawk (*nui lusango ntare*). Seven leaf-cutting ants (*dúndu munántoto*), which should be collected as they carry food on the way to their nest. (Clearly, all of this is powdered.)

Those who receive this talisman will memorize the following prayers: the Juez Justo, the Santos Evangelios, the Santo Sepulcro, the Guía de Caminantes, and the Cruz de Caravaca. These prayers are burned, then the ashes are wrapped in a little cotton and put inside the bag. (Some swallow them, since they are good protective charms inside the body.)

Once the amulet has been constructed and fed, a candle is lit and prayers are recited: an Our Father, a Hail Mary, and a Credo. "Speaking to it, one always says (before entering into the subject at hand) that the dead follow the cross and the cross follows the dead. The living Christian person goes behind the cross."

"The Guayacán with ceiba, *majagua, yamao, amansaguapo, cambia voz,* and verbena is unbeatable for controlling a situation or dominating a person. You also add a small snake and earth from three graves."

On the other hand, healers believe the *guayacán* tree is unrivaled for treating syphilis.

Baths infused with its leaves "cleanse" and invigorate; decoctions purify the blood, and its resin is well known among certain beggars who—in a practice that is "now somewhat out of fashion"—ask for handouts in the name of Babá, showing their *ileanos*, reddish and caramel-colored sores that are not real, but are faked remarkably well with *guayacán* resin.

GUAYARU

OWNER: OCHOSI.

("In Mayombe, we call it Uéke.")

For ritual work with this orisha.

It is a disinfectant. Objects used by an infectious sick person are washed with the leaves and roots, which have been boiled well, in order to avoid contagion.

---

129 DF-N: Cabrera's inconsistent use of both *guayakán* and *guayacán* has been reproduced here. Regardless, the *u* is pronounced in both (i.e., *güayacán*).

GÜIRA

Crescentia cujete, L.

ENGLISH: CALABASH, GOURD.

LUCUMÍ: EGWA, IGBA, AGBE.

CONGO: MPUTO, GUÁNKALA.

"The calabash! Oh, damn. It has all kinds of mysteries!"

Its fruit "is the world, sky and earth when they weren't separated, because once upon a time the sky was up against the earth."

Odua or Obatala, the creator of the human race, and his wife Yemu lived inside a calabash with sixteen snails. "One day they quarreled and Obatala took out her eyes." "Inside the *Igba*, the wife of Obatala decided to lift the lid, and she was blinded."

Some calabashes are never opened, such as the one containing a particular San Lázaro of the Arará.

"When they opened *igba*, they had to make petitions and offerings, because of the many calamities they had caused."

The calabash is divided into two parts: "The top one was the sky, and the bottom one was the earth." These parts are called *jícaras*, and "they are the true home of the Ocha, even though they now live in tureens. Sacred objects used to be kept in a closed calabash or a *jícara*. Orula keeps his *odus* in a calabash, Osain his secret, the *Santos* their cowrie shells."

"I've heard humans came down to earth, or they came out of calabashes."

"The rain depended on a calabash that was broken in two and had to be put back together, but it couldn't be put back together. The earth became dry, the crops, the fields; people were dying of thirst and hunger. After a great deal of suffering, when the calabash was closed, the rain fell and *oyoro* ended the drought."[130]

There were three calabash trees in the world. The place where they grew was very sad, and the people who lived there were tormented. Until the Ibeyi were born, each with an axe over their shoulder. They gave the axes to their mother so she would keep them, but a few days later, they asked for the axes back so they could break open those calabashes.

"*Atu-atú-tú-ñara. Atún-atún-ñara-a tú-tú-agongoró, ñara atú góngoro!*" They both sang as they walked down. And from the trunk of the first calabash tree that the *ibeyis* split with their axes, a man, a woman, and a cat emerged before being quickly swallowed by the earth. The next day they split the second one, and two hunchbacks came out of that one before the earth swallowed them too. The third day a man and a woman holding a sick boy in her arms emerged from the third calabash tree, all of them well formed. These were not swallowed by the earth. They built a house. The man went far away to work, and as soon as he finished his work, he would return home. The boy remained sick, and the man would ask the woman.

"And Maboni?"

"Not well."

"And Maboni?"

"He died."

Then the man said, "*Maboni sini mabómbo.*" He carried the boy to the middle of *el monte* to bury

---

130 DF-N: Various metaphors are at work here in terms of mythology and natural cycles, including reproduction (the calabash as womb, water/rain as fertility, etc.).

him. But the world got brighter, because those calabash trees blocked the rays of light.

"The calabash tree is really diabolical," Jesús Santos tells us. "The devil gets inside her. It's the calabash tree's fault that we have little monsters in the world. Cachano is called through the mouth of a calabash . . ."

At the beginning of the world, a *kianboba* (elderly woman) was clearing the earth in front of her house. She saw a seed and said to herself, "I'm going to plant it and see what comes out." But is it good to plant the seed of a tree one doesn't know?

A very large tree came from that seed. The tree produced a round fruit on a branch that kept growing and growing. The old woman saw that the branch kept growing and growing, and she said to it, "If you keep growing like that, you're going to take up the whole sky and all of my land." And she cut the branch and the calabash. She cut the calabash gourd into three pieces and said to one of the pieces, "This one will make a good *dilonga* (plate)."

"I'm not a plate," it answered, then it transformed itself into a man holding an axe in one of his hands.

The man said, "I'm a *castrador de abejas* [beehive harvester]!"

"Fine, then," replied the old woman. "There's a beehive over there. Bring it down and we'll eat honey."

He went straight to the tree, but the hive was high up. He sang, "*Tanguñao pánkeré, kián kián pankeretekian!*"

The hive fell down on him, and the bees stung him. He ran away and disappeared.

The old woman yelled at him, "You're not a beehive harvester! You're nothing!"

And she grabbed another piece of gourd.

"With this one I'll make a skimming ladle (*espumadera*)."

The piece of gourd said, "I'm not a ladle. I'm a fisherman."

"Well, then let's go to the sea."

That other piece of gourd turned into a fisherman holding his net and singing at the edge of the water.

"*Timereko mandórimá, venga pá lante má!*"

A huge fish came out of the water and hit him with its tail. He got scared, ran away, and disappeared.

Then the old woman picked up the third piece of gourd and said to it, "I'll make you into a spoon."

"No, ma'am, I'm not a spoon. No, I'm Koko the hunter." And the hunter started setting traps, traps, and more traps, all over, until he got to the land of the devil. When he arrived at the border, the devil's watchman saw him setting up his traps, arrested him, and turned him over to the devil.

The devil said to him, "Who gave you permission to hunt in my lands?"

"No one. I entered your territory unintentionally."

"Leave your *kabulaso*, your snares, in place. But the first bird that falls is for me."

Then Koko went to look for the old woman and said to her, "When I call you, come. There'll be birds in all the traps that I've set."

The old woman gathered a great many of her people to collect the birds that would fall in the traps when Koko sent word.

G

But he didn't give the devil the first bird that fell in a trap, and Koko kept placing more traps in the devil's lands.

The devil reminded him of the debt.

"This time I'll give you two birds."

Then the devil made evil creatures, and he put them in the traps, singing, "*Koko yaré yaré kówongo Koko . . .*"

And the old woman went with all of her people to get the birds, because Koko had told them to go and collect more birds. But the woman and everyone else saw those horrible creatures and ran away, and the creatures ran after the old woman and the people. They all ran away, screaming, with nowhere to hide. And Koko disappeared in the calabash tree.

"There are marvels inside calabashes."

Omí bobo ikala emi bobo ika emíbo kuasa omi bo ikala Olu omi. There was no water in the world. The only one who had water was the Crab, Akan. He was the owner of the *ofí,* the well, and he sold and bartered water in exchange for other things.

Ekuaro, the quail, was very poor. She sent her son Okure to get water. The young man presented himself, plump, covered in feathers, and holding a clay pot. The Crab, bald and cold, was envious and said to him, "I won't give any more water. If your father wants it, then he'll pay for all of the water in my well."

"If I go back home without water, my father will punish me and rip out all my feathers."

"My water belongs to San Pedro. Go and ask him for it."

"Where is San Pedro?"

"How am I supposed to know where San Pedro is!"

That *omode kuaro* went to look for San Pedro. He asked everyone he met where San Pedro might be. He knocked on the door of a house, and an old woman opened.

"Wo le!" (Enter!)

"Mamita, where does San Pedro live?"

The old woman did not answer, but she asked him to pluck a hen.

He was so hungry that he ate the feathers, then he returned the *abua's* hen clean.

"Mo lo . . ."

And he left, *chon, chon, chon.* He came across an *adete,* a leper.

The leper saw that the *omode* was hungry, and he gave him a yam.

"Tani ichu." (Take this yam.)

The young man ate the peel and returned the inside of the yam.

And he continued on his way, *ká, ká, ká, ká . . .*

In a *monte,* he found a man who had a great many iron tools. It was San Pedro himself.

"Where does San Pedro live? We don't have any *owo* to pay the Crab for water."

There was a calabash tree nearby, and that blacksmith said, "Look at those three gourds hanging from that branch. Don't take the biggest one. Cut three small ones, and when you leave *el monte,* throw one to the ground. Halfway along your trip, smash the other one. And when you arrive at your home, at the doorway, toss the third one."

Okuro did as he was told, and when he arrived at his *ile* and tossed the last little gourd, a deep well opened up in the middle of his patio, and it flowed quickly.

His house then filled up with slaves, animals, and treasures.

Crab was no longer able to abuse poor people because now there was enough water for everyone.

Then the water in his well started drying up. Full of envy, he sent his son to go see San Pedro.

And San Pedro showed him the gourds, telling him that the big ones were dead and the small ones were the good ones. But the son of Crab took the big ones. It's true that, previously, when the old woman had asked him to peel the hen, just as she had asked Okure, the son of Crab had given her back the feet, the head, and the feathers, eating the best parts of the hen himself. And he had given the leper only the peel of the yam. When he broke the first gourd, the road became very long. When he broke the second one, three rabid black dogs came out of the gourd and chased him to the door of his house. And when he threw the third one down, the well disappeared. His house filled up with deformed animals: blind birds, frogs and tarantulas, one-eyed goats with two legs, and one-legged bits and pieces of horses and dogs.

Thanks to the gourds, the Crab's tyranny over the water on earth ended. *Omitutu* is a gift from God. Like the light of the sun, it is meant for all his children.[131]

A very poor man went, like all those in need, to seek out the diviner's advice. The diviner simply warned the poor man to be careful when he bathed in the river because he would lose an object that would cause his happiness or misfortune. The man burned the words of Ifa into his memory, and when he went to bathe, he placed the only coin he owned in his mouth as a precaution. But when he lost his balance when he put his weight on a loose stone, he accidentally opened his mouth. The coin fell out of his mouth and into the river, then the swift current carried it away before he could get it back. He couldn't reach it, but he kept swimming after it until the river flowed out into the sea. The sun was setting, and it was getting dark quickly. Out there, he asked Olokun permission to spend the night among their reefs.[132] He couldn't rest at all that night, much less get a moment of sleep, waiting there among the spikes and barbs of the reef. But the next morning, when Olokun asked how he had rested in his prickly reef, the man gave thanks for Olokun's hospitality and said that he had slept very well. Perfectly! Then Olokun pointed out where he could find a couple of gourd trees near the shore and said to him, "The gourds from the tree on the right don't talk. The ones from the one on the left do talk. Take three from the tree on the left.

---

131 DF-N: In Cabrera's original, the end of the story about the gourds and the Crab is marked by a closed quotation (although the beginning is not marked clearly by an open quotation mark), and the following section opens a new story (presumably told by a different narrator) with an open quotation mark ("A very poor man went . . .").

---

132 DF-N: In the original, Cabrera's description of Olokun employs a series of conspicuously neutral gender formulations. For example, the phrase "allí pidió permiso a Olokun" does not identify either character as male or female.

G

When you leave, toss one on the ground and another halfway on your journey. You'll throw the last one when your house comes into view."

He did so. When he saw his house and threw down the last gourd, his poor *ile* transformed into an *ile oba*, a palace. The palace had a room packed with treasure, floor to ceiling. Everyone in town had witnessed these miracles, wide-eyed and open-mouthed, and they welcomed him back, refusing to leave—as usual—until they had showered lavish praise on the man who was rich that day, even if no one had given him a second thought the previous day."

The theme of miraculous gourds is inexhaustible in the folklore preserved by Cuba's Black Creoles.

In this world, there were a man and woman who adored each other.

One day, under a calabash tree, she said, "If I *kúfuá* (die), would you look for another woman?"

"No. You'll be my only woman. And if I *kufuá?*"

"I'd kill myself."

"If you die, I'll castrate myself."

And that is what they swore under the calabash tree they had in their *dikanga di nso* (patio).

Time went by. The woman died. More time went by. The man was going to get married, but the calabash tree that kept the oath started singing on the morning of his wedding:

Ndúmba que fué Mamá, kiyénye
Ndúmba que fué táta, kiyénye
E é é kiyényé
Tabulo que tiene tabulenke
Kiyénye tabulo que tiene cuenda
E é é kiyénye . . .

The children of the dead woman came to hear what the tree was saying. They took their father, and the man, who had forgotten his oath, took his knife out right there and castrated himself.

Only the king over there in the land of Guiní had the privilege of raising a *chelerá* (flag) at the door of his house.

An *awo* arrived in that town. In order to announce himself, he placed a flag at his own door. The people immediately went to tell the king that a stranger had arrived, and he must be the king's equal because the man dared to flaunt a mark of such high distinction.

The king sent for the *awo*, who explained that his flag meant that he was a diviner. Oba prepared a secret to investigate the truth and know whether or not the man was nothing more than a *fefe*, and he divided that secret among three gourds. The king said that if the *awo*, in the presence of the king's whole court, failed to divine what he had placed inside the gourds, he would pay for his lies with his life. Then he ordered that the *awo* immediately be taken to meditate in *ilewon*, the jail, and that they lock him in a cell. Fortunately, the *awo* had fed his head.[133] He kept thinking and thinking, but nothing came to him, until they brought a woman and put her in the same cell with him. When they were alone, this woman, who was a little *Ogun obini* (masculine) started bother-

---

133 DF-N: This is a reference to *ebori*, ritual offering and care for a person's head (spirit, soul, destiny).

ing him, asking him for *acho* and *omi* all the time, until she finally fell asleep. When she woke up, the woman said, "I dreamed that the Oba has you here *aratubu* so you can divine what he has hidden in three *panchaku*, and I have seen that one has *epa*, another *eku*, and another *eya*."

On the third day, they took the *awo* to the king. The *awo* pointed to the three gourds hanging from the ceiling and said what they contained.

The king authorized him to use a flag, and later called on him often for consultation on his businesses. Eventually, the king named him chief of the palace *babalawos*. Once upon a time, Orula was strolling in *araoko* when he saw the calabash tree, and he told it to make *ebo*.[134]

"I don't see what need I have to make *ebo*," the tree answered. "I have a happy, peaceful life here with all of my children!"

Orula shrugged his shoulders and continued on his way.

A short time later, a man showed up who owned the land on which the calabash tree lived so happily and peacefully. The tree was full of fruit, and the man began cutting them with his *obe*.

Later, Orula came across a half of one of those gourds, and he advised the half gourd to make *ebo* so he would not drown, so he would be able to serve everyone and the whole world would appreciate him. He made *ebo*. That is why he floated so well when anyone threw him in the water. This is

the *jícara*. On the other hand, the whole gourd, who did not make *ebo*, was thrown in the water and fell to the bottom."

And since then, it is true, everyone appreciates the *Igba*.

The fruit of the calabash—emptied of its innards or pulp, well scraped, with its shell polished, and split in two—provided for humble peasants, slaves, and the people as a whole. This is the extremely useful *jícara* (or *jigüera*, as it is called around Vuelta Arriba), which had, and sometimes still has, so many uses in rustic households.

Black people used the *jícara* to take water from barrels and clay pots. They ate and drank from the *jícara*. It was their tableware. In plantation houses, a big spoon made from a piece of gourd was used to serve rice, cornmeal, and jerky—that is, if they were fed well.

They made offerings to their orishas in *jícaras*. And before they had tureens (*gorishas*) made from ceramics, the orishas were kept in *jícaras*. ("The orishas weren't kept in *canastilleros* [cabinets]. They were in their *jícaras*, on the floor, in a corner of the room. And more often than tureens, they were kept in *tazas bolas* [round bowls] with striped borders in the *santo*'s color.") To this day, in many *bohíos*, *jícaras* are still the home of the orisha. Such a humble and economical receptacle also has a very personal and intimate use.

The *jícara* was not absent from well-appointed, wealthy homes. Mounted on silver tripods, their use to drink chocolate and coffee following a meal became generalized. Some among our people maintain the habit of drinking coffee in a *jícara*—particularly the people of Pinar del Río. A prominent *iylaocha* from Pinar del Río brings her *jícara* to drink coffee from it when she travels to the capital.

134 DF-N: *Aroko* (analogous to *ara oko*) refers to *el monte*.

G

Decorated with fanciful images and themes, marked with names or initials engraved by a punch or painted on, generally with red and blue, they were often used in bathrooms as washbasins or soap dishes, or side by side with solid silver basins and soap dishes. Light and easy to handle, they worked well for scooping water from wooden troughs or large metal basins (which preceded the long iron clawfoot bathtubs from the age of enlightenment), and pouring it over one's body in streams that flooded the floor, which would later be mopped by a docile and patient slave.

It was a very comfortable accessory, the predecessor of today's showers. Baths made with tile from Triana, Valencia, or Catalonia were still in use in the middle of the previous [nineteenth] century, until the American intervention. They were found, in many houses and country villas, within a freestanding room at the rear or center of the patio, and the bather always carried to it a *jícara* holding the soap and washcloth to rub their body, letting it float in the bathwater if they took an immersion bath.

What child, now in their fifties, did not delight in playing with these *jícaras* in their bath? They made such excellent boats, sailing obediently in their fantasies, through tranquil or stormy seas, until they foundered in an enormous whirlpool or wave created by the child's hands or feet, despite the protests of the "manejadora" [nanny] who would get soaked by that sudden splashing.[135]

The *jícara* is no longer found in Havana homes—except in the houses of Black people, which are more conservative, where they have not been given up.

In the city of Trinidad and other towns in Las Villas, widows and hooded figures still travel mysteriously in the dark nights—*tenorios* [womanizers] who disguise themselves as "ghosts" in black *dominó* [cloaks] to keep secret their compromising romantic appointments. And, before a wedding that has already been agreed upon and announced, the groom-to-be steals away his fiancée. Also there, on All Souls Day, it was customary to simulate the figure of a dead person in the patios of houses with a gourd, a candle, and a bedsheet. Five holes representing the eyes, nose, and mouth gave it the unmistakable aspect of a skull. A candle was lit inside, the body was formed with the white sheet, and the deceased was laid out on a table in the darkest corner of the patio. The objective was to frighten the children of the house. At *el toque de ánimas* [eight o'clock at night],[136] the children were shown the horrifying figure of the dead person at a distance, emitting an otherworldly light from its eyes and with every exhalation of its breath. The children were obligated to buy it sweets and cigars, which the adults smoked.

Indeed, fear of that dead body, the lugubrious annual visitor, tended to curb the impetus of the naughtiest, most indomitable children. On the night of All Souls Day, cattle bones were tied to the feet of the worst-behaved children as they slept. The adults solemnly swore these bones were from dead people, brought from the cemetery by the deceased, so that when they awoke, they

G

---

135 DF-N: The word *manejadora* translates literally as "handler."

---

136 DF-N: *Toque de ánimas* is an idiomatic term with origins in medieval Spain. It refers to the ringing of bells (*toque*) to announce nightfall, akin to a curfew announcement (*toque de queda*), often followed by a prayer for souls (*ánimas*) in purgatory.

would be scared (which they always were) and obey the deceased, who told them to go to school and be more obedient and restrained.

GÜIRA CIMARRONA

OWNERS: OSAIN AND ELEGUA.

The leaves are used for fortifying baths.

The bark and roots are used in an infusion to purify the liver, the kidney, and the bladder.

Juice from its fruit is applied in the treatment of gangrenous sores. ("If gangrene appears, put a poultice on it, and the *güira* will eat away the gangrene.")

"For venereal diseases, I let the *güira* rot, then I squeeze it out and add oil and a small spoonful of sulfur. I administer all of this as a purgative."

"Charo, the midwife, would give mothers who had recently given birth a purgative decoction with *güira cimarrona*."

The fruit of the *güira cimarrona*—the real one belonging to Osain and Elegua—is smaller than the creole one, which belongs to Yemayá. This gourd—*egwa pikuti*—is preferred by Osain and Elegua for their amulets and protective charms. As we know, Osain—the talking Osain—is put inside one of these.

The *güira cimarrona* is used to make a cough syrup that the old Africans used to prepare in the following way: "Three little gourds from the *güira cimarrona* for two liters of liquid. They're boiled with *lengua de vaca* (*we we*); mango sprouts (*igokooro*) that were pulled upward, because if they're pulled down they could cause hemoptysis; roots and leaves of *naranja agria* (*olombo*); a little *miel de purga* (sugarcane syrup); ten centavos' worth of ointment made from whale sperm, which can be bought in a pharmacy; and a pound of brown sugar. All of this is boiled until it becomes a syrup. It is cooled and bottled. Many call this concoction *amedol de güira*, and it is still highly regarded by the people." "It's an African remedy, the best there is for colds and pneumonia."

(Spoonfuls of cockroach—white roaches are preferable—fried in olive oil are no less effective "to push out the froth of pneumonia.") And why not this other formula? Woodlouse, cockroach, and pig excrement in oil; a spoonful of this oil on an empty stomach followed by a decoction of oregano and pennyroyal.

The small *güiro espinoso* (*Solanum mammosun*, L.)—is excellent for asthma.

The gourd is used to make countless *edis* (spells). In order to avoid making this note too extensive, we will give two examples.

"*Edi* to attract a person: You clean out a Güira Cimarrona, removing the insides. You pour a liter of *aceite de carbón* [fuel] and another liter of cooking oil into it. Open a hole in the ground a half yard deep and a hand's width across. Above this hole, you make a bridge with *caña de millo*. You write down the name of the person who is being aloof on a piece of paper, then place the paper on the bridge (it is important that it does not touch the bottom of the hole). The gourd is placed over the paper, halfway across the bridge. Counting the days, this is where you invoke and *chiche* (work) the person. A lamp remains lit continually for the length of the ritual."

"*Edi* to make a person insane: The same process as the previous example, but at the end of the ritual period, the gourd is taken to a river that flows out into the sea. The person is invoked and a request is made to make them insane. Be careful not to spill it when it is put in the river.

G

And since it is a delicate ritual, whoever delivers it is paid $0.75."

"Having someone hanging from a gourd in the wind—continuously moving, with their name, hair, nails, their handkerchief, whatever you have of theirs, including the necessary ingredients to do this—is certain to drive them out of their mind. They'll wind up crazy."

(Among the ingredients for this curse, quicksilver is at the top of the list.)

GÜIRA CRIOLLA

A woman who has lost a child in the womb will drink a decoction made with the roots, bark, leaves, and fruit of this tree as if it were regular water.

The fruit is used to work in *mayombe* and bury (or "plant") a malevolent curse with the name of the person intended to be harmed.

Regarding the *güiro*, a *ñáñigo* tells us, "When the Obones in Usagare consecrated their sacred tools, an evil spirit appeared. The Iyamba feared punishment, so he consulted with Nasako, the diviner. Nasako investigated the matter and told the Iyamba that the apparition was, indeed, a dark spirit. But he used his power to drive the evil shadow away. He put seven seeds inside a gourd, shaking it hard and saying, "*Obiasa Abasi ona Ekue.*" Then he gave it to Iyamba and advised him that whenever he walked with the *Fundamento*, he should always move the gourd and repeat "*Obiasa Abasí ona Ekue.*" Another *ñáñigo* told us that in Efí land, during the course of the various tests undertaken to capture the Divine Voice, a gourd was used along with a fish skin and a canvas tarp.

We have already explained that the results of all of these tests were fruitless because the Divine Voice was muted by the skins of the fish and the ram.

The large gourds with long necks (*ato*) are emptied, adorned with a net of beads, and filled with seeds to make music for Baba, San Lázaro.

"That is his true musical instrument, and his favorite ritual music is made with *güiro.*"

GUISASO DE CABALLO

Xanthiub chinense Mill.

ENGLISH: COCKLEBUR.

LUCUMÍ: EMO.

OWNER: OGUN.

In decoctions, for the kidneys. Also cures ulcers and is beneficial for tuberculosis.

HELECHO OR LECHO DEL RIO

Osmunda regalis L.

ENGLISH: RIVER FERN.

LUCUMÍ: IMOSHUN, IMO, ITI, IBU.

CONGO: VITITI LÁNGO, NFITA MASA.

"It grows at the bottom, and for Ocha people it is one of the first plants they use for the *omiero* of the *Asiento*. We *mayomberos* call it alúmamba.

"In some *palo* houses, it is used to give clairvoyance. The eyes of the *yimbe* are washed with the river fern, honey from a hive in the cavity of a rotten tree, anisette (*ojén*), marjoram, *geranio*, and yellow *moya* flowers [*moyas amarillas*]." "The godfather washes the eyes, while the Mayordomo stands behind the *perro*"—the neophyte. "And when the godfather finishes washing them, he smashes a coconut on the floor. The *perro* gets scared, and in that moment, acquires a vision with his eyes closed, and they can see everything."

The river fern allows them to see while they are mounted—that is, possessed. "Otherwise, with other types of visions, like the ones provoked by the rheum from a dog or a *mayimbe*, they suffer a great deal in the dark." (Because they see too much, and all the time.)

HENEQUEN

Agave fourcroydes, Lemaire

ENGLISH: HENEQUEN, AGAVE.

LUCUMÍ: KUNWEKO.

Woven *henequén* is used to make the clothing of those who make vows to Baba, since Babalu Ayé wears fabric made from agave fiber.

Some sorcerers wear a sack made from agave over their shoulders when they fly around on their nocturnal adventures.

HICACO

Chrysobalanus icaco L.

LUCUMÍ: KINSEKE.

CONGO: MUNGAOKA.

OWNERS: THE IBEYI.

It is used in a decoction to treat dysentery.

HIGUERA

Ficus caica L.

ENGLISH: FIG.

LUCUMÍ: POTO, POPO, OPOPO.

Hot figs are an excellent poultice for boils and tumors.

They are a laxative (either dry or in decoctions) for the chest, and they are "bone builders." After a massage with ram's tallow, a fig leaf is placed over a fracture or dislocation, and then it is tied on with a piece of fabric of the color associated with the healer's or the patient's *Santo*.

The famous Aniceto Abreu had a secret way to grow figs on his patio that were so big and sweet that they compared with the figs from the Balearic Islands. One of his "goddaughters," astounded by the taste of the figs, asked him how he managed to grow such wonderful figs in Cuba. The old man said, "Enjoy the taste and don't ask so many questions."

HIGUERETA

Ricinus communis L.

ENGLISH: CASTOR BEAN, CASTOR OIL PLANT.

OWNER: OBATALA.

The seeds ground up, mixed with wild flowers and fried in castor oil, *cubiertas con cutré*, are used in poultices to cure diphtheria. "It is extreme."

A leaf is stuck on the forehead to avoid sunstroke and treat headaches.

HINOJO

Foeniculum vulgare Mill.

ENGLISH: FENNEL.

LUCUMÍ: KORIKO.

"Obatala works with fennel to end a *karkámbuka*" (to obliterate the effects of sorcery).

"It is a tree related to death." It is used in ceremonies that are performed on the bodies of deceased *mayomberos judíos* before burying them.

HOJA MENUDA

Pithecolobium berterianum (Balbis.) Benth.[137]

OWNERS: THE IBEYI AND OSHÚN.

---

137 DF-N: The Spanish name, *hoja menuda*, can be translated literally as "small leaf," "common leaf," or "regular leaf."

For children with cholic.

HUEVO DE GALLO

Tabernaemontana citrifolia L.

OWNERS: ELEGUA AND OSAIN.

"A two-colored chameleon, similar to the American iguana, lives in this tree. The tree and the chameleon are both useful in work to make people sick and kill them.

"The decoction returns vigor and virility to a manhood in decline, and the sap helps contain bleeding."

(The old man José del Rosario used to call it Chotón.)

It is used a great deal in witchcraft.

HUMO

Pithecellobium ovovale A.Rich.

LUCUMÍ: EYEREYO.

CONGO: CHONÁ.

OWNERS: OBATALA, ODUA.

It is used to prevent unforeseen circumstances that might prevent the celebration of a marriage.

It is also used for other "work." An excrescence from its trunk is turned into a charm. If the charm is for good, it is taken from the side of the trunk facing east; if the charm is for ill, it is taken from the west side of the trunk.[138]

"For hexes, it is especially effective to use an Humo that has *bereke*" (thorns).

---

138 DF-N: In the original Spanish, Cabrera writes *oriente* (the Orient, or the east) and *poniente* (the side of where the sun sets, or the west). The rhyming, idiomatic turns of phrase in this passage are properly poetic, suggesting mystical qualities associated with the four cardinal points or directions (north, south, east, and west). *See also* LAUREL.

These thorns, like all other thorns, defend against the evil eye. One herbalist calls it *Amloi*.

I
....

INCIENSO

Artemisa arbrotamum L.

ENGLISH: SOUTHERNWOOD.

LUCUMÍ: TURAREM, MINSELO.

OWNER: BABALÚ AYÉ. IT IS ALSO ATTRIBUTED TO OBATALÁ.

For cleansing rituals and baths.

In a decoction, it regulates the menstrual period and calms stomach pain. Inhaled, its incense "clears the mind and wards off bad influences."

It takes away headaches.

INCIENSO DE GUINEA (?)

LUCUMÍ: EWE TURERE.

OWNER: OCHOSI.

"It must only be cut at three in the morning. It grows at high altitudes, and it's powerful. It can get anyone out of jail, delinquents and innocent people alike, by making them invisible. It's prepared with other apparently anodyne ingredients, like cumin powder and cinnamon. But if it is scattered in a jail inconspicuously . . . and if the prisoner is brave, then they can escape without any problem, because no one will see them."

Other informants call this plant (which they say is not "incienso de Guinea" but rather "incienso de costa") *Lokode*.

INCIENSO DE PLAYA

Tournefortia gnaphalodes (L.) R.Br.

LUCUMÍ: EGBADO.

OWNER: YEMAYA.

The branches are used for a spiritual cleansing, wetting them in the seawater.

In massages, it is used for rheumatism.

It is one of the herbs the *ñáñigos* use to purify their sacred objects in the *Batamú*.

J

....

JABONCILLO

Gouania polygama (Jacq.) Urb.

LUCUMÍ: OBUENO, KEKERIONGO.

CONGO: KÁNGUI.

OWNER: OSHÚN.

The sap is used to clean ivory objects. A toothpick made from it is used to whiten teeth. It was a natural tooth-brush and toothpaste for sailors. It was used a great deal in the past; a toothpick made from *jaboncillo* was chewed to produce a frothy saliva that was considered excellent for dental hygiene.

See also BEJUCO DE CUBA.

JAGUA

Genipa americana L.

ENGLISH: GENIPAP.

CONGO: GÓOTONGO, DIAMBULA.

The smoke from this plant will "cloud the vision" of sorcerers, distracting and mocking them. ("But it also cures blindness.")

It blinds *ngangas judías*. The smoke from its wood envelops the "fumbis"—the car-riers of the sorcery of the *ndongo*—in a darkness so thick that it impedes their path, preventing them from delivering the "bilongo" to its destination.

The Jagua also "offers a drink to a per-son who is thirsty and lost in *el monte*."

"Inside, it has an *ache* of clear, fresh water." It is said that it counteracts im-potence, that it is an aphrodisiac, and that it cures gonorrhea.

JAGÜEY

Ficus membranacea C.Wright.

LUCUMÍ: FIAPABA, AFOMA, UENDO.

CONGO: NKUNIA BRACANONE OR BARACANONE, NKUNIA SANDA SANDA, OTAKONDO.

OWNER: OGUN.

Musi *Nganga*.

"It is so powerful that it can swallow an *aguacate* (avocado) tree. It challenges the ceiba and dominates it. It can overcome all the other trees. If the *jagüey* cov-ers the ceiba, it is because the ceiba is a mother and the *jagüey* and the ceiba are husband and wife."

It cannot conquer the *palma real* [royal palm], which is topped with Siete Es-trellas, Nsasi, Cabo-Guerra.

"The *jagüey* sometimes likes to get in the river, because it likes to grow on the shore and in caves. But it doesn't tangle with the *guamá* along the shore, because Yemaya is in the *guamá*, and Madre Agua [Mother Water] is very strong. That's why the *guamá* will defeat the *jag-üey* in a challenge."

"There are *jagüey kalayánga* and *jagüey iyákara* (female and male). The male has a small heart, the female a big one. It has a little poison, and the leaf-cutting ants don't attack it."

"This tree works just as well in *mayombe judío* or *mayombe cristiano*, and it is highly venerated by the faithful of all sects of Af-rican origin. In the countryside, a hole in the trunk of a *jagüey* is often a natu-ral sanctuary, the abode of an orisha that receives sacrifices, offerings, and libations there, such as the guardian Elegua at the sacred lagoon of San Joaquín in Matanzas.[139]

San Lázaro often goes to rest in the shade of the *jagüey*. And like the ceiba and the laurel, *makutos* are also buried in its shade.

A *mayordomo nganga* confesses to me that the mysterious and treacherous *jagüey* terrifies him (and many others). It is a sort of octopus, a plant vampire that embraces, then devours, the tree that lives next to it. He understood that a *jagüey* that grew along the river where he bathed with his friends at Puentes Grandes "wanted to swallow" him. He resisted the terrible fascination with the *jagüey* that "called him from its roots," which sank into the water, and he trembled when he got out of the water. He swore he would not return, and he had dreamed that the roots wrapped around him like snakes and kept him in the depths of the river. But the next day, his own fear took him back to the river. He was convinced that he could not oppose the imperious will of the tree, which "was waiting" for him:

"I knew the *jagüey* wanted me, and that it was more powerful than me. I had to obey it. I was trembling, but my Angel is very strong, and it saved me. One of my mother's friends stopped me along the way. She said, 'Listen, don't go there to bathe in the river. One of these days, one of you is going to get tangled in the roots of that *jagüey*. I've been warned: there'll be lamentation.' The old woman kept me occupied, talking about other things, and while we were there, a man came up to tell us that one of my friends had drowned, and

his cadaver had been found in the roots of the *jagüey*. It took a lot of effort to free myself from that tremendous *jagüey*, that kept calling me, driving me to obey it. I never went back to that river, and, for a while, nobody went back to bathe there. Every year, lots of people would drown in that area. Every time I see a *jagüey*, I have to recover my composure and overcome my feelings again ...

"I feel a strange sensation. My knees shake. That tree commands me. To this day, now and again, I dream that it's embracing me under the water. That time, it was impatient to grab me, and it took that poor boy."

Nonetheless, baths with *jagüey* leaves— seven baths—improve one's luck. With either good or bad intentions, the *mayombero* uses these leaves to bewitch the shadow or double of a person. (These hexes on shadows are performed by both *babalochas* and *ngangas*.)

The bark is also useful for cures. It is ripped off, and the inside is placed over an inflamed organ, which yields good results, most especially for swollen hands. It cures hernias.

JAIMIQUI

Manilkara jaimiqui C.Wright

ENGLISH: WILD DILLY.

Similar to caoba (mahogany). It is useful for doing ill and doing good.

JAYAJABICO

Colubrina reclinata L'Her, Brongn.

CONGO: YÓMMO.

OWNER: (?).

It is administered in a highly concentrated decoction made with the roots,

139 DF-N: The lagoon is the setting for Cabrera's *La laguna sagrada de San Joaquín* ([1973] 1993).

the bark, and the branches so that the witchcraft or *bilongo*, which has been [458] ingested and is acting directly on the body, can be expelled by the victim.

JAZMIN DE LA TIERRA

Jasminum grandiflorum L.

ENGLISH: SPANISH JASMINE, ROYAL JASMINE, CATALAN JASMINE.

LUCUMÍ: ALENYENYEN.

OWNER: OBATALA.

The juice from its flower is used to keep breasts youthful and smooth.

JIA AMARILLA

Casearia ramiflora Vahl.[140]

LUCUMÍ: ERERE, YASE.

CONGO: MOSÚMBILA, TÓTÓCONGO.

OWNER: OSHÚN.

It is used to make the *omiero* for washing the animal bones that are employed in amulets and relics.

JIA BLANCA

Casearia alba A.Rich.

LUCUMÍ: EREREFUN, UNKUA.

CONGO: MOSÚMBILA.

It is used in the Regla Mayombe for "loading" some *npakas*.

Powdered well, it is dispersed in unhygienic and fetid places to combat negative "spiritual and physical" influences and to neutralize bad odors.

JIA BRAVA

Casearia aculeata Jacq.

CONGO: MOSÚMBILA.[141]

OWNER: BABALU AYÉ.

"Wasps are born prodigiously from this tree."

"The *Jía* gives birth to Luguakame (the wasp). *Kuikuimafinda!* It's one of the great mysteries of nature: a tree that gives birth to an animal!"

On the contrary, Calazán believes that it is a tree that is born from the wasp.

Its shadow is evil, since only dark, evil spirits that lack knowledge go to this tree. "At the trunk of this tree, one talks with those miserable ghosts, making deals with their desperate, earth-bound souls."

Unscrupulous *mayomberos* use *Mosúmbila* for much of their work, preparing terrible curses, particularly with its thorns.

In Ocha, the *Jía brava* is used to cover Baba.

JIBA

Erythroxylum havanensi Jacq.

OWNER: ORISHAOKO.

"It wards off witchcraft, and its roots contain good secrets."

"But you need to be very specific and very clear when you're going to cut it," a young herbalist tells us. "You need to tell it, 'Va ti va bonga atu kuenda nsímbo kunán toto ntoto Sambianpungu güiri kuenda yari yari.' And you need to present it with an offering of seven centavos. Otherwise, its roots will break or you won't be able to collect the tree's virtues. The *Jibá* is effective for helping people, for curing them."

---

140 DF-N: In the separate entries for three varieties of *jía*, each entry describes distinct ritual associations and uses. The *-fun* suffix in the Lucumí name for *jía blanca* corresponds literally to the word "white."

141 See Cabrera ([1984] 2001, 231).

J

"This *igi* is Okoga. It is a healer, and it doesn't give its virtue to anyone unless they pay for it. A little cross made from *jibá* wood and *nuez moscada* [nutmeg] wards off the bad winds that can cause illness, the evil eye, and sickness."

A decoction made with its roots lowers fevers. To expel bile, healers recommend boiling its leaves to make an infusion that the sick person will drink for some time instead of regular water. It is always found in the teas that are prepared to cure syphilis and other venereal diseases.

This tree truly cures anything. It is good for tuberculosis, to control hemoptysis, and for all pulmonary infections.

That is why Capé says, "A *prendero* can't cure anything without the *jibá* root."

It dissolves internal tumors and, in poultices, tumors on the skin. It is also an abortive.

And the *Aye* stay away when they see a cross made from *jibá* wood. That is why many Centros Espirituales (Spiritualist Centers) place these crosses at the four corners of the room where they celebrate their sessions, preventing the arrival of dark spirits.

JICAMA

Calopogonium coeruleum, Hemsl.

(MY OSAINISTA CLAIMS THAT JÍCAMA IS AN AFRICAN WORD, "BECAUSE THE LUCUMÍ CALLED IT THAT, AND OTHERS, CONGO WHO WERE 'SORT OF LUCUMÍ,' CALLED IT TÚAKAO.")

OWNER: OBATALA.

Its roots, bark, and leaves are used in an infusion whose curative vapor is inhaled by those who suffer from polyps, itching, or rawness on the inside or edges of their nose.

JIQUI

Pera bumelifolia Gris.[142]

LUCUMÍ: IGISORO.

CONGO: NTUENKE, BOTTA.

OWNER: OGUN.

It is used to fire up Ogun by covering him with its leaves.

Baths prepared with a decoction of these leaves transfer the tree's strength and stamina to the person's own body.

It dispels *ndiambos* and extinguishes sorcery.

Mayomberos employ its leaves for cleansings, and its roots and the core of its trunk to "warm up," making their *ngangas* more vigorous.

JOBO

Spendias membin L.

ENGLISH: YELLOW MOMBIN, HOG PLUM.

LUCUMÍ: ABBA, OKINKAN, WAKIKA, KINKAO.

CONGO: GRENGUERENGUÉ KUNANSIETO, GUENGUÉ, MENGUÉNGUÉ.

OWNER: CHANGÓ. (SEVERAL SANTEROS FROM MATANZAS ALSO ATTRIBUTE IT TO ELEGUA.)

"This is the home of the *hutia, ekuté,* just like the *caña brava* is the home of Nanu, Nanabuluku, wife of Daidajuero,[143] the home of *inioka,* the sacred boa." (Nana is a great *vodu* of the Arará that takes the

---

142 DF-N: The plant is also known as the *corazón de paloma.*

143 DF-N: The proper name of the *vodu* might be transliterated in a variety of other ways (e.g., Daidawero, Huedo, etc.).

form of the boa and, like other orishas, lives in rivers and springs.)

Jobo leaves are used to baptize the stone of Changó and the cedarwood figure that represents him. "It is washed with an *omiero* in which *jobo* leaf is a primary ingredient. It is mashed with the other leaves of the *santo*, then they are placed in a basin with water, holy water, and coconut water."

"To baptize the stone, I leave it in the *omiero* for a day or a night. Later, I spill the blood of a rooster over it, I clean it again with *omiero*, and I rub it with palm oil. I feed it an offering of cornmeal, okra, etc. And afterward, I take all of this, including the *omiero* and the blood it drank, to a palm tree or a *jobo* tree, and I leave it there with a lit candle."

The fruit of the *jobo*, which is very similar to that of the plum, "is very much to Changó's taste," just like pitahaya and *mamey*.

Mayomberos also value it a great deal, and they use it to consecrate *kangome* (bones) in a cauldron or *mulunguanga*.

In baths, it dissolves witchcraft that is picked up through one's feet, after stepping distractedly in a *malembo mpolo*, a *wanga bangabi mpolo wabbi*, by adding *rompe zaragüey*, *piñón*, *botija*, and *cedro verde* to *jobo*. Many sorcerers use it to cure madness in the following way: pieces of clothing and nails (*mioko*) from the right foot of the sick person are boiled with the roots, bark, and leaves of the *jobo* in seven cups of water. This is boiled down to three cups, and the decoction is administered by drinking throughout one day: once in the morning, once in the afternoon, and once at night. They will recover their sanity when they start drinking the third cup and reject it, warning that the liquid has a special taste and realizing that they were not drinking pure water.

In the Regla *palo-cruzado*, *jobo* leaves are used to baptize Matari-Nsasi, or the type of figure known as Chicherekú, which will be called Kini-Kini or Batalla-Tondá.

A ram that is going to be killed for Changó is offered a *jobo* leaf before cutting its throat, although the *alamo* leaf is preferable.[144] The animal will chew the leaf if Changó accepts the sacrifice.

Jobo is used to make protective charms and Osain.

Aside from being able to reduce swelling of the feet, a decoction made with its leaves helps to expel gas. And a purely domestic application: old washerwomen, who are still protective of their professional integrity, know that washing colored fabrics with a decoction from these leaves prevents cloth from fading.

JOCUMA

Sederoxylon foetidissimum Jacq.

ENGLISH: FALSE MASTIC, YELLOW MASTIC.

OWNERS: CHANGÓ AND OGUN.

It is used to mix in an herbal infusion for the treatment of leprosy.

Elders "help ease their *canchila* (hernias) with *jocuma*."

JUCARO BRAVO or JUCARO DE UÑA

Bucida buceras Jacq.[145]

ENGLISH: GREGORYWOOD, BULLET TREE, BLACK OLIVE TREE, ANTIGUA WHITEWOOD, GEOMETRY TREE.

---

144 DF-N: In the original Spanish, it is unclear as to whether the *alamo* or *jobo* is preferable.
145 DF-N: Also known by the botanical name *Terminalia buceras* (L.) C.Wright.

OWNERS: CHANGÓ AND OYA.

When a person suffers an electric shock, a bonfire is made with *júcaro bravo*. Abundant smoke from its wood (which is excellent for charcoal) neutralizes the terrible effects of Oya's rage—because the lightning bolt, or electrical current, is nothing more than a manifestation of the rage of these orishas. The smoke of the *júcaro* revives the victim and gives them strength.

"When there's a hurricane, this tree—because it belongs to Oya—lies down, waiting for the storm. The hurricane doesn't break it. After the storm passes, it comes back up."

In Baró's opinion, it is not a bad tree for making *nganga*.

JUNCO MARINO

Parkinsonia aculeata L.

LUCUMÍ: HUNEO, ATEKUN-IFEFE.

CONGO: KALÚNGA, MADDIADA.

OWNER: YEMAYA.

Yemaya prescribes a cure for cancerous ulcers with a powder made from this plant.

JURUBANA or JURABAINA

Hebestigma cubense Urb.

OWNERS: ELEGUA, CHANGÓ, AND OGUN.

Used against Diambo. It removes the "bilongo" from a person's body after they have consumed it. It is one of the great plants in *mayombe*. When it is necessary to harm a *gangulero*, to defend oneself from their attacks, or to kill the *nganga* that serves them, it is enough to dust them with *jurubana*. That is why the sorcerer does not consent to have just anybody near their *Prenda* . . .

"What *palo* dances more than Ngruba?"

L
....

LAUREL

Ficus nitida Thumb.

ENGLISH: INDIAN LAUREL FIG.

LUCUMÍ: IGINILE ITIRI (?), IGGI GAFIOFO.

CONGO: OKEREKE.

OWNER: CHANGÓ.

The spirit goes from the laurel to mount its horse.

> *Abajo lauré villumba me llevó,*
> *Abajo laurel yo tengo mi confianza.*
> *Debajo lauré yo tengo mi*
> *confianza.*[146]

And this is how the *gangulero* proclaims its eminence, invoking the spirits inside it with this *mambo*:

> *Lauré lauré. Vamos, lauré, ié,*
> *lauré . . .* [147]

By saying that they put their trust under the laurel tree, they mean that his work is guaranteed and carried out under the auspices of the great spirit or *mfumbi* that lives in the tree, and that nobody would be capable of taking their *boumba* or killing them.

---

146 DF-N: Translation of *mambos* like these is fraught and often counterproductive, leading to a flattening of the ambiguity, multidimensionality, and nuance of their text and context. Roughly speaking, the singer of this *mambo* is proclaiming that a *villumba* (spirit) called, pulled, or took them to the *laurel*, and that they have a consecrated ritual object under the tree. In this context, the singer's *confianza* means, variously: trust; faith; an ally; power; and/or a consecrated object (*nganga, fundamento, prenda*, etc.).

147 DF-N: *Vamos* (let's go) suggests going to the *laurel*, activating its spiritual power, and so on.

BOTANICAL ENCYCLOPEDIA

L

448

Amo tumba su caballo abajo lauré
Donde tengo mi confianza.[148]

This is the chorus of the "canutillos," devotees and believers gathered by the *nkisi* (*juego*), until a spirit from the laurel—Yimbiri-gwágwa Cobayende [Coballende], for example—responds by taking possession of the "vasallo" [vassal, subject]. Then, in another *mambo*, they begin boasting about the victory they will gain over all the *fumbis*, *diambos*, or *ndundus* who might oppose their will.

> *Yimbiri Gwákwá*
> *Yimbirigwá Cobayende*
> *Arriba truena*
> *Abajo ponde (responde)*
> *Guínguiríngomba*
> *Matende bana*
> *Siete Hueso*
> *Kalunga Manga*
> *Saya Coba raya*
> *Mbele y cota Cambiriso*
> *Yo entra finda*
> *Yo sale finda*
> *¡Voto vá dió soberano!*
> *Salamaleko maleko nsala.*
> *Yimbiri Cobayende*
>
> *Yo coge la tuna sin zapato*
> *Palo verde tá cayendo*
> *Palo seco tá parao*
> *Nsulo (el cielo) son moquitero*
> *Tu sube Nsulo tu cae Ntoto*
> *Medio fuete no dá cambio*
> *Remolino Revuelo*
> *La doce del día no se cuenta*
> *Mira gúnga ta yambulando*[149]

---

148 DF-N: *Amo* (owner, master, boss) *tumba* (knocks down, defeats, overcomes, posseses [as in a trance]) *su caballo* (horse, possession mount, spirit medium, subject) under the *laurel*, where I have my *confianza*.

149 LC: The sugar refinery bell that sounds at twelve noon.

Abajo Mamá Kalungo son genio malo
Como Yimbirigwá Cobayende
Si Kalunga sube Kalunga baja
Si río crece yo paro río
Si yo llega fondo son cosa malo.

Yimbiri Gwákwá
Yimbirigwá Cobayende
When it thunders above
Down below responds
Guínguiríngomba
Matende bana
Seven Bones
Kalunga Manga
Saya Coba raya
Mbele y cota Cambiriso
Salamaleko maleko nsala.
Yimbiri Cobayende
I enter *el monte*
I leave *el monte*
I praise God almighty!
Salamaleko maleko nsala.
Yimbiri Cobayende

I catch the moon barefoot
The green tree is falling
The dry tree is standing
The sky is my mosquito net
You go up to the Sky, you go down to the Earth
A half (whip / riding crop / strength / source) doesn't change anything
A whirlwind/whirlpool stirs up a commotion
You don't talk (at/about) twelve noon
Look, the bells are ringing
Under Mamá Kalunga, they're bad genies (spirits)
Like Yimbirigwá Cobayende
If Kalunga goes up, Kalunga comes down
If the river rises, I stop the river
If I get to the bottom, it's a bad thing.

"The laurel tree is thick with spirits," Ceferino says. "There are so many of them, and they're so strong—*sambia tori*, great *santos*, like in the *ceiba*. It has so much

L

mystery and authority that it is as powerful as Mamá Ngúndu. The *fumbis* congregate there."

"There's a very strong concentration of spirits in the laurel tree."

A piece of the roots from the east side of the tree,[150] the *munifüisi* [necessary critters], earth from a crossroads or four paths, and other substances are used to fill the *mpaka* (horns). A piece of mirror is embedded in its base, the *vititi-mensu*, where, as we already know, the sorcerer is able to see the invisible after their vision has been prepared. (According to C.P., this tree belongs to the Cuatro Vientos [Four Winds], and it controls the four cardinal points.)

In one hand, the Yimbi holds this *mpaka* made from a bull or goat horn. It is an amulet and a talisman. And just like the *kinsegueré* (tibia), it attracts the spirit "guide" to the *yimbi* medium and indicates what they must do.[151]

---

150 DF-N: The Spanish original (*el naciente*) is more evocative: "the birth side," meaning the east, where the sun rises, renewing plant and animal life. The tree's orientation in space is metaphorical (as in turning things "around" or "upside down"), geographic, and cosmic.

151 DF-N: The revelational logic of spiritual mediums and possession trance is capable of establishing tradition instantaneously. For example, a song sung "through" a credible medium can be understood as a historical precedent: if the "singer" is an ancestor or primordial deity, then the song itself is understood simultaneously in both mythical and historical terms. In this context, ritual authority is contested as individuals try to discern fact from fiction, keenly attuned to the possibility of deceit, fakery, and self-interest in the guise of mysticism. Cf. the references to "Santicos" (false spirit possession) in chapter 2. *See also* COCO.

The shade of the laurel tree is extraordinarily magical. "It's comparable to that of the ceiba." Accordingly, contact with it is vivifying. The leaves and roots, boiled together, fortify the body of the Mámbi and their godchildren, purifying them of witchcraft. Additionally, the leaves of the laurel are used to prepare the water with which the sorcerer washes their initiate's eyes to make them clairvoyant. The leaves are mixed with those of the *salvadera* and *yaya cimarrona*, then left with the *nganga* for seven days, or buried in a bottle under the laurel tree. Once the right amount of time has passed, the *ngombe* is brought there in order to "extend their sight," then the spirit is called.

When they are possessed of their *ngombe*, the Father takes a white plate and makes a cross on it with the flame of a burning candle. They sit the *ngombe* in front of the *nganga*, making them hold the *mpaka* in their right hand.

Using the water prepared with the laurel tree, their eyes and forehead are washed. The flame of the candle is brought near each of their pupils, tracing the form of a cross in front of each eye. The *mpaka* is taken from their hand, placed on the plate, then the burning candle is placed next to the plate. After having the candle put in front of their eyes, they are asked what they saw.

"Vititi Mensu ke kuenda Ngonga musi-musi."

The *ngombe* explains what they saw when they opened their eyes: sometimes an animal, a strange figure that is not of this world, or an unidentified being. The Father who has given them sight sees what the *ngombe* has seen, and according to their own experience confirms that "now those eyes open to see the other world too."

Yo le entro a Finda
Yo sale Finda | ¡Vola va Dio Soberano!
YIMBIRIGUA COBALLENDE
Sala Maleco | Maleco Ensala | yo coge la tuna sin zapato |
Palo verde tá cayendo | Palo seco tá parao | En sulo son
mosquitero | tu sube en sulo | Tu cae en toto | Medio
fuente no da cambio | Remolino resuelto la doce del día No
se cuenta | Mira gunga tá yambulando | abajo MAMA Ka-
lunga es malo genio | ¡Como yimbirigua Coballende | Si
Kalunga sube Kalunga baja | Si rio crece yo pararío,
si yo llega fondo son cosa malo!

X por levantado

Palo Ganga-   Ban
Canto   Canto de "yimbi"   (del se trabaja
                            "espiritual" cargado
                            o matado)
Canto
        Yimbiriguagua
        Yimbirima Coballende
        Arriba truena
        Abajo responda.
        Guinguiringombe
        Matendabana
        7 hueso Kalunga Manga
        Saya- Coba-raya-
        Vela y cota cambiriso   vuelta

"Yo le entro a Finda…" and "Palo Gangá."
Index cards with Cabrera's handwritten
notes. Courtesy of the Cuban Heritage
Collection at the University of Miami.

"There's no good Nganga without the laurel tree."

One elder who puts his trust in the laurel recalls, "I slept under a laurel tree for seven days in *el monte*. That's how us real *paleros* take our oath. Because being scratched in *palo* is a very profound and serious thing: dying, being with the dead, then resurrecting with an agreement with the dead.

"After I came back from *el monte*, they presented me to the *nganga* at my godfather's house, dressed in the clothes I had buried for seven days in *kambónfinda*."

For adherents of the Regla Lucumí, it is one of the trees belonging to Obakoso, and it figures prominently among their most venerated trees.

Baths with laurel leaves dispel negative or harmful influences, and are also as invigorating as those of the ceiba. This tree has the power to immunize against typhoid. Using the roots, *santeros* prepare a liquor that invigorates and returns energy to bodies weakened by grave illness.

The branches ward off the *aye*. For a cleansing incense: the leaves with *incienso*, *comino*, a grain of salt, oregano, and *pata de gallina*. (The body will then be cleansed with a candle, which will be left lit for the neediest spirits.)

LECHUGA

Lactuca sativa L.

ENGLISH: LETTUCE.

LUCUMÍ: ILENKE, YEYE.

OWNERS: OSHUN AND YEMAYA.

It refreshes Oshun and Yemaya. They are used to cover the *egwa* (gourd) or tureen that contains the sacred *otan*, the stones of these goddesses. These might even be wrapped in lettuce leaves.

To cleanse homes of negative influences, the floors are washed with lettuce, parsley, cinnamon, eggs, Agua de Florida perfume, and bee honey.

LEGAÑA or LAGAÑA DE AURA

Plumbago scandens L.[152]

ENGLISH: PLUMBAGO.

LUCUMÍ: EWE IWAGO, IKOLEKOKE.

OWNER: OSHÚN.

"They call it a vine, but we have both vines and grasses." "It smells like *mayibe nsuso* (turkey vulture), it grows among rocks, and yields a purple seed that looks like a grape and is administered in concoctions to 'tie down' a person."

It is used for cleansings. Its boughs are used to sweep negativity, and that is why it is also called *yerba bruja* [witch leaf]. Others call it *malacara* [bad face].

Mixed with alcohol, it is good for rheumatism. "It stings a little." (It is caustic.) "In a decoction, it is also used to cure children's diarrhea."

LIMO DE MAR

ENGLISH: SEAWEED.

LUCUMÍ: EWE OLOKUN.

To soothe and make amends to Yemaya, the stone in which she is adored is wrapped in "limo de mar" and submerged in a pail full of seawater.

She is petitioned during seven days. The first, pouring seven bottles of molasses over her *otan*. The second, offering her black-eyed peas. Third, *fruta bomba* [papaya]. Fourth, coconut candy. Fifth, cornmeal and a sprin-

---

152 DF-N: The plant's name, *lagaña aura*, refers literally to the mucus (rheum) around the eye of a vulture.

kling of indigo wash. Sixth, fourteen *palanquetas* [sweet pastries]. Seventh, a melon.

From these offerings, one portion is taken to the ocean, another to the river or a hilltop, and a third is thrown in the garbage.

LIMO DE RIO

Potamageton lucens L.

ENGLISH: SHINING PONDWEED.

LUCUMÍ: IMO, OSHUN, EWE ODO.

OWNER: OSHUN.

To soothe Oshun or obtain her favor, her *kotan* is placed in bee's honey and offered two hens. The next day, the stone is taken out of the honey and wrapped in *limo de río*. The following day, it is fanned with five different fans (*abebe fele fele*). She is offered five different fine sweets. And on the fifth day of gifts and contemplation, the stone is submerged in river water, then wrapped in a yellow cloth with a small piece of gold. The person who finances these offerings places them in a basket (*agbon*) and puts five bracelets on their wrist to attract Oshun's attention so the goddess will follow them.

This offering is taken to the middle of the river, where she is called by ringing a small bell. (This is one of the *ewes* for the *omiero* of the *Asiento*.)

LIMON

Citrus limonum Risso.

ENGLISH: LEMON.

LUCUMÍ: OROKO, OROMBOUEUE [OROMBOWEWE], OLOMBO.

CONGO: KORONKO, KIANGANA.

The lemon, which is so good for health, is used to treat fever, flu, uric acid, to destroy intestinal parasites, etc. etc. But it also has a very bad "path," lending itself to terrible curses.

"A lemon is stabbed with fifty needles while saying, 'Just as I pierce this lemon, I pierce the heart of So-and-So.' Or saying, 'Heart of So-and-So, I pierce you,' etc. You make a mound of ashes and red powder from Changó, then mix the lemon in the ashes."

The lemon should be cut in two halves or three pieces. J.E. advises me against cutting it in four pieces: "Be careful to never do that, because it is very bad."

Some witchcraft using lemons is greatly feared. For example, this one, which condemns a man to impotence for life: "The written name and essence of the person are placed in a small cooking pot. The juice from three lemons is poured in. *Aceite de palo, bálsamo tranquilo, adormidera, amansa guapo,* and earth from a cemetery are added. The cooking pot is kept at the feet of Elegua for three days, then it is taken to a cemetery and buried in an empty grave.

LIRIO

LUCUMÍ: PEREGUN FUN FUN, MEREFE, OSUMARE.

CONGO: TUNKANSO.

OWNER: OBATALA.

Its juice is an emetic. "It rips out *bilongo*." It is also prepared in a syrup for whooping cough.

LLANTEN CIMARRON

Echinodorus grisenbachii Small.; *Echinodorus cordifolius* Gris.

ENGLISH: AMAZON SWORD PLANT.

LUCUMÍ: CHECHERE.

OWNER: OSHUN.

L

453

It is used in decoctions to treat the liver and kidneys.

Its juice is used to treat the little "sores" on the gums. To reduce inflammation, "one leaf is thoroughly covered in palm oil, heated and placed over a swollen belly to decrease the swelling."

LLEREN

Galathea allouia (Aubl.) Lindl.

ENGLISH: GUINEA ARROWROOT, SWEET CORN ROOT.

OWNER: OSHUN.

The juice is used to alleviate toothache.

M
....

MABOA

Cameraria latifolia L.

LUCUMÍ: LECHÚ IBAYÉ.

CONGO: MALEMBE.

OWNERS: OBATALA AND OGGUN.

It is used to make poisons.

Its sap is used to destroy calluses on the skin and cavities in teeth.

MACAGUA

Psendolmedia spuria (Sw.) Griseb.

ENGLISH: FALSE BREADNUT.

An extremely powerful *nganga* is made using the *macagua* and a "yalumbo di-moana," the right hand of a woman "who doesn't miss a thing and doesn't let go once she has grabbed on." Many sorcerers contend that the hand of a woman's cadaver is incomparably more valuable than the *kiyumba*, or cranium.

The leaves and root are used in a decoction to rejuvenate the elderly. "The scent of the *macagua* vivifies a tired body."

MADRESELVA

Lonicera japonica Thumb.[153]

ENGLISH: JAPANESE HONEYSUCKLE, GOLDEN-AND-SILVER HONEYSUCKLE.

It is used for cleansing baths.

It is used for *omiero*.

MAGUEY

Furcraea hexapetala, Vent.

LUCUMÍ: IKERI.

OWNER: YEMAYA.

"When the *magüey* falls in the river, the Turtle and the fish who live there have to say 'kikiribu.'" (They die.) From this, one can judge for themselves how "good" the *magüey* is for doing "evil."

MAIZ

Zea mays L.

ENGLISH: CORN.

LUCUMÍ: AGUADO, ABADDO, OKA.

CONGO: MASANGO.

It belongs to all of the *Santos*. The roasted cobs are offered to Babalú Ayé. Toasted kernels for Elegua, Ogun, and Ochosi. Cut into pieces, the cob is offered to Oshun and Yemaya. "Ground" for Yemaya. All of the orishas enjoy popcorn, especially Obatala and the Ibeyi.

"Ika was selfish and greedy. He didn't give anybody anything. One day, he was sitting on top of a pile of corn and Tere—the mouse—introduced himself and asked for a few grains of corn.

"Listen to the thin little voice of the tiny mouse, who says,

---

153 DF-N: The plant's name, *madreselva*, can be literally translated as "mother jungle," "mother of the jungle," or "jungle mother."

Emi o yeun lo o mi. (I haven't eaten today.)

"Listen to the big thick voice of Ika, who says,

Emi koye, emi koye. (Well, I ate.)

"Listen to the even thinner little voice of the hungry mouse, who replies,

Emi tiri. (I saw, I saw you eating.)

"But Ika refused the grains of rice the poor little Tere Tere was asking for.

"A little later, Olobo—the cat—arrived, and he was hungry too. He stuck out his paw, but Ika didn't give him anything either. But then Eshu arrived in the middle of all of this, and without blinking, he struck down Ika. All the corn was scattered over the floor, and in the shake-up that ensued, a great many who were hungry and needy were saved."

"The first one to grind corn was Changó. On one of his adventures, he made a deal with some men who were not from Africa. He carried it in his shoulder bag, and when he got hungry, he ground it and ate it as cornmeal.

"He arrived in Takua country, and he taught the Takua to eat it. They had never tasted it before. And Changó turned corn into the gold of the Takua country."

......

The bread (*akara*) of the Orissa and a sort of *tamal* (*eko*), consumed at celebrations and *bembes*, are both prepared with corn. The corn is soaked overnight, then ground very well. The following day, it is cooked in a bain-marie so that it becomes a soft, white dough. This is strained and divided into shapes, like loaves of bread, then dried on plantain leaves.

The *Eko*, diluted in cold water and sweetened with sugar, is considered a healthy and tasty beverage.

The *Eko* is one of the most important elements in the *ebo* (*saraeko*) sometimes required by *muertos*.

A "sara" is made for the *ñangale, saraeko ñangale*, or *ñangare*—a ceremony celebrated before the *ita*, the morning of an *Asiento*, or after an important sacrifice. "Those of us who keep the old customs as direct descendants of the Lukumí Oyo perform *ñangare* after the sacrifice. With this ceremony, we salute and give thanks to the sun, to the sky, to Olodumare. In the middle of the courtyard, we use ashes to draw a circle with a cross inside on the ground, then we cover the center of it with dried plantain leaves and place on those a big cooking pot or basin—what we call the *barika*—with the *denge*." *Denge* is another name for this beverage made with dried corn, sugar, and a few drops of bee's honey.

The Iyalocha that distributes the *ñangeri* (or *denge*) stands inside the circle of *bebeina* or *eru* (ashes) next to the basin and serves as *gallo* of the song:[154]

Ñangare, ñangare Oloru . . .

The chorus answers:

Ñangareo
Ñangale ñangale odudu koto yu
Ñangareo oloyu oloreo . . .

Each *santero*, each child, presents their *jícara* to the rising sun, spilling a little of the liquid in a circle, then drinks. A separate batch is separated beforehand in a different *jícara* that is taken to *el monte* for the ancestors. Turning in a circle around the circumference of the ashes, "going round and round, *poriri poriri*, because the earth is round, and so is the sun that gives life, and singing,

Barika barika Olonu kwa mi
Akere Olodumare akere Olodumare

M

---

154 DF-N: *Gallo*, which literally means "rooster," refers idiomatically to a lead singer.

Ota yiyi olo o . . .

"We drink three times and give thanks to Orún and Olóddumare. We ask for their blessings."

The gods receive their offering of *denge* before this ritual begins.

Olorisas and *aborisas* cover their heads with a white fabric to greet the new sun, imploring for Olorun's favor, to dispel the spirits of the dead and Eshu, and drink from the *denge*.

When *ñangale* is done as part of an *Asiento*, the *iyawo* and their godmother, who fills the *jícaras*, are in the middle of the circle.

This ceremony lasts approximately one hour. When it is over, everyone goes to salute the *orisas*.

 Da yo salu orisa
 Da yo salu Legba, etc.

Those from Havana, who are less meticulous than those from Matanzas, make a small circle with sand rather than ashes, and they even omit the cross that should be drawn in the circle. And instead of using a basin capable of containing an abundant amount—"because you need to drink plenty of the *ñangare* for Olofi, so He can see that His *eko* is good"—they only offer a *jícara* of it. They spill a little at the edge of the circle then, beginning with the elder *santeros*, they lift the *jícara* to the sky, but they only wet their lips. "They make the gesture, pretending to drink, and they don't care about the time of day. They don't care whether it's twelve noon or four in the afternoon. What an atrocity! The *ñangale* is done at daybreak, when the sun comes up, to receive its grace at the dawn of a new day."

To ask whether or not the sky is satisfied with its *ñangare* and confirm it will be propitious, four pieces of coconut (*obi*) are not used for divination. Instead,

crust from a loaf of bread is removed, and four pieces are cast on the ground, just as the coconut is cast.

When *saraeko* is made, a little sugar and pinches of cocoa butter and *cascarilla* are added to the *eko*. When it is offered to the orishas, white sugar is replaced with bee honey.

Oftentimes, the *olocha* is required to wash and mop their home temple with *eko* and *lino de río*—or *verdolaga, orodigiosa,* or *bledo blanco*—to avoid an accident that might happen there to the detriment of the good order and personal reputation. *Santeros* always have—or should have—*eko*.

Toasted corn—which Elegua, Ogun, Ochosi, and Babaye can never be without, and which is so often used for cleansings—should be scattered throughout homes, though only when it is indicated by an orisha.

A drink called *chekete* is prepared with toasted corn, water, bitter orange, and molasses. This is traditionally served at *santo* feasts with popcorn, *ekru aro, olele,* and *eko*.

(Also, a very strong *oti*—moonshine—is made for Elegua and Changó using dry, ground corn in water and sugar. It is allowed to ferment for thirty days in a bottle or a demijohn, depending on the desired quantity, and which is buried in the process.)

Although it is not customary in Havana's Santeria, according to an *iyalocha* from Villa Clara "it is very beneficial to scatter corn straw throughout the home." The goal of this procedure is to appease and purify the house. At the same time, the residents will take seven centavos in coins in their hands and run them over their bodies; these coins will be placed in a *jícara*, the contents of which are then tossed out at the corner of the street.

Corn straw, as we have seen, is used to make the *nkanges*, *masangos*, and *makutus* in the *mayombero's* house.

When an *iyalocha* or *babalocha* dies, a ceremony called *itutu* (an appeasement, "a ceremony that calms and refreshes the deceased") is celebrated.

The very same day that the individual dies, a group of *santeros* gathers at the mortuary to fulfill the will of the deceased and their tutelary orisha, interrogating them by way of the cowrie shells to determine who might inherit the stones of the deceased's patron *santo* and the other orisha they have worshipped during their life, as well as other sacred objects that belonged to them. Upon death, the orishas often want to "leave with their child," or else the child wants to take them along to the grave.

One of the *babalochas*—never the godfather or godmother of the *Asiento*—serves as *oriate*, directing the ceremony. Everybody remains seated around as the *oriate* interrogates the orishas using the sets of shells to which they belong.

In this way, the tutelary orisha and other orisha that the deceased worshipped in life declare with which blood relative or ritual relation—child, sibling, aunt or uncle, nephew or niece "in *Santo*"—of the deceased they wish to remain.

Once the election within the natural or spiritual family of the departed has been made, some *santos* stay on earth, but others leave because "they want to go with *iku*."

Sometimes, only the Angel or principal *ocha* follows the deceased to the land of shadows. Other times, especially in the case of old *olochas* who are the owners of ancient and delicate *santos*, all of the *santos* want to leave. The deceased takes them if it is judged that no one among his own people is fit to have them.

(The person who inherits one of these stones in which an orisha has materialized will later celebrate another ritual "to remove the hands of the deceased from the *otan*.")[155]

The eighteen shells belonging to an orisha—each has their own, and Elegua has twenty-one—that has expressed their desire to accompany the deceased *santero* are put in a small bag along with small pieces of smoked fish, hutia, and grains of corn. The bag is placed over the heart of the cadaver. The *otán*, the stone of the orisha, is tossed into the river—as it is done by some groups in Guanabacoa—or it is thrown into the grave or put inside the coffin ("according to the customs of each *fundamento* or *santo* family").

The tureen of the orisha, a plate, and one of its necklaces are broken. A *jícara* is placed on the floor on top of a white cloth and a black cloth, then *santeros* place the powdered red, yellow, white, and blue paints that were used to paint the head of the deceased when it was consecrated.

The *oriate* breaks the comb the deceased took to the river before their initiation and which, at the end of the sixth day of their *Asiento*, the *oyubona* or second godmother, after performing a *moyuba*, gave to the primary godmother along with the paints, the razor, the scissors, the cut hair, and the four cloths which had been used as a type of canopy over the head

---

155 DF-N: Cabrera's parenthetical note offers a formula regarding the inheritance of ritual objects: as the hands of the deceased must be "removed" from the stones, a late priest's ownership and agency are ritually nullified without necessarily removing their presence, spirit, and/or prestige. In other words, while the inherited orisha is placed exclusively in the hands of the inheritor, the orisha is neither entirely nor exclusively their own.

M

of the deceased when they received the *santos*. The *oriate* places the broken comb in the *jícara*.

"This is the comb we used to comb our child's hair," the *oyubona* says to the *iyare*. "This is the razor we used to shave them." (She first hands over the white cloth, then the red, the blue, and the yellow.)

The braid or tuft of hair that had been cut off to make their *Santo* is placed in the coffin. The cadaver is dressed in the initiation outfit, which *santeros* store carefully for the day of "their surrender"— that is, death.

The *itutu* ceremony "should be done with maximum scrupulousness, so the deceased can leave peacefully, so they don't return later to cause trouble or punish those who failed to fulfill their obligations properly." All of the *olochas* present at the *itutu* ceremony shred corn straw, and they break small pieces of dry okra, which are placed in a *jícara* with the corn straw and charcoal ashes. After this procedure, by which the deceased is meant to be separated from everything and able to leave "*tuto*, cool," the *santeros* turn their backs and the *oriate* takes a black chicken, kills it by smashing its head on the ground, and places it in the *jícara*.

This *jícara*, which contains the *ebo* of the *itutu*, is taken to the mortuary and placed next to the cadaver until just before departing for the burial. It should enter the cemetery before the cadaver, then be thrown into the end of the open grave corresponding to the head of the coffin.

The *itutu* is performed behind closed doors in the room farthest from the center of the home. Afterward, all of the *santeros* are led by the *oriate*, who marks time by striking the floor with a stick decorated with ribbons. They sing and dance around the cadaver, which is already in the coffin. They call the deceased by their secret name, singing to the dead, family ancestors and religious forebears. Later, they do "oro," singing for each orisha, and these "come down," sometimes crying, and purify the cadaver, "cleaning" the coffin with colored kerchiefs.

A son or daughter of Oya ("a goddess associated with death") is necessarily present. She possesses her horse right away, uses her *eluke* (fly whisk) to perform cleansing, and presides over the funerary ceremony.

To bid the *santos* farewell at the *itutu*, their horses are turned to face the wall and struck with three sharp blows.

On the road to the burial, a small clay pot is smashed behind the coffin, and plenty of water is scattered "so the deceased is cool" when they go to the kingdom of Yansa.

Nine days after the death, after the *oro ile olofi*—the sung mass celebrated in the church for the eternal rest of the late *olocha*—the *santeros* gather again to offer coconut to their spirit.

After one year, if possible, the "levantamiento del plato" [lifting or raising of the plate] ceremony is carried out. It consists of the sacrifice of a pig or (according to "the path"—god—of the deceased) a ram or a goat. And a drumming ceremony that goes on all night is given in honor of the deceased and all ancestors. (If the deceased is a *babalawo*, a pig is not killed.)

To perform this delicate and transcendental ceremony, a table is covered with a white sheet to serve as an altar or burial mound. The plate on which the deceased used to eat is placed on the table, along with another plate holding salt, candles (there will be no skimping on candles), and a bottle of Agua de Florida perfume. A religious picture card of San Pedro and another of Santa Teresa tend to be obligatory. And no flowers; not a single one. The Agua de Florida stands in for them because flowers "are for spiritist masses. In the Regla de Ocha, neither the *santos* nor the *iku* are given flowers."

On the wall behind the table, another white sheet is hung, this one with a cross made of black cloth applied to the center. A *jícara* is placed on the floor in front of the table for the attendees at the *levantamiento* (lifting ceremony) to leave whatever amount of money they are willing and able to contribute toward the expenses occasioned by the ceremony. A pot containing the blood and head of the pig or other sacrificial animal will be placed under the table, which will remain there "so the deceased can drink the blood and see the head" throughout the entire ritual, between the afternoon of the slaughter and the next day.

Everyone attending the ceremony will have the well-known lines drawn on their cheeks with *cascarilla*, "a visual password, so death doesn't take them."

Prayers and songs in praise of the *ikus* accompany the sacrifice. Outside the house, an elder *santero* (women cannot perform this task) uses *cascarilla* to mark a line on a tree for every family ancestor. In order to not get confused or forget, they mark the number of indispensable individuals who must be invoked and "begged." Each time one is named, the *santero* strikes the ground with the staff and prays for the peaceful rest of their soul.

Once the sacrifice has concluded, the person directing the ceremony—which began with an offering of coconut—deposits the blood and head of the victim below the altar, as we have already described. At this moment, when *obi* is offered, all of the other participants should turn their faces away and avoid looking. At twelve midnight, "when the people of the otherworld dance and run around freely," the drumming and dancing and singing begin; on this occasion, they are only for the dead. Except for Oya and Elegua, the *santos* do not usually come down. The songs are sad, different from those heard at a celebration.

At midnight, the food for the dead is sent to the cemetery, a ceiba, or the bush. If it is difficult to enter the cemetery, it will be left at one of the corners of the cemetery. A stew is prepared for them using the legs, ribs, and innards of the pig, ram, or goat. (The *santeros* share this food, called *osun*, with the dead at midnight.)

The meat is fried and eaten with unsalted white rice by everyone who attends the wake. And, unlike the custom at an *ocha* celebration, no one can take home so much as a morsel of the meat, which "has been shared with the deceased."

Before dawn, around three in the morning, "what has been put under the table" (the blood and head) is removed from the house mysteriously and sent to the deceased at their grave or a ceiba. But the drumming, singing, and dancing continue. Later, everyone attends a mass in a church, then return to the home to begin the purifying, cleansing, and washing. The leftover food is scattered all over, then it is swept up from the back of the house to the front door, "so the deceased follows the food and leaves the house. The corners need to be swept very well, so they don't hide." Not a single particle of the funerary food should remain.

Finally, the sheet hanging on the wall is taken down. Four *olochas* hold the sheet covering the table and place it, along with the plate, on the floor. "Premia lagguemi ayaba dide," then the name of the deceased is intoned, "*iku, iku unlo*, the deceased, So-and-So, has been lifted up and has left." Immediately the plate is

M

taken to the street corner and smashed. By virtue of this last rite, the deceased becomes completely unbound from life and its necessities.

"In Havana, since it is no longer possible to break the plate of the *iku* in the street, the *santeros* lift the sheet and take it to the courtyard, then they lower it next to the gutter. There, at the gutter, they break the plate."

In an *ebo* for departure, *eko* is indispensable. "By that I mean an *ebo* of release, removing the spirit from a moribund body. For that, the *eko* is cut into three pieces and offered to their orisha with palm oil and grains of toasted corn. A chicken (which should not have black and white patches) is passed over the body of the person who's dying, then it is taken to a crossroads."

Corn, in fact, appears continually in *ebos* and magical procedures of *mayombe*. To ensure good luck, a Madre in *palo* tells me she buys three pounds of corn and three pounds of sesame seeds. She wraps them separately in white cloths and keeps them within reach and sight of everyone who lives in her house and visits and goes in and out constantly. She toasts the grains, also separately, being careful to not burn a single one, then mixes them together. She goes out and scatters handfuls of them as she walks down the main street in town while praying: "Justice, favor me and help me rather than harming me. Let the most powerful men in town come to me and serve me. Let white people, Black people, Chinese, and *mulatos*, young and old, favor me. Never let misfortune find its way to my home," etc.

During this entire journey, she never turns her head to look back, nor does she return the same way she went out. (This is what messengers from an *ile orisa* should also do, when they take an *ebo* to the bush or go out to fulfill any other duty of this kind: never returning the same way that they left, nor looking back, even if they're called or threatened, as so often happens in vacant lots at night.) This curious pilgrimage should begin near a park, moving in the direction of the home, always going forward, and returning by way of a different main street.

Back at her home, this *palera* keeps two pairs of pigeons, one black and one white. She uses one pair to trace the form of a cross over the heads of all her family and intimate relations who live with her and benefit from this ritual, then she runs the pigeons over their bodies, asking that fortune favor them. When they have all formulated their petition, "I squeeze the birds so they die over one of them. The birds pick up the evil, and that's why they die." The birds remain facedown on the floor until sunset, when she herself picks them up, puts them in a paper bag, and takes them to a crossroads. Meanwhile, a candle remains lit in her room at home, and the door is left wide open.

At a crossroads, the *palera* again asks for health, luck, money, and power for herself and her people. ("You should never ask for work. It's not advisable to say that word out loud.")

The next day, the same cleansing and petitions are usually repeated with another pair of pigeons. To win over someone's love, sympathy, or confidence, others form a triangle using three corn husks. They write the first name of the person on a piece of paper, the surname on another, then they place each paper in the shape of a cross at the center of the triangle. On top of all of this, they place a lit candle and say three times, "Nfuriri."

"Nobody in this world knows what they swallow. Nor why people of good character live as subjects of others. To be dominant in this way, there is one very reliable ritual (*trabajo*) that is done often

M
—

and gives the best results. With your permission, I'll tell you about it. Whoever wants to have someone underfoot will swallow some grains of raw corn. Once the grains have passed through their body, they collect them. The grains are toasted, ground into powder, and prayed over, then given—dissolved in a drink—to the person they want to enslave." (The same witchcraft is also performed with peanut; we will omit others that are similarly nauseating but very common.)

The following formula pertains to hunters. R.A. says, "To hunt every kind of bird that eats grains, you put sweet corn in a bottle of pure alcohol. The corn will stay in the bottle of alcohol for three days and three nights. Then you take it to *el monte*, to a place where lots of birds come down, and you say this: 'King of the birds, with your permission and the will of Sambianpúngo, give me the power to overcome anyone who would oppose the act I am going to carry out so that I can take all the birds I want.' Pay the *derecho* and scatter the corn. After eating it, the birds fall down drunk and your only job is to pick them up."

It is not unusual for a worried mother or wife to turn to *santeros* so they will perform effective "trabajo" [work] to stop their son or husband from stealing, if they have chosen theft as a trade, which is so dangerous when it is practiced by a person of humble means.[156] The *iyalocha* or *oluo* will quickly determine their tutelary Angel and request the requisite number of corncobs. They toast the grains and pour them out around Ogun's cauldron. They speak to him— "Ogun, alahere owo kobo kogun"—and

write the name of the thief on a corncob that is "jailed" (placed among the iron tools in the cauldron), asking the orisha to "keep the hands of So-and-So bound so they cannot steal, just as the corncob is imprisoned." Three days later, Ogun receives the blood of a rooster, which is spilled over the corncob. This is then deposited where the orisha dictates.

The stone of San Lázaro is covered completely with grains of toasted corn in its tureen or bowl. A pot full of all kinds of beans is placed next to this, along with a plate with palm oil and a *jícara* of dry wine.

A corncob, toasted and decorated with a red ribbon to keep illness away and "keep San Lázaro happy," is always placed behind the doors of homes. Along with the corncob, there are those who also place two small crutches made of cedarwood and a small bag made of *henequén* fiber. The bag is filled with centavo coins, which are gathered until they reach a certain quantity—ten, seventeen, or seventy-seven centavos.

"Corncobs belong to Babalu Ayé and to Oshun." Therefore, the children of Babalu Ayé cannot eat cornmeal without first offering a portion to the orisha. Oftentimes, the *omo* who forgets this rule will pay for their lack of courtesy with poor digestion or a strong stomachache.

San Lázaro invariably recommends carrying seven grains of toasted corn rubbed with palm oil and a small ball of camphor in a small bag made of red cloth or *henequén* fiber during seven or seventeen days to avoid becoming ill during an epidemic.

In short, when corn grows spontaneously in the courtyard or garden of a home or sprouts between paving stones, those who live there will quickly experience the effects of an unexpected prosperity.

---

156 DF-N: Cabrera offers an incisive social commentary: while privileged people might steal with impunity, people of modest means necessarily risk their lives by stealing.

M

The medicinal properties of the corn silk strands are well known and employed constantly by the people to treat kidney disease, and they are also a truly excellent diuretic.

Mixed with *borraja* leaves, a decoction made from corn silk causes measles outbreaks.

Corn is fundamental to the diet of the Cuban people, and it is used to prepare some of the most exquisite and typical dishes of the excellent old Creole cuisine.

MAJAGUA

Pariti tiliaceum (L.) St Hil.

ENGLISH: SEA HIBISCUS.

CONGO: MUSENGUENÉ, GÚSINGA, MUSINGA.

OWNERS: OGUN AND YEMAYA.

"*Tutan tu koko* . . . Ogun asked the *awos* for a rooster. They didn't give it to him. He asked the ceiba for a rooster. She didn't give it to him. He went to the *majagua* tree. The *majagua* felt pity for Ogun and gave him a rooster. (But Ogun took two roosters.) For a while, the ceiba was in bad shape because Ogun took his revenge."

There is no *okun igi* nor any *amarre* (binding ritual) more solid and long-lasting than the one made with strips of the phloem from this gorgeous tree. The shadow or "trace" of a person buried wrapped in strands from the *majagua* will never be free.

We are continually reminded that whatever belongs to an individual, for the purposes of magic, is treated "as if it is the individual themselves," and it will remain so. It is enough, then, to possess a small piece of cloth that they have worn, a handkerchief, or whatever object that has been in contact with their body in order to take control of them and tie them down. The shadow that is their spiritual double

can be captured by collecting the dust or earth upon which it is projected. Likewise, Capé tells us, rope from *majagua* is more powerful than rope made from corn, which is commonly used to bind a shadow and bewitch it.

Seven fibers of *majagua*, seven tablets of indigo, a new *obe* (knife), one or two cow tongues (if there are two people gossiping), and candles: this is what a *babalocha* requests to punish an ill-spoken person (or group of people) whose slanderous curses hound those who have asked for protection.

The tongue is sliced deeply from one side to the other. One of the candles is broken in half, then the name of the slanderer is called before the stone of the *orissa* (or before the *nganga*), and the candle is lit backward. It is allowed to burn for seven minutes, then it is put out by inserting it into the knife wound that was made on the tongue. The tongue is stabbed seven more times, and a little ball of indigo is put inside each of the holes while invoking the power of Yemaya to destroy whoever bears false witness or speaks against the interests of the person binding their tongue. Along with the remaining wax from the candles, this tongue that has been "worked" is taken to the ocean by the *santero*, but it is not tossed into the water. They take three steps forward and another three steps back, imperiously calling the name of the sorcery's subject. The matter is handed over to the power of Yemaya and left at the shoreline so that the waves reach it without violence, then drag it around and toss it around, destroying it slowly and prolonging its torture.

Sometimes the goddess of the sea punishes the guilty or indiscreet person within seven hours. This "work" also done by other orisha, especially Ogun, is hung from a post out in the open, so the person with the gossiping tongue sees their own tongue hanging there, becoming carrion for vultures. This sorcery is often displayed deliberately for all to see among our people in order to strike terror. The psychological shock inevitably experienced by someone who thinks they are the object of the sorcery explains its efficacy. The combination of fear and suggestion invariably ensure a positive result.

The *majá* [Cuban tree boa] does not go near the *majagua* tree, because the tree is able to dislocate its bones and destroy it. To paralyze a *majá*, it is sufficient to throw a branch of this tree at it. (Its bones can also be dislocated by grabbing it with the left hand.)

The *ngangula* who owns a *prenda* containing a piece of *majagua* cannot have one of these venerable reptile "guardians" of *ngangas* in their home, because the *majagua* would kill it.

If one holds a *musena* (rope) made from Majagua in their hand, an alligator will not attack.

Used in the medicine of the *onichogun* and the *gangantare*, the root and bark dissolve internal tumors, and the strands are used to bind dislocated wrists and ankles, producing a different effect on humans than it does on *mboma* (the *majá*). It also gets rid of muscle cramps. The flower is used to prepare decoctions or syrups to treat bronchitis, asthma, and colds. In alcohol, the flowers relieve rheumatic and muscle pain. Oddedei claimed that they were very beneficial, mixed with juice from *berro* (watercress), for treating "juku juku" (those suffering from tuberculosis).[157]

MALACARA

Plumbago scandens L.[158]

ENGLISH: DOCTORBUSH.

LUCUMÍ: MUBINO.

Often used for "work" to instigate divorce or to provoke quarrels and anger.

MALANGA

Xantosoma sagitifolium Schott.

ENGLISH: ARROWLEAF ELEPHANT EAR, AMERICAN TARO.

LUCUMÍ: IKOKO, MARABABO.

CONGO: NKUMBIA, MBI NKANDA, GÁNKUA.

OWNER: YEMAYA.

The "derecho," the money that the *iyare* will receive to "give Santo" in the *Asiento* ceremony, is kept in a leaf from the *malanga*.

The culminating moment is the "Parada," when the initiate is thrown to the ground, possessed by their orisha in response to the songs of invocation. In this ceremony, at least four *olochas* each hold together the corners of four cloths in the form of a canopy—one white, one red, one blue, and one yellow, while the sacred stones of the orishas are "raised up" from the floor in their respective tureens, each one held, one after another, by the Godparents over the head of the *iyawo*. The *oyubona* or second Godmother of the *Asiento* alone holds the tureen of the principal *santo*, owner of the *iyawo*, the last raised to their head. In a state of trance, they then receive the *ache*, which consists of marking the form of a cross on their tongue with the flat side of a razor blade (in the

---

157 DF-N: The term *juku juku*—an exception to the overall transliteration of Spanish orthography in this edition—is pronounced with an *h* sound (HOO-koo HOO-koo), not a fricative *j* sound.

158 DF-N: In keeping with Cabrera's description of its primary ritual uses (sowing conflict and discord), the Spanish name of this plant translates literally as "bad face."

past, a small cut was made), then immediately putting bee's honey, three pepper seeds, and small bits of smoked fish and hutia. Almost simultaneously, they are presented with the bleeding neck of a chicken whose head the *oyubona* ripped off as quickly as possible so the god incarnated in the *iyawo* can drink the blood. Later, after the *iyawo* has become themself again and "has now become a king and a *santo*," a newborn and someone born again, they are literally "the husband of the deity." They sit—on a *pilón* if they are a child of Changó or Yemaya, or a chair if they are a child of Obatala, Ochun, or Oya—on a throne erected for this ceremony in a corner of the *igbodu* (sanctuary). They are present for the slaughter during the great sacrifice, tasting the blood of the recently cut head from each of the animals presented by the *oyubona*.

In these moments, the *iyawo* is already sitting over the "secret of the *Santo*": four concentric circles have been painted on the floor—white, red, blue, and yellow, with four blue points along the outside edge of the circle—which reproduce the very same that are painted (*Orififi*) on the shaved head of the *iyawo* with *osu* (a seed imported from Africa whose powder is red), indigo, *cascarilla* chalk made from egg shell, and red ocher.[159] Or, "in the modern style," water paints are used. The *oriate* is generally a man, a *babalocha*, who directs the ceremony, or an elderly and very experienced *iyalocha* such as Latuá, Guillermina Castel, or Oni Olá. They paint the head, singing "fifi o kán winiki de kun" or accompanying themselves with other songs to which

the *oyubona* and other *iyalochas* respond as a chorus.

Oso loddo awo ori efun dache ewao sula uro.

The money for the *Santo* is wrapped in a *malanga* leaf and covered in a piece of cloth of the color associated with the orisha that is "being made." To be specific: *fun*, white for Obatalá; *pupa*, red for Changó; *oferere*, blue for Yemayá; *iyeye*, yellow for Oshún. And they add a bit of "ache" and powder of the *ewes* that belong exclusively to the orisha being consecrated. These leaves are ground by the *oyubona*, who grinds with a stone, the *oke* of Obatala. They are not taken from the bunch in which all the various orishas' other leaves are mixed together. Once this procedure—carried out slyly, so neither the *iyawo* nor anyone else sees it—has been completed, it is placed on the straw mat, then the *pilón* is placed over the money and the *ache*, thus keeping the "derecho" (monetary offering) a well-hidden secret.

The feathers of birds offered to one or several (as is more common) orishas are included in the offerings. The *olocha* makes a solid, wrapped bundle containing the offerings (although it is sometimes necessary to prepare several packets).[160] In exchange for a "derecho" of $1.05, the messenger (the *onche*) deposits these bundles at the specific locations indicated by the god or gods whose protection is being implored.

Before the *onche* heads out with their inconspicuous cargo, they and the *olocha* recite the following while raising their arms up in the most archaic posture of adoration, presenting the palms of their

---

159 DF-N: *Cascarilla* (white egg shell chalk) is often mixed with red ocher to produce yellow.

160 LC: The bundle of offerings is also called *ebo*. "*Ebbó* or *egbó* means the root of the religion." ("The most important thing is to make *ebbó*.")

hands to the sky: "Okana sa be lari Eshu agua te te te ebo fí boada."

("Assuming this attitude," my *babalocha* tells me, "we need to speak to Olofi and tell him: *Kosi obikan tu wo che afa mara wa oke kentu kiyo firie ki yo Olofi.* And the same with the sun, when we greet him in the morning: *Okun ye dun paba dodu emi ke ka fi re oku ade.*")

Every prayer, every *ebo*, is a purification, a "cleansing" and salvation for the person who performs it from the moment the orisha accepts it. "Ebo fiye osa." A person who makes *ebo* can do anything. "They can sit and wait calmly."

"After making offerings, we're clean and under their protection: a *sarayeye* frees us from all evil.[161] For it to work, the *taita* or *iya* chant as they're cleaning us, 'Feti la toke, fetilatoke.' The response: 'Aye un bai bai.' This means: 'May all the *santos* protect you.'"

"*Iku latigwa aya un bai bai . . .* May death never reach us, may evil spirits keep away.

"*Eye latigwa, iku latigwa, ye un bai bai.* May tragedy never visit your home, may blood never spill in it.

"*Ofo latigwa, ofo latigwa, aya un bai bai.* May disgrace never visit you.

"*Oge oge lasako oge oge aya un bai bai . . .* May the pick and the shovel dig deep, and may we carry them down a good road."

Naturally, the same orisha that is being consulted will indicate the ingredients and plants necessary for the offering, an indispensable process in every "trabajo." These ingredients are placed with the "derecho" in front of the tureen, or "*gorisha.*" The santo is called and petitioned and begged. The cloths of different colors that are so often necessary for offerings and *ebos* are placed over the shoulders of the devotee, and each one of the objects and materials—fruits, eggs, plants, birds, meat, etc.—is used to cleanse the person (running them over their body), then they are placed in front of the orisha's stone for hours or days.

Malanga leaves are tools for the work of Yemaya.

Ducks sacrificed for this goddess are blindfolded with a *malanga* leaf.

Some *iyalochas* reduce the leaves to powder and mix them with *espuela de caballero* and baking soda for specific ends.

To refresh Elegua, one bathes him with Malanga. To make an offering to him, a small piece of *eko* is covered with palm oil and *ache* (*yefa*) from Orula, then placed on a *malanga* leaf.

Water from the stalk fortifies the brain and is recommended for anyone who suffers from mental weakness.

In the Regla Kimbisa de Santo Cristo del Buen Viaje, it is used to do harm, and it is taboo for all of its members.

161 DF-N: Miguel "WIllie" Ramos offers two translations for the Lucumí term *sarayeye*: in a literal vein, "putting the body (*ara*) at ease"; in a more figurative vein, "a cleansing that will protect us from all evil" (personal communication, 2018). Correlating contemporary orisha liturgy in Cuba and Nigeria, Kone (2016) writes, "Asking a Cuban, I was told this means 'to wash the body (Yor. *ara*), so that there is no death (Yor. *ikú*).' Visiting Nigeria, I heard exactly the same song in a ritual and was explained that this is really sung to the body—to the body of the bird—so that it sprouts its feathers (Yor. *iyé*) smoothly (to take away the bad influences) and '*ba ikú n lọ,*' accompanies the death in going away."

M

The daughters of Oya should not eat it in this *Regla*.

The yellow *malanga*, which has identical properties, belongs to Oshun.

MALOJA

LUCUMÍ: EWE ECHIN.[162]

OWNER: ELEGUA.

"Would you believe that I don't know of any kind of *trabajo* that uses this plant?"

MALVA (White)

LUCUMÍ: LANLA, DEDE FÚN.[163]

CONGO: DUBUE.

OWNER: OBATALA.

Decoctions made with it are refreshing. Those made with the leaves are used for vaginal washes, and those made with the roots are used to purify the blood.

Excellent for refreshing the head: white *malva* with *mariposa*, *yerba de la niña*, *bledo blanco*, coconut water, *cascarilla*, coconut butter, an egg from a white dove, cotton, and pulp from a dry coconut.

MALVA TE

Corchorus siliquosus L.

LUCUMÍ: DEDE.

CONGO: DUBUE.

OWNER: OSHUN.

It is used for baths for cleansing and purification.

It is used to wash the stones and attributes of the orisha.

An infusion with *malva té* is recommended to wash the heads of those whose hair is "*malagazo*, which is neither kinky nor straight, but suspicious."[164]

MALVIRA

Baubinia megalandra Gris.

LUCUMÍ: KIYO (?).

CONGO: KÓNLÓBANTO.

OWNER: OSHUN.

It is used to prepare medicinal washes for the head in order to treat acne and seborrhea.

MAMEY

Achras zapota L.

LUCUMÍ: EMI.

CONGO: NYÚMBA, MACHAFIO, NINI YÁNGA, MACHAFIO BONGOLÓ (MAMEY DE SANTO DOMINGO).

OWNER: CHANGÓ.

The seed is used for many curses. For example, the object of this one is to make a hated person sick: The seed of the *mamey* is powdered and mixed with *pimienta de china*, *pimienta de guinea*, and cooking oil. The name of the victim is written seven times on a piece of paper and placed inside the *mamey*, together with a lock of their hair. During a certain number of days, the person is cursed and a candle is lit at twelve noon and twelve midnight, so they are consumed by the evil intended for them.

---

162 DF-N: The plant's Spanish name, *malhoja*, translates literally as "badleaf."

163 DF-N: Cabrera's original transliterates the first Lucumí name as *lánlá*, which might imply an emphasis on the *a* vowel sound, a soft nasalized *n* sound, and/or a tonal or melodic contour.

164 DF-N: The quote captures a snapshot of aesthetic racism: the word "suspicious" indicates a dubious, mixed, racial identity, meaning that the person's hair causes others to "suspect" African ancestry.

The cooked seed is also recommended to cure colitis.

MAMONCILLO

Melicoccus bijugatus L.

ENGLISH: SPANISH LIME, ACKEE, GUINEP, KENÈP, QUENEPA, HUAYA.

LUCUMÍ: OMOYLA, OMU.[165]

OWNERS: THE IBEYI.

In a decoction, it is used as a salve to treat gangrene: "It removes the heat from it."

The sap, fruit, and roots are used to prepare a digestive liquor that has a pleasant taste and works as a very effective treatment for stomach ulcers. It is recommended for liver ailments.

MANAJU

Rheedia aristata Gris.

ENGLISH: CUBAN MANGOSTEEN.

LUCUMÍ: NERI.

CONGO: MOPÚSÚA.

OWNERS: THE IBEYI.

One blow struck with wood from this tree, even without violent force, will dislocate the bones of the recipient.

"It is eminently able to dislocate bones." The *majá* (Cuban tree boa) will not go near the *manajú* tree.

It is a purgative, and its sap extracts splinters buried deep in the skin.

MANGLE

Rhizophora magle L.

ENGLISH: MANGROVE.

---

165 DF-N: The Spanish and Lucumí names both refer literally to sucking (the root verbs *mamar* and *mu*, respectively).

LUCUMÍ: EWE ATIODO, KASIORO.

CONGO: MUSI KWILO.

OWNERS: YEMAYA, INLE, AND OSHUN.

The juice from its leaves is highly recommended for rheumatism. A decoction made with its roots is administered as an aphrodisiac. It purifies the blood.

MANGO

Mangifera indica L.

ENGLISH: MANGO.

LUCUMÍ: ORO, ELESO, ORUN BEKE.

CONGO: EMÁ BENGÁ, TUÑÉ MACONDO.

OWNER: OSHUN. ENJOYED BY ALL OF THE ORISHAS.

When it yields too much fruit, it presages misery.

The seed is crushed in alcohol and used as a very handy disinfectant.

A decoction using *mango macho con travesera* is recommended for hernias.

MANI

Arachis hypogaea L.

ENGLISH: PEANUT, GROUNDNUT.

LUCUMÍ: EPA, EFA.

CONGO: MINDO, GÚBA.

OWNER: BABALU AYÉ.

During epidemics, *santeros* forbid eating peanuts.

"Toasted with brown sugar, it is an offering for Oshun. The peanut is associated with the *santa*, because it has certain particular virtues."

It is believed to be an aphrodisiac.

"*Mindo* was one of our ancestors' favorite foods. Lukankansa, the Devil, planted and harvested *loso* (rice) and taught humans that it was good for *uddia* (eating). He told them to bring him peanuts and he would give them rice in exchange. But it turned out the Devil kept the peanuts, the rice, and the people who brought him the peanuts.

"A king in Congo territory, Luanda, went to negotiate with the devil, alone and carrying a sack of peanuts on his own shoulders. This king went along singing, 'Kimene-kimene nganga, kimene kumena taita nganga.' He had to cross a river, so he put his sack of peanuts on a raft. That is how he navigated his way to the territory where Lukánkansa had his rice field. Lukánkansa greeted the king with a laugh that gave him cause for concern.

"The king exchanged his sack of peanuts for a sack of rice. The king left, but before leaving the rice field, a black cow mooed, 'Burrié! Ya sángara amarra buey!' And a little rooster in the same pen sang, 'Kikirikí, carne se va!'

"The king put his hand in the sack and threw a handful of rice at the little rooster, who choked on it as the Congo king ran back over to his raft.

"'Arruyénye . . . arruyénye . . . arruyénte yo va yo!' The raft was pulled along by the current, and it slid over the water, quickly and smoothly.

"Lukankasa saw the man, the first to escape from him, and he unleashed his iron chain, which ran along—*famayáyarú, famayáyarú, famayáyarú*—through the *munseke* (savanna). It reached the shore, threw itself in the water, swam through the water, and tied up the raft. But the Congo king said, 'Yo tiene mi Zarabanda. A luchar pecho con pecho!' (I have my Zarabanda. Let's fight, chest to chest!)

"Zarabanda appeared, and he grabbed a metal file. Curíngángá, curí, curi, cúri con tu maña. And Zarabanda cut the chain.

"Arruyénye . . . arruyénye . . . arruyénye. The raft moved forward, free. The broken chain stayed at the bottom of the river.

"The king arrived at his land. He ate the rice. It was good. The people then began to plant and cultivate it, just like the devil.

"One day Lukankanza showed up at the kingdom of the Congo, looking for a fight. But the king defeated him with Buán Buru and Zarabanda, and that put an end to the devil's abuse. Everyone who wanted to could plant rice, and rice could be exchanged for peanut, or peanut for rice."[166]

The peanut from the savanna is used in a salve (by boiling the whole plant) as a remedy for hemorrhoids.

MANOPILON

Mouriri valenzuela Gris.

LUCUMÍ: MORELE, OWODON.

OWNER: OGUN.

It is used to make "tools"—symbolic objects—and decorations for the orishas, as well as small objects used as amulets.

MANTO DE LA VIRGEN

Coleus blumei, Benth.

ENGLISH: COLEUS, PAINTED NETTLES.

LUCUMÍ: OCHARE.

OWNER: OBATALA.

It is used to wash the *otan* and relics of the orisha.

---

166 DF-N: This passage epitomizes the inconsistent ways Cabrera transliterates Afro-Cuban terms: the name of "the Devil" (el Diablo) is written three different ways (Lukankansa, Lukánkansa, and Lukankanza).

MANZANILLA

Chrysanthellum americanum (L.) Valke.

LUCUMÍ: NIKIRIO (!).

CONGO: DÚNBUANDE.

OWNER: OSHUN.

It is used in decoctions to aid the stomach and intestines. It fortifies hair's roots, and it revives the body.

MARAÑON

Anacardium occidentale L.

ENGLISH: CASHEW.

OWNERS: OSHUN, INLE, AND CHANGÓ.

A belt made with the green seeds of the *marañon* worn constantly will cure hemorrhoids. As the seeds dry out, the hemorrhoids are reduced and disappear forever.

MARAVILLA

Mirabilis jalapa L.

ENGLISH: MARVEL OF PERU, FOUR O'CLOCK FLOWER.

LUCUMÍ: EWE EWA, INKUALLO.

CONGO: BODDULÉ.

OWNERS: OBATALA, YEWA, AND OYA.

"The seeds of the white *maravilla* are toasted and ground into powder. This powder is placed on a cotton plant leaf with *cascarilla* and cocoa butter, then covered with a white kerchief. A *prodigiosa* leaf is used to cover the kerchief. This is left on Obatala's stone. For eight days, a little of this *afoche* is blown on the front door, then luck will visit the house."

When the eyes of a cadaver have remained open, they are covered with *maravilla* leaves, which have the ability to close them softly and slowly.

A decoction made with its root is very good for the digestion, and it helps control tenesmus and bloody vomit.

The juice of the whole plant bursts external tumors.

("The *maravilla* doesn't like mosquitoes. It doesn't let them come near.")

MARIPOSA

Hedychium coronarium, Koenig.

ENGLISH: WHITE GINGER LILY.

LUCUMÍ: BALABA,[167] AROAO.

CONGO: KÁNDA, FITITI NKANGRISO.

In decoctions meant to be gargled, it is used to treat tonsillitis and other ailments of the throat. The roots are used to expel phlegm caused by a cold.

MASTUERZO

Lepidium virginicum L.

ENGLISH: PEPPERWORT, VIRGINIA PEPPERWEED.

LUCUMÍ: ERIBO.

OWNER: ELEGUA. IT IS ALSO ATTRIBUTED TO BABA.

At the break of dawn on Good Friday or another Friday, before the sun has come out, you go out to look for this plant. You touch it three times with your hand, talk to it, then pull it up and run it over your face. You need to be careful that it is not hit by sunlight. You take it home and let it dry. You pulverize it and put it in a bottle with perfume containing valeriana, metal powder from a magnet, and powder from a *zún zún* [hummingbird].

---

167 DF-N: The plant's names in Spanish (*mariposa*) and Lucumí (*balaba*) both translate literally as "butterfly." *Balaba* is analogous to the Yoruba *labalába* (Crowther [1854] 1913, 20) and the Lucumí *labé labé* (Cabrera [1957] 1986, 198).

M

"With this perfume, women drive men wild." And vice versa.

To cure a cold, the root is boiled and strained. It is administered as a drink three times a day without telling the recipient what it is.

It is very refreshing. It reduces the amount of sugar in the blood and also cures the kidneys and liver. It reduces or cures hernias.

If the hernia is recent and not too severe, and a doctor's intervention is inevitable, then you gather a good handful of *mastuerzo* seeds, put them in a glass, and take them to a dairy farmer when he is milking his cow early in the morning. (You pay him to fill the glass, since one of the virtues of this remedy consists of the milk falling on the *mastuerzo* directly from the udder, then drinking it next to the cow.)

During nine days, continue the same treatment at the same early hour of the day.

To heal on old hernia, it is worth trying this recipe: "For that intractable *canchila*, make jockstraps of strong cloth and put some grinding stone mud on there. Change the cloth twice a day.

"When the testicles get hard like rocks, stop using the mud. Make new jockstraps and put sterilized cotton inside so the testicles will soften. Once they're soft, get rid of the jockstraps, because the hernia will be cured." (Literal quote.)

MATANEGRO

Rourea glabra Kth.

LUCUMÍ: KONRI. (SOME CALL IT KUKENKELEYO.)

OWNER: YEMAYA.

"The *santa* that defeats all sorcerers and subdues all the *abikus* uses this tree to fight.

"In slavery times, the stalks of this shrub were used as whips to punish slaves.[168]

"It is used in *mayombe* to make *chicherekus* move more quickly."

(It is the *bejuco Baracoa*.)

MEJORANA

Origanum marjorana L.

ENGLISH: MARJORAM.

"It is best to gather the San Juan variety. It is allowed to dry. Then you take advantage when swallows pass by. You hunt one, and remove its heart. All of this is ground into a powder, and the powder helps you do whatever you want."

San Ciprián and the *congos de nación* [African-born Congos] used it a lot.

When the marjoram grows in abundance, it is an augur of prosperity; when it withers, of ruin.

A little stick on its own, without performing any incantations, has the power of an *igide*, an amulet, and it should always be carried in one's pocket.

"The marjoram is very jealous, and you should not add any other plants to decoctions made with it."

In a decoction, it is given to women in labor. It brings on contractions.

"For a hysterical person—or spasms of the mouth of the stomach [esophagus]— I run my hand over them while praying the Apostles' Creed three times, and I give them a decoction to drink three days in a row which is prepared with marjoram, *carquesa*, and three shoots from an *anón* [custard apple] tree."

---

168 DF-N: The plant's Spanish name translates literally as "kills Black (people)" or "Black killer."

MELON DE AGUA

Citrullus citrulls (L.) Karst.

ENGLISH: WATERMELON.

LUCUMÍ: AGBEYE, AGWE TUTU, ITAKUN, OYE, OGURE.

CONGO: MACHAFIO SURI MAMBA.[169]

OWNER: YEMAYA.

One of the favorite fruits of the goddess.

The devotee offers a whole melon (if their means allow for it), or seven pieces, which are placed—like all offerings—before the tureen of the orisha. After seven days, they are taken to the ocean.

Decoctions made with the roots and leaves are used to refresh the eyes or to alleviate irritability and fatigue. The seed is used to prepare a sugary paste which is very nutritious and has diuretic properties.

MELON DE CASTILLA

Cucumis melo L.

LUCUMÍ: EGURE, LESEITAKU.

CONGO: MACHAFIO SURI YANGA.

OWNER: OSHUN.

After five days, the melon that has been offered to Oshun is turned over to the river, where the goddess passes by in her *okweri* (boat).

These offerings of fruit are often distributed among the neighborhood children by order of the gods, who sometimes require they be given fruits and sweets, because "the Ibeyi are children."

Likewise, Obatala adores children.

MIERDA DE GALLINA

Bunchosia nitida Jacq.

LUCUMÍ: ADIE IGBEMI.[170]

OWNERS: THE IBEYI.

It is used to "cleanse," liberating children who are born sick from evil influences or spirits.

"To purify sick blood, boil three roots of the plant—not the trunk—with a little aguardiente made from sugarcane, then you drink one cup when you wake up and another cup when you go to sleep."

MIJE

Eugenia rhombea (Berg) Krug & Urb.

ENGLISH: RED STOPPER, SPICEBERRY.

OWNERS: OSHUN AND ESHU.

"Oshun likes seeing it on her altar. It is hers just as much as the *canela* tree."

Many *santeras* use it to prepare an amulet with the caul of a newborn.

"It's very fortunate to keep the caul from one's birth! People who do that are assured good luck."

The first edition of the *Diccionario de Autoridades* tells us, "The caul is the cloth-like covering in which a baby is sometimes born, which is kept and considered very valuable and useful for many things."

They assure us that there is no better talisman, "nothing better" for "many things," than a small piece of this tissue, since those who are born in their caul are exceptionally lucky.

Oftentimes, "receivers" (midwives) with little or no conscience steal them from their clients and sell them at a high price. Above all, sailors will pay any

---

169 DF-N: The Spanish, English, Lucumí, and Congo names are all literal analogs: "(fresh) water" and "fruit," "gourd," or "melon."

170 DF-N: The Lucumí and Spanish names both translate literally as "chicken shit."

M

price for the cauls of baby girls. Stealing this membrane from a newborn deprives them of good luck: "It spoils their destiny." Like A.M., who was born covered entirely in her caul, only to have it stolen by one of her mother's neighbors who did not even leave a single fragment of it for the poor little one. The life of A.M. has not been a happy one, and she blames all of her misfortunes on that hateful theft.

Referring to a lucky person, one often hears others saying, "Surely they were born in their caul." It is a sign of Obatala's favor. He is the owner of the caul, and will accompany the child on its journey in the world. Like those who are born with a cross on the roof of their mouth or on their tongue, those who are born standing up, or those who cry before being born, they will be diviners, "great heads."

MIL FLORES

Clerodendrum fragans, Vent.

ENGLISH: CASHMERE BOUQUET.

OWNERS: OYA AND YEWA.

It is used for cleansings and baths for good luck.

If evil spirits pursue us, the thought of death obsesses us, we have anguished dreams about the dead, or we have dreams in which we see death in the form of a skeleton, then baths with *mil flores* will free us from them.

It is very beneficial to avoid harm and "hexes."

Mil flores and seven types of albahaca leaves.

MILLO

Hulcus sorghum L.

ENGLISH: SORGHUM GRASS.

LUCUMÍ: OKABLEBA, OKUARE.

OWNER: BABALU AYÉ.

So that epidemics and illness do not enter the home, a small broom made from sorghum grass is decorated with a red ribbon and nailed behind the front door, along with a dried corncob covered in palm oil and a printed Catholic card of San Lázaro or a prayer to this *santo*.

Obatala, the mother of Changó, was going through hard times. In fact, times were so tough that she decided to ask Ifa for advice. He told her to go visit the home of her son Changó, who was a king, and that she should make *ebo* with a sprig of sorghum grass (*okableba*). He also warned her that she would suffer three great challenges along the way, but she needed to stay quiet and keep moving forward.[171]

When Obatala headed out, she came across Eshu disguised as a coal vendor. Begging for Obatala's help, he put his hands on Obatala's white robe and stained it. She was going to complain, but she remembered Ifa's words and continued on her way.

Farther along, she encountered Eshu again, this time disguised as a market woman with a basket of fruits on her head.

"Help me!" she said, bringing the basket down.

Obatala, *funfun wemo*, helped the woman, who then flipped over the basket and stained her all over with palm oil. Still, Obatala said nothing. Controlling her indignation, she cleaned herself off and kept going, still holding her sprig

---

171 DF-N: Note the complex gender markers in this Lucumí mythical tale (*pataki*): Obatalá ("king of the white cloth") is a mother and a "she" (*ella*).

M

of sorghum grass under her arm. She crossed a *monte* ("which was *aeru*") in the midst of terrible drought.

Changó's horse had been missing for twelve years, lost inside that *monte*. Because of the drought, the horse saw the sorghum grass Obatala was carrying and followed her to eat it. Obatala tried to shoo the horse away, but it kept coming back. Walking together like that, they reached a checkpoint where Changó's soldiers recognized the horse, tied him up, and took the woman with the grass prisoner.

They took her to Changó. Bakoso was *ite oba*, sitting on his throne, but when he recognized his mother, he jumped up and went to her, doing somersaults, and landed at her feet. It had been many years since he had seen her, and he was overjoyed: "Omuyu! Iya etie kekere!"

Changó built her an *ile*. And since that encounter, his red necklace was mixed together with his mother's white beads.

MIRAGUANO

Thrinax wendlandiana, Becc.

ENGLISH: FLORIDA THATCH PALM.

LUCUMÍ: MARIWÓ.

OWNERS: CHANGÓ AND AGAYU.

Strands of the thatch palm fronds are used to make fringes—*malipo*—that adorn the *igbodu* when the "Asiento" is performed for Yewa, a very secret ceremony to which a very limited number of people are invited.

The fringes also decorate the homes of *santos*, hanging from the inside of the door frame in honor of Agayu.

The oil made from its seed stops hair from falling out.

MIRTO

(Muralla) Murraya exotica L.

ENGLISH: ORANGE JASMINE, CHINA BOX, MOCK ORANGE.

LUCUMÍ: URARI.

OWNER: OSHUN.

It is used for soaking baths when the skin is irritated and parched from being exposed to the sun for too long.

MORURO

Pithecellobium arboreum (L.) Urb.

ENGLISH: LORITO TREE, WILD TAMBRAN.

LUCUMÍ: ORUDAN, EFUNKOKO.

CONGO: KASAOASA, KINPASE.

It is used for *prendas* in Mayombe.

"It has the authority to do whatever is wanted, good or bad, like the laurel or the ceiba."

It is covered in leaves for six months. Mayimbe lays its eggs in the *moruro* tree. The rain does not wet them, out of respect.

It is used to do harm when it is naked, without leaves:

> To ruin a person or obstruct everything they set out to accomplish, you go to a *moruro* tree at twelve noon on the dot and give it three whacks with the flat side of a machete, then drive it into the trunk. The next day, at the same time of day, you pull out the machete and invoke that person, cursing them, then you take a small piece of paper with their name written on it and put it inside the wound in the trunk. You cover the hole with three handfuls of ash stolen from their fireplace and the resin coming out of the bark.

The *moruro* tree will take revenge on the person who caused the harm it has endured.

Illness and death itself can be transferred to a tree, communicating a feeling of hatred and a desire to exact revenge for others.

The *moruro* tree has the ability to help wounds heal and to harden gums.

Its wood—like that of the *cocuyo*, *Ramón*, and *sabicú* trees—is used by the Lucumí, the Congo, all the Africans and their descendants, to make statues, which they keep to terrorize people. "Muñeco con píritu de mueto muchacho, que nelle metía dentro." [A doll with the spirit of a *muerto*, which they put inside it.]

One old man recalls the Siete-Ngúnga [statue] belonging to a sorceress who was his *comadre*: "Parao arriba caparate, e mimo baja bucá mi comare pa que lo aprepara, lo víti, echa agua cañangano, y vuébve figurín, montá caparate y pone otra ve tieso." [He's standing up in the the rafters, then he comes down himself, looking for my friend to prepare him, dress him, and pour sugarcane liquor on him, then turns back into a doll, climbs back up into the rafters, and goes back to being stiff.]

We have reports of many other harmless statues that move themselves from one place to another. For example, a Changó statue made by the carver Juan Kilate out of cedarwood, and belonging to a *santera* from Pogolotti, sometimes descends from his altar to pull off some innocent prank, and he constantly moves from one position to another on it.

Pedro G's Twins (*meyi, simba*) "come out at night to get some fresh air, and they often wake him up, because they climb up onto his bed."

The Virgen de Regla "escapes from the chapel to bathe in the sea, and she returns at dawn in wet clothes."

NARANJA

ENGLISH: ORANGE.

LUCUMÍ: OROLOKUN, OROMBO, OLOMBA, OSAN, OBURUKU, OSAEYIMBO, ESA.

CONGO: BOLO MÁMBA, MÁAMBE, MBELIA KALA, MBEFO MALALA, NKIÁNKÁN.

OWNER: OSHUN.

It is the fruit that Yeye so often demands when she comes down to dance with her *omos* and devotees.

"*Chi chi olombo kini mo guase olombo yeye*, says the Santa Mulata."

"Yalode likes nothing better than finding a beautiful basket of oranges at the shore of the river."

After bathing, the goddess always savors the sweet golden fruit with delight, "which is sweet like her."

The orange has many applications for the healer. Using the dried, mashed leaves, they prepare a cigarette that is considered effective in correcting hoarseness and bronchitis. A decoction made with its flowers is given to children when they suffer from acidosis. A decoction made with its leaves is recommended for colds, and another made from scraped bark is used as an after-dinner drink to aid digestion.

"Often, the skin of *obiri oloñu* (pregnant women) becomes discolored. After they give birth, these blemishes can be removed with their child's first excrement, which is rubbed on to stay on quite a while, then we wash it off with orange leaves and coffee."

You can also cure indigestion with orange, oil, and salt.

For hiccups, an infusion made with orange blossom: "To treat gas that forms in the belly and irritation, massage it softly with an orange blossom salve and sip the decoction."

NARANJA AGRIA

Citrus aurantium L.

ENGLISH: BITTER ORANGE, SOUR ORANGE.

LUCUMÍ: KOROSAN.

To treat erysipelas: "I stop it with the leaf of the bitter orange. Three days in a row, I cut, sanctify it, and pray the Apostles' Creed."

ÑAME

Dioscorea alata L.

ENGLISH: PURPLE YAM, UBE, GREATER YAM.

LUCUMÍ: ICHU, OSURA.

CONGO: IMBIKU, LOATO.

OWNER: ELEGUA.

Like the coconut and corn, it belongs to all of the orishas. It is offered to all of them.

The *babalawo* uses the core of the yam (*ichu*) to prepare the "ache" or "yefa," the white powder that is full of virtues and used to cover the divination board of Orumila.

Whoever has been the subject of witchcraft should rub palm oil on a yam, using it to scrub their door for three days along with salvia, *piñon botijo*, basil, and ginger, and they should take baths with ocean water, river water, and *verdolaga*.

"What better offering is there for Obatala than eight balls of yam prepared with *efun* and *ori* (*cascarilla* and cocoa butter), presented during eight consecutive days, then deposited in the bush?"

A yam on a white plate or in a small clay pot represents Elegua in many houses.

For many reasons, the yam—like the coconut—is blessed:

Olofi Orula was very poor. (Orula was suffering great hardship.) Olofi had a party, and all of the *santos* took him luxurious gifts. Orula didn't want to arrive empty-handed. He had farmed a plot of yams, so he chose the best one and took it to Olofi. It was all he had. All of the *santos* laughed at the poverty of the gift. They mocked Orula and his yam, but Olofi said, in front of everyone and loud enough for all to hear, "The yam will be blessed!"

Time went on. Plague, pestilence, and adversity came, and the wealthy were ruined. To eat, the wealthy had to go to ask for a yam from the one they had mocked so much. Orula, at that exact moment, was harvesting his crop, and he was able to help them. All the *santos* ate yam!

It is placed raw on the ground and next to the door of the house in order for it to be born spontaneously near Elegua. This sprouting of shoots is considered a precursor to good fortune, a promise of prosperity, when this yam, (called *ñame volador* [flying yam]) propagates abundantly.

R.S. recommends an effective offering, "mo la ichu odun." You bake a beautiful yam and place one end, "the head," in front of Elegua's stone with *alubosa* (onion), black-eyed peas, palm oil, honey, four pesetas, and a *medio* [five-centavo coin]. The rest of the yam is divided into four

Ñ

pieces that are covered in honey, palm oil, and a little salt.

This tuber is full of mystery: "It's the only fruit, along with the *bejuco jimagua*, that the earth births in pain." Although it represents and can substitute the *okunla* of Elegua, it belongs to Oko, San Isidro Labrador, the owner of all agriculture who was highly revered in Havana during colonial times, especially by women, and remains so in Matanzas and rural areas.

The characteristic attributes of this old *orisa*—"a güajiro"—and the service of its cult is transmitted from mothers to daughters. "The *santo* is hereditary, and it is obligatory that the daughter of the *iyalocha* must keep it and care for it." The particular cult of Orisha Oko (or Osaoko, as many elders call it), "who ensures the prosperity of the earth," has largely been abandoned in Havana. "Here, people do not obey Osaoko like they did before. They only do the bare minimum that is necessary . . . They just muddle through. They don't feed him as often as they should. And Orisaoko is the very ground that sustains us! It's the earth that gives food."

Thanks to Oko, sterile women can conceive, and many daughters of Yemaya—because she is the mother of the *abikus*—make offerings to him and implore him to not let the child they carry in their belly be miscarried.

The emblems of the god are a statue representing a farmer, a cart with an umbrella pulled by two oxen (which a wealthy *santero* will have sculpted in silver), an old terra-cotta roof tile, two dry coconuts, and sometimes a wheel. The god of food and the fertility of the earth can also fulfill the role of judge (*oniyade*) in disputes between the *santos*.

Without the yam it would be impossible to swear an oath (initiate) in the Abakuá society. It is one of the principal attributes.

"The elders would prepare a *fufu* (pounded yam dish) made from yam that they called *eura*."

ÑAME VOLADOR or ÑAME CIMARRON

Dioscorea pilosiuscula Gris.

ENGLISH: BULBOUS YAM.

LUCUMÍ: ICHU.

CONGO: IMBÍKUA SALÁLÁLÁ.

This wild, climbing vine is enjoyed by horses and cows. Like the *ruda*, it has the excellent ability to repel the *ndokis* and flying sorcerers. E.H. affirms, "The Ndoki won't land where there is *ñame volador*."

The vine is used to make harmful powders.

With the *ñame volador*, the *santero* is able to enact wicked deeds, inducing Elegua to do them.

....

OCUJE

Calophyllum antillanum Britton (C. calaba, Lacq.)

ENGLISH: ANTILLES BEAUTY LEAF, ALEXANDRIAN LAUREL, GALBA, MAST WOOD, WEST INDIAN LAUREL.

LUCUMÍ: YENYE.

CONGO: SIMANO.

In Mayombe "cristiano," the leaves are mashed and used in poultices to treat swollen knees. The roots, combined with other roots in a rubbing oil, is used to combat rheumatism.

OFON or OFÚN (?)

"IT IS MEREMIYÉ. I DON'T KNOW ANY OTHER NAME FOR IT."

OWNER: OBATALA.

It is used to wash relics. It is used in the ceremonies carried out during the *Asiento*.

OJO DE BUEY

Mucuna urens (L.) D.C.

ENGLISH: OX-EYE BEAN, HORSE-EYE BEAN.

LUCUMÍ: HUMIYI.

OWNER: CHANGÓ.

This pretty seed is used to prepare protective charms of indisputable power. It acquires the appearance of a jewel when it is polished.

OJO DE PROFETA

LUCUMÍ: RECHEYE'E (?).

CONGO: MIKÁMBO.

OWNER: ORULA.

The *babalawo* "works" with this plant. A decoction with the leaves is used for cleansing baths. The sap is recommended for use in salves on the head to treat headaches and, above all, feelings of heaviness, congestion, or "heating up."

OJO DE RATON

Rivina humilis L.

CONGO: MODOBO.

OWNER: ELEGUA.

The *santero* will use this plant to make their adversary's business fail.

OREJA DE PALO (Guindavela or Palo Caballero)

Coriolus maximus (Mont.) Murril.[172]

With this tree, the spirit of a *muerto*, and the customary critters, one is able

to construct a very good *prenda* for self-defense and protection.

OROZUZ DE LA TIERRA

Lippia dulcis, Trec.

ENGLISH: AZTEC SWEET HERB, BUSY LIPPIA, HONEYHERB.

LUCUMÍ: OROSUN KIKIO SIMAWA (?), EYEFO'O.

CONGO: IMEYEMO (?).

OWNER: OSHUN.

This plant extends itself like *yerba buena*, and it is similar in appearance to it, except its leaves have a longer shape. These leaves are so sweet that infusions made with them are prepared without sugar, and they are highly recommended for the stomach and asthma. The entire plant is used to prepare protective charms for drug traffickers.

"*Orozúz* is used to wash houses of gambling and ill repute, and it's also very good for spraying to cleanse the atmosphere in elegant salons.

"When Orozúz has been used to prepare an amulet for drug smugglers or businessmen who work in the kinds of dirty or risky businesses that are so popular these days, the charm is given the name of Judas."

ORTIGUILLA

Fleurya cuneata (A.Rich) Wedd.

LUCUMÍ: EWE NE, INA, AIÑA.

CONGO: IYEN.

OWNER: BABALU AYÉ.

Boiled to be drunk like regular water, it does not itch and it cleanses the blood of impurities. In an infusion mixed with *canutillo* and *rabo de zorra*, it cures impotence. (It is first drunk on an empty stomach in the morning, then at midday, and at night.)

---

172 DF-N: Another botanical name for it is *Trametes maxima* (Mont.) A.David & Rajchenb.

To cause impotence: "You grab Mamá-Tété Oromí. Seven spiders, seven leaf-cutting ants, and seven flies. A hummingbird. You give a rooster to Elegua. You take the head of the rooster, and the two nails from the middle fingers. These ingredients are taken to *el monte*, where you find a tree in the shape of a cross. You say: 'After God and the earth, I come to greet you. The day you move from this place where you are and go make a cross somewhere else, my work will be ruined. But as long as you have your cross, my work will remain.' If the work is being done to one person, you pay the tree three centavos. If it is several people that will be ... then you give seven centavos."

(The same harm can be wrought with seven pumpkin shoots, nails from the victim, scraped toward the base, hair from all the parts of their body, *ortiguilla*, and a *narigón* [nose ring] from an ox. You say to the pumpkin: "You and all the other plants asked the Santísimo Sacramento that wherever you hang, you won't let go of whomever you grab.")

To "ruin" a home, take every type of misfortune: the head of a black dog, *ortiguilla*, seeds from an *aromo* plant, toasted sesame seeds, the head and feathers of a guinea fowl, and the indispensable guinea pepper.

P

....

PALO AMARGO

Picramnia reticulata Gris.

ENGLISH: BITTERBRUSH.

LUCUMÍ: IGI KIKAN.

CONGO: MÓMBOCO.

OWNERS: CHANGÓ AND OGUN.

Without the bark, it is used in "works" for *santo*. ("And to make someone's life bitter.")

The bark, roots, and leaves are boiled and administered when it is necessary to expel a cursed beverage that has been unknowingly ingested.

"It takes out the witchcraft from critters or from any *bilongo* the person has inside them."

The *santero* also prescribes these decoctions for some stomach ailments. Drunk like regular water, it cures the vice of drunkenness.

A decoction made with the roots is used to treat gout and arthritis.

"If it doesn't rid a drunk (*omo'oti*) of their vice entirely, I guarantee that it will at least relieve the stomach pains, cramps, acid reflux, and other maladies suffered by all *guarapetas* [drunks]."

PALO BATALLA

This name is given to any strong tree used to "*nasrande*"—do mayombe witchcraft. It is also given to branches or trunks that brush against others in the same tree, "those that do battle, one against the other."[173]

PALO BLANCO

Simarouba glauca D.C.

ENGLISH: PARADISE TREE, DYSENTERY-BARK, BITTERWOOD.

LUCUMÍ: IGGI-FÚN.

CONGO: MUSI MINDOLA.

An infusion made with the leaves, roots, and bark is used to treat diabetes. The leaves by themselves are used to whiten teeth.

---

173 DF-N: *Palo batalla* translates literally as "*palo* for battle," "battle tree," etc.

PALO BOBO

LUCUMÍ: INABIRI, IYUMO.[174]

CONGO: NKUNI MBI MACHAFIO, GUAÉKO.

OWNER: OBATALA. (SOME ATTRIBUTE IT TO CHANGÓ OR OGUN.)

"It's used to weaken a decoction made from the leaves of other trees. When it is too strong, this neutralizes it a little." It is also mixed with poisonous trees or plants if it is necessary to utilize them.

PALO BOMBA

Xilopia glabra L.[175]

LUCUMÍ: OLÚNIPA.

CONGO: MUBÓN.

OWNERS: CHANGÓ AND OGUN.

The leaves, bark, and roots are combined with other plants by the *agugu* or *alafoche* to procure a very discreet poison. "They say the person that takes it will explode, without a doubt. Although they die from internal hemorrhaging, it doesn't leave any sign of poison in the guts or stomach. It has the same advantage as the witchcraft that is made with a fish bone (?) and put in coffee."

It is only used for *malambo* (or *ika*).

PALO BRONCO

Malpighia biflora Sw.[176]

ENGLISH: BARBADOS CHERRY, ESCOBILLO.

---

174 DF-N: *Palo bobo* translates literally as "stupid *palo*," "dumb tree," etc.

175 DF-N: *Palo bomba*, translates literally as "bomb *palo*," "bomb tree," etc.

176 DF-N: The plant's name, *palo bronco*, translates literally as "rough *palo*," "coarse tree," etc. It is closely related to *yagé* (*Banisteriopsis caapi*), the plant used in the entheogenic brew known as *ayahuasca*.

CONGO: MORUAMBO.

OWNER: OSAIN. (IT IS ALSO ATTRIBUTED TO ELEGUA, OGUN, AND CHANGÓ.)

The *ngangula* or *osainista* uses it as an amulet for safe travel, to penetrate the thicket of an unspoiled *monte*. A walking stick or dry branch of *palo bronco* liberates one from all mishaps: you will not get lost; wasps and ants will not sting you; you will not come across any harmful animal (the *majá* snake with dangerous eyes will run away from the *palo bronco*); you will not be pricked by venomous thorns; evil spirits will not chase you; you will not breathe the terrible emissions of malignant trees and waters where *ndokis* live. The *palo bronco* will guide and defend you.

Some *santeros* will not venture into unfamiliar forests without gripping this magical wand in their hand. These protective walking sticks, loaded with magic, are also made with wood from the olive and *avellano* [hazel] trees. When it is necessary, or perhaps simply convenient, for the stick to not be too strong, it is made with *caña de castilla*. (Andrés Petit's famous walking stick, the subject of many miraculous stories, was made from the wood of an olive tree.)

PALO CABALLERO

Phoradendron rubrum Gris.

ENGLISH: MAHOGANY MISTLETOE.

CONGO: BUTEKIE.

OWNER: CHANGÓ.

It is also called *guinda vela*. It is found on *guásima*, *granadillo*, and other trees. Its power is used for all purposes. "It was one of the *palos* that Marigwánga used to play with, and it became well known in Matanzas."

It protects against witchcraft and all manner of negative influences. With a little piece of its stalk kept in a pocket over one's chest, "it works just like a *detente* (protective amulet)."

It is recommended for washing the head (it prevents hair loss) and to regulate menstruation. Its stalks are used for poultices.

PALO CACHIMBA

LUCUMÍ: ACHO IKOKO.

OWNER: CHANGÓ. MANY ATTRIBUTE IT TO OSAIN, OTHERS TO OYA.

It has the power to dispel squalls. It protects against electrical discharge.

"Its wood is used to make a bonfire in *el monte* or near the *bohío* to keep *bokoso*"—lightning—"from striking."

PALO CAFE

Amaious corymbosa H.B.K.

LUCUMÍ: IGIFERE, APO.

CONGO: AN HERBALIST CALLS IT IRINKAO OR POPOLU.

"The aroma released by its wood when it is burned serves as an African religious incense. And like incense, it carries away *ikiniku*, all evil. It eliminates harmful fetid odors, and it purifies the rooms of sick people."

C.P. adds, "It was the incense used by the *negros de nación*. They insisted that the smoke from this tree would rid a house of illness. And when a sick person got healthy, they burned it so the illness wouldn't grab them again. The incense made with its dried leaves and mixed with leaves from the *plátano guineo* [banana] is better than the one made with its stalks. It clears away the illness in bad smells."

PALO CAJA

Allophylus cominia Sw.

LUCUMÍ: ORIN, MEREMBA.

CONGO: NGUENGE.

OWNER: CHANGÓ.

It is used for cleansing baths. It kills witchcraft.

"It's a very noble tree in Mayombe. It likes to do good. It's a healer." Indeed, a decoction made from its bark contains hemorrhaging and works as an abortive. It regulates or causes a menstrual period if it is delayed.

Boiled with *raíz de china*, *bejuco congo* (or *garañón*), *bejuco jaboncillo*, *bejuco jimagua*, and *batalla*, it strengthens the body. This preparation is drunk like normal water until its beneficial effects are felt.

It combats tuberculosis.

It suppresses toothaches. "With a mouthful of the juice from *palo caja*, Black people used to alleviate toothaches. Their teeth were so good that they seldom hurt, and they would go to *kambon sila* with all of their teeth.[177] You see how Black people these days lose their teeth? And they go around acting so proud of their toothbrushes!"

PALO CAMBIA VOZ or CAMBIA CAMINO[178]

CONGO: KISIAMBOLO.

It is one of the names *paleros* give the *cuaba* tree.

"Because it makes people change their opinion and direction. In Congo, we call it Nkunia Bondansua."

---

177 LC: The cemetery.

178 DF-N: *Palo cambia voz* translates literally as "*palo* changes voice," "voice-changing tree," etc. *Palo cambia camino* translates literally as "*palo* for changing course," "change path tree," etc.

PALO CENIZO or HUMO DE SABANA[179]

Pithecolobium obovale (A.Rich.) C.Wright

LUCUMÍ: IGBELEFIN.

CONGO: NCHUNGO, CHUNGORA, MIFOTOTO.

"It might appear to be an insignificant log . . . But it is important in the *nkunia*"—the bundle of wood in Mayombe—"and the *ngangas* and the *nbanis*"—horns. "It's the one that balances all of the energies."

PALO CHINCHE

Amomis odiolens Urb.

CONGO: INSEGUA.

It is characterized by its excessive smell . . . like *chinche* [chinch bugs]. My informant does not know of any medicinal applications for it.

Another plant with the same smell is used to cure diarrhea.

PALO CLAVO

Eugenia caryphyllata Thumb.

ENGLISH: CLOVE.

OWNER: OGUN.

Decoctions using the root, the leaves, and the heart of this tree are administered to this who have drunk a potion made with animals, such as those made with lobster, scorpion, centipede, etc. They expel the *bilongo* and save the person from a deadly curse before it is too late.

PALO COCHINO[180]

Tetragastris balsamifera (Sw.) O. Ktze.

LUCUMÍ: EPOTO (?), IGILEDE, EWIMAMARO.

CONGO: FUMASI.

OWNERS: CHANGÓ, YEMAYA, OR OGUN. (OPINIONS ARE DIVIDED. THE MAJORITY ATTRIBUTE IT TO YEMAYA.)

The leaves are consumed to make *ebo* or perform a cleansing.

The bark and roots are boiled then drunk to purify and enrich the blood. A highly concentrated decoction made with the roots is drunk like regular water and recommended for diarrhea.

PALO DIABLO[181]

Capparis cynophallophors L.

ENGLISH: JAMAICAN CAPER.

LUCUMÍ: BIESHU, BURUBU, KINSONKO (?).

CONGO: MEKUEMBRI, WABI.

OWNER: ESHU.

Lucumí supposedly do not use this small shrub because, as its name implies, it is so maleficent that its powder is used to enliven *ngangas* "judías" during Holy Week.

Sorcerers in "kunanchet"—the country, the bush—plant it far from their huts. Instead of watering it, they nourish its roots with the blood of animals that belong exclusively to Lugambe.

The natural wickedness of this shrub is intensified by the "menga"—blood—of these diabolical animals, which infiltrates

---

179 DF-N: *Palo cenizo* translates literally as "ash *palo*," "tree of ashes," etc. *Humo de sabana* translates literally as "savanna smoke," "smoke from the savanna," etc.

180 DF-N: *Palo cochino* translates literally as "pig *palo*," "tree of swine," etc.

181 DF-N: *Palo diablo* translates literally as "devil *palo*," "devil's tree," etc.

the plant and nourishes it from the day it first sprouts from the ground.

For this reason, sorcerers who have "sworn an oath to a *nganga*" next to it prefer not to speak of its nefarious properties or the sinister spirits that inhabit it. It is difficult to imagine just how demonic this *palo diablo* might be if it only shelters *nfumbis* of killers, cruel souls of criminals and suicides who are tormented and torment others.

PALO GUITARRA

Citharexylum caudatum L.

ENGLISH: FLORIDA FIDDLEWOOD, SPINY FIDDLEWOOD.

LUCUMÍ: ALARE.

CONGO: OSONKO.

OWNERS: OBATALA, CHANGÓ, AND OGUN.

Its wood is used to make musical instruments.

Decoctions made with its leaves and roots are used to wash ears in cases of deafness or purulent secretions, or when a patient is disturbed by strange noises or buzzing. Perhaps due to the fine resonance of its wood, *palo guitarra* has the virtue of curing illness of the ears and overcoming deafness.

It is considered just as effective in the treatment of disrupted menstrual cycles.

PALO HACHA[182]

LUCUMÍ: IGI NIKA.

CONGO: MUSI BELE LOASIA.

OWNER: OYA.

"This tree is used to rile up Oya." (For Oya's "Battles.")

PALO HEDIONDO[183]

Cassia emarginata L.

LUCUMÍ: IKIHARA-HARA.

CONGO: SEKENSE, BAYE, BITONDO.

When the painful agony of a dying person is prolonged, it is because the soul clings to a useless body and refuses to abandon it.

"In these cases, if the dying person has orisha, a sage person *lo baja* [brings it down, performs divination]. If not, they make *suchungara*. They burn a branch of *palo hediondo* with feathers from a hen near their headboard of the deathbed to send their spirit on its way."

The properties of the aroma facilitate the release of the soul and bid it farewell, "making it believe that the substance of the body it is determined to continue occupying have already decayed. That smell makes it decide to abandon the body and leave it in peace. When this person—*alamuriuku* or *oteribacho*—becomes a cadaver, salute it with these words: *leni odegu odocha oda kulebo*. This means: you are now a spirit and I kneel before you."

PALO JERINGA or TEKEN-TEKE

OWNER: YEMAYA.

Despite its prosaic name, sorcerers employ this wood as a powder for its aphrodisiac properties.[184] "The powder is spread around the bedroom of a married couple whose intimate relations are apathetic, and the result is always satisfactory."

See also PARAISO.[185]

---

183 DF-N: *Palo hediondo* translates literally as "fetid *palo*," "foul-smelling tree," etc.

184 DF-N: The term *jeringa* (literally, injection needle) in the plant's name is euphemistic.

185 DF-N: There is no entry for PARAÍSO FRANCÉS in the encyclopedia.

182 DF-N: *Palo hacha* translates literally as "axe tree," etc.

P

PALO JICOTEA[186]

LUCUMÍ: IKI AYA URA.

OWNERS: OSAIN AND CHANGÓ.

"When a sorcerer takes it out of *el monte* and prepares it in small pieces, it talks just like we do, and it can talk with another tree that has the same strength and virtue. A *prenda* that is prepared with *palo jicotea* contains a lot of ingredients, including a lot of critters."

A small piece of this tree—along with a *mate* seed, *sacú-sacú*, *bejuco boniato*, and *espuela de caballero* (*Ensubo*)—make a very reliable amulet for Changó's protection.

PALO MALAMBO

Canella alba, Murr.

CONGO: NKUNIA MPEKA.

(One of my informants also calls it Korokoyo.)

It is one of the strong, enchanted trees manipulated by sorcerers with Congo affiliation. It dispenses benevolent or maleficent effects equally. It can attack or defend. "But it is excellent for doing harm, so when it sets out to be *judío*, it's as wicked as any other *palo*, and when it sets out to be *cristiano*, it's as good as it gets."

Let us highlight some of its secondary, "cristiano" qualities: it cures tetanus, if we give credence to one *palero's* optimism. And it cures all spasms and cramps.

A decoction made with its roots and bark is always given to new mothers to prevent complications.

The water that this tree exudes has an abortive effect.

---

186 DF-N: *Palo jicotea* translates literally as "turtle tree," etc.

PALO MANGA SAYAS (?)

"This *palo* protects *novios* [lovers]."

"It is used for *ichepanchagara* (prostitutes) and everyone who deals with matters between men and women. It's *palo mayombe*, but it also works for the *oluo* when they need to do work for a . . . *saranbadya*."

"Saran- . . . ?"

"A clandestine woman."

PALO MORO

Psychotria brownei Spreng., *P. obovalis* A.Rich.

ENGLISH: BROWNE'S WILD COFFEE.

"I DON'T KNOW WHAT THIS TREE IS CALLED IN LUCUMÍ. OR IN CONGO. (BUT, IF THEY'VE TOLD YOU IT'S CALLED MIÑO IN LUCUMÍ, THAT DOESN'T SOUND RIGHT TO ME. AND DONSONKO IN CONGO? WELL, LET'S JUST LEAVE IT AT THAT . . .)"[187]

OWNER: ELEGUA.

It is used to be fortunate in love—to attract and charm by treacherous means.

One of the authorities I consulted claims that the soil around this tree is marvelous for taking control of a person's "rastro" ("trace," "footprints," or "track")—that is, a human shadow and, consequently, the person.

Over and over, we have already been warned that our theurgists of all shades and colors spend their whole lives "picking up people's traces and tying them up." Enchanting, possessing, and controlling are the eternal objectives pursued by

---

187 DF-N: With this quotation, Cabrera makes the contested and layered nature of this linguistic and botanical knowledge extravagantly legible.

sorcerers' magic and occupation, good or bad, all around the world. Having taken control of so many "traces" throughout his life, let the *Taita* himself explain his technique once again:

> A person's footsteps leave the emanation of their life in the earth or the floor. The essence of a person is left in their footprint. It's enough to take a small handful of earth where they stepped. There's nothing better for this than the earth itself. If they walked on a floor, you pick up the dust.
>
> When you want to control someone, you need to bind them, tie them up. And to do that, the first thing you need to do is take control of their footsteps. When you have their footsteps—the trace—you already have the person in your hands. The life and destiny of that man or woman belongs to you, because then we can work (bewitch) them easily. Why? I already told you. They left their essence in the footprint.
>
> Because the earth is more pure out in the country and rural towns, it's easier to tie people up out there, where their trace is more intense.

For his part, Murillo says, "We always try to gain control. And to control someone, you need something of theirs. What does it matter what it is? As long as it formed a part of their body, near them, soaked in their heat, their sweat. In case you don't even have a single hair from the person. Or nails. Or blood. Or a picture. Or used clothes. If you have so much as a little piece of fabric that they bought in a store to make a shirt or a slip, even if they never made it, but they thought about making it and touched the fabric, handled it, then you can rob their trace. Then you can grab hold of them really, really well. Their heat is in there,

their life force, and you get a direct emanation of the person. You can also steal their Guardian Angel."

"Their Guardian Angel?"

"Yes, the shadow that walks behind the body. The Angel in their head is facing forward, looking ahead. You need to get the shadow after the person has gone by. Otherwise, the Angel (*Eleda*) would see what was happening and defend them. That's if they're on good terms. After we take the shadow, we work on that person who's been left without a shadow."

"The Angel . . . It only faces forward? It doesn't occur to them to look around?"

"If the Angel's happy with the person, then yes, it'll look out for everything. But when it's not satisfied, it turns to the side. And when it's really upset, it turns its back completely. In that case, they're actually in favor of the harm intended for the person they accompany. That's how, if they're angry, they'll look for an opportunity to let the person they defended get hurt, leaving their head on the chopping block. Or they'll leave the head entirely. Many times, madness is nothing more than that. A head that's been left without its Angel. Those attacks that sometimes make the *ochiwere*—crazy person—sane, then, other times, crazy: that's the Angel leaving, coming back, and leaving them again.

"We have to win over the Angel of the person who we're going to work. We do it with food, flattering them, praising them a lot, so they leave the head where they reside, getting them out of there or pushing them aside. That's the most important thing: knowing the name of the Angel on whose day that person first saw the light of day, to establish a relationship with them, to call on them and summon them. That's why you shouldn't say the person's first name they were given or the name that came from their *Asiento* or *nganga*, because you'll lose them with those names. Those names that you shouldn't say carry a sort of trace, the essence of a life. The true name of the person and the person, they are the same thing. The name is a very sacred thing. It needs to be truly silenced." Anyone can distract someone else's Angel by offering them food and taking advantage of that moment they're distracted or enjoying their favorite meal. (Some Angels are less vigilant or easier to tempt with sweets. Yemaya is renowned for taking good care of her children. To "take the shadow" of a child of Yemaya, the sorcerer runs into serious difficulties, and their efforts usually fail.)[188]

I recall that an aunt of the *santera* R. never took a nap, because—literally—"the Angel disconnects itself from body. And because she had enemies, she did not give them a chance for them to work her." Neither did she allow anyone around her to sleep at the wrong time— that is, during the day. Her advice and explanation for her fears were well founded: "The *Congo de nación* used to say, '*Tango yángonda tó mundo son manito.*, When the moon shines, all men sleep. And asleep, they are all brothers. But during the day, some are brothers and other are enemies: the one who's awake wants to hurt the other one, and in a moment of carelessness, they take advantage of the moment when their enemy's Angel separates itself from their body. The person's

Eleda leaves while they sleep, going for a stroll, or even traveling far away, and the body is left alone. That little nap— combined with people coming in and out of a house, a half-shut door, or an open window—is an opportunity. Anyone can take advantage of it while the body has no one to keep watch over it, and it will receive all the garbage, the *ebora* they toss at them. At night, people take better precautions."

In short, if a person who has been chosen to be enslaved is skillfully led to one of these trees and leaves their footprint imprinted in the earth, which is so propitious for this sort of theft, they will be tied up right there and then, becoming a captive at the thief's mercy.

"Two lovers voluntary bound together at the Donsoko tree will never separate."[189]

PALO MULATO

Exothea paniculata (Juss.) Radlk.

ENGLISH: BUTTERBOUGH.

LUCUMÍ: KUKUNDUKU.

CONGO: POUNKORO, BANDUNDU.

OWNER: OSHUN.

It belongs to both *mayombe cristiano* and *mayombe judío*. "It is equally good and bad: it dances to whatever tune you play for it."

In baths, it cleans away negative influences. In incense, it purifies the atmosphere and dispels witchcraft. In decoctions, it invigorates the body.

Like another very magical tree— *manajú*—it has great magnetic power. It is used with the brain and eyes of

---

188 DF-N: Since Cabrera herself was a "child" of Yemaya, the passage can be interpreted as a sharp-edged act of rhetorical and mystical self-defense—a warning meant to preempt and/or neutralize potential ritual malice. In letters that shifted between French and Yoruba, her friend and collaborator Pierre Fatumbi Verger often addressed Cabrera affectionately as "Chère Yemoja." See Cabrera and Verger (2011).

189 DF-N: This consensual binding ritual is a counterpoint to other ritual formulas in this volume that violate any semblance of consent. See chapter 2.

beautiful animals like horses and peacocks to make a powerful talisman intended for those women who are pretty but lack "*sandunga*" and have no luck in love or friendship.

Supplied with this talisman, attention will be focused on them, allowing them to effortlessly attain whatever their heart or vanity desire.

PALO NEGRO

LUCUMÍ: IGI ERU.

CONGO: MASENSE, MUFUITA.[190]

OWNER: ELEGUA.

"Its heart is very, very black. A little powder from this tree, properly consecrated and prayed over, flies like the wind. Elegua, who handles all the *mayomberos'* trees, likes working with it.

"You need to keep it on hand in case Elegua asks for it. Just like *abre camino*, *amansa guapo*, and *quita-saco*, it's a tree that belongs to him, and it's hard to find."

"It's also used by Ogun Achibiri Ki, who is San Miguel Archangel."

PALO RAMON

Trophis racemosa (L.) Urb.

ENGLISH: WHITE RAMOON.

CONGO: KUARIBAO, NKITAN KITAN, MOLUYABA, NKENTO.

Another one of the principal trees in Mayombe. According to the expression used by C., it "is good for catching and holding the *muerto*."

One of the wonders of this tree is described to us as "the gift of menstruating like a woman, and giving milk during the waxing moon." That is why so many mothers drink water boiled with the leaves, roots, and bark of this tree while they nurse their children—which, among our people, is sometimes prolonged past the age of three years. The decoction is used to increase lactation and prevent its disruption.

In the old days, Black people would use the *palo Ramón* tree when one of their teeth was in bad shape, filling the cavity with its sap, which destroyed the tooth and—after some time—let them extract the tooth in pieces, without pain.

"It's very mysterious. At certain times . . . that one will *soro soro* . . . he talks. It is one of those that makes itself invisible, and the *palero* doesn't dare to make a sound in its presence."

Sandoval affirms that *palo Ramón* and *bejuco cochino* "can kill twenty-four hours a day, if one needs to do harm."

Some *babalochas* attribute it to the god Ogun. An Iyalocha assures me that "it belongs to Changó." And an *osainista* says it belongs to Obatala.

Chicherekus are made with its wood.

PALO ROMPE HUESO[191]

Casearia sylvestris Sw.

LUCUMÍ: ICHIEGU, BOROKOMA, OR (?).

CONGO: BEBERICO, KULOMBE.

OWNERS: CHANGÓ, OYA, AND OGUN.

"It has a strong *muerto* that breaks bones when it mounts someone."

A cross made from this bush's resistant wood and "prayed over" contains a mystery, a profound *ache* (grace). It is held

190 DF-N: The Spanish, Lucumí, and Congo names have roughly the same literal meaning. See Cabrera ([1957] 1986, 122; and [1984] 2001, 234).

191 DF-N: *Palo rompe hueso* translates literally as "bone-breaker *palo*," "bone-breaking tree," etc.

up to ward off a tornado or storm that is threatening to come near. The storm goes away as soon as it sees the cross.

Additionally, the ritual performed in these cases can induce the elements to divert their trajectory away from *bohíos* and crops. The storm is stunned, or it goes in the opposite direction. And if it should pass, it will avoid dwellings and farm plots without causing the slightest damage.

PALO SANTO

"It is the Holy Father of all the trees in *el monte*. *Mpungu funan kunia*. If it's mistreated, the other trees start to dry out. If it's burned, its wood smells the same as the burning flesh of a *cristiano* [human]."

PALO TENGUE

Poeppigia procera, Presl.

LUCUMÍ: ADEBESU.

CONGO: NKITA, NKUNIA CHECHE KABINDA.

Mentioning it is enough to make a *palero* salute its name: "*Malembe ngei malembe mpolo*. Tengue is the strongest of all the trees."

Sikiri mato boba ngei ntukua. Tengue, nkisi kensi guatuka? Tengue bugule nkunia. Nkunia sandu. Lumbendon Sambia guatuku dundu mabaka. ("Listen to what I'm saying. Tengue is my father. Tengue is great. What family do I belong to? I am a *fundamento* of Tengue, a *santo* tree with the great power of God. Amen.")

PALO TOCINO

Acacia paniculata Willd.

LUCUMÍ: ORE.

CONGO: YIGUAYEO, FUNKULERE.

"Well, for certain kinds of work, I can tell you. It's the best! And to bring on a delayed period (menstruation), a decoction using its leaves, fuzz from a coconut shell, and leaves from a two-faced *croto*."

To cure gonorrhea, it is mixed with a decoction made with leaves from the Don Carlos, leaves from the *sén*, coconut water, and a handful of Epsom salts. This is one of the best-known infusions ("chicha").

It neutralizes witchcraft and confers good luck.

Its "iru" or "kerebende"—like all thorns—are used to do harm or to protect someone who is afraid of being harmed.

PALO TORCIDO

LUCUMÍ: OTITIE, MITONLO.

CONGO: ALUBENDE DIANFINDA, OTUTUA.[192]

OWNER: ESHU.

"It's used to twist someone's luck, to jinx them. It's twisted and it twists.[193] Used in an *afoche* or simply using one of its branches, it will block an enemy's path, delay them, or turn them around."

See also MANOPILON.

PALO VERRACO[194]

Hypericum styphelioides A.Rich.

LUCUMÍ: TENI-TENI, LEDE.

CONGO: FUMASI, DOKIRONGO.

---

192 DF-N: Note the similarity between two of the Lucumí and Congo names (*otitie* and *otutua*, respectively).

193 DF-N: The plant's name, *palo torcido*, translates literally as "twisted, bent, and/or crooked tree."

194 DF-N: *Palo verraco* translates literally as "boar *palo*," "male pig tree," etc.

OWNER: YEMAYA.

A purifying infusion made with its bark, branches, and roots is well known among all Cuban people as a cure for syphilis and other venereal diseases.

PAPO, PAPITO, ZAPATICO DE LA REINA[195]

Fagelia bitaminosa D.C.

LUCUMÍ: OYI, BATAYABA.

CONGO: MUKANDA.

OWNER: OSHUN.

It is used in baths to cleanse negative influences, as well as in some amulets. A decoction made from the entire plant is very fortifying.

PARAISO

Melia azedarach L.

ENGLISH: CHINABERRY.

LUCUMÍ: IBAYO, YIYA.

OWNER: CHANGÓ.

Extremely sacred. As sacred as *cedro.* "It might," Hernández believes, "contain even more mysteries than *cedro.*"

It protects and gives good luck. Among the people, it is one of the most sought after and most admired trees.

Its branches should be collected on Mondays and Fridays, leaving a tribute of five centavos at its roots or offering it to the tree's owner.

For cleansing baths, one must tear off segments of it by pulling upward while saying, "*Paraíso,* just as you are so tall, make me grow and rise up."

"To clean your house, clear out the bad luck, and attract good luck, it's one of

a kind." Whoever has a *paraíso* in their garden knows this: they receive constant requests from the whole neighborhood, who just "need a little piece of it for a remedy."

The floors of homes are washed from the inside toward the door with water and *paraíso* leaves. The branches are used to sweep the ceiling while saying, "*Paraíso santo,* I want to rise up the same way you do." "First, you clean the front gate or entrance to the house. After it's been used, the branch carries away all the negativity it finds. It's tossed in the street, and you use another branch to sweep out the rest of the house. All the garbage is picked up and deposited in an open field."

Its leaves are placed over the chest to cure or protect an ailing heart. They calm dyspnea and tachycardia, and they should be replaced when they dry out.

The shoots are prepared in a decoction to alleviate retching, and the seeds crushed in alcohol are used often in Trinidad to kill lice.

The owner of a *paraíso* should take good care of it. If it dries out, they will surely suffer serious unpleasantness, or the course of their life will be altered in some other way.

With a flowering branch, some invoke the Anima Sola.

PARAMI[196]

CONGO: KAGUANGACO.

It is used to influence, possess, and control a person.

The *paramí* and *amansa guapo* trees always "work" together to secure these sorts of conquests. The recipe is very

195 DF-N: *Zapatico de la reina* translates literally as "the queen's little shoe."

196 DF-N: *Paramí* translates literally as "mine," "give me," etc.

common: clippings from the chosen person's fingernails and toenails, and some of their hair. The hair is not burned; it is ground carefully (burning it would cause that person great harm). All of this is used to make a powder that is added in small batches to coffee every day until it is all consumed.

"Everyone uses this tree: Lucumí *santeros*, spiritists, *congueros* . . . When one of their goddaughters offers a four-legged animal to an *iyalocha*'s guardian angel, they put some of the animal's bones aside and crush them into powder. They pray over it at the feet of the *santos*, then they save the powder. Then, if the goddaughter quarrels with her husband, the godmother mixes that powder with powder made from *paramí* and *vencedor*, and, for an even more powerful effect, hair. And the husband is bound. From then on, he'll be very, very tame, and he'll yield."

PATA DE GALLINA

Eleusine indica (L.) Gaerth.

ENGLISH: INDIAN GOOSEGRASS.

LUCUMÍ: EWE ERAN, DEDE, ARAOGU.

CONGO: KIMBANSA, BEBEKE.

OWNER: ELEGUA.

After a *taita dibamba* has—like *olochas*—asked his dead ancestors for permission to celebrate his "juego" [ritual], he proceeds to tie up the four corners of his house. Using *pata de gallina*—known in all of the *Reglas* with Congo affiliations as *Kimbansa*—they "linga" or "nkanga" the *mundele* or *mukuaputo*,[197] the white man that represents the authorities, the Orden Público, as my older informants insist on referring to the police. (*Dundu tonga, masoriale.*)

---

197 DF-N: The verbs *linga* and *nkanga* refer to binding and tying down (Cabrera [1957] 1986, 251), and *mukuaputo* refers to police (235).

The initiation and oath-taking rituals, invocations, conjuring, casting of spells, and all of the sorcery—*gualonampulu*, as Juan Lara calls it—takes place in the room that is farthest toward the back of the house and dedicated exclusively to the *prenda*, the *nso mpungu* or *nso ndoki* (if they are an evil sorcerer). Invariably, the rituals of Mayombe begin this way: The Father, Fumo Sangu—supported by his *mayordomo* or assistant, the *wanga nkise*—sounds three sharp whistles or forcefully strikes the floor in front of *kalubanga* (magic receptacle) three times with his fist or foot. Until that moment, the *kalubanga* had been covered with white, red, or black fabric, depending on the type of spirits they serve and the kind of work they will carry out. These strikes alert the spirit that sleeps in the cauldron. Following the copious spraying of *Chamba* and blowing of tobacco smoke used to gratify his *nganga*, the Father takes a handful of *kimbansa* ("the plant that clears the way and guards the door") and *mpolo-ntoto* (earth or dust from the four corners, which had already been collected by his godchildren), then mixes it with a little of the earth contained inside the *nganga*.

A small amount of earth with fibers from the *kimbansa* are placed in the center of two corn husks (*masango*) arranged in the shape of a cross. The sorcerer rolls up and twists the corn husk containing the earth and *kimbansa*, praying and imploring the support of the "fuiri" while the *bakuyula-ngangas*—the godchildren and godbrothers of the temple—sing a chorus in a monotone whisper:

Arruru nkanga nsila
Como nkangala Kangala sila

The sorcerer ties three or four knots in each *masango*. (Each of these small packages is called a *masango*, which is the name given to packages made with corn, *kangris*, or *makutos*.) When he

P

finishes the four packages, he steps on them hard with his left foot. Then the *mayordomo* steps on them, followed by the *mayombero*'s other godchildren and the participants in the "juego."

The *masangos* are placed on a board, where they are sprayed with *chamba* and covered with tobacco smoke (*nfute* or *sunga*). Immediately afterward, three small mounds of gunpowder (*fula*) are lined up on the same board to ask if the *muertos* and spirits dwelling on the corner are ready and willing to block the way of any intruders. (Gunpowder is only used in the Regla de Palo or Mayombe, never in Lucumí rituals.) If the fire makes the gunpowder explode by "sweeping it all at once"—that is, if the three small heaps explode in succession—then it is understood that there is nothing to fear. They are on the right path: the spirits have responded with an emphatic yes. Otherwise, they need to start over because some element of the *nkanges* has been neglected.

The two godchildren who brought the *mpolo nsila* (dust from the street) go out to deposit a *masango* at each corner. But they take great care to place the one containing dust from the south corner at the north corner, the one from the east at the west, the one from the west at the east.

The police or enemy will be disoriented, and they will be unable to find the sorcerer's house. (On other occasions, in order "to frighten away the police," various powders are scattered at each corner: red ocher, *cascarilla*, shavings from a deer antler, or the excrement of a broody hen, hutia, and fish.)[198]

The *kimbisas* often work with *kimbansa*, and orisha devotees put it over the small clay vessel for Elegua, the owner of the roads who uses this plant to "bind or tie up."

A "*niche*" used to find employment is made with *pata de gallina* and spools of white and black thread. The threads and plant are used to sew the name of the person who can grant the job into a piece of paper, which is then left under Elegua.

PEGA PEGA

LUCUMÍ: KIRIMEKO.

CONGO: INI INAGO (ACCORDING TO AN HERBALIST IN THE PLAZA DEL VAPOR).

OWNERS: THE IBEYI.

"The leaves and roots are used by *santeros* to unite broken marriages or relationships."[199]

PENDEJERA

Solanum torvum Sw.

ENGLISH: TURKEY BERRY, DEVIL'S FIG, PEA EGGPLANT, PLATEBRUSH.

LUCUMÍ: ISIAMI, EWE ODUYAFUN, INYELO.

CONGO: MILISIA.

OWNER: ESHU.

"This shrub is used in petitions to foster conflict and legal trouble involving an official or leader who needs to appear before tribunals and will benefit from the dispute being drawn out and ever more entangled."

A decoction using the roots is very good for treating ailments of the kidneys and the urethra. It soothes the burning sen-

198 DF-N: Compare this to the PIMIENTA entry, which includes a ritual formula with a very similar list of ingredients.

199 DF-N: The plant's name, *pega pega*, translates literally as "stick stick"—as in adhering or binding.

sation. It purifies the blood. Among its other virtues, it helps avoid impotence, "and an illness the Lucumí used to call *oko okuo*. Write that down. And the Congo called it Nfia languan."

"*Oko Okuo?* Mary, mother of God! Write . . . *epon aro*."[200]

PEONIA

Abrus abrus (L.) W.F.Wright (*Abrus precatorius* L.)

ENGLISH: PEONY.

LUCUMÍ: EWEREYEYE OR IGEREYEYE, KUPA.

Every *ikoko*—the clay pot that is filled with plants, to shred them and prepare *omiero* for *kariocha*—includes peony leaves, and the basin for the *omiero* includes its seeds. Outside the context of the *omiero*, the seed is extremely dangerous: if it is stepped on, it provokes arguments and disorder. It is used to make powerful curses.

PERALEJO DE MONTE

Brysonima crassifolia (L.) H.B.K.

OWNER: OSHUN.

When it is burned, it "blocks vision." To extract vengeance, it is pulverized, mixed with other ingredients, and diluted in the coffee or other beverage of a man in order to take away their virility prematurely.[201]

PEREGRINA

Jatropha diversifolia A.Rich.

LUCUMÍ: ERO.

CONGO: NTINGORO.

OWNER: OSHUN.

It is used for cleansing.

The leaves are used to make offerings for those adults who cry over insignificant matters or for no reason at all.

PEREJIL

Petroselinum Beth. & Hook.

ENGLISH: PARSLEY.

LUCUMÍ: ISAKO, IYADEDE.

CONGO: NTUORO, VITITI KAMATUYA.

OWNER: OSHUN.

It is used to sanctify and to make cleansing baths.

Its power is often used to gain employment. "The parsley is ripped into very small pieces, then mixed in a basin with water, honey, and powdered cinnamon. This is used to wash the door of the house. Then, in the same space that has been cleansed, you scatter raw cornmeal [515] and say, 'Caridad del Cobre, I give you parsley, *oñi*, cinnamon, and cornmeal. In exchange, you'll help me find a way to earn a living.' You don't ask her to give you work. Instead, you ask for her benevolence, a way to put food on the table, etc."

Parsley appears in many formulas for cleansing the body. And here is one employed in a cleansing ritual for a person

> who is stagnant because someone else hexed them to impede their good fortune. They're made to chop the parsley very fine with a pair of scissors. The entire time

---

200 DF-N: In this context, the Lucumí name offered by one informant (*oko okuó*) can be translated literally as "dead penis" or "dead testicle." A second informant suggests a less vulgar term: *epon aro* (analogous to the Yoruba, *ɛp`ɔn àrùn*), meaning "sick testicles." Cf. Cabrera ([1957] 1986, 250, 251) and Crowther ([1854] 1913, 96, 49).

201 DF-N: Other names for the plant are changunga, muruci, nanche, golden spoon, and (in Jamaica) hogberry.

P

they do this, they say, "Parsley, don't let me be lazy, and give me what I'm asking of you." Then the parsley is kept in a bottle with alcohol and put next to the *santo*.

That person needs to go to the river to make *ebo*, cleanse themselves, and leave it there. They're sent to buy a candle that will be cut into three pieces. When they head out to the river, at the moment they're walking out, they light one piece of the candle behind the door. They'll light another one at the river, and the last one when they've finished bathing.

They'll go to the river wearing the oldest clothes they own, but taking a set of new clothes, Castile soap, and two plants besides parsley to fully clean themselves: *apasote* and salvia. Once they're in the water, they destroy the used clothes, ripping them to shreds. They should position themselves so they're facing downstream in a way that lets them light the piece of candle. They soap themselves and rub their skin with the parsley, salvia, and *apasote*. And they should keep a close watch, never taking their eyes off what's being washed away (the *ebo*). Then they rinse themselves, dress in the new clothes and leave the burning candle.

Three days later, they take the bottle with the parsley and alcohol they've kept next to the orisha. They rub their body with it every night until the bottle runs out, saying, "The ram defecates and forgiven. The dog defecates and forgiven. The cat defecates and covers it up."

"Is there anything better for attraction, conquest, and triumph than a bath with parsley, a white carnation flower, honey, cinnamon, and dust from a magnet?"

Business people will attract more clients to their shops or offices with parsley leaves that are toasted, then ground, and mixed with cassava flour (*maricuyé*), cornmeal, a magnet, and the stone of La Caridad del Cobre. These are scattered around the store or workshop. Outside the front door or on the sidewalk, cinnamon extract, water, and Agua de Florida perfume are poured on the ground.

To rip witchcraft out of someone's stomach, the victim of the curse is given a decoction with parsley root, *sacu-sacu*, *romero* flowers, and raw milk for seven days. Milk can be substituted with dry wine or wine vinegar.

If parsley is not available from herbalists, the juice from the leaves can be used. It is mashed separately in a mortar, then its juice is poured into a decoction made with *sacu-sacu* and *romero* flowers.

PICA PICA

Stizolobium pruritum (Wight) Piper[202]

LUCUMÍ: SIS, ISELIYE, RIRA, AGUANARA, AINA.

CONGO: OTE (ACCORDING TO AN HERBALIST WHOSE LANGUAGE CANNOT BE IDENTIFIED BY MY MOST COMPETENT INFORMANTS).

OWNERS: BABALU AYÉ AND ELEGUA.

"It is a transmitter for something evil, which leads it and guides it, along with the *muerto*."

In powders used for curses, it is combined ("married") with Pimienta, and it causes arguments and quarrels which have grave consequences.

---

202 DF-N: Another botanical name is *Mucuna pruriens*.

In a decoction, it soothes itching.

PIERDE RASTRO

It is used to ward off an undesirable person or to erase someone's tracks, aiding a fugitive to avoid or hide from the law so they cannot be found.[203]

The vine or tree used to obtain this result is given the name *Pierde Rastro*, Griwasu, or *Tapa Camino*, like the parasitic plants on some trees, such as *Guinda Vela*.

(It is also used to ward off a person, magically obligating them to stay away from the place they most frequent. A powder made with red ocher, *cascarilla*, and ashes or shavings from a deer antler. Or dried hen excrement, fish, smoked hutia, and corn.)

PIMIENTA

Pimenta pimenta (L.) Cockerell

ENGLISH: PEPPER.

LUCUMÍ: ATA.

CONGO: ESAKUKAKU.

OWNER: OGUN.

It is used in harmful *mpolos*, to seed and feed *prendas* and *makutos*.

Pepper is a necessary ingredient for making *chamba*, the drink offered to *ngangas*. It works as a tonic and stimulates the *nganga*. As we already know, it is prepared with aguardiente, *ají guaguao*, powdered *palo canelo*, *genjibre*, a lot of pepper, *ajo*, and *cebolla blanca* [white onion]. In order for these ingredients to dissolve, the bottle of aguardi-

---

203 DF-N: This entry does not necessarily describe a specific plant. Rather, it identifies a type of plant that is named and classified according to its esoteric ritual characteristics and functions: *pierde rastro* can be translated as "gone without a trace" or "footprint eraser."

ente containing them should be buried underground for three days.

(*Ngangas* also drink Agua de Florida perfume, which "refreshes it," with ginger, dry wine, and cognac.)

Chamba that is poured over a "Fundamento" comes into contact with the magical substances and associated spirits, thereby acquiring miraculous curative properties. In Mayombe temples, what remains of these libations in the cauldron is given the name Agua Ngongoro or Kimbisa. It shares that name with the sacred and equally beneficial water gathered from a hole in the ground or among the roots of a ceiba.

All *Padres* and initiates, and all those who have been presented to a *nganga* have drunk Kimbisa, which contains, along with aguardiente and spices, the blood of successive and frequent sacrifices. "The *kimbisa* protects their body from witchcraft, cleans them, and gives them strength."

It contains so much vital energy, power, and virtues! For the recovery, a "repair" to lift the spirits of a despondent soul and "clear the way," the *Taita* often uses *kimbisa*, under the auspices of the *fumbi*. He lifts and tilts his cauldron, pouring a little bit in a *jícara* and gives a drink of it to the sick, bewitched, or downcast person.

A request has been made of the spirit:

Pá curá cristiano, Catimabuey
Saca remedio pá curá cristiano
Catimabuey
Tú saca remedio, Catimabuey . . .

To cure a person, Catimabuey
Take the remedy to cure a person
Catimabuey
You take the remedy, Catimabuey . . .

The spirit, always ironic, comments:

Si cabeza m'enduele

Bamo la casa Mundo
Si barriga m'enduela
Bamo la casa Mundo[204]
Si brazo m'enduela
Bamo la casa Mundo . . .

If my head hurts
Let's go to the Home World
If my belly hurts
Let's go to the Home World
If my arm hurts
Let's go to the Home World . . .

He already knows the illness. They have "seen," and they do not delay in formulating their medicine.

Cosita yo vá hacé
Tenga corazón.
Agua Ngóngoro
Buena pa remedio
Agua Ngóngoro
Tenga corazón
Buena pa remedio . . .

I'm going to do a little something
Take heart.
Ngóngoro water
Is a good remedy
Ngóngoro water
Take heart
It's a good remedy . . .

and he makes them take a few sips of the incomparable elixir.

Every certain number of years, the magical receptacles are washed, and the water from the washing is saved because "it's holy water for remedies. It cures all *mamenga yari yari*, any sickness that shows up."

Insambie! Analyzing the components of *kimbisa* is enough to make anyone tremble with revulsion. And one needs to have real heart [i.e., courage], as the *nfumbi* advises in the *mambo*, to drink a mouthful of this putrid liquid. Aside from the blood rotting in the cauldron or clay pot, one always finds common offerings like bugs, lizards, or frogs that are decaying slowly inside there, because "the *nfumbi* eats them little by little."

But what is a man capable of doing to save his life? And my elders claim that "agua ngongoro" has never killed anyone; on the contrary, it has saved a great many.

In some temples (including one with numerous "godchildren" in the neighborhood of Azul), this brew of miraculous filth—blood, saliva, carrion—is called Agua de San Roque, and it is used as a medicine and a beverage for communion on particular days of the year.

T.A. declares that the Lucumí do not possess anything resembling *kimbisa*: "*Omiero* is not that strong."

This is nothing more than an opinion. It is more than a little boastful, and—given the space to do so—an *olorisa* would certainly argue against it.

All the different types of pepper are used in Mayombe: *malagueta*, *china*, *de costa*, *de playa*. Although their magical properties "should only be known by those who have been scratched," they are widely known among all the people, who frequently benefit or suffer from those properties.

Upon initiation, the Padre *nganga* gives the neophyte seven grains of pepper with a sip of holy water and a piece of a rooster's heart. ("So their body will stay healthy and protected when they're attacked by the *wembas* and all the *ntufi* sent by sorcerers.") After that, Baró says, they can drink poison, which they would surely expel right away. The godchild has truly become a "cuerpo nfumbi" [the body of *nfumbi*], protected by forces that do not assist ordinary mortals.

Like the *Yamao*, pepper "calls and brings." That is why the sorcerer re-

P

204 LC: The home of the *mayombero*.

sorts to pepper when one person has distanced themselves from another. For example, a husband who has left home, or a boyfriend who stubbornly refuses any efforts at reconciliation and stays away from a girlfriend with whom he has quarreled. If the subject still desires the love or friendship of the person who has abandoned them, the sorcerer prepares the number of grains they deem necessary on the *nganga* to ensure that the person returns to them resolutely. The subject leaves their house, takes the first grain, and says to it, "Call So-and-So, make him respond to my call, make him happy to see me, make him follow me and return to my side." At each corner along the way, they will drop the little grains of pepper and give them the same command. Lastly, they will toss it at the door of the person's house, "who the pepper has predisposed in their favor, and who is sure to be waiting. Hearing their voice, the person will say something like, 'What took you so long?' And they'll go back to the way they were before they argued or drifted apart."

They will also keep a toothpick made from *canela de monte* in their mouth, and another made from *cuabaliri* or *guachinango*. Each time they pronounce the name of the beloved and distant person, they will spit on the ground and step on their saliva with their left foot. (They are symbolically stepping on the other person, because "the name is the person," and they will overcome them and "have them at their feet.")

"Experience proves that pepper is so good for reconciliation that people who go back to loving each other and get back together, thanks to this work, won't even notice the change. The day before, they might be talking trash about somebody, and they really won't want to see them again. Then, if they run into them the next morning in the street, or if that person they hated so much goes to find them at their own house, they'll welcome them with open arms and follow them around like a little dog, as if nothing had happened between them."

But pepper does not work without the intervention of a *nfumbi*, a supernatural energy. Pepper—both *pimienta china* (black pepper) and *pimienta de guinea*—is an agent of discord. Sorcerers use it as a medium to provoke the most violent altercations, fights that often end with blood being spilled. This is well known and feared by everyone. For this purpose, it is mixed with salt, egg shell, spider, *mosca verde* [green fly], sulfur, saltpeter (if it is available), soil from a cemetery, teeth and nails from a dog and a cat, shavings from a human skull (taken from the sorcerer's *nganga*), and tibias and phalanges. All of this is powdered and mixed with ashes from three coals that were ground down to powder while they were still burning. All the while, the names of the people whom one wishes to make enemies are recited out loud, and the spirit—who "goes" in the bones and the dirt from the cemetery—is ordered to ignite their moods until they all lose their minds. Nothing will be able to contain them, and they will insult, attack, wound, and kill each other.

These powders act immediately when they are stepped on or inhaled. In order to not belabor the point further, it should suffice to say that the magical formula for the pepper *mpolo* above, by virtue of being traditional and genuine, "can start revolution."

In any case, while it is *pimienta de guinea* that unleashes tragedy and "carries the *muerto* and the spirit of a critter," it does not seem prudent to step on any pepper, even if it is not enchanted. It could predispose one to anger, harshness, or curtness that are out of place. It is always a dangerous irritant.

P

In a tenement, the mere suspicion that someone has scattered *ata* is enough to heat up the atmosphere and cause one fiery argument or another.

To make a *musi* (*palo*) "go far," one gives it pepper ground together with *pica pica*. An old *palera* with a very good reputation shares the following: "To make a living person rot away, you steal their excrement. You grind two kinds of pepper, add salt to the excrement, and boil it with a little aguardiente and a little water. Then you take it to a tree *de mala sombra* [with an evil shadow], where you *nkangri* and bury it."

With five little grains and the favor of the goddess Oshun—who is so fond of sorcery in one of her "paths" or aspects, "the Oshun that has a mortar and pestle to prepare her *afoche*"—a person can be bewitched at a distance.

These powders are used to invoke and conjure at high noon, pouring five drops of honey on them. The person carrying out this sorcery also needs five yards of fabric of various colors— blue, white, red, and yellow. Following the invocation, the yellow fabric will be used to cover a container full of bee honey, camphor, quicksilver, and *adormidera* leaves, all of which will be placed under their bed "to tame and control them."

Twenty-one grains of common pepper from a kitchen, gunpowder, mustard, guinea pepper, and sea salt bought in three different shops are all crushed and dissolved together. Then it is left between Monday and Friday in the home or place—a park, theater, traffic circle, etc.—where you want to cause a tragedy that will result from a violent argument. (Or powdered *mayimbe*, dog, cat, *macao*, soil from a grave, and pepper.)

In order to "break apart," ruin, or sow discord in the core of a family, a lizard is "worked," making it swallow several bewitched grains of pepper, then leaving it free to roam in the family's home.

The *kimbisas* "load" a fearsome *mpaka* using dirt from Oya (the cemetery) and three kinds of black *pimienta de guinea*, quicksilver, the footprints of a black dog, and powdered vulture, sacrificing a black *pollo grifo* [chicken with curly feathers] and invoking Nkuyo.

In order to propose and present a business deal, or to demand or suggest a demand of any sort, many people keep a grain of pepper in their mouth which a *mayombero* has effectively sweetened and prepared in a *nganga*. Pepper facilitates speech. As they begin their predictions, diviners will often place a grain of pepper on their tongue.

Devotees offering a sacrifice of a ram, goat, young bull, pig, or deer to the orisha will chew three, seven, five, or nine grains of pepper with small pieces of coconut. In this case, only the individual making the offering chews the pepper, which they will spit into the eyes and each ear of the animal, entrusting it with a request which the animal will transmit to the deity. And if the offering involves an *ebo* by an eminent *babalawo*, a "work" or sacrificial offering as important as the one made by Awo Bolo "to ward off a war that was coming to Cuba," then all the *babalawos* (or *babaniguas*) present at the moment of offering the animal to the orisha will chew coconut and pepper to spit on the victim.

Those who carry their protective charm on the inside—that is, those whose *awo*, or godfather, has made them swallow a talisman that "will live" in their belly— feed it with grains of pepper. (Sometimes a cut will be made in the skin to insert a very small talisman, such as a small stone or a tiny piece of gold.) The number of grains that should be consumed without chewing them depends on the hallmark number associated with their orisha.

PIMIENTA CHINA

ENGLISH: BLACK PEPPER.

LUCUMÍ: OSEI.

CONGO: TUOLA.

OWNER: OGUN.

The juice, roots, and leaves are used to prepare an aguardiente for *mayombe* cauldrons. The powdered grains are used as a condiment, which has a strong effect on the stomach, cleans the liver and kidneys, and cleans away witchcraft.

"Black pepper works to do harm, like *mekua*, the Guinea pepper. As you already know, they can all be used.

"It's served in alcohol to bring down swelling. For decoctions, put three seeds in a cup of water to repair the stomach and open up the appetite. For the heart, uremia, aches in the belly, or colds.

"Ground with petroleum jelly or oil, you rub it on the chest for pneumonia. And . . . everybody knows, pepper helps men preserve their vigor."

The people believe it is an aphrodisiac.

PIMIENTA MALAGUETA or PIMIENTA PRIETA

ENGLISH: CHILI PEPPER.

OWNER: OGUN.

The crushed grains are prescribed as a poultice when, due to poor circulation of the blood, the feet get cold in an unpleasant way.

The leaves and grains are used in food offerings given to Ogun.

The roots are used to make liquors that are strong in flavor and aroma.

PINIPINCHE

Metopium toxiferum (L.) Kr. Urb.

ENGLISH: POISONWOOD, FLORIDA POISONTREE, HOG GUM.

OWNER: ESHU.

It is scattered with other powders that are equally harmful.

It causes sores on the skin.

P . . . DE GATO

Dieffenbachia seguine (Jacq.) Schott[205]

ENGLISH: DUMBCANE.

OWNERS: ELEGUA AND OGUN.

The whole plant is used in the "work," whose objective is to transform virility into impotence.

(Innumerable potions and spells accomplish this task. Some women's hatred and desire for vengeance often lend themselves to unimaginable methods. Such curses are preceded by a sacrifice to La Potencia, or whichever spirit that promises its protection. At the new moon, for example, the woman will invoke whichever orisha endorses the curse. Standing on their bed, they will use some pretext to step over the body of their husband or lover, who they thereby condemn to incurable impotence for the rest of his days.)

PINO

Pinus tropicalis Moric., *Pinus coribea* Morel.

ENGLISH: PINE.

LUCUMÍ: OKILAN, ORUKONYIKAN, YEMAO.

CONGO: MABA NLONBE.

---

205 DF-N: Propriety seemed to demand that Cabrera redact the plant's full name, *pinga de gato* (cat's cock).

P

OWNER: CHANGÓ.

The roots possess great virtues conferred by Nsasi Nkita (Santa Bárbara).

"The pine tree is the earth's level. It grows until it can see the ocean. When it's planted for good luck, it's paid its *derecho* of four or six centavo or *real* coins, and it's given four eggs and the blood of a rooster. The person planting it works squatting down, and they end the ceremony standing upright, invoking Santa Bárbara all the while. The tree is given a rooster every year. The pine will rise up, and the person who planted will rise too. As it grows, the person pleads with it, praying and feeding it year after year. The pine will be grateful and offer its benevolent shade. Its owner will not allow anyone to cut its branches, because it would hurt him. These matters should not be divulged. You don't tell anyone when you consecrate a tree." Eshu often lives in the pine tree, and he can be heard whistling up in its branches.

A decoction made with its roots is used to treat pyorrhea and to wash the head, since it makes hair grow.

PIÑA BLANCA

Ananas ananas (L.) Cock.

ENGLISH: WHITE PINEAPPLE.

LUCUMÍ: EGBOIBO, OPOYIBO.

CONGO: MERENTEN MINGE.

OWNER: OBATALA.

The juice from the roots and the shell is mixed in equal parts and drunk to clean the vocal cords and digestive tract.

The shell is used to prepare the beverage known as *chicha*. Foreigners believed that it prevented yellow fever, back in the days when that illness claimed so many victims in the new world. ("It's very invigorating in the hot parts of the Americas. They drink it as a preventive against yellow fever and other diseases that boil the blood.")

Like all juicy fruits, it is used in offerings to *ori*.

PIÑA DE RATON

LUCUMÍ: OMO IGI BOIBO, MAIMAI.

CONGO: EKENI, MUINGE.

OWNER: ELEGUA.

Its sap and an infusion made with its roots are used to prepare an elixir to improve digestion, and it is also nutritious.

PIÑA DE SALON or PIÑA DE ADORNO

LUCUMÍ: IYE, KOROYIMA, OGBA EWEKO.

CONGO: MABA NLONBE.

OWNER: OSHUN.

"Prendas"—talismans—are buried in its roots so they can be concealed in the parlor room of a home, exerting their influence "without exposing some highly regarded white family's *Prenda* to the curiosity of their visitors or the criticism of their peers who would label them as practitioners of witchcraft."

Many amulets are buried among the roots of trees and bushes in gardens, and under the plants decorating parlors—for good luck, for the prosperity of the head of the household, to maintain the unity of a marriage (and arrangements among common-law spouses), to preserve health, etc.

Nobody suspects the "secret," the intelligent and active force often hidden beneath a beautiful plant, nor the misfortune that will befall anyone who allows it to die or does away with it, unaware of what lives inside it.

"Many individuals' luck and health depend on a nondescript little tree or plant." (And how many of the successes of the fabulous salons that open their doors to the appetites of an undiscriminating society!)

It is interesting to observe the respect inspired by plants and trees that grow in the home of a *santero*, or those that are suspected of having been planted for magical ends by a *babalao* or *babalocha* who performed the obligatory rituals.

PIÑI PIÑI

OWNER: ESHU.

Like the *guao*, which is just as formidable, it figures prominently among the *palos* that the old man Calazán designates as "*palos* that are genuinely used by the devil to *ona ti ti ti*" [punish, accomplish his wickedness].

It is a shrub rather than a tree, but *paleros* and the people in general call many shrubs or plants *palos*.

The *piñi-piñi*, like others of the same kind, "is so evil that it's harmful to the very same man who has made a pact with Cachica. It poisons them by getting inside their nose or ears."[206]

PIÑON BOTIJA

Curcas curcas L.

LUCUMÍ: ADO, ALUMOFO, AKUNU.

CONGO: PULUKA, MASOROSI.

OWNERS: ELEGUA AND CHANGÓ.

This wild tree is among the most common in Cuba. It grows in any type of soil, and it is a great help in protecting oneself from treacherous attacks by sorcerers.

"It is, basically, *cristiana* [humane, benevolent]," and it repels and stops *ndiambos*

[hexes, curses, witchcraft]. Fortunately, everyone knows this.

Two piñón leaves are placed in the form of a cross inside shoes. If the person wearing those shoes steps on *malambo* powders or some other substance animated by a malevolent occult energy, they will not penetrate the body.

It cannot be placed inside *ngangas* because it would ward off the spirits that perform their dark work there. The sorcerer only uses it when he needs it for self-defense.

If a possession mount in the Congo tradition (*caballo de prenda conga*) is hit on the head with a piñón branch, the *nfumbi* will never "mount" again, nor will an *omo orisha* be "struck" by *santo* again.

If it is taken to a spiritist session—as the *iyalocha* Rosalía enjoyed doing, putting a few leaves on her chest or in the soles of dancing slippers—no spirit will manifest at the session, which will need to be suspended due to the complete absence of the "brethren from outer space."[207] They will not appear, even if they are invoked and summoned patiently all night long.

This virtue of the piñón is put to use in the washing of doors, when there are fears that witchcraft has been sent, or to immunize the home from possible "harm." In this case, it is recommended that piñón be mixed with salvia, albahaca, *ñame*, palm oil, and *jengibre*. Piñón leaves are also mixed with *ciguaraya*, *curujey*, *rompe zaragüey*, *saco-saco*, *alamo*, *raspa lengua*, and *trébol*, then boiled and added to water from a turtle's enclosure, crushed garlic, ammonia, ashes, and hydrochloric acid. (All our elders agree

---

206 DF-N: This entry describes a dangerous poison without offering its botanical, Lucumí, or Congo names.

207 DF-N: In the terminology of spiritism, the original Spanish term *hermanos del espacio*—translated literally as "brethren from outer space"—refers to spirits, otherworldly beings, etc.

on this point, however: "To annihilate witchcraft, piñón, urine, and the butt of a cigar are enough.")

After this washing, the person who feels directly threatened bathes with verdolaga [purslane] leaves, river water, seawater, and holy water.

If witchcraft has penetrated the body, three piñón seeds will be eaten, which have laxative and emetic properties. Three seeds will not produce any discomfort whatsoever. Two seeds can be fatal. (Another of this tree's mysteries.)

When the bark is scraped, boiled with the root of the *altea*, and applied in a poultice, it puts an immediate stop to swelling of an ailing limb. Swelling of the feet, invariably caused by contact with an *ogun* scattered on the ground, will ease immediately with a bath of piñón leaves, *anamú*, and *caisimón*. If witchcraft has caused a "ñáñara" [sore], this decoction is used to wash it, then the leaves are toasted, reduced to powder, and applied liberally to cover the sore.

Small pieces of wood from the trunk of the tree are used to make crosses that are nailed behind doors, thereby protecting the home's door and its residents. These talismans inspire absolute confidence.

The sap from the *piñón botijo* turns into blood on Good Friday. Therefore, during Lent, it should only be used in the pursuit of cures.

PIÑON DE PITO

Erythrina Berteroana Urb.[208]

LUCUMÍ: EFELEKE, YIRIN.

CONGO: FOSONOGAKO.

OWNER: ELEGUA.

It is used to wash the relics of *santos*, make offerings, and do "work."

Its *pitillos* are used to make a syrup that is very beneficial to emaciated children, "those skinny *mokekere* that don't step firmly, whose feet bend like molasses."[209] To make them stronger, their mothers shake them, singing and making them dance: "Ika pupo mulanganga hia."

The roots are prepared in a decoction and drunk as a treatment for constipation.

PIÑON LECHOSO

LUCUMÍ: EWEA, ADO.

CONGO: MASOROSI, PULUKA.

OWNERS: ESHU AND OGUN.

As an antidote to a love potion, three leaves of this piñón and its black seeds are boiled, and a cup of the brew is drunk at breakfast every morning. Then, two leaves are boiled for a fresh brew that should be drunk for another three days. Alternatively, in the absence of seeds, three small pieces of different branches, then two from other branches, can also be used to carry out the treatment.

PISCUALA

Quiscualis indica L.

LUCUMÍ: MOMON.

OWNERS: CHANGÓ AND OYA.

In folk medicine, the seed is used to treat parasites (*ilu kokoro*), and an infusion made from its leaves, flowers, and roots are used to bathe the legs upon returning from long, tiring walks.

P

208 DF-N: Another botanical name is *Erythrina cubensis* C.Wright.

209 DF-N: In this context, the term *pitillo* remains obscure, although it probably refers to the plant's long, thin flowers (which are like drinking straws, sometimes known as *pitillos*).

PITAHAYA

Hylocereus triangularis (L.) Britton & Rose

ENGLISH: PITA, PITAHAYA, DRAGON FRUIT.

LUCUMÍ: ESOGI.[210]

CONGO: BELONGO.

OWNER: CHANGÓ.

The flower and fruit are enjoyed by the god of drums and thunder, Changó Oniyo.

Decoctions made with the flower are "prescribed as soon as the *dilogun* announces the onset of cancer, or when one first sees its symptoms."

PLATANILLO DE CUBA

LUCUMÍ: OLUBO.

It is used in Santeria for cleansing baths and "work."

In a decoction, the roots purify the blood. It is very medicinal. It is used to combat discharge and gonorrhea.

"This plant's beauty is equaled by its gift for work. For *edi* (tying up), you get nails and hair from the person you want to capture. If you can get some fuzz from the pulvis (*sic*), that's even better. The nails are crushed into powder. You uproot the *platanillo* plant, open up the onion at its base, and put the person's hair and powdered nails inside it. You cover the plant back up with soil, which needs to be done carefully. And that's where you have them in *ilemba* [prison], whoever it is. All you need to do is take care of your *platanillo*, and make sure nobody steals or kills it. But whoever destroys a plant or tree that has something like that . . . I don't envy them."

---

210 DF-N: *Esogi*—like *eso*, *isogi*, and *asogi*—is a generic Lucumí word for "fruit." See Cabrera ([1957] 1986, 124).

There is nothing easier to achieve, if it is convenient or desirable, than making someone leave a home: eight *platanillo* leaves are toasted with the tail of a black dog, another from a white dog, and *pica pica*. "Some powders can't be resisted. That person will, inevitably, leave their house."

PLATANO

Musa paradisiaca L.

ENGLISH: PLANTAIN.

LUCUMÍ: OGEDE.

CONGO: MAKONDO.

OWNER: CHANGÓ.

"The plantain controls the wind because its trunk contains all the secrets of the *santos* and nature. Especially the *plátano indio*, which is the top one. All humans need the plantain, not only to feed themselves, but to make *ebo* for their health or to save their lives."

Makondo minganga is what the Congo used to call the *plátano indio*. The *plátano enano* ("el ciento en boca") is called *mbaka*. The *plátano guineo* is called *biekerer* and *ntiba*.

"Makondo was born with clothes, although he decided he would discard it for the sake of humankind. He asked Nsambi to let his fruit thrive more than any other, although it would be left naked when its fruit was eaten. That's where the saying comes from: *pelado como un plátano* [as naked as a plantain]. It gives its bark and blood for remedies and its meat—its fruit—for food. It's benevolent, like sugarcane. If somebody's poor, they won't starve to death as long as they can eat sugarcane or plantain."

Its fruit is enjoyed by all the orishas, but Changó and Yansa are the ones who enjoy and eat it the most. Especially Changó. "He likes it so much that *ogede* [plantain] is the first thing

P

he asks for when he arrives at a house where they're going to ask him to do good works. He might also ask for *aguado* (corn), and—of course—*akuko* (rooster) and *ayakua tiroko* (turtle). In that case, everything's already been prepared, because he had already asked for it through the cowrie shells."

Changó sometimes comes back, mounting the *iyalocha* who is going to make the offering, and says, "Oyireo . . ." (Good morning.) The response is, "Ohh." And he is given the bunch of plantains and his food. "He loves plantains," Calazán tells us. "Let me tell just how much. Once upon a time, the *santas* were all gathered together, chatting. Each one was bragging about how much their children loved them. Yemaya said quite earnestly: 'Mine loves with *kokan* (his heart).'

"The others asked her, 'Are you sure?'

"'*Kokan*. Of course I believe it. It's the truth!'

"'Your son loves you, but not with *kokan-kokan*,' said Oba.

"'How could you convince me that he doesn't love me the way I say?'

"One of the *santas* answered, 'Yalode . . .'"

(Yalode means very great lady, and although you often hear Oshun referred to as Yalode, Yemaya and elder *iyalochas*—that is, any doyenne among *iyalochas*—can also be given this courtesy, which is another way of saying the elder, the queen . . .)

"'Yalode, go home. Pretend to be *aro* (sick) and we'll take care of telling Changó. You'll see that your *omo* likes *yeun* (eating) and *añaga* (dancing) more than he likes you . . .'

"'Bah!'

"'Ofunilara!'

"But she did go to her *ile*, lay down in her *oyudo* (dais, bed), put her head down on her *irori* (pillow) as if she were really sick, and the *santas* went to tell Changó.

"'Alafia, yara yara! Iya tie aro!' (Come quickly; your mother's sick.)[211]

"'Iyami are? Etemi chon, miri Iyami aro.'

"He said, 'If my mother's sick, I'll go see her.' And he hit the road. But they saw him coming and prepared a party with a lot of the food he likes. When Changó approached, they started drumming and came out to meet him.

"'Etie mi suku suku.' He said, 'I'm crying.'

"'Kiche, Alafi?' They asked, 'Why?'

"'I'm crying because my mother is sick. Etie mi funyuru.'

"But as soon as the drums tightened up their rhythm and he heard *kimban, kimban, kimban*, he started dancing. And when he got tired of dancing, he remembered his mother. Then, *yo ko yeun.*

"He sat down to eat. He ate until he was stuffed, and with his *ifiin* all full, he hung two *akuko* and two bunches of *ogede* from his belt to take them as a gift for his sick mother.

"*Cherin-cherin-cherin*, he walked, walked, walked, but Changó never fills his *ino*: he never has enough in his belly. He looks at the plantains and sits, *unyeun!* And he eats a rooster. He keeps going down the road, but then he gets hungry again. *Ebin kua mi! Ogede?* And he eats a bunch of plantains. Yes, child, Changó is such a glutton that he can eat an *ogutan* (ram) all by himself.

---

211 DF-N: It is unclear whether or not *Alafia* is a typographical error. Contextually, it most likely refers to Alafi or Alafin (as in the sovereign of Oyo, Changó), not Alafia (an Arabic-derived Lucumí greeting meaning "peace," a sign in *obi* coconut divination, etc.).

"He's very happy and says, '*Oda!*' He drinks water at the river. *Cherin-cherin-cherin*, and after another hour on the road, he looks at the remaining bunch of plantains and rooster. They're for Yemaya, his mother, who is sick, but when he gets to her house, he only has half a rooster and seven plantains.

"Yemaya had been seeing everything Changó did along the way. She said, 'My son, it's true what they say: you like *ogede* and *anyaga*, eating and partying, more than you care about your own mother.'"

Therefore, when it is necessary to calm Changó, the *mamaocha* or *baba* prepare a type of ointment with palm oil, cocoa butter, and *cascarilla*. They rub this ointment on their hands and call and pray to Changó as they rub four green plantains from top to bottom. Once they have been covered and "prayed over," the plantains are tied up with a red ribbon and taken to a ceiba so Obatala can pacify him.

To prevent something grave from happening, the plantains are placed on the west side, facing the setting sun.

If the opposite is desired, they are placed on the east side.

"When Orula received the power to control the winds, he saw a gorgeous bunch hanging from the plantain tree. He cut it down and took it to Changó.

"And he won him over with that bunch of plantains."

Changó does not forgive his children taking so much as a single plantain from the bunches they continually offer him. María Andó Cárdenas, whose father is the Takua Changó named Ogodo Ma Kulenkue ("Takua, like Igese Adomaye"), tell us, "My father is a brutish *santo*. He doesn't recognize cars or trains. He thinks he's still in Africa." Once, she was unable to resist the temp-

tation, or rather the necessity of taking eight Plátanos Manzanos from him. "That same arm I stretched out to take Changó's plantain, he really messed it up badly." Poor María, who was unaware of the gravity of a theft that seems innocent to us, suffered terrible pain in her hand and arm which were definitely not due to "romatism" [rheumatism]. When she asked the *orisa* himself for a remedy, he let her know that he had punished her because "nobody can take something sweet out of his mouth when he's eating it." And the food of a *santo* must be respected, even if someone is starving to death.

To enliven a party or any gathering, or to simply cheer up a house, whether it is humble or comfortable, there is nothing better than scattering ground green plantain mixed with *anduyo* (chewing tobacco paste) from time to time.

According to some *mayomberos*, "Plantains are one of the favorite foods of Lukunkansa, the devil. He's always wandering around plantain groves," which are very dangerous at night.

His guardians and messengers—like the woodpecker, "who works in *nfinda* for Kachana"—also visit the tree and eat its fruit.

"Lundu Makondo"—*cepa de plátano*, the underground portion of the tree's trunk—"and *cascarilla* made from egg shells are the first things a *taita* needs to remove death from a sick person."

My elderly informants believe that "the *cepa del plátano* contains a living being,[212] and it therefore is better than a statue

---

212 DF-N: Cabrera refers to "mis viejos," which I translate as "my elderly informants." While this is literally correct, using "elderly" (rather than "old") deliberately (re)frames Cabrera's possessive form to a more honorific, deferential posture.

for absorbing a grave illness," which—in extreme cases—is transferred from a person to an object. "We put the illness in the *cepa* to do *mutambia fuiri bamba*. We dress it in all the clothes the sick person was wearing, then we bury it. The Lucumí bargain for a person's life using a statue"—although, in the countryside, this operation is always performed with a *cepa*—"a statue that looks like the sick person, that is, a portrait of them, and we take the illness out of the person and put it in the statue. Then we mourn it like a *muerto*, with four candles around it, and bury it in the cemetery.

"In Mayombe, this ceremony is done by the Nkita himself, mounted.

"In Ocha, the *babalawo* does it. It is very secret, very solemn, and astonishing.[213] And it's expensive! The statue is put between four candles and laid down next to the sick person, who—if they have deep knowledge—will bear witness to everything that is done. Their face is painted with *cascarilla*, then they are covered with a white sheet. A stick with nine small bells is shaken over them to frighten death away, then nine eggs and nine pieces of coconut are passed over their body. The items used in these cleansings—which also include cleaning the sick person with birds—are buried in the cemetery, along with a *derecho*. The *onche* or messenger in charge of delivering this *ebo* needs to be prepared properly and cleansed both on the way out and when they return. When they come back, I cleanse them with *escoba amarga* and three kinds of albahaca, because the evil often returns to the house by following their footsteps."

The *plátano morado* is taboo for *nganguleros*.

"And the *guineo* too."

The sap contained in the *cepa* of the *plátano manzano* "is the salvation of those with tuberculosis." We are assured that many have been cured after suffering advanced stages of the disease.

This *agua de plátano* [plantain juice]—which old Calazán considers one of nature's great wonders because "*levanta muertos*" [it raises the dead]—is just as effective in healing stomach ulcers and curing jaundice.

And "a decoction made with the peel of a green plantain with urine from a black bull, a live lizard, and *ciguaraya* is guaranteed to work. It also prevents hemorrhaging in women."

Plátano guineo or *manzano*, aguardiente, corn, and brown sugar are used to make an "oti" [liquor] that Elegua appreciates very much.

The vessel that contains the *denge* [porridge] in the *nangale* is placed over dried plantain leaves.[214]

POMARROSA

Jambos jambos (L.) Millsp.

ENGLISH: ROSE APPLE, PLUM ROSE.

LUCUMÍ: YILEBO, ECHIKACHO.

CONGO: KOLOMAFA.

OWNER: OSHUN.

The *pomarrosa* is greatly feared by *mayomberos* who own a *nganga judía*. Baró considers it a terrible "mata brujo" [witchcraft killer]: he confesses to me that if *pomarrosa* and urine from a black mare are scattered on the ground so a *mayombero* walks over it, or if it is scat-

P

213 DF-N: The translation of the Spanish word *impresionante* is meant to resonate with MacGaffey and Harris's use of "astonishment" as their preferred gloss on the Ki-Kongo word *ngitukuru*. See MacGaffey and Harris (1993).

214 DF-N: *See also* MAIZ, and its discussion of the *ñangale/nangareo*.

tered around their home, the *nganga*
will escape and never return to its
munan sungu (cauldron). "It will make
us lose everything we have." It is the
only thing that voids one of those evil
ngangas; that is why those who work with
them cannot even bear to look at a *pomarrosa* seed. It is not even mentioned out
loud in the home of a *ngangulero* so that
the *nfumbi* does not flee. If it is cunningly
introduced into the food of a *nkombo falo
nganga* (medium), "the evil *muerto* will
never mount them again; it won't come
anymore."

Its sap is used via inhalation to counteract bad smells in the nose.

The roots "have a gift" for curing gonorrhea, leukorrhea, and diabetes.

PONASI

Hamelia patens Jacq.

ENGLISH: FIREBUSH, HUMMINGBIRD
BUSH, SCARLET BUSH, REDHEAD.

CONGO: NFITA SUNDA MOKNA.

OWNERS: CHANGÓ AND NSASI.

The leaves are used in a decoction for
cleansing baths, as well as for the treatment of eczema and the swelling of the
legs and feet.

PRINGA HERMOSA

LUCUMÍ: OKORERE.[215]

CONGO: NAKATO.

OWNER: OSHUN PANCHAKARA.

An *afoche* is made with powder from
its roots and leaves. Following the
usual *ebo*, it is used to construct an
amulet that will protect prostitutes
from being beaten, shot, or stabbed.
With this protective charm, they will
not be abused.

"It's a terrible plant. Even its smell
causes a desperate itching. To exact
revenge by disfiguring the *bundi* (face)
of a woman who's hated for some reason or other—because she betrayed
her husband or spurned a suitor—
the sorcerer makes a very fine powder
with *Pringa-Hermosa*, vulture excrement, *yaba* or *ortiguilla*, and tobacco
ashes. The powder is spread over the
woman's bed and pillow, making sores
appear on her face, making her hair fall
out, and transforming her into a para-
gon of ugliness."

Q

QUIEBRA HACHA

Copaifera hymenaefolis Moric.[216]

LUCUMÍ: EDU, IGI, ELE, ARUDIKI.

CONGO: MBELE MUKUA NKETETE.[217]

OWNERS: OYA AND OGUN.

"Ogun works with *quiebra hacha* a lot."

The leaves, roots, and bark are used in a
decoction to expel intestinal gas.

---

215 DF-N: The word *pringa* is a thin veil that
(barely) obscures the more vulgar word *pinga*
(cock). Therefore, the name *p(r)inga hermosa*
can be translated—more or less literally—as
"gorgeous cock." Cf. P . . . DE GATO. Similarly,
the Lucumí word *okorere* can be translated
as "very good cock," and the plant's putative
owner is a *camino* (path, avatar) of the Oshun

associated with prostitution and sexual licen-
tiousness. See also the references to *panchakaras* and Oshun *panchagara* in chapter 2 and
Cabrera ([1957] 1986, 296).
216 DF-N: The plant's name, *quiebra hacha*,
literally translates as "axe breaker."
217 DF-N: In *Vocabulario Congo*, the word *mbele*
is translated as "axe" or "knife," and it is used
figuratively to refer to guns, knives, and other
lethal weapons. See Cabrera ([1984] 2001, 224).

The juice from its crushed leaves is a purgative.

QUIMBOMBO

Hibiscus esculentus L.

ENGLISH: OKRA.

LUCUMÍ: LILA, ALILA.

CONGO: GONDEI, BANYE.

OWNER: CHANGÓ.

It is one of the favorite foods of the orisha Changó.

"Let's remember that his legitimate wife, Oba Labi, received treacherous advice, then she cut one of her own ears and gave it to him in a plate of okra. Instead of enchanting him by these means, she made the god distance himself from her."

Okra has the distinctive feature of being very harmful to sorcerers—like Baró, his siblings, children, and religious kin—who avoid having it in their homes and do not eat it.

"Because it's slippery, the work I do would slip. They wouldn't be firm, and they'd slip and fall off."

If a *mayombero* needs to "chalanga" (perform sorcery that necessarily requires binding), they will not eat okra under any circumstances whatsoever. If they would leave their house to cure a sick person or to deliver a *bilongo*, they would slip along the way.

As we have seen, *mayomberos* generally abstain from using any plant or tree that is slippery, and the wisest and most prudent also abstain from eating them.

Witchcraft is obliterated with okra mixed with ashes and menstrual blood.

Changó's objects and tools are washed with dried okra that is soaked with *malvate*.

"The Baby Jesus had a sore on his navel. Nobody could cure the child's sore.

"An old woman told the Virgin, 'That sore can be cured with okra.' But the old woman disappeared, and the Lady couldn't find her.

"Okra is a flexible plant that produces flowers which look like sunflowers, but there were none to be found.

"Then the Virgin sent the Deer out into the world to look for the okra she could use to cure her son. And it was the Deer that went *juye-juye-juye-juye*, and when he arrived at the edge of a *monte*, he saw an old woman sitting next to an enormous okra plant. And he said, 'Mama, I'm a servant of the Virgin, and I'm looking for two okra plants to cure the navel of the Baby Jesus.'

"And the old woman said, 'Yes, child. The okra is mine. Look at it. Climb up and take some.'

"That old woman—a demon!—was the same one who had told the Virgin about the remedy.

"When the Deer climbed up, the plant rose up with him, and he got lost in space . . .

"The old woman had put a cauldron next to the trunk, and she moved a fan over it as she sang,

> *Fe e e . . .*
> *Fegrinya mufegere*
> *Ndan saramo!*

"And the okra hit the ceiling of the firmament. The Deer's head was smashed, and it fell next to the old woman, who hung it in her hut and ate it.

"Meanwhile, the Virgin waited and the Baby cried.

"Then, a wild pig arrived at the foot of the okra.

"'Will you give me two okras for the child of the Virgin to help his sick navel?'

"'Go ahead.'

"And the old woman fanned her cauldron. 'Fenigriya, mfegere, ndan salamo.'

"Oh, how the old woman really enjoyed peeling the skin from the pig and frying up pork rinds in its lard!

"The servants of the Virgin who went out looking for okra didn't come back.

"The Tiger went out. When the old woman saw him approach, she jumped in a hole, stuck her head out, and shouted to him, 'To cure the Virgin's baby boy, you can take it all!'

"But when she saw that the Tiger had climbed up, she took out her *nfu* [fan] and her cauldron, and she sang her song. The okra shot up into the sky, the branch bent in half, and the Tiger fell down.

"The Virgin was becoming desperate. The Baby Jesus kept crying and crying because his navel wouldn't heal.

"The Virgin only had two servants left.

"One of them, who nobody paid much attention to as it dragged its belly around, was Matenga, Turtle.

"Turtle searches, investigates, thinks, moves slowly, thinks, moves even more slowly, hides, learns, and then decides.

"The old woman saw him and greeted him with a mouth full of *mbisi* (meat): 'Good afternoon, turtle!'

"Ah, Mama. I'm looking for okra . . .'

"'Climb up the tree and take a branch for *nkento yande* (the Lady).'

"'Ntandala moana (thank you), but I can't climb up. My legs are short and they're no good for climbing. And they have sores on them; the doctor said I would get gangrene if I touch them. Please climb up for me, cut a branch,

and give me a little okra. I brought *simbo nkuto* to pay you.'

"'Very well,' the old lady said. Seeing how unimpressive he was, the old lady suspected nothing. 'I'll get them down for you.'

"'And I'll pay you.'

"As soon as the old woman leaned on the tree trunk and turned her back: *Nflu nfu salanga*.

"Turtle fanned the cauldron and sang the same mambo that the old woman sang to her okra:

"'Fediya mufe musegere . . .'

"The okra rose up, and with its roots sticking up out of the ground, took the old woman up with it.

"'Get out of here you snooty, low-down, shameless Black woman! Shut your mouth!'

"' . . . en kenda salanga fediyamufe . . .'

"The old woman was smashed against the sky. Turtle buried the cauldron, cut the okra, and took it to the Virgin Mary, who cured the Baby's navel by putting a poultice on it. And they planted the okra all over so it could be a remedy for people who were constipated, asthmatics, people with liver disease, and to annihilate the evil dispatched by sorcerers."

QUITA MALDICION

It is crucial in the *omiero* for the *Asiento*.

Its name reveals its virtue.[218]

See also ROMPE ZARAGÜEY.

---

218 DF-N: This is a curiously brief entry for a plant whose name translates as "removes curse," "curse remover," "hex breaker," etc.

Q

R

RABO DE GATO

OWNERS: ELEGUA AND THE IBEYI.

It is used to magically tie up a baby inside its mother's womb so it has difficulty being born . . . "o se ñequee" (or the pregnancy is ruined).

A great deal of vengeance is visited on the child of a hated person. The child is born "bound up," subject to the power of an enemy who becomes the author of their days and destroys them little by little unless they are saved by the prompt "vision" and expertise of a *babalawo*.

RASCA BARRIGA

Espadea amoena A.Rich[219]

LUCUMÍ: OMA, EKA ORE.

OWNER: ELEGUA.

"It is used to hit Elegua during the *Asiento*." An *Iyawo* of Elegua is beaten, sometimes roughly, by their godparents.

"Nine switches are made with *rascabarriga* [sic], decorated with nine colors and a jingle bell on the end of each one. The *santero* paints seven lines on their cheeks with *cascarilla* and spends the whole night performing the cleansing, running the switches over the body of the gravely ill person and ringing the bells, which scare death away. Then, early in the morning, they perform the exchange of lives, a ceremony that should end by twelve noon."

The exchange of lives is a removal of illness and harm, and it replaces death with life, "transferring it from one body to another. The evil is removed from the body and taken by an animal or a statue of the same size as the sick person, which is mourned and buried in a cemetery."

RASPA LENGUA

Cesearia hirsuta Sw.

LUCUMÍ: EWE ELENU, YEREOBO.[220]

CONGO: NKANGA, NKUFINDULA, LUEKELONI.

OWNER: ELEGUA.

All the authorities agree that it is "very valuable for winning legal disputes in court. It's powdered and mixed with *cascarilla*, *canela*, and white sugar, then scattered on the seat of the opposing attorney or prosecutor. The thing is, this *afoche* holds back people's tongues."

If a lawyer steps on or breathes in these seemingly harmless powders, they are made mute, speak clumsily, or get confused. Even more simply, they might withdraw their accusation or fail to defend their client.

It is also useful, in all fairness, "to tie up the tongues of foul-mouthed people."

RESEDA

Reseda odorata L.

ENGLISH: GARDEN MIGNONETTE.

ONE HERBALIST IN HAVANA CALLS IT DINKUYERO.

OWNER: YEMAYA.

Cockroaches flee from *reseda*, just as mosquitoes flee from *maravilla*. It is used in a decoction to cure intestinal flu, and to wash and darken hair.

"*Reseda* always deserves a place on a list of aromatic medicinal plants. For example,

---

219 DF-N: *Rasca barriga* translates literally as "belly scratcher."

220 DF-N: The names in Spanish (*raspa lengua*) and Lucumí (*ewe elenu*) are virtually synonymous; loosely translated, they mean "tongue scraper" and "tongue leaf," respectively.

you use it to prepare that aguardiente that's good to have in the house during the rainy season, to prevent the spread of an epidemic, or for any chronic illness that may present itself. You take a half liter bottle of aguardiente made from pure sugarcane and you add *reseda* flowers, marjoram, *toronjil, caña santa, yerba buena,* albahaca, *romero, naranja* [orange] or *limón* [lemon] leaves, *geranio, coate,* a small piece of *palo guaco* (only a little, because it is very bitter), *manzanilla, canela* on a branch, prunes, and brown sugar or candy. The bottle is buried for thirty days. A spoonful is enough to tone the stomach and get rid of the chill in the body. Take it in moderation, because it can make you drunk."

RETAMA

Neuroleana lobata (L.) R.Br.

ENGLISH: JACKASS BITTERS.

LUCUMÍ: CHACHARA, EWE ALE.

OWNER: BABALU AYÉ.

It is used in decoctions to reduce fever.

("It's also called Teikoyo and Nkorimanfo.")

Some say that a branch of *retama* helps the recitation of the prayer to the Anima Sola.

REVIENTA CABALLO

Isotoma longiflora (L.) Presl.[221]

ENGLISH: STAR OF BETHLEHEM, MADAMFATE.

LUCUMÍ: ERAN OPANI CHIN.[222]

CONGO: FITA FWA KOMBO.

(ON THE LIST OF AN *OSAINISTA* IN THE HAVANA MARKET, IT ALSO APPEARS AS MANSOKATO AND EFINLORO.)

OWNER: OYA.

It is only used to do harm. It is used to make a strong poison.

ROBLE

Tabebuia pentaphylla, Hemsl.

LUCUMÍ: AKOGI.

"No monta" (it doesn't mount), and Talaví believes it merits consideration as a tree that is exclusively beneficial and only used to cure epilepsy.[223] Its leaves and flowers are burned, and their smoke is inhaled by children suffering from this malady.

It is also highly recommended in a poultice to reduce swelling.

ROMERO

Rosmarinus officinalis L.

ENGLISH: ROSEMARY.

LUCUMÍ: EWE RE, "EWE PAGWABIMA" (FOR GIVING BIRTH). ONE INFORMANT, WHO DOES INSPIRE CONFIDENCE, CALLS IT LUNNUO AND SEREMI.

OWNER: YEMAYA.

Its branches are used for cleansings.

A young *santera* in the capital responds that the virtue of the Romero's aroma is a secret that should be kept quiet.

A decoction and the prayer to San Ramón will ease childbirth.

---

221 DF-N: It is more commonly known as *Hippobroma longiflora.*

222 DF-N: The literal meanings of the Spanish, Lucumí, and Congo names seem to be analogous.

223 DF-N: Talaví is more commonly spelled as Talabi. It is a common Lucumí and Yoruba *orisha* name given to a person born covered in a caul.

R

It is taken at the onset of labor pains. It is used in alcohol for massages to treat rheumatism and headaches.

Its juice blackens hair, and a decoction is recommended for cases of bronchitis.

The Abakuá call it *ifan mkere*.

ROMPE ZARAGÜEY

Eupatorium odoratum L.[224]

ENGLISH: SIAM WEED, CHRISTMAS BUSH, DEVIL WEED.

LUCUMÍ: TABATE.

CONGO: NTEMA DIAN FINDA.

OWNER: CHANGÓ.

"*Kata kata!* Rompe Zaragüey breaks bad luck."

It is one of the most popular and precious plants belonging to this orisha.

For cleansing baths and the purification of homes, "Rompe Zaragüey removes hexes and witchcraft. A single bath of *zaragüey, ruda, perejil, apasote, piñón, paraíso,* and alacrancillo (all of it boiled) will free a body from a *manyunga*."

Together with guara and yaya, many *Ramas* of Palo Monte use it for the seven baths that prepare and purify an individual who will be "scratched" or initiated. Before pouring the liquid over their body, they will make the sign of the cross over themselves with it and take three long sips of it to cleanse and fortify themselves internally. After each bath, they will avoid drying themselves with towels so their body is covered and penetrated by the magical properties of these three powerful vegetable forces.

To defend a home from any sort of *wanga* or *ndiambo*, a cross made from *rompe zaragüey* is placed on the door, and another cross is drawn underneath it with cocoa butter.

"It is very useful for *apuntadores*"— those who partake in gambling that is, in theory, prohibited. Just as it is able to repel and chase away *ndiambos* sent by enemy sorcerers to attack a clandestine gambler or hustler, it also stops the police (*achelu* or *agane*), which are sometimes more fearsome than evil shadows (the *egun*) or the hypothetical harms (*bilongos*) launched by a *musambu*."

ROSAS

ENGLISH: ROSES.

LUCUMÍ: IDON, DIDO.

OWNER: OSHUN.

They are used in baths for attraction: five yellow roses, quicksilver, bee honey, and cinnamon.

They are used in a bath for *lowo* (to attract money): five yellow roses, parsley, basil, five different perfume essences, and bee honey.

ROSA DE JERICO

Rosa centifolia L.

Boiled, it is used to contain hemorrhaging.

ROSA FRANCESA (Miniatura and mimosa)

LUCUMÍ: TETELI, DIDE KERE.

CONGO: MENI-MENI, IMPOINKO, KONKOSOTI WANGO UBEKON.

OWNER: YEWA.

It fortifies the bones and brain.

Its flowers are used to make a very effective cough syrup.

---

224 DF-N: It is also known as *rompe saragüey* and by the botanical name *Chromolaena odoratum*.

RUDA

Ruta chalepensis L.

LUCUMÍ: ATOPA KUN.

OWNER: CHANGÓ.

Sorcerers detest it: it is their worst enemy. "Mata que mata brujo." (It is a real witchcraft killer.)

Ndokis cannot penetrate a house where this plant grows.

"Although the *ndoki* from the Canary Islands doesn't nourish itself on human blood, the African *ndoki* only wants blood. Like the ones from the hills near Cuzco and the late Tona Jorrín, who was a *ndoki*. She sucked the blood of all her neighbor's kids, and the neighbor moved away to avoid losing her last little girl."

"Tona was known to be a *ndoki*. Like the old man Tá Lucas, and Má Viviana in Corral Falso. Tá Lucas cost my grandfather his life."

"One night, my grandfather ran into him. He was so horrified by seeing Tá Lucas fly that he lost consciousness and died from the shock."

"Having a *ruda* plant in your patio is a precaution. You never know who's living next door. *Indokería* causes a lot of misfortune. And children are the ones who are most exposed to the most danger."

The healer or the *iya* alleviate or cure earaches with *ruda* fried in oil, and *el mal de madre* with a decoction.[225]

Among innumerable "works" that are carried out using the witchy *ruda* plant, we will select this "strong binding" as an example:

Five hairs each from the person who is going to be bound and the person who will bind them. A tenacious Má recommends that you buy "a small loaf of fresh bread. You cut it in half with a clean knife—if possible, a new one. The hairs are placed inside the bread: the hairs of the person doing the binding are placed on top of the hairs of the person who will be captured. The two halves of the loaf of bread are put together and skewered with three spikes from a *palo mirto* so the two halves stay together firmly. When the plants start withering, you pick the best branch and plant it.

"You shouldn't give anybody leaves from this plant, and you shouldn't touch them on Fridays."

RUIBARBO

ENGLISH: RHUBARB.

LUCUMÍ: ERUKO EWE KAN.

CONGO: FUTUAKO.

OWNER: OSAIN.

It is used to treat bile disorders, intestinal ailments, and liver disease.

S
....

SABE LECCION

Lepidium virginicum L.

ENGLISH: PEPPERWORT, VIRGINIA PEPPERWEED.

LUCUMÍ: ICHINI-CHINI, ERIBOSA.

CONGO: SOBUNORO.

Powdered and mixed with filings from a magnet, it is a talisman to make others fall in love with you. The leaves are placed on the head to preserve your memory.

See also MASTUERZO.

---

225 DF-N: *El mal de madre*—literally, "the mothers' malady"—refers to hysteria and/or disorders of the female reproductive system.

SABICU

Lysiloma sabicu Benth.

ENGLISH: HORSEFLESH MAHOGANY, WILD TAMARIND.

OWNER: BABALU AYÉ.

The ashes from its wood are scattered in the house of a sick person to prevent contagion.

SABILA

Aloe vera L.

ENGLISH: ALOE.

OWNER: YEMAYA.

It is used to purify the liver, kidneys, and bladder. It also combats asthma. Healers recommend it in hot water for vaginal washes to treat cases of gonorrhea and leukorrhea.

"It scares sickness away" if a few stalks are placed behind the door.

SABINA

Juniperus lucaya, Britton

OWNER: YEMAYA.

It is also very medicinal. A decoction made with the wood is used to treat syphilis. A decoction made with its roots is recommended every two or three hours to stop menstruation. The oil from the seeds stimulates hair growth and it prevents balding if it is applied in time.

SACU-SACU or MALANGUILLA

OWNERS: INLE AND OSAIN.

It is very vigorous and magical, and it is a great resource for sorcerers. "The spirit will never leave the cauldron that contains Sacu-Sacu." "It's real *bilongo!*" "It works in emotional sorcery . . .

Tima con tima[226]
Ahora sí verá
Tima con tima
Mpangi son verdá.
Bialosa sí verá . . .
Heart (to/with) heart
Now you'll (really) see
Heart (to/with) heart
Brethren/family (are/for) real/true
Bialosa will (really) see . . ."

SAGU

Maranta arundinacea L.

OWNERS: THE IBEYI.

It is used for cleansing baths.

A decoction made with the root is used to curb a baby's kicking in their mother's belly.

SALVADERA

Hura crepitans L.[227]

ENGLISH: SANDBOX TREE, POSSUMWOOD.

LUCUMÍ: EWE GUNA, ARONIKA.

When a cadaver has left the house or when friends and relatives are gathered for a burial, they are "cleansed"— purified—with small sticks of *salvadera* and *escoba amarga.*

Like the *siguaraya*, it yields a fruit similar to the *almendrilla.* Three of these fruits produce a very strong purgative effect. Mixed with almond oil, it is a terrible [very effective] purgative. Aside from working as a purgative, its boiled leaves also work as an emetic.

---

226 LC: Heart.

227 DF-N: It is also known by the name *jabillo.*

SALVIA

Pluchea odorata Cass.

ENGLISH: SAGE.

OWNER: BABALU AYÉ.

A decoction made with its leaves, or even a leaf simply placed on the temple or forehead, is used to treat headaches. It is also used for washing hair when one has a cold. The steam of an infusion prepared with it eases muscle pain. "Neuralgia is cured by drinking and bathing in a decoction of salvia and *nuez moscada*. Two leaves can also be placed in the form of a cross in the bottom of a cup, pouring unsweetened coffee over the cross; this should be drunk outside rather than inside the house, in the fresh air, so it won't be harmful."

SALVIA DE CASTILLA

Salvia officinalis L.

ENGLISH: GARDEN SAGE, COMMON SAGE.

LUCUMÍ: KIRIWI (?).

CONGO: VITITI LEKA.

OWNER: OBATALA.

It is used to combat insomnia.

SALVIA MORADA

OWNER: BABALU AYÉ.

Its juice is used to massage the joints of invalids and cripples.

Rubbed into the roots of hair, it does away with dandruff.

SAN DIEGO

Gomphrena globosa L.

ENGLISH: GLOBE AMARANTH.

OWNER: ELEGUA.

The herbalist from the Havana market, who has been cited so many times, calls this plant *maitoko* and *foyinkaro*.[228]

---

228 DF-N: Although the Havana market has only been mentioned once before, Cabrera makes it clear that the particular herbalist (*osainista*, *yerbero*, etc.) cited here is the source of a great many other bits and pieces of information in *El Monte*. Presumably, this anonymous individual spent many hours with Cabrera, requested to remain unidentified, and provided numerous quotations in the encyclopedia. The individual's depth of knowledge and singular contributions to Cabrera's project are emphasized by the acknowledgment that he is the *only* source for African names in this entry. He is very likely the same individual pictured in the second photograph in the collection of images at the end of the book, in which Josefina Tarafa's camera captures an elegant figure, dressed impeccably all in white and a straw hat. The camera angle in the picture contrasts sharply with the more formal portraits of other individuals who are cited in the text and identified by name in captions. Yet the image offers enough of a profile view of the man's face to see the length of a cigarette in his mouth and make him roughly identifiable. The photograph—notably, undated—is a study in artful ambiguity, a vivid illustration of an anonymous ethnographic source: if you knew the location and that the man was smoking a cigarette, they would be instantly and easily identifiable; otherwise, the individual remains conspicuously unidentified (and maintains a plausible deniability as an "informant"). Yet Cabrera makes it perfectly legible that the anonymous subject of the photograph—in this researcher's opinion, almost certainly the same person mentioned in this note on "the herbalist from the Havana market"—deserves a singular prominence in *El Monte*: the caption reads, simply, "El yerbero." (That is, not merely *an* herbalist, but *the* herbalist.)

It contains one of the great secrets of Elegua.[229]

SANGRE DE DONCELLA, CARNE DE DONCELLA, or PALO SEÑORITA[230]

Byrsonima lucida D.C.

LUCUMÍ: IGI UNDIA, AKERI.

OWNER: OSHUN.

This *igi* should be pulled by a maiden. Thanks to a ritual in which it is used—a petition performed next to the *orisa* or over the *nganga*—and thanks to the way a competent *iyalocha* will use its branches, many women recover their virginity, even if it has been lost for a long time, and as many times as might be necessary.

"In the old days, we had to work a lot with the blood of a virgin. These days, only in certain cases . . . but now virginity is not so important. The men aren't so demanding; nowadays, they don't care about that."

It is used often in amulets and potions.

To make women love and submit to someone: baths with its leaves, parsley, marjoram, honey, and a fine perfume.

SAPOTE

Sapota achras Mill.

LUCUMÍ: NEKIGBE.

CONGO: KOBANKO.

OWNERS: THE IBEYI.

It is used for "work." Its leaves are mashed and mixed with ashes to stop a hex.

Its dried leaves are used in a decoction used to treat insomnia and to recover one's strength after long and difficult everyday work. A powder made from its resin helps reduce bleeding.

"If a period [menstruation] is too heavy, sit in the shade of this tree."

SARGAZO

Sargassum vulgare, Ag.[231]

LUCUMÍ: AYARAYERE.

OWNER: YEMAYA.

They are the grapes of the sea, "como iyó, la sal, es su azúcar" (just as *iyo*, salt, is its sugar).

It is used to treat emaciated and scrofulous children. It cures sores and rashes.

SASAFRAS

Bursera graveolens, Triana & Planch.[232]

A decoction is made with the peel from wild *zarzaparrilla* gathered in a *monte* (or, if that is unavailable, bought from a pharmacy) and roots from *palo jiba* to cleanse impurities from the blood.

SENSITIVA or VERGONZOSA

Mimosa pudica L.

LUCUMÍ: ERAN KUMI, ERAN LOYO, OMIMI, YARANIMO.

OWNER: YEWA (?).

It is used for cleansings, purification.

---

229 DF-N: This is an explicit provocation, compelling curious readers to ask, "What is the 'great secret'?" The plant's extraordinary chemical and medicinal properties are well known.

230 DF-N: The plant's Cuban Spanish names translate literally as "maiden's blood" or "virgin's blood," "maiden's meat" or "virgin's flesh," and "young lady's *palo*" or "young [unmarried] lady tree."

231 DF-N: *Sargassum vulgares* is only one among numerous types of seaweed that wash up on the shores of Cuba.

232 DF-N: *Bursera graveolens* is commonly known as *palo santo*, while sassafras is part of the *Lauraceae* family of plants.

"We use it to work with the sensitivity of the person."

It is used for spells to hinder and inspire romantic love.

"When you're getting ready to pull it, you rub your hand over it softly, caressing it, then you say to it three times, 'I want you to make So-and-So love me,' or 'I want you to help me tame someone,' or whatever you desire. The *sensitiva* needs to hear you clearly. Then you should take it and keep it away from sunlight. When it's dried out, put it inside a good perfume. Then you're ready to go conquer!"

"You pray over it, grind it into a powder, and mix it with crushed *girasol* and *benjuí*, as well as powdered *valeriana* and *rosa*. Then you put it inside a bottle of perfume that's been left out for three days, taking in the goodness of the sun and the night dew. You use it on a handkerchief to get somebody to fall in love with you."

We are assured that you can use the *sensitiva* to "do whatever you want." The thorny variety is no good. (There are also both female and male *sensitiva* varieties.) The thorny one is used "for things having to do with sweetness, love." Capé insists that "the other is no good for anything."

This plant, "which lives on the ground and feels everything," is extraordinarily sensitive. In the hands of our theurgists, it is an agent of priceless magical value.

Negros de nación [African-born Black Cubans] used to call it *morí-viví*.

SESO VEGETAL[233]

Blighia sapida, Koen.

ENGLISH: ACKEE, ACHEE, ACKEE APPLE, AYEE.

OWNER: OBATALA.

In cases of madness, its fruit is eaten as a "rogation" for the head, taking care to remove the seeds, which contain a poison.

("It cures madness . . . and, if one so desires, it can also drive someone mad.")

SIETE CABEZAS[234]

"It is a vine that should be pulled by someone who is nude, and it should be paid its price beforehand."

SIGUARAYA or CIGUARAYA

Trichilia havanensis Jacq.

LUCUMÍ: ATORI.

CONGO: INSO OR TINSO, EBORA, NSINBA DIAN FINDA.

OWNERS: CHANGÓ AND ELEGUA.

An old *Mayombero* tells us, "It's the first *palo* I salute after greeting the Four Winds in *El Monte*. It's the principal one for my *Nganga*, and when it's time to cover *Ngando*"—when an adept falls into trance—"you put its leaves on the *mulunda* (head), so the spirit grabs them with a strong hold."

It is called *Rompe-Camino*, *Abre-Camino*, and *Tapa-Camino*.[235]

---

234 DF-N: *Siete cabezas* translates literally as "seven heads."

235 DF-N: *Rompe-Camino*, *Abre-Camino*, and *Tapa-Camino* can be loosely translated as "Break-the-Way" or "Destroy-the-Way," "Open-the-Way" or "Clear-the-Way," and "Block-the-Way" or "Hide-the-Way," respectively. In addition to meaning "way," *camino* can also be usefully understood as "road" or "path."

---

233 DF-N: *Seso vegetal* translates literally as "brain plant" or "brain vegetable/fruit."

Rompe-Camino because the *fumbi* destroys the road ahead of our enemies. *Tapa-Camino* because it prevents our enemies from getting in the way of one's *nfumo* and obstructing it.

"That's why we sing:

> *Siguaraya rompe camino*
> *Nsiguaraya rompe camino*
> *Abre la Nfinda, abre*
> *Siguaraya*
> *Camino Casa Grande, camino Mama*
> *Ungunda Rompe Siguaraya!*

> *Siguaraya* break(s)/destroy the path/ road
> *Nsiguaraya* break(s)/destroy the path/road
> (Open) *el monte* (opens), open(s) *Siguaraya*
> The path/road to the Big House, the path/road (to/of/from) Mama Ungunda break(s) *Siguaraya!*[236]

"*Siguaraya* lays waste to evil, and it crushes witchcraft. If you bathe in it and wash your house with it, there won't be any *munbanda* left in your body or your house: Siguaraya, Agua de Florida Murray perfume, and a *real* worth of aguardiente, *ponasí* leaves, and an egg white. Mix it well. Rub it on the walls, mop the floor with it, then sweep from the back of the house to the front door, sweeping and singing:

> *Siguaraya bota pá*
> *Fuera Siguaraya*
> *Bota pa fuera . . .*

". . . and the evil will leave. Then you can burn a little *mirra* [myrrh] and sulfur. The Siguaraya already opened the

way." (Incense—*Sambia mpolo*—cannot be burned in the house of *mayombero judío*, because the *nganga* will leave immediately.)

"It's a holy scent, and no *mujamba judía* can stand it." And, as the *ñáñigos* say, nobody has ever seen a *judío* make the sign of the cross. When a hurricane lashes *el monte*, "the *siguaraya* is very wise, and it doesn't fight. She lies down and doesn't get back up until the wind has calmed down." Because "it has the authority to weather hurricanes better than any other tree."

Its oily resin can be consumed in small doses to safely evacuate any witchcraft that might have been ingested. Administered imprudently, it becomes such a drastic purgative that, according to José Santos, "if you overdo it by just a hair, it'll completely empty out the person." And there is no doubt that large doses will remove a *bilongo* immediately, and possibly take a person's life as a side effect. Its effects can be so decisive that it can simultaneously annihilate the *wemba* and the person afflicted by it. Baró confesses to me, "Once, cleansing an old lady who had some very bad witchcraft inside, my *bakulu* and I overdid it and, instead of giving her a half glassful, we pushed a full glass of it on her. The old lady died on us. She was spilling her guts out. Her son was not happy about what happened."

To purify a body and free it from the influence of a *ndiambo*, a person takes nine baths with the leaves of its sprouts, its root, and its bark boiled with cloves of *ajo* [garlic], and *flor de agua*. These lustrations are recommended by an *iyalocha* who was a "*caballo*" (horse, mount) in Palo Mayombe before being initiated in the Regla de Ocha. The baths should begin on a Friday, "which is a day belonging to all the *santos*, and never on Tuesday" (when Eshu is in charge).

---

236 DF-N: While the inherent grammatical ambiguity of the text of the *mambo* makes it practically impossible to translate literally, it offers insight into the various, sometimes contradictory ritual functions suggested by these different names.

Three sips of the mixture should be drunk before the first bath.

And here is another formula considered very effective in the expulsion or breaking up of any sort of *moruba*: Three shoots are placed in aguardiente made from sugarcane, three small Siempre-Viva leaves, three grains of *pimienta de guinea*, and a little honey. This liquid is kept in a bottle, in addition to three large mouthfuls of tobacco smoke blown into the bottle before sealing it. It is left outside in the sunlight and night dew for three days, "picking up the strength of the sun and the stars, the virtues of the day and the night. Before beginning to drink it and bathe in it, it should also be left out for a while in a place where everyone can see it."

The old man Pichardo, whose vocabulary is so charming, discusses the *siguaraya*—just as our contemporary healers—in terms of its excellent medicinal properties: "Among its most outstanding virtues is its influence on the urogenital tract. In both alcohol and decoctions, it discharges gallstones and kidney stones, mending hematuria." Our people still consider it the best specific remedy for venereal diseases and syphilis, which it "cures" in combination with *guaguasí*. There are female and male varieties of *siguaraya*, and, as usual in medicinal and magical procedures, the female variety is administered to men, while the male variety is administered to women. ("You need to pay very close attention to this. So many people get twisted around or run into misfortune, or the "work" just fails, because the plants aren't used the way they should be. If you make a preparation for a man using a male plant, or use a female plant for a woman, they get twisted around and reversed!")

To induce sows to come into rut, you feed them *siguaraya* leaves—presumably, leaves belonging to the male variety of *siguaraya*.

SIGUELE RUMBO or SIGUELE RASTRO, or CAMINO-RUMBO[237]

The peasants in the countryside in Oriente province believe that the Cuban boa extracts this plant's juice to acquire the hypnotic powers it uses on the hutia. "The boa wraps itself around the trunk or a branch of the *síguele rumbo*, and it blends into the tree.

"The hutia will climb up, but it won't be able to distinguish the snake from the tree. Birds will settle on a branch without seeing it. Then the boa fixes its eyes on its victim, hypnotizes it, and eats it."

If the boa is cut, it is cured with the leaves of this tree. If the wound is so large that the snake cannot get the leaves itself, he whistles, and his fellow boas bring the medicine to him.

SOPLILLO

Lysiloma bahamensis, Benth.

ENGLISH: FALSE TAMARIND, WILD TAMARIND.

LUCUMÍ: AKI.

OWNER: OSHUN.

It is used to treat resistant fluxes and to "restore young ladies' virginity."

T

....

TABACO

Nicotiana tabacum L.

ENGLISH: TOBACCO.

---

237 DF-N: The plant's names translate literally as "follow (its/their) path," "chase after (its/their) trail/footprints," and/or "journey-path."

LUCUMÍ: EWE WTABA, ACHA.

CONGO: SUNGA.

OWNERS: OSAIN, ELEGUA, OGUN, AND
OCHOSI.

Processed, it is, as we have seen, one of
the offerings most appreciated by the
masculine deities. All of the male orishas smoke and chew *anduyo*. "They love
snuff."

The juice from its roots, its leaves, its
flowers, and its green stalks is used—
along with a few other plants—to make
a great emollient. A decoction made with
its leaves cures *el pasmo* [shock]. Spoonfuls of an infusion made with chewing
tobacco are used as an emetic.

TABANO

Pavonia typhalea (L.) Cav.

It is used in decoctions to combat rheumatism, bronchitis, and kidney ailments. "There's no better medicine for
inflammation than bathing with *tábano*
and drinking the decoction."

TAMARINDO

Tamarindus indica L.

ENGLISH: TAMARIND.

LUCUMÍ: IGI IYAGBON.

OWNER: OBATALA (?).[238]

"In Santa Clara, at least, Nuestra Señora
del Carmen first appeared inside a tamarind tree. It falls asleep at three in the
afternoon, and it is advisable to cut its
branches before it gets sleepy. To sleep
well, put the branches under your pillow.
It gives peaceful dreams."

Its fruit is very good for digestion, and it
is an excellent remedy for constipation

and liver disease. A decoction made with
the roots and bark is combined with
other plants to make a diuretic.

TENGUE

Poeppigia procera C.Presl.

LUCUMÍ: SONGA, LABARI.

CONGO: INKITA, LINGA, NKUNI,
CHECHE KABINDA.

OWNER: ESHU.

"It is the strongest and witchiest of all
the strong, witchy *palos*."

It is excellent for stupefying.

"You do everything in Mayombe with
tengue. It intercedes in a lot of work
that can be done to get people to be in
harmony."

It is among the most sacred in *el
monte*. *Isa* (it raises, lifts up), *monta* (it
mounts),[239] and—along with Paramí—
it gives strength to the *vititi mensu* and
talismans. "Tengue is a big deal. He travels a long way, all the way to the ends of
the earth. It's a tree with *fundamento*."
And it is "one of the most serene," like
the Yaya. For the old man Baró, it is
"the most *mayombero*" of all of the
trees in Anabutu. It can fight, knock
things down, and spoil things. But it
also repairs things and puts them back
together, putting things in harmony.

> *Tengue, yo te llamo*
> *Tengue ié Tengue*
> *Tengue malo*
> *Vamos la loma*
> *Tengue vamo a guerrea*
> *Sube Tengue la loma*
> *Tengue wángara*
> *Wángara simandié . . .*

T

---

238 DF-N: According to several *olorisha*, it is
also closely associated with Changó.

239 DF-N: In *Vocabulario Congo*, Cabrera
translates *isá* as "a state of trance" and *isa* as
"rising or lifting" (*subir* and *levantar*) ([1984]
2001, 189).

Tengue, I'm calling you
Tengue *ié* Tengue
Bad tengue
Let's go up in the mountains
Tengue let's go to war
Tengue go up the hill . . .
Tengue wángara
Wángara simandié . . .

To definitively "spoil" something, "it offers the best guarantees":

Téngue salió la Bana
Cayó en Matanzas
Palo Monte Tengue
Palo mío
Tengue palo
¡Acaba cuento Tengue malo!

Tengue left Havana
And landed in Matanzas
Palo Monte Tengue
My *palo*
Tengue *palo*
(Put an) end/stop (to the) story/
    talk, bad Tengue!

Severina was a great Madre de Palo. When she died—one of her godchildren tells me, "she was *akufila*, dead, and tears were still coming from her closed eyes"—they mourned with this *mambo*:

Arriba Tengue Severina tiene valor
Tiene valor ariba Tengue
Tu arriba Tengue Severina
Dame valor Severina, dame valor
Arriba de Mariata Severina tiene valor
Tu arriba Mayimbe Severina tiene
    valor.

Atop Tengue, Severina has courage
(She) has courage atop Tengue
You're atop Tengue, Severina
Give me courage, Severina, give me
    courage
You're atop Mayimbe, Severina, you
    have courage.

The spirit of tengue makes it possible to carry out any sorcery imaginable. Any enemy can be stupefied, all obstacles can be smoothed over, and one can obtain the impossible.

TIBISI

Arthrostylidium capillifolium Gris.

OWNER: CHANGÓ.

I copy this down word for word:"It is made into powder and scattered in workshops, corners, parks, salons, elegant receptions lobbies, conference rooms, and political meetings, wherever a person wants to be likable, shine, and be the object of everyone's gaze. In the native tongue, it is called Koroleo or Igbe Kambo."

TITONIA

Tithonia ritundifolia (Mill.) Blake.

ENGLISH: RED SUNFLOWER, MEXICAN SUNFLOWER.

LUCUMÍ: SEREIYE.

CONGO: MONIKUANA.

OWNER: OSHUN.

It is crushed at the doorway when one wishes to ward off the inopportune child of a neighbor, who insists on being a nuisance with his insufferable visits.[240]

TOMATE

Lycopersicum esculentum Will.

ENGLISH: TOMATO.

LUCUMÍ: ICHONA, IKAN.

CONGO: KOROGONDO.

OWNERS: CHANGÓ AND IBEYI.

Its juice is used to combat constipation. Drops of the sap from its roots are used to treat toothache.

The fruit enriches the blood and strengthens eyesight.

TOMATE DE MAR

LUCUMÍ: IKAN OLOKUN.[241]

CONGO: KOROGONDO DE KALUNGA, FORONKO.

"There are male and female varieties. To know which sex they belong to, the seeds are submerged in a glass of water. The seed that floats is female, and it should be given to a man. The one that sinks to the bottom is male, and it is meant for a woman. They cure hemorrhoids."

They are talismans that remedy this ailment. Tied together with a cord from the order of San Francisco (Saint Francis), they are carried in one's pocket, wallet, or purse, or wrapped around the waist. "If it doesn't make [hemorrhoids] disappear, the *tomate de mar* will at least soothe them."

TORONJIL

Melissa officinalis L.

ENGLISH: LEMON BALM.

LUCUMÍ: EWETUNI.

It is used for the stomach in a decoction by itself or mixed with candied sugar, marjoram, *yerba luisa, albahaca morada, yerba buena,* and *geranio.* It can also be boiled with milk and sugar.

Mixed with *yerba buena, yerba luisa,* and the peel of *naranja de China del país* [(Cuban) China orange], it is boiled in three cups of water and given to a sick person in order to stop diarrhea or vomiting.

TRAVESERA

Eupatorium villosum Sw.[242]

ENGLISH: FLORIDA KEYS THOROUGHWORT.

LUCUMÍ: AFOSI.

OWNERS: ELEGUA AND CHANGÓ.

"I know it in the native language as Afosi. To defend myself or to cut off an enemy's path, I pull it and mix it with *espuela de caballero, aromo, pimienta de guinea,* and *ortiguilla.* All of that is gathered to do harm, which I explain clearly to the plants. I tell it: *Travesera,* I've come to get you because I need you, and you're coming with me to block and interfere with everything So-and-So is thinking of doing and anything he might think of doing later. I go to the *espuela de caballero* and tell it: *Espuela del diablo,*[243] I've come to get you before twelve noon so that, just as you have nothing to grab hold of, So-and-So should be restless and swallow thorns. By the power of Osain. *Ortiguilla* (over in Cienfuegos we call it *ewe isa*), before twelve, just as you prick and sting, prick and sting So-and-So, and leave without a place of their own.

"To the *Pimienta,* you say: *Pimienta,* I grind you and mix you with *espuela del diablo* and *ortiguilla* so you all fight, and So-and-So should also fight and rave every day, as soon as the sun comes up.

"The counter to everything that can be done with this work is *ewereyeye (peonía)* with *ewe oni bara (meloncillo), ewe dudu (siempre viva), omi olorun (holy water),* and white sugar. This *omiero* is poured around the house of the victim whose life has turned bitter and miserable, and

T

241 DF-N: The Spanish, Lucumí, and Congo names are literal analogs ("sea tomato," "tomato of the sea," "tomato of the ocean," etc.).
242 DF-N: The plant is also known as *albahaca de sabana, abahaquilla, rompezaragüey,*

rompezaragüey de sabana, yerba amarga, and *zanca de grullo. Chromolaena odorata* is sometimes also known as *zanca de grullo.*
243 DF-N: *Espuela de diablo* ("devil's Spur") invokes a less amiable aspect of the plant's potential than *espuela de caballero* ("gentleman's spur").

then you send them to bathe three times with leaves from *majagua, yaya blanca,* and *ewe dudu (siempre viva)."*

See also ALBAHAQUILLA.

TREBOL

Trifolium repens L.[244]

ENGLISH: WHITE CLOVER.

LUCUMÍ: EWE ETAMERI.

CONGO: KANDA TATU.

OWNER: OBATALA.

Its water [sap, juice] belongs to Yemaya.

Trébol irritates the most senior orisha.

The aquatic variety cures scrofula and anemia.

TRIPA DE JUTIA[245]

OWNER: ELEGUA.

It is used to construct the relics of this orisha.

Decoctions made with its branches and roots are used for cleansing baths.

"It's used to treat dropsy. It's a purgative and an emetic. Along with this one and *yerba mierda de gallina,* you boil leaves of *naranja agria, guanábana, sén,* and a little bit of tea in five pitchers of water. This decoction should be drunk like regular water to reduce swelling in the belly. Then you take three purgatives made with Le Rúa from France, or four of them with intervals between each one. After this purging, you should drink as many as forty cups of a decoction made with *garro morado."*

(This is from the notebook of an old healer who assures me that all of her clients were cured with this remedy.)

Many veterans of the War of Independence experienced this plant's attributes when they were holed up in the bush.

TUBA TUBA

If it is pulled up, it works as an emetic. If it is pulled down, it works as a purgative. It is used as an antidote to the *guao.*

TUNA

Euphorbia lactea Haw.

ENGLISH: MOTTLED SPURGE.

LUCUMÍ: EGUN, WEGUN, IKIKIGUN.

OWNER: OBATALA.

It is gathered on the fifth day of a new moon during three consecutive lunar cycles to cure asthma. The skin of the sick person is rubbed with almond oil, then the leaves are rubbed with garlic and used to cover the chest, then the person is bundled up to keep them warm.

For any sort of swelling, the leaf is rubbed with almond oil and stuck to the swollen body part. To ward off enemies, a branch of the wild, thorny variety of *tuna* is hung behind the door.

U

....

UÑA DE GATO[246]

Momisia iguanale (Jacq.) Rose & Standl.[247]

---

244 DF-N: In eastern Cuba, *trébol* is also known as *trebolillo* or *trébolo.*

245 DF-N: *Tripa de hutia* translates literally as "hutia guts."

246 DF-N: *Uña de gato* translates literally as "cat's nail/claw."

247 DF-N: *See also* ZARZA BLANCA.

"It is maleficent." Crushed and mixed with powders from the heart of the *yaba*, it is used to blind.

V
....

VACABUEY

Curatella americana L.

OWNER: CHANGÓ.

The juice from its leaves is used in a lamp made for the purpose of "setting back" or "jinxing" a person.

VAINILLA AMARILLA

Epidendrum facutum Lindl.

OWNER: OSHUN.

It is used to nourish Oshun amulets.

VAINILLA ROSADA

Epidendrum atropurpurenum Willd.

OWNER: OSHUN.

It is used to nourish Oshun amulets intended to be used by men.

VARITA DE SAN JOSE

Althea rosea, Cav.

LUCUMÍ: OFUN DARA, DIDEFUN.

OWNER: OBATALA.

It is used for cleansings and rogations.

VERBENA

Verbena officinalis L.

ENGLISH: VERBENA.

LUCUMÍ: EWE ORUKAN, ORIOYO.

OWNER: YEMAYA.

It is used in a decoction to treat the liver. Its juice can be used as an emetic. Its sap is also mixed with olive oil for hair care.

Verbena gathered at dawn on June 24 is dried out and mixed with the heart of a swallow—"if you can manage to find one in Havana"—to make a talisman that will help acquire anything one might desire.

VERDOLAGA

Tanilum paniculatum Goertn., *Portulaca oleoracea* L.

ENGLISH: FLAMEFLOWER, JEWELS-OF-OPAR, PINK BABY'S-BREATH.

OWNER: YEMAYA.

It is used to cover and refresh the orisha. It is also used in cleansings and washings for good luck.

VETIVER

Chrysopogon zizanoides L.

ENGLISH: VETIVER, KHUS.

LUCUMÍ: ORUFIRI, KURUBI.

OWNER: OSHUN.

Its roots are steeped in alcohol to make a rubbing oil that treats neuralgia and rheumatism. For good luck, it is used in baths with marjoram, *yerba buena*, and albahaca.

VIBORA[248]

Bryophyllum calycinum, Salisb.

LUCUMÍ: EWE NIOKA, FATU-FATU. (IT IS CALLED FUKOROROKO AND MONGAO BY AN HERBALIST WHOSE LANGUAGE CONFOUNDS MY OTHER INFORMANTS.)

OWNER: ESHU.

It is very good for sorcery. It is used to poison, "spoil," and set back—that is, to cause any sort of harm one desires.

---

248 DF-N: *Víbora* translates literally as "viper," "adder," and/or "snake."

VICARIA or PURISIMA BLANCA Y MORADA

Vinca rosea L.

OWNER: OBATALA.

"To refresh the eyes, you place their cool freshness (*frescura*) over the eyes."

The roots are used to treat fever.

VIGUETA

Chione cubensis A.Rich.

CONGO: FORUMBO.

OWNER: CHANGÓ.

It is used for fortifying baths.

A decoction made with its bark is used to treat malaria.

VIOLETA

Violeta odorata L.

ENGLISH: SWEET VIOLET.

LUCUMÍ: LUKO.

OWNER: YEMAYA.

Its flowers—or, in the absence of flowers, its leaves—alleviate any kind of pain.

Y
....

YABA

Andira jamaicensis (W.Wright) Urb.

LUCUMÍ: IGI SOIKU, YABA.

CONGO: NKASA KADIAMPEMBA.

OWNER: CHANGÓ. IT IS ALSO ATTRIBUTED TO OGUN.

Capé maintains that it only produces maleficent effects. "It belongs to Ogun, and it's from the middle of *el monte*. Ogun blinds with *yaba*, covering the eyesight of other warriors so they can't see him.

In one war he fought, he poisoned the river water with *yaba* and blinded all of his enemies so they wouldn't be able to see him escape from the opposite shore.

"He uses *yaba* when he fights Changó. Even though these *santos* are blood brothers and brothers in arms, they're always fighting each other over women, family troubles . . . Changó doesn't forgive Ogun for coming home drunk and beating his mother, Yemaya."

A powder made from its bark is used to treat ringworm, and a decoction made with the same powder is used to treat intestinal parasites.

Yaba is also used to make poisonous powders and beverages.

When it flowers, bees will not settle on its flowers. The bee will die if it sips the flower's nectar. Its crushed bark is used to magically compel an inconvenient neighbor to move away. Ashes from its trunk are mixed with powder made from the spiny and witchy *uña de gato* to afflict someone's eyes.

"The yaba has a terrible spirit that you can't mess around with because it likes to blind people's eyes."

Bewitched and crushed when it is still green, it is often used for precisely this purpose—to blind others—by *mayomberos judíos*.

All of the work done with yaba is ill fated.

YABU

OWNER: CHANGÓ.

"This *yabú* is the same plant as *apónao*, and it's also called *bélenc*. The *imbanda* uses it to warm up his *kimbango*." (It is used by the sorcerer to strengthen his *prenda*.)

YAGRUMA

Ceropia peltata L.

ENGLISH: TRUMPET TREE, SNAKEWOOD.

LUCUMÍ: IGI OGUGU, LARO.

CONGO: MATITI. (THE HERBALIST AT THE PLAZA DEL VAPOR CALLS IT KANDOLAO, MARATAFO, AND FENILIYE.)

OWNER: OBATALA.

For *mayomberos*, it is the lookout tower for Susundamba, the owl, who waits there, ready to gather and deliver messages. It is the messenger bird of death, and it works with the *yagrumo*.[249]

"It is the watchman of *el monte* by virtue of being the tallest, the one that lifts its head above all the others." In Africa, the tallest trees were indeed like watchtowers, and our *paleros* often refer to the *yagrumo* as a sentinel, because it is also where *susundamba* or the *fumbi* "*aguaita*" (awaits, keeps lookout for) enemies' movements.

Capé says, "The *perro de Mayombe* (possession mount) goes to the *yagrumo* with a knife and a piece of paper that carries the sorcerer's request written on it. Then he leaves the paper nailed onto the tree with the knife.

"The paper disappears. The knife remains, nailed there in the tree. Susundamba picks up the paper and delivers it to whomever it's sent."

Considering it from a "purely medicinal" point of view, Sandoval thinks there is nothing better for treating a bad cold or an asthma attack than a decoction made with *yagrumo* leaves and hermit crab shell, brown sugar, *miel de Castilla*

[honey from *Melipona* bees], and violet leaves. He assures us that many asthmatics owe their recovery to the *yagrumo*.

A very effective and pleasant decoction is made with its leaves and *bejuco ubí*, *cuajaní*, *zapatón*, *higo*, *cordován*, *cañita santa*, *naranja*, *sandoval*, and brown sugar. And, of course, *romerillo*.

YAMAO or YAMAGUA

Guarea trichilioides L.[250]

LUCUMÍ: FENDEBILLO.

CONGO: NKITA, MORINBANKUO, MACHUCHO.

It is very important.

A *mayombero* will always call it *yamao*, because "it is used for calling."[251] A chip of its wood is placed in a container along with an egg and dry wine. If someone longs for the return of a distant person, or if someone separated from their lover wants to return to them, they call the person with this wood, saying the person's name three times. The third time, the person will hear them, and they will not delay in returning, submissive to the will and enchantment of the *yamao*.

The *agugu* or *alafoche* also makes use of this *palo* to cast spells at a distance. They can order a fire at a businessman's shop, destroying anything with flames, or take away someone's eyesight.

Whoever wants to become wealthy— "making *owo* come into their home"— will blow *yamao* powder into that home, mixed with *sóngue* (magnetic stone), *bejuí*, corn, and egg shells, say-

---

249 DF-N: The title and text of the entry both indicate that the tree is known as *yagruma* and/or *yagrumo*. *See also* ARRIERO.

250 DF-N: More commonly known as *Guarea guidonia* (L.) Sleumer.

251 DF-N: The plant's names include wordplay. *Yamao*: *llamar* (to call), *llamador* (caller, one who calls). *Yamagua*: *llama agua* (to call water, one who calls water).

ing, "Talismán de Portugalete, bring money to my home."

Like the royal palm, the *yamao* is also used to invoke and plead with Changó during times of drought, asking him to make it rain and to strike down an enemy with his lightning.

Cut during the waning moon, the *yamagua* directs "the diviner to the place where they'll find water by pointing the tip down and touching it to the ground, where it will immediately get wet. It finds water where nobody knows to look for it. That is its gift."

YAREY

Copernicia Sp.

LUCUMÍ: OPE.[252]

OWNER: CHANGÓ.

Santeros use its powdered bark and mix it with the blood of animals that eat its green leaves to change the color of a person's skin, helping them to "become like a chameleon" and escape justice.

It is useless to the *mayombero*. "It's no good for a *Prenda*."

YAYA

Ozandra lanceolata (Sw.) Benth.

LUCUMÍ: YAYA, ECHI.

CONGO: KOROMENI, MBEKESE.

OWNER: CHANGÓ.

It is one of the fundamental *palos* for the *Nganga*. "Palo muerto y para wangara" (and to wage war).

It is powerful for both making and deterring sorcery. Like all *palos* in a *nkunia anabutu*, it is equally effective in serving the good or ill intentions of a *Taita Kindamba*. We constantly hear the praises of the magical virtues of the *yaya*, *yayita*, "which destroys everything bad."

It invigorates, cleanses, and "removes hexes." It purifies even the most tainted blood, and its *nkanda* (bark) cures the scabs and sores on the legs and feet of someone who has stepped on witchcraft.

"It's a strong *Prenda* for the *paleros* in Vuelta Arriba.[253] There's no *mayombero* who doesn't have it. *Yaya* is female. It knocks down and lifts up. It can kill or cure anything."

Its leaves, without mixing them with those of any other tree, are used in cleansing baths.

"*Yaya* means mother. I am her son. I swore an oath to *Yaya*. Ambekese ambekese yaya, Nyaya gidi ngidi nke nkema. Kumba nkumba nkumbansa nsa kunanbeta mbeta beta lenge ema lembe yaya . . . That's how you pray to *yayita* in Congo."

YAYA CIMARRONA

Mouriri acuta Gris.

Like the previous entry, it is another of the strong and basic *palos* that a *gangulero* cannot do without.

> Yaya Yaya
> Con campo alegre
> Son palo malo
> Yaya con campo alegre
> Yaya yaya tu mimo Nsambia
> Yaya lucero mundo . . .
>
> Yaya Yaya
> With *campo alegre*
> It's a bad *palo*
> Yaya with *campo alegre*

---

252 DF-N: *Ope* is also a generic Lucumí name used for palm trees, and *Copernicia* is a genus of fan palms.

253 DF-N: Vuelta Arriba refers to tobacco-growing areas in central and eastern Cuba.

Yaya yaya, you're Nsambia
Yaya *lucero mundo* . . .

"Every sorcerer looks for it. To fight and win wars, there's nothing better."

Tumba, tumba Yayita!
Mi Nganga yatumba
Como tumba Yayita!
Mi siete rayo,
Tumba Yayita . . .

"*Yaya* can defeat any palo." It is a panacea in the hands of the healer. It cures *pasmo* [shock] and dysentery, and midwives give women a decoction made with its leaves at the onset of labor pains.

"Nsasi is its owner. Its leaves purify even the most tainted blood, and its bark cures sores and gangrene. It is a powerful tonic."

It attracts the *fumbi* with so much force that the *kisengere*—the tibia that a *mayombero* holds to call the *muerto*—is wrapped in its leaves. Baró says, "*Yayita* is a fierce *prenda* belonging to the *paleros* in Vuelta Arriba." Additionally, "*Yayita* is just as strong working in Vuelta Abajo,[254] because all the *mayomberos* in Cuba need her."

In the Regla Kimbisa del Santo Cristo del Buen Viaje, a good *nganga* is prepared with *yaya* and *alegre caminante*.[255]

YEDRA

Auredera spicata Pers.

ENGLISH: IVY.

LUCUMÍ: ITAKO.

OWNER: OBATALA.

The *yedra* [ivy] sticks to whatever it touches, and it is difficult to detach it.

"When you want to stay stuck to a person you love like the *yedra*, you find *yedra, amor seco, sacu-sacu, paramí, jobo, valeriana,* and *amansa guapo*, bright red silk floss, two bottles of Amor Vencedor perfume, and a pair of scissors."

All of this is handed over to a competent *iyalocha*, who will do what is necessary to realize the client's dreams . . . *de amor y de yedra* [of love and ivy].[256]

In a decoction, it is given to children with whooping cough to drink like regular water, and it also helps contain hemorrhaging.

"It removes bad ideas."

The root is steeped in alcohol to make a rubbing oil to treat the rheumatic pain.

YERBA BRUJA

LUCUMÍ: EWE ICHOCHO.

OWNER: YEMAYA.

It is used to call the spirit of a person who is far away.

"You go out to the country, and wherever you find a *yerba bruja* plant whose branches are facing west toward the setting sun, you say, 'With the permission of God and the *santos*, and with your permission, I'm going to pull you.' You pull it out and bury it in the ground upside down, branches and all, with its roots sticking up, taking great care to bury it at least a hand's length to the east from where it was pulled up. You light a candle at the spot where you found it. Then you walk in the direction of the setting sun, kneel down with your back to the plant, and call the spirit of the missing person. You immediately light a candle and take out a new mirror in which nobody has seen themselves.

---

254 DF-N: Vuelta Abajo is a renowned tobacco-growing area in the western Pinar del Rio province.

255 DF-N: See Cabrera (1977).

---

256 DF-N: The idiomatic reference remains obscure.

With your left hand, you hold the candle behind your head so its light is reflected in the mirror, and you will see the image of the person you called. After contemplating them, you bid them farewell in the name of God and all the *santos*. This procedure should only be performed at twelve noon or midnight."

This plant is used in binding spells for women who are unfaithful to their husbands.

YERBA BUENA

Mentha sativa L.[257]

ENGLISH: CORN MINT, FIELD MINT, WILD MINT.

LUCUMÍ: EFIRIN EWE KA, AMASI.

OWNER: YEMAYA.

It is crushed and mixed with rum and applied to troublesome sores. "It stings badly. By the second application, the pain starts going away. And by the third or fourth, it will get rid of the sore."

"The Virgin Mary and Santa Ana went to *el monte* to gather plants. Santa Ana pulled one, smelled it, tasted it, and said, 'Esta es yerba buena.' [This is a good herb.] But the Virgin Mary had pulled a different one at the same time, and she answered, 'Esta es mejor, Ana.' [This one's better, Ana.] Ever since then, the herb found by Mary is called *mejorana*, and the one Ana found is called *yerba buena*."

YERBA CAIMAN

LUCUMÍ: EWEDO.

CONGO: NSEKE GANDO, BAMBA.

OWNERS: YEMAYA AND OSHUN.

"Yemaya is a *santa* that really likes to cure people. With *yerba caimán*, she

cures hemorrhoids that bleed a lot. It also prevents blood in the urine."

In strong decoctions, it is used to treat gonorrhea.

YERBA DE DON CARLOS

Sorghum halepense (L.) Pres.

ENGLISH: JOHNSON GRASS.

A decoction is prepared with its root to expel kidney stones.

It should be drunk in great quantities at all hours.

"This herb is also called *cañuela*. Mixed with *quita maldición*, coconut water, Epsom salts, and a pinch of sugar, a small cup of it in the morning and another in the evening will cure gonorrhea."

YERBA DE GUINEA

LUCUMÍ: OKOERAN-ERANGINI, EDI EDI.

CONGO: VITITI, MARIARE, MAOMA, BOLONGO.

OWNER: BABALU AYÉ.

A decoction from it is drunk like regular water at the first appearance of an outbreak of measles, smallpox, or chicken pox. Its juice is used to wash the skin.

At the beginning of springtime, it is mixed with *canutillo* to make an *omiero* that is used to wash Changó.

YERBA DE LA NIÑA[258]

Phyllanthus niruri L.

ENGLISH: GALE OF THE WIND, STONEBREAKER, SEED-UNDER-LEAF.

LUCUMÍ: EWE NENE OR EWE NANI.

BOTANICAL ENCYCLOPEDIA

Y

---

257 DF-N: It is better known as *Mentha arvensis* L.

258 DF-N: *Yerba de la niña* translates literally as "the girl's herb."

It is used for cleansing baths and washes.

It is also used for decoctions to treat irritation of the ovaries and uterus.

YERBA DE LA SANGRE[259]

Cordia globosa H.B.K.[260]

ENGLISH: BLOODBERRY, BUTTERFLY-SAGE, CURACAO BUSH.

LUCUMÍ: EWEYE.

OWNER: YEMAYA.

It is purifying for the blood and all types of hemorrhaging.

YERBA DE LA VIEJA[261]

Flaveria trinervia (Speng.) Mohr.

ENGLISH: CLUSTERED YELLOWTOPS, SPEEDYWEED, YELLOW TWINSTEM.

LUCUMÍ: EWE ABGUA.

CONGO: KIAMBOBA.

It is used in a decoction to treat the liver and kidneys. It is also used to treat people who excrete too much.

YERBA DE PLATA[262]

Peperomia pellucida B.H.K.

ENGLISH: PEPPER ELDER, SHINING BUSH PLANT, MAN TO MAN.

LUCUMÍ: EWE SADAKA.

"Because its leaves look like little silver coins, and it shines like the moon when it's covered in dew."

It heals the heart.

(This herb is also called *corazón de paloma*.)[263]

YERBA DE SANTA BARBARA

These and other plants belonging to Changó are used to overcome obstacles and enemies through an old ritual that has favored many political figures and financiers during both the colonial and republican eras.[264] The individual who is interested in obtaining the resolute protection of the gods in legal disputes or other very important matters plays a very active role in this ritual—or, in some cases, a member of the person's family, such as their father, son, or brother.

In the middle of the *ile-orisa*, the *santero's* room, a mortar a meter or more in height is placed on a straw mat. The *santero* helps the subject climb up on the mortar. After planting their feet on the mortar's edge with their heels sticking out, the subject is passed an enormous bunch of plants which they will pound with a large pestle. The operation is long and tiring, and it should be concluded before twelve noon. While they crush and pound the mound of plants between their feet, trying to keep their posture as erect as possible, two large white porcelain vessels are placed on the straw mat, side-by-side, in front of the mortar. Each vessel contains oil and sixteen *akara* (cotton

---

259 DF-N: *Yerba de la sangre* translates literally as "the blood's herb."
260 DF-N: It is also known as *Varronia globosa*.
261 DF-N: *Yerba de la vieja* translates literally as "the old woman's herb."
262 DF-N: *Yerba de plata* translates literally as "silver herb."

263 DF-N: *Corazón de paloma* translates literally as "dove's heart."
264 DF-N: The entry discusses a type of plant whose taxonomy is based on ritual and mythology—plants that "belong" to Santa Barbara, Changó, and (presumably) Nsasi—rather than a specific, distinct botanical species.

wicks). The wicks are lit, starting a true firefight between the two vessels, which represents the struggle between two opposing parties—the person performing the ritual and his enemies or opponents. The wicks jump from one vessel to the other and fight; whichever wick extinguishes the others and burns the longest symbolizes the winner.

Two corncobs and spools of various colors of thread have already been prepared. Having completed the difficult task of pounding the large heap of herbs, the subject should wrap the corn with the thread, then cover the wrapped cobs in a white cloth. The *santero* helps them get down from the mortar, then the subject picks up the mortar with their hands and uses it to cover the plants, saying, "Just as I overturn this mortar, I overcome my enemies (or whatever one wants), and nothing can overcome me."

Often the person determined to emerge triumphant will stagger and be unable to stay on the mortar very long. If they do not falter or pass out—like a certain very well-known banker, who lost consciousness and fell from his high perch (the mortar)[265]—and if their strength does not fail them, allowing them to remain firm and active in such an uncomfortable pedestal until the conclusion of the ceremony, then, when one wick defeats the wicks representing their rivals or enemies, their success is guaranteed.

The interested party will keep one of the corncobs in their home as a protective talisman, hidden somewhere, possibly behind a picture frame or a piece of furniture.

YERBA DE SAPO[266]

LUCUMÍ: EWE POLO, OKUALE.

CONGO: NFITA NYOKAPEMBE.

It purifies the Blood.

See also YERBA DE LA NIÑA.

YERBA DEL PARAL[267]

LUCUMÍ: EWE GUGU, MASEKA (?).

CONGO: BIROFO.

OWNER: OCHOSI.

Its ashes are used to ripen fruit quickly.

YERBA DIEZ DEL DIA

Portulaca pilosa L.

ENGLISH: PURPLE PURSLANE, KISS-ME-QUICKLY, HAIRY PIGWEED.

OWNER: OGUN.

"Its little purple flowers open at ten in the morning." It is used to treat malarial fever. Its roots and flowers are mixed with *lagrimonia* to treat cases of fever caused by typhoid,[268] as well as other types of fever, regardless of their cause.

---

265 DF-N: In Cabrera's day, the full name of a real banker must have been attached to this bit of gossip, an embarrassing anecdote in which Cabrera mocks the subject of the story, not for engaging in the elaborate ritual, but rather for his spectacular failure, which revealed a conspicuous gap between ambition and tenacity.

266 DF-N: *Yerba de sapo* translates literally as "frog's herb."

267 DF-N: *Yerba del paral* translates literally as "the post's herb" ("post" meaning a column, support, or prop).

268 DF-N: This probably refers to *Agrimonia eupatoria*, also known as common agrimony, church steeples, and sticklewort.

"Egbado tani ewe la unye eweni? What was the first herb the Egbado pulled to make *santo?* The *diez del día."*

YERBA HEDIONDA[269]

Cassia occidentalis L.

ENGLISH: SEPTICWEED, COFFEE SENNA, COFFEEWEED, STYPTIC WEED.

LUCUMÍ: HARA-HARA.

It is a purgative. It is good for treating bloody colitis.

YERBA INCIENSO DE GUINEA (?)

It is used to treat colic: "Nine sprouts of *incienso de Guinea,* three round slices of *mamey colorado* boiled in three large cups—the old-fashioned ones—of water, and you boil it until it's reduced down to a cup and a half.

This decoction is consumed very hot, and it will relieve pain immediately.

"It needs to be gathered at three in the morning. Only at that hour. It grows at the top of hills. We use it to get prisoners out of jail. We burn it, prepare it with ashes from *comino cimarrón* [wild cumin] and store-bought powdered cinnamon. Everything gets mixed together and scattered at the jail. Then the prisoner escapes, because nobody can see them."

YERBA JICOTEA[270]

LUCUMÍ: OKONYANIGBO, EWE AYA, ILINKALE.

CONGO: MOFOROYO "NFLU".

OWNER: CHANGÓ.

It is used to work the orisha. "It is an *ewe* with a lot of secrets."

And this informant will not, nor should they, reveal its "mysteries" in passing to an indiscrete layperson.

YERBA JURUBANA or ... SURBANA?

It is similar to the *dormidera,* and it helps sterile women conceive.

YERBA LECHOSA[271]

OWNER: OBATALA.

It is applied to wounds to disinfect them. And if it is placed in the form of a cross, it contains bleeding, although all herbs placed in the form of a cross possess this virtue.

YERBA LUISA

Aloysia triphyla (L'Her.) Britton

ENGLISH: LEMON VERBENA.

OWNER: OSHUN.

It is used in decoctions to treat stomach pains, colic, and discomfort caused by a nervous disorder.

Mixed with *marilope* and *maravilla,* it is used to treat dyspepsia.

YERBA MARAVEDI

LUCUMÍ: BANAIBANA. ONE PARTICULAR HERBALIST ALSO CALLS IT MOKOLOIMAO OR TENKENIA.

OWNER: OSHUN.

It is used for cleansing baths and for washing a house.

It is also used to make talismans for thieves and prostitutes ("those poor girls

---

269 DF-N: *Yerba heidonda* translates literally as "fetid herb." *See also* PALO HEDIONDO.
270 DF-N: *Yerba jicotea* translates literally as "turtle/tortoise herb."

---

271 DF-N: *Yerba lechosa* translates literally as "milky herb."

really struggle"), with which they will make good profits.

YERBA MORA

Salanium nigrum L.

ENGLISH: BLACK NIGHTSHADE, BLACKBERRY NIGHTSHADE.

LUCUMÍ: ATORE, EFODA.

OWNERS: OGUN AND YEMAYA.

It is very sorcerous.

La Piedra Imán (the Magnetic Stone) is baptized with *yerba mora* and holy water.

It is used to make a decoction that is good for tonsillitis and other illnesses of the throat.

It is also used to wash sores and to combat dandruff.

It calms the nerves and cures rashes.

YERBA MULATA

OWNER: OSHUN.

It is used in a decoction to treat colitis and dysentery.

YERBA RABO DE RATON or YERBA RABO DE ALACRAN[272]

OWNERS: ELEGUA AND OSHUN.

For pustules.

Its leaves are crushed and mixed to form a paste with pigeon excrement, Castile soap, and the insides of a pumpkin. The mixture is applied over the pustule. Then a yam is harvested from deep in the soil—"a real local *magüey*"—and its peel is removed carefully, grated, and boiled in a new clay pot with *rabo de*

---

272 DF-N: *Yerba rabo de ratón* translates literally as "rat's tail herb." *Yerba de alacrán* translates literally as "scorpion's tail herb."

alacrán and a little white sugar. The sick person is administered three cups of this decoction per day. The liquid from the poultice is put in a bottle and taken to a hill."

YUA or AYUA

CONGO: LUNGA-KUMA.

OWNER: OGUN.

It is among the most fearsome *palos*: "To go near a Yúa, you need to be brave."

Sorcerers work with *yúa* to perform curses—to destroy, divide. If it is combined with black *cuaba*, *jobo*, and *soyanga* (critters) like wasps, termites, and woodworms, the damage it causes is irreparable.

The protective talismans made with *yúa* are very reliable.

To obtain whatever one desires, especially in love:

> You take three little wax candles of any kind. You go to the foot of the *yúa* tree on a Thursday or Friday. You clear the ground around the tree a little bit and say, "Santa, Santa, good day. How are you? I'm the one that's not well, and I come to you because I need you." If it's a man in love with a woman, they declare their desire: "Santo pini, what I want is for So-and-So to look at me, fall in love with me, and take care of me. For her to not want any other man other than me. For her to return my love right away and only think of me. If you give me what I want, I will come back and clear away all of the other plants and vines that make your life difficult. And you'll become very beautiful and strong, and I'll bring you fresh water and other good things." It's very important, essential, that the

yúa is old. The hour to visit it is twelve o'clock. You scatter a little bit of white sugar around its roots and tell it, "But if you don't give me what I want, I'll come back and hack you to pieces so you dry out and die all at once!"

The old Yúa, who wants to live and be beautiful, will give you what you want.

YUCA

ENGLISH: CASSAVA, MANIOC, YUCA.

LUCUMÍ: KOKOMADOKO, IBAGUDAN, BAGUDAN.

CONGO: NKUMBIA, MANDIOKA.

OWNER: OGUN.

Grated *yuca*, *quimbombó*, ashes, water, and menstrual blood will annihilate the worst witchcraft if this disgusting compound is scattered over the person in which it is found, or at the place where one suspects the substances constituting the "harm" were deposited. The witchcraft will have no effect. It is believed that this is the most effective "counterspell" of all.

Z

....

ZARZA

Pisonia aculeata L.[273]

ENGLISH: DEVIL'S-CLAW, COCKSPUR, PULL-AND-HOLD-BACK, OLD-HOOK.

LUCUMÍ: EGUN IGI EGUN.

CONGO: NKUNIA NTUTA, NKUNIA KEREBENDE, MPUKO, TILINKO.

OWNER: OGUN.

---

273 DF-N: In Spanish, it is also known as *garabato prieto*.

"It is the shirt of Ogun." It is used in all of the ceremonies for this orisha.

A great war was being waged by the Warrior *Santos*. In order to impose peace, Yemaya, Bilu Omi, made the oceans overflow. Ogun, along with everyone else, was forced to abandon the fight. Ashamed of having been seen feeling the waves by a woman, he hid out in the jungle. When the messengers of Olofi came to him and asked him, in the name of his father, to return to living with humans, they always found him covered in *zarza*. Oshun found him wrapped up to his neck in *zarza*, but she finally rubbed honey on his lips and took him from *el monte* to the house of Olofi, who tied him up with a chain.

Zarza is also used to cover Baba and Elegua.

During epidemics, the offerings made for cleansings and petitions to Babalu Ayé are deposited in two saddlebags, as well as all the money collected to pay him his *derecho*. In this case, the food offerings are not cooked inside the house. Babalu Ayé receives them at a *zarza* plant.

Its thorns are mixed with turtle shell, vulture feathers, *cambia voz*, and dry wine and used to make an amulet that helps with anything one might want. It is called Agongo Nigue. If the owner of this protective charm needs to escape from the police, they will carry a *Kole* [vulture] feather. The *iyalocha* will burn and powder the feathers and rub their forehead with a little bit of the ashes and a pinch of *pimienta*.

Women who suffer from trouble with their ovaries are cured with *zarza* root, *palo de añil*, *nuez moscada*, and Epsom salts, all of which is boiled with an old *medio* [five-centavo] coin.

ZARZA BLANCA

Momisia iguanaea Jacq.

OWNERS: OGUN AND ESHU.[274]

As a magical tool, it can be used to make a rational, sane person entangle themself regrettably in courts of law, ensnaring them in conflict so much that they lose their freedom.

---

274 DF-N: *See also* UÑA DE GATO.

ZARZAPARRILLA

Smilax havanensis Jacq.

LUCUMÍ: ATEWE EDIN OR ATEKE DIN.

OWNER: CHANGÓ (SOME ATTRIBUTE IT TO ORISAOKO).

It is used to agitate the *orisa*, who sometimes requests it for certain work.

"It's a medicinal *ewe*. It cleans the blood, cures arthritis, syphilis, and mental problems. If you inhale it (burning the root) when you're having trouble breathing, it provides great relief."

Osain. Photo by Josefina Tarafa.

El yerbero (The herbalist). Photo by Josefina Tarafa.

Sacrifice of a rooster to Elegua at a sacred *jagüey* tree. The *babaocha*, two *santeras*, and the devotees salute the *jagüey*. Photos by Josefina Tarafa.

Top left: José de Calazán Herrera, Bangoché, alias El Moro. Photo by María Teresa de Rojas. *Top right:* Calixta Morales, Oddedei. Photo by María Teresa de Rojas. *Bottom:* The temple of the son of Changó, with the appearance of a castle and painted red, the color of that orisha. Photo by Teresa de la Parra.

Top left: Juan O'Farrill, great narrator of Gangá tales. *Top right:* Manuela Mariate (Boisaddé). *Bottom left:* J. S. Baró. *Bottom right:* Saturnino (Nino) from Cárdenas. Photos by María Teresa de Rojas.

Top left: Marcos Domínguez. *Top right:* Francisca Ibáñez from Corral Falso. *Bottom left:* Enriqueta Herrera (*center*) with her son (*left*) and husband Domingo Hernández (*right*). *Bottom right:* The honorable *iyálocha* Conga Mariate next to her Ogun. Photos by J. Tarafa.

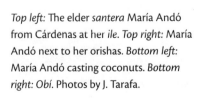

Top left: The elder *santera* María Andó from Cárdenas at her *ile*. *Top right:* María Andó next to her orishas. *Bottom left:* María Andó casting coconuts. *Bottom right: Obí.* Photos by J. Tarafa.

Opposite top, from left to right: Osain, Oyá, Yemayá. *Opposite middle, from left to right:* Changó, the Ibeyi. *Opposite bottom, from left to right:* Ochosi, Oshun, Ogun. Photos by María Teresa de Rojas.

Top: The altar of a *babaocha* with the Niño de Atocha, Elegua. *Bottom left:* Elegua. *Bottom right:* The cauldron of Ogun. Photos by Josefina Tarafa.

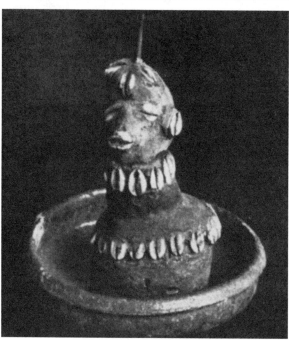

Eleguas. Photos by Josefina Tarafa.

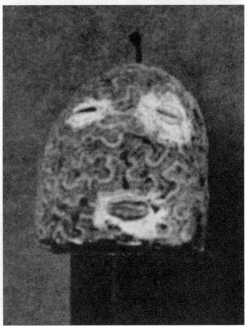

Top left: Elegua, made from cement. *Top right:* The warriors Ogun and Ochosi, made from cement, a fanciful modern creation of Havana *santería*. *Bottom left:* A carved Elegua in a flat stone. *Bottom right:* Elegua in coral rock. Photos by Josefina Tarafa.

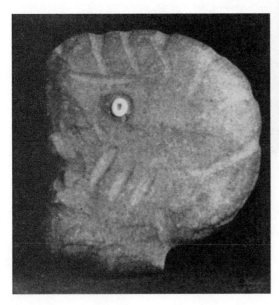

Otan orishas. Photos by Josefina Tarafa.

Top left: Stones and attributes of Yemayá. *Top right:* Oshún Kolé, a gourd decorated with four turkey vulture feathers that hangs in the orisha shrine room, representing the goddess in one of her avatars. *Middle left:* Attributes of Aggayú. *Middle right:* Orisha óko, San Isidro Labrador. *Bottom left:* Orisha óko, San Isidro Labrador. *Bottom right:* Osu. Photos by Josefina Tarafa.

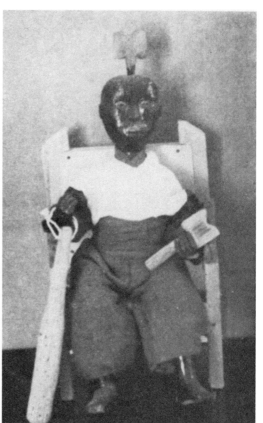

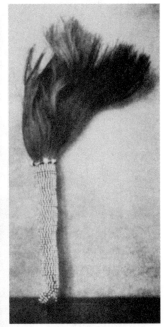

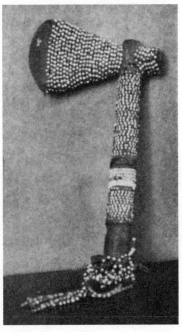

Opposite, top: Changó (Obakosó and Oggoddó ma kulenkue). *Opposite, bottom:* Attributes ("tools") of Changó. Photos by María Teresa de Rojas.

Top left: Altar for Changó with a painted cedarwood vessel, topped with a castle and containing the god's stone. Photo by J. de Dobrony. *Top right:* A horsetail fly whisk decorated with white and red beads, Eluké. Photo by María Teresa de Rojas. *Bottom left:* Yánsa. Photo by María Teresa de Rojas. *Bottom right:* Axe (*Changó aké*), attribute of the orisha. Photo by María Teresa de Rojas.

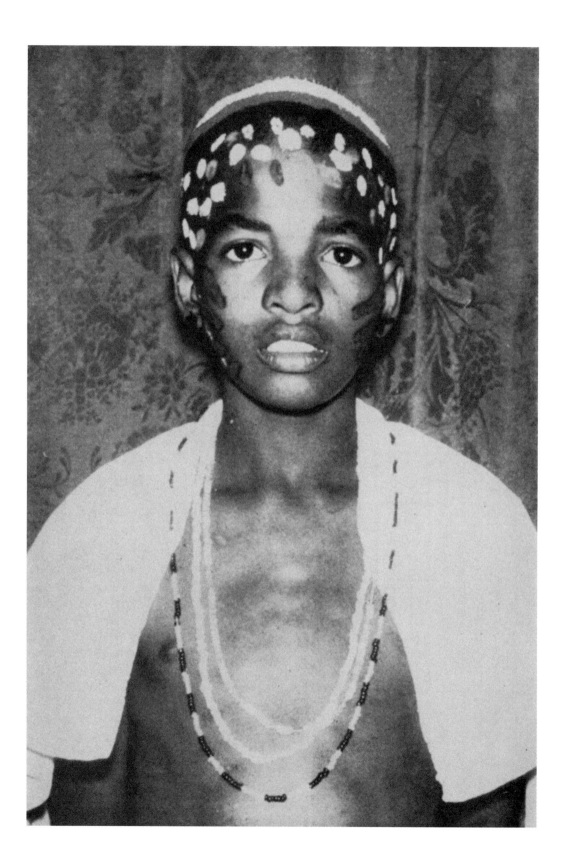

Opposite: The head of the *iyawó* (*ori fiyi ocha,* or *fifí okkan*) painted to receive the orishas in the Asiento ceremony. Photo by J. de Dobrony.

Above: Olorí Iyawo Orissá. Photo by J. de Dobrony.

Top: The "fulfillment of an oath," an offering at a sacred lagoon in the province of Matanzas: the moment a *santero* intones a chant calling Yemayá, one of her "horses" falls to the ground, possessed by the goddess. Photo by Josefina Tarafa. *Bottom:* The presentation of *iyawos* to the drum. Photos by J. de Dobrony.

Top left: The *nganga* of J. S. Baró, Camposanto Media Noche. Photo by María Teresa de Rojas. *Top right*: Brucoso, a Congo guardian at the doorway, a dart with feathers and magical contents, which falls to the floor spontaneously to warn its owner of impending danger. Photo by Josefina Tarafa. *Bottom*: The *nganga*.

Top: An exposed common grave in the
Guanabacoa cemetery. *Bottom:* Gravediggers.
Photos by Josefina Tarafa.

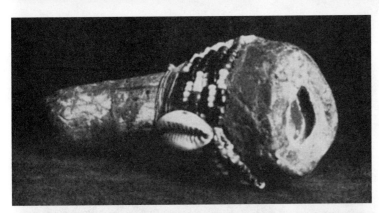
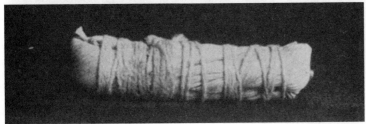

Top left: *Mayombe* talisman. *Top right:* Magic nails to protect the home. *Middle:* The *mayombero's* *vititi mensu,* or magical mirror. Bottom: *Masango, nkangue.* Photos by Josefina Tarafa.

Top: Ekue. *Bottom:* Coconut, which some Abakuá lodges (*potencias ñáñigas*) display as a symbolic representation of Ekue. Photos by María Teresa de Rojas.

Opposite, top and middle: Iremes. *Opposite, bottom:* Itón (staffs) of the Four Heads (chiefs) of a *potencia* (Abakuá lodge). Photos by María Teresa de Rojas.

Traditional processions in honor of Our Ladies, La Virgen de Regla and La Caridad del Cobre. Photos by Josefina Tarafa.

Photo by Josefina Tarafa.

References

Abiodun, Rowland. 1994. "Understanding Yoruba Art and Aesthetics: The Concept of Ase." *African Arts* 27, no. 3: 68–78, 102–3.

Akiwowo, Akinsola, and David Font-Navarrete. 2015. "*Awo Ayan*: Metaphysical Dimensions of the Yoruba Divinity of Drumming." In *The Yorùbá God of Drumming: Transatlantic Perspectives on the Wood That Talks*, edited by Amanda Villepastour, 35–50. Jackson: University Press of Mississippi.

Angarica, Nicolás Valentín. n.d. [1955]. *Manual de Orihate*. N.p.: self-published.

Arenas, Reinaldo. 1987. *Graveyard of the Angels*. Translated by Alfred J. MacAdam. Originally published as *La loma del ángel*. New York: Avon Books.

Bakhtin, Mikhail. (1975) 1983. *The Dialogic Imagination: Four Essays*. Edited by Michael Holquist. Translated by Caryl Emerson and Michael Holquist. Austin: University of Texas Press.

Baquero, Gastón. 1982. "Carta para Lydia Cabrera." *Noticias de Arte*, May 1982.

Barrera y Domingo, Francisco. 1953. *Reflexiones Histórico Físico Naturales Médico Quirúrgicas*. Havana: Ediciones C.R.

Bascom, William. 1954. "Four Functions of Folklore." *Journal of American Folklore* 67, no. 266: 333–49.

Bascom, William. (1969) 1991. *Ifa Divination: Communication between Gods and Men in West Africa*. Bloomington: Indiana University Press.

Bascom, William. 1976. "Oba's Ear: A Yoruba Myth in Cuba and Brazil." *Research in African Literatures* 7, no. 2: 149–65.

Bascom, William. (1980) 1993. *Sixteen Cowries: Yoruba Divination from Africa to the New World*. Bloomington: Indiana University Press.

Baumgartner, Albert. 2002. *Sacrifice in Religious Experience*. Boston: Brill.

Bedia, José, Judith Bettelheim, and Jane Catherine Berlo. 2011. *Transcultural Pilgrim: Three Decades of Work by José Bedia*. Los Angeles: Fowler Museum at UCLA.

Bilby, Kenneth. 1994. "The Caribbean as a Musical Religion." In *Caribbean Contours*, edited by Sidney W. Mintz and Sally Price, 181–218. Baltimore: Johns Hopkins University Press.

Blackwell, Anna. 1873. *Spiritualism and Spiritism*. Glasgow: Printed for the writer by H. Nisbet.

Blanc, Giulio. 1988. *Amelia Peláez, 1896–1968: Una retrospectiva*. Miami: Cuban Museum of Art and Culture.

Bowen, Eleanor Smith [Laura Bohannon]. 1954. *Return to Laughter: An Anthropological Novel*. New York: Doubleday / American Museum of Natural History.

Brandon, George. 1997. *The Dead Sell Memories: An Anthropological Study of Santeria in New York City*. Bloomington: Indiana University Press.

Braude, Anne D. 2001. *Radical Spirits: Spiritualism and Women's Right in Nineteenth-Century America*. Bloomington: Indiana University Press.

Bremer, Fredrika. 1853. *The Homes of the New World: Impressions of America / Hemmen i den Nya verlden*. New York: Harper and Brothers.

Bretón, André. 1942. *Fata morgana*. Buenos Aires: Éditions des Lettres Françaises.

Brown, David H. 2003a. *The Light Inside: Abakuá Society Arts and Cuban Cultural History*. Washington, DC: Smithsonian Institution Press.

Brown, David H. 2003b. *Santeria Enthroned: Art, Ritual, and Innovation in an Afro-Cuban Religion*. Chicago: University of Chicago Press.

Cabrera, Lydia. 1936. *Contes negres de Cuba*. Paris: Gallimard.

Cabrera, Lydia. 1940. *Cuentos negros de Cuba*. Havana: La Verónica.

Cabrera, Lydia. 1950. "La ceiba y la sociedad secreta Abakuá." *Orígenes* 7, no. 25: 16–47.

Cabrera, Lydia. (1954) 1992. *El monte: Igbo, Finda, Ewe Orisha, Vititi Nfinda (Notas sobre las religiones, la magia, las supersticiones y el folklore de los negros y el pueblo de Cuba)*. Miami: Ediciones Universal.

Cabrera, Lydia. 1955. *Refranes de negros viejos: Recogidos por Lydia Cabrera*. Havana: Ediciones C.R.

Cabrera, Lydia. (1957) 1986. *Anagó: Vocabulario Lucumí (El Yoruba que se habla en Cuba)*. Miami: Ediciones Universal.

Cabrera, Lydia. 1959. *La sociedad secreta Abakuá: Narrada por viejos adeptos*. Havana: Ediciones C.R.

Cabrera, Lydia. 1970. *Otán iyebiyé: Las piedras preciosas*. Miami: Ediciones C.R.

Cabrera, Lydia. 1971. *Ayapá: Cuentos de Jicotea*. Miami: Ediciones Universal.

Cabrera, Lydia. (1973) 1993. *La laguna sagrada de San Joaquín*. Photographs by Josefina Tarafa. Miami: Ediciones Universal.

Cabrera, Lydia. (1974) 1980. *Yemayá y Ochún: Kariocha, iyalorichas y olorichas*. New York: Ediciones C.R.

Cabrera, Lydia. 1975. *Anaforuana: Ritual y símbolos de la iniciación en la sociedad secreta Abakuá*. Madrid: Ediciones C.R.

Cabrera, Lydia. 1976. *Francisco y Francisca: Chascarrillos de negros viejos*. Miami: Ediciones C.R.

Cabrera, Lydia. 1977. *Itinerario del insomnio: Trinidad de Cuba*. Miami: Ediciones C.R.

Cabrera, Lydia. (1977) 1986. *La Regla Kimbisa del Santo Cristo del Buen Viaje*. Miami: Ediciones Universal.

Cabrera, Lydia. (1979) 1986. *Reglas de Congo: Palo Monte Mayombe*. Miami: Ediciones Universal.

Cabrera, Lydia. 1980. *Koeko iyawo: Aprende novicia; Un pequeño tratado de regla lucumí*. Miami: Ediciones C.R.

Cabrera, Lydia. 1982a. "A Conversation with Lydia Cabrera." By Suzanne Jill Levine. *Review: Literature and Arts of the Americas* 16, no. 31: 13–16.

Cabrera, Lydia. 1982b. "Cuban Writer Lydia Cabrera Reads from Her Prose and Is Interviewed." Sound recording, two reel-to-reel tapes, 7-1/2 ips, 7 in. RXA 2512—RXA 2513, LLCN 93842590, Library of Congress, Washington, DC. https://www.loc.gov/item/93842590/.

Cabrera, Lydia. 1983. *Cuentos para adultos, ninos, y retrasadas mentales*. Miami: Ediciones C.R.

Cabrera, Lydia. 1984. *La medicina popular de Cuba: Médicos de antaño, curanderos, santeros y paleros de hogaño*. Miami: Ediciones C.R.

Cabrera, Lydia. (1984) 2001. *Vocabulario Congo (El Bantú que se habla en Cuba)*. Edited by Isabel Castellanos. Miami: Ediciones Universal.

Cabrera, Lydia. 1988a. *La lengua sagrada de los Ñáñigos*. Miami: Ediciones C.R.

Cabrera, Lydia. 1988b. *Los animales en el folklore y la magia de Cuba*. Miami: Ediciones Universal.

Cabrera, Lydia. 1994. *Páginas sueltas*. Edited by Isabel Castellanos. Miami: Ediciones Universal.

Cabrera, Lydia. 2003. *Le fôret et les dieux: Religions afro-cubaines et médecine sacrée à Cuba*. Translated by Beatrice de Chavagnac and Erwan Dianteill. Originally published as *El Monte* (1954). Paris: Jean-Michel Place.

Cabrera, Lydia. 2005. *Afro-Cuban Tales*. Translated by J. Alberto Hernandez-Chiroldes and Lauren Yoder. Originally published as *Contes negres de Cuba* (1936). Lincoln, NE: Bison Books.

Cabrera, Lydia. 2020. *The Sacred Language of the Abakuá*. Edited and translated by Ivor L. Miller and Patricia González Gómes-Cásseres. Jackson: University Press of Mississippi.

Cabrera, Lydia, and Josefina Tarafa. ca. 1956. *Música de los cultos africanos en Cuba*. Boxed set of fourteen LP discs and liner notes. Havana: Ediciones C.R. / Burgay y Cía.

Cabrera, Lydia, and Josefina Tarafa. 2001a. *Havana, Cuba, ca. 1957: Rhythms and Songs for the Orishas*. Smithsonian Folkways Recordings SFW 40489, compact disc.

Cabrera, Lydia, and Josefina Tarafa. 2001b. *Matanzas, Cuba, ca. 1957: Afro-Cuban Sacred Music from the Countryside*. Smithsonian Folkways Recordings SFW 40490, compact disc.

Cabrera, Lydia, and Josefina Tarafa. 2003. *Havana & Matanzas, Cuba, ca. 1957: Batá, Bembé, and Palo Songs from the Historic Recordings of Lydia Cabrera and Josefina Tarafa*. Smithsonian Folkways Recordings SFW 40434, compact disc.

Cabrera, Lydia, and Pierre Verger. 2011. *Cartas de Yemayá a Changó: Epistolario inédito de Lydia Cabrera y Pierre Verger*. Transcribed and translated by Jesús Cañete Ochoa. Alcalá, Spain: Archivo de la Frontera.

Cabrera, Ramiro. 1922. "Los cantos populares de Cuba." Text from a conference presentation delivered at the Teatro Capitolio, August 12, 1922. *Diario de la Marina*, October 6, 1922.

Cacchione, Richard. 1988. "Lydia Cabrera: The Evolution of a Legacy." In *En torno a Lydia Cabrera*, edited by Isabel Castellanos and Josefina Inclán, 325–35. Miami: Ediciones Universal.

Cámara, Madeline. 2015. "Para llegar a Lydia Cabrera. Conversación con Isabel Castellanos: Las ceremonias de adiós entre Lydia Cabrera y María Teresa Rojas." *Revista Surco Sur* 5, no. 8: 28–30.

Capone, Stefania. 2000. "Entre Yoruba et Bantou: L'Influence des stéréotypes raciaux dans Afro-Américaines." *Cahiers d'Etudes Africaines* 40, no. 157: 55–77.

Carpentier, Alejo. 1936. "Los cuentos de Lydia Cabrera." *Orígenes* 28, no. 41: 40.

Carpentier, Alejo. (1960) 1963. *Explosion in a Cathedral*. Translated by John Sturrock. Originally published as *El siglo de las luces*. Boston: Little, Brown.

Castellanos, Isabel, and Josefina Inclán, eds. 1988. *En torno a Lydia Cabrera*. Miami: Ediciones Universal.

Castellanos, Jorge, and Isabel Castellanos. 1992. *Cultura afrocubana*. Vol. 3, *Las religiones y las lenguas*. Miami: Ediciones Universal.

Castellanos, Jorge, and Isabel Castellanos. 1994. *Cultura afrocubana*. Vol. 4, *Letras, música, arte*. Miami: Ediciones Universal.

Cernuschi, Claude. 2019. *Race, Anthropology, and Politics in the Work of Wifredo Lam*. New York: Routledge.

Césaire, Aimé. (1939) 1943. *Retorno al país natal*. French-Spanish bilingual edition of *Cahier d'un retour au pays natal*. Translated by Lydia Cabrera. Introduction by Benjamin Péret. Illustrations by Wifredo Lam. Havana: Molina y Cía.

Césaire, Aimé. (1939) 2013. *Cahier d'un retour au pays natal*. French-English bilingual edition of *Cahier d'un retour au pays natal*. Translated and edited by Clayton Eshelman and James Arnold. Middletown, CT: Wesleyan University Press.

Chávez-Álvarez, Ernesto. 1991. *El crimen de la niña Cecilia: La brujería en Cuba como fenómeno social*. Havana: Editorial de Ciencias Sociales.

Chaviano, Daína. 2008. *The Island of Eternal Love*. New York: Riverhead Books.

Chemeche, George, Donald J. Cosentino, and Vagner Gonçalves da Silva. 2013. *Eshu: The Divine Trickster*. Woodbridge, UK: Antique Collectors' Club.

Chief FAMA [Farounbi Aina Mosunmola Adewoae-Somadhi]. 1993. *Fundamentals of the Yorùbá Religion (Òrìsà Worship)*. San Bernardino, CA: Ile Orunmila Communications.

Chief FAMA [Farounbi Aina Mosunmola Adewoae-Somadhi]. 2001. *FAMA's Èdè Awo: Òrìsà Yorùbá Dictionary*. San Bernardino, CA: Ile Orunmila Communications.

Christopher, Emma. 2013. "Josefa Diago and the Origins of Cuba's Gangá Traditions." *Transition*, no. 111, 133–44.

Conde de Rivero [Nicolás Rivero y Alonso]. 1922. "El Monasterio de Santa Clara de Asís: Narración Documentada." *Diario de la marina*, Suplemento literario, November 5, 1922.

Corbitt, Roberta Day. 1950. "A Survey of Cuban Costumbrismo." *Hispania* 33, no. 1: 41–45.

Cros Sandoval, Mercedes. 1977. "Santería: Afro-Cuban Concepts of Disease and Its Treatment in Miami." *Journal of Operational Psychiatry* 8, no. 2: 52–63.

Cros Sandoval, Mercedes. 1979. "Santeria as a Mental Health Care System: An Historical Overview." *Social Science and Medicine* 13B, no. 2: 137–51.

Cros Sandoval, Mercedes. 2006. *Worldview, the Orichas, and Santería: Africa to Cuba and Beyond*. Gainesville: University Press of Florida.

Crowther, Samuel. (1854) 1913. *Dictionary of Yoruba Language*. Lagos, Nigeria: Church Missionary Society Bookshop.

Cruz, Celia, and La Sonora Matancera. 1955. *Yerbero Moderno*. Composed by Néstor Milí Bustillo. Musart 16-83. 45 RPM 7".

Cuervo Hewitt, Julia. 2007. "Aché, ewe, guedes, nganga, vititi nfinda y Orichas en 'La jungla' de Wifredo Lam." *Afro-Hispanic Review* 26, no. 1: 59–74.

Cuervo Hewitt, Julia. 2009. *Voices out of Africa in Twentieth-Century Spanish Caribbean Literature*. Lewisburg, PA: Bucknell University Press.

Curtin, Philip D. 1967. *Africa Remembered: Narratives by West Africans from the Era of the Slave Trade*. Madison: University of Wisconsin Press.

Daniel, Yvonne. 2010. "The Economic Vitamins of Cuba: Sacred and Other Dance Performance." In *Rhythms of the Afro-Atlantic World: Rituals and Remembrances*, edited by Mamadou Diouf, 19–40. Ann Arbor: University of Michigan Press.

Davis, Ben. 2018. "Why Hilma af Klint's Occult Spirituality Makes Her the Perfect Artist for Our Technologically Disrupted Time." *ArtNet News*, October 23, 2018. https://news.artnet .com/exhibitions/hilma-af-klints-occult-spirituality-makes-perfect-artist-technologically -disrupted-time-1376587.

De Ley, Margo, and James O. Crosby. 1969. "Originality, Imitation, and Parody in Quevedo's Ballad of the Cid and the Lion ('Medio día era por filo')." *Studies in Philology* 66, no. 2: 155–67.

Deren, Maya. 1953. *Divine Horsemen: The Living Gods of Haiti*. New York: Thames and Hudson.

Dianteill, Erwan. 1995. *Le savant et le santero: Naissance de la science des religions afro-cubaines (1906– 1954)*. Paris: L'Harmattan.

Dianteill, Erwan, and Martha Swearingen. 2003. "From Hierography to Ethnography and Back: Lydia Cabrera's Texts and the Written Tradition in Afro-Cuban Religions." *Journal of American Folklore* 116, no. 461: 273–92.

Diario de la marina. 1923a. "Comité de propaganda." February 9, 1923.

Diario de la marina. 1923b. "El sepelio de Don Raimundo Cabrera." May 23, 1923.

Díaz, Johnny. 2021. "Two Men Are Accused of Stealing Skulls from Florida Cemetery." *New York Times*, January 11, 2021. https://www.nytimes.com/2021/01/11/us/florida-graves-theft-arrests.html.

Díaz Fabelo, Teodoro. 1998. *Diccionario de la lengua conga residual en Cuba*. Santiago de Cuba: Casa del Caribe.

Diccionario de la literatura cubana. 1967. Havana: Academia de Ciencias de Cuba, Departamento de Investigaciones Literarias.

Digital Library of the Caribbean. n.d. Website. Accessed April 11, 2022. http://dloc.com.

Digital Portobelo. n.d. Website. Accessed April 11, 2022. http://digitalportobelo.org.

Diop, Birago. 1975. "Breath." In *Poems of Black Africa*, edited by Wole Soyinka, 44–46. Ibadan, Nigeria: Heinemann.

Doris, David T. 2011. *Vigilant Things: On Thieves, Yoruba Anti-aesthetics, and the Strange Fates of Ordinary Objects in Nigeria*. Seattle: University of Washington Press.

Drewal, Henry J., John Pemberton III, and Rowland Abiodun. 1989. *Yoruba: Nine Centuries of African Art and Thought*. New York: Center for African Art / Henry N. Abrams.

Drewal, Margaret Thompson. 1992. *Yoruba Ritual: Performers, Play, Agency*. Bloomington: Indiana University Press.

Duany, Jorge. 1988. "After the Revolution: The Search for Roots in Afro-Cuban Culture." *Latin American Research Review* 23, no. 1: 244–55.

Elebuibon, Yemi. 1994. *Apetebii: The Wife of Orunmila*. Brooklyn, NY: Athelia Henrietta.

Elebuibon, Yemi. 1999. *Iyere Ifa (Tonal Poetry, the Voice of Ifa)*. San Bernardino, CA: Ile Orunmila Communications.

Elebuibon, Yemi. 2000. *The Healing Power of Sacrifice*. Brooklyn, NY: Athelia Henrietta.

Epega, Afolabi. 2003. *Obi Divination*. Brooklyn, NY: Athelia Henrietta.

Epega, Afolabi, and Philip John Neimark. 1995. *The Sacred Ifa Oracle*. San Francisco: HarperSanFrancisco.

Espirito Santo, Diana. 2015a. *Developing the Dead: Mediumship and Selfhood in Cuban Espiritismo*. Gainesville: University Press of Florida.

Espirito Santo, Diana. 2015b. "Turning Outside In: Infolded Selves in Cuban Creole *Espiritismo*." *Ethos* 43, no. 3: 267–85.

Espirito Santo, Diana. 2018. "Telegraph Spirits and 'Muertos Chinos': Technologies of Proximity and Distance in the Material Commemoration of the Dead in Cuba." *Journal of Africana Religions* 6, no. 2: 208–31.

Evans-Pritchard, E. E. 1937. *Witchcraft, Oracles, and Magic among the Azande*. Oxford: Clarendon.

Faulkner, William. (1931) 2011. *Three Famous Short Novels: "Spotted Horses," "Old Man," "The Bear."* New York: Vintage Books.

Feld, Steven. 2011 "My Life in the Bush of Ghosts: 'World Music' and the Commodification of Religious Experience." In *Music and Globalization*, edited by Bob W. White, 40–51. Bloomington: Indiana University Press.

Ferrer Castro, Armando, and Mayda Acosta Alegre. (2012) 2015. *Fermina Gómez y la casa olvidada de Olokun*. Havana: Ediciones Cubanas Artex.

Figarola, Joel James. 2009. *La brujería cubana: El palo monte; Aproximación al pensamiento abstracto de la cubanía*. Santiago de Cuba: Editorial Oriente.

Figarola, Joel James. 2012. *Cuba la gran nganga: Algunas prácticas de la brujería*. Havana: Editorial José Martí.

Finch, Aisha K. 2015. *Rethinking Slave Rebellion in Cuba: La Escalera and the Insurgencies of 1841–1844*. Chapel Hill: University of North Carolina Press.

Font, Mauricio A., and Alfonso W. Quiroz, eds. 2005. *Cuban Counterpoints: The Legacy of Fernando Ortiz*. Lanham, MD: Lexington Books.

Font-Navarrete, David. 2018. "Inside, Outside, and Between: On Translation and the Study of Afro-Cuban Music." *Musicology Now*, February 2, 2018. https://musicologynow.org/inside-outside-and-between-on-translation-and-the-study-of-afro-cuban-music/.

Font-Navarrete, David. 2021. "Writing Orisha Music: Text, Tradition, and Creativity in Afro-Cuban Liturgy." *Religions* 12, no. 11: 964–87. https://www.mdpi.com/2077-1444/12/11/964.

Font-Navarrete, David. 2022. "Beyond the Archive: The Cabrera-Tarafa Collection of Afro-Cuban Music, ca. 1956." CUNY, December 20, 2022. http://cuny.manifoldapp.org/projects/musicadelosocultos.

Fouchet, Max-Pol. 1976. *Wifredo Lam*. New York: Rizzoli.

Galvin, Joseph C., and Michael Spiro. 2020. *Music of the Arará Savalú Cabildo: Songs and Rhythms from Matanzas, Cuba*. Petaluma, CA: Sher Music.

García, David F. 2006. *Arsenio Rodríguez and the International Flows of Latin Popular Music*. Philadelphia: Temple University Press.

García, David F. 2018. *Listening for Africa: Freedom, Modernity, and the Logic of Black Music's African Origins*. Durham, NC: Duke University Press.

García Rodriguez, Gloria. 2011. *Voices of the Enslaved in Nineteenth-Century Cuba: A Documentary History*. Translated by Nancy Westrate. Chapel Hill: University of North Carolina Press.

Gilroy, Paul. 1993. *The Black Atlantic: Modernity and Double Consciousness*. Cambridge, MA: Harvard University Press.

Glassie, Henry. 2010. *Prince Twins Seven-Seven: His Art, His Life in Nigeria, His Exile in America*. Bloomington: Indiana University Press.

Gleason, Judith. 1973. *A Recitation of Ifa, Oracle of the Yoruba*. New York: Grossman.

Gleason, Judith. (1987) 1992. *Oya: In Praise of an African Goddess*. New York: HarperCollins.

Gómez, Déborah. 2019. *Azúcar agridulce: Memoria, discursos, y paisajes en la nación y la cultura cubana (1791–2017)*. Madrid: Editorial Verbum.

González, Laura. 1984. *Piante e magia: Religioni, medicina e folclore delle culture afrocubane*. Milan: Rizzoli Editore.

González Echevarría, Roberto. 1984. "Socrates among the Weeds: Blacks and History in Carpentier's 'Explosion in a Cathedral.'" *Massachusetts Review* 24, no. 3: 545–61.

Gonzalez-Pando, Miguel, dir. 1992. *Y los quiero conocer: Historia de Cuba en vivo 1902–1959*. Miami: Florida International University. Video, 73 minutes. http://ufdc.ufl.edu/AA00061141/00001.

Goodman, Walter. 1873. *Pearl of the Antilles, or An Artist in Cuba*. London: Henry S. King.

Granda, Germán de. 1977. *Estudios lingüísticos hispánicos, afrohispánicos y criollos*. Madrid: Gredos.

Guridy, Frank Andre. 2010. *Forging Diaspora: Afro-Cubans and African Americans in a World of Empire and Jim Crow*. Chapel Hill: University of North Carolina Press.

Gutiérrez, Mariela. 1991. *El cosmos de Lydia Cabrera: Dioses, animales, y hombres*. Miami: Ediciones Universal.

Gutiérrez, Mariela. 2008. *An Ethnological Interpretation of the Afro-Cuban World of Lydia Cabrera (1900–1991)*. Lewiston, NY: Edwin Mellen Press.

Hagedorn, Katherine. 2000. "Bringing Down the Santo: An Analysis of Possession Performance in Afro-Cuban Santería." *World of Music* 42, no. 2: 99–113.

Hagedorn, Katherine. 2001. *Divine Utterances: The Performance of Afro-Cuban Santeria*. Washington, DC: Smithsonian Institution Press.

Helg, Aline. 1995. *Our Rightful Share: The Afro-Cuban Struggle for Equality, 1886–1912*. Chapel Hill: University of North Carolina Press.

Herzberg, Julia. 1992. "Wifredo Lam: The Development of a Style and Worldview: The Havana Years 1941–1952." In *Wifredo Lam and His Contemporaries*, edited María R. Balderrama, 30–51. New York: Studio Museum in Harlem.

Hiller, Susan. 1991. *The Myth of Primitivism: Perspectives on Art*. New York: Routledge.

Hiriart, Rosario. 1978. *Lydia Cabrera: Vida hecha arte*. New York: Eliseo Torres and Sons.

Hodges, Stephen, and Bradley C. Bennett. 2006. "The Ethnobotany of *Pluchea carolinensis* (Jacq.) G. Don (Asteraceae) in the Botánicas of Miami, Florida." *Economic Botany* 60, no. 1: 75–84.

Hoffman-Jeep, Lynda. 2005. "Creating Ethnography: Zora Neale Hurston and Lydia Cabrera." *African American Review* 39, no. 3: 337–53.

Holbraad, Martin. 2012. *Truth in Motion: The Recursive Anthropology of Afro-Cuban Divination*. Chicago: University of Chicago Press.

Hurston, Zora Neale. (1938) 1990. *Tell My Horse: Voodoo and Life in Haiti and Jamaica*. New York: HarperCollins.

Irizarry, William J. 2012. *Ewé Osaín: 221 Plants, Herbs, and Trees Essential to the Lucumí Tradition*. Self-published, CreateSpace.

Iseman, Fred. 1984. "Robert Farris Thompson: Canons of the Cool." *Rolling Stone*, November 22, 1984.

Jay, Nancy. 1992. *Throughout Your Generations Forever: Sacrifice, Religion, and Paternity*. Chicago: University of Chicago Press.

Kalvig, Anne. 2017. *The Rise of Contemporary Spiritualism: Concepts and Controversies in Talking to the Dead*. New York: Routledge.

Kardec, Allan, and Emma A. Wood. 1874. *Experimental Spiritism*. Boston: Colby and Rich.

Kaser, Richard T. *African Oracles in 10 Minutes*. New York: HarperCollins.

Kone, Moussa. 2016. "The Incomplete Yorùbá Guide to Lukumí." OrishaImage, June 25, 2016. Accessed December 4, 2018. https://www.orishaimage.com/blog/yoruba-lukumi-guide.

Kubayanda, J. Bekunuru. 2002. "Notes on the Impact of African Oral-Traditional Rhetoric on Latin-American and Carbbean Writing." *Afro-Hispanic Review* 21, no. 1/2: 113–20.

LaGamma, Alisa, and Josiah Blackmore. 2015. *Kongo: Power and Majesty*. New York: Metropolitan Museum of Art.

Lam, Wifredo. 1992. *A Retrospective of Works on Paper*. New York: Americas Society.

Latchatañeré, Rómulo. (1938) 1992. *¡¡Oh, mío Yemaya!! Cuentos y cantos negros*. Havana: Editorial de Ciencias Sociales.

Latchatañeré, Rómulo. (1942) 1995. *Manual de la santería: El sistema de cultos lucumís*. Havana: Editorial de Ciencias Sociales.

Latour, Bruno. 1993. *We Have Never Been Modern*. Translated by Catherine Porter. Cambridge, MA: Harvard University Press.

Latour, Bruno. 2010. *On the Modern Cult of the Factish Gods*. Durham, NC: Duke University Press.

La vanguardia. 2019. "Encuentran 42 cráneos, 31 huesos, un feto y un altar en una casa de Ciudad México." *La vanguardia*, October 28, 2019. https://www.lavanguardia.com/sucesos/20191028/471236675400/mexico-cartel-narcotrafico-traficantes-huesos-satanico.html.

Law, Robin. 1997. "Ethnicity and the Slave Trade: 'Lucumi' and 'Nago' as Ethnonyms in West Africa." *History in Africa* 24: 205–19.

Leighton, Alexander H., T. Adeoye Lambo, Charles C. Hughes, Dorothea Cross Leighton, Jane M. Murphy, and David B. Macklin. 1963. *Psychiatric Disorders among the Yoruba: A Report from the Cornell-Aro Mental Health Research Project in the Western Region, Nigeria*. Ithaca, NY: Cornell University Press.

Leiris, Michel. (1934) 1988. *L'Afrique fantôme*. Paris: Gallimard.

Leiris, Michel. 2017. *Phantom Africa*. Translated by Brent Hayes Edwards. Kolkata: Seagull Books.

Lipski, John M. 1987. "On the Construction *ta* + Infinitive in Caribbean *Bozal* Spanish." *Romance Philology* 40, no. 4: 431–50.

Lipski, John M. 2001. "From *Bozal* to *Boricua*: Implications of Afro-Puerto Rican Language in Literature." *Hispania* 84, no. 4: 850–59.

López, Francisco. 1998. *La Selva*. Rotterdam: V2_Archief V228. Compact disc.

Lovejoy, Henry B. 2018. *Prieto: Yorùbá Kingshop in Colonial Cuba during the Age of Revolutions*. Chapel Hill: University of North Carolina Press.

Lovejoy, Henry B. 2019. "Mapping Uncertainty: The Collapse of Oyo and the Trans-Atlantic Slave Trade, 1816–1836." *Journal of Global Slavery* 4, no. 2: 127–61.

MacGaffey, Wyatt. 1983. *Modern Kongo Prophets: Religion in a Plural Society.* Bloomington: Indiana University Press.

MacGaffey, Wyatt. 1991. *Art and Healing of the Bakongo Commented by Themselves: Minkisi from the Laman Collection.* Bloomington: Indiana University Press.

MacGaffey, Wyatt. 2000. *Kongo Political Culture: The Conceptual Challenge of the Particular.* Bloomington: Indiana University Press.

MacGaffey, Wyatt. 2016. "Constructing a Kongo Identity: Scholarship and Mythopoesis." *Comparative Studies in Society and History* 58, no. 1: 159–80.

MacGaffey, Wyatt, and Michael D. Harris. 1993. *Astonishment and Power: The Eyes of Understanding; Kongo Minkisi / The Art of Renee Stout.* Washington, DC: Smithsonian Institution Press.

Madrid, Alejandro, and Robin Moore. 2013. *Danzón: Circum-Caribbean Dialogues in Music and Dance.* Oxford: Oxford University Press.

Maguire, Emily. 2013. "Two Returns to the Native Land: Lydia Cabrera Translates Aimé Césaire." *Small Axe* 42: 125–37.

Maguire, Emily. 2018. *Racial Experiments in Cuban Literature and Ethnography.* Gainesville: University Press of Florida.

Marcuzzi, Michael D. 2005. "A Historical Study of the Ascendant Role of Bàtá Drumming in Cuban Òrìshà Worship." PhD diss., York University.

Marcuzzi, Michael D. 2007. Review of *Lydia Cabrera and the Construction of Afro-Cuban Identity*, by Edna Rodríguez-Mangual. *Canadian Journal of Latin American and Caribbean Studies / Revue canadienne des études latino-américaines et caraïbes* 32, no. 63: 254–56.

Marcuzzi, Michael D. 2008. Review of *Havana and Matanzas, Cuba, ca. 1957: Batá, Bembé, and Palo Songs*, by Lydia Cabrera and Josefina Tarafa. *Latin American Music Review / Revista de música latinoamericana* 29, no. 1: 112–15.

Marks, Morton. 1987. "Exploring El Monte: Ethnobotany and the Science of the Concrete." In *En torno a Lydia Cabrera*, edited by Isabel Castellanos and Josefina Inclán, 227–45. Miami: Ediciones Universal.

Marta, Karen, and Gabriela Rangel, eds. 2019. *Lydia Cabrera: Between the Sum and the Parts.* New York: Americas Society.

Martinez Betancourt, Julio Ismael. 2013. *Yerberos en La Habana.* Havana: Jardín Botánico Nacional / Universidad de Cuba / Fundación Fernando Ortiz.

Martínez-Fernandez, Luis. 2018. *Key to the New World: A History of Early Colonial Cuba.* Gainesville: University Press of Florida.

Martínez-Ruiz, Bárbaro. 2013. *Kongo Graphic Writing and Other Narratives of the Sign.* Philadelphia: Temple University Press.

Marvin, Thomas F. 1996. "Children of Legba: Musicians at the Crossroads in Ralph Ellison's *Invisible Man*." *American Literature* 68, no. 3: 587–608.

Mason, John. 1992. *Orin Òrìṣà: Songs for Selected Heads.* New York: Yoruba Theological Archministry.

Mason, John. 1996. *Olóòkun: Owner of Rivers and Seas.* New York City: Yoruba Theological Archministry.

Mason, John. 2002. *Àdúrà Òrìṣà: Prayers for Selected Heads.* Brooklyn, NY: Yoruba Theological Archministry.

Mason, Michael Atwood. 1994. "'I Bow My Head to the Ground': The Creation of Bodily Experience in a Cuban American Santería Initiation." *Journal of American Folklore* 107, no. 423: 23–39.

Mason, Michael Atwood. 2002. *Living Santería.* Washington, DC: Smithonian Books.

Matory, J. Lorand. 1994. *Sex and the Empire That Is No More: Gender and the Politics of Metaphor in Oyo Yoruba Religion.* Minneapolis: University of Minnesota Press.

Matory, J. Lorand. 1999. "The English Professors of Brazil: On the Diasporic Roots of the Yoruba Nation." *Comparative Studies in Society and History* 41, no. 1: 72–103.

Matory, J. Lorand. 2005. *Black Atlantic Religion: Tradition, Transnationalism, and Matriarchy in the Afro-Brazilian Candomble*. Princeton, NJ: Princeton University Press.

Matory, J. Lorand. 2008. "Free to Be a Slave: Slavery as Metaphor in Afro-Atlantic Religions." In *Africas of the Americas: Beyond the Search for Origins in the Study of Afro-Atlantic Religions*, edited by Stephan Palmié, 351–80. Boston: Brill.

Matory, J. Lorand. 2018. *The Fetish Revisited: Marx, Freud, and the Gods Black People Make*. Durham, NC: Duke University Press.

McNeil, Donald G., Jr. 2019. "Diagnoses by Horn, Payment in Goats: An African Healer at Work." *New York Times*, March 4, 2019. https://www.nytimes.com/2019/03/04/health/traditional -healer-africa-ebola.html.

Meadows, Ruthie. 2021. "Tradicionalismo Africano in Cuba: Women, Consecrated Batá, and the Polemics of 'Re-Yorubization' in Cuban Ritual Music." *Ethnomusicology* 65, no. 1: 86–111.

Metraux, Alfred. 1960. *Haiti: Black Peasants and Voodoo*. New York City: Universe Books.

Millay, Amy Nauss. 2005. *Voices from the Fuente Viva: The Effect of Orality in Twentieth-Century Spanish American Narrative*. Lewisburg, PA: Bucknell University Press.

Miller, Ivor. 2000a. "Religious Symbolism in Cuban Political Performance." *TDR: A Journal of Performance Studies* 44, no. 2: 30–55.

Miller, Ivor. 2000b. "A Secret Society Goes Public: The Relationship between Abakua and Cuban Popular Culture." *African Studies Review* 43, no. 1: 161–88.

Miller, Ivor. 2004. "The Formation of African Identities in the Americas: Spiritual 'Ethnicity.'" *Contours* 2, no. 2: 193–222.

Miller, Ivor. 2009. *Voice of the Leopard: African Secret Societies and Cuba*. Jackson: University Press of Mississippi.

Miller, Ivor. 2016. "Cuban Abakuá Music." La Médiathèque Caraïbe. http://www.lameca.org /publications-numeriques/dossiers-et-articles/cuban-abakua-music/.

Miller, Ivor. 2020. "Solidarity and Mutual Aid through Abakuá." *Calabar Mgbè*, no. 20, 1–4.

Minh-ha, Trinh T. 1991. *When the Moon Waxes Red: Representation, Gender, and Cultural Politics*. New York: Routledge.

Miomandre, Francis de. 1933. *Theophanie: Exposition de livres manuscrits*. Paris: Galerie Myrbor.

Moore, Robin D. 1997. *Nationalizing Blackness: Afrocubanismo and Artistic Revolution in Havana, 1920–1940*. Pittsburgh: University of Pittsburgh Press.

Moreman, Christopher M. 2013. *The Spiritualist Movement: Speaking with the Dead in America and around the World*. Santa Barbara, CA: Praeger.

Murphy, Joseph M. 1988. *Santería: An African Religion in America*. Boston: Beacon.

Murphy, Joseph M. 2015. *Botánicas: Sacred Spaces of Healing and Devotion in Urban America*. Jackson: University Press of Mississippi.

Murphy, Joseph M., and Mei-Mei Sanford, eds. 2001. *Òṣun across the Waters: A Yoruba Goddess in Africa and the Americas*. Bloomington: Indiana University Press.

Museum of Modern Art. n.d. "The Jungle (La Jungla)." Accessed April 11, 2022. https://www.moma .org/learn/moma_learning/wifredo-lam-the-jungle-1943/.

Obuke, Okpure O. 1978. "The Poetry of Wole Soyinka and J. P. Clark: A Comparative Analysis." *World Literature Today* 52, no. 2: 216–23.

Ocasio, Rafael. 2012. *Afro-Cuban Costumbrismo: From Plantations to the Slums*. Gainesville: University Press of Florida.

Ochoa, Todd Ramón. 2010. *Society of the Dead: Quita Manaquita and Palo Praise in Cuba*. Berkeley: University of California Press.

Okri, Ben. (1991) 1993. *The Famished Road*. New York: Anchor Books.

Olupona, Jacob, and Terry Rey, eds. 2008. *Òrìṣà Devotion as World Religion: The Globalization of Yoruba Religious Culture*. Madison: University of Wisconsin Press.

Ortiz, Fernando. (1906) 1973. *Hampa afrocubana: Los negros brujos (Apuntes sobre un estudio de etnología criminal)*. Miami: Ediciones Universal.

Ortiz, Fernando. 1920. "La fiesta afrocubana del Día de Reyes." *Revista Bimestre Cubana* 16, no. 1: 5–26.

Ortiz, Fernando. 1940. *Contrapunteo cubano del tabaco y el azúcar: Advertencias de sus contrastes agrarios, económicos, históricos y sociales, su etnografía y su transculturación*. Havana: Jesús Montero.

Ortiz, Fernando. (1940) 1947. *Cuban Counterpoint: Tobacco and Sugar*. Translated by Harriet De Onís. New York: Alfred A. Knopf.

Ortiz, Fernando. 1943. "Por la integración cubana de blancos y negros." *Ultra* 13, no. 77: 69–76.

Ortiz, Fernando. 1950. *La africanía de la música folklórica de Cuba*. Havana: Ministerio de Educación.

Ortiz, Fernando. 1952–55. *Los instrumentos de la musica afrocubana*. 5 vols. Havana: Ministerio de Educación / Cárdenas.

Ortiz, Fernando. 2018. *Fernando Ortiz on Music: Selected Writings on Afro-Cuban Culture*. Edited by Robin D. Moore. Translated by Robin D. Moore, David F. Garcia, Cary Peñate, and Sarah Lahasky. Philadelphia: Temple University Press.

Otero, Solimar. 2015. "Entre las aguas / Between the Waters: Interorality in Afro-Cuban Religious Storytelling." *Journal of American Folklore* 128, no. 508: 195–221.

Otero, Solimar. 2020. *Archives of Conjure: Stories of the Dead in Afrolatinx Cultures*. New York: Columbia University Press.

Otero, Solimar, and Toyin Falola, eds. 2013. *Yemoja: Gender, Sexuality, and Creativity in the Latina/o and Afro-Atlantic Diasporas*. Albany: State University of New York Press.

Oyelami, Muraina. 1991. *Yoruba Bata Music: A New Notation with Basic Exercises and Ensemble Pieces*. Bayreuth, Germany: Iwalewa Haus.

Palmié, Stephan. 2002. *Wizards and Scientists: Explorations in Afro-Cuban Modernity and Tradition*. Durham, NC: Duke University Press.

Palmié, Stephan, ed. 2008. *Africas of the Americas: Beyond the Search for Origins in the Study of Afro-Atlantic Religions*. Boston: Brill.

Palmié, Stephan. 2013. *The Cooking of History: How Not to Study Afro-Cuban Religion*. Chicago: University of Chicago Press.

Parra, María Teresa de la. 1982. *Obra (Narrativa, ensayos, cartas)*. Caracas: Ayacucho.

Petry, Ann. 1946. *The Street*. Boston: Houghton Mifflin.

Quintero, Alberto, and Michael Marcuzzi. 2015. "The Making of Aña in Venezuela." In *The Yorùbá God of Drumming: Transatlantic Perspectives on the Wood That Talks*, edited by Amanda Villepastour, 23–52. Jackson: University Press of Mississippi.

Ramos, Miguel. 2003. "La Division de La Habana: Territorial Conflict and Cultural Hegemony in the Followers of Oyo Lukumi Religion, 1850s–1920s." *Cuban Studies* 34: 38–70.

Ramos, Miguel. 2012. *Obí Agbón: Lukumí Divination with Coconut*. Miami: Eleda.org Publications.

Ramos, Miguel. 2014. *On the Orishas Roads and Pathways: Oshún, Deity of Femininity*. Miami: Eleda.org Publications.

Richards, Paulette. 1988. "Wifredo Lam: A Sketch." *Callaloo*, no. 34, 91–92.

Rivera-Barnes, Beatriz. 2014. "Detrás de la puerta: Una aproximación ecocrítica a *El monte* de Lydia Cabrera." *Revista de crítica literaria latinoamericana* 40, no. 79: 121–40.

Roche y Monteagudo, Rafael. 1925. *La policía y sus misterios en Cuba*. 3rd ed. Havana: La Moderna Poesía.

Rodríguez Coronel, Rogelio. 1992. "Marginalidad y literatura en textos afrocubanos de origen Yorubá." *Hispamérica* 21, no. 61: 95–100.

Rodríguez-Mangual, Edna M. 2004. *Lydia Cabrera and the Construction of an Afro-Cuban Identity.* Chapel Hill: University of North Carolina Press.

Roig, J. T. 1928. *Diccionario botánico de nombres vulgares cubanos.* Havana: Editorial Nacional de Cuba.

Roig, J. T. 1945. *Plantas medicinales, aromáticas o venenosas de Cuba.* Havana: Editorial Científico-Técnica.

Rojas, María Teresa de, ed. 1947. *Índice y extractos del Archivo de Protocolos de la Habana, 1578–1585.* Havana: Burgay.

Román, Reinaldo L. 2008. "Governing Man-Gods: Spiritism and the Struggle for Progress in Republican Cuba." In *Africas of the Americas: Beyond the Search for Origins in the Study of Afro-Atlantic Religions,* edited by Stephan Palmié, 107–40. Boston: Brill.

Sánchez, Reinaldo, José Antonio Madrigal, Ricardo Viera, and José Sánchez-Boudy, eds. 1978. *Homenaje a Lydia Cabrera.* Miami: Ediciones Universal.

Sanford, Mei-Mei. 2001. "Living Water: Osun, Mami Wata, and Olokun in the Lives of Four Contemporary Nigerian Women." In *Òṣun across the Waters: A Yoruba Goddess in Africa and the Americas,* edited by Joseph Murphy and Mei-Mei Sanford, 237–50. Bloomington: Indiana University Press.

Schwegler, Armin, and Constanza Rojas-Primus. 2010. "La lengua ritual del Palo Monte (Cuba): Estudio comparativo (Holguín/Cienfuegos)." *Revista internacional de lingüística iberoamericana,* no. 15, 187–244.

Schweitzer, Kenneth. 2013. *The Artistry of Afro-Cuban Batá Drumming: Aesthetics, Transmission, Bonding, and Creativity.* Jackson: University Press of Mississippi.

Slave Voyages. n.d. Digital database. Accessed April 11, 2022. https://slavevoyages.org.

Sogbossi, Hyppolite Brice. 1998. *La tradición ewé-fon en Cuba.* Havana: Fundación Fernando Ortiz.

Sontag, Susan. 1977. *On Photography.* New York: Delta.

Sosa Rodríguez, Enrique. 1982. *Los Ñáñigos: Premio casa de las Américas 1982; Ensayo.* Havana: Ediciones Casa de las Américas.

Sotheby's. 2020. "Wifredo Lam, Omi Obini." https://www.sothebys.com/en/buy/auction/2020/impressionist-modern-art-evening-sale/wifredo-lam-omi-obini.

Soyinka, Wole. 1967. *Idanre and Other Poems.* London: Methuen.

Stokes Sims, Lowery. 1992. "Myths and Primitivism: The Work of Wifredo Lam in the Context of the New York School and the School of Paris, 1942–1952." In *Wifredo Lam and His Contemporaries, 1938–1953,* 71–88. New York: Studio Museum in Harlem.

Stoller, Paul, and Cheryl Olkes. 1987. *In Sorcery's Shadow: A Memoir of Apprenticeship among the Songhay.* Chicago: University of Chicago Press.

Sublette, Ned. 2004. *Cuba and Its Music: From the First Drums to the Mambo.* Chicago: Chicago Review Press.

Szwed, John. 2005. *Crossovers: Essays on Race, Music, and American Culture.* Philadelphia: University of Pennsylvania Press.

Thompson, Robert Farris. 1975. "Icons of the Mind: Yoruba Herbalism Arts in Atlantic Perspective." *African Arts* 8, no. 3: 52–59, 89–90.

Thompson, Robert Farris. 1981. *The Four Moments of the Sun: Kongo Art in Two Worlds.* Washington, DC: National Gallery of Art.

Thompson, Robert Farris. 1983. *Flash of the Spirit: African and Afro-American Art and Philosophy.* New York: Random House.

Torres, J. T., and Jill Flanders Crosby. 2018. "Timeless Knowledge, Embodied Memory: The Performance of Stories in Ethnographic Research." *Etnofoor* 30, no. 1: 41–56.

Torres, Ramón. (2015) 2018. *Abakuá: (De)codificación de un símbolo.* Panama City, Panama: Aurelia Ediciones.

Tsang, Martin. 2016. "Have You Got Memory? Martin Tsang Writes about Religious Knowledge Transfers via 'El Paquete.'" *Cuba Counterpoints*. https://cubacounterpoints.com/archives/712 .html.

Tsang, Martin. 2019. "A Critical Biography of Lydia Cabrera." In *Twentieth-Century Literary Criticism*, vol. 380, 1–102. Farmington Hills, MI: Cengage Gale.

Tsang, Martin. 2021. "Write into Being: The Production of the Self and Circulation of Ritual Knowledge in Afro-Cuban Religious Libretas." *Material Religion* 17, no. 2: 229–61.

Turnbull, Colin. 1961. *The Forest People*. New York: Simon and Schuster.

Tutuola, Amos. 1952. *The Palm-Wine Drinkard*. New York: Grove.

Tutuola, Amos. 1954. *My Life in the Bush of Ghosts*. New York: Grove.

Tutuola, Amos. 1986. *Yoruba Folktales*. Ibadan, Nigeria: Ibadan University Press.

Vaughan, Umi. 2012. *Carlos Aldama's Life in Batá: Cuba, Diaspora, and the Drum*. Bloomington: Indiana University Press.

Vega, Marta Moreno. 2000. *The Altar of My Soul: The Living Traditions of Santería*. New York: One World.

Verger, Pierre. 1956. "Oral Tradition in the Cult of the Orishas and Its Connection with the History of the Yoruba." *Journal of the Historical Society of Nigeria* 1, no. 1: 61–63.

Verger, Pierre Fatumbi. (1955) 2002. *Orixás: Deuses iorubás na África e no Novo Mundo*. Salvador, Brazil: Fundação Pierre Verger.

Verger, Pierre Fatumbi. 1967. *Awon ewe Osanyin: Yoruba Medicinal Leaves*. Ife, Nigeria: University of Ife, Institute of African Studies.

Verger, Pierre Fatumbi. 1995. *Ewé: The Use of Plants in Yoruba Society*. Rio de Janeiro: Odebrecht.

Verger, Pierre Fatumbi. (1995) 2007. *Ewé: The Use of Plants in Yoruba Society*. Montclair, NJ: Black Madonna Enterprises.

Verger, Pierre Fatumbi. 2007. *Articles*. Vol. 1. Montclair, NJ: Black Madonna Enterprises.

Villaverde, Cirilo. (1882) 1935. *The Quadroon: A Romance of Old Havana*. Translated by Mariano J. Lorente. Originally published as *Cecilia Valdés o La loma del Angel*. Boston: L. C. Page.

Villepastour, Amanda. 2010. *Ancient Text Messages of the Yorùbá Bàtá Drum: Cracking the Code*. Burlington, VT: Ashgate.

Wangüemert, Gómez. "Crónicas de Arte: El Salón 1922." *Diario de la marina*, April 27, 1922.

Warner-Lewis, Maureen. 1990. "Trinidad Yoruba: A Language of Exile." *International Journal of the Sociology of Language*, no. 85, 9–20.

Warner-Lewis, Maureen. 1996. *Trinidad Yoruba: From Mother Tongue to Memory*. Tuscaloosa: University of Alabama Press.

Warner-Lewis, Maureen. 2018. "The African Diaspora and Language: Movement, Borrowing and Return." In *Tracing Language Movement in Africa*, edited by Ericka A. Albaugh and Kathryn M. de Luna, 321–41. Oxford: Oxford University Press.

Waxer, Lise. 1994. "Of Mambo Kings and Songs of Love: Dance Music in Havana and New York from the 1930s to the 1950s." *Latin American Music Review / Revista de música latinoamericana* 15, no. 2: 139–76.

Wenger, Susanne, and Gert Chesi. 1983. *A Life with the Gods in Their Yoruba Homeland*. Wörgl, Austria: Perlinger Verlag.

Wirtz, Kristina. 2005. "'Where Obscurity Is a Virtue': The Mystique of Unintelligibility in Santería Ritual." *Language and Communication* 25, no. 4: 351–75.

Wirtz, Kristina. 2007a. "Divining the Past: The Linguistic Reconstruction of 'African' Roots in Diasporic Ritual Registers and Songs." *Journal of Religion in Africa* 37, no. 2: 242–74.

Wirtz, Kristina. 2007b. *Ritual, Discourse, and Community in Cuban Santería: Speaking a Sacred World*. Gainesville: University Press of Florida.

Wirtz, Kristina. 2011. "Cuban Performances of Blackness as the Past Still among Us." *Journal of Linguistic Anthropology* 21, no. S1: E11–E34.

Wirtz, Kristina. 2013. "A 'Brutology' of Bozal: Tracing a Discourse Genealogy from Nineteenth-Century Blackface Theater to Twenty-First-Century Spirit Possession in Cuba." *Comparative Studies in Society and History* 55, no. 4: 800–833.

Wirtz, Kristina. 2014. *Performing Afro-Cuba: Image, Voice, Spectacle in the Making of Race and History*. Chicago: University of Chicago Press.

Wirtz, Kristina. 2016. "The Living, the Dead, and the Immanent: Dialogue across Chronotopes." *HAU: Journal of Ethnographic Theory* 6, no. 1: 343–69.

Index

gourds: Elegua and, 105; güira criolla
tree, 440; güira plant, 432–39; magic
of, 107–8; *nganga* and, 137; Osain and,
103–4, 106; secrets of, 105. *See also jicara*
Gregorian masses for the dead, 64–66
Guerra: de los Diez Años, 35, 35n26; La
Guerra Chiquita, 35n26; La Guerra
del 14 (World War I), 402
Gurunfinda. *See* Osain

Haitian: Vodun, religion, xi, xix, xvi;
witchcraft of, 18
head, 391; blessing of, 393; cleansing, 189;
rogation, 328, 393–95, 409, 421, 515
herbalist: on amor seco plant, 333; on
ceiba tree, 183; diviner, xii; and Havana Market, 91, 513, 513n228; on jiba
plant, 445; on medicine, 67; Osain as,
107, 109; *osainista*, 108, 121; on plant
knowledge, 189; and ritual plants, 118;
santo, 103
Hernández, Domingo, 71, 98, 112; on
Elufe, 99
Herrera, José de Calazán (Bangoché),
liii, xlviii, 220; Chinese sorcery and, 17;
Clementina and, 73
Holy Saturday, 129, 197–200; folk medicine and, 188; water of God, 199
Holy Thursday, 197; and the devil, 199; in
el monte, 200; *kimbiseros judios* sorcery,
199–200; *mayomberos judios*, 199; and
Satan, 199; and sorcerers, 199; sorcery
and, 199–200
Holy Week: activity during, 202; arbol
de la vida, 336; and Black people, 197;
Eshu, influence of, 201; *judio* and, 379,
481; Kadiempemba, influence of, 201;
spells during, 379
horse: as divinity, 34; fake *santo* as, 35;
possessed person, 23–24; to remove
the *santo*, 26–27

Ibeyi, 255–56, 272–73, 280, 389, 432
Ifa, 72; initiation into, 87, 87n25; as
supreme oracle, 44
iku (death), 74–75, 327, 380, 386, 403,
460; and *awo*, 104; and Changó,
258–60; and Day of the Dead, 64;
Eyife, coconut configuration, 382; *Itutu*

ceremony, 459; waning moon, 125.
See also muertos
illness: *aguinaldo blanco* and, 309; of
Black people, 18; cabima plant, 353;
caña fistula plant, 369; cedro (cedar
tree), 374; coconut tree, 398–99;
escoba amarga plant, 413–14; and
plantains, 504; as punishment, 45;
as work of *bilongo*, 15–16
incense, 231, 299, 311, 516; Abakuá rituals, 218–19; African religious, 480;
albahaca, 316; arabo, 335; cebolleta,
374; copalillo de monte, 405; incienso,
442; laurel, 452; palo mulato, 485; and
santos, 14; stone, cleaning of, 150
incest, 76, 173, 249–55
indiseme, 225–27; Abakuá initiate,
218–19; tributes paid by, 224
initiations, 36, 87, 87n25, 108–9; of Abakuá society, 217–18, 224–25, 227, 231;
asiento ceremony, 224–25; of Isunekue,
401; offerings, 224; into Palo Monte,
183–86, 266; Regla de Mayombe del
Santo Cristo de Buen Viaje, 424–25;
ritual, 218–19; trials of, 20
Inle, 45, 57–58, 87; children of, 383;
coming down, 58, 58n49; Itagua
coconut configuration signs, 386; La
Zumbao, 57; patron to lesbians, 57;
and San Juan Bautista, 58; as *santo*,
57–58
ireme, 212, 316; Aberinan, 302; Anamangi,
300; caña de azucar plant, 369; and
comecara tree, 404; Embakara, 299;
Emboko Fembe, 216, 226; Embokoro,
222; Enkoboro, 219, 225, 301; Eribangando, 218, 228, 294–95; guard of the
drum skins, 299; Llanto ceremony, 221,
221n19; Mariba Kankemo, 224; masquerades, 69; plaza of, 216; Tenkama,
296–97. *See also diablito*
Iroko (ceiba), 159–62, 188, 205; and Black
people, 204; cadavers at, 172–75; celebration of, 197; dance and, 160, 166;
and deceased souls, 161; gender of,
191; global drought and, 162; offerings
to, 166–67; pledge to ceiba, 166–67;
protection by, 190; savior of the species,
162; water and, 162. *See also ceiba*

lightning, 234; Santa Bárbara, 234.
See also palm tree
rumba, 181–82, 181n19